W0036601

Praise for
Developing Business Applications for the Web

"As an IT professional, I see the value in forward-thinking developers and business analysts, who are prepared to take their company to the next level. Laura and Christian have created a unique book that outlines a logical process for Web development in today's challenging Web environment. Students will find that this book easily traverses the skills required to create an effective Web interface, access databases, and provide valuable business applications."

Lisa Bock
Computer Information Technology Assistant Professor
Pennsylvania College of Technology

"A great overview of business application Web development. Experienced application developers on enterprise systems can use this text to get started with the different Web technologies ... the book pulls it all together. It is also a great resource for young IT professionals just getting started in business application development. The book can be used by seasoned IT managers to help them understand the complexities of developing Web applications for their business."

Jim Buck
IBM i educator and coauthor of *Programming in ILE RPG, Fifth Edition*

"An intelligent resource for any serious business-minded Web developer."

Charles Guarino
President, Central Park Data Systems

"Today's successful business developer must be well-versed in both Web development skills and in how to connect these skills to dynamic business environments. *Developing Business Applications for the Web* addresses both of these vital components by providing technical coverage of a vast array of development tools while keeping the focus on real-world business applications. "Get down to business" with *Developing Business Applications for the Web*!"

Char Parker
Computer Information Systems Instructor
Muskegon Community College

"Business developers now have a step-by-step guide to HTML, CSS, JavaScript, and more, and can complete their learning with the exercises provided. The journey to developing business applications for the Web starts with this book."

Alan Seiden
Seiden Group

"*Developing Business Applications for the Web* provides a great way to learn how to take business to the Web with exercises and examples to guide you through the process. It not only teaches basic Web development skills, but also how to take existing business applications to the Web to reach a broader audience. A great starting point for developing business Web applications!"

Amanda Walsh
Senior Programmer/Analyst (IBM i and Web developer)
Consultech Services, Inc.

Developing Business Applications for the Web

With HTML, CSS, JSP, PHP, ASP.NET, and JavaScript

Laura Ubelhor

Christian Hur

MC Press Online, LLC
Boise, ID 83703 USA

Developing Business Applications for the Web:
With HTML, CSS, JSP, PHP, ASP.NET, and JavaScript

Laura Ubelhor and Christian Hur

First Edition

First Printing—March 2017

© 2017 Laura Ubelhor and Christian Hur. All rights reserved.

Printed in USA. *All rights reserved.* This publication is protected by copyright, and permission must be obtained from the publisher prior to any prohibited reproduction, storage in a retrieval system, or transmission in any form or by any means, electronic, mechanical, photocopying, recording, or likewise. For information regarding permissions, contact *mcbooks@mcpressonline.com.*

Every attempt has been made to provide correct information. However, the publisher and the author do not guarantee the accuracy of the book and do not assume responsibility for information included in or omitted from it.

The following are trademarks of International Business Machines Corporation in the United States, other countries, or both: DB2, Domino, IBM, Lotus, Rational, and WebSphere.

Adobe, Dreamweaver, and Photoshop are registered trademarks of Adobe. Chrome is a trademark of Google. Firefox is a registered trademark of The Mozilla Foundation. Java, and all Java-based trademarks and logos, are trademarks or registered trademarks of Oracle and/or its affiliates. JBuilder is a registered trademark of Embarcadero Technologies. Bing, Internet Explorer, Microsoft, SQL Server, and Windows are trademarks of the Microsoft Corporation in the United States, other countries, or both.

Linux is a registered trademark of Linus Torvalds in the United States, other countries, or both. Safari is a registered trademark of Apple. SlickEdit is a registered trademark of SlickEdit. TextPad is a registered trademark of Helios Software Solutions. UltraEdit is a trademark of IDM Computer Solutions. UNIX is a registered trademark of The Open Group in the United States, other countries, or both. Yahoo! is a registered trademark of Yahoo.

All other product names are trademarked or copyrighted by their respective manufacturers.

MC Press offers excellent discounts on this book when ordered in quantity for bulk purchases or special sales, which may include custom covers and content particular to your business, training goals, marketing focus, and branding interest.

MC Press Online, LLC
Corporate Offices: 3695 W. Quail Heights Court, Boise, ID 83703-3861 USA
Sales and Customer Service: (208) 629-7275 ext. 500;
service@mcpressonline.com
Permissions and Bulk/Special Orders: mcbooks@mcpressonline.com
www.mcpressonline.com • www.mc-store.com

ISBN: 978-1-58347-348-1

Acknowledgments

I'd like to thank Christian Hur for working with me on this project. We had a great experience and worked well together. Christian made this large project a pleasure, and I greatly appreciate the knowledge, insight, experience, and effort Christian put forth. Thank you also to Anne Grubb, MC Press Book Editor.

I'd also like to thank my family for their support. A special thanks to Paul for his love and patience. Writing this book would not have been possible without the support my family provided. This effort is dedicated in loving memory of my beloved nephew Brent. We miss him so, and he will always live on in our memories. Brent was known to say "the sky's the limit." These words are so true; they're definitely inspirational words to live by. Don't hesitate to reach for the sky.

My hope is that this book inspires experienced business developers to feel comfortable learning Web skills and those new to development to dive in and learn how to get down to business with Web tools. I've been fortunate to have a career that I enjoy and am very passionate about. I hope this book inspires others to realize the same career satisfaction.

Laura Ubelhor

First and foremost, I'd like to thank Laura Ubelhor for the opportunity to be a part of this project and for the learning opportunities she has provided. The completion of this project could not have been accomplished without her experience, encouragement, and guidance. I'd also like to thank Anne Grubb for her support and encouragement. Truly, I've been blessed to have worked with Laura and Anne on this project, and I'll remain forever thankful.

I cannot express enough thanks to Jim Buck for his encouragement and advice. Jim has led me to places I never thought I would go, and I offer my sincere appreciation for introducing me to this project. I'd also like to thank all my colleagues at Gateway Technical College for their support. A special thanks to all my students at GTC for giving me inspiration to keep on writing and teaching.

I'd also like to thank my family for their support and encouragement. Most of all, I want to thank my wife, Kelly, for her incredible heart and invaluable support. Thanks for giving me the strength to believe in my passion and pursue my dreams.

Christian Hur

Contents

Introduction

Developing business applications for the Web is a topic of great interest. Getting down to business with Web application development, in our opinion, is even more interesting and is a topic that's highly relevant to any business developer. We have enjoyed writing this book and have worked hard to provide an inclusive resource for business developers who want to expand their skill set into developing Web applications for business.

Why Another Book About Web Application Development?

With so many books already written about Web application development, why write another? We felt that few, if any, books capture the real needs of business application programmers. Too often, Web development books focus on a single technology or language. Learning to write HTML, JavaScript, and Cascading Style Sheets (CSS) is only half the battle. We're reminded of a commercial from years ago, in which a young programmer excitedly shows off his latest company Web page, complete with flaming, spinning logos, to his boss. The boss nods in appreciation, and then says, "Great, now can you integrate it with accounts payable?"

How many veteran application developers, with many years' experience building complex and productive applications, have suddenly been thrown off balance when asked to develop an application for the Web? How many students trying to find their way into the work world are unsure of what it takes to develop skills fitting to a career as a business Web developer? And where does someone who wants to become a business application developer begin?

To address such questions, we wrote this book. It provides a comprehensive guide not only for HTML, but for many aspects of browser-based applications. In short, this book is written by business application developers and educators for business application developers. You will learn to do much more than create Web pages with flaming logos: you will learn to actually deploy real-time data to Web-based applications and create fully interactive modern applications.

How Is This Book Arranged?

The early chapters of the book introduce HTML, the foundational language for browser-based applications. The HTML covered within this book is extensive, but also focused. Rather than trying to teach every possible feature of HTML, we focus on those portions most useful to business programmers. Later chapters introduce common methods for integrating real application data into Web applications.

When we review specific coding techniques, you will see the commands/tags and any pertinent parameters separated with borders, like this:

Tag:

```
<a
   parameter 1
   parameter 2
   parameter 3
>
</a>
```

Consistently displaying commands in this way makes it easier for you to use this book as a reference, so you can easily skim the book looking for the command you need.

You'll review simple HTML pages for a hypothetical business, Belhur Publishing. The first examples show the creation of a home page for the business, which provides a Web presence and contact information. Later pages add more content and more sophisticated design techniques. After that, browser-based application programs are reviewed. You will see example applications that present practical, day-to-day business uses. Use these examples to help develop your own applications. After reading and learning from the examples, you'll gain confidence in your ability to develop a business Web application.

The screenshot below shows our starting point for the Belhur Publishing website: a simple Web page. It's not much—just a simple, static HTML document. Very little is happening on this Web page, as far as images, formatting, or style sheets. These features will be added later in the book, but since we're application developers, not graphic designers, the focus is on the code involved, not on design and creating aesthetically pleasing Web pages. (That said, it's a good idea to acquaint yourself with at least the fundamentals of Web page design. A quick Internet search will reveal many resources to guide you in this area.)

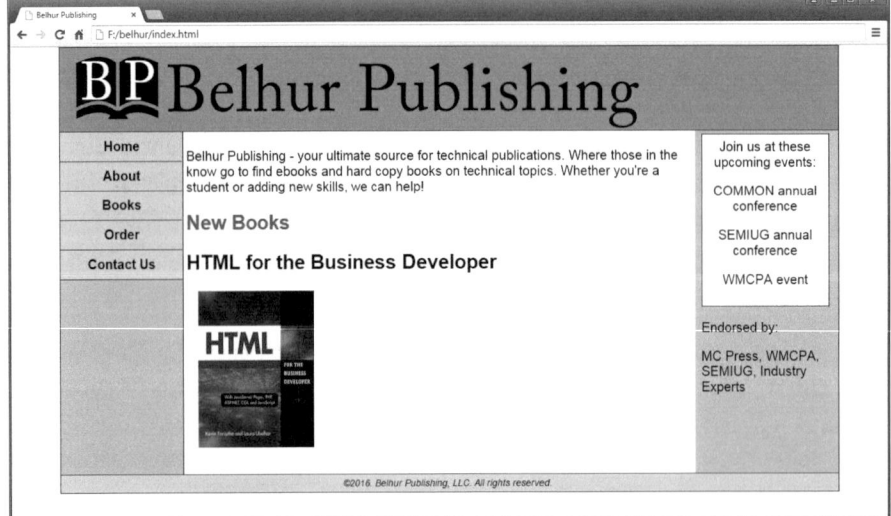

Once we've covered the basics of the HTML, we'll discuss other languages that interact with HTML. It's inconceivable to have a business Web application created with only HTML. Virtually every Web application incorporates other elements, such as languages, to produce the necessary dynamic content. We've selected several of the most common languages used to develop Web applications. Each one has its own chapter in this book.

Intended Audience

The intended audience for this book is business developers or those who are considering or are interested in becoming business developers. Many books teach Web development, each focusing on a specific language or technology. This is not just another book about Web application development: this book focuses on getting down to business. Building a static site is one thing, but accessing databases and providing business applications is another. Many developers have extensive experience in developing business applications. These developers might be very familiar with traditional mainframe/midrange programming environments, but know little about Web-based applications. The world is ever changing, and many business programmers find themselves needing to learn about doing business on the Web. Possibly you're a student being introduced to the Web and/or business applications, pondering where you should start and how you can develop the skills needed to be a successful business Web developer.

In larger shops, the business application developer might not be the one to create and support the organization's website, but may still be expected to develop new business applications to deploy through the site. This kind of collaborative environment is nothing new. Most IT staffs are comfortable with team-based development and collaborative effort. Do you need to know all the website development bits and pieces to code business applications? No, probably not. We intentionally included many of the pieces for a traditional site to help you see how they work together; this insight can help you make better decisions throughout the application development process. We cover the basics and then dive into the fun stuff, always with the business developer in mind.

As a business developer or someone studying to become a business developer, you likely already have a programming language or languages with which you are very literate and comfortable. It might be RPG on IBM i, COBOL on a mainframe, or C++ on a PC. While traditional developers often work on a single platform, Web development might require using more than one platform. The thought of stepping outside of the box—and your comfort zone—can be overwhelming. Our intention for this book is to make you feel more comfortable with Web application development and also to help you learn new skills that you can apply within your organization (or prospective organization) to become more productive, versatile, and valuable.

Do I Need to Start from Scratch?

Does going to the Web mean starting from scratch? Do you need to scrap your existing business applications and start over? Absolutely not! Doing so would be inefficient and cost-prohibitive. A more sensible approach is to continue to use what you have and learn some new tools to reach a broader audience or provide broader access to your applications. In this way, you can retain much of your organization's existing investment in complex business logic.

Does Web development mean new hardware? Not necessarily. Many of the tools we discuss can be used with a variety of platforms. Java technologies can be used on any platform that supports use of the Java Virtual Machine (JVM). Often, a separate server is used for hosting sites. Is this necessary? No, not always; depending on the size of your servers, available capacity, security issues, and application workloads, you might be able to host your applications on existing servers. Since opening applications up to the Web often creates new security considerations, however, you might need separate servers, even if your existing servers have sufficient capacity.

Choosing Development Tools

How to choose the best technology for a development project is a complicated subject. There is a lot of debate on which tools are the best tools. Often, arguments seem biased based on the technology comfort zone of those providing opinions. The bias also lies in the thought that a single technology needs to be used. The further a business programmer delves into Web application development, the clearer it is that a wide variety of tools are available. All these tools have beneficial features and functionality, as well as limitations.

If a business developer is looking for a quick way to generate dynamic Web content, PHP might be the right solution, as it is easy to learn, inexpensive, and available on many platforms. On the other hand, advocates of Microsoft .NET technology are satisfied with their development tools and the resulting solutions, even though they are generally constrained to a Windows-based environment. Java-related technologies are very robust and are available for use on a wide variety of platforms and servers, but developers are often deterred from using Java because of its learning curve. Many tools have been around a long time, but there seems to be a trend in replacing some tools with other easier, established, more flexible technologies.

Which is the right fit for your organization? It might well be a combination of these or other technologies.

Summary

This book introduces HTML, covering the basics and enabling you to begin developing Web pages. Then we add CSS, JavaScript, and form processing to these basic skills. Once we've covered the basics, we are ready to delve into the really fun areas of application development! We'll first introduce you to browser-based applications, then introduce technologies including JavaScript, PHP, JSP, and ASP.NET, which transform HTML into a useful business application development language.

Which of these is the correct choice for your needs? After reading this book, you might see that it takes a combination of languages and tools to satisfy your development requirements. Upon completion of this book, you'll have enough knowledge to "get down to business" yourself and start developing your own business Web applications.

An Introduction to Browser-Based Applications

This book is written for business programmers, by business programmers and educators. Since HTML is the foundation language for all browser-based business applications, we'll start with HTML. However, any browser-based application almost certainly involves languages or tools in addition to HTML. In later chapters, you'll see many examples of how those other languages and tools integrate with HTML.

What exactly is a **browser-based application**? Application development in the 21st century can be broken down into two categories: *legacy* and *modern*. (These terms are commonly used by business application developers, but they can be a bit misleading, as legacy applications are sometimes quite modern in their design, while some so-called modern applications have horribly archaic designs.) Modern application development splits further into two sub-categories: *browser-based* and ***client-based***. Client-based applications are typically deployed as executable files loaded onto each computer that needs the application. This often involves one or more installation files typically downloaded from a website. A browser-based application, the topic of this book, is quite different.

A **Web browser** is a program such as Google Chrome, Microsoft Internet Explorer or Edge, or Mozilla Firefox. It is designed as a generic **Web page** presenter, accepting complex streams of commands and data from remote Web servers and composing them into visually appealing Web pages. A browser can typically process instructions written in a number of different languages, but by far the most common language is **HTML**, which stands for *Hypertext Markup Language*.

HTML is one of many markup languages. All of them rely on small snippets of code called **tags** that are intermixed with the content being processed. In the case of HTML, a tag is recognized by the less-than and greater-than signs that surround it. For example, to create a large page heading, you might code <h1>MY PAGE HEADING</h1>. The <h1> tag signals the browser that the text that follows appears very large, as shown in Figure 1.1.

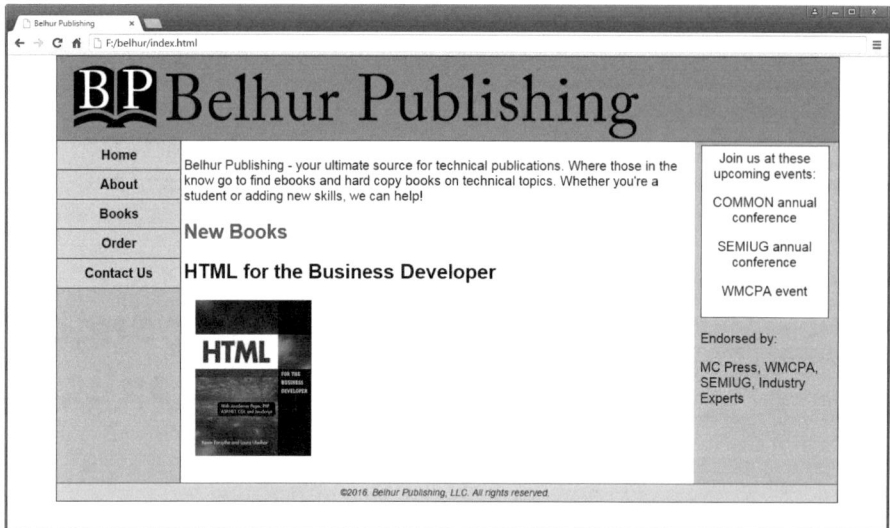

Figure 1.1: An example of an HTML page heading

The </h1> tag is called an **end tag**. The slash indicates that this tag ends the previous heading tag. Any text processed after the end tag appears in the default size and style. Most, but not all, HTML tags have corresponding end tags.

HTML is a relatively simple language. While it has some quirks, it should not intimidate anyone. Generally, the most complex aspects of Web page design come from integrating **other languages** into the HTML code, such as **JavaScript** and Cascading Style Sheets (**CSS**).

Additional Languages

Initially, you'll learn how to incorporate JavaScript and CSS into your Web pages. Then, you'll see how to combine those pages with other languages, such as JSP, **PHP**, and ASP.NET, to provide database integration.

Each language has its own strengths and weaknesses. JavaScript is a powerful Java-based language modeled on **C++**, but simpler and with key design changes to make it easier to deploy on a variety of computers. PHP is a popular scripting language designed specifically for database integration. This HTML preprocessor runs on a **Web server** and creates dynamic HTML content that is returned to the remote user via the browser. ASP.NET is similar in concept to PHP, but the syntax is similar to **VB.NET**, the version of Microsoft's Visual Basic (VB) implemented on Microsoft .NET Framework. Both PHP and ASP.NET rely on specialized Common Gateway Interface (**CGI**) programs. CGI programs can be written in many languages and provide a powerful and flexible method for developing dynamic Web pages.

Which language you choose is up to you, and will be the product of a decision that considers many factors, such as your current skill sets, your coworkers' skill sets, skill sets of available resources, executive mandates, existing applications, and personal preference. Our goal is to provide complete, clear, and functional examples of browser-based applications written with each of these methods, enabling you to be productive immediately upon completion of this book.

What Is a Client?

The **client** is the **hardware** device that will be used to access the **Web application**. The client is probably a laptop or desktop computer, but it might be a handheld device such as a **PDA/smartphone**, **tablet, iPad**, or even a mobile phone. Which devices your application will need to support usually depends on who your application users are and what devices they use to access the Internet. These devices will also likely use a variety of operating systems. While the most common **operating system** is Microsoft Windows, there are many other possibilities, such as Mac OS and Linux.

Even if all your website's visitors will be using Windows on PCs, they might be using different screen sizes and resolutions, which will affect the appearance of the site and applications. Those differences may or may not affect how applications are coded. For example, if your visitors will use **handheld devices**, your application might need to be designed and coded to easily fit displayed data on a smaller screen. If your application has a lot of graphics, the need to consider performance and appearance will be more important. (Considerations based on device types, operating systems, screen sizes, and resolution are discussed in more detail in chapter 12.)

What Is a Browser?

A browser is **software** that acts as an interface between the user client and the Web. The browser is also sometimes referred to as a **Web client**. The browser sends requests for information, receives that information, and displays it on a user client.

You are probably already familiar with some of the available browsers. They include, but are not limited to, Chrome, Edge, Firefox, Internet Explorer, Opera, and Safari. The browsers used to access applications can affect appearance and impose other considerations for **Web development**. Browsers are free of charge and change in popularity. If your application provides access to the general Internet community, many different browsers will probably be used to access your site and applications. (Browsers are discussed in more detail in chapter 12.)

What Is HTML?

If you are creating a Web application, you almost certainly will use HTML. HTML has been around quite a while and is likely to be used for a long time to come. It is the language of the Web, so you must have at least a basic understanding of it. HTML has changed since its initial inception to include functions and features that make it more flexible and easier to use for Web application development. HTML5 was released in October 2014 and includes significant enhancements. You will be introduced to HTML in the following chapters.

A document in pure HTML is static, meaning it exists in a constant state. **Client-side scripting** can be embedded within HTML to make a Web application dynamic. Most often, the language used for client-side scripting is JavaScript. You'll learn about JavaScript and client-side scripting in chapter 8.

HTML forms are often used as the means to incorporate CGI within a Web application. As mentioned earlier, CGI is a protocol for interfacing with applications on a Web server. This involves **server-side scripting**. You will learn about CGI and server-side scripting in later chapters.

What Is a Web Server?

The term *Web server* can refer to the program that is responsible for communicating with client browsers. A Web server accepts HTTP requests from client browsers and serves HTTP responses, including optional data content, which is usually in the form of an HTML document and linked objects. The term *Web server* can also refer to the system that runs Web server programs. There are really two components of a Web server: hardware and software.

Writing Web applications doesn't necessarily mean that you'll need to purchase new hardware. Many platforms can be used to serve websites. Some are more compatible and better suited to Web development than others, but most can accommodate Web development. Most organizations probably already have a system that can be used for serving a website and Web applications.

A decision will need to be made whether additional hardware is required to serve your site and Web applications. Additional hardware may add another layer of security. Data and applications can reside on the same system, or you might want to separate data to add yet another layer of security. On the other hand, having additional hardware requires additional support and administration. Using a Web hosting service or cloud solution should also be considered.

What Database(s) Are Used?

Nearly any database management system (DBMS, or **database**, for short) could have been used for the examples in this book. Web programming is generally very inclusive, and most databases are supported. The examples in this book use primarily IBM DB2 and MySQL databases, but chapter 7 includes a brief discussion of connecting to different databases. Later chapters use examples of connecting databases and include several examples of connections that can be used to incorporate dynamic database content within your Web applications.

Where Can I Find Sample Code?

The code examples and supplemental material for this book are available for download on the book's Web page in the MC Press Bookstore, *https://goo.gl/2uYjHb.* Feel free to download and use the examples. We are confident that using this book and the examples included will help you to develop your own Web-based applications as quickly and easily as possible. The downloadable materials include corresponding code files for all the code examples provided within this book.

The Development Process

The tools and techniques may be different for Web development than for traditional **business programming**, but the process is very similar. Developing applications still requires information gathering, analysis, design, coding, testing, documentation, implementation, and support. Web development also requires looking at the application life cycle and building flexibility into the design so it can adapt to business process changes.

An organization's **development standards** should be updated to provide developers a structure and process to follow as a standardized guide. Like development with legacy code, having predefined standards for Web development keeps code consistent, organized, easily maintained, and manageable.

All environments have their own unique challenges, just as all programmers have their own unique methods of coding. You can ask a number of programmers to code the same solution, and none of the applications will be coded exactly the same. Having a defined **development process** minimizes the effects of development differences. This holds true for Web applications as well as other applications. Organizations may also have internal requirements, such as Sarbanes-Oxley or HIPAA compliance, which cannot be overlooked and need to be accounted for in the development process. Web applications may add another twist, as additional hardware is often introduced into the mix. For example, application databases and some of the application code might reside on one system, and the browser-based components and server on another.

Take the time to consider how Web development fits into the process, and have a defined process to follow. This will be time well spent. When learning a new language, developers will try to stick to a comfortable coding style. If a process is not predefined, developers will define their own process. Having a defined process and coding style will result in more consistent code and a more organized application. This kind of application is much easier to support in the long term, whether you or someone else has to go back and change, maintain, or debug code.

Once decisions have been made about the tools, technology, and hardware infrastructure that will be used for Web development, and prior to actually beginning the development, consider the development process. This process should be revisited periodically. Changes will be made as a result of business requirements, business needs, and technology changes, among other reasons. The development process, like any other, can be defined, revisited, and enhanced to fit an organization's environment. How informal and flexible the process is depends on an environment's specifics.

IT Staff

As with legacy applications, development tasks for Web applications may be the responsibility of several groups or departments. This holds true especially in larger organizations. One group might be responsible for the **application design and graphics**, another for database support, another for administration, and another for business **application logic** and development. Responsibility might also be structured by platform, as Web applications often involve more than one platform. This does not mean that Web development requires more staff than legacy development, but it does mean you must consider the components, tasks, and **IT staff** structure. Staff structure will be based in part on resource skill sets and project requirements. In smaller organizations, the developer may also be responsible for configuration, Web design, and coding. However, you'll often find that experts in design or coding are not necessarily experts in configuration or hardware infrastructure. Therefore, tasks are often spread among different staff members and departments.

The size of the organization and the skill sets of development resources can have a great impact on the structure of an IT staff. As shown in Table 1.1, small organizations require individuals with very diverse skill sets and an understanding of the complete realm of requirements. One of the interesting challenges of Web development is that it enables business developers to try their hand at design. Often, developers with strong analytical skills, who are able to tackle complex business requirements and turn them into well-functioning applications, aren't nearly as intuitive at designing the look of an application. This might mean stepping outside of a comfort zone, but it does not mean a business developer cannot fulfill this role within an IT staff structure.

Table 1.1: Size of Organization and IT Staff	
Organization Size	IT Staff Roles
Large	Often structured with multiple departments segmented by various roles required for Web development tasks. Departments may include, but are not limited to, management, project leaders, hardware and operations support, security and administration, design and graphics, database administration, and development. The size of Web projects tends to be large in regard to scope and timeline.
Medium	Often structured with multiple departments, but fewer than larger organizations. A combination of structuring is often based on staff skill sets.
Small	Often structured with few, if any, departments. Staff members fulfill many roles, as "jacks of all trades."

While this book focuses on business programming, it also includes other topics to provide insight into the many areas of Web development. Whether you will be responsible for many Web application tasks or for programming only, an understanding of the related tasks will help you develop solid Web programming skills and better prepare you to determine where you fit. Trying to be a jack of all trades may result in your being a master of none. Don't overwhelm yourself. We have intentionally focused on the business developer and on coding **dynamic business applications**, so that you will have an understanding of the technical skills required. You'll find, after you've gained some experience, there are often similarities in the languages and tools used for Web development. Learning HTML is valuable no matter what role you will fill as a developer. Learning common languages to create business applications is always beneficial.

So what does this mean to you as a developer? You can focus your effort on coding only, or you can decide to develop expanded Web skills to fulfill a role requiring a diverse skill set. Your personal goals, job status, and skill set will affect where you fit within an organization's IT staff structure. A developer with diverse skills will have more flexibility in the roles and organizations that are a good fit. If your desire is to learn other skills in addition to business application Web development, you might be more content within a small to medium organization. If you want to focus your skills on application coding and development, and not learn design, administration, or other related skills, a large organization will likely be a better fit.

Platforms

Creating Web applications does not necessarily mean an organization will need to change or add new **platforms**. Often, existing hardware can be used, if it is fit for Web development. Most organizations already have clients set up with Web browser support. Browser support is a necessity. The back-end hardware will probably not be the same as the client devices that users employ to access the Web. The configuration will also include a Web server. One of the most popular platforms for a Web server is a PC. This might be the same PC-based server used for the organization's intranet, or for security purposes, it might be a server dedicated to Web applications.

Legacy code may be reused with Web applications and will likely continue to reside on the legacy platform. Databases will also likely continue to reside on their current platform. So, will you need to learn new hardware operating systems? Probably not, unless the platforms currently used do not support Web applications.

If the decision is made to use Java-based technology, any platform that supports Java Virtual Machine (JVM) can be used. If the decision is made to use ASP.NET, a Microsoft server will probably be used. Some languages are better suited to specific hardware, but most languages used for Web development are supported by a variety of platforms. Web development is much more open than legacy application development. Its flexibility makes platform decisions easier.

Cost, resource skills, and staff knowledge will also be factors in deciding which platforms to use for Web development. Most organizations already have platform knowledge of PC-based client hardware with Web browser support, as well as platforms that can be used as a Web server.

Devices

Web applications open up the ability for the application to support additional **devices**. Any device that can connect to the Internet and provides a browser-based emulator can be used for Web applications. The decision to create and use Web applications enables you to provide user access through a variety of devices, including PCs, tablets, iPads, PDAs, smartphones, and other mobile devices.

The key to using **non-traditional devices** is application design. The design needs to accommodate the screen size, keyboard, and operating system of the devices to be used. With **Wi-Fi** making it possible for field staff or shop-floor staff to easily access and use applications, you can breathe new life into your old applications. (*Wi-Fi* is an abbreviation for *wireless fidelity*, a wireless technology often used for Internet connectivity.) An organization's sales staff could use their smartphones or other mobile devices to determine inventory quantities. Shop-floor staff could use handheld devices to easily inquire about manufacturing requirements. While this book does not focus on building applications using unconventional devices, it does put you on the path to making these Web-based applications a reality. Many technology changes have occurred in recent years, and what may be considered unconventional today may well be the standard tomorrow.

Ajax

Web applications are fun to build. However, some Web applications are slow and sometimes frustrating for users. Because Web applications are made up of several components, even well-coded sites sometimes require the user to wait for data and pages to be loaded. You've probably seen the hourglass or percentage of completion display on a website that appears when, behind the scenes, the application goes through the processing steps to evaluate input, respond to the request, retrieve information, and format it for display through your Web browser.

Ajax (Asynchronous JavaScript and XML) is a buzzword, and for good reason. It is a way of programming for the Web that gets rid of the hourglass and slower response time. It is not new technology; it is a new way of looking at technology that is already mature and stable.

Ajax is a group of interrelated Web development techniques for creating dynamic, interactive Web applications. Using Ajax, data, content, and design are merged together. The primary advantage and reason for using Ajax is the increased responsiveness and interactivity of Web pages that its use enables. The improvement is realized by exchanging small amounts of data with the server so that the entire Web page does not have to be reloaded each time the user performs an action. Because the Ajax engine is handling requests, the information can be held by the Ajax engine and allow interaction with the application and user to happen independently of any interaction with the Web server. When a user clicks on something in an Ajax-driven application, very little response time is required. The page simply displays what the user is asking for. The result is speed, functionality, usability, and increased Web page interactivity.

Web applications are usually coded so that the interactions between the user and the server are *synchronous*, meaning one step has to follow another. If a user clicks a link and initiates a request, the request is sent to the server, which then processes the request and returns the results back to the user's Web browser.

Ajax is *asynchronous*, in that extra data can be requested from a server and loaded in the background, without interfering with the display and behavior of the current Web page. JavaScript is usually the scripting language used for Ajax function calls. The JavaScript is loaded when the page loads and handles most of the basic tasks on the client side, including data validation, data manipulation, and data display, without making a trip to the server. At the same time, the Ajax engine is sending data back and forth to the server. The data transfer does not depend on user actions and occurs concurrently. Data within an Ajax site is retrieved using the XMLHttpRequest object available to all scripting languages that are compatible with modern Web browsers. **XML** is often used with Ajax, but it is not a requirement that the asynchronous content be formatted in XML.

Ajax is a flexible technique based on cross-platform usability. It can be used with a variety of platforms, operating systems, and Web browsers. Ajax is based on open standards such as JavaScript and the Document Object Model (**DOM**). While Ajax itself is beyond the scope of this book, you'll learn more about JavaScript and the DOM throughout this book. Free, open source Ajax examples are available that are suitable for most Web-based application projects.

A great example of an Ajax site is Google Maps (*www.google.com/maps*). Visit the site and check it out. There really is very little wait time when maneuvering around the site and enlarging or moving around the maps.

SOA

Another important technology is *Service-Oriented Architecture (***SOA**). SOA defines how two or more entities interact in such a way as to enable one entity to perform a unit of work on behalf of the other. The unit of work is referred to as a *service*.

SOA is really a collection of services that communicate with one another. The communication can include services either simply passing data or coordinating some activity. The service interactions use a well-defined description language. SOA is an evolution of distributed computing based on the request-and-reply paradigm for asynchronous and synchronous applications.

Using SOA, an application's business logic or individual defined functions are modularized and presented as services for user applications. The key is that each interaction is self-contained and has a loosely coupled nature. Each interaction remains independent of any other interaction. The service interface is independent of the implementation. Application developers can build applications by composing one or more services without knowing the service or the underlying implementations of the service. For example, a service can be implemented in .NET or **Java** on a Windows server, and the application consuming the service could be in **RPG** running on an IBM i.

SOAP-enabled Web services are the most common implementation of SOA. **SOAP**, or *Simple Object Access Protocol*, is a standard that defines the application-level structure for messages. For applications to integrate, they must agree on the message structure used. SOAP provides an application-level message structure for use over many communication protocols. Applications that speak SOAP can easily exchange information with each other; thus SOAP facilitates integration between completely different systems.

The protocol independence of SOA means that different consumers can use a service by communicating with it in different ways. Service orientation is a method of architecting systems of autonomous services. Using SOA, services are built to be functional, flexible, reliable, and available. New service topologies may evolve over time, so systems using SOA are also built to accommodate changes.

This book does not focus on SOA, but it does introduce skills and tools that can be used to develop SOA applications.

Web Services

Many environments make use of more than one hardware platform, software systems, and databases. Different software may use different programming languages, posing the need for a method of communication between multiple systems that isn't dependent on a specific programming language. Using a **Web service** is a frequently employed solution for enabling the systems to exchange data with each other over the Internet. A Web service includes a service requester and a service provider. The system initiating the exchange is called the *service requester*, and the system that receives and processes the request to provide data is called the *service provider*. The Web service uses parameters to pass data back and forth between the requester and provider.

Most systems can interpret and use XML tags. Web services can use XML files to exchange data. A Web service is a standardized way of integrating Web-based applications, one that makes use of Extensible Markup Language (XML), SOAP, Web Service Definition Language (**WSDL**) and Universal Description, Discovery, and Integration (**UDDI**) open standards over an Internet Protocol (IP) backbone. In a Web service, XML is used to tag data, SOAP is used to transfer data, WSDL is used for describing the services available, and UDDI lists what servers are available. A Web service is a software function provided at a network address over the Web.

Within this book, we mention Web services, as most environments have more than one platform and can make use of Web services. As a beginner in Web application development, once you learn the basics of Web development, you'll be ready to explore using Web services.

Other Languages

This book starts with HTML and continues to introduce other programming languages used for Web development. Not all the possible languages that may be used for Web development are introduced here. However, careful thought has been given to introduce some of the more common ones. You'll find many options and examples that can be used to create dynamic Web applications.

Although Web development has been around for quite a few years, it is still in its infancy compared to non–Web-based business application development. The growth has been like wildfire, and by no means is Web development for business applications a mature technology. As with any other growing technology, new Web development languages and tools continue to be developed and introduced. There is a lot of debate about which are the best tools and what will be popular in the future.

Many languages and tools used for Web development are quite similar. Often, a combination of languages is used to create a Web application. Web development tends to be much more open than traditional development in regard to mixing things up. Traditionally, for example, RPG is used to code on an IBM i, COBOL is used on a mainframe, and Visual Basic is used on a Microsoft server. Web development, on the other hand, typically does not lock an organization into a specific platform or a single language.

So, what are some of the languages that can be used for Web development? In addition to the tools covered in this book (HTML, CSS, JavaScript, PHP, ASP, and JSP), many other languages may be used for Web development, including A, ActionScript, Ada 95, AppleScript, **C**, C++, CCI, CMM, Dylan, Eiffel, Fantom, GEL, Glyphic Script, Guile, HyperTalk, Icon, Java, jQuery, KQML, Linda, Lingo, Lisp, Logo, ML, Modula-3, NewtonScript, Obliq, **Perl**, **Python**, REXX, **Ruby**, ScriptX, SDI, Self, SiMPLE, SLOTH, Smalltalk, SMSL, Synergy, Tcl, Telescript, Tycoon, UserTalk, Viola, VBScript, WebScript, VRML, XHTML, and XML. This is by no means a complete list, but it gives you an idea of the extent of tools available for Web development. Each of the languages has its own unique features, advantages, and disadvantages. This book focuses on some of the most mature, proven, and popular tools for Web development.

Fear of Web Technology

Many business application developers who are experienced and comfortable with so-called legacy applications are a bit intimidated by the thought of coding an application using Web technology. Applications written in non-Web technology can also easily be written with Web technology. For intensive data entry tasks, it may be argued that non-Web applications are best. This is very debatable, however; a well-designed and well-coded Web application can be a great fit for intensive data entry needs. It is more likely the comfort level of a developer speaking rather than an unbiased opinion. Given that many younger programmers were exposed to Web-based applications at an early age and thus are comfortable with the technology, developer preference is shifting toward Web applications.

This doesn't necessarily mean you should rewrite all your non-Web applications using Web technology. Doing so isn't realistic or practical. For example, consider an organization that has a considerable investment in a non–Web-based ERP package with in-house add-on applications. It does not make sense to undertake rewriting the ERP package and its add-ons just for the sake of having a Web-based application. However, when you're already heavily enhancing or rewriting an application, developing a new one, or modernizing applications, don't fear the Web. (We discuss reusing legacy applications in chapter 7.)

There are many practical reasons to consider and employ Web technology for business applications. Business application development is changing and may one day be dominated by Web applications. It can even be argued that Web applications have already established dominance within the business environment.

While those new to business application development are likely to be already using Web tools, those who have been staff developers for years might consider Web development to be outside their comfort zone. If that description fits you, then it's time to step out of the box and expand your skills. Learning Web development isn't as scary as it might seem at first glance. As with any other technology, once you've learned Web development, used it, understand how it technically works, and are comfortable with it, you're off to the races.

We've met many developers over the years who have been exposed to Web development in a variety of ways. A classic example of the *wrong* way to introduce Web development is that a developer is tasked with creating a Web application and sent off to a Java class, with the expectation that he or she will return with the tools and knowledge needed to start pumping out code. This scenario isn't likely to have a successful outcome, and can even backfire, instilling in the developer a fear of Web application development. Java in itself is not scary. It is a very robust, powerful, and useful language. It is also, however, a complex language that takes time to learn.

In this book, we intentionally do not focus on a single technology; rather, our approach is to introduce and provide examples of combinations of tools, so that you can develop business applications upon completion of this book. If you are a bit afraid of Web development, we are confident that, upon finishing this book, you'll be over your fear and eager to use the tools you've learned.

Expanding Your Skill Set

With organizations becoming more global—expanding, merging, and changing—everyone needs to keep their skills updated. Should you be scared? Not at all. Being open to change and expanding skills is a fact of life.

Technology has changed significantly over the years in regard to development. It's amazing what has been accomplished. Business thrives on technology. Technology provides a framework for keeping a business running smoothly and provides opportunities to improve the business. Such opportunities can take the form of resource savings or other cost savings. They can also be take the form of fulfilling basic business requirements, including reaching others outside of an organization.

Not that long ago, it was possible to argue that the Web might be a short-term fad. Time has shown this is definitely not the case. The Web is here, it's bigger than ever, and it hasn't stopped growing. Similarly, not many years ago, it was unusual to have a PC at home connected to the Internet. Now, most households have some sort of Internet connectivity. In fact, individuals are introduced to computers and the Web at a very young age, resulting in a broader comfort with Web-based technology. Technology has changed rapidly, making it possible for almost anyone to have Internet access, almost anywhere. As a business application developer, this means if you intend to continue to advance in your career, you will need to include Web technology as a part of your skill set.

Where can you learn Web skills? Many learning resources and options exist. Some options are less expensive and time-consuming than others. There are many books and classes available on a variety of Web topics. Our experience, however, has been that most education sources focus on a specific segment of Web development and are not always based on the viewpoint of the business developer. Care has been taken in writing this book to focus on you, the business developer. Upon completing this book, you will have the tools you need to start coding business Web applications.

The Job Market

Today's **job market** still provides a place for legacy coders, but more often than not it requires the job-seeking developer to have Web skills. Most businesses have evolved significantly. Buyouts, consolidations, and global business infrastructures are commonplace today. The ever-present climate of change in the business world has had a significant impact on today's business application developers. Change is a constant within the business infrastructure, but don't be misled into thinking it is such a moving target that you cannot safely determine where your time is best spent in developing your skill set.

The future promises to be strong for IT job seekers with the right technical skill sets. The retirement of baby boomers, along with continuing business demand for skilled technology professionals, fuel a strong job market for developers. The aging IT population may spell trouble for some organizations in regard to their global competitiveness, as they lose veteran programmers to retirement. However, the need for programmers is good news for those who wish to move up within their IT departments or are new to the job market. The supply is down and the demand continues to grow for IT workers. Between 2012 and 2022, the Bureau of Labor Statistics projects employment for the industry, which already boasts more than 300,000 professionals, to grow 8.3 percent. The profession's strong expected growth (as well as high median salary) helped software developers and Web developers place well in ranking of *U.S. News & World Report*'s Best Jobs of 2016 (see *money.usnews.com/careers/best-jobs/rankings/the-100-best-jobs*).

Organizations are still investing in IT projects. The outlook for IT careers and demand for developers continues to be favorable. The trends show a strong need for business analysts and developers. Salaries for IT professionals have increased significantly in recent years. According to *Forbes*, the value and demand for experts who can help businesses keep up with the rapid pace of technology will grow with the exponential pace of tech innovation (see *www.securityinfowatch.com/article/12050413/ rapid-technology-advancements-in-security-may-out-pace-users*). The competition for tech talent is fiercer than ever.

Organizations are continuing to Web-enable their existing applications and to pursue Web-based solutions, making Web-based skills very hot. Business developers with Web skills including Ajax, Java, .NET, JavaScript, HTML, and PHP are in high demand. According to Business Insider (see *www.businessinsider.com/programming-languages-in-highest-demand-2016-1*), some of the popular programming languages that can help you land a job include Java, PHP, Perl, C, JavaScript, .NET, Ruby, Python, CSS, and HTML.

Business knowledge is important as organizations strive to align IT services with the businesses they support. Demand remains strong for application developers with business-specific knowledge and system analysis skills. Organizations also want developers who are familiar with the entire software development life cycle and are well rounded in terms of leadership and communication skills. Organizations are looking for individuals with broader sets of development skills.

Today's business market is global. The Web and technology have played an important role in global markets. Even small organizations are affected by the globalization of business. The Web has made it possible for both large and small businesses to expand their reach to a very distant base of clients.

Outsourcing

Outsourcing is commonplace today within the business environment. The intent of introducing this topic is not to debate the advantages and disadvantages of outsourcing. As a business developer, you should simply be aware of it.

Organizations look at outsourcing for several reasons. One reason might be budget considerations. Another reason might be that available in-house resources do not have the required skills to complete a project. When an organization makes the decision to take applications to the Web, if the necessary skills aren't available to the organization, outsourcing may well be considered. If you are an experienced staff business developer, contractor, or someone just getting your feet wet in business development, having the appropriate skills to fit business needs will improve your career prospects. The fact that you are reading this book shows you have the desire to advance your skills.

The topic of outsourcing is controversial. Outsourcing opponents' claims that IT jobs are being shipped in droves offshore are usually exaggerated. The conclusion for most organizations that track such statistics is about five percent of all IT jobs have been displaced by foreign workers. Most of these are lower-level coding jobs, technical support positions, or call center work. The jobs requiring more advanced skills are likely to remain within an organization. Skills that will be in declining demand in the near future are routine coding and systems testing, application maintenance, technical support, data continuity, and data recovery. These skills are among the jobs that are being increasingly outsourced and offshored. IT jobs related to customer service and helping a business grow tend to remain within an organization. Organizations are coming to the realization that it takes a lot of work in interfacing and managing projects to have outsourcing work effectively.

Outsourcing doesn't necessarily mean the resource will be overseas. Outsourcing may also include consultants and independent contractors. Technology advancements in Wi-Fi connectivity, security, and improvements in remote connections have made it possible to connect to a remote server from almost anywhere at any time. The improvements have opened up opportunities for employees and contractors to work remotely. Although not everyone is cut out for working remotely, and it may not be a fit for all organizations, a remote workforce is another possible resource.

What does this mean to you as a business developer? It is important that your skill set is advanced and fits the industry's needs. This, of course, includes Web development skills. It also means that as a business developer, you may also want to consider a career as a consultant.

Summary

We have covered a lot of information within this chapter and hope it has inspired you to think through some of the considerations that affect you as a business developer. You can do what you set your sights on, if you really want to. The stronger the desire, the more successful you will likely be. Taking the first step is essential. This book will help make that first step into Web development much easier. If you already have some Web development knowledge, you'll benefit from this book as well. We've made an effort to present information here that will reduce the time you spend learning and prepare you as quickly and efficiently as possible to code a business Web application.

Key Terms

Ajax	hardware	server-side scripting
application design and graphics	HTML	smartphone
application logic	iPad	SOA
browser-based application	IT staff	SOAP
business programming	Java	software
C	JavaScript	tablet
C++	job market	tags
CGI	legacy	UDDI
client	non-traditional devices	VB.NET
client-based	operating system	Web application
client-side scripting	organization size	Web browser
CSS	other languages	Web client
database	outsourcing	Web development
development process	PDA	Web page
development standards	Perl	Web server
devices	PHP	Web service
DOM	platform	Wi-Fi
dynamic business applications	Python	WSDL
end tag	RPG	XML
handheld devices	Ruby	

Discussion/Review Questions

1.   What is a browser-based application?
2.   What programming languages are commonly used for Web-based business applications?
3.   What is the development process?
4.   What databases are used for Web-based business applications?
5.   What is HTML?
6.   What is a client?
7.   What is a browser?
8.   What is a Web server?
9.   What are the differences in an IT staff structure within a small, medium, and large organization?
10.   Research and provide examples of some of the common platforms used for Web-based business application development.
11.   What types of devices are used for Web-based business applications?
12.   What is Ajax?
13.   What is SOA?
14.   What is a Web service?
15.   What are some of the languages used for Web development?
16.   What is the difference between legacy and modern applications?
17.   What is the job market potential for a Web application developer? What are some of the considerations for a career as a Web developer?
18.   Does outsourcing have an impact on the Web application development market? Why?
19.   What is the difference between client-side and server-side scripting? How are each used?

Exercises

1.   Develop a list of common tools used for business Web application development.
2.   Provide an example of a business Web application that makes use of a client-side and server-side application.
3.   Investigate and provide information about the current job market and future job market outlook for Web application developers. Cite reference information sources.
4.   Research and create a list of databases used for business Web applications. Rank the databases in order by usage.
5.   Create a list of available Web browsers and rank in order by usage.

CHAPTER 2

An Introduction to HTML

Why should you, as a business programmer, take the time to learn HTML? What is it all about, anyway? In this chapter, you will find the answers to those questions, as you learn the basics of this standard language for building Web pages.

Why Learn HTML?

HTML is the *lingua franca* of the Web. It is the common tongue of the Web that is understood by all computers and devices on the planet. While it's true that other tools are available for creating Web pages, every website that you visit today is written in HTML. It is almost inconceivable that a programmer could deploy a browser-based application without using HTML at some point in the process.

HTML is a relatively simple language to learn. These days anyone can publish anything on the Web without even having to really learn HTML. As a result, programmers who do not continue to update their skills risk professional obsolescence.

Generally, there are different dimensions to computer languages, such as compiled versus interpreted, low-level versus high-level, and general versus specific. Although one could argue that HTML is not truly a programming language, it is an interpreted, high-level, and specific language. In case you hadn't noticed, our industry is in the midst of a huge transition. In the past, many business applications were written and customized to run on a particular platform, using the language most common to that platform: COBOL on mainframes, Visual Basic on Windows, C++ on UNIX, and RPG on IBM. All these languages are optimized for the environments in which they run. By definition, however, they are tied to that specific environment. Porting one of these applications to another platform or deploying it in a different way is a serious challenge.

Well, that answers half the question. Learning something is necessary, but why HTML? As mentioned, HTML is the most common language used in browser-based application development. It is platform independent. That means that no matter what type of platform a Web page was created on, the page can be rendered by any browser running on any operating system.

What Is HTML All About?

HTML is the acronym for **Hypertext Markup Language**. Hypertext refers to the ability to create links to other Web pages. Markup means it's used for creating pages of formatted text, images, and other resources embedded in the page. HTML was created by Tim Berners-Lee in 1990. He also invented the term "World Wide Web" and the first Web browser, and went on to found the World Wide Web Consortium, also known as the **W3C**. Among other things, the W3C acts as a shepherd watching over the development of Web technologies. It provides guidelines, standards, recommendations, and education on many aspects of Web-related technology. You can find out more about the W3C at *www.w3c.org*.

Perhaps the most fundamental guideline that the W3C produces is the HTML specification document found at *www.w3.org/TR/2014/PR-html5-20140916/*. This document provides information about the HTML language and recommendations as to its correct usage. While these guidelines in no way prevent developers from coding as they like, it is wise to be aware of them. As the language continues to evolve, changes could make the code obsolete in Web pages you have written. For example, the W3C guidelines indicate which HTML language elements are *deprecated*. Deprecated features remain in the standard, but with the understanding that they might be removed in the future. At the very least, their use is discouraged. Since many existing pages contain these deprecated elements, we'll cover them here. Review the W3C guidelines for clear documentation on this issue.

HTML5

Several major revisions of the HTML standard have been endorsed by the W3C since its founding in the early 1990s. At the time this book was written, **HTML5** was the official successor to HTML4 and replaced XHTML. A bonus feature for HTML5 is that it is backward compatible. Features of both HTML4 and XHTML were incorporated into HTML5, in addition to its own set of new elements and features. In a nutshell, HTML5 provides standards-based development technologies for modern Web 2.0 applications with highly visual effects and user interactions. This chapter introduces you to the syntax of HTML5. The sample Web pages and HTML codes used throughout the rest of this book are based solely on the HTML5 standard.

A Basic HTML Page

HTML coding is based on a set of markup symbols placed in an HTML document or Web page. These markup symbols identify **structural elements** or **tags** that tell a Web browser (and other user agents) how to render and display a Web page. A Web page is a plain-text file that consists of only text and HTML elements.

Each tag has a meaning and serves a very specific purpose, with the exception of the <div> tag, which we will discuss later in this chapter. Thus, HTML is often referred to as a *semantic* language because tags describe the document content. In the next chapter, we will learn Cascading Style Sheets (CSS), which is the *presentational* language of the Web.

Each HTML tag is enclosed in angle brackets, the less-than (<) and greater-than (>) signs, as you've just seen above with the <div> tag. Most tags come in pairs: a start tag and an end tag. The content is encapsulated by the start and end tags. Tags that come in pairs are sometimes referred to as *container tags*. The syntax of a container tag looks like this:

```
<tagname>Content</tagname>
```

The *tagname* is the name of the element, and *Content* is the content of the element. Consider the following example:

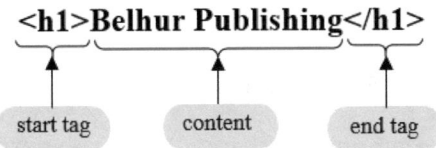

The <h1> tag is one of six heading tags that will be explained in more detail later in this chapter. The <h1> is called the start tag, and the </h1> is called the end tag. The text that is between the container tags is what would be displayed on a browser. The <h1> tag signals the browser that the text that follows appears larger and darker than the default text, as shown here:

Belhur Publishing

The end tag always starts with a forward slash. The forward slash in the </h1> tag indicates that this tag ends the previous <h1> tag. Any content placed outside of these container tags will not be affected.

There is a major distinction between the start tag and end tag. In the next few sections, you'll learn that every HTML **element** can include attributes that modify and describe the function of the element. For example, the **attribute** lang in <html lang="en"> denotes the spoken language for the document. Attributes can only be included in the start tag, not in the end tag. In fact, white spaces or other characters or symbols are not permitted in the end tag, except for the name of the HTML tag.

Tags that do not come in pairs are often called empty, self-contained, or single-sided tags. They are referred to as *void elements* in HTML5. For example, a <br/> is an empty tag that configures a line break on a Web page. Empty tags can be coded with or without the forward slash: **
** or **
**. Notice the forward slash in an empty tag, which must come immediately before the close angle bracket, not before the tag name. The forward slash is only used for backward compatibility and is optional in HTML5. In this book, we will always use a forward slash to terminate an empty tag.

Let's start learning HTML by looking at a very basic Web page. Consider the simple Web page shown in Figure 2.1.

Figure 2.1: A simple Web page

Any HTML novice could create this simple Web page. Its code is shown in Figure 2.2. This is the complete source code to display the basic HTML5 Web page template (found in the downloadable files on the book's Web page at *https://goo.gl/2uYjHb*, in the folder *chapter2/template*.html). The name of a static HTML document usually ends with the extension *.html* or *.htm*, as in *template.html*. The word *static*, as opposed to *dynamic*, refers to the fact that HTML documents are stateless. A static Web page cannot retain its values when a browser reloads it. We will revisit stateless and dynamic Web pages later when we learn Web development using server-side languages such as PHP, ASP.NET, and JSP. Throughout the rest of this chapter and the subsequent chapters leading to chapter 8, we will work with only static HTML documents.

HTML is a very flexible language and not case-sensitive. This means that even if you code your Web page with errors, the browser will still render and display the page correctly to the end user. Nevertheless, we will follow the convention to use lowercase letters for all HTML tags (with the exception of <!DOCTYPE html>, as shown in Figure 2.2).

```
<!DOCTYPE html>
<html>
    <head>
        <title>Belhur Publishing</title>
        <meta charset="utf-8" />
    </head>
<body>
    <h1>Belhur Publishing</h1>

    . . .

    <footer>&copy;2016.  Belhur Publishing, LLC.  All rights reserved.</
footer>
</body>
</html>
```

Figure 2.2: The HTML5 code for the page shown in Figure 2.1

As shown in Figure 2.2, every Web page you create will usually contain these six HTML elements: **DOCTYPE**, html, head, title, meta, and body. The first seven lines and the last two lines will usually be common throughout all Web pages. A Web page is divided into three major sections: **doctype declaration**, head, and body. In the next section, we will explore each of these sections and what each of these tags mean.

DOCTYPE tag:

```
<!DOCTYPE html>
```

Line 1 of the code in Figure 2.2 contains the <!DOCTYPE html> tag. It's called the doctype declaration, or DTD statement. DTD stands for **document type definition**, which is a W3C standard for identifying a Web document. It defines the doctype declaration section, and it's the first statement in every Web page. The exclamation mark (!) at the beginning of the tag name is required. As HTML tags are not case-sensitive, it's only a convention that the DTD statement uses all uppercase letters for the word DOCYTYPE and lowercase letters for the word html. Thus <!DOCTYPE HTML>, <!doctype html>, or <!Doctype Html> will work just as well. Also, this is the only self-contained tag that we won't use a forward slash with, as we did with the <br/> tag earlier.

As we've already learned that there are multiple versions of HTML, there are also multiple versions of Web browsers—and not all browsers support HTML5. However, at the time this book was written, most modern Web browsers were capable of rendering HTML5 elements. Thus, the DTD statement is required to identify the HTML version contained in the document for the browsers to render the Web page correctly. The *html* identifies the HTML version used in the document. HTML5 documents require only this short DTD statement: <!DOCTYPE html>.

There's one important reason why <!DOCTYPE html> should be coded as the first statement of a modern Web page. This has to do with how the layout engine of Web browsers displays a Web page using **quirks mode** and **strict mode** (aka s*tandard mode*). Back in the 1990s, most websites were written to work with two dominant Web browsers: Netscape and Internet Explorer (IE). Each Web browser had its own set of standards until W3C was formed to set a more common set of standards for all Web browsers. Thus, quirks mode refers to the legacy standards set by Netscape and IE. Standard mode follows the modern HTML and CSS specifications set by W3C. A Web page developed with quirks mode does not have a doctype declaration as its first HTML tag. Thus, any HTML code placed above the <!DOCYTPYE html> declaration will trigger quirks mode, which may cause the Web page to be rendered incorrectly in most modern browsers.

If you choose to code your Web page with an earlier version of HTML (such as XHTML or HTML4), you will need to code the correct doctype statement. Following is an incomplete list of DTD statements that a programmer must use to identify the HTML version used in a Web page. As you review these DTD statements, we hope that you will appreciate the much simpler doctype for HTML5.

XHTML 1.0 Strict:

```
<!DOCTYPE html PUBLIC "-//W3C//DTD XHTML 1.0 Strict//EN" "http://www.w3.org/TR/xhtml1/DTD/
xhtml1-strict.dtd">
```

XHTML 1.0 Transitional:

```
<!DOCTYPE html PUBLIC "-//W3C//DTD XHTML 1.0 Transitional//EN" "http://www
.w3.org/TR/xhtml1/DTD/xhtml1-transitional.dtd">
```

HTML 4.01 Strict:

```
<!DOCTYPE HTML PUBLIC "-//W3C//DTD HTML 4.01//EN" "http://www.w3.org/TR/html4/strict.dtd">
```

HTML 4.01 Transitional:

```
<!DOCTYPE HTML PUBLIC "-//W3C//DTD HTML 4.01 Transitional//EN" "http://www
.w3.org/TR/html4/loose.dtd">
```

HTML tag:

```
<html lang="en">
</html>
```

Line 2 of the code in Figure 2.2 contains the **<html>** tag. This is a container tag and instructs the browser that the text after it is HTML code. Since browsers must be able to process data written in many different languages, Web pages typically identify their primary language at the beginning of the code. A matching </html> as the last line in Figure 2.2 ends the source code. As mentioned earlier, the main purpose of the lang attribute is to denote the primary spoken language for the Web page. The values for the lang attribute are either a two-letter subcode (ISO 639-1) or a two-letter subcode followed by the ISO country code. For example, lang="en" (for English) identifies English as the primary language, lang="en-US" as U.S. English, lang="fr" as French, and so on. By default, the lang attribute is set to English and therefore is not required to be defined explicitly. Other purposes for using the lang attribute are for search engines and screen readers. The lang attribute is not restricted to only the <html> tag but can also be included in other tags.

HTML elements can be nested inside other elements. As illustrated in Figure 2.2, the **<title>** and <meta> tags are nested within the **<head>** container tags, the <h1> and **<footer>** tags are nested within the **<body>** container tags, and all these tags are nested within the <html> container tags. While most HTML elements can be nested inside other elements, there are some elements that can't be nested or the page will break. We will explore these tags later in this chapter.

Head tag:

```
<head>
</head>
```

Line 3 of the code in Figure 2.2 contains the <head> tag that begins the **head section**, and ends with the </head> tag in line 6 of the code. The <head> container tags must be placed after the </html> tag and the <body> tag. The head section contains elements that describe the Web document. Typical elements that are contained inside the head section include title, meta, link, and script. These elements are not visible or useful to the user but are crucial to user agents such as screen readers and search engines. The <title> and <meta> tags are discussed next, while <link> and <script> are discussed later in this chapter.

Title tag:

<title>Belhur Publishing</title>

Line 4 of the code in Figure 2.2 contains the <title> container tags. Every Web page should have a page title. The <title> element is required for an HTML5 document. The text between the <title> and </title> tags is used as the title of the Web page. The <title> tag configures the text to be displayed in the title bar or tab of the browser window but not in the browser window, also called the browser viewport. For example, let's look at the title page of our Web page template in Figure 2.2.

Figure 2.3 shows the page title in the title bar of the window containing the Web page template, as viewed with Microsoft Edge, Google Chrome, and Mozilla Firefox.

Figure 2.3: Examples of a page title in a Web page's title bar in Microsoft Edge, Google Chrome, and Mozilla Firefox

---

Meta tag:

<meta charset="utf-8"/>

Line 5 of the code in Figure 2.2 contains the <meta> tag. The <meta> tag is a self-contained tag and describes the characteristic of a Web page. For example, the attribute charset="utf-8" describes the **character encoding** using the 8-bit Unicode Transformation Format (UTF), which is the preferred encoding for Web pages and email. There are many other types of meta tags, such as description, keywords, author, robot, and refresh.

The <meta> tag is extremely important for search engine optimization (SEO) because it provides information about the Web page to browsers and Web crawlers. A *crawler* or *e-bot* is software used by search engines such as Yahoo! and Google to systematically crawl and examine the content of Web pages on the Internet. Crawlers evaluate and index these Web pages for inclusion in search engines.

Crawlers are constantly scouring the Internet, examining page after page. The <meta> tags in your Web page can affect your placement within these search engines. You'll learn more about search engines and SEO in chapter 13. The <meta> tags' usefulness is subject to change as the Internet continues to evolve. Tags that were useful last year might not be useful this year, and ones we don't use today might become useful next year. It's an area that needs periodic reevaluation.

Body tag:

```
<body>
</body>
```

Line 7 of the code in Figure 2.2 contains the <body> tag. The <body> tag marks the beginning of the **body section** of the Web page and ends with the matching end </body> tag, which appears immediately before the </html> tag at the end of the source code in line 11. The <body> container tags must be placed after the </head> tag and </html> tag. The body section contains displayable content such as text, images, and multimedia. Everything visible on the browser window is contained in the body section, and it is in the body section that a programmer will spend the most time writing code.

Comment tag:

```
<!-- This is a comment... -->
```

Comments are an important feature for any language, and HTML is no exception. You will find that comments are particularly useful in clarifying the more complex, less intuitive portions of your Web pages. Comments are not intended to be displayed on the Web browser window. Comment tags start with the <!-- tag and end with the --> tag. Any content contained within the comment tags is ignored by the browser. While comment tags can be inserted anywhere within your document, they should only be placed within the <html> tags to prevent some Web browsers from going into quirks mode. For example, the following code snippet inserts three comments in three different areas of a Web page, shown in Figure 2.4.

```
<!DOCTYPE html>
<html>
  <!-- This is the Index page of our website -->
  <head>
     <!-- This is the head section -->
     <meta charset="utf-8"/>
     <title>Belhur Publishing</title>
  </head>
                                              Continued
```

```
<!-- This is the body section. This is where all visible content
     Should be placed. -->
<body>

   .

   .

</body> </html>
```

Figure 2.4: The HTML code for the comment tag

Congratulations! You've just learned the basic structure of a Web page and the necessary requirements for creating a valid HTML5 document. Next, we'll explore some of the many HTML elements used to develop a more robust and content-rich Web-based application.

Block-Level and Text-Level Elements

HTML elements are categorized by the W3C into seven broad categories: metadata, flow, sectioning, phrasing, embedded, interactive, and heading. There are other categories that are used for specific purposes. Then there are some that do not fit into any particular category at all. Even though these elements are categorized into their particular categories, you'll see that many of them also belong to the same group based on how they affect the appearance of the Web page. Next, we're going to learn about the two major element group classifications: block-level and text-level.

Block-Level Elements

The first group of elements is called *grouping* or *block-level elements*. Most block-level elements come in pairs and contain content that is viewed as a distinct block within the Web page. This group of elements starts their content on a new line. Table 2.1 lists some of the block-level elements that are commonly used in a Web page.

Table 2.1: Block-level Elements	
Element	**Description**
p	A paragraph
hr	A horizontal rule to separate topics within a section
pre	A block of preformatted text (usually displayed in a fixed-width font, and all white space and special characters are retained)
blockquote	Content quoted from another source (indented from left and right margins)
h1, h2, h3, h4, h5, h6	Heading elements with a given rank number (h1 has highest rank, and h6 has the lowest rank)
div	A division useful for stylistic purposes or wrapping multiple paragraphs within a section
ol	A list of ordered items
ul	A list of unordered items
li	A list item from an ordered or unordered list
dl	A description list (formerly a definition list)
dt	A definition term, name, or part of a term-description group in a description list

Table 2.1: Block-level Elements (continued)	
Element	Description
dd	A definition, description, or value from a description list
address	Contact information for author or owner (text is usually rendered in italics)

Let's explore some of the common block-level elements and see how they are rendered by the Web browser.

Heading tags:

```
<h1>content</h1>
```

The heading elements come in six levels and contain the text of the main headings on a Web page. They define the text within the tags from the heaviest weighted or largest heading (<h1>) to the smallest or lightest heading (<h6>). Each Web browser has some control over the actual size of text displayed, so that users with limited eyesight, for example, can define their preferred size of text. Web developers refer to a "logical" size of text. Rather than specifying an exact size, such as 12 pixels (or 12px), the developer indicates a relative size, such as h1 (big), h3 (medium), or h6 (small). Although heading tags can be used to configure text to be big and bold, they should not be used for that purpose. Instead, you should use them for headings only, so that search engines can properly index your Web pages. Figure 2.5 shows the various heading levels, h1 through h6.

Figure 2.5: Examples of <h1> through <h6> headings

Paragraph tag:

```
<p>content</p>
```

Paragraph tags are block-level elements and are very important. If the browser can recognize a section of text as a paragraph, it can better render the text onto a page. The content that is contained within the **<p>** and </p> tags is displayed as a block with empty spaces above and below it. For example, without paragraph tags, you must explicitly code line breaks between paragraphs.

By default, all text is left justified. To force the alignment of the text to left, right, or center, you use the align attribute. For example, to center-align the text of a paragraph, you would use the align="center" attribute. Note that the align attribute is deprecated in HTML5. In the next chapter, you will learn how text alignments can be set more efficiently using CSS.

The code sample in Figure 2.6 shows text from a sample Web page written to use paragraph tags. The result, shown in Figure 2.7, is rendered in a Web browser.

```
<p>Belhur Publishing takes pride in providing learning solutions for
students and those who want to advance their Web development skills. First
steps are important, and we have taken great care in offering materials,
education, and inspiration to assist individuals to move forward and
learn.</p>

<p>Our primary customer base includes educational institutions,
individuals, and organizations wanting to further their growth in
technology-based Web development careers.</p>

<p>Established in 2015 in collaboration with Christian Hur, Laura Ubelhor,
and MC Press.</p>
```

Figure 2.6: HTML code for a sample page with paragraph tags

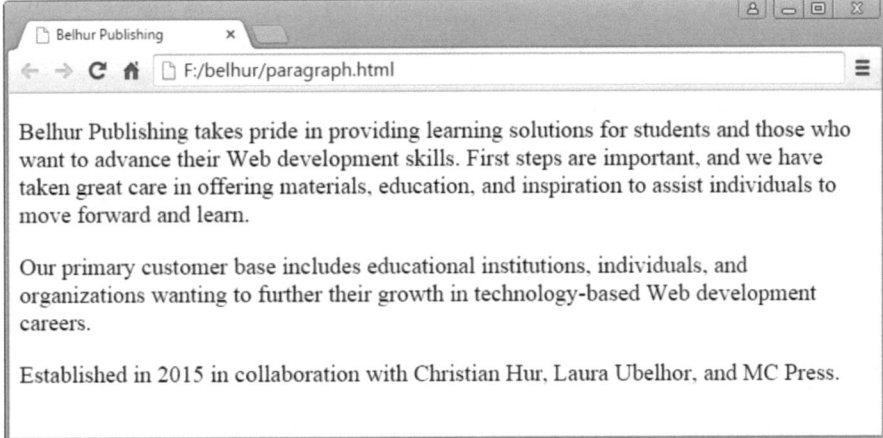

Figure 2.7: A sample page rendered in a Web browser with paragraph tags

---

Preformatted tag:

<pre>content</pre>

Preformatted text is placed between the **<pre>** and </pre> tags. This tag overrides the browser's ability to compress white space and blank lines as it sees fit. Any white space and carriage returns included between the tags are preserved by the browser when the Web page is displayed. For things such as addresses or sets of data that have specific formatting, the <pre> tag can be quite useful. The code sample in Figure 2.8 shows text from a sample Web page written to use <pre> tags. The result, shown in Figure 2.9, is rendered in a Web browser.

```
<p>Belhur Publishing takes pride in providing learning solutions for
students and those who want to advance their Web development skills. First
steps are important, and we have taken great care in offering materials,
education, and inspiration to assist individuals to move forward and
learn.</p>

<pre>Our primary customer base includes educational institutions,
            individuals, and organizations wanting to further their
                growth in technology-based Web development careers.</pre>

<p>Established in 2015 in collaboration with Christian Hur, Laura Ubelhor,
and MC Press.</p>
```

Figure 2.8: HTML code for a sample page with <pre> tags

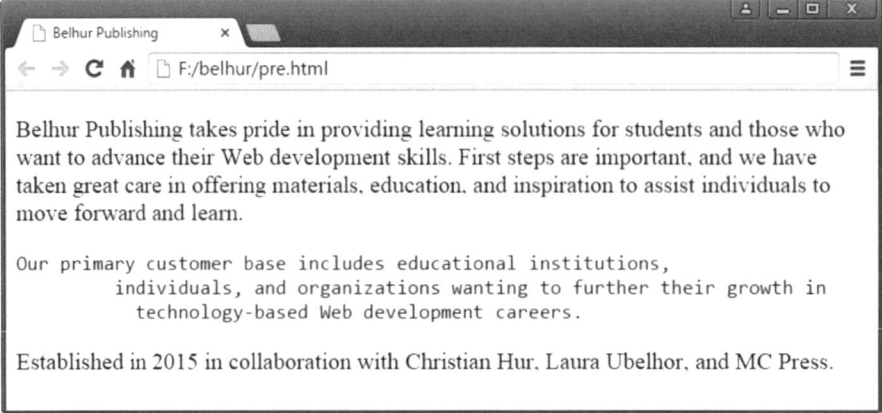

Figure 2.9: A sample page rendered on a Web browser with <pre> tags

---

Horizontal rule tag:

<hr/>

The **<hr>** tag is a self-contained tag that simply draws a line, or rule, across the Web page. The width attribute defines how far across the page the line should extend. The value for width can be expressed either in pixels or as a percentage of the page width. The align attribute determines whether the line is centered, left justified, or right justified. The align attribute is deprecated in HTML5; instead, alignment is controlled by CSS rules. The size attribute determines the line's thickness in pixels, and pixels only. The noshade attribute removes the 3D effect from the line, resulting in a "flatter" look. The code snippet in Figure 2.10 shows the HTML code needed to create the three horizontal lines, shown in Figure 2.11.

```
<hr/>
<hr width = 80% />
<hr width = 50% size=4 noshade />
```

Figure 2.10: The HTML code to create two horizontal rules

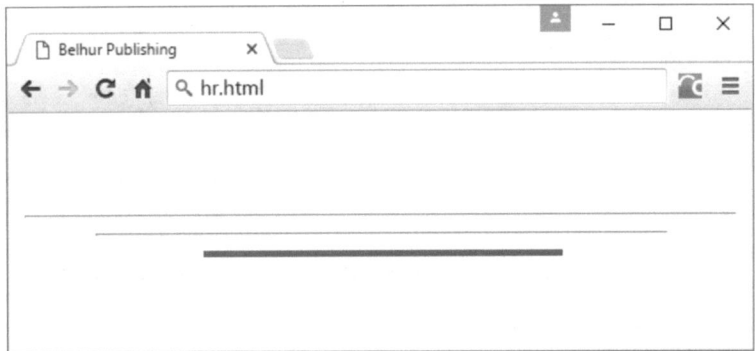

Figure 2.11: The horizontal rules

You can use <hr> to add some structure to a Web page, by defining different sections.

Blockquote tags:

```
<blockquote>content</blockquote>
```

To define a section of text as a quotation to a Web page, use the **<blockquote>** tag. The <blockquote> tag is used to display a block of quoted text indented from both the left and right margins of the Web page. Let's use the same code snippet in Figure 2.8 and replace the second <p> tags with the <blockquote> tags. The code snippet in Figure 2.12 uses these tags to produce the output shown in Figure 2.13.

```
<p>Belhur Publishing takes pride in providing learning solutions for
students and those who want to advance their Web development skills. First
steps are important, and we have taken great care in offering materials,
education, and inspiration to assist individuals to move forward and
learn.</p>
```
                                                                      Continued

```
<blockquote>Our primary customer base includes educational institutions,
individuals, and organizations wanting to further their growth in
technology-based Web development careers.</blockquote>

<p>Established in 2015 in collaboration with Christian Hur, Laura Ubelhor,
and MC Press.</p>
```

Figure 2.12: HTML <blockquote> code

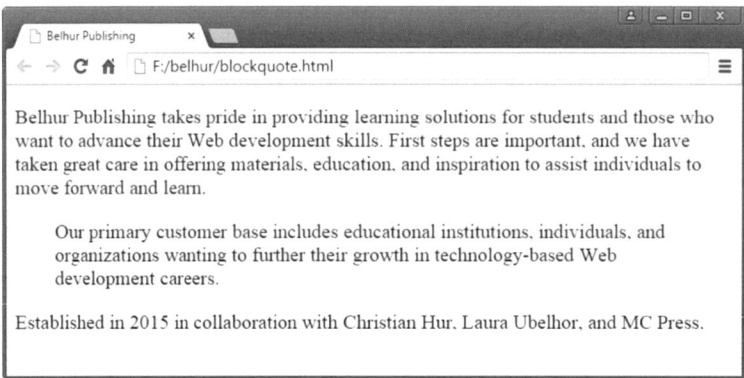

Figure 2.13: A sample Web page that uses the <blockquote> tags

Unordered list and list item tags:

```
<ul>
  <li>content</li>
  <li>content</li>
  ...
</ul>
```

Unordered lists are commonly referred to as bullets. Unordered list tags are used to display a list of items in no significant order. Unordered lists begin with the **<ul>** tag and end with the closing </ul> tag. Each item is contained within the **<li>** and </li> tags. The list can be displayed as one of three types: disc (the default), square, and circle. To change the default type to a square or circle, insert the type attribute within the <ul> tag. The HTML code in Figure 2.14 generates the catalog text shown in Figure 2.15.

```
<h2>Our New Books:</h2>

<ul>

    <li>Web Services for Everyone</li>
    <li>PHP Hot Scripts</li>
    <li>The IBM i Programmer's Guide to PHP</li>
```
Continued

```
        <li>jQuery Uplifts Your Web Application</li>
    </ul>

    <h2>More Cool Books:</h2>

    <ul type="square">
        <li>How to Make a Great Website</li>
        <li>Advanced ASP.NET Programming</li>
        <li>Application Design 101</li>
    </ul>
```

Figure 2.14: The HTML code to create Figure 2.15

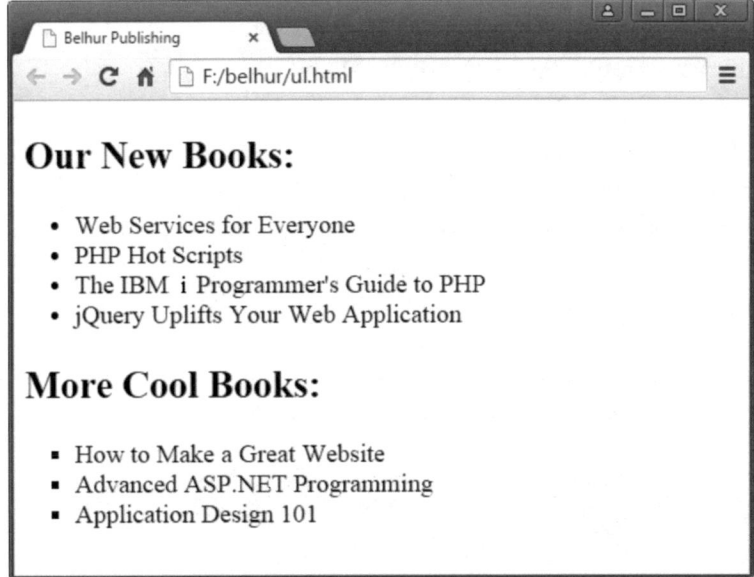

Figure 2.15: An example of an unordered list

Ordered list and list item tags:

```
<ol>
   <li>content</li>
   <li>content</li>
   ...
</ol>
```

Sometimes, bullets are not appropriate for the items you're listing. Yes, they worked fine for the catalog shown in Figure 2.15, but what if we had a series of instructions to follow in a specific sequence? This type of requirement is where an **ordered list** shines. Ordered lists are used to list items in an organized order. Both unordered and ordered lists use the <li> tags to list items. Each item is contained within the <li> and </li> tags. The ordered lists can be itemized using numerals (the default), lowercase letters, uppercase letters, lowercase Roman numerals, or uppercase Roman numerals. The valid values for the type attribute are 1, a, A, i, and I. The start attribute sets the beginning value for the type attribute. The valid value for the start attribute is always numeric, even if the type is not. For example, a value of 2 for start yields "b" for type a, "ii" for type i, and so on.

Figure 2.16 shows the same items in Figure 2.14 with ordered lists. The resulting lists are shown in Figure 2.17.

```
<h2>Our New Books:</h2>
<ol>
    <li>Web Services for Everyone</li>
    <li>PHP Hot Scripts</li>
    <li>The IBM i Programmer's Guide to PHP</li>
    <li>jQuery Uplifts Your Web Application</li>
</ol>
<h2>More Cool Books:</h2>
<ol type="A" start=3>
    <li>How to Make a Great Website</li>
    <li>Advanced ASP.NET Programming</li>
    <li>Application Design 101</li>
</ol>
```

Figure 2.16: The HTML code to create Figure 2.17

Figure 2.17: An example of an ordered list

As you can see in this example, the list automatically starts at 1 and increments by one. There are only a few supported options. If you need something else, you can create it manually using the value attribute of the <li> tag. For example, to number the items by twos (silly, but it's just an example), see Figure 2.18. The value attribute is similar to the start attribute, in that the number represents the sequence of a specific value in a list. In a lowercase alphabetical list, 2 represents "b," not the number 2.

```
<ol>
    <li value="2">Web Services for Everyone</li>
    <li value="4">PHP Hot Scripts</li>
    <li value="6">The IBM i Programmer's Guide to PHP</li>
    <li value="8">jQuery Uplifts Your Web Application</li>
</ol>
```

Figure 2.18: An ordered list with specific numeric values

Description list, term, and description tags:

```
<dl>
    <dt>Term1</dt>
    <dd>Definition1</dd>
    <dt>Term2</dt>
    <dd>Definition2</dd>
      ...
</dl>
```

The third type of list is the **description list** (formerly definition list). It is designed for assigning a definition or description to a list of terms. Obviously, this is useful if you are publishing a dictionary, but where else does it work? In our example Web page, we might want to add a description of some important terms. The code to do that is shown in Figure 2.19, and the resulting Web page in Figure 2.20.

```
<h2>HTML Elements:</h2>
<dl>
    <dt>html</dt>
    <dd>The html element represents the root of an HTML document.</dd>
    <dt>body</dt>
    <dd>The body element represents the content of the document.</dd>
    <dt>header</dt>
    <dd>The header element represents introductory content and typically
contains a group of introductory or navigational aids.</dd>
    <dt>footer</dt>
    <dd>A footer typically contains information about its section such as
who wrote it, links to related documents, copyright data, and the like.</dd>
</dl>
```

Figure 2.19: The HTML code for a description list

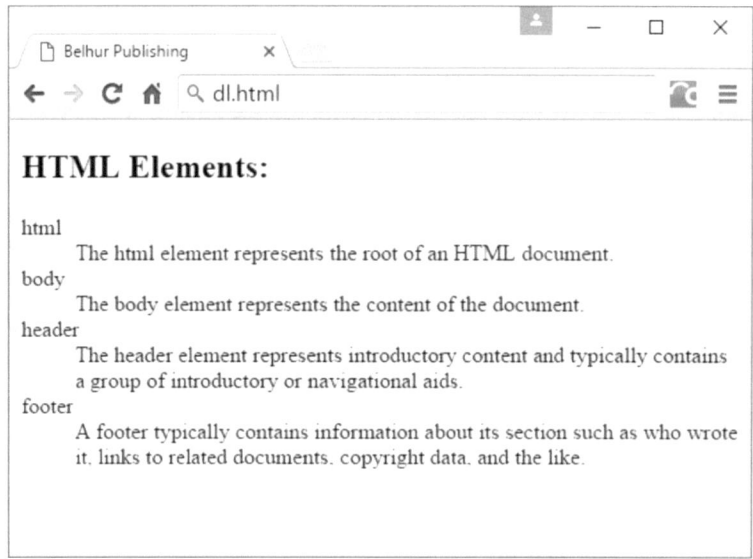

Figure 2.20: An example of a definition list

The browser aligns and positions text in lists as well as it can, depending on a variety of factors, such as screen resolution and window size. In a large window, the descriptions shown in Figure 2.20 flow across the entire screen. If the window size shrinks, the browser will shorten the width of the page and add more lines if needed.

Text-Level Elements

The second group of elements is called text-level or inline elements. This group of elements does not start out on a new line, but instead flows inline with the rest of the characters in the block-level elements. Table 2.2 lists some of these text-level elements.

Table 2.2: Text-Level Elements	
Element	Description
abbr	An abbreviation or acronym
em	Indicates emphasized text (usually displayed in italics)
cite	A reference to a creative work (usually displayed in italics)
code	A fragment of computer code
mark	Text that is highlighted for reference purposes
span	Group or markup inline elements or content for styling and configuration
sub	A subscript
sup	A superscript
strong	Strong importance or seriousness for its contents
b	Bold text
i	Renders text in italics

Subscript and superscript tags:

```
<sub>
</sub>
<sup>
</sup>
```

The subscript (**<sub>**) and superscript (**<sup>**) tags allow you to deal with things such as exponential notation and footnotes. The code snippet in Figure 2.21 shows how to use these tags to create the output shown in Figure 2.22.

```
<p>The sum of (x<sup>2</sup> + 2x<sup>2</sup>) is 3x<sup>2</sup></p>
<p>Today's temperature is 67<sup>o</sup>F.</p>
<p>The chemical formula for water is H<sub>2</sub>O.</p>
```

Figure 2.21: HTML code using the superscript and subscript tags

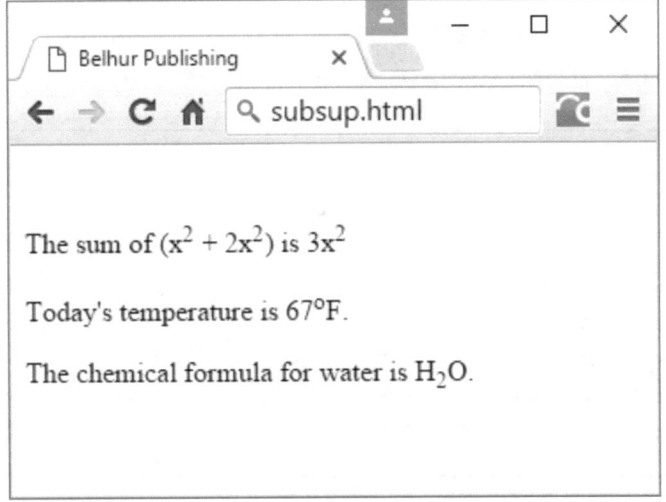

Figure 2.22: The result of the <sub> and <sup> tags

Italics, underline, and bold tags:

```
<i>content</i>
<u>content</u>
<b>content</b>
```

Use the <i>, <u>, and <b> tags to create text that is italicized, underlined, or bold. These are inline-level tags and can be used to mark up a group of text without causing the line of text to break. For example, you can use them in the short code snippet shown in Figure 2.23 to produce the result in Figure 2.24.

```
<p><b>Belhur Publishing</b> - your <u>ultimate</u> source for
<i>technical</i> publications.</p>
```

Figure 2.23: The HTML <b>, <u>, and <i> tags

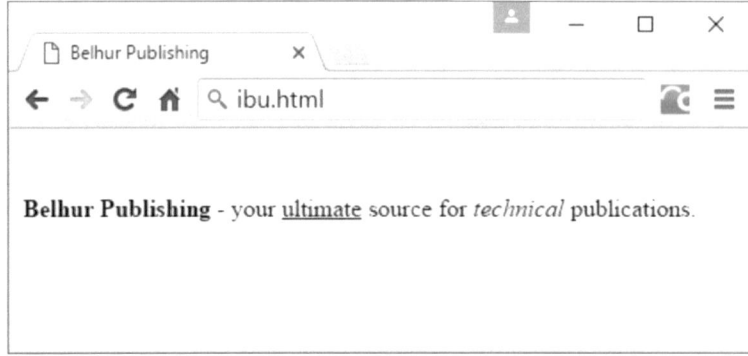

Figure 2.24: The result of the <b>, <u>, and <i> tags

These tags are deprecated in HTML5 and should only be used as a last resort. Instead, you should use CSS rules, as you'll learn in the next chapter.

Line Break tag:

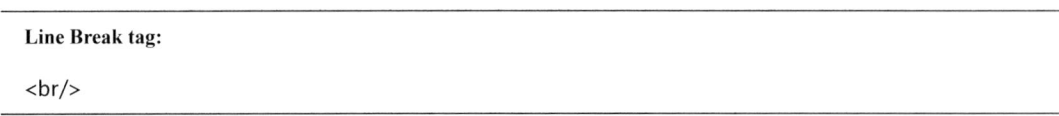

The break tag, <br>, has no end tag. It forces the browser to insert a line break at that location. By default, a browser compresses white space in the Web page and arranges content as the browser deems best. This can sometimes create discrepancies in how a Web page is displayed. Figure 2.25 illustrates how break tags are used to force blank lines between paragraphs, and Figure 2.26 shows the resulting page. Other, more advanced methods for dealing with this are discussed later.

```
<h3>Without line break:</h3>
1. Web Services for Everyone
2. PHP Hot Scripts
3. What is PHP?

<h3>With line break:</h3>
1. Web Services for Everyone<br/>
2. PHP Hot Scripts<br/>
3. What is PHP?<br/>
```

Figure 2.25: The HTML for <br> tags

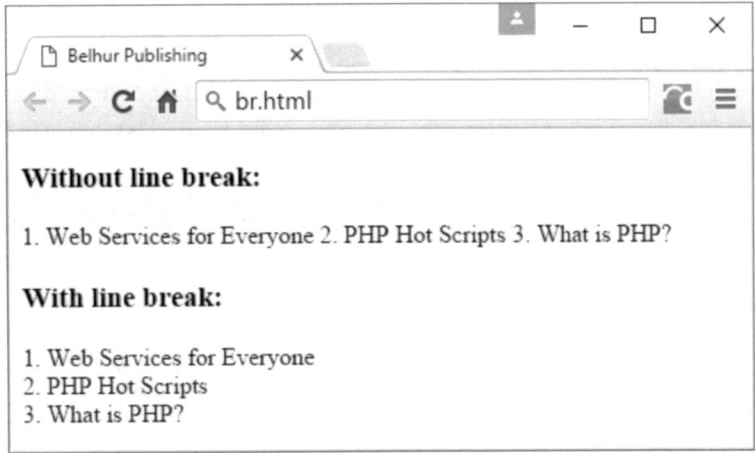

Figure 2.26: The result of the <br> tags

Special Characters

In addition to special codes for colors, there are special codes for characters. The previous examples have used fairly simple text. What if we wanted to include quotation marks ("), the greater-than symbol (>), the less-than symbol (<), the copyright symbol (©), or other special characters? Many of these characters are available through the use of *escape codes*, sometimes called *character references*. Table 2.3 lists these common special characters and their corresponding descriptions and codes. For a complete list of special characters, see Appendix B, included in the downloadable book materials available at *https://goo.gl/2uYjHb*.

Table 2.3: Special Characters in HTML			
Character	Description	Named Code	Numeric Code
"	Double quotation mark	&quot;	&#34;
'	Single quotation mark	&rsquo;	&#39;
<	Less than	&lt;	&#60;
>	Greater than	&gt;	&#62;
©	Copyright symbol	&copy;	&#169;
&	Ampersand	&amp;	&#38;
white space	Non-breaking space		

The semicolon (**;**) is part of the code and is required. For example, if you want to add a copyright symbol to the copyright statement in the footer of your Web page, like this:

©2016. Belhur Publishing, LLC. All rights reserved.

Use either the HTML named code © or numeric code © to display the copyright symbol, as shown below:

```
&copy;2016. Belhur Publishing, LLC. All rights reserved.
```

It's important to note that while these special characters can be useful, some of them can be misinterpreted by user agents as computer codes instead of plain text. For example, the less-than (<) and greater-than (>) symbols could be misinterpreted by the Web browser as the start and end of an HTML tag. Let's suppose that you want to mark up your Web page to display the text shown in Figure 2.27.

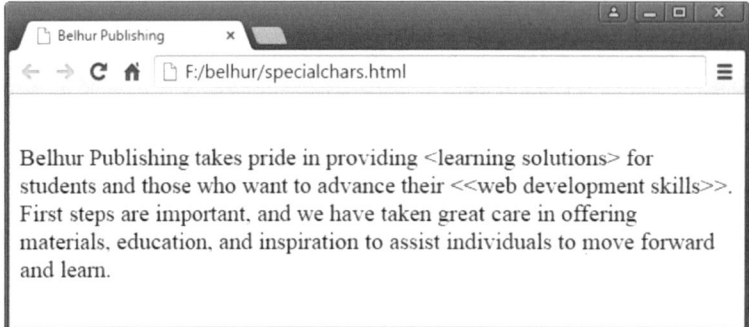

Figure 2.27: A Web page displaying special characters

You code your Web page as shown in Figure 2.28.

```
<p>Belhur Publishing takes pride in providing <learning solutions> for
students and those who want to advance their <<Web development skills>>.
First steps are important, and we have taken great care in offering
materials, education, and inspiration to assist individuals to move forward
and learn.</p>
```

Figure 2.28: HTML code without using escape codes for special characters < and >

When you render the Web page in your Web browser, you get something like Figure 2.29.

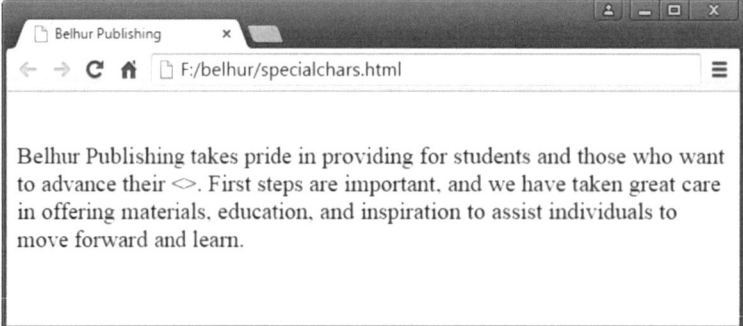

Figure 2.29: A Web page rendered without encoding the special characters < and >

What happened? The text within the less-than and greater-than symbols did not display because those symbols were not encoded. Therefore, they were treated as special computer codes and rendered incorrectly by the Web browser. To prevent this from happening, you should encode these special characters with either their corresponding named codes or numeric codes, as shown in Figure 2.30.

```
<p>Belhur Publishing takes pride in providing &lt;learning solutions&gt;
for students and those who want to advance their &lt; &lt;Web development
skills&gt;&gt;. First steps are important, and we have taken great care in
offering materials, education, and inspiration to assist individuals to
move forward and learn.</p>
```

Figure 2.30: HTML code using escape codes for special characters < and >

Another very important special character is the non-breakable space, . This character appears as a blank on the screen, but unlike a typical blank, a blank space character is preserved. The non-breakable space controls the indention of text on a page. Remember that, as the browser displays your Web page on the user's screen, it only preserves one white space character. Any extra blanks in HTML code are simply ignored, even if you hit the space bar, Enter key, or Tab key a hundred times. The code snippet in Figure 2.31 shows how to use   to indent the text a specific number of spaces; Figure 2.32 shows how the code is rendered in the browser.

```
<h2>Our New Books:</h2>
1.  Web Services for Everyone<br/>
2.  PHP Hot Scripts<br/>
    a.  What is PHP?<br/>
    b.  PHP Uplifts Your Web Application<br/>
```

Figure 2.31: HTML code with non-breakable spaces as indentation

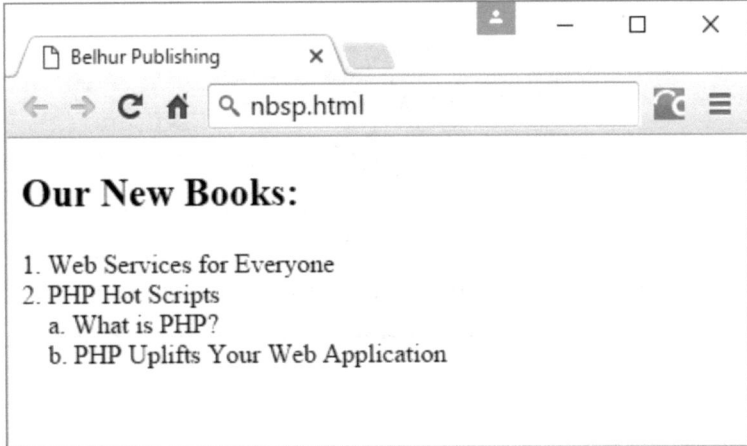

Figure 2.32: An example of using   to control spacing

Structural Elements

The structure of the page body of a Web page is constructed with HTML structural elements. In this section, we will discuss some of these important elements, which enable you to build Web pages in a more meaningful way.

Division tag:

<div>content</div>

For many years, the generic **<div>** element has been one of the most widely used tags in constructing Web pages. The <div> tag is a block-level element that is used to section out different page divisions (such as header, navigation, main content, sidebar, and footer) by assigning a unique id attribute to each division. It's one of the few widely used structural elements that is not a semantic tag. Another such element is the **<span>** tag, which we'll discuss next. Figure 2.33 shows a typical Web page **wireframe** outlining the structure of the page body using the <div> elements, and Figure 2.34 shows a sample code snippet of the wireframe. A wireframe is a diagram that Web developers use to show the layout of a Web page, and how each section of the page can be configured with structural elements.

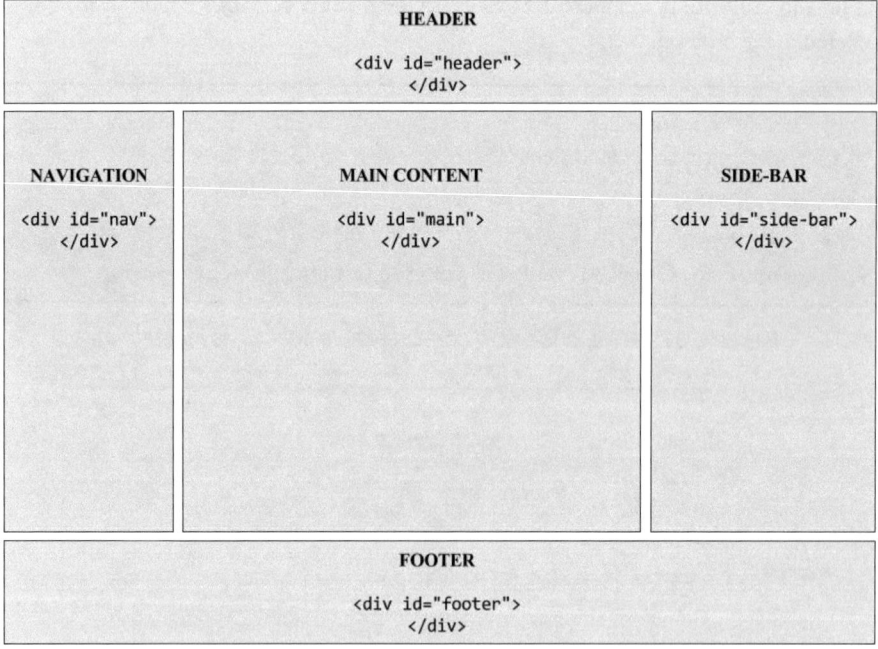

Figure 2.33: A Web page wireframe using HTML 4.01 structural elements

```
<body>
    <div id="header">
    </div>

    <div id="nav">
    </div>

    <div id="aside">
    </div>
                                                    Continued
```

```
    <div id="main">
    </div>

    <div id="footer">
    </div>
</body>
```

Figure 2.34: HTML code using the div elements

Span tag:

```
<span>content</span>
```

The `<span>` tag is a non-semantic tag that is used to define and format a section on a Web page or an area that is contained within another element. The `<span>` is an inline element that appears exactly where you code it and does not perform a line break. It doesn't do anything unless an attribute or CSS is applied to it. So, `<span>` is typically used for styling content by using CSS rules, as we'll see in the next example.

To see this in action, let's take the same code snippet from Figure 2.23 and use only the `<span>` tags in place of the `<b>`, `<u>`, and `<i>` tags to produce the same result. The modified code snippet is shown in Figure 2.35, and the resulting Web page is shown in Figure 2.36.

```
<p><span style="font-weight:bold;">Belhur Publishing</span> - your <span
style="text-decoration:underline;">ultimate</span> source for <span
style="font-style:italic;">technical</span> publications.
</p>
```

Figure 2.35: HTML code with `<span>` tags

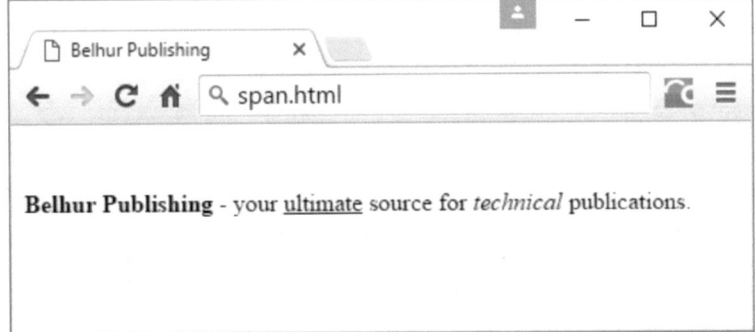

Figure 2.36: A Web page using `<div>` and `<span>` tags

If you compare the result shown in Figure 2.24 with that shown in Figure 2.36, you probably can't tell the difference. The only differences are in the HTML code. Notice the attribute style in each of the opening <span> tags in Figure 2.35. This is called a CSS *inline style*, which we will discuss in the next chapter.

To see <div> and <span> working as intended, you must incorporate CSS into your Web page. By assigning class names and id names to the <div> and <span> tags, you can assign positioning, alignment, and other formatting properties to these tags.

Many of the tags discussed thus far directly affect the appearance of the content on the Web page. This was fine in earlier days of HTML coding, but as mentioned earlier in this chapter, many of these HTML codes have been deprecated. Their use is discouraged, and they are not considered acceptable for HTML5 documents. Instead, they're being replaced by CSS, as you've just seen in the example with the <span> tags. Eventually, support for these tags may be dropped completely. However, many existing pages still use them, so some knowledge of them is essential.

HTML5 Structural Elements

HTML5 introduces a whole new set of structural elements that are more functional and meaningful. These elements are also more friendly to search engines and easily accessible to various user agents such as screen readers. Table 2.4 shows some of these structural elements and their purposes. In this section, we'll explore some of these elements and their purposes.

Table 2.4: HTML5 Structural Elements	
Element	**Description**
header	Introductory or navigational aids content
nav	A section with navigational links
main	Main content of the page
section	A generic section of content in the page
article	A complete, self-contained composition in the page
aside	Content that is tangential and considered separate from the page's main content
footer	Contains information about its section and is placed at the bottom of the page

Header tag:

<header>content</header>

The **<header>** tag is a semantic element that's used to contain the heading content of either a Web page or the headings of an area of a section or an article. The **header elements** begin with the <header> tag and end with the </header> tag. This tag is commonly used to contain the masthead of the Web page, which typically consists of the company or website logo and other small elements that are displayed consistently at the top of the page.

Nav tag:

<nav>content</nav>

The **<nav>** tag is used to contain the navigation links on the page. The <nav> tag can be used multiple times within the same page where sections of navigation links are necessary. Typically, navigation links are created with the unordered list element, and the links are styled and configured with CSS. Figure 2.37 shows a sample code snippet of a section of navigation links. You can see what this navigation section looks like after it is styled with CSS in the Updated Sample Page section, near the end of this chapter.

```
<nav>
    <ul>
        <li><a href="index.html">Home</a></li>
        <li><a href="about.html">About</a></li>
        <li><a href="books.html">Books</a></li>
        <li><a href="order.html">Order</a></li>
        <li><a href="contact.html">Contact Us</a></li>
    </ul>
</nav>
```

Figure 2.37: HTML code using the <nav> and <ul> tags

Main tag:

<main>content</main>

The **<main>** tag is used to contain the main content of the Web page. Sometimes this tag is also called the wrapper tag because the Web page's main content is wrapped within these tags. There can be only one <main> tag on a Web page.

Footer tag:

<footer>content</footer>

The <footer> tag is typically used to contain the Web page's footer content. The footer content usually includes copyright information, contact information, the sitemap, authorship information, and related documents.

Now that we've learned the importance of some of these HTML5 structural elements, let's see how they're put together in a Web page. Figure 2.38 shows sample code for the sample Web page wireframe.

```
<body>
    <header>
    </header>
                                                    Continued
```

```
    <nav>
    </nav>

    <aside>
    </aside>

    <main>
    </main>

    <footer>
    </footer>
</body>
```

Figure 2.38: HTML code using the HTML5 structural elements

Figure 2.39 below shows the sample Web page wireframe from Figure 2.33, outlining the structure of the page body using the HTML5 semantic elements after applying CSS rules.

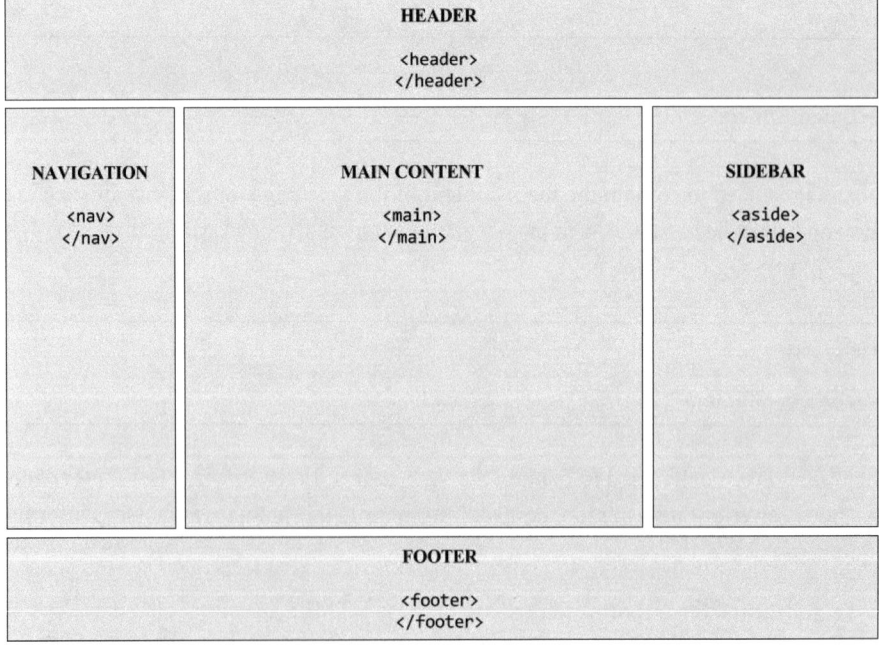

Figure 2.39: A Web page wireframe using HTML5 structural elements

Even though HTML5 has introduced a few new semantic structural elements in place of the <div> tag, this tag is still being used in conjunction with the new HTML5 structural elements to structure Web pages. In the next few chapters, we will learn how to construct a Web page using CSS to style and configure the structural elements to produce a result something like Figure 2.39.

Updated Sample Page

Let's add the HTML code we've looked at in this chapter to our Web page. The modified code shown in Figure 2.40 creates the updated Web page in Figure 2.41.

```html
<!DOCTYPE html>
<html>
<head>
        <title>Belhur Publishing</title>
        <meta charset="utf-8" />
        <link rel="stylesheet" href="main.css"/>
</head>
<body>
    <div id="main-container">
        <header>
            <h1>Belhur Publishing</h1>
        </header>
        <div id="left-side-bar">
            <nav>
                <ul>
                    <li><a href="index.html">Home</a></li>
                    <li><a href="about.html">About</a></li>
                    <li><a href="books.html">Books</a></li>
                    <li><a href="order.html">Order</a></li>
                    <li><a href="contact.html">Contact Us</a></li>
                </ul>
            </nav>
        </div>
        <aside>
            <div id="conference">
                Join us at these upcoming events:
                <p>COMMON annual conference</p>
<p>SEMIUG annual conference</p>
<p>WMCPA event</p>
            </div>
            <p>Endorsed by:</p>
                MC Press, WMCPA, SEMIUG, Industry Experts
            <br class="clear" />
        </aside>
```

Continued

```
        <main>
            <section>
                <article>
                    <p>Belhur Publishing - your ultimate source for technical
publications. Where those in the know go to find ebooks and hard copy books
on technical topics. Whether you're a student or adding new skills, we can
help!
                    </p>
                    <h2 id="new-books">New Books</h2>
                    <h2>HTML for the Business Developer</h2>
                    <img src="images/9781583470794-thumb.jpg" alt="HTML for
the Business Developer">
                </article>
            </section>
            <br class="clear" />
        </main>
        <footer>&copy;2016.  Belhur Publishing, LLC.  All rights
reserved.</footer>
    </div>
</body>
</html>
```

Figure 2.40: The HTML code to create the Web page in Figure 2.41

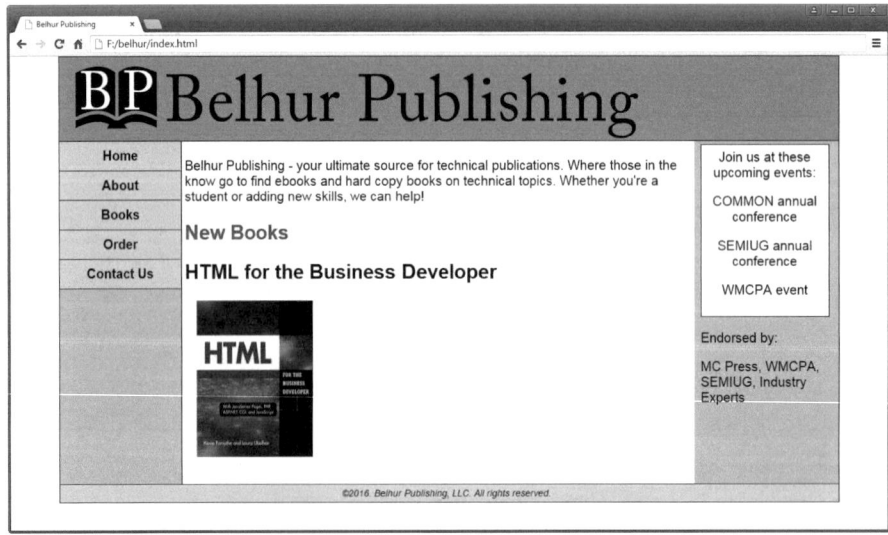

Figure 2.41: An updated Web page

This page won't look like this without the CSS style sheet. If you look at the code carefully, the style sheet is linked to the page through Line 6: <link rel="stylesheet" href="main.css"/>. In the next chapter, we will explore in more detail the CSS used to style the sample Web page you've just seen.

Summary

Is this all there is to HTML? Certainly not! This is just the tip of the iceberg. We've covered many of the basic tags in HTML, but there are many more to discuss. Some are fairly simple and straightforward, while others are much more complex. You'll see all these tags in the remainder of this book. Also, remember that some of the tags discussed here are considered deprecated by the W3C and may fall into disuse. However, you will still find them on some Web pages today, so some familiarity with them is necessary. Later in the book, you'll learn about alternatives to some of these deprecated options.

Key Terms

<!DOCTYPE>	<ol>	document type definition
<article>	<p>	(DTD)
<aside>	<pre>	element
<blockquote>	<section>	head section
<body>	<span>	header element
 	<sub>	HTML 4.01
<div>	<sup>	HTML5
<dl>	<title>	Hypertext Markup Language
<footer>	<ul>	(HTML)
<head>	attribute	ordered list
<header>	body element	structural elements
<hr>	body section	tag
<html>	character encoding	unordered list
<li>	description list	W3C
<main>	div element	wireframe
<nav>	doctype declaration	XHTML 1.0

Discussion/Review Questions

1. What is an HTML document?
2. What is Hypertext Markup Language (HTML)?
3. Who created HTML, and when was it created?
4. Why should you learn HTML?
5. What is the purpose of the document type definition (DTD) or DOCTYPE declaration?
6. What is an HTML element?
7. In what language is a Web document written?

8. What is the name of the organization that takes a proactive role in developing recommendations and prototype technologies related to the Web?
9. Where should <meta> tags be placed in a Web document?
10. What is the purpose of the <title> tag?
11. What are the major differences between an HTML 4.01 and HTML5 document?
12. When should you use an ordered list instead of an unordered list?
13. Why do you need to encode special characters in a Web page?
14. What are structural elements?
15. What do the following terms mean: head element, head section, header element, and heading element?
16. What are five HTML5 structural elements?
17. What are block-level and text-level elements?
18. In which section of the HTML document are elements that describe the Web page placed?
19. In which section of the HTML document should visible contents be placed?
20. What is a Web page wireframe?

Exercises

1. Write the HTML code for a basic HTML5 document.
2. Create an unordered list to display the following:
   Favorite Books
   - HTML5
   - JavaScript
   - PHP
   - ASP.NET
   - JSP
3. Write the HTML code to display the title of your favorite movie with the second largest heading element.
4. Write the HTML code for a horizontal rule that has a length of 90% and a thickness of 5 pixels.
5. Write the HTML code to render the following paragraph: HTML can be used to format and display special character symbols such as &, ©, °F, H_2O, and N^2.
6. Create a Web page wireframe for a simple website.
7. Write the basic HTML code for the Web page wireframe you created in Exercise 6.
8. Write the HTML code for a comment.

Using Cascading Style Sheets

Cascading Style Sheets (CSS) provide a flexible way to control the look or presentation of your Web pages. Small changes to a single CSS style sheet can dramatically change the appearance of many Web pages. This easy method for controlling the design of your pages allows you to rapidly implement changes to the look and feel of your website. The CSS elements are often called style rules and can be inserted directly in a Web page or separately in an external file.

There are three different methods by which CSS styles can inserted in a Web page: inline style, embedded or internal style, and external style. There is a fourth method that uses the @import directive to import an external style sheet into another style sheet, similarly to how the include statement is used in PHP. Although we will not discuss this method in detail, we'll show an example of using it later in this chapter. Each method has its own advantages and disadvantages. However, the rule of precedence is an important concept, and CSS rules must be coded in a logical order, as CSS styles will cascade down from one style sheet to another. In this chapter, we will discuss and learn some of the most common CSS styles and how they can be inserted into a Web page using the three different methods.

What Is CSS?

In a nutshell, CSS is a simple language that defines style constructs to format the appearance of a Web page. The style rules define a set of formatting instructions (one or more property-value pairs) that affect the HTML elements in a Web page. CSS is a *presentational* language, in contrast with HTML, which is a *semantic* language. CSS is a presentational language because it configures, formats, and styles the HTML elements to give the Web page its visual appearance. HTML, in contrast, is a semantic language, which means that an element describes its meaning associated with the content to a user agent such as a Web browser, a screen reader, or a Web crawler (discussed in Chapter 13). In other words, you will not find a loop statement or a function in CSS. It is the perfect complement language to HTML and was designed primarily to work with HTML.

The CSS style rules and standards are set and maintained by the World Wide Web Consortium (W3C), which introduced the first version (or level) of CSS, CSS1, in 1996 followed by CSS2 in 1998 and CSS3 in 2005. Each newer level of CSS is built over the previous level. At the time this was written, CSS Level 3 (CSS3) was still the most up-to-date version used in today's Web development. Even though CSS3 was released more than a decade ago, many new properties and rules have been gradually introduced. This chapter covers many of the standard CSS properties and rules and some of the new CSS3 properties.

How Cascading Style Sheets Work

A CSS style rule contains two parts: **selector** and **declaration**. A selector can be any HTML tag (such as p, h1, or div) or a user-defined selector such as a *class* or an *id*. We will discuss **class** and **id selectors** later in this chapter. The declaration is a list of property-value pairs that are associated with the selector. A **property** is any construct such as font-size, color, or **position** with values like 12px, red, or relative, respectively.

Figure 3.1 shows the syntax for defining a CSS rule.

```
selector { property : value; }
```

Figure 3.1: Syntax for a CSS style rule

A selector can have more than one property-value pair. Each pair must be separated by a semi-colon (;) and should start on a new line, as shown in Figure 3.2.

```
selector {
        property1 : value1;
        property2 : value2;
        property3 : value3;
}
```

Figure 3.2: Syntax for a CSS style rule with multiple property-value pairs

When defining the style for an element (such as a <p> tag), the element's tag is listed without the angle brackets (<>) and followed by braces ({}). Within these braces, any available property can be defined. Each property is followed by a colon (:) and then by its associated value. Each value is followed by a semicolon (;). You may list additional properties as needed. The ending brace is coded after all the listed properties. The example in Figure 3.3 defines style rules for the paragraph (p) and heading (h1) selectors.

```
p {
   color: purple;
                                                          Continued
```

```
    padding: 7px;
    text-align: center;
}
h1 {
    color: green;
    padding: 7px;
    text-align: center;
}
```

Figure 3.3: CSS style rules for the p and h1 selectors

CSS is a flexible language and follows similar rules to those of HTML. As you've seen in the previous examples, style rules can be written in a single line or multiple lines because white spaces are ignored. In addition, style rules can be applied to more than one element. To apply the same style rules to multiple elements, simply separate each selector with a comma. If you look at our example in Figure 3.3, you see that both selectors have an identical list of properties. Since they are the same, we can apply the style rules to both selectors and save a few lines of code. Figure 3.4 shows the result of combining both selectors within the same style rules.

```
h1, p {
    color: green;
    padding: 7px;
    text-align: center;
}
```

Figure 3.4: A CSS style rule applied to two selectors

If you want the h1 selector from the previous example to have a different **font-style** (such as italics) but want to retain the same rules, then you can define h1 again as a separate selector and apply just the font-style, as shown in Figure 3.5.

```
h1, p {
    color: purple;
    padding: 7px;
    text-align: center;
}
h1 { font-style: italic; }
```

Figure 3.5: Multiple CSS style rules applied to the same selector

A question you might have is "How does the Web browser know which selector to use?" What's really happening behind the scenes is that the Web browser collects all the CSS style rules created for each selector and regenerates a new complete virtual set of rules for that selector. The resulting style sheet is a *virtual style sheet* that contains all the selectors and their associated declarations, as shown Figure 3.6.

```
p {
    color: purple;
    padding: 7px;
    text-align: center;
}
h1 {
    color: purple;
    padding: 7px;
    text-align: center;
    font-style: italic;
}
```

Figure 3.6: A virtual style sheet rendered by the Web browser from the CSS in Figure 3.5

Applying Style Sheets to Web Pages

Now that you know and understand how Cascading Style Sheets work, let's learn how to apply them to a Web page using the methods discussed earlier. CSS style rules are applied to a Web page based on the orders of precedence in which style rules cascade down, from rules with lowest precedence to highest precedence. So the concept of cascading is synonymous to a series of waterfalls, as shown in Figure 3.7.

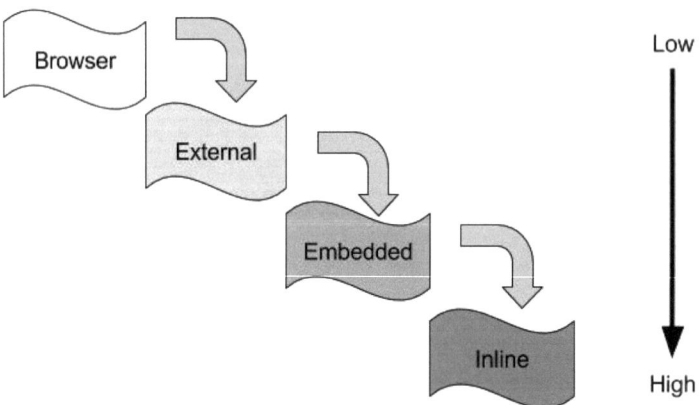

Figure 3.7: How CSS styles cascade and the orders of precedence

As illustrated in Figure 3.7, a Web browser applies style rules from the top down, or from lowest to highest precedence. Generally, all modern Web browsers have their own style rules built into them. This ensures that any Web pages that do not have any custom styles created could still be rendered in a manner that is presentable to the end user. Thus, an embedded style will override any styles defined before it but will be superseded by an inline style. Of course, there are always exceptions to some rules, and such is the case with CSS orders of precedence. Even though precedence is applied here, the manner in which one style sheet overrides another is dependent on how the style sheets are placed logically within the Web page. We'll discuss this topic in more detail later in this chapter. Next, we will learn how to apply style rules using the inline, embedded, and external styles.

Note: Since the Web browser has its own set of default styles built into it, its built-in styles will automatically be applied to a Web page—the programmer has no control over these styles. Thus, we will not discuss how to apply these styles to a Web page.

Creating an Inline Style Sheet

Inline styles have the highest orders of precedence, and they are the last to be interpreted by the browser. Inline styles are applied directly and specifically to only a single element using the **style attribute**. For example, Figure 3.8 shows how a style rule is applied to a <p> tag to display the content in Georgia font in color purple.

```
<p style="font-family: Georgia; color: purple;">This is an Inline Style.
</p>
```

Figure 3.8: An inline style rule applied to a p element

An advantage of inline styles is made clear during the development phase, in which style rules can be applied quickly and directly to the tags. Doing it this way saves the developer the time of scrolling up and down the HTML document or switching between the external style sheet and HTML document to write the style rules in the style sheet. Another advantage of inline styles is that they enable you to override a remote style rule that you don't have access to or control over. The main disadvantage of inline styles is that, because they can be applied only to a single tag, making changes to such styles can be tedious and inefficient for the programmer. It's no easy task when there are tens and hundreds of individual tags that need to be changed. For this reason, using inline styles is not the preferred method of styling a Web page.

Creating an Embedded Style Sheet

An **embedded style sheet** is a list of style rules that are embedded internally within the Web page and can only be applied to a single document. Although a style sheet can be inserted anywhere within the head or body sections of the Web page, the style sheet is typically inserted in the head section using the **<style>** element. Don't confuse the <style> element with the style attribute discussed earlier. Style rules are encapsulated between the <style> and </style> tags. Figure 3.9 shows how an embedded style sheet is incorporated into a Web page, and Figure 3.10 shows the result rendered in the browser.

```
<!DOCYTYPE html>
<html>
  <head>
    <title>Belhur Publishing</title>
    <meta charset="utf-8"/>
    <style>
      p {
          padding: 7px;
          text-align: center;
      }
      h1 {
          text-style: italic;
          font-family: Georgia;
          text-align: center;
      }
    </style>
  </head>
  <body>
    <h1>Belhur Publishing</h1>
    <p>Belhur Publishing was established in 2016 as a joint effort between
MC Press, Laura Ubelhor, and Christian Hur.</p>
  </body>
</html>
```

Figure 3.9: An embedded style sheet

Figure 3.10: A Web page result of the embedded style sheet shown in Figure 3.9

Style rules can be embedded multiple times within a Web page. For example, the embedded style sheet in Figure 3.9 could be separated out to two separate sections and inserted at two different locations within the same document, as shown in Figure 3.11. However, the Web page would be formatted and displayed exactly the same as shown in Figure 3.10. Although the Web page appears flawlessly on the browser window, it's bad practice to include embedded style sheets within the body section. In an HTML5 document, embedded style sheets must be coded within the head section only.

```
<!DOCYTYPE html>
<html>
  <head>
    <title>Belhur Publishing</title>
    <meta charset="utf-8"/>
    <style>
      h1 {
         text-style: italic;
         font-family: Georgia;
         text-align: center;
      }
    </style>
  </head>
<body>
   <h1>Belhur Publishing</h1>

   <style>
      p {
         padding: 7px;
         text-align: center;
      }
   </style>

   <p>Belhur Publishing was established in 2016 as a joint effort between
MC Press, Laura Ubelhor, and Christian Hur.</p>
  </body>
</html>
```

Figure 3.11: Two style rules embedded in separate locations within the same Web page

The embedded style is much more convenient and efficient than the inline style because it can be applied to multiple elements from one central location. While an inline style is more targeted to a specific tag, the embedded style is targeted to multiple tags at once.

Creating an External Style Sheet

An external CSS style sheet is a text file that ends in the *.css* suffix. The main advantage of using an external style sheet is that it can be applied to any Web pages on the site. Programmers appreciate this single point of control. An external style sheet is often named theme.css or main.css. "Theme" is a good choice for the filename, since a style sheet can create the visual theme for a website. All you need to do is have all the pages in your website reference the same CSS style sheet.

You can attach an external style sheet to your Web page using the **<link>** tag. The code snippet in Figure 3.12 shows an example of such a link. When the HTML page is opened, the browser will search the theme.css style sheet to find rules for handling the content of the page.

```
<link href="theme.css" rel="stylesheet" />
```

Figure 3.12: Linking to an external style sheet

To see how this works, let's create a very simple external style sheet called theme.css. Like HTML, an external style sheet can be created by using any text editor tool, such as Notepad++, or by using a sophisticated tool in a Web design product such as Adobe Dreamweaver or Microsoft Expression. Figure 3.13 shows the code for a basic theme.css style sheet using NotePad++.

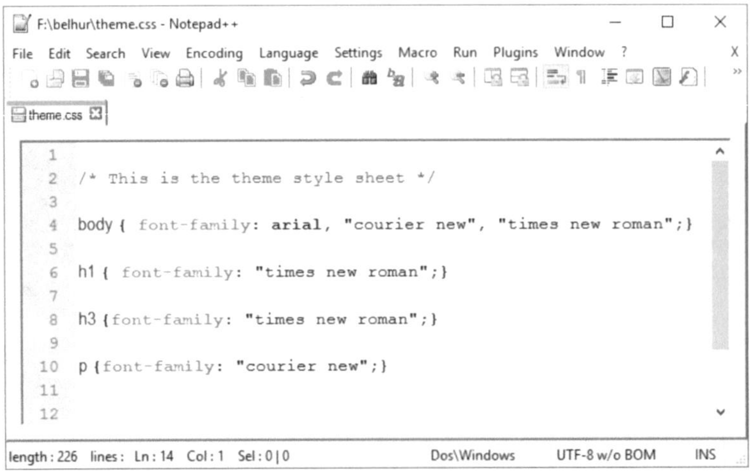

Figure 3.13: A basic style sheet for four HTML tags

The example in Figure 3.13 shows an external style sheet with five lines of code. The first line of code illustrates how comments are coded. Any text between the /* and */ tags is ignored by the Web browser. The other four lines of code are style rules for the HTML <body> element, the <h1> and <h3> heading elements, and the paragraph <p> element. As discussed earlier, HTML elements are commonly used as CSS selectors but without the "<>" brackets. Notice also that the <style> and </style> tags are not present, as discussed earlier. This is because HTML tags are not allowed. The <style> tags are used only within an HTML page to embed an internal style sheet. An external style sheet can contain only comments, style rules, and special directives (such as *media query* and *import*, which will be discussed briefly later in this chapter). As the HTML document is rendered, the styles are read in from the style sheet and applied. There other ways to define styles, such as using style classes, which we will discuss later in this chapter.

In theme.css, each of the four element styles sets the default font family for that element. In the body style, the font family is set to Arial. If Arial is not available on the user's computer, one of the alternate fonts listed will be used. Simply list all the fonts in order of preference. The first one available on the user's computer will be used. If none of the listed fonts are available, the default font of the user's browser will be used. The h1 and h3 styles define the font family as Times New Roman. When the name of a font family contains two or more words, such as "Times New Roman," it should be enclosed with a pair of double quotation marks. The fourth style is for the paragraph tag (p). This style sets the default font to Courier New.

A wide variety of fonts is available. Monospace fonts such as Courier New use the exact same width for every letter. This makes them very attractive when you need to get text to line up a certain way.

Figure 3.14 shows the code for a sample Web page that links to the theme.css style sheet. The Web page is shown in Figure 3.15.

```
<!DOCTYPE html>
<html>
<head>
    <title>Belhur Publishing</title>
    <meta charset="utf-8" />
    <link rel="style sheet" href="theme.css"/>
</head>
<body>
    <h1>Belhur Publishing</h1>
    <h3>Corporate Overview</h3>
    <p>Belhur Publishing takes pride in providing learning solutions for
students and those who want to advance their Web development skills. First
steps are important, and we have taken great care in offering materials,
education, and inspiration to assist individuals to move forward and
learn.</p>

    Belhur Publishing was established in 2016 as a joint effort between MC
Press, Laura Ubelhor, and Christian Hur.
</body>
</html>
```

Figure 3.14: The HTML code for a Web page using an external style sheet

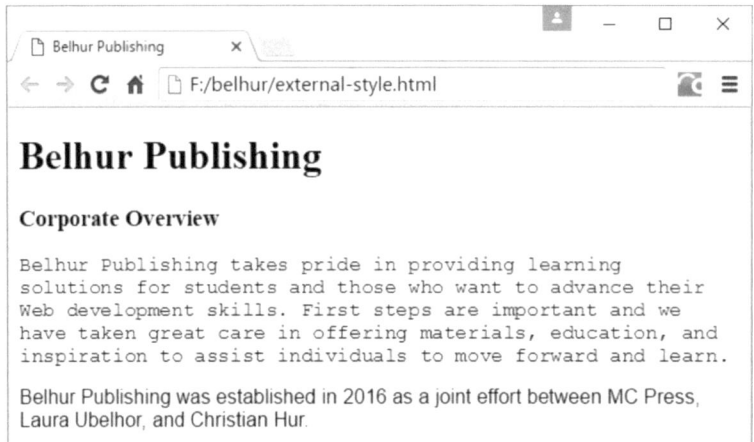

Figure 3.15: Sample font families using an external style sheet

Notice in Figure 3.14 that within the <body> element, there are three child elements (h1, h3, p) and a paragraph. In general, the innermost, or *child*, element will inherit properties from a parent element, but the child also has the option to override those properties. For example, both <body> and <p> element styles attempt to change the font family, but the <p> tag takes precedence, since it is the innermost tag. Therefore, the text in the <p> tag appears in Courier New instead of Arial.

Importing Style Sheets

Briefly, a fourth method of incorporating style sheets in a Web page is to import an external style sheet into the Web page by using the @import directive. The external style sheet being **imported** must be inserted into either an embedded style sheet or into another external style sheet. Also, the @import directive must be inserted before all other style rules in the style sheet. While external style sheets can be incorporated into a Web page using <link> tags, the reason a developer would instead want to import an external style sheet is to combine multiple external style sheets into a single style sheet.

The advantages of combining multiple style sheets into one are portability and maintainability. For example, you might want to develop a Web application to accommodate multiple languages. This example involves style sheet dependency where one style sheet depends on another style sheet. Thus, the most logical approach is to create a master (or default) style sheet (for formatting the overall layout of the site) and individual language style sheets (for formatting different language texts). Then instead of incorporating the master and language style sheets into the Web document using two separate link tags, the developer could just import the master style sheet into the language style sheet, thereby maintaining only a single link tag.

The disadvantage of using @import is that it can have a negative impact on Web page performance. Style sheets that are incorporated using the <link> tags are downloaded and processed simultaneously (in parallel); therefore, page loading time is much faster. On the other hand, style sheets that are incorporated using the @import directive are downloaded and processed sequentially, thus preventing other style sheets from loading and causing the page to load much more slowly. Figure 3.16 shows how two external style sheets are incorporated into a Web page via the @import directive.

```
<!DOCYTYPE html>
<html>
  <head>
    <title>Belhur Publishing</title>
    <meta charset="utf-8"/>
    <style>

      @import url(theme.css);
      @import url(shop.css);
      h1 { color: blue; }
      p  { font-family: Arial; }

    </style>
  </head>
  <body>
```

Figure 3.16: Importing two external style sheets via the @import directive

Exploring CSS Style Rules and Properties

By now, you should be familiar with how CSS works and the methods of incorporating style sheets into a Web page. Now that we've taken these first steps into CSS, the next step is to explore some of the major CSS style rules and their properties that developers use to configure and format Web-based applications.

How Do You Style Text Using CSS?

In addition to the **font-family property**, you can also set the font size, font style, or font weight. Alternatively, you can set the font property, which has several values, including style, variant, weight, size, and family.

```
{font-family: font1,font2,...
 font-size:size
 font-style:normal
     italic
     oblique
 font-weight:normal
     bold
     bolder
     lighter
     number
 font:style weight
   size family
 }
```

Most of the properties have specific options to choose from. For example, **font-weight** can use relative terms such as lighter, normal, bold, or bolder. These choices are displayed here in **bold** text. Other properties allow more varied values. These are displayed here in ***bold italics***. For example, font-weight accepts a numeric value that is a multiple of 100, from 100 to 900. A value of 100 is the lightest (thinnest) font weight, while 900 is the heaviest (thickest).

The **font-size** property requires a value that may be followed by a code such as 12px, which means 12 pixels wide. The available size codes are:

- **em**: the width of the letter m in the current font
- **ex**: the width of the letter x in the current font
- **cm**: centimeters
- **mm**: millimeters
- **pc**: picas (1 pica = 4.216 mm)
- **pt**: points (1 point = 1/12 pica)
- **in**: inches
- **px**: pixels

Using the **em** and **ex** sizes allows you to define the size of certain portions of text without needing to know the underlying size of the font. Specifying a value of .5em, for example, means you want the font to be 50 percent smaller than the current text size for the letter m. Similarly, to define a size 20 percent greater than the current text size of the letter x, use a value of 1.2ex. Avoiding hard-coded font sizes provides better support for users who have adjusted their own font sizes.

Use the font-style to determine whether the text should be printed in its normal form, italics, or as oblique text. (Oblique prints "slanted" text that, to the untrained eye, looks the same as italics.)

There are a number of other text properties not directly associated with a font. These include color, direction, line-height, letter-spacing, text-align, text-decoration, text-indent, text-shadow, text-transform, Unicode-bidi, white-space, and word-spacing.

```
{color:color
    rgb(r,g,b)
    #rrggbb
direction:ltr
    rtl
line-height:normal
    number
    percent
letter-spacing:normal
    number
```

```
text-align:left
     right
     center
     justify
text-decoration:
     none
     underline
     overline
     line-through
     blink
text-indent: number
       percent
text-shadow: color
horizontal-distance
vertical-distance
blur radius
text-transform:none
       capitalize
       uppercase
       lowercase
white-space: normal
       pre
       nowrap
word-spacing:normal
       number
Unicode-bidi:normal
       embed
       bidi-override
 }
```

Color may be coded as a specific name, such as blue or red, as an RGB hexadecimal (hex) value, or as RGB decimal values. Color names are easy to use, but not all browsers present the colors in exactly the same way. The 16 standard HTML colors are shown in Table 3.1, together with their hex values. You can find more colors in Appendix E, included in the downloadable book materials available at *https://goo.gl/2uYjHb*.

Examples of hex values are #000000 (black), #C0C0C0 (silver), and #FFFFFF (white). Each hex code is made up of a pound sign (#) followed by three hex values (00 through FF), representing the red, green, and blue values of the color. Most programmers know that hex is a base-16 number system, where 0=0 and F=15. So, a hex code of #3366CC has 33 for the red value, 66 for the green, and CC for the blue, resulting in a medium grayish-blue.

Table 3.1: Standard color names and hex codes	
Color Name	Hex Code
Aqua	#00FFFF
Black	#000000
Blue	#0000FF
Fuchsia	#FF00FF
Gray	#808080
Green	#008000
Lime	#00FF00
Maroon	#800000
Navy	#000080
Olive	#808000
Purple	#800080
Red	#FF0000
Silver	#C0C0C0
Teal	#008080
Yellow	#FFFF00
White	#FFFFFF

The direction property can be set to left-to-right (ltr) which is the default, or right-to-left (rtl). Line-height can be set to normal, a specific number, or a percentage.

Letter-spacing controls the space between text characters. This property can be set to either normal or a specific number.

The **text-align property** can be set to left, right, center, or justify.

Text-decoration lets you add an underline or overline effect to the text. You can also cause the text to appear with a line through it. This is often used to represent deleted text. A blinking effect can also be added.

The text-indent property sets the amount of indention for the first line of text in the paragraph. It can be entered either as a fixed amount or as a percentage.

Text-shadow sets the color for a shadow effect added to the text. Horizontal and vertical distance properties indicate the offset distance of the shadow effect from the text. This property is not supported by many browsers at this time.

Use the text-transform option to force the text to appear in upper case or lower case, or to capitalize the first letter of every word.

White-space controls the way in which the browser handles the white space within the HTML text. Setting it to pre causes the text to be handled as if the HTML <pre> tag were specified. Using the nowrap value indicates that the text should never wrap down to the next line. It will continue on the same line until the end of the text or a line-break tag (<br/>).

The word-spacing property sets the distance between each word in the text. Set this to a specific size.

If you use the rtl directional text, you can set the Unicode-bidi property to bidi-override, causing the first letter of text to be printed at the right margin, with each following character moving closer to the left margin. Otherwise, rtl will simply cause the text to be aligned on the right margin. For an example of this, consider the code in Figure 3.17. If the style sheet in Figure 3.18 is applied, the sentence is printed right to left, as shown in Figure 3.19. The text is aligned on the right margin by default.

```
<p>this text prints right to left</p>
```

Figure 3.17: The HTML code to print a line of text

```
p {direction:rtl; unicode-bidi:bidi-override;}
```

Figure 3.18: The style sheet code that controls the text in Figure 3.17

Figure 3.19: Right-to-left text

This example might be a bit silly, as it is rare that you would need to print text right to left. However, most of the other font properties, such as color assignment and weight, don't show up well in printed material.

What Properties Control the Arrangement of an Element?

Typically, each element on a Web page is assigned a rectangular section or "box" known as the **CSS box model**, as shown in Figure 3.20. The box model is composed of four concentric boxes: content, padding, border, and margin. Properties that affect the general positioning and arrangement of content on the page manipulate the format of these boxes. As a general rule, these boxes are not visible.

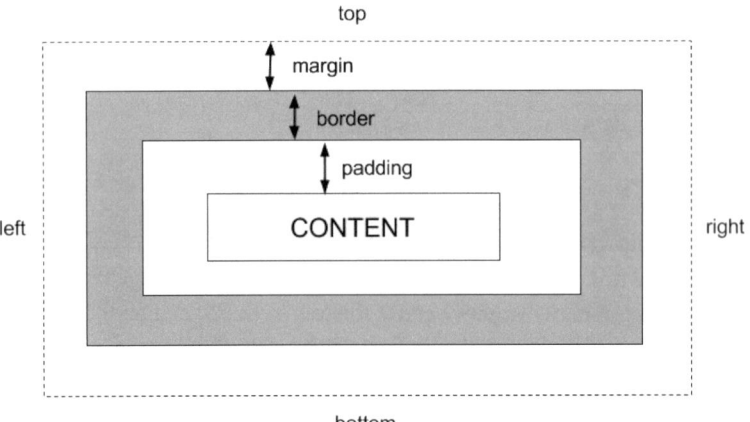

Figure 3.20: The CSS box model

The content box is the actual content of an element, such as the text or content between the <p> and </p> tags. The padding box is the space between the edge of the content and the inner edge of the border. The border box extends from the outer edge of the padding area to the inner edge of margin. Finally, the margin box is the space between the outer edge of the border and the next element on the page. The following tags describe how these four sections can be manipulated to control the size and appearance of elements on a Web page.

Use the padding properties to control the spacing around an element.

```
{padding-bottom: size
     auto
 padding-left: size
     auto
 padding-right: size
     auto

 padding-top: size
     auto
 padding: top right
   bottom left
}
```

Padding refers to the internal space between the content of an element and the element's border. You can control the padding values for each of the four sides of the element, or if you specify the **padding property**, you can set all four at once.

If padding contains just a single value, such as {padding:3px;}, that value applies to all four sides of the element. If two values are given, such as {padding:3px 2px;}, the first value is for the top and bottom, and the second value is for the left and right. When three values are given, the first is for the top, the second for the left and right, and the third for the bottom. When four values are given, such as {padding:3px 2px 4px 5px;}, the values apply to all four sides of the element in a clockwise direction starting at the top. Therefore, the first is for the top, the second for the right, the third for the bottom, and the fourth for the left. This is also called using shorthand notation.

```
{height:size
    auto
width: size
    auto
 max-height: size
        auto
max-width: size
        auto
 min-height: size
        auto
min-width: size
        auto
 }
```

The height and width properties refer to the size of the element itself. Use a size in one of the formats discussed earlier for the font-weight property. The max-height and max-width properties refer to the maximum size that an element can expand to. Rather than specifying an exact size, these properties set a limit on the element's size. The min-height and min-width properties control the minimum size the element can be shrunk to.

As the browser integrates a variety of elements on the same page, some will be placed beside others. If necessary, you can force the browser to leave either one side or both sides free of adjacent elements. For example, if you wanted to keep the right side clear, you would set the clear property to right.

```
{clear: none
    both
    left
    right
 bottom:number
    auto
 float: left
    right
    none
 visibility: visible
    hidden
    collapse
 top: number
 auto
 right: number
    auto
 left: number
    auto
 position: static
    relative
    fixed
    absolute
```

```
clip: auto
   rect(top,right,
     left,bottom)
overflow: visible
     hidden
     scroll
     auto
vertical-align:
     number
     baseline
     sub
     super
     top
     text-top
     middle
     bottom
     text-bottom
  z-index: auto
     number
  }
```

The bottom property sets the distance that an element is above the bottom edge of its block area. Left, right, and top properties define the distance of the element's content from the edge of that block.

Use the float property to identify how the element should be arranged with other elements. Set it to right if it should float to the right, left to float left, or none to prevent it from floating at all.

Visibility controls whether an element can be seen or not. Set this to visible for elements that should be seen, hidden for ones that should remain in the background, and collapse if the element is to be hidden away from view, but available for quick display if needed.

Overflow determines how the browser handles content that will not fit in the defined space for the object. Set overflow to visible to guarantee that the content will be visible despite overflowing the element's maximum size. Use hidden to cause the overflow content to become invisible. Use scroll to indicate that scrollbars should be added to the element to allow access to its entire contents. Clip sets the size of the clipped area of an element with overflow. It accepts four values—the top, right, left, and bottom positions, which identify the top right corner of the object and the bottom left corner of the visible portion of the element.

Use the position property to control the way in which the browser places the element on the page. If the property is set to absolute, the element's position (top, right, left, and bottom) is relative to the page itself and independent of any parent elements on the page. If the position property is set to relative, the position of the element is adjusted from the location at which it would normally appear. So, an element that would normally appear 10 pixels from the top of the page and 20 pixels from the left, with position set to relative, and 5px for both the top and left properties, would appear 15 pixels from the top of the page and 25 from the left.

Use **z-index** to define layers within the Web page. By default, all the content is at the "0" index layer. Content placed at z-index 1 will overlay that, and content at z-index 2 will overlay the z-index 1 content. This provides an easy mechanism to overlay content. To avoid layering and keep all content at the same layer as the parent element, specify auto as the z-index.

The vertical-align property controls the alignment of elements in line with each other within a containing box. Baseline is the default value. It causes all the elements in the line to align with each other along the baseline of the containing box. Sub and super cause elements to align as if they were subscript and superscript, respectively. Top, bottom, and middle cause the elements to align along the top of the highest element, the bottom of the lowest element, or the middle of all the elements. With text-bottom or text-top, the elements are lined up with the bottom or top of the parent item's font property.

What Properties Control the Display of an Element?

The cursor and display properties provide the ability to customize the look of the cursor and the text of the page. The cursor can be modified to appear as a variety of pointers, arrows, or crosshairs. The display property affects text in numerous ways. For example, it can force text to appear in line with other text, or force the text to appear in vertical lists.

```
{cursor: auto
    crosshair
    pointer
    default
    move
    e-resize
    ne-resize
    nw-resize
    n-resize
    se-resize
    sw-resize
    s-resize
    w-resize
    text
    wait
    help
 display: none
    inline
    block
    list-item
```

```
        run-in
        compact
        marker
        table
        inline-table
        table-row-group
        table-header-group
        table-footer- group
        table-column-group
        table-row
        table-column
        table-cell
        table-caption
    }
```

Reformatting the mouse pointer may be a useful tool for communicating with users. For example, you could use the cursor to indicate that a certain link provides help information. The **cursor property** sets the appearance of the mouse pointer. Set it to crosshair to change the mouse pointer into a targeting crosshair. Use move to create a mouse pointer that indicates the element can be moved. This looks similar to the crosshairs, but includes arrows on the end of each line.

The resize values of cursor switch the pointer to a sizing arrow that points in the given direction. So, the e-resize cursor is an arrow that points east-west, and the nw-resize cursor is an arrow that points northwest-southeast.

Use the text value of cursor to change the mouse pointer to the vertical line commonly used in text areas. Wait causes the cursor to change to an hourglass, and help changes it to a question mark.

The display property has a wide range of options and an even wider range of support from the major browsers. Rather than going over all of these, we'll focus on a few of the more useful options. Set display to none to cause an element to not be displayed. This is different from the hidden value, which was discussed earlier. A hidden element occupies space on the page, and other elements will move as if it were there. The {display:none} property causes the element to be ignored by the browser, so other elements on the page may be placed in the space that the non-displayed element would have occupied.

The block value essentially behaves like paragraphs have always behaved, advancing to a new line and avoiding placing other elements to its right or left. The inline option causes an element to display on the current line of the current block.

The code sample in Figure 3.21 creates a series of hypertext links. Figure 3.22 shows how they would normally appear in the browser. The links appear one after another until the right margin is reached, at which point the text moves down to the next line.

```
<a href="abc.html">Link to page 2</a>
<a href="def.html">Link to page 3</a>
<a href="ghi.html">Link to page 4</a>
```

Figure 3.21: HTML code to show three hypertext links

Figure 3.22: Links formatted inline with each other

If you wanted each link to advance to the next line, similar to the way paragraphs behave, you could use the display:block property. To accomplish this, you could add the code in Figure 3.23 to a CSS style sheet. The output would change, as shown in Figure 3.24.

```
a {display:block;
}
```

Figure 3.23: A style sheet for block format

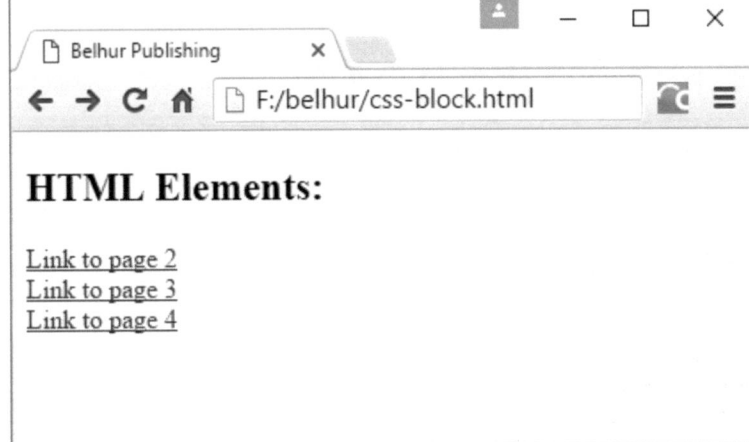

Figure 3.24: Links presented in block format

Margins define the space between the border and the edge of a containing box.

```
{margin-bottom:size
     auto
  margin-left: size
     auto
  margin-right: size
     auto
  margin-top: size
     auto
  margin: top right
    bottom left
}
```

Each margin can be set to a specific size, as for the font-size property described earlier. The **margin property** lets you set all four margins at once. If only one value is given, all four margins use that value. If two values are given, the top and bottom margins use the first value, and the right and left margins use the second. If three values are given, the first value is for the top margin, the second for the left and right, and the third for the bottom.

Use the **border property** to set the width, style, and color of the border. Set the width to a specific size, as for the font-size property. The style can be set to values such as dashed, groove, inset, or outset. The default border style is none. The color may be coded as a color name, a hex value, or an RGB value.

```
{border: width
     style
     color
  border-color: color
     rgb
     hex
  border-style: none
     hidden
     dotted
     dashed
     solid
     double
     groove
     ridge
     inset
     outset
  border-width:size
     thin
     medium
     thick
  border-radius: size
  border-top-left-radius: size
  border-top-right-radius: size
```

```
border-bottom-left-radius: size
border-bottom-right-radius: size
border-top-color: as above
border-top-style: as above
border-top-width: as above
border-top: as above
border-bottom-color: as above
border-bottom-style: as above
border-bottom-width: as above
border-bottom: as above
border-left-color: as above
border-left-style: as above
border-left-width: as above
border-left: as above
border-right-color: as above
border-right-style: as above
border-right-width: as above
border-right: as above
}
```

By default, no border is shown for an element. Use border-color to set just the **color property** for the border. Similarly, the **border-width property** defines just the width of the element's border. The **border-style property** can be set to none to indicate that no border be displayed, or hidden to indicate that the border be rendered on the page, but invisibly. The dotted, dashed, and solid values obviously describe the appearance of the border.

The groove border style appears like a channel cut into the surface of the Web page. Ridge creates a 3D raised border that surrounds the element. Double creates a border within a border. The inset border appears sunken into the surface of the Web page, while the outset value makes an element appear to be elevated, as if on top of a button.

Use border-top, border-left, border-right, and border-bottom to set the border properties for just that section of the element.

To make the links from Figure 3.24 more visually distinct, we could add a border. In this case, the code in Figure 3.25 adds an outset border to make them appear raised above the surface of the Web page, as shown in Figure 3.26.

```
a {display:block;
    border-style:outset;
    width:14ex;
    text-align:center;
}
```

Figure 3.25: The style sheet code for anchor tags with special borders

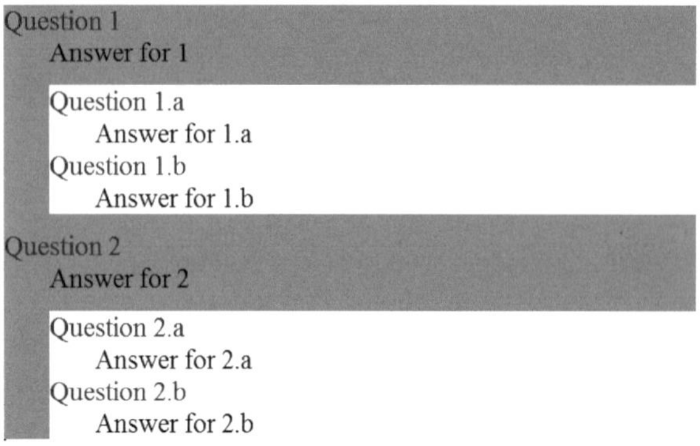

Figure 3.26: Centered links with outset borders of a specific width

The code in Figure 3.25 keeps the block attribute from the earlier example and adds the outset border. It also sets the width to 14ex (fourteen *x*'s) so that the outset borders would not continue all the way to the right margin of the page. The text was also centered within the block so that it lined up neatly within the borders. This makes the links look like buttons.

Before CSS3, it was impossible to easily add rounded corners to the border of an element with just HTML tags or CSS style rules. For years, that task had been a developer's nightmare. To add rounded corners, a developer or graphics designer would have to design the rounded corners in a graphics program, such as Adobe Photoshop, then slice and splice them into separate images. The challenge was stitching them together so that the rounded corners would display seamlessly on the Web page. An alternative solution to that problem was to just forgo rounded corners altogether and stick with the rectangular boxes. Fortunately, CSS3 comes with a whole new set of border properties that have made the developer's job much easier.

To create rounded corners of a box for an element, use the border-radius property. It takes a numeric value using the px, em, or % unit. You can also style each of the four corners individually using the border-top-left-radius, border-top-right-radius, bottom-left-radius, or bottom-right-radius properties. Although these properties may not fully support all browsers, most modern browsers should render them without any problems. The code snippet in Figure 3.27 shows how the rounded corners of the boxes for two elements are created, with the resulting page shown in Figure 3.28.

```
<style>
.border1 { border: 1px solid #000;
          border-radius: 25px;
          height: 50px;
          width: 200px;
          padding:10px;
}


.border2 { border: 1px solid #000;
```

Continued

```
                    border-top-left-radius: 10px;

                    border-top-right-radius: 20px;

                    border-bottom-left-radius: 25px;

                    border-bottom-right-radius: 40px;

                    height: 50px;

                    width: 200px;

                    padding: 10px;

}
</style>
<div class="border1">
   Belhur Publishing
</div>
<br/><br/>
<div class="border2">
   Belhur Publishing
</div>
```

Figure 3.27: CSS border-radius properties to configure rounded corners

Figure 3.28: A sample Web page of border-radius properties

What Properties Control the Background of an Element?

Use the **background-image property** to indicate the URL of an image file you want to use as the background of the element. When specifying the URL, be sure to code it within the url('…') wrapper, as shown in the syntax below.

Set the background-attachment property to fixed if you want the background image to remain in exactly the same position within the viewable area of the Web page. If this property is set to scroll, the image will move with the content as the user scrolls through the element.

If you are not using a background image and would rather set the background to a solid color, use the background-color property. Set it to the desired color name, a hex code, or an RGB value.

```
{background-attachment: fixed
    scroll
background-color: color
    rgb(r,g,b)
    #(rr,gg,bb)
background-image: url('url')
background-position:
    x y
    top left
    top center
    top right
    center left
    center center

    center right
    bottom left
    bottom center
    bottom right
background-repeat: repeat
    repeat-x
    repeat-y
    no-repeat
background: color
    image
    repeat
    attachment
    position
}
```

If you want a background image to repeat (tile) to fill the element, set the **background-repeat property**. The property's default is repeat, which causes the image to tile as many times as needed to fill the available space. If it is set to repeat-x, the image repeats across the element horizontally, but only one row is tiled. If the property is set to repeat-y, the image repeats vertically, but only one column is tiled. To cause the image to only appear once, use the no-repeat value.

The **background-position property** identifies the starting position of the background image. Specify the *x* and *y* distances, where *x* is the offset distance from the left border, and *y* is the offset from the top border. Use the standard size values discussed earlier in this chapter. To avoid hard-coding a specific distance, you can specify one of the special values, such as top left or center center. As you would expect, the image is anchored to the element at the specified location. To set all the background image properties at once, use the **background property** and provide the values in the order shown.

To update the background of our sample Web page, we might remove all the background properties set in the <body> tag in the HTML code and add the code in Figure 3.29 to the style sheet. The result is shown in Figure 3.30.

```
body {background:url(Belhur-Publishing-Logo.jpg);
      background-repeat:no-repeat;
      background-position:top right;
}
```

Figure 3.29: The style sheet code for the body of a Web page

Figure 3.30: The result page for the body of a Web page shown in Figure 3.28

This style defines the background as a single image (Belhur-Publishing-Logo.jpg), positioned in the upper-right corner of the page. This doesn't change the look of the page at all, but it does move the control of the background image into the style sheet and out of the HTML code. There is another advantage to this that we'll discuss at the end of this chapter.

What Properties Control the Appearance of Elements?

The **list-style-type property** sets the specific symbol to use for ordered and unordered lists. The disc, circle, and square values create the standard symbols discussed in chapter 2. Set the type to lower-roman to use lowercase Roman numerals in an ordered list, or upper-roman for uppercase Roman numerals. Upper-alpha creates an ordered list with uppercase alphabetic characters, and lower-alpha uses lowercase alphabetic characters. **List-style-position** has two values: inside indents the list items, while outside (the default) prints them aligned to the current text.

```
{list-style-type:
  disc
  circle
  square
  decimal
  decimal-leading-zero
  lower-roman
  upper-roman
  lower-alpha
  upper-alpha
  lower-greek
  lower-latin
```

```
    upper-latin
    Hebrew
    armenian
    georgian
    cjk-ideographic
    hiragana
    katakana
    hiragana-iroha
    katakana-iroha
  list-style: type position image
  list-style-position: inside
         outside
  list-style-image: url(url)
  marker-offset: length
       auto
}
```

If the standard symbols are not sufficient for your needs, use the list-style-image property to specify a URL containing an image file of a symbol. Be sure to wrap the URL using url(...). Many people report having difficulty in getting list-style-image to work correctly and consistently in multiple browsers. If you have this problem, first try setting the position to outside. If that does not fix the problem, you might need to consider attaching a background image to the text instead of using an <li> tag.

The marker-offset property exists in the CSS definition from the W3C, but few, if any, browsers support it at this time.

To set the style, position and/or image at the same time, use the **list-style property**, then specify a type, position, and URL. Any of these items may be omitted, as needed.

The page properties affect the way an HTML document is printed. The two most common properties are page-break-before and page-break-after. Add either of these properties to an element to control how it handles page breaks.

```
{marks: crop
   cross
 orphans: number
 page-break-after: auto
       always
       avoid
       left
       right
 page-break-before: (as above)
 page-break-inside: auto
       avoid
size: length width
   auto
   landscape
   portrait
 widows: number
}
```

To force a page break before a given element prints, set its page-break-before property to always. This forces a page break to occur no matter how far down the page it is. Set a page-break-inside property to prevent page breaks from occurring within a given element.

Use the orphans property to set the minimum number of lines that must print at the bottom of a page before advancing to the next page. Similarly, the widows property defines the minimum number of lines that may print on a new page after a page break occurs in the middle of an element.

Set the marks property to crop if you want to allow images to print all the way to the edge of the paper, ignoring margins. Set this property to cross if you want to print alignment crosses on the paper, which are special symbols used by certain printers to guarantee correct alignment.

You may define the basic layout of the page by setting the size property to either landscape or portrait. Auto uses the default page size. If you want to manually set the page size, simply provide the length and width sizes.

There are also specific CSS properties for working with tables. For example, table-layout can be set to fixed if you have consistent row and column sizes. The sizes of the cells in the first row of the table provide the template that all subsequent rows use. This can result in a performance improvement when loading large tables, as the browser does not need to calculate the size of each cell as it is displayed.

```
{border-collapse: collapse
        separate
 border-spacing: length
        horz vert
 caption-side: bottom
       left
       right
       top
 empty-cells: show
       hide
 table-layout: auto
        fixed
 }
```

Use the empty-cells property to control how empty table cells are handled. Set this to hide if you want empty cells to be hidden from view, or show (the default) to indicate that all cells should be visible.

The border-collapse property compresses two adjacent borders into a single border, creating a more compact table. Setting this value to separate (the default) displays the two adjacent borders with a small space between them. Use the border-spacing property to control the size of the space between the borders when they are separated. Set border-spacing to a single value, and that length will be used as the size for both the vertical and the horizontal borders. Alternatively, provide the horizontal and vertical border sizes separately. The caption-side property simply determines the side of the table on which the caption appears. This can be set to top, right, left, or bottom.

Defining Style Classes

So far, you have seen ways to change the properties of standard HTML elements. There is a far more powerful option within CSS, however. You can define something called a *class*, which is a set of properties that can be used by one or more types of elements. You can define a class as a subclass of a specific element, as shown in Figure 3.31.

```
p.question {font-weight:bold;
}
p.answer {font-weight:normal;
}
```

Figure 3.31: Examples of subclasses

You can then write some HTML code that uses the style sheet, as in Figure 3.32. As you can see, the style sheet defines two types of paragraph tags: the question class and the answer class. Questions will be displayed in bold, while answers will be displayed in normal text.

```
<p class="question">How do we define style classes?</p>
<p class="answer">Using the ".class-name" syntax in the style sheet</p>
```

Figure 3.32: HTML code controlled by subclasses

The beauty of this method is that if you decide you want to display all questions in, say, blue, and the answers in green, you would only have to update the style sheet, and all pages that reference it would be updated. The HTML code references the class by adding the class property to a tag. If there is a paragraph class defined with that name, its properties will be used on this element.

You also have the option to define classes that are completely independent of all elements. The code for this is shown in Figure 3.33. As you can see, a class is defined with a period (.) as its first character.

```
.question {font-weight:bold;
}
.answer {font-weight:normal;
}
```

Figure 3.33: Examples of classes

Since the question class in Figure 3.33 is not associated with a specific HTML tag, any tag could inherit its properties by simply referring to it. This allows multiple elements, such as paragraphs and headings, to acquire the same properties.

How Do Elements Inherit Properties from a Parent Element?

Elements inherit any properties they can from their parent. So, if the <body> tag has its font-family set to Arial, every element within the body that prints text will acquire that font property by default. However, any child element that defines its own font-family property supersedes the value in the <body> tag.

It's also possible to use classes in style sheets to define properties for child elements. For example, suppose you created a list of questions and answers using the definition-list HTML tags. You could use the style classes shown in Figure 3.34 to define the look of the definition terms and the definition descriptions. You could also provide a separate look for the major and minor questions.

```
.major {background:#999; font-size:120%; width=200px;
}
.minor {background:white; font-size 90%;
}
.question {color:blue;
}
.answer {color:#000;
}
```

Figure 3.34: Styles for a question-and-answer page

The styles in Figure 3.34 define the major topics as having a gray background and larger text, while the minor topics have a white background and smaller text. Each cell within the row will inherit these properties from its parent. They will also define their own class as being either a question, which is printed in blue, or an answer, which is printed in white. The code for an HTML table that uses these classes is given in Figure 3.35.

```
<dl class="major">
<dt class ="question">Question 1</dt>
<dd class ="answer">Answer for 1</dd>
<dl class="minor">
<dt class ="question">Question 1.a</dt>
<dd class ="answer">Answer for 1.a</dd>
<dt class ="question">Question 1.b</dt>
<dd class ="answer">Answer for 1.b</dd>
</dl>
<dt class="question">Question 2</dt>
<dd class ="answer">Answer for 2</dd>
<dl class="minor">
```

Continued

```
<dt class ="question">Question 2.a</dt>

<dd class ="answer">Answer for 2.a</dd>

<dt class ="question">Question 2.b</dt>

<dd class ="answer">Answer for 2.b</dd>

</dl>

</dl>
```

Figure 3.35: The HTML code for a question-and-answer page

The <dl> tag defines the beginning of a new definition list. In this case, it also selects the class as being major or minor. The <dt> tag identifies a term, or in this case a question, and defines the class as question. The <dd>, or definition description, tag uses the answer class. The text that appears in the list acquires the properties of both of the classes set in the <dt> and <dd> tags, as well as the class set in the <dl> tag. This is because the <dt> and <dd> tags are within the <dl>, making them child elements that inherit properties from their parent.

The code in Figure 3.35 creates the page shown in Figure 3.36. All the questions appear in blue, while the answers are in black. The major questions appear in a larger text with a gray background. The **width property** in the major class limits the width of the element to 200 pixels. Without this, the gray background would extend all the way across the page.

You might be thinking that the list in Figure 3.36 is pretty ugly. While that's true, it provides a fairly simple way to illustrate the inheritance we're discussing, and that is our primary goal.

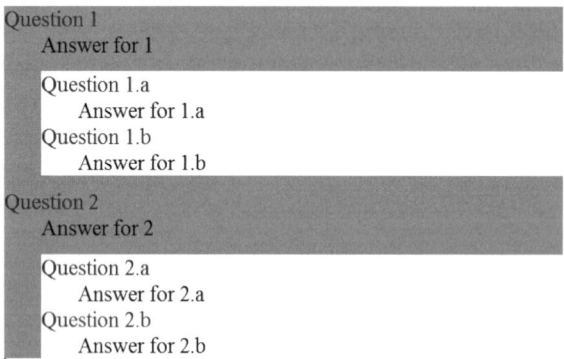

Figure 3.36: A question-and-answer HTML page, showing definitions with inheritance

Rather than using inheritance to provide the flexibility needed in the question-and-answer list, we could have assigned multiple classes to a single element. The code for the style sheet remains the same as in Figure 3.36, but the HTML changes to that in Figure 3.37.

```
<dl>

<dt class ="question major">Question 1</dt>
```
Continued

```
<dd class ="answer major">Answer for 1</dd>
<dl class ="minor">
<dt class ="question minor">Question 1.a</dt>
<dd class ="answer minor">Answer for 1.a</dd>
<dt class ="question minor">Question 1.b</dt>
<dd class ="answer minor">Answer for 1.b</dd>
</dl>
<dt class ="question major">Question 2</dt>
<dd class ="answer major">Answer for 2</dd>
<dl class ="minor">
<dt class ="question minor">Question 2.a</dt>
<dd class ="answer minor">Answer for 2.a</dd>
<dt class ="question minor">Question 2.b</dt>
<dd class ="answer minor">Answer for 2.b</dd>
</dl>
```

Figure 3.37: Alternative HTML code for the question-and-answer page

In this version of the definition list, all the decisions about question versus answer and major versus minor have been moved into the specific <dt> and <dd> tags. To improve the look of the list, we also included the minor class for the inner (minor) definition lists. As shown here, more than one class may be listed for the class property of an HTML tag. Simply list all the relevant classes, with a space between each. The result of this modified code, shown in Figure 3.38, is noticeably different from the previous example.

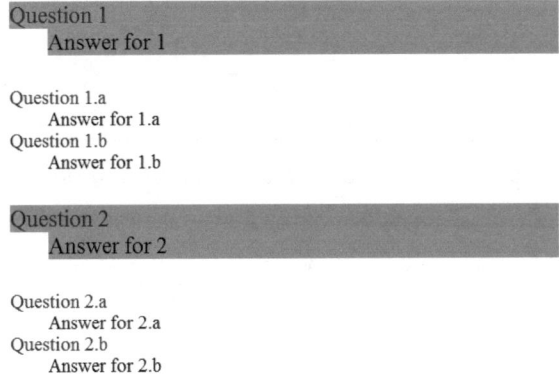

Figure 3.38: A definition list with multiple classes

Because we moved the major class out of the <dl> tag and into the <dt> and <dd> tags, only those specific question-and-answer sections have a gray background. Since the answer is indented beneath the question, and both have a fixed length of 200 pixels, the gray shading for the answer boxes sticks out further than the questions. We might want to set a smaller width for the answer so that all the answers align on the right side, but that is a cosmetic change that we don't need to worry about here. You can do it on your own, if you want.

It is also possible to define the style for elements that are the child of other specific elements. For example, you could define the look of the <li> tag when it is within an ordered list as being different from when it is within an unordered list. The CSS code might look like Figure 3.39.

```
ul li {color:blue; font-size:120%;
}
ol li {color:green; font-size:100%;
}
```

Figure 3.39: Styles for list items within unordered and ordered lists

Using this style sheet, the sample HTML code shown in Figure 3.40 creates the output in Figure 3.41.

```
<ul>
<li>Major Topic A</li>
  <ol>
  <li>Minor topic a.1</li>
  <li>Minor topic a.2</li>
  </ol>
<li>Major Topic B</li>
  <ol>
  <li>Minor topic b.1</li>
  <li>Minor topic b.2</li>
  </ol>
</ul>
```

Figure 3.40: The HTML code to create the Web page in Figure 3.41

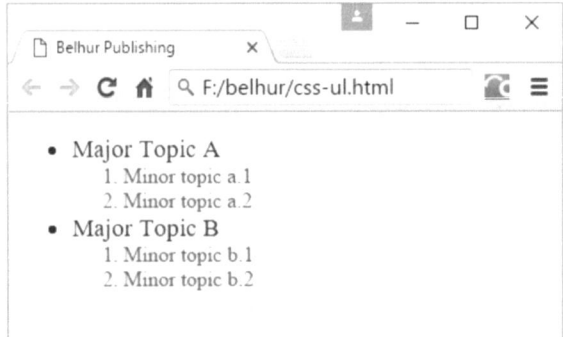

Figure 3.41: Nested lists with subclass styles

Remember that in this example all six lines of code are generated within the <li> tag. The different behavior comes from the parent element, in this case, the <ul> or <ol> tag. This type of subclass is called a **child selector**.

Another type of a subclass is the **descendant selector**, which identifies an element that is descended from another element, but not necessarily an immediate descendant. For example, if you added definition lists within the minor topics in the previous examples, you would have several layers of elements. You would have an <ol> containing a <ul> containing a <dl>. To assign a style to a definition list contained somewhere inside an ordered list, you would use the code shown in Figure 3.42.

```
ol>dl {color:green; font-size:100%;
}
```

Figure 3.42: The style for a definition list somewhere within an ordered list

If you needed to define the style of a definition list that was the grandchild or later descendant of another element, you would use the code in Figure 3.41 in the CSS. In this example, if the definition list were immediately beneath the ordered list in the HTML code, this style would not apply. There would have to be at least one other element between them for this style to apply.

```
ol*dl {color:green; font-size:100%;
}
```

Figure 3.43: The style for a definition list that is at least a grandchild of an ordered list

If you needed to identify sibling elements, such as a paragraph that immediately follows an <h3> tag, you could define a style sheet as shown in Figure 3.44. In this case, the plus sign indicates that the <p> tag must follow the <h3> tag. It is important to note that as opposed to the earlier examples, the <p> tag is not inside the <h3> tag, but adjacent to it, within a larger element such as the page body.

```
h3+p {color:blue; font-size:100%;
}
```

Figure 3.44: The style for a paragraph that immediately follows an <h3> tag

Once you understand these basic methods of identifying various selectors based on their relationships, an even more complex method of identifying elements in relationships to one another is to string together multiple dependent selectors. For example, if you wanted to identify only those ordered lists that existed somewhere within a paragraph and immediately after an unordered list, you could write the CSS code shown in Figure 3.45.

```
p>ul+ol {color:blue; font-size:100%;
}
```

Figure 3.45: An example of nested subclasses

This might seem at first like an odd and not terribly useful ability. However, what if you wanted to nest one unordered list inside another, such as shown in Figure 3.46?

```
<ul>
<li>Major Topic A</li>
  <ul>
  <li>Minor topic a.1</li>
  <li>Minor topic a.2</li>
   <ul>
   <li>Tertiary topic a.2.1</li>
   <li>Tertiary topic a.2.1</li>
   </ul>
  </ul>
</ul>
```

Figure 3.46: The HTML code for nested lists

Normally, for nested lists like this, the browser will assign different symbols such as disk, circle, and square to the list items at each level. But what if you wanted to change more than the symbol? What if you wanted to change, say, the text color and size as well? You could use the CSS code in Figure 3.47 to define the behavior for each layer of nested, unordered lists.

```
ul {color:blue; font-size:120%;
}
ul ul {color:green; font-size:100%;
}
ul ul ul {color:Red; font-size:80%;
}
```

Figure 3.47: Styles for nested lists

The first style is for the top-level unordered list. If you didn't code anything else, it would apply to all levels. The second style applies to the second level of nested unordered lists. The third style applies to all unordered lists that have been nested at least three levels deep. When this CSS code is combined with the previous HTML code, it generates the output shown in Figure 3.48. To continue defining different looks for deeper levels such the fourth or fifth levels, simply add additional styles with either four or five ul identifiers at the beginning.

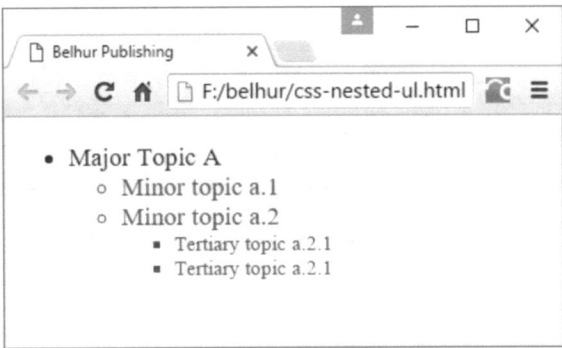

Figure 3.48: Three nested, unordered lists

Whenever more than one selector applies to an element, the one that is most precise takes precedence. There is a formula for determining this, but it's a bit more complicated than we want to try to explain here, so the overly simplified rule is this:

The selector that refers to the most IDs (discussed next) takes precedence. If the selectors refer to the same number of IDs (or none), then the number of classes referenced determines the selector that takes precedence. If the selectors refer to the same number of classes (or none), then the number of HTML tags referenced determines the selector that takes precedence. If two selectors refer to the same number of HTML tags, then the one listed last in the style sheet takes precedence.

What Is an ID?

So far, we have been talking almost exclusively about classes. But there is another entity called an *ID*. Where classes are used to define styles for one or more HTML elements, IDs are exclusively designed to uniquely identify a single element. So, if a page had three paragraphs, you might assign the same class to all three, but also assign a unique ID to each one, as shown in Figure 3.49.

```
<p id="p1" class="notes">Some misc information</p>

<p id="p2" class="notes">More misc information</p>

<p id="p3" class="notes">The last misc information</p>
```

Figure 3.49: Paragraph tags with IDs

Any attributes that are common to all three paragraphs can be assigned via the class's style. If you wanted only the second paragraph to print in italics, however, you might create CSS code such as that shown in Figure 3.50. The .notes entry defines the style for the notes class, which then applies to all three paragraphs. All ID tags referenced in a CSS precede the id identifier with a pound sign (#). So, the entry starting with #p2 defines the style for the second paragraph. Because the HTML code has both a class and an ID, both styles apply. The entry for the id tag overrides any conflicting values from the notes class.

```
.notes {font-style:normal; width:60%;margin-left:20%;
}


#p2 {font-style:italic
}
```

Figure 3.50: The style for the notes class and the p2 ID

The three paragraphs in Figure 3.49, with the CSS code in Figure 3.50, create the output in Figure 3.51. Remember that when you use an id tag, it should be unique within the HTML document.

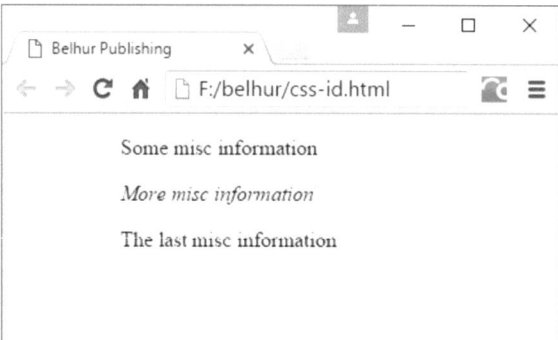

Figure 3.51: Three paragraphs with classes and IDs

What You Can Do with a Cascading Style Sheet

You can define style rules for virtually every HTML element, even if some are pointless, such as a font assignment for an embedded video file. All the examples you've seen so far are fairly simple. This is appropriate, because you are just beginning to understand how style sheets work.

One of the main uses for style sheets is to control the arrangement of content on the page. By *arrangement*, we mean not just setting properties such as font sizes and colors, but to actually move elements all over the page. One of the neat things you can do is create pages that can wildly change their looks and layouts, simply by changing the style sheet they use. We'll discuss this further in chapter 6. For now, let's look at a revised version of our Web page that incorporates a style sheet. We'll change the page to pull in the barn image as a background.

The HTML code shown in Figure 3.52 is for the Belhur Publishing About page. We'll use the same wireframe design from chapter 2. The sample Web page uses a three-column structure. Below the header are the navigation (left column), main content (middle column), and aside (right column). The footer section at the bottom of the page is similar to the header and expands across the entire width of the page. The page is styled using an external style sheet called main.css, which we link to the head section of the document.

```
<!DOCTYPE html>
<html>
<head>
  <title>About Belhur Publishing</title>
  <meta charset="utf-8" />
  <link rel="style sheet" href="main.css"/>
</head>
<body>
<div id="main-container">
  <header>
      <!-- Belhur Publishing Logo -->
  </header>
  <div id="left-side-bar">
    <nav>
        <ul>
          <li>Home</li>
          <li>About</li>
          <li>Books</li>
          <li>Order</li>
          <li>Contact Us</li>
        </ul>
    </nav>
  </div>
  <main>
    <section>
      <article>

        <h2>Corporate Overview</h2>

        <p>Belhur Publishing was established in 2016 as a joint effort
between MC Press, Laura Ubelhor, and Christian Hur.</p>
        <p>Our mission is to bring world-class learning material to those
who want to learn! </p>

        <p>Belhur Publishing takes pride in providing learning solutions
for students and those who want to advance their Web development skills.
First steps are important, and we have taken great care in offering
materials, education, and inspiration to assist individuals to move forward
and learn.</p>
```

Continued

```
        <p>Our primary customer base includes educational institutions,
individuals, and organizations wanting to further their growth in
technology-based Web development careers.</p>


        <p>Established in 2016 in collaboration with Christian Hur, Laura
Ubelhor, and MC Press.</p>

    </article>
  </section>
 </main>
  <footer>&copy;2016.  Belhur Publishing, LLC.  All rights reserved.</footer>
</div>
</body>
</html>
```

Figure 3.52: The modified HTML code for the Belhur Publishing About page

The entire body of the Web page is wrapped within a container called main-container. The first container elements are the header elements, which make up the page's masthead. Notice there is no content between the <header> and </header> elements. For now, they're just there as placeholders for our logo image. We are going to use CSS to style these tags to put our logo image as a background. The CSS style rules will also set the background color to a dark gray and the height just enough to accommodate the height of our logo image.

The left column is <div> tag that holds the navigation links. The navigation links will be created using the unordered list. The <div> container tags are to be floated to the left of the page. The center column is created with the <main> tags and holds the page's main content. The right column is wrapped within the <aside> tags and will float to the right. Finally, the footer is placed outside of the <main> tags so it can expand across the entire page.

The new style sheet for our About page is shown in Figure 3.53. This style sheet defines the picture of the Belhur Publishing logo as the background for the header of the page, positions it in the upper-left corner, and prevents it from repeating, so only one logo is shown.

```
/* CSS Document */

body {
        margin-left:auto;
        margin-right:auto;
        font-family:Arial, Helvetica, sans-serif;
        margin-top:0px;
}
                                                            Continued
```

```
header {
        background-color: #999;
        background-image:url("Belhur-Publishing-Logo.png");
        background-position:left;
        background-repeat:no-repeat;
        height: 115px;
        padding: 5px;
        border-bottom: 1px solid #000000;
}
#main-container {
        min-width: 700px;
        max-width: 1024px;
        margin-left: auto;
        margin-right: auto;
        width: 90%;
        border: 1px solid #000000;
        background-color:#C0C0C0;
}
main {
        background-color: #ffffff;
        margin: 0 200px 0 191px;
        padding: 10px;
        border-left: 1px solid #000000;
}
h2 {
        font-family: "Palatino Linotype", Georgia, serif;
        padding:0px;
        margin:0px;
}
#left-side-bar {
        width: 190px;
        margin-bottom: 0;
        float: left;
        text-align:center;
}
nav ul {
        list-style:none;
        padding:0px;
        margin-top:0px;
}
```

Continued

```
nav {
      margin:auto;
      text-align:center;
}
nav li {
      display:block;
}
footer {
      font-size: .70em;
      font-style: italic;
      text-align: center;
      padding: 5px;
      background-color: #ccc;
      color: #000;
      border-top: 1px solid #333;
}
```

Figure 3.53: The style sheet for the Belhur Publishing About page

We added a series of font types to the heading <h2> with the first choice being "Palatino Linotype", second Georgia, and third serif. The navigation links are placeholders only and have no actual links created. (In the next chapter, we will learn how to create hyperlinks.) We remove the bullets from the unordered list by setting the property list-style:none. The footer contains a copyright symbol, and the entire text is italicized and center with a font size of .70em. The resulting Web page is shown in Figure 3.54.

Figure 3.54: The updated Web page using a Cascading Style Sheet

Summary

CSS style sheets provide a tremendous amount of flexibility and expand your options for designing Web pages. Combining HTML with style sheets creates vastly more sophisticated Web pages.

The topics covered in this chapter only begin to scratch the surface of the CSS topic. To expand your knowledge of CSS, it is a good idea to partner with an experienced Web designer to create the layout and look of your Web pages. If you don't have an experienced designer to learn from, consider investigating some of the many online tutorials and books on CSS. With a little research and effort, you can build on this introduction to CSS, and you'll be on the road to becoming an experienced Web developer yourself!

Key Terms

@import	CSS box model	list-style property
<link>	cursor property	list-style-position
<style>	declaration	list-style-type property
background property	descendant selector	margin property
background-image property	em unit	padding property
background-position property	embedded style sheet	position property
background-repeat property	ex unit	pt unit
border property	external style sheet	px unit
border-color property	font-family property	rule
border-style property	font-size property	rule of precedence
border-width	font-style property	selector
Cascading Style Sheets (CSS)	font-weight property	style attribute
class attribute	id attribute	text-align property
class selector	id selector	width property
child selector	imported styles	z-index
color property	inline style	

Discussion/Review Questions

1. What is a Cascading Style Sheet (CSS)?
2. What are three common methods of incorporating style sheets into a Web document?
3. What are style rules?
4. A CSS style rule is comprised of what two parts?
5. How is CSS a presentational language?
6. What is an inline style, and how is it coded on a Web page?
7. What is an embedded style sheet?
8. What is an external style sheet?
9. How do you incorporate an external style sheet into a Web page?
10. What are CSS orders of precedence?
11. What is a CSS selector?

12. An external style sheet can be incorporated into a Web page using which HTML tag?
13. What is the main advantage of using external style sheets?
14. What should not be included in the body of a style sheet?
15. Why is it not recommended to import external style sheets using the @import directive?
16. What are parent, child, and descendent selectors?
17. Why are class and id selectors essential?
18. When should you use a class selector?
19. If you want the font-size of a paragraph text to be resized automatically relative to the font-size of its parent tag, which font-size unit should you use?
20. What is the CSS box model?
21. The padding property of an element is bordered between which two properties?

Exercises

1. Write the HTML code for incorporating an external style sheet called main.css.
2. Write the HTML code for a div tag that uses an inline style to configure the font-size to be 1.2em and text color to be blue.
3. Write the HTML and CSS code for an embedded style sheet that configures a class called detail to have green text, a size of 12px, and be in Arial, Georgia, Verdana, or a sans-serif font.
4. Provide a CSS style rule to configure a div tag as follows:
   a. a solid red border type with 1px thickness
   b. a non-repeating background image called bg.png with a top center position
5. Describe the item selected by the following selector:

   ```
   p.detail { color: blue; text-decoration: italic;}
   ```

6. Write the CSS code to configure only the <p> descendent elements of the <div> elements (as shown below) to have blue text and 1.2em in size:

   ```
   <p>I am a sibling element of div.</p>
   <div>
       <p>I am a descendent element of div.</p>
       <aside>
           <p>I am also a descendent element of div.</</p>
       </aside>
   <div>
   ```

7. Create an external style sheet to format a Web page as follows:
   a. Set the document background color to yellow
   b. Set the document default font family list to Arial, Helvetica, Verdana, and sans-serif
   c. Set the document default font size to 12px
   d. h1 selector to be 2em in size with blue text color
   e. Hyperlinks to have a background color of black, text color of white, and no text decoration

4

Adding Links and Anchors

Links are an essential ingredient on any Web page. They provide a means by which users can easily navigate from one page to another with a simple click of the mouse. If moving between Web pages required constantly typing URLs, far fewer people would surf the Web.

Because links are so easy and intuitive to use, they have become an important tool for interacting with the public. For many Web pages, links have few requirements beyond being clear and simple to use. For businesses, however, the needs can be far more significant. Links between Web pages affect placement in Web search engines. (For more information about search engines, see chapter 13.) Linking to a Web page deep inside another website ("deep linking") might be attractive, but it has its pitfalls. Using anchors wisely can dramatically improve navigation through a large Web page. These and other important topics are discussed in this chapter.

How to Place a Link on a Page

The key to placing a link onto a Web page is the **anchor tag**. This tag defines a clickable hyperlink on your page, and then acts as an anchor or point for the user to return to when he or she is done viewing the linked-in page.

Anchor tag:

```
<a
    href
    hreflang
    name
    id
    target
```

```
   charset
   title
>
</a>
```

The anchor tag has many attributes. The **href attribute** is the most important attribute because it defines the target of the link. Typically, the target is another Web page, but it could be a different place on the current page or on another **domain**, or even a file of a different type, such as a Word document, PDF, or movie file. If your browser can render the file type, you can just click the link to process it through the browser. Files that your browser cannot render may still be right-clicked on and saved to your local PC.

The **hreflang** attribute sets the language ID for the Web page. The purpose of the hreflang attribute is to show search engines what the relationship is between Web pages in alternative languages, so the search engines can display the result to users searching in a particular language. Search engines support the ISO 639-1 format, which uses two-letter codes. For example, for American English, set this to en-US; for British English, use en; and for Japanese, use ja. There are approximately more than 200 different language codes, so it is not possible to list them all here. You can find a complete list at *www.loc.gov/standards/iso639-2/php/code_list.php*.

Both the **name** and the **id** attributes provide a mechanism for naming the anchor. Within the anchor tag, name has been deprecated in HTML5 and replaced by the id attribute, which is more commonly used. Links in other documents or even at other locations within the same document may navigate directly to a named anchor, as discussed later in this chapter. **Target** controls the behavior of the link. The following list explains the options for the **target attribute**:

- **_self** opens a link in the current frame.
- **_blank** opens a link in a new window.
- **_parent** opens a link in the frameset parent frame (discussed in chapter 7).
- **_top** opens a link in the topmost window.

Title defines the pop-up tooltip text for the link, which will appear when the user's mouse hovers over it. **Charset** indicates which character set should be used. The most common character set is ISO-8859-1, which is used for English and many European languages. A complete list is available at *www.iana.org/assignments/character-sets*.

The code snippet in Figure 4.1 shows the HTML code to create a link to our fictitious Belhur Publishing site, shown in Figure 4.2. This is one of the easiest and most basic links that can be created.

```
<a href="http://www.belhurpublishing.com" title="Go to Belhur
Publishing">Belhur Publishing</a>
```

Figure 4.1: A basic example of the HTML anchor tag

Figure 4.2: The link created from the code in Figure 4.1, showing tooltip text

To change this link so that it opens in a separate window, use the target parameter, as shown in Figure 4.3.

```
<a href="http://www.belhurpublishing.com" title="Go to Belhur Publishing"
target="_blank">Belhur Publishing</a>
```

Figure 4.3: A hypertext link to Belhur Publishing that opens in a new window

The code snippet in Figure 4.3 shows the target entered in lower case. This is important, as some browsers might not support this value in upper case. If you're designing an application that opens a link in a new window, it might be useful to set the size of the window smaller than the original, so that it is clearly a "child" window displayed above its "parent." Chapter 8 includes some JavaScript that can be used to open a child window in a specific size.

How Links Affect Search Engines

Links do more than just provide connections to other documents. They can affect the placement of your Web page in search engines. In general, the inbound links to your site have a much greater effect on your website's search-engine ranking than the outbound links you write in your Web pages' code. So, one of the best things you can do to improve your Web page's placement in a search is to get other reputable sites to link to yours. Focus on getting sites in your industry to link to your site—perhaps business partners' sites, or those of clients or vendors. The anchor text in those links should relate to your website's *keywords*, which are special key terms that describe the content and nature of your website. For example, the anchor text "Learn Web Development with HTML, CSS, and JavaScript" contains keywords that relate to this book. In contrast, the anchor text "Our New Book" contains keywords that aren't relevant to this book at all. Likewise, the anchor text for your outbound links should include relevant keywords pointing to reputable sites to give your Web page a slight bump in its perceived quality. In both situations, a search engine compares the anchor text with the actual content of the target page, then determines the relevancy and quality of your Web page, which in turn can improve the page's search-engine ranking. We will discuss keywords and how search engines rank your Web pages in more detail in chapter 13.

It is also important to note that different search engines use different rules, and these rules are constantly evolving. Therefore, what works today might not work tomorrow. Thus, it's important for

Web developers to stay current on algorithm updates to search engines such as Google, Bing, and Yahoo!.

Deep Linking

Deep linking refers to the practice of linking to a particular Web page or other document located in another website. This site might belong to a company you do business with, or it might just be a site that provides useful information for the public. An example of a deep link appears in Figure 4.4.

```
<a href=" http://www.mcpressonline.com/application-software/microsoft/
analyze-db2400-data-with-excel.html"
target="_blank">Analyze DB2/400 Data with Excel</a>
```

Figure 4.4: An example of deep linking

This link is valid only until MC Press reorganizes its website or removes that file. Once the site is restructured, your link to its page will no longer work. Therefore, the safest way to link to another site is by linking to its home/main page rather than using deep linking. Although avoiding deep linking entirely might be more convenient for you as a developer, the downside is that by doing so, you lose the ability to have your links to attach directly to relevant content.

To minimize the risk of broken links occurring with deep linking, it's a good idea to contact the owner of the website you want to link to and ask if they can provide you with a URL that is unlikely to change regardless of what happens with their internal structure. However, it's more likely that they will allow you to link to their site while providing the warning that there is no guarantee that the link will continue to work for any period of time. If you do have deep links, test them periodically to ensure they continue to work correctly.

How to Use Anchors

So far in this chapter, you've seen how to use anchors as links. Now, let's discuss using them as … anchors! An anchor is a location within the body of a Web page that can be linked to. Traditionally, the key to making an anchor tag function as an anchor has been the name attribute and the anchor (<a>) tag, as shown in Figure 4.5. As discussed earlier, this method has been deprecated in HTML5, and the id attribute should be used instead.

As you can see, this anchor tag does not contain an href attribute. Because it is not acting as a link, no such attribute is needed. There is also no anchor text between the begin and end tags (<a> and </a>). Since all we are doing is marking a section of the page, this is fine. Another Web page or even another section of the same Web page might link to this anchor to position the browser at that specific place in the Web page.

```
<a name="location"></a>
```

Figure 4.5: An anchor tag with the name attribute using the traditional method

The code snippet in Figure 4.6 demonstrates how to link to a specific anchor on a page. This link opens the requested Web page in the current window and positions it at the anchor named location. As you can see, the anchor name comes after the HTML file's name and is prefixed by a pound sign (#).

```
<a href="your-document.html#location">Anchor-Text</a>
```

Figure 4.6: A hypertext link to the anchor in Figure 4.5

The preferred method is by using an id attribute attached to another element such as a <div> or a <span>, or to any tag within the document. Virtually, any id attribute can be used as an anchor for a hyperlink. Figure 4.5 can be modified to anchor the location to a <div> tag, as shown in Figure 4.7. The hyperlink in Figure 4.6 would still have the same effect.

```
<div id="location"></div>
```

Figure 4.7: An anchor location with the id attribute in HTML5

Links such as these are invaluable on long pages, which include features such as a table of contents or a "Frequently Asked Questions" (FAQ) section. In such cases, anchors mark specific sections of a page, and a list of links at the top of the page points to the various anchors. For example, the code in Figure 4.8 is for an FAQ page that answers questions a new HTML programmer might have.

```
<!DOCTYPE html>
<html>
    <head>
        <title>HTML FAQs</title>
        <meta charset="utf-8" />
    </head>
<body>

<h1>HTML FAQs</h1>

<h2>Questions?</h2>
<ul style="list-style:none; padding:0px;">
    <li><a href="#mean">What does HTML mean?</a></li>
    <li><a href="#do">What does HTML do?</a></li>
    <li><a href="#style">What is a style sheet?</a></li>
    <li><a href="#link">How do I link to another Web page?</a></li>
    <li><a href="#tool">What tool do we use to edit HTML?</a></li>
</ul>
                                                    Continued
```

```
<h3 id="mean">What does HTML mean?</h3>
<p>HTML stands for HyperText Markup Language.
There are many markup languages, of which HTML is one.
The language is designed to send a mix of text content and
links to other content to the user's web browser.</p>

<h3 id="do">What does HTML do?</h3>
<p> HTML defines the method in which text and images can be
integrated by a Web browser. The browser is responsible for
interpreting the document correctly and displaying it in a
fashion that integrates text with other content such as images.</p>

<h3 id="style">What is a style sheet?</h3>
<p>A style sheet is a document containing one or more style
definitions. These definitions control the look of a Web
page. The same style sheet can be linked to multiple
documents, allowing a single point of control for the look
of your Web page.</p>

<h3 id="link">How do I link to another Web page?</h3>
<p>As discussed earlier in the chapter, the anchor tag (&lt;a&gt;)
provides the mechanism by which a Web page makes clickable links
to other Web pages. The href attribute is the key to defining
the link.</p>

<h3 id="tool">What tool do we use to edit HTML?</h3>
<p>Numerous tools exist for editing Web pages. You can use something
as simple as NotePad++, Bracket, Microsoft's Expression, or Adobe
Dreamweaver.</p>

</body>
</html>
```

Figure 4.8: HTML code to create the FAQ page shown in Figure 4.9

This HTML code creates the Web page shown in Figure 4.9. The questions near the top are displayed as anchors. Each one uses an id name to create a link to the specific section lower on the page that answers that question. Therefore, the <a href="#style"> link connects to the <h3 id="*id-name*"> anchor.

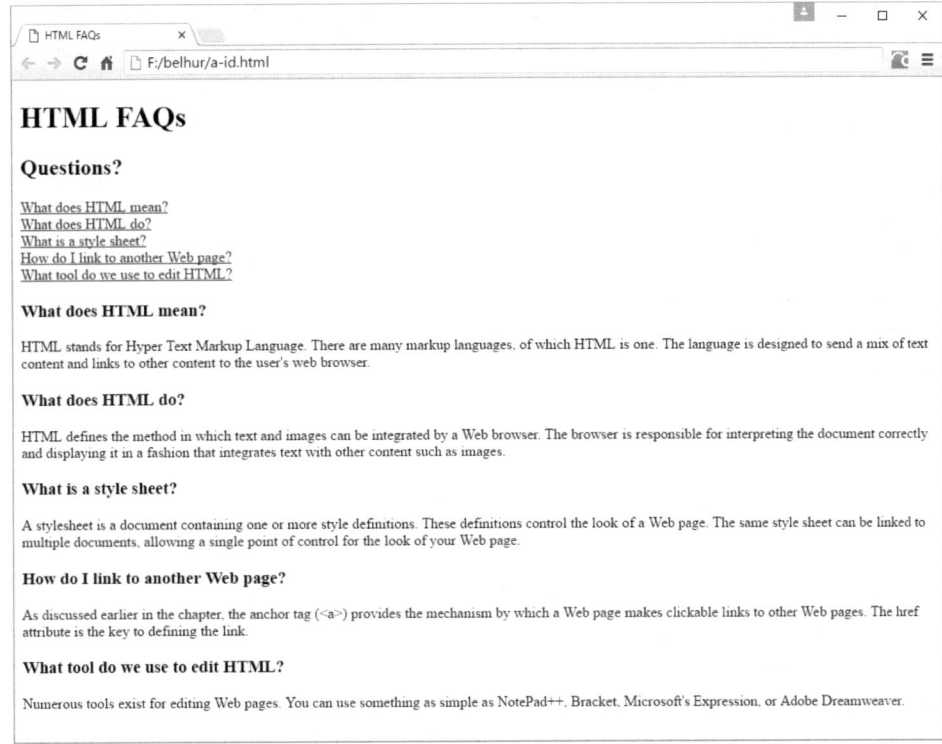

Figure 4.9: An FAQ page using named anchor tags

Types of Hyperlinks

HTML supports several types of hyperlinks. The two most popular types of hyperlinks are **absolute** and **relative**. An **absolute hyperlink** (or absolute link) is one in which the **full path** (called the *Uniform Resource Identifier*, or *URI*) to the targeted file or content is specified in the href attribute. An absolute path contains the URI (also often referred to as **URL**), which is a string of characters that represents the Internet Protocol (IP) address of a device or server connected to the Internet. The exact location of a Web page stored on a Web server can be identified and then accessed with a URI. Figure 4.10 shows the absolute path to an anchor position on a Web page.

Figure 4.10: An absolute hyperlink (full path URL) and its components

The "http" portion of the URL is the *protocol* (or *scheme*), a set of rules that instructs networking devices how to transfer data. Websites always use **Hypertext Transfer Protocol (HTTP)**. When linking to a subfolder, it's a good idea to end the URL with a slash (/)—for example, href="http://www.mycompany.com/download/". This simplifies handling of the link for the server, which otherwise will have to do additional processing to add the slash for you. Similarly, whenever you link to other files in the same folder, use a local reference, such as href="mywebpage.html", instead of href="http://www.mycompany.com/mywebpage.html". The local reference requires less work for the server and improves response time.

By default, hyperlinks are rendered by the browser with an underline and a blue color text. If you want to create links that do not have underlines, try adding the style attribute to the anchor tag, as shown in Figure 4.11.

```
<a href="http://www.mycompany.com" style="text-decoration: none">
some-anchor-text</a>
```

Figure 4.11: A hypertext link without an underline

Periodically test your links to ensure that they are still valid. Bad links will lower the quality of your Web page, both in the eyes of site visitors and in search-engines' rankings.

Absolute links are necessary if you want to link to a Web page or content outside of your website's domain. If you do not specify the protocol and server name, the Web browser will treat the target page as a local file residing on the local server. A link that does not contain a protocol scheme and a server name is considered a **relative hyperlink**. Hyperlinks that are linked to files that reside on the same domain as the Web page should use relative links to speed up processing time. An example of a relative path is the *Path* portion of the URL shown in Figure 4.10. The relative path is relative to the location of the file that contains the hyperlinks. Figure 4.12 shows how three relative links are created.

```
<a href="about.html" title="About Us Page">About Us</a>
<a href="images/logo.gif" title="Logo Image">Logo Image</a>
<a href="../ch3/example/index.html">Chapter 3 Example</a>
```

Figure 4.12: Creating three different relative hyperlinks

Line 1 in Figure 4.12 links to a file that is on the same directory as the current page. In this example, the About page is located in the same directory as the current page; thus, we specify just the filename as the value for the href attribute. Line 2 links to an image file that is located one directory down from the current page. The forward slash (/) after the directory name signifies a directory level. Line 3 links to the index page of a subdirectory that is in another directory above the directory in which the current page resides. The two periods followed by a slash (../) signify a directory above the current directory.

Other Kinds of Links

The previous examples have all worked with typical HTML files. The links simply move the browser through Web pages, or perhaps to an image file. There are other kinds of links as well. One of the more common examples is the **mailto** link. The code in Figure 4.13 illustrates an example use of mailto: it provides a clickable link that opens a new email message and fills in some of the message's content.

```
<a href="mailto:christian.hur@belhurpublishing.com?subject=HTML">
Send an e-mail to Christian</a>
```

Figure 4.13: Using mailto to create a link to the default mail client

This sample creates the link shown in Figure 4.14. When the link is clicked, the opened email message has its destination address and subject already filled in.

Figure 4.14: The mailto link on a Web page

If you wanted to have mailto links for multiple recipients, your HTML code would list all the email addresses, with commas separating them, as shown in Figure 4.15.

```
<a href="mailto:user@whoknows.com,another@whoknows.com?cc=boss@yourcompany.
com,secretary@yourcompany.com">Send Some Mail</a>
```

Figure 4.15: An example of a mailto link with additional data predefined

A more sophisticated example loads all the parts of the email that can be filled in. As shown in Figure 4.16, the link includes more email addresses for the CC (carbon copy) and BCC (blind carbon copy) sections, and even adds some text in the body of the email. The link created by this HTML code looks exactly the same as that in Figure 4.13, but its behavior after it is clicked is different. It simply fills in more fields than the first example.

```
<a href="mailto:christian.hur@belhurpublishing.com?cc=sales@company1.
com&bcc=IT@company1.com&subject=HTML%20Book&body=Christian,%0A%0AHello!">Se
nd an e-mail to Christian</a>
```

Figure 4.16: An example of a mailto link with embedded blanks and new-line characters

Notice the %20 code. It is used to represent a blank. In fact, coding a blank between HTML and Book would create an error in the mailto link, so the %20 escape character is used instead. This code translates as a blank when it is displayed in the email's subject line. Similarly, the escape character %0A moves to the next line. When used together (%0A%0A), the two escape characters create a single blank line after other text.

Also notice that after the first email address, a series of parameters is passed. The first parameter is preceded by a question mark (?). The remaining parameters are preceded by ampersand characters

(&). In more complex URLs, these codes are very important in allowing more flexible processing of Web content. The mailto link from Figure 4.16 creates an email message like the one in Figure 4.17.

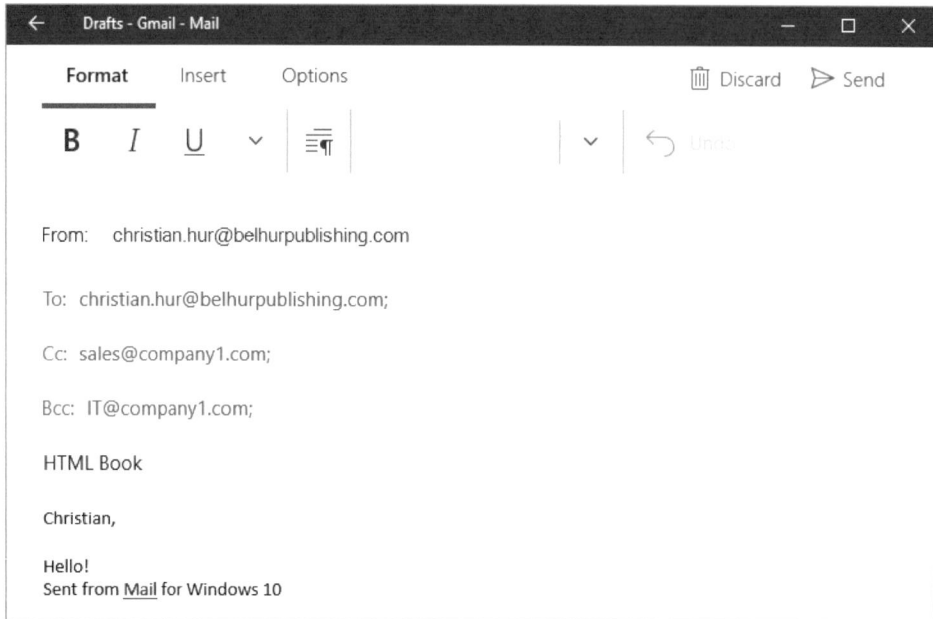

Figure 4.17: A mailto email message

Mailto Drawbacks

While the mailto link is a simple way to generate emails from a Web page, it has some drawbacks. First, the remote user must have a mail client installed. Without one, the mailto link will not know what program to execute to open a new email. This is out of our control, as Web developers.

A second drawback is that spammers scour the Internet looking for email addresses in mailto links to add to their directories. Some developers suggest using the escape sequence @ in place of the "at" sign (@) in an email addresses. Using this sequence will still render the @ symbol correctly in the email message, but (supposedly) it will prevent the address from being read by spammer robots searching for new email addresses.

Finally, site visitors may perceive a mailto link as less businesslike than using a form to create an email. (We'll discuss this more in chapter 10, PHP programming.) Using mailto might give some users the impression that you're new to HTML—which you may be, but you might not want anyone else to know that!

Using an FTP Link

Another type of link is an FTP link (ftp). This type of link automates a **File Transfer Protocol (FTP)** transfer of the specified file from the given website and downloads it to your system. The target website does not need to be the one that hosts your Web page.

The code in Figure 4.18 shows a simple example of an ftp link.

```
<a href="ftp://ftp.yoursite.com/yourfolder/yourfile.txt">
```

Figure 4.18: An example of an FTP link

Using Invisible Links

Another kind of link involves the **<link>** tag. Notice that there is no end tag for <link>. It simply defines the related documents, with no visible content to display.

Link tag:

```
<link
  href
  hreflang
  rel
  rev
  target
  type
  media
  charset
  lang
>
```

This tag can be used to define a variety of connections to other documents. For example, you can define the relative position of a document within a series of documents using the <link> tag's rel attribute, as shown in Figure 4.19.

```
<!DOCYTYPE html>
<html>
<head>
  <meta charset="utf-8"/>
  <title>Second Page</title>
  <link rel="prev" href="page1.html">
  <link rel="next" href="page3.html">
</head>
```

Figure 4.19: An example of invisible links to other pages

These links should be coded within the heading section of the document. Certain tools, such as book readers, may look for tags like these, allowing readers to easily navigate through a series of HTML documents that make up a larger document, such as a book.

Another (and very practical) use of the <link> tag is to define a style sheet. (Style sheets are discussed in detail in chapter 3.) For now, Figure 4.20 shows a simple link to a style sheet. This link identifies the style sheet file as being a Cascading Style Sheet (CSS), which is in use for this Web page. In short, the style sheet contains a series of formatting definitions. These could be anything from the default font and size to the background color of the page, and more.

```
<!DOCYTYPE html>
<html>
<head>
  <meta charset="utf-8"/>
  <title>Sample Page</title>
  <link rel="stylesheet" href="stylesheet.css" />
</head>
```

Figure 4.20: A link to a Cascading Style Sheet

It's also possible to define an alternate style sheet, as in Figure 4.21, so that users might someday be able to choose what format they'd like to see the page displayed in. For now, an alternate style sheet is of little value, but as browsers continually improve, it may become more useful.

```
<!DOCYTYPE html>
<html>
<head>
  <meta charset="utf-8"/>
  <title>Sample Page</title>
  <link rel="stylesheet" href="stylesheet.css" />
  <link rel="alternate stylesheet" href="stylesheet2.css" />
</head>
```

Figure 4.21: A link to both a main style sheet and an alternate style sheet

The <link> tag also lets you define alternate-language versions of a page. To do so, simply add code such as that in Figure 4.22 to point to language-specific versions of your page.

```
<link rel="Alternate" href="page1.fr.html" hreflang="fr" title="Page1 -
française">
<link rel="Alternate" href="page1.ja.html" hreflang="ja"
charset="Shift_JIS"
  title="page1 - Japanese" lang="ja">
<link rel="Alternate" href="page1.pdf" type="application/pdf" media="print"
  title="page1 - PDF">
```

Figure 4.22: Linking to alternate HTML and PDF documents for printing in different languages

The rev attribute defines the link from the document in the href to this document. In other words, it is the reverse of the rel attribute. The rev and rel attributes identify the link type being defined. Many of the choices for link type are defined in Table 4.1.

Table 4.1: Link Types	
Link Type	**Description**
Alternate	A replacement document for the one with the link
Stylesheet	A Cascading Style Sheet used by this document
Start	The first document in a series
Copyright	The copyright statement for a series of documents
Contents	The table of contents for a series of documents
Next	The next document in a series
Prev	The previous document in a series
Chapter	A chapter in a series of documents
Section	A section in a series of documents
Subsection	A subsection in a series of documents
Glossary	The glossary for a series of documents
Appendix	An appendix for a series of documents
Index	The index for a series of documents
Help	An additional information resource for this document
Bookmark	A bookmark to a specific part of a document

As cool as these link types seem, remember that support for them is a bit thin. So, check the tools and browsers that you work with to see if there is any advantage to be gained from using these options.

What About Our Example Page?

In chapter 3, we created our example Web page to include a photo of our logo as a background image for the header. We also created placeholder navigation links, which are not clickable. How can we improve the site by adding links?

The About page really isn't long enough to warrant using internal links to jump to various sections. Instead, let's create all the other pages that are currently listed on the navigation section: home, books, order, and contact pages. Then we will modify our navigation links to link to those pages. The modified code for the About page is shown in Figure 4.23.

```
<!DOCTYPE html>
<html>
<head>
        <title>About Belhur Publishing</title>
        <meta charset="utf-8" />
```

Continued

```
        <link rel="stylesheet" href="main.css"/>
</head>
<body>
<div id="main-container">
  <header>
        <!-- Belhur Publishing Logo -->
  </header>
  <div id="left-side-bar">
        <nav>
         <ul>
           <li><a href="index.html">Home</a></li>
           <li><a href="about.html">About</a></li>
           <li><a href="books.html">Books</a></li>
           <li><a href="order.html">Order</a></li>
           <li><a href="contact.html">Contact Us</a></li>
         </ul>
        </nav>
  </div>
  <main>
    <section>
      <article>

        <h2>Corporate Overview</h2>

        <p>Belhur Publishing was established in 2016 as a joint effort
between MC Press, Laura Ubelhor, and Christian Hur.</p>
        <p>Our mission is to bring world-class learning material to those
who want to learn! </p>

        <p>Belhur Publishing takes pride in providing learning solutions
for students and those who want to advance their Web development skills.
First steps are important, and we have taken great care in offering
materials, education, and inspiration to assist individuals to move forward
and learn.</p>

        <p>Our primary customer base includes educational institutions,
individuals, and organizations wanting to further growth in technology-
based Web development careers.</p>

        <p>Established in 2016 in collaboration with Christian Hur, Laura
Ubelhor, and MC Press.</p>
```

Continued

```
        </article>
      </section>
    </main>
    <footer>&copy;2016.  Belhur Publishing, LLC.  All rights
reserved.</footer>
  </div>
</body>
</html>
```

Figure 4.23: The HTML code for the sample About page, including links

Notice that we did not specify the targets of the links with the reference _blank. Since these are only internal links, they should not cause each of the three sections to open in their own new windows or tabs. In other words, we want our visitors to stay on our site for as long as possible. We wouldn't want our visitors to click away from our site. So, only external links should be opened with their own windows or tabs, so that our site always remains visible for the user to return to.

The code for the home page (index.html) is shown in Figure 4.24. Notice that the same navigation links are created to link back to any of the other pages. The user can click to any page at any time by clicking the links.

```
<!DOCTYPE html>
<html>
<head>
<title>Belhur Publishing</title>
<meta charset="utf-8" />
<link rel="stylesheet" href="main.css"/>
</head>
<body>
<div id="main-container">
  <header> </header>
  <div id="left-side-bar">
    <nav>
      <ul>
        <li><a href="index.html">Home</a></li>
        <li><a href="about.html">About</a></li>
        <li><a href="books.html">Books</a></li>
        <li><a href="order.html">Order</a></li>
        <li><a href="contact.html">Contact Us</a></li>
      </ul>
```

Continued

```
      </nav>
    </div>
    <aside> </aside>
    <main>
      <section>
        <article>
          <p>Belhur Publishing - your ultimate source for technical
publications.
            Where those in the know go to find e-books and hard copy books on
technical topics.
            Whether you're a student or adding new skills, we can help! </p>
          <h2 id="new-books">New Books</h2>
          <h2>HTML for the Business Developer</h2>
        </article>
      </section>
    </main>
    <footer>&#169;2016.  Belhur Publishing, LLC.  All rights
reserved.</footer>
  </div>
</body>
</html>
```

Figure 4.24: The HTML code for the Home page

The code for the Books page (books.html) is listed in Figure 4.25. Notice that each book title is wrapped inside the <p> tags, which are then nested inside the <div> tags. We assign two class ids for the book titles. The book class selector will be used to define the width and height for the content of each title, such as the title, description or tagline, and image of the book. For now, the book class selector is only a placeholder. We will not format it until chapter 5, when we learn to add images. The book-title class selector is for formatting the book title only.

```
<!DOCTYPE html>
<html>
<head>
<title>Belhur Publishing - Books</title>
<meta charset="utf-8" />
<link rel="stylesheet" href="main.css"/>
</head>
<body>
<div id="main-container">
```

Continued

```
<header> </header>
<div id="left-side-bar">
  <nav>
    <ul>
      <li><a href="index.html">Home</a></li>
      <li><a href="about.html">About</a></li>
      <li><a href="books.html">Books</a></li>
      <li><a href="order.html">Order</a></li>
      <li><a href="contact.html">Contact Us</a></li>
    </ul>
  </nav>
</div>
<aside> </aside>
<main>
  <section>
    <article>
      <div class="book">
        <p class="book-title">Web Services for Everyone</p>
      </div>
      <div class="book">
        <p class="book-title">PHP Hot Scripts </p>
      </div>
      <div class="book">
        <p class="book-title">The IBMI i Programmer's Guide to PHP</p>
      </div>
      <div class="book">
        <p class="book-title">jQuery Uplifts Your Web Application </p>
      </div>
      <div class="book">
        <p class="book-title">Modernize Your Applications with Ruby
on Rails </p>
      </div>
      <div class="book">
        <p class="book-title">Application Modernization </p>
      </div>
      <div class="book">
        <p class="book-title">Integrating Legacy Code on the Web </p>
      </div>
```

Continued

```
      </article>
    </section>
    <br class="clear" />
  </main>
  <footer>&copy;2016.  Belhur Publishing, LLC.  All rights
reserved.</footer>
</div>
</body>
</html>
```

Figure 4.25: The HTML code for the Books page

The code for the Order page (order.html) appears in Figure 4.26.

```
<!DOCTYPE html>
<html>
<head>
<title>Belhur Publishing - Order</title>
<meta charset="utf-8" />
<link rel="stylesheet" href="main.css"/>
</head>
<body>
<div id="main-container">
  <header> </header>
  <div id="left-side-bar">
    <nav>
      <ul>
        <li><a href="index.html">Home</a></li>
        <li><a href="about.html">About</a></li>
        <li><a href="books.html">Books</a></li>
        <li><a href="order.html">Order</a></li>
        <li><a href="contact.html">Contact Us</a></li>
      </ul>
    </nav>
  </div>
  <aside> </aside>
  <main>
    <section>
      <article>
```

Continued

```
          <h2>Place your order with us.</h2>
          <br/>
          <br/>
          <br/>
          <br/>
          <br/>
          <br/>
          <br/>
          <br/>
          <br/>
          <br/>
          <br/>
        </article>
      </section>
      <br class="clear" />
    </main>
    <footer>&copy;2016.  Belhur Publishing, LLC.  All rights
reserved.</footer>
  </div>
  </body>
</html>
```

Figure 4.26: The HTML code for the Order page

Finally, the code for the Contact Us page (contact.html) appears in Figure 4.27. In chapter 6, we will add a form for the user to fill in.

```
<!DOCTYPE html>
<html>
<head>
<title>Contact Belhur Publishing</title>
<meta charset="utf-8" />
<link rel="stylesheet" href="main.css"/>
</head>
<body>
<div id="main-container">
  <header> </header>
  <div id="left-side-bar">
    <nav>
```
Continued

```
      <ul>
        <li><a href="index.html">Home</a></li>
        <li><a href="about.html">About</a></li>
        <li><a href="books.html">Books</a></li>
        <li><a href="order.html">Order</a></li>
        <li><a href="contact.html">Contact Us</a></li>
      </ul>
    </nav>
  </div>
  <aside> </aside>
  <main>
    <section>
      <article>
        <h3>CONTACT US</h3>
        <h4>WRITE US</h4>
        Belhur Publishing<br>
        123 Sunshine Drive<br>
        Big Town, MI 97568<br>
        Phone: 313-264-3975<br>
        Email: info@belhurpublishing.com<br>
      </article>
    </section>
    <br class="clear" />
  </main>
  <footer>&copy;2016.  Belhur Publishing, LLC.  All rights
reserved.</footer>
</div>
</body>
</html>
```

Figure 4.27: The HTML code for the Contact Us page

The code for our external CSS style sheet (main.css) appears in Figure 4.28. We will keep adding more code to this form as we build our pages. We have added a few new selectors, particularly the nav, a, and .book-title selectors.

```
/* CSS Document */

body {
        margin-left:auto;
```
Continued

```
        margin-right:auto;
        font-family:Arial, Helvetica, sans-serif;
        margin-top:0px;
}
header {
        background-color: #999;
        background-image:url("images/Belhur-Publishing-Logo.png");
        background-position:left;
        background-repeat:no-repeat;
        height: 115px;
        padding: 5px;
        border-bottom: 1px solid #000000;
}
#main-container {
        min-width: 700px;
        max-width: 1024px;
        margin-left: auto;
        margin-right: auto;
        width: 90%;
        border: 1px solid #000000;
        background-color:#C0C0C0;
}
main {
        background-color: #ffffff;
        margin: 0 200px 0 191px;
        padding: 10px;
        border-left: 1px solid #000000;
}
h2 {
        font-family: "Palatino Linotype", Georgia, serif;
        padding:0px;
        margin:0px;
}
#left-side-bar {
        width: 190px;
        margin-bottom: 0;
        float: left;
        text-align:center;
}
```

Continued

```
nav ul {
      list-style:none;
      padding:0px;
      margin-top:0px;
}
nav {
      margin:auto;
      text-align:center;
}
nav li {
      display:block;
}

nav a:link {color: #000;}
nav a:hover {color: #000; background:#fff;}
nav a:visited {color:#000;}

nav a {
              text-decoration:none;
              padding: 10px;
              background-color:#ccc;
              border-bottom:1px solid black;
              display:block;
              font-weight:bold;
}

.book-title {
              font-weight: bold;
      font-size: 1.2em;
      font-family: "Palatino Linotype", Georgia, serif;
      margin:5px;
}

footer {
      font-size: .70em;
      font-style: italic;
      text-align: center;
      padding: 5px;
      background-color: #ccc;
```

Continued

```
        color: #000;
        border-top: 1px solid #333;
}
```

Figure 4.28: Our main external style sheet

All five pages can be viewed at once. Figures 4.29 through 4.33 show what the website might look like with our five pages.

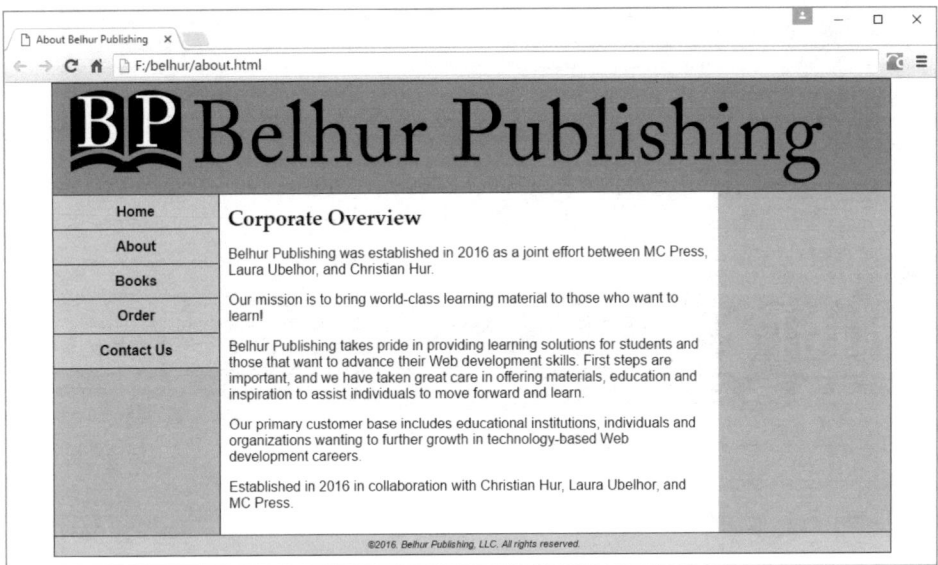

Figure 4.29: About page example

Figure 4.30: Home page example

Figure 4.31: Books page example

Figure 4.32: Order page example

Figure 4.33: Contact Us page example

Summary

When creating links, keep in mind their purpose. Typically, people digest information better when it's given in small pieces. If you create a single, gigantic page with massive amounts of data, it might overwhelm and confuse users, or at least make finding any specific thing much more difficult. It might be better to create a smaller main page that has links to other pages, which provide additional information on specific topics. Each page should contain only about one screen's worth of data. Ideally, a Web page should not be too deep with too much content, as this will tremendously affect processing time. The page should be broken down into smaller pages. Then those smaller pages can still be linked to by creating hyperlinks. Additional pages can be added to further break up the content into appropriately sized pages. An exception to this might be lists of data, where a larger number of rows of similarly formatted data is not terribly confusing.

Also, remember that no matter what tips and guidelines we or anyone else gives you, you are responsible for managing your users' experience when they view your pages. Take the time to think about how they might use your site, what they might be looking for, and what they might be trying to accomplish. If you keep those thoughts in mind as you develop your Web pages, you will greatly enhance their effectiveness.

Key Terms

_blank	anchor tag	Hypertext Transfer Protocol
_parent	charset	(HTTP)
_self	deep linking	mailto link
_top	domain	relative hyperlink
<a>	File Transfer Protocol (FTP)	target attribute
<link>	full path	title attribute
absolute hyperlink	href attribute	URL

Discussion/Review Questions

1. What is a hyperlink?
2. What is the difference between an absolute hyperlink and a relative hyperlink?
3. What is an anchor?
4. What is a Uniform Resource Identifier (URI)?
5. What are the five parts of a URL?
6. Which HTML tag is used to create a hyperlink?
7. What does the value "#location" for the href attribute in a hyperlink target mean?
8. Which components are included in an absolute hyperlink?
9. An anchor is created by assigning a unique name to an HTML element using which attribute?
10. Which type of hyperlink do you need to use when linking to a document on an external site?
11. What does a mailto link do?
12. What is the purpose of deep linking?
13. What is the risk of using deep linking?

14. What are the three drawbacks of using a mailto link?
15. What purpose does a File Transfer Protocol (FTP) link serve?
16. What other link types does a <link> tag define?
17. What are the four options for the target attribute of a hyperlink?
18. Which attribute of the anchor tag contains the destination of the link?

Exercises

1. Write the HTML code for marking the text "Back to Top" as a hyperlink link to a location in the same document with an anchor named top.
2. Write the HTML code for marking the text "Contact Us" as a hyperlink link to the contact. html file, which resides in the same folder as the current document.
3. Provide the HTML code to link the text "MC Press Online" to the URL *http://www. mcpressonline.com* and display the destination document in a new browser window or tab.
4. Write the HTML code to link the text "Email Us" to the email address *contact@ belhurpublishing.com* with a subject of "Please add me".
5. Write the HTML code to link to a named anchor called html within the programming.html file in the languages directory on the domain www.belhurpublishing.com.

CHAPTER 5

Visual Elements and Web Multimedia

Visual elements and multimedia such as graphics, audio, and videos are a key form of Web page content. A media-rich website not only brightens up your site, but also provides an interactive user experience and makes your site sticky. Browsers are inherently visual, so effective, clear graphics are crucial for your Web page. Business applications often include images in product catalogs and other types of Web pages. What kinds of image files are there? How do we incorporate them into Web pages? What about video and audio? What tools are there for working with these types of elements? What are the dos and don'ts of image processing? What types of video files are supported? We'll answer these questions and more in this chapter.

Video Graphics Overview

Nearly since the moment of the PC's inception, the push began for better graphics. IBM's first graphics card for its new PC, the Color/Graphics Monitor Adapter (CGA), was a rather limited card that provided support for up to 16 colors and a 640×200-pixel screen resolution. This was supplanted in 1984 by an Enhanced Graphics Adapter (EGA). This graphics card supported up to 64 colors and a maximum resolution of 640×350 pixels (px). Although some third-party vendors offered additional options beyond EGA, it dominated the market until 1987, when IBM released the new Video Graphics Adapter (**VGA**) card.

VGA is a standard for graphics that is still in use today. Typically, all types of graphics hardware and software support VGA or better graphics modes. While VGA is not sufficient for most modern graphical applications, it does provide a safe "fallback" option for manufacturers and developers. VGA supports up to 256 colors and a maximum resolution of 640×480. It is important to note that to achieve maximum resolution, the number of colors must be reduced, and to display the maximum number of colors, the screen resolution must be reduced. Eventually, IBM replaced VGA with XGA, but that standard did not dominate the marketplace.

Both VGA and XGA were supplanted by **SVGA**, also known as Super VGA, in 1989. Its maximum resolution started at 800 × 600 and increased to 1024 × 768 px (high-definition). The number of supported colors became almost limitless, due to improved techniques. Enhancements and improvements in graphics cards continued after the development of SVGA.

High-definition (HD) entered the video graphics market in early 2000. HD, a digital standard, is the top-level resolution for computer monitors. Monitors have also been redesigned from the previous 4:3 aspect ratio screen sizes to the wider 16:9 aspect ratio screen sizes. Some common resolutions for HD computer monitors and displays are 1366 × 768, 1600 × 900, and 1920 × 1080. As computer monitor manufacturers began building better and higher-resolution monitors, many websites were redesigned to the layouts optimized for HD. Today, the 16:9 aspect ratio is becoming the standard display for most computer monitors and laptops.

Types of Image Files

As confusing as the different video standards may be, the number of different image formats is even more staggering. Each format has its own strengths and weaknesses. Table 5.1 shows a list of common formats and their respective strengths and weaknesses.

Table 5.1: Image Format Strengths and Weaknesses			
Format	Name	Strengths	Weaknesses
FH	Freehand	Excellent for scaling and complex images	Not commonly used in websites, requires specific editors
SWF	Flash File	Excellent for animation	Owned by Adobe
GIF	Graphics Interchange Format	Common in websites and a good choice for simple images	Lacks sharpness and clarity in complex images
JPG, JPEG	Joint Photographic Experts Group	Excellent compression for pictures, common in websites	No transparency support
JP2, J20	JPEG 2000	Provides more sophisticated progressive downloads than JPEG	Longer decompression times than JPEG, not an open standard
PNG	Portable Network Graphics	Common in websites, provides enhanced transparency	File sizes larger than GIF or JPEG
PSD	Photoshop Document	Excellent editability	Owned by Adobe, generally only used in editing applications
PSP	Paintshop Pro	Excellent editability	Owned by Corel, generally only used in editing applications
TIFF	Tagged Image File Format	Often used in printing, better quality than JPEG. Excellent scalability	Larger size than JPEG
BMP	Windows Bitmap	Good quality	Large size, slow download
SVG	Scalable Vector Graphics	Vector based, resolution independent, very scalable while maintaining quality	Not all browsers support it, not ideal for complex objects
WebP	Google's Graphics	Lossless/lossy compression algorithm, small file size	Still in development and currently works only with Google Chrome and Opera

Compression describes how relatively small the files are. *Transparency* is a feature that allows one image to be superimposed on top of another. The background color of the transparent image is not displayed. *Scalability* reflects the ability of an image to retain its clarity as its size is increased.

For simple images, **GIF** has been the standard for many years. However, **PNG** provides better functionality, and you might find that PNG images perform better than GIFs. While it is true that GIF has been the most common format for animation in the past, more recently it is often replaced by Flash image files.

For complex images and photographs, **JPEG** has been and remains the standard format of choice. **TIFF** files provide a higher-quality image than JPEG, particularly when images are being scaled up, but they are also dramatically larger and so take longer to download. This slows the display of your Web page and generally diminishes the perceived quality of your website. Also, some browsers might not have support for TIFF files by default. Still, for certain specific functions, particularly if the primary function of an image is downloading for printing, the extra download time of TIFFs might be worth the improved quality of the printed image.

Some browsers, particularly older ones, may not have good support for PNG files. If that presents a problem, you might need to use GIFs instead. While PNGs are generally thought of as a replacement for GIFs, they can also replace JPEG images. In certain situations, the "lossless" compression of the PNG format provides significant improvement in quality over JPEG's "lossy" compression method, which can lose image data.

The lossless graphics **SVG** is an XML-based vector image format. Although it has been around for more than a decade, SVG really hasn't caught the attention of developers. One reason is that SVG is vector based, which means it's made up of coordinates in an XML format. A simple object such as a polygon is easy to create and only requires a few sets of coordinates. In fact, SVG objects can be drawn directly on a Web page with HTML5 and JavaScript. And because it is comprised of only vectors, an object would never lose its quality regardless of what you do to the image. SVG is a perfect choice for interactivity and animation on a Web page. However, the downside to SVG is that a really complex image, such as a car or a forest, can require up to hundreds of thousands of coordinates. Drawing something that complex with vectors can be a nightmare. Fortunately, many vector graphics editors (for example, CorelDRAW, Adobe Illustrator, and Microsoft Visio) are available that make it much easier for developers and graphics designers to draw complex objects and export them to be displayed on a Web page.

The newest type of Web graphic is Google's **WebP** (pronounce "weppy"), which was still in development at the time this book was written. The format is a derivative of Google's own VP8 codec, which is a video compression format. WebP lossless images can be about 25 percent smaller in size compared to PNGs, and its lossy images are 25 to 35 percent smaller in file size than JPEGs. Like its PNG counterpart, WebP supports transparency. In the media-rich environment of the Web, anything that speeds CPU processing time and reduces page-loading time is highly favored by both programmers and Web surfers. Does this mean that Google's WebP could eventually become the format of choice for Web development, potentially rendering PNG, JPG, and most of the older formats obsolete? We'll just have to wait and see.

Incorporating Images into Web Pages

Images can easily be inserted into HTML code with the <img> tag.

Image Tag:

   Align
   Alt
   Border
   Height
   Width
   Hspace
   Vspace
   Ismap
   Src
   Usemap

The image tag <img> places an image on the page. It's a single-sided tag. The various attributes can be used to modify the image as desired; however, most of them are now deprecated and replaced by Cascading Style Sheets (CSS). For example, the align, border, height, and width attributes are replaced with CSS properties. The hspace and vspace attributes are also replaced with the CSS padding and margin properties. So, we will not discuss them further.

Figure 5.1 shows the syntax for placing an image on a Web page using the <img> tag.

```
<img src="image-file" alt="short image description" />
```

Figure 5.1: The syntax for placing an image on a Web page

The only attributes required for creating an image link in HTML5 are src and alt. Everything else is optional. The example shown in Figure 5.2 displays the Belhur Publishing logo on the Web page.

```
<img src="Belhur-Publishing-Logo.png" alt="Belhur Publishing Logo" />
```

Figure 5.2: The HTML for creating an image tag on a Web document

Src is the most important attribute for the <img> tag. It defines the location of the image. This can be a physical location on the server, or a Universal Resource Locator (URL) to another location on the Internet. If no path is given before the image name (C:/ ... or http://), then it is assumed the image is in the same location as the Web page. To indicate that the image is stored in a folder one level up from this one, use the syntax "../filename". Alt provides an alternate text for the image, and it is required in HTML5 for accessibility, such as for visually impaired users, and by some search engines when evaluating a page's contents. The effect of the alt attribute on the Web page is that when the mouse hovers over the image, this text is displayed as a tool tip below the cursor. In addition, if the image is broken (not found), the text is displayed in place of a broken image placeholder, as shown for Google Chrome, Mozilla Firefox, and Microsoft Edge (and also Internet Explorer) in Figures 5.3, 5.4, 5.5, and 5.6.

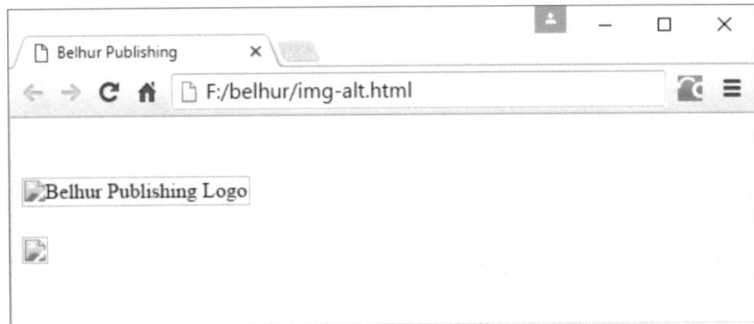

Figure 5.3: Broken images with and without the alt attribute in Google Chrome

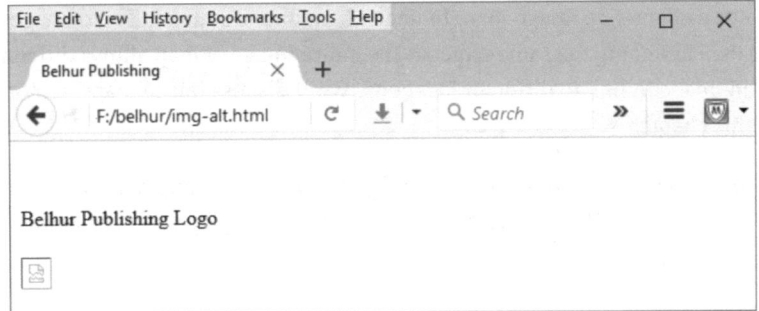

Figure 5.4: Broken images with and without the alt attribute in Mozilla Firefox

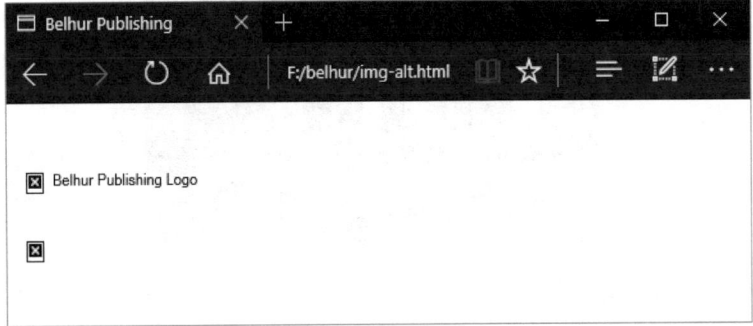

Figure 5.5: Broken images with and without the alt attribute in Microsoft Edge

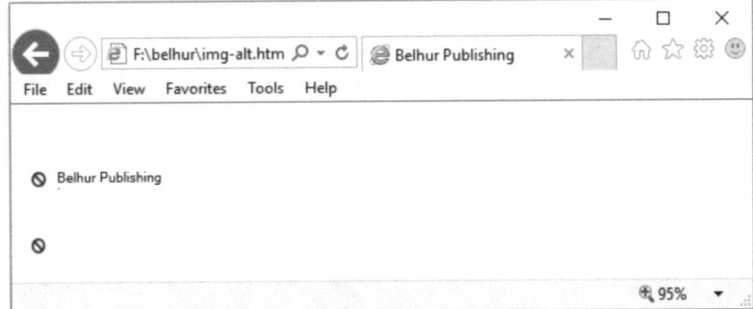

Figure 5.6: Broken images with and without the alt attribute in Internet Explorer (IE11)

Ismap indicates that the image has a corresponding server-side image map. When an image is used with the ismap attribute, the selected coordinates are sent to the server using the GET method. Figure 5.7 shows an example of a server-side **image map**.

```
<p href="http://www.belhurpublishing.com/map.php" src="location.png"
ismap="ismap">Our location</p>
```

Figure 5.7: The HTML for creating a server-side image map using the ismap attribute

The entire image is an active region that is linked to a server-side PHP file. A click anywhere on the image will send the coordinates to the PHP file for processing.

Usemap indicates a client-side image map. In general, an image map applies to images that are used as links. Rather than assigning the same target to the entire image, a map allows different sections, or *hotspots*, of an image to link to different locations. We'll discuss image maps in more detail in the next section of this chapter.

As mentioned, images can be resized from their original size. For example, if you have an image of your product taken at 300×250, such as the Belhur Publishing logo shown in Figure 5.8, it could be placed on a Web page at various sizes.

Figure 5.8: An image of the Belhur Publishing logo at 300 x 250 resolution

The sample Web page code in Figure 5.10 redisplays the image from Figure 5.9 at 150×150, 50×100, and 100×50 px.

Figure 5.9: The Belhur Publishing image logo at various sizes

The sample Web page shown in Figure 5.9 was created using the code in Figure 5.10.

```
<!DOCTYPE html>
<html>
<head>
  <title>Belhur Publishing</title>
  <meta charset="utf-8" />
  <style>
div {
        float:left;
        text-align:center;
        padding:5px;
        margin:10px;
}
img {
        border:1px solid black;
}
body {
        margin-left:auto;
        margin-right:auto;
}
  </style>
</head>
```

Continued

```
<body>
  <div> 150x150<br/>
     <img src="images/bh-logo.jpg" height=150 width=150>
  </div>
  <div> <img src="images/bh-logo.jpg" height = 50 width = 100> <br/>
        50x100
  </div>
  <div> <img src="images/bh-logo.jpg" height = 100 width = 50> <br/>
        100x50
  </div>
</body>
</html>
```

Figure 5.10: The HTML code to scale an image to various sizes

Once you know the resolution of an image, maintaining its proportions as you shrink or expand it is easy. Some applications might require images of specific sizes. Remember, as mentioned earlier, some image types scale better than others. Therefore, important images, such as those of products, are often best stored in exactly the same resolution and file type. This will give a clean, consistent look on the Web page. Of course, if you are building pages specifically for certain items, the images can be managed independently.

An image's quality is generally better maintained by shrinking it rather than expanding it. The results you get may vary widely, however, depending on factors such as the image's file format and density, measured in dots per inch (dpi).

Figure and figure caption elements:

```
<figure>
    content
    <figcaption>caption</figcaption>
</figure>
```

Two new structural elements were introduced in HTML5 for displaying figures such as images on a Web page in a more meaningful way. The <figcaption> element is optional and is used to represent a caption or legend for the contents of the <figure> element. The code in Figure 5.11 creates a figure box containing the image of the previous edition of this book and a caption, shown in Figure 5.12.

```
<figure>
  <img src="images/html.jpg" alt="HTML for the Business Developer">
<figcaption>$31.95</figcaption>
</figure>
```

Figure 5.11: The HTML code for displaying an image with a caption

Figure 5.12: Sample Web page using figure and figcaption tags

Creating Image Hyperlinks

Previous examples showed how to embed an image directly into your Web page. The discussion on handling videos also showed how to create a link to a video file. Chapter 4 reviews linking in detail, but this section provides a brief overview of linking to an image.

Images can also be used as hyperlinks. To create an image hyperlink, simply encapsulate the <img> tag between the <a> tags and configure the anchor tag to link to a target page, as shown in Figure 5.13.

```
<a href="http://www.mc-store.com/HTML-Business-Developer-Kevin-Forsythe/
dp/1583470794" target="_blank"><img src="images/html.jpg" alt="HTML for the
Business Developer"></a>
```

Figure 5.13: The HTML code for creating an image link

That's it! The image is now a hyperlink that links to the book's detail page on MC Press's online bookstore. Some older Web browsers might display a blue border around the image by default, which is similar to how text links are also blue and have a blue underline. You can remove the border by adding a CSS style rule that includes the value border:none; to the image's border property.

The code sample in Figure 5.14 shows how we might create a link to the full detail page of the products in our "books" catalog page, which is shown in Figure 5.15.

```
<div class="books">
  <p class="book-title">HTML for the Business Developer</p>
```
Continued

```
    <figure> <a href="9781583470794.html"> <img src="images/html.jpg"
alt="HTML for the Business Developer"> </a>
      <figcaption>$31.95</figcaption>
    </figure>
</div>
```

Figure 5.14: The HTML code to link to products detail page

Figure 5.15: A page with images as links

Image Maps

The previous example showed how to use an image as an anchor to another image or Web page. What if you had a large image with numerous features, each with its own associated target? That is an *image map*.

Consider, for example, a Web page about a car. It might have a picture of a car, and then allow the users to click on different parts of the car, such as its door, windows, lights, tires, and engine. Each click could act as a different link, taking the user to a Web page with details on that particular part of the car.

For our example Web page, the catalog section could have handled the images differently by presenting a single image of a table, nicely arranged with all the items displayed. The user could then click on the product he or she was interested in, causing the larger image to display.

The image map, or *usemap*, identifies which parts of an image link to what pages or files.

Map **and** area **tags:**

```
<map
  name
>
  <area
    shape
    coords
    href
    alt
  >
  </area>
</map>
```

A client-side image map is created using three elements: **<image>**, **<map>**, and **<area>**.

- The <img> tag must include the usemap attribute, preceded by a pound sign (#), defining the image map to use.
- The <map> tag, along with its attributes, must define a series of areas within the image that are clickable links to other content.
- The <area> element defines the hotspots on the image map.

The primary attribute of a map is its name. The name should match the one specified in the usemap attribute of the associated image. The <area> tag is subordinate to the <map> tag. Each <area> tag defines a clickable area that has a shape. Valid shapes are rect for rectangular shapes, circle, and poly for polygons, as shown in Figure 5.16. Depending on which shape is used, the coordinates in the coords attribute are specified differently.

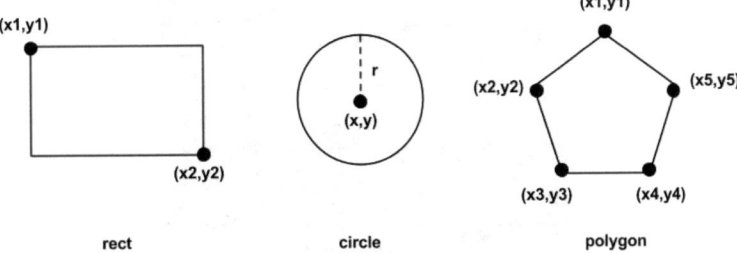

Figure 5.16: Types of shape coordinates for the <area> element

For rectangles, the cords attribute needs four values: the x and y coordinates of the upper-left corner of the rectangle, and the x and y coordinates of the lower-right corner. These two points are all that is required to define the shape of the rectangle. For circles, only three coordinates are needed: the x and y coordinates of the center of the circle, and a third value to specify the radius of the circle. Polygons are more complex, as they can be any number of points defining the outside border of an area. The coordinates should be presented as a series of paired x and y coordinates.

The href attribute identifies the target of each clickable area, and the alt attribute provides alternate text associated with each clickable area. One benefit of the alt attribute that is particularly useful with image maps is that it will be displayed as the user moves the mouse over the image. If each clickable area has its own alt text, it is much easier to see where the boundaries between clickable areas are, and where they might lead.

The example in Figure 5.17 shows how an image map might be implemented with a rectangle area type. The coordinates mark the rectangular area around Laura Ubelhor's name on the book cover as a hotspot so that when clicked, it sends an email to her.

```
<img src="images/htmlbook.jpg" alt="Belhur Publishing Logo" border="0"
usemap="#Map">


<map name="Map">
  <area shape="rect" coords="147,350,232,378" href="mailto:laura.ubelhor@
belhurpublishing.com" alt="HTML book">
</map>
```

Figure 5.17: The HTML for creating a hotspot using a client-side image map

If we map out the coordinates onto the book cover, the imaginary rectangular area around the name Laura Ubelhor would be precisely marked, as shown in Figure 5.18. Figure 5.19 shows the result on the Web page.

Figure 5.18: An illustration showing coordinates of a rectangle hotspot

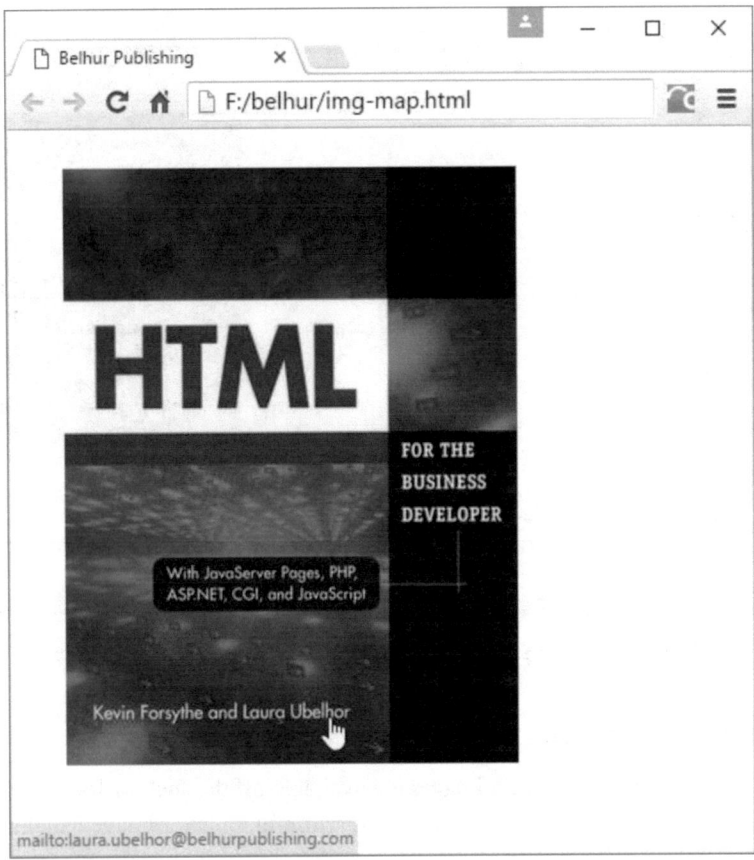

Figure 5.19: The sample Web page with a hotspot from Figure 5.17

One of the first questions programmers have about image maps is how to determine the coordinates you need, such as those in Figure 5.16. Many Web-page authoring tools, such as Adobe Dreamweaver, provide graphical user interface (GUI) wizards to assist in creating image maps. Simply open an image in Dreamweaver, and as shown in Figure 5.20, click on the image, select the desired shape from the lower left corner, and start clicking to create the coordinates with the mouse. You don't need to be perfect; just be close enough so that the user can identify what visual element in the picture distinguishes this area from the others.

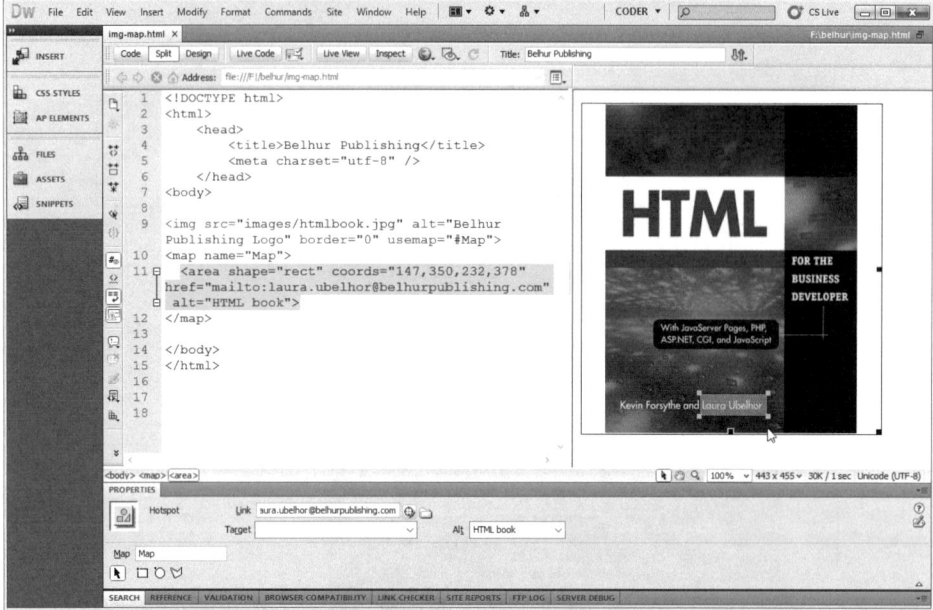

Figure 5.20: Using Adobe Dreamweaver to create an image map

Tools for Working with Images

A great variety of tools for working with images are available off the shelf or for download from the Internet. Here is a rundown of some of the more popular/useful tools for image handling:

- Photoshop CS6—Generally considered the king of photo editing software, this product is not low-priced. But as the saying goes, you get what you pay for.
- Photoshop Elements—This is a more moderately priced version of the popular Photoshop tool and is useful for general editing.
- Photo Impact—At a fraction of the price of Photoshop, this feature-rich tool gives you a lot of value, but with less ease of use.
- Photosuite—This is one of the lowest-priced tools on the market, though it has far fewer features than the previously mentioned tools.
- Paint Shop Pro Photo—This is another tool with a price in the low to middle range, but with high-end capability.
- Gimp—Originally designed for UNIX/Linux, this open source freeware tool for photo editing has been ported to Windows.
- Paint.net—Another open source photo tool, this one was developed with help from Microsoft.
- Web design tools—If you use a Web page design tool, it might well include at least some basic photo editing capability. Some include GIF animation wizards and other such tools.

For typical business applications, you probably won't need extremely high-end photo editing software. If you're doing graphical design work or dealing with particularly demanding graphics-based applications, such as computer-aided design (CAD), you might. If you're not sure what you need, start with some of the free/inexpensive options and then upgrade to something better, if necessary.

The Dos and Don'ts of Working with Image Files

Here are some tips to keep in mind when working with image files:

- First, be sure you know the format(s) of the files you are working with and why each format was chosen. Don't assume that the image files you receive are always in the most appropriate formats for browser-based applications.
- Consider the images' sizes. Larger images typically take more time to load, although this can be mitigated to a great degree depending on the file format you are using. You'll need to determine whether the images you're using should be sized consistently with one another, or whether each image can be uniquely sized.
- In general, avoid displaying bitmaps (BMP) and TIFF files on your Web pages. These are probably better handled by providing links to the images, allowing the users to download them to their PCs and work with them locally.
- It's always best to use an image's native dimensions. However, remember that it's generally better to shrink a large image to a certain size rather than starting with small images and expanding them. Expanding images usually degrades their quality.
- Avoid placing a large number of images on one page. Reducing the number of images reduces page load time and makes the page easier to work with.
- Use transparency in images, so they appear better integrated with the Web page. If an image has a background different from the Web page's color, it typically results in an ugly square block around the image. This cheapens the feel of the application.
- For images requiring a large amount of scaling, the PNG format might work better than JPEG. Remember that JPEG uses a "lossy" scheme for encoding the image, meaning that it is subject to losing data as it changes, either by being saved again and again or by scaling. PNG images use a "lossless" scheme for encoding the data, which makes them a better choice when scaling.

Web Multimedia

Video and audio files are often included in a Web page as either advertisements or promotional materials. Some Web pages automatically play video when the page is loaded, creating an "introduction" to the page. Audio and video content can be embedded on a Web page on the fly with the new HTML5 **<video>** and **<audio>** elements. Many tasks related to handling of audio and video files fall into the area of Web design rather than programming, at least as we see the distinction. So, we'll confine our discussion to some basic and practical uses for video and audio that you might find in business today.

Embedding Audio on Web Pages

Audio files can be embedded to be played directly on a Web page or linked to the audio file to be played on the browser by using a **plug-in**. A plug-in is a special helper program that plays audio and video files, and resides on the user's local machine. There are many types of audio formats available, but not all formats are supported by all Web browsers. Table 5.2 lists some of these common audio formats.

Table 5.2: Common Audio Formats for the Web		
Format	Name	Description
.aiff, .aif	Audio Interchange	Audio format on the Mac
.mp3	MPEG-1 Audio Layer-3	The most popular audio format used for music files. Excellent compression rate and has nearly universal support, which makes it ideal for the Web.
.wav	Wave	Microsoft's audio standard format and primary format for the PC. File sizes are too large and impractical for the Web.
.ogg	OGG	An open source and royalty-free file compression format designed for the Web. Not supported by most browsers.
.m4a	MPEG-4 Audio	An audio-only format that uses the AAC codec. Supported mainly by Apple's QuickTime, iTunes, iPod, and iPad.

You can create an audio hyperlink just like you would any regular hyperlink. The example in Figure 5.21 creates a hyperlink to an audio file using the <a> tag.

```
<a href="audio/congratulations.ogg">Congratulations!</a> (OGG)
```

Figure 5.21: The HTML code to create an audio hyperlink

When the hyperlink created in Figure 5.21 is clicked, the browser looks for the proper plug-in to run the audio file in a new window or tab, as shown in Figure 5.22. If the user's local system doesn't have a plug-in that supports the audio format, it will prompt the user to search and download one from the Internet.

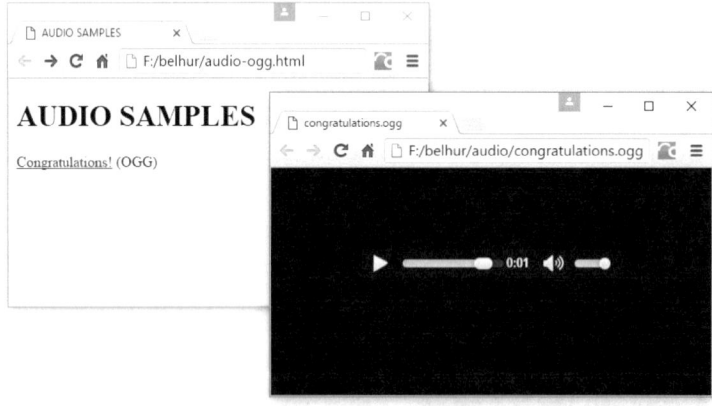

Figure 5.22: The sample Web page with an audio hyperlink from Figure 5.20

Audio tag:

```
<audio
  controls
  src
  title
  type
  autoplay
  loop
  preload
>
  <source src="source1_url" />
  <source src="source2_url" />
  ...
  <a href="source1_url"></a>
  <a href="source2_url"></a>
  ...
</audio>
```

The <audio> tag has some functional attributes, which are all optional. The only attribute that is more a "nice to have" than required is controls, which displays the audio player and its menu control buttons, such as play, pause, and stop. By default, the controls attribute is turned off, so you must have it turned on to see the audio player on the browser that supports the <audio> tag. Table 5.3 lists all the audio attributes and their functions.

Table 5.3: Audio Element Attributes (Optional)		
Attribute	**Value**	**Description**
controls	controls	Displays the audio player and its controls and is disabled by default; enabling this attribute is recommended.
src	media filename	The audio source (filename) to be played
title	text	Text description of the audio file displayed by browser and assistive technologies such as screen readers
type	MIME type	Audio MIME types in the form audio/format, such as audio/mp3, audio/ogg, or audio/wav
autoplay	autoplay	Plays the audio file automatically when the page loads
loop	loop	Provides a continuous loop
preload	none, auto, metadata	None, the default, requires no preloading; auto—download the media file; metadata—download only the metadata content of the media file.

The code in Figure 5.23 shows how to embed an audio with the <audio> tag; Figure 5.24 shows the result.

```
<audio controls="controls" src="audio/congratulations.ogg">
    <a href="audio/congratulations.ogg">Download the file</a> (OGG)
</audio>
```

Figure 5.23: Another method to embed an audio file on a page

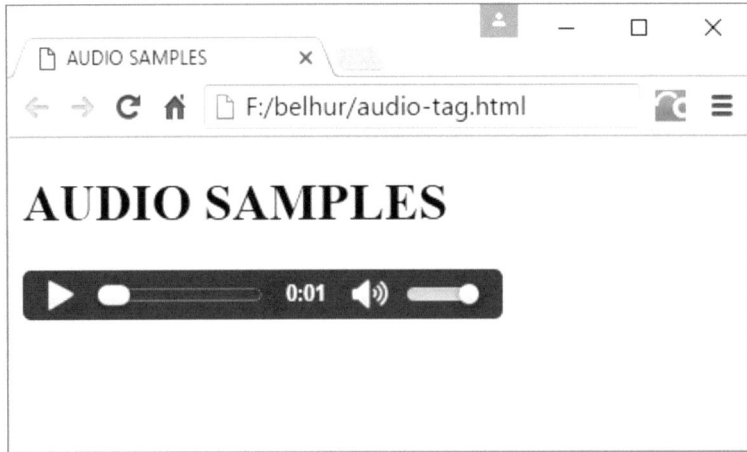

Figure 5.24: The sample Web page with an embedded audio player

The <audio> start tag on line 1 of the code in Figure 5.23 embeds the audio player. Notice all the attributes are not used except for controls and src. Controls instructs the browser to display the audio player so that it is visible on the Web browser window, as shown in Figure 5.24. Src points to the media file congratulations.ogg, which is stored in a directory called audio. The term *media file* pertains to any digital image, audio, or video files on an electronic device such as a computer or flash drive. Line 2 is a direct link to the media file for download. This is used for browsers that do not support the <audio> tag, such as IE8 or IE9. Instead of the audio player being displayed, the link in line 2 will be displayed for the user to click and download, as shown in Figure 5.25.

Figure 5.25: The result of the code in Figure 5.23, as shown on an IE8 emulator

So, what happens when the user's Web browser doesn't support an .ogg audio format? To accommodate this possibility, you may want to supply as many formats as you can, to ensure that all visitors can play and listen to the audio. The sample code in Figure 5.26 will resolve this issue.

```
<audio controls="controls"`>
   <source src="audio/congratulations.ogg" type="audio/ogg">
   <source src="audio/congratulations.mp3" type="audio/mpeg">
   <source src="audio/congratulations.wav" type="audio/wav">
   <a href="audio/congratulations.ogg">Download the OGG file</a>
   <a href="audio/congratulations.mp3">Download the MP3 file</a>
   <a href="audio/congratulations.wav">Download the WAV file</a>
</audio>
```

Figure 5.26: The HTML code to embed an audio file on a page

Notice that we removed the src attribute from the <a> tag and include it in line 2 as one of the **<source>** tags within the body of the <audio> tags. The <source> element is a self-contained element used to specify a media format. It is commonly used with the <audio> and <video> elements, which we will discuss in the next section.

Lines 2, 3, and 4 use a <source> tag to include three different media formats. If the src attribute is not used in the <audio> tag, at least one <source> must be specified to load the audio into the player. If the src attribute is used in the <audio> tag, then the additional <source> tags should only be used for a different media format. You can provide as many or as few media sources as you'd like. Again, lines 5, 6, and 7 are used to display clickable links to download the media sources in case the <audio> tag is not supported by the user's Web browser.

Embedding Videos on Web Pages

Video files can also be downloaded to play locally on the user's system or played on the Web browser with a plug-in. The code in Figure 5.27 shows how to create a video link; Figure 5.28 shows the result.

```
<a href="videos/test_video.mp4">Test Video</a> (MP4)
```

Figure 5.27: Creating a video link

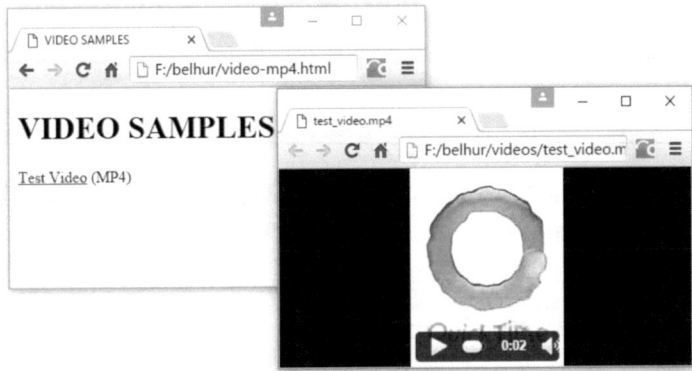

Figure 5.28: The sample Web page with a video hyperlink from Figure 5.27

Embedding Videos with the <video> Element

Rather than providing a hyperlink to the video, it is preferable to embed the video directly into the Web page. Embedding a video on a Web page is just as simple as and a similar process to embedding an audio file. As with audio, many types of video formats exist. Table 5.4 shows a partial list of video formats used on the Web.

Table 5.4: Common Video Formats for the Web		
Format	Name	Description
.avi	Audio Video Interleaved	Microsoft's standard video format for the PC
.mp4, **.m4v**	MPEG-4 H.264	Apple's proprietary video format, which is supported by QuickTime, iTunes, and mobile devices
.webm	WebM	Google's open source and royalty-free video format
.ogv	Ogg Theora	An open source and royalty-free video format developed by Xiph.org
.flv	Flash Video	Adobe video format, which uses the Adobe Flash Player to deliver video on the Web
.mov	QuickTime	Apple's movie format used on the Mac

Video tag:

```
<video
  controls
  src
  title
  type
  autoplay
  loop
  preload
  height
  width
  poster
  muted
>
  <source src="source1_url" />
  <source src="source2_url" />
  ...
  <a href="source1_url"></a>
<a href="source2_url"></a>
...
</video>
```

The <video> tag works just like the <audio> tag discussed earlier. All the attributes are optional. In addition to three new attributes, most of the attributes for the <audio> tag are the same as for the <video> tag and serve the same purpose. Table 5.5 lists all the video attributes and their functions.

Table 5.5: Video Element Attributes (Optional)		
Attribute	**Value**	**Description**
controls	controls	Displays the video player and its controls and is disabled by default; enabling this attribute is recommended.
src	media filename	The video source (filename) to be played
title	text	Text description of the video file displayed by browser and assistive technologies such as screen readers
type	MIME type	Video MIME types in the form video/format, such as video/mp4, video/ogg, or video/webM
autoplay	autoplay	Plays the video file automatically when the page loads
loop	loop	Provides a continuous loop
preload	none, auto, metadata	None, the default, requires no preloading; auto—download the media file, metadata—download only the metadata content of the media file.
height	numeric value	Video height in pixels; supplying a height value is recommended.
width	numeric value	Video width in pixels; supplying a width value is recommended.
poster	image filename	An image to display over the video player or if browser cannot play the media file
muted	none, muted	Mutes the audio output of the video

The code in Figure 5.29 shows how to embed a video with the <video> tag; Figure 5.30 shows its result.

```
<video controls="controls" src="videos/test_video.mp4" width="200"
height="200">
    <a href="videos/test_video.mp4">Download the MP4 file</a>
</video>
```

Figure 5.29: Another method to embed a video on the page

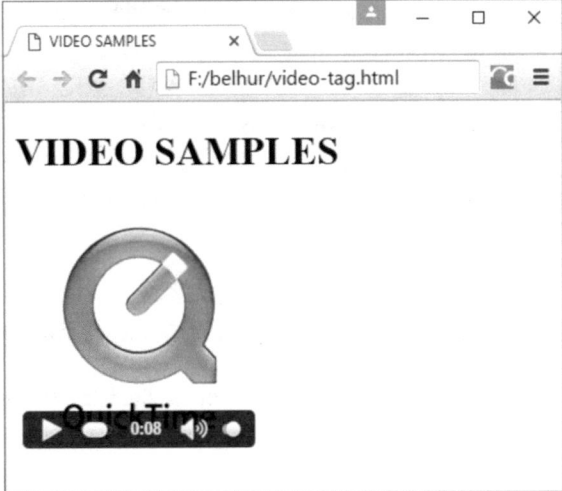

Figure 5.30: The sample Web page with an embedded video player

The <video> start tag on line 1 of the code in Figure 5.29 embeds the video player. Not all the attributes are required, but you should use the controls, width, and height attributes, otherwise the embedded video player is not visible on the page. Src points to the media source file, which is stored in the videos directory. Line 2 is a direct link to the media file for download if the Web browser does not support the <video> tag.

As shown earlier in our discussion of audio formats, you can also embed multiple video formats to ensure that all visitors can play and watch the video. The sample code in Figure 5.31 shows how to supply multiple video formats using the <source> tag discussed earlier.

```
<video controls="controls" width="200" height="200" poster="videos/video-
poster-qk.png">
    <source src="videos/test_video.mp4" type="audio/mp4">
    <source src="videos/test_video.avi" type="audio/avi">
    <source src="videos/test_video.ogv" type="audio/ogv">
    <a href="videos/test_video.mp4">Download the MP4 file</a>
    <a href="videos/test_video.avi">Download the AVI file</a>
    <a href="videos/test_video.ogv">Download the OGV file</a>
</video>
```

Figure 5.31: The HTML code to embed an audio on the page

We supplied three media formats and three links for download. The poster attribute is also added to the <video> start tag, so that the image is displayed over the video player before it starts. Once the user clicks and plays the video, the poster will be replaced with the actual video content. If you have the same content in a Flash shockwave file (**.swf**), it can also be embedded within the <video> container tags by using either the **<embed>** or **<object>** tags, as shown in Figure 5.32.

```
<video controls="controls" width="200" height="200" poster="videos/video-
poster-qk.png">
    <source src="videos/test_video.mp4" type="audio/mp4">
    <source src="videos/test_video.avi" type="audio/avi">
    <embed type="application/x-shockwave-flash"
     src="videos/test_video.swf" quality="high" width="200" height="200"
     title="Test Video">
</video>
```

Figure 5.32: The HTML code to embed a Flash media file on the page

For browsers that don't support the HTML5 <video> element, there are two methods for embedding videos on a Web page that can be displayed by those browsers: the <embed> and <object> tags.

Embedding Videos with the <embed> Element

The <embed> tag in HTML allows you to "push" the content of the video and the video player into the surface of the Web page, making it feel much more integrated into the page.

Embed tag:

```
<embed
   src
   width
   height
   align
   autostart
   loop
   playcount
   volume
   controller
   pluginspage
 >
 </embed>
```

The code in Figure 5.33 shows how to embed the videos in Figure 5.34. This code sample uses a few attributes of the <embed> tag. Src identifies the location of the video file being played. Height and width perform as they do with other HTML tags, setting the object's size. Align controls the flow of text around the video player. (See chapter 2 for more information about the align attribute.)

```
<style>
  div {
      float:left;
      text-align:center;
      margin:10px;
  }
</style>
<div>
  <h3>QuickTime</h3>
  <embed width ="200" height= "200" src="videos/test_video.mp4"
      autostart ="false"></embed>
</div>
<div>
  <h3>Weather</h3>
```

Continued

```
    <embed width ="200" height= "200" src="videos/test_video2.mp4"
        autostart = "false"> </embed>
</div>
<div>
   <h3>Blackberry</h3>
   <embed width ="200" height= "200" src="videos/test_video3.mp4"
        autostart = "false"></embed>
</div>
```

Figure 5.33: HTML code to embed videos

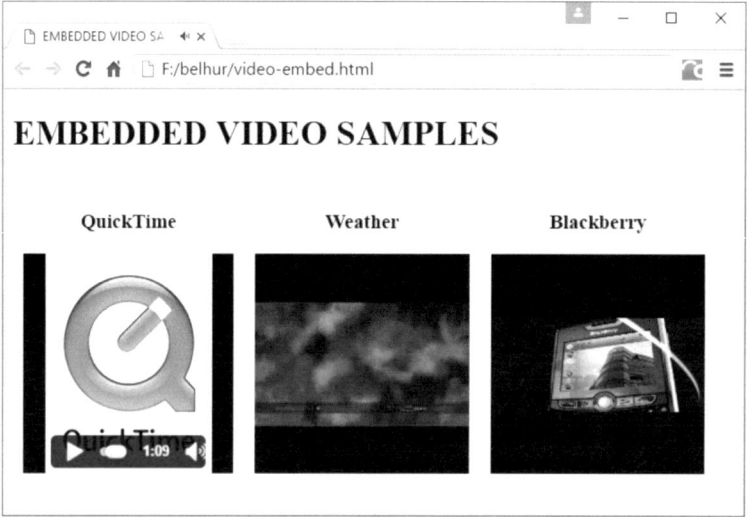

Figure 5.34: The embedded video files

Autostart controls whether an embedded video file should automatically begin playing when the page is displayed. This attribute defaults to "true" but can be set to "false". Loop controls how many times the video will be played. It can be set to a specific number, "true", or "false". "False" is the default, meaning that the movie will play once and then stop. If set to "true", the video will loop continuously until stopped. Playcount also controls how many times a video will be played and takes precedence over the loop attribute.

Volume is set to a range from 0 to 100, with 50 being the default. As you would expect, this controls the playback volume of the audio portion of the video file. Set the controller attribute to either "true" or "false" to indicate whether the controls for the video player should be displayed for the user. "True" is the default. If "false" is specified, the user can still right-click the video player and use the control options included in the pop-up menu. If the user does not have the necessary player installed, the pluginspage attribute identifies the Web page where it can be found, providing the user with an easy mechanism for installing the necessary player.

Embedding Videos with the <object> Element

Another method to embed videos so that Web browsers that do not support the HTML5 <video> element can still play videos is by using the <object> element.

Object tag:

```
<object
  data
  form
  height
  name
  type
  usemap
  width
>
  <parameters>
  ...
</object>
```

The <object> tag works similarly to the <embed> tag, as discussed earlier. All the attributes for the <object> tag are listed on Table 5.6.

Table 5.6: Object Element Attributes		
Attribute	**Value**	**Description**
data	media filename	The video source (filename) to be played
form	text	The name of the form the object belongs to
type	MIME type	Video MIME types in the form video/format, such as video/mp4, video/ogg, or video/webM
name	text	A unique name for the object
height	numeric value	Video height in pixels. Supplying a height value is recommended.
width	numeric value	Video width in pixels. Supplying a width value is recommended.
usemap	URL	The link to a client-side image map

The code in Figure 5.35 shows how to embed a video with the <video> tag.

```
<object data="videos/test_video.mp4" type="audio/mp4" height="200"
width="200">

</object>
```

Figure 5.35: Another method to embed a video on the page

Different browsers parse the media file in different ways. For this reason, a **<param>** tag is also used to ensure that all browsers are able to retrieve the media file correctly. In addition, the <object> tag can be used to embed Flash videos. With the <object> tag, a Flash SWF file can be inserted, as shown in Figure 5.36.

```
<object data="videos/test_video.swf" type="audio/swf" height="200"
width="200">

    <param name="src" value="videos/test_video.swf">

    <embed type="application/x-shockwave-flash"

    src="videos/test_video.swf" quality="high" width="200" height="200"

    title="Test Video">

</object>
```

Figure 5.36: Embedding a Flash SWF file within an <object> tag

While certain video files, Flash animations, and multimedia presentations typically fall under the responsibility of Web designers, those closely tied to products, human resources, and internal training often become the responsibility of programmers.

What About Our Example Page?

Although we aren't graphic designers, it's time we updated the look of our books catalog page. How would we expand the use of images on our sample Web page? An obvious improvement is adding images to the catalog of items for sale. Figure 5.37 shows a new layout for our books catalog page. It also demonstrates that we are not Web designers!

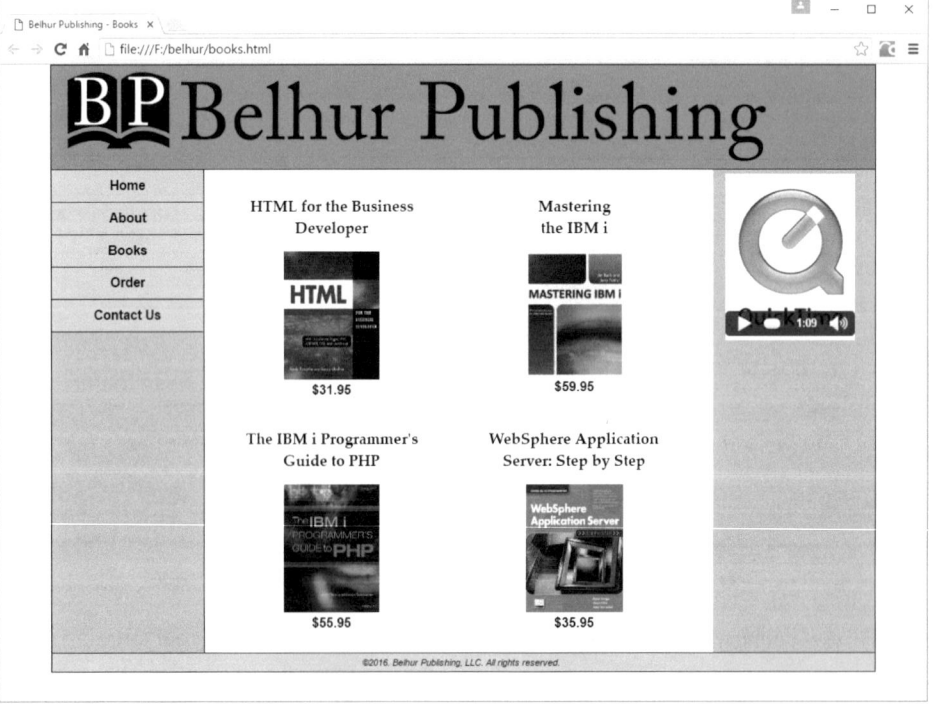

Figure 5.37: The updated books catalog Web page from chapter 4

Figure 5.38 shows all the HTML code for the final page in Figure 5.37.

```
<!DOCTYPE html>
<html>
<head>
<title>Belhur Publishing - Books</title>
<meta charset="utf-8" />
<link rel="stylesheet" href="main.css"/>
</head>
<body>
<div id="main-container">
  <header> </header>
  <div id="left-side-bar">
    <nav>
      <ul>
        <li><a href="index.html">Home</a></li>
        <li><a href="about.html">About</a></li>
        <li><a href="books.html">Books</a></li>
        <li><a href="order.html">Order</a></li>
        <li><a href="contact.html">Contact Us</a></li>
      </ul>
    </nav>
  </div>
  <aside>
  <video controls="controls" width="170" height="200" poster="videos/video-
poster-qk.png">
        <source src="videos/test_video.mp4" type="audio/mp4">
        <source src="videos/test_video.avi" type="audio/avi">
        <source src="videos/test_video.ogv" type="audio/ogv">
        <a href="videos/test_video.mp4">Download the MP4 file</a>
        <a href="videos/test_video.avi">Download the AVI file</a>
        <a href="videos/test_video.ogv">Download the OGV file</a>
    </video>
  </aside>
  <main>
    <section>
      <article>
        <div class="books">
```

Continued

```
        <p class="book-title">HTML for the Business Developer</p>
        <figure>
        <a href="9781583470794.html">
        <img src="images/html.jpg" alt="HTML for the Business Developer">
        </a>
        <figcaption>$31.95</figcaption>
        </figure>
    </div>
    <div class="books">
        <p class="book-title">Mastering<br/>
          the IBM i </p>
        <figure>
        <a href="9781583473566.html">
        <img src="images/Mastering_IBM_i.jpg" alt="Mastering the IBM i">
        </a>
          <figcaption>$59.95</figcaption>
        </figure>
    </div>
    <div class="books">
        <p class="book-title">The IBM i Programmer's Guide to PHP</p>
        <figure>
        <a href="9781583470831.html">
        <img src="images/ibmi_php.jpg" alt="The IBM i Programmer's Guide
to PHP">
        </a>
          <figcaption>$55.95</figcaption>
        </figure>
    </div>
    <div class="books">
        <p class="book-title">WebSphere Application Server:  Step by
Step</p>
        <figure>
        <a href="9781583470619.html">
        <img src="images/websphere.jpg" alt="WebSphere Application
Server:  Step by Step">
        </a>
          <figcaption>$35.95</figcaption>
        </figure>
```

Continued

```
        </div>
      </article>
    </section>
    <br class="clear" />
  </main>
  <footer>&copy;2016.  Belhur Publishing, LLC.  All rights reserved.</
footer>
</div>
</body>
</html>
```

Figure 5.38: The HTML code for the books catalog page

Summary

There is a lot more to image handling than we have covered here, but those more sophisticated aspects typically fall into the realm of designers. These are truly artistic professionals whose careers encompass working with photographic images and design tools and incorporating the images into print media, video, and websites.

Most programmers, whose concerns and experiences revolve around data and business management, are not talented graphical artists. That's not to say they can't be, but most people would agree that artistically talented computer programmers are rare. So, this chapter has focused on the more practical and "data-centric" aspects of managing images in HTML. We are much more concerned with applications like online catalogs than background images, audio and video elements, and the look and feel of a Web page.

We hope that this chapter has provided you with useful insights and tools for incorporating various kinds of visual elements and multimedia into your Web pages. Obviously, it's just the tip of the iceberg, but once you know enough to get started, it's relatively easy to move forward on your own.

Key Terms

.avi	<audio>	ismap
.flv	<embed>	JPG/JPEG
.m4v	<object>	media file
.mov	<param>	plug-in
.mp3	<source>	PNG
.mp4	<video>	SVG
.ogg	compression	SVGA
.ogv	GIF	usemap
.swf	high-definition (HD)	VGA
.wav	image map	WebP

Discussion/Review Questions

1. What type of files are .wav and .mp3?
2. Which HTML tag is used to incorporate an image into a Web page?
3. What are three common image types?
4. What is a plug-in?
5. What happens when the alt attribute is not used with a broken image?
6. What causes a broken image icon to be displayed on a Web page?
7. What are the two attributes required for creating a valid image link in an HTML5 document?
8. Which image format should be used for complex images and photographs?
9. Which image format supports transparency?
10. What is an image hotspot?
11. Why is the alt attribute important for an image link?
12. What does it mean when an image is broken?
13. Which three HTML elements do you use to create an image map?
14. How many valid shapes can be used to create a hotspot, and what are they?
15. What happens when a JPEG file is resized from its native dimensions?
16. Videos and audios can be embedded on a Web page using which HTML5 elements?
17. What happens when a user's Web browser doesn't support the audio or video element?
18. What is the purpose of the poster attribute in the video tag?
19. What are the differences between the <object>, <embed>, and <video> tags?
20. What is an image map, and when is it used?

Exercises

1. Provide the HTML code to display an image called mcpresslogo.gif on a Web page.
2. Provide the HTML code for creating a hyperlink to an audio file called demo.mp3.
3. Write the HTML code to embed the audio file named demo.mp3 on a Web page.
4. Write the HTML code to display and play the following video on a Web page:
   a. Video files: demo.mp4, demo.ogg, demo.webm
   b. Dimensions: 480 pixels wide, 320 pixels high
   c. Autoplay: On
   d. Controls: On
   e. Poster: demo.jpg
5. Provide the HTML code for creating an image hyperlink link to the about.html page when the image named home.png is clicked.
6. Write the HTML code to embed the following audio file on a Web page:
   a. Audio file: learn_html.mp3
   b. Preload: auto
   c. Controls: On
   d. Autoplay: On
   e. Loop: True

Arranging Content

Now that you're armed with a fair command of HTML, and you've learned to incorporate CSS, you're ready to tackle the last major hurdle in Web page design: arranging the content of the page. This might seem simple and straightforward, but there are a number of subtle issues at work here. How easily maintained is your Web page? How smoothly will users be able to navigate through your website? Is the overall design of all the Web pages and their links clear and intuitive, so that untrained users can easily find what they need? In this chapter, we'll answer these and other questions about the arrangement of Web page content.

Content-Arrangement Methods

There are many methods for controlling the arrangement of content on our pages. You can use tables to align text and images into neat rows and columns. Historically tables have been used to control the overall framework of the entire page, but doing so is not now generally recommended.

Frames were designed specifically to control the overall framework of Web pages. They have some great features that are very useful for arranging content, but their use is diminishing in favor of other methods. We'll still discuss frames in this chapter, because you need to understand them to work with the many websites that still do use them.

The <div> and <span> tags are the most up-to-date HTML tags for controlling the arrangement of content on your Web pages. Those tags, in conjunction with CSS, are currently the most accepted way to arrange the content of your Web pages.

The Purpose of Arranging Content

Before you can arrange the content of a Web page, you have to understand what the goal of your website is. What do you want the page to accomplish? Here are some possible goals you might have for the pages at your website:

- Tell potential customers about your company.
- Generate sales leads.
- Sell a product.
- Communicate with business partners.
- Provide resources.

Your requirements for arranging content on a page will depend on the focus of your website. So, before you worry about arranging the content on a page, consider what your website's ultimate goal is. Keep that goal in mind as you design the site.

Tell Potential Customers About Your Company

Telling the public about your company is a relatively easy task. You can accomplish this with a static website that may be what is commonly called "brochure-ware." Literally, you could take the artwork that you used in your company's print marketing materials and incorporate that look into your website. This is useful in that it maintains a consistent look across all your marketing material. Basically, this treats the website as an extension of your marketing program.

Generate Sales Leads

Generating sales leads requires some form of two-way communication with visitors to your site. It could be something as simple as an email link that lets visitors send a message to your sales department for follow-up. It could be an input form that allows visitors to provide information about their interests, then sends that information to a Common Gateway Interface (CGI) program (discussed later) on the server so that it can be entered directly into your database.

Sell a Product

Selling a product (or products) requires even more interaction with your users than generating leads. Not only do you need to obtain information from your visitors, you also must provide a fair amount of detail about your available products. This information might include prices, descriptions, and even pictures. It's not practical to put that kind of dynamic information into a static Web page. How would you handle keeping the prices current and accurate? How would you handle adding new products or removing obsolete ones?

Because of these types of issues, any website that needs this level of interaction must get data from a database. You probably already maintain up-to-date product information in a database, so there is minimal extra overhead there. There are many ways to deliver dynamic content from your database to a Web page. For example, a CGI program, Java Server Page, PHP, or an Active Server Page could perform this task. These four common methods are discussed later in this book.

When you sell a product via a website, your goals involve getting users to come to the site, optimizing its placement in search engines, generating a large number of hits, and keeping visitors on the site as long as possible.

Communicate with Business Partners

Communicating with business partners requires basically the same techniques as selling a product. The focus changes, though, from presenting catalogs and taking orders to expanding your company's Internet presence. You will typically be presenting information from multiple databases through this type of website. The information could be such things as order statuses, shipping schedules, and inventory levels.

Business partners need to come to your website to fulfill their own business requirements. You don't need to advertise or entice them to come to the site. In fact, you might want to prevent the public from accessing the site, and allow only trusted business partners to gain access.

Provide Resources

Providing resources is almost as simple as producing brochure-ware. Resources are relatively static collections of information such as Frequently Asked Questions (FAQs), user manuals, technical support documents, how-to videos, software downloads, and links to other useful websites. Rather than focusing on marketing, a resource site is more likely to feature a large number of links to documents and other websites.

As with sales sites, search-engine optimization (SEO) would be very important for a resource site. However, the focus would be on delivering useful and easy-to-find content to your visitors, without concern for how often they visited or how long they stayed.

A Web Page Structure

In chapter 2, you learned how to construct a Web page wireframe using HTML structural elements such as div, section, main, article, and nav. Although we will cover mostly the table and form elements in this chapter, table elements are less widely used than they once were. Today's mobile-friendly Web pages should be constructed with structural elements, which better accommodate Web browsers and search engines, are easier to maintain and modify, and are more flexible with CSS and JavaScript. Nonetheless, table elements still have their place on the Web when used strictly for displaying tabular data. So we will start our exploration of a Web page's structure by learning how to create tables.

Tables

In business programming, we often need lists. We produce lists of items, orders, inventory, and more. Tables are a great tool for arranging lists of data. Therefore, it's likely that tables will become a common tool for you in developing Web pages.

Table tag:

```
<table
  align
  bgcolor
  border
  cellspacing
```

```
    cellpadding
    frame
    rules
    summary
    width
  >
  </table>
```

Simply put, **tables** are just grids of data. You specify some number of rows and columns, perhaps define a heading, a footer, and other properties, and the browser takes care of the rest. If you don't provide specific instructions to do otherwise, the browser will expand or contract the sizes of the rows and columns to fit the content within them. So, you can have some columns that contain relatively large text blocks or images, while other columns contain minimal information, like a yes/no flag (Y/N).

Even though browsers handle much of a table's formatting, a programmer still has plenty of options for defining a table. Therefore, the **<table>** tag has many properties. For example, you can define the alignment as left, center, or right. Use the bgcolor property to set the table's background color, as either a color name or a hex code. The total width of the table is controlled by the width property, which can be set to a specific size in pixels or a percentage of the page width. **Cellspacing** refers to the distance between cells in the table, while **cellpadding** refers to the distance between the border of a cell and its contents.

To show the borders between cells, set the border attribute to one or more pixels. When this is set to zero (the default), no border is shown. The rules attribute defines which borders/rules to show within the table. When rules is set to none, only the outside border is shown. Alternatively, rules can be set to cols, indicating that only the vertical rules between the columns are shown, or "rows" to display only the horizontal rules between the rows.

The frame attribute defines the behavior of the outside border/frame. Set it to void to prevent the frame from being displayed. If this attribute is set to box or border, the frame on all four sides of the table is shown. Setting it to lhs or rhs displays, respectively, the frames on the left side or right side only. Use hsides to show only the top and bottom sides of the frame, or vsides to show only the right and left sides. Set the frame attribute to either above or below to show the top or bottom frames, respectively. The summary attribute provides a text description of the table, useful for visually impaired users.

Even with all these attributes, the <table> tag by itself is not enough to create a table. The simplest of tables will include tags for both rows and data. These tags define the rows and columns within the table. Other tags also affect the row and column definitions. We'll discuss these tags later in this chapter.

Table row tag:

```
<tr
  align
  bgcolor
  valign
>
</tr>
```

The **<tr>** tag defines a row within a table. This tag should always be coded between the <table> and </table> tags. Its align and bgcolor attributes provide the same options as those for the table itself. The valign attribute lets you define the vertical alignment for the entire row. The options are top, middle, and bottom. Whichever is chosen, the content of each cell in the row will be aligned to that point.

Table data tag:

```
<td
  align
  bgcolor
  valign
  width
  height
  abbr
  scope
  nowrap

  colspan
  rowspan
>
</td>
```

The **<td>** tag defines each separate cell within the row. It has the same align, bgcolor, and valign attributes as the <tr> tag. Use the height and width properties to define the size of each cell. The abbr attribute provides an abbreviated description of the contents of the cell. Use the **scope attribute** to assign headings to cells for use in screen readers (discussed later in this chapter). The nowrap attribute prevents the text within a cell from automatically wrapping to the next line. This can result in very wide cells. The **colspan** and **rowspan** attributes are used to define how many columns wide or rows high the cell is.

With these three tags, we can create a basic table. The code in Figure 6.1 creates a table that has one row and three columns. The total width of the table is 200 pixels, and the second cell uses the nowrap attribute to force its text to appear in a single line. The table also has its border property set to 2 to create an obvious border around the table and between the cells. The output from the code sample is shown in Figure 6.2.

```
<table width=200px border=2>
  <tr>
    <td>HTML for the Business Developer</td>
    <td nowrap>Mastering the IBM i</td>
    <td>The IBM i Programmer's Guide to PHP</td>
  </tr>
</table>
```

Figure 6.1: The HTML code for a table

Figure 6.2: A simple table with one row

This clearly shows the behavior of the `nowrap` attribute in the second cell. Remember, however, that managing the look of content such as this is best done with a style sheet, rather than with HTML itself. (Style sheets are discussed in chapter 3.)

Now let's add a couple of rows of data to the table, remove the `width` attribute of the `<table>` tag, and remove the `nowrap` attribute of the second `<td>` tag. The code for these changes is in Figure 6.3, and the output is shown in Figure 6.4.

```
<table border=2>
  <tr>
    <td>1,254 titles in Programming</td>
    <td>763 titles in Database</td>
    <td>2,751 titles in Operating Systems</td>
  </tr>
  <tr>
    <td>323 titles in Programming</td>
    <td>982 titles in Database</td>
    <td>1,200 titles in Operating Systems</td>
  </tr>
  <tr>
    <td>769 titles in Programming</td>
    <td>255 titles in Database</td>
    <td>3,100 titles in Operating Systems</td>
  </tr>
</table>
```

Figure 6.3: The HTML code for a multi-row table

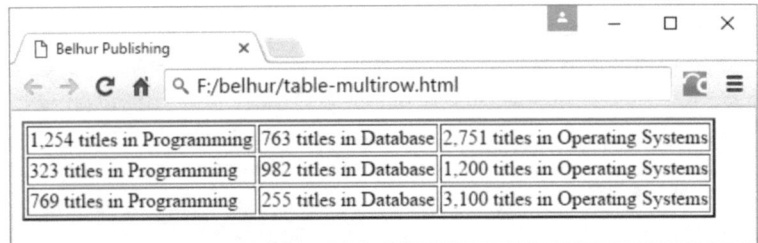

Figure 6.4: A table with three rows

This example illustrates how the browser will adjust the size of each cell to fit its contents, and adjust the size of the table to fit all the cells. Sometimes this is fine, but often we need to control some aspect of the table's size to better manage the way the table is presented to users.

The table in Figure 6.4 is missing both column headings and row headings. There is a special tag just for column headings: the table column header (<th>) tag.

Table column header tag:

```
<th
  align
  bgcolor
  valign
  width
  height
  abbr
  scope
  nowrap
  colspan
  rowspan
>
</th>
```

The <th> tags create a row of cells specifically designed as headings for the other rows in the table. The modified code for a table with headings is shown in Figure 6.5. You can see the table it creates in Figure 6.6.

```
<table border=2>
  <tr align=center>
    <th>Programming</th>
    <th>Database</th>
    <th>Operating Systems</th>
  </tr>
  <tr>
    <td>1,254 titles</td>
```

Continued

```
    <td>763 titles </td>
    <td>2,751 titles </td>
  </tr>
  <tr>
    <td>323 titles </td>
    <td>982 titles </td>
    <td>1,200 titles </td>
  </tr>
  <tr>
    <td>769 titles </td>
    <td>255 titles </td>
    <td>3,100 titles </td>
  </tr>
</table>
```

Figure 6.5: The HTML code for the table in Figure 6.6

Programming	Database	Operating Systems
1.254 titles	763 titles	2.751 titles
323 titles	982 titles	1.200 titles
769 titles	255 titles	3.100 titles

Figure 6.6: A table with column headings

The headings in this table have been centered inside each cell. The browser is still automatically adjusting the size of the cells, rows, and the table itself. You can begin to see the table taking shape as we add more and more code to it. To make the cells a bit larger, giving the content more room, we could use the cellpadding attribute. We could also add additional column and row headings. The code sample in Figure 6.7 includes an enhanced version of the table, which is shown in Figure 6.8.

```
table border=2>
  <tr align=center bgcolor=gray>
    <th colspan=4>Books (in Titles)</th>
  </tr>
  <tr align=center bgcolor=gray>
    <th>Warehouse</th>
```

Continued

```
      <th>Programming</th>
      <th>Database</th>
      <th>Operating Systems</th>
   </tr>
   <tr>
      <td bgcolor=gray>Michigan</td>
      <td>1,254</td>
      <td>763</td>
      <td>2,751</td>
   </tr>
   <tr>
      <td bgcolor=gray>Wisconsin</td>
      <td>323</td>
      <td>982</td>
      <td>1,200</td>
   </tr>
   <tr>
      <td bgcolor=gray>Idaho</td>
      <td>769</td>
      <td>255</td>
      <td>3,100</td>
   </tr>
</table>
```

Figure 6.7: The HTML code for the table in Figure 6.8

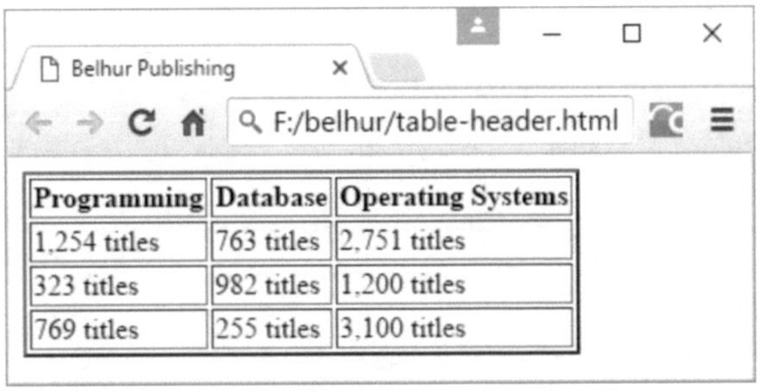

Figure 6.8: A table with more complex headings

As you can see in this example, the cells are a little less cramped, as there is now a little extra space between the content and the borders of the cells, and the headings are automatically emphasized in a darker print. We added a gray background to the two heading rows and the first cells in each of the data rows. The top cell uses the colspan attribute to extend itself four columns wide.

Now that we've removed the word *titles* from the data cells, we can see that the left-aligned text doesn't work well for numbers. The title counts would look better if they were aligned to the right side of the cells. Since we only want to adjust the alignment of the data cells, and not the entire row, we'll add the alignment to the cells themselves. We can also add a column on the right side that contains some legend information for the table. Because we want this cell to extend down across all four rows, we'll use the rowspan attribute and set it to 5. The code in Figure 6.9 contains these changes, creating the table shown in Figure 6.10.

```
<table border=2 cellpadding=2>
  <tr align=center bgcolor=gray>
    <th colspan=5>Books (in Titles)</th>

  </tr>
  <tr align=center bgcolor=gray>
    <th>Warehouse</th>
    <th>Programming</th>
    <th>Database</th>
    <th>Operating Systems</th>
    <th rowspan=4 width=10>2 0 1 6</th>
  </tr>
  <tr align=right>
    <td bgcolor=gray align=left>Michigan</td>
    <td>1,254</td>
    <td>763</td>
    <td>2,751</td>
  </tr>
  <tr align=right>
    <td bgcolor=gray align=left>Wisconsin</td>
    <td>323</td>
    <td>982</td>
    <td>1,200</td>
  </tr>
  <tr align=right>
    <td bgcolor=gray align=left>Idaho</td>
    <td>769</td>
    <td>255</td>
    <td>3,100</td>
  </tr>
</table>
```

Figure 6.9: The HTML code for the table in Figure 6.10

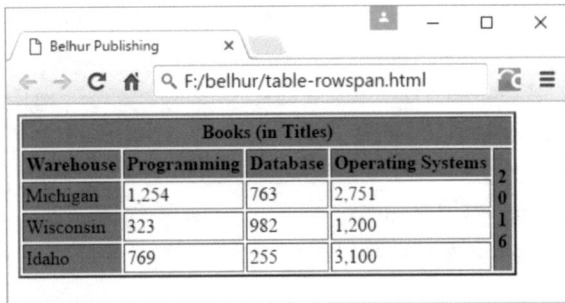

Figure 6.10: A table using the align, rowspan, and colspan attributes

Notice in Figure 6.9 that the year is entered with a space between each number. This allows the browser to insert line breaks between each number, and the width of 10 pixels is too narrow to let more than one number in the year print on the same line. Making the alignment as easy as possible to manage, we added the align=right attribute to the <tr> tag beginning each data row. Then we added an align=left attribute to the warehouse state name cells.

Tables can be split into three sections: header, body, and footer.

Table header tag:

```
<thead
  align
  valign
>
</thead>
```

Table body tag:

```
<tbody
  align
  valign
>
</tbody>
```

What this table needs now is a total line. This can be created using a table-footer section. Unlike the headings, which can be created with <th> cells, the footer cells must be defined using the **<tfoot>** tag, which defines the footer section of a table.

Table footer:

```
<tfoot
  align
  valign
>
</tfoot>
```

The code in Figure 6.11 modifies our table to take advantage of these sections. It creates the image shown in Figure 6.12.

```
<table border=2 cellpadding=2>
  <thead>
    <tr align=center bgcolor=gray>
      <th colspan=5>Books (in Titles)</th>
    </tr>
  </thead>
  <tbody>
    <tr align=center bgcolor=gray>
      <th>Warehouse</th>
      <th>Programming</th>
      <th>Database</th>
      <th>Operating Systems</th>
      <th rowspan=4 width=10>2 0 1 6</th>
    </tr>
    <tr align=right>
      <td bgcolor=gray align=left>Michigan</td>
      <td>1,254</td>
      <td>763</td>
      <td>2,751</td>
    </tr>
    <tr align=right>
      <td bgcolor=gray align=left>Wisconsin</td>
      <td>323</td>
      <td>982</td>
      <td>1,200</td>
    </tr>
    <tr align=right>
      <td bgcolor=gray align=left>Idaho</td>
      <td>769</td>
      <td>255</td>
      <td>3,100</td>
    </tr>
  </tbody>
  <tfoot>
    <tr align=right>
```

Continued

```
        <td bgcolor=gray align=left>Total</td>
        <td>2,346</td>
        <td>2,000</td>
        <td>7,051</td>
        <td bgcolor=white></td>
      </tr>
    </tfoot>
  </table>
```

Figure 6.11: The HTML code for the table in Figure 6.12

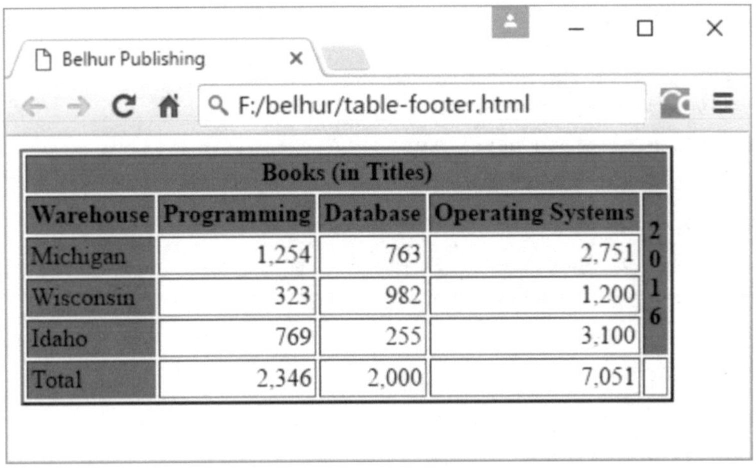

Figure 6.12: A table with a header and footer

In the first section, <th> tags define the cells within the heading. In the footer section, the cells are defined using the standard <td> tags. To make the total even more visually distinct, we could choose to define the footer row with a different color of text or a background color. For our purposes, though, this is good enough.

Screen Readers

To improve the accessibility of Web pages for visually impaired users, HTML includes the ability to define supplemental information by a specialized type of software called a *screen reader*. Such software packages read the content of Web pages and provide an alternative presentation to the user. For example, they might magnify or speak the text.

Caption tag:

```
<caption
  align
>
</caption>
```

To improve the accessibility of our table, we might make some changes, such as replacing the top row with a caption and providing an abbreviation to explain that the oddly formatted cell on the right side of the table is a year. We'll also change the state name cells to table **headers** and add the scope attribute to all the table header cells. The sample code in Figure 6.13 shows the HTML for the table in Figure 6.14 with these modifications.

```
<table border=2 cellpadding=2>
  <caption>
  Books (in Titles)
  </caption>
  <thead>
  </thead>
  <tbody>
    <tr align=center bgcolor=gray>
      <th scope=col>Warehouse</th>
      <th scope=col>Programming</th>
      <th scope=col>Database</th>
      <th scope=col>Operating Systems</th>
      <th rowspan=4 width=10 abbr="Year 2016">2 0 1 6</th>
    </tr>
    <tr align=right>
      <th bgcolor=gray align=left scope=row>Michigan</th>
      <td>1,254</td>
      <td>763</td>
      <td>2,751</td>
    </tr>
    <tr align=right>
      <th bgcolor=gray align=left scope=row>Wisconsin</th>
      <td>323</td>
      <td>982</td>
      <td>1,200</td>
    </tr>
    <tr align=right>
      <th bgcolor=gray align=left scope=row>Idaho</th>
      <td>769</td>
      <td>255</td>
      <td>3,100</td>
    </tr>
  </tbody>
```

Continued

```
    <tfoot>
      <tr align=right>
        <th bgcolor=gray align=left scope=row>Total</th>
        <td>2,346</td>
        <td>2,000</td>
        <td>7,051</td>
        <td bgcolor=white></td>
      </tr>
    </tfoot>
  </table>
```

Figure 6.13: The HTML code for the table in Figure 6.14

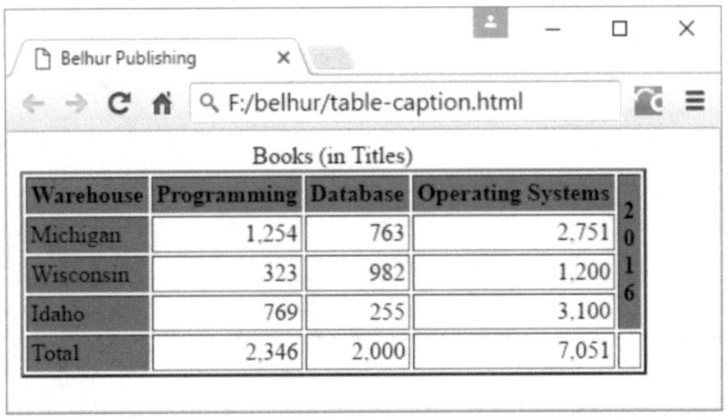

Figure 6.14: A table with a caption and table headers

The scope attribute used in the table headers is an important tool for screen readers. It helps to identify which pieces of data belong to what headings. Most of us are able to easily grasp that relationship visually, but when the table is being described verbally, it's much more challenging. Also notice that the scope was applied to both columns and rows. The caption, if one is provided, must immediately follow the <table> tag. With the exception of the caption, none of the changes made any difference in the way the table was displayed. Hopefully, though, these changes would improve the experience of visually impaired users.

Accessibility is a difficult issue to pin down. Different browsers support different tags, different readers use different tags, and different users have vastly different needs. We've tried to focus on practical examples in introducing this topic, but an in-depth review is beyond the scope of this book. If accessibility is a concern for your organization, you will need to do additional research in that area.

Columns and Column Groups

Earlier in this book, you saw how row groups (**<thead>**, **<tbody>**, and **<tfoot>**) can better define a table. Similarly, column groups can better define the columns in the table. There are two tags used to define columns: <col> and <colgroup>. Use <col> to define a single column and <colgroup> to define multiple columns.

Column tag:

```
<col
  align
  span
  width
  bgcolor
>
</col>
```

Column group tag:

```
<colgroup
  align
  span
  width
  bgcolor
>
</colgroup>
```

The primary role of both these tags is to provide attributes for all the cells in their column(s), not the content. The updated table appears exactly as it did in Figure 6.14. However, as the code in Figure 6.15 shows, the <col> and <colgroup> tags now contain most of the cell formatting attributes.

```
<table border=2 cellpadding=2>
  <caption>
  Books (in Titles)
  </caption>
  <col bgcolor=gray align=left>
    </col>

  <colgroup span=3 align=right>
  </colgroup>
  <col width=4>
    </col>

  <thead>
  </thead>
```

Continued

```
<tbody>
    <tr align=center bgcolor=gray>
        <th scope=col>Warehouse</th>
        <th scope=col>Programming</th>
        <th scope=col>Database</th>
        <th scope=col>Operating Systems</th>
        <th rowspan=4 abbr="Year 2016">2 0 1 6</th>
    </tr>
    <tr>
        <th scope=row>Michigan</th>
        <td>1,254</td>
        <td>763</td>
        <td>2,751</td>
    </tr>
    <tr>
        <th scope=row>Wisconsin</th>
        <td>323</td>
        <td>982</td>
        <td>1,200</td>
    </tr>
    <tr>
        <th scope=row>Idaho</th>
        <td>769</td>
        <td>255</td>
        <td>3,100</td>
    </tr>
</tbody>
<tfoot>
    <tr align=right>
        <th scope=row>Total</th>
        <td>2,346</td>
        <td>2,000</td>
        <td>7,051</td>
        <td bgcolor=white></td>
    </tr>
</tfoot>
</table>
```

Figure 6.15: The HTML code for a table with columns and column group definitions

In this example, the first <col> tag defines the attributes of the first column, which holds the city name. The <colgroup> tag spans three columns, providing the alignment for all the data cells in the table. Some of the heading cells were also affected, but those will have their alignment corrected within the <tr> tag.

Nested Tables

Sometimes one table is just not enough, and you might find a need to nest one or more tables inside another table. Our example so far in this chapter lists inventory for various locations. What if each location stocked different categories of books? Sure, we could simply add more columns to the table, but then we wouldn't have an excuse to nest one table inside another.

Look at the table in Figure 6.16. It is actually two tables. The outer table contains a row for each location, and within the data cell for each location, another table lists that location's inventory. Review the code in Figure 6.17, which generates Figure 6.16.

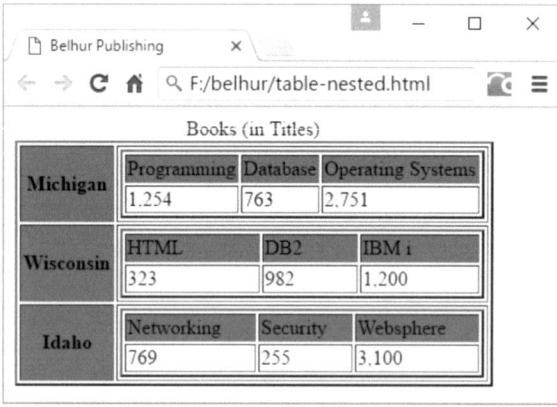

Figure 6.16: Nested tables

```
<table border=2 cellpadding=2 margin-top=2px>
  <caption>
  Books (in Titles)
  </caption>
  <col bgcolor=gray align=left>
    </col>

  <colgroup span=3 align=right>
  </colgroup>
  <col width=4>
    </col>

  <thead>
  </thead>
```
Continued

```
<tbody>
  <tr>
    <th scope=row>Michigan</th>
    <td><table border=2  width=100%>
        <tr bgcolor=gray>
          <td>Programming</td>
          <td>Database</td>
          <td>Operating Systems</td>
        </tr>
        <tr>
          <td>1,254</td>
          <td>763</td>
          <td>2,751</td>
        </tr>
      </table></td>
  </tr>
  <tr>
    <th scope=row>Wisconsin</th>
    <td><table border=2  width=100%>
        <tr bgcolor=gray>
          <td>HTML</td>
          <td>DB2</td>
          <td>IBM i</td>
        </tr>
        <tr>
          <td>323</td>
          <td>982</td>
          <td>1,200</td>
        </tr>
      </table></td>
  </tr>
  <tr>
    <th scope=row>Idaho</th>
    <td><table border=2 width=100%>
        <tr bgcolor=gray>
          <td>Networking</td>
          <td>Security</td>
          <td>Websphere</td>
        </tr>
        <tr>
```

Continued

```
            <td>769</td>
            <td>255</td>
            <td>3,100</td>
        </tr>
      </table></td>
    </tr>
  </tbody>
</table>
```

Figure 6.17: The HTML code for nested tables

As you can see, there are many options for working with tables. You can define columns and rows, format the cells, and even nest one table inside another. The code given here should provide good examples for the majority of tables you're likely to create.

Anywhere that you need to organize content into clearly defined rows and columns, columns are likely to be useful. Remember, though, to avoid using tables to define the layout of your entire Web page. This is better handled with <div> and <span> tags, discussed later in this chapter.

Frames

Frames are vaguely similar to tables. They define blocks of content that can be organized into rows and columns, if desired. However, frames, or *framesets* as they are sometimes called, were specifically designed to control the layout of Web pages, as opposed to tables, which should not be used for that task. The major downside to framesets is that they are not compatible with most assistive technologies, such as screen readers; they are also not search-engine friendly. Therefore, framesets are now deprecated and no longer supported in HTML5. For this reason, we will limit our discussion of frames in this chapter.

Inline Frames

A more flexible type of frame is the *inline frame*. It is called an inline frame because the frame and its contents are placed on the Web page as if they were an inline element, such as an image. This enables you to pull content from other pages into frames placed on the current page. You might do this if you have a common document that contains information that you want to present on multiple pages. Each of those pages might include an inline frame that displays the same information. The advantage of this is that the information is stored in a single document, so it is more easily maintained. Otherwise, keeping the same information consistent across multiple changes is difficult and time-consuming.

Inline frame tag:

<iframe-, end tag
  name
  src
  scrolling
  width

```
    height
    align
    frameborder
    marginwidth
    marginheight
>
</iframe>
```

The attributes of the inline frame are similar to those for the <frame> and <frameset> tags. The src attribute identifies the document being displayed within the frame, while the other attributes control various aspects of how it is displayed.

Figure 6.18 shows the code for a simple example of an inline frame. Figure 6.19 shows the resulting Web page.

```
<h3>An iframe of our book's page.</h3>
<iframe src="books.html" width="80%" height="350">
If you see this, your browser does not support iframes.
</iframe>
```

Figure 6.18: The HTML code for an inline frame

Figure 6.19: A Web page with an inline frame

As you can see, the inline frame is placed in the middle of the second paragraph, with a width of 80 percent of the page and a height of 350px. Because the HTML document is too long to fit in the area for the inline frame, a scrollbar is added. Also notice, in Figure 6.23, the text between the **<iframe>** and </iframe> tags. The sentence "If you see this, your browser does not support iframes." should only display if the user's browser does not support inline frames.

Web Forms

Web forms are present on virtually every website you've ever visited: search engine sites, social media sites, e-commerce sites, college and university websites, and many more. One particular type of Web form that is found on every large website is a *search form*, or *search bar*. While some search forms are more prominent than others, they all serve one purpose: to give site visitors the quickest way to find something on the site. Figure 6.20 shows examples of some search forms.

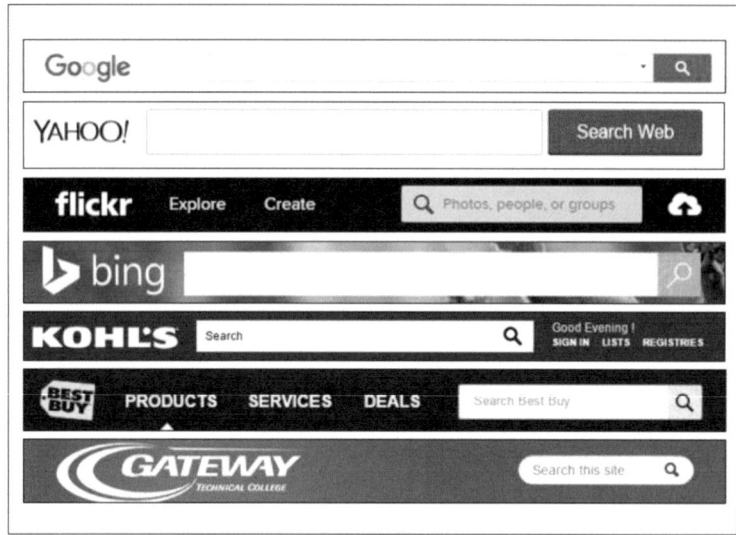

Figure 6.20: Examples of search forms

Generally, a Web form is created with an HTML element that contains objects called *form controls* that can be organized into various topical areas.

Form tag:

```
<form
   accept-charset
   action
   autocomplete
   enctype
   method
   name
   novalidate
   target
   id
   class
   style
>
</form>
```

A Web form is created with the **<form>** and **</form>** tags. The form contains *fields* or *form controls* in which users can enter data, make selections from a list, click a radio button, or enter text in a text area box. A Web page can have multiple forms, but a form cannot be nested within another form. Each form on the page is a separate entity. Although a name and ID are not required for a form, it is recommended that a unique name and ID should be assigned in order for JavaScript and CSS to interact with it more efficiently. Table 6.1 lists the attributes that can be used to configure a form.

Table 6.1: Form Attributes		
Attribute	**Value**	**Description**
accept-charset	Character-encoding name	List of character-encoding names used for character encoding for the submission
action	URL	Specifies the form-submission action for the element
autocomplete	On, Off	Specifies whether values are sensitive or insensitive. On indicates the value is not sensitive, so data can be entered by the user. Off indicates the value is sensitive, so the user has to re-enter the value each time.
enctype	Application/x-www-form-urlencoded, multipart/form-data, text/plain	Specifies a MIME type to associate the element for submission
method	Get, post	Specifies the HTTP method for transfer form to the server. GET appends form key-value pairs to the URL, which are visible. POST sends form key-value pairs through the message, which are hidden from the user.
name	Text	Gives the name of the form. Used by JavaScript to, for example, edit, access, and validate the form information.
novalidate	True, false	Indicates that the form is not to be validated during submission
target	Context names or keywords (e.g. _self, _blank, _parent, _top, or an iframename)	Specifies a name or keyword that represents the target of the control after submitting the form. In HTML5, it is the name or keyword for a browsing context (e.g. tab, window, inline frame).
id	Text	A unique ID name, used primarily for styling with CSS
class	Text	A class name used primarily for styling with CSS

Figure 6.21 shows how a simple Web form is created; Figure 6.22 shows the result.

```
<h3>SEARCH</h3>
<form method="post" action="#">
    Enter Phrase:
    <input type="text" name="key" id="key" required="required">
    <input type="submit" class="formButton" value="Search">
</form>>
```

Figure 6.21: The HTML code for a simple Web form

SEARCH

Figure 6.22: A simple Web form

Without much effort, our simple form in Figure 6.22 looks similar to the search forms listed in Figure 6.20. The form is easy to design; it can be as simple as our example or as complex as a financial form. The difficult part is the processing part, which is the programmer's responsibility. Thus, it is important for programmers to understand how Web forms are designed and how they work.

Typically, Web forms are not used just for performing a search; they're often used to collect visitors' information. For example, an owner of a business consulting firm might want to collect information about potential clients for her company's services, or a marketing manager for an e-commerce website wants to gather information about people who are interested in the products for sale on the site.

A typical Web form usually has more fields than just a search box and a submit button. A form might even have several sections that are organized into topic areas, such as a registration section, a customer information section, a survey section, and so on. These sections might have different types of controls for users to interact with, such as buttons, check boxes, input boxes, lists, or a comments box. All these controls and more can be inserted within a Web form. Table 6.2 lists the different types of form controls and the elements that create them.

Table 6.2: Types of Web Form Controls		
Type	Element	Description
Input box	<input type="text"/>	Boxes for user input
Password box	<input type="password"/>	Input text box where entered text is replaced with asterisks or other symbols
Option button	**<option>**</option>	A combo box for selecting a single or multiple items from a list of items
Check box	<input type="checkbox"/>	For selecting a yes/no response
Radio button	<input type="radio"/>	For selecting a single option from a list of options
Selection list	**<select>**</select>	A drop-down list of items for selection
Text area	**<textarea>**</textarea>	A comments box for extended text input
Fieldset	**<fieldset>**</fieldset>	A visual cue element that groups similar form controls together by enclosing the controls with an outline or border
Legend	**<legend>**</legend>	Works in conjunction with fieldsets to provide a text description for the fieldset group
Label	**<label>**</label>	Text description for a form control
Image	<input type="image"/>	Used to replace the standard buttons with custom buttons
Button	**<button>**</button>	Buttons with clickable events, especially for submitting the form
Hidden input	<input type="hidden"/>	Stores data that is hidden from the browser window
Reset button	<input type="reset"/>	Resets the form fields to their initial values
Submit button	<input type="submit"/>	Submits the form for processing

An **input box**, or **text box**, is one of the most widely used control elements in a Web form. Examples of text boxes on a form include username, email, address, phone number, and so on. A **password box** is a special input box that allows the user to type in a secret password but replaces the text with a symbol such as an asterisk. **Options** are combo-boxes in which a list of items is displayed and one or more items can be selected. Usually, multiple items can be selected by pressing the Shift or Ctrl key and clicking the items on the list. A **select list** is a drop-down box in which only a single item can be selected from the list.

A **check box** is a control element that holds a yes or no response. Check boxes are independent of each other, so users are allowed to select one or more at the same time. Unlike check boxes, **radio buttons** are usually grouped together by a unique name, so that only one option is allowed to be selected.

A **text area** configures an extended input box for user to input text. It is commonly used to allow users to type in comments or feedback, or request information in writing.

Fieldset and **legend** controls are visual cue elements that group together control elements that serve a similar purpose. **Label** is used to label or describe a control element. Its purpose is to provide assistance to people who are visually challenged and for search engine optimization (SEO).

An **image button** is used to replace the standard button with an image. For example, you might use an image button in place of the standard button so it matches the rest of the control elements. The **button** element is used to configure a button with an image as well as a block of text outside of the button. The button is triggered whenever either the button or the block of text is clicked.

Hidden inputs are useful for storing data that is not meant for the user to select but is crucial for the form as a whole. For example, a hidden input control might be used to store a tracking ID for a specific form or page to see where the data was submitted from.

The reset and submit buttons are usually the last two visible control elements on a form. The **reset button** does only one thing: it resets the entire form controls to their initial values. The **submit button** submits the Web form to the server for processing. It causes the Web browser to transmit the form data to the Web server via the method specified in the form's method attribute.

What About Our Example Page?

Now that we know how tables and Web forms are created, let's update our sample website to have a contact form on our "contact" page. Figure 6.23 shows a new layout for our contact page from chapter 5 for the final page shown in Figure 6.24.

```
<!DOCTYPE html>
<html>
<head>
<title>Contact Belhur Publishing</title>
<meta charset="utf-8" />
<link rel="stylesheet" href="main.css"/>
</head>
<body>
<div id="main-container">
<header> </header>
<div id="left-side-bar">
<nav>
  <ul>
    <li><a href="index.html">Home</a></li>
    <li><a href="about.html">About</a></li>
    <li><a href="books.html">Books</a></li>
    <li><a href="order.html">Order</a></li>
    <li><a href="contact.html">Contact Us</a></li>
  </ul>
</nav>
</div>
<aside> </aside>
<main>
<section>
  <article>
    <h3>CONTACT US</h3>
    <form method="post" action="process.php">
      <fieldset>
        <legend>Your Contact Information <em>(All fields
required)</em></legend>
        <label for="FirstName">First Name:</label>
        <input type="text" name="FirstName" id="FirstName"
required="required">
        <br>
```

Continued

```
        <label for="LastName">Last Name:</label>
        <input type="text" name="LastName" id="LastName"
required="required">
        <br>
        <label for="Email">E-mail:</label>
        <input type="email" name="Email" id="Email" required="required"
placeholder="youremail@domain.com">
        <br>
    </fieldset>
    <fieldset>
        <legend>Comments</legend>
        <textarea name="Comments" id="Comments" rows="3"
cols="45"></textarea>
    </fieldset>
    <input type="reset" class="formButton" value="Clear">
    <input type="submit" class="formButton" value="Submit">
    </form>
    <h3> WRITE US </h3>
    <table>
      <tr><td> Belhur Publishing</td></tr>
      <tr><td> 123 Sunshine Drive</td></tr>
      <tr><td> Big Town, MI 97568</td></tr>
      <tr><td> Phone: 313-264-3975</td></tr>
      <tr><td> Email: info@belhurpublishing.com</td></tr>
    </table>
  </article>
</section>
<br class="clear" />
</main>
<footer>&copy;2016.  Belhur Publishing, LLC.  All rights
reserved.</footer>
</div>
</body>
</html>
```

Figure 6.23: The HTML code for the books catalog page

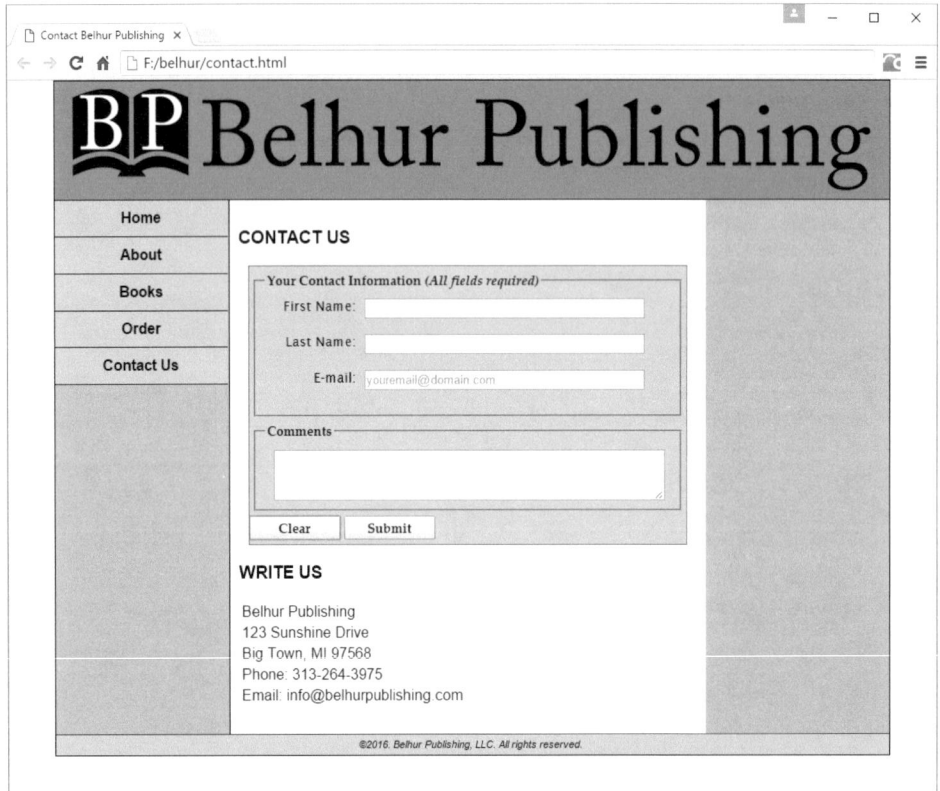

Figure 6.24: The updated contact Web page from chapter 5

Summary

Today, nearly all existing websites are being redesigned to conform to the new HTML5 structural and semantic elements and CSS3. As mobile devices and tablets are becoming more affordable and powerful, more people than ever are relying on these smaller devices to shop, collaborate, and conduct business. To accommodate their increasingly mobile visitors, website owners are adopting more flexible websites that are designed to be more responsive and adaptive, providing an optimum user experience on all types of devices.

Even as websites evolve, tables remain a useful way to present data since virtually all business applications need to display content in neatly defined rows and columns. Although framesets are obsolete and no longer supported by most modern Web browsers, inline frames are still useful for providing additional capabilities to blend content from various documents into a single Web page. Using the frame tags to control the presentation of content is discouraged, however, in favor of the <div> and <span> tags. Finally, Web forms are an invaluable way for any website owner to collect visitors' information and to allow users to contact the business via its website.

We'll leave you with a final reminder: keep in mind the ultimate purpose of your Web page, and arrange your content in a way that supports that purpose.

Key Terms

<button>	<td>	method attribute
<caption>	<textarea>	password box
<fieldset>	<tfoot>	radio button
<form>	<thead>	reset button
<iframe>	<tr>	rowspan attribute
<input>	button	scope attribute
<label>	cellpadding attribute	select list
<legend>	cellspacing attribute	submit button
<option>	check box	table
<select>	colspan attribute	text box
<table>	headers attribute	
<tbody>	hidden input	

Discussion/Review Questions

1. Where should the <caption> tag be placed if it is used in a table?
2. What are tables in HTML?
3. Which attribute is set to show the borders between table cells?
4. What is the difference between cellspacing and cellpadding?
5. What tag defines each table cell within a table row?
6. Between which HTML tag pair are the contents of a table cell placed?
7. If you want to group rows in the table footer, which HTML tag pair should you use?
8. Which HTML tag pair is used to display table headings?
9. Which HTML tag pair is used to create a table row?
10. Table headings are placed between which HTML tag pair?
11. What are nested tables?
12. When might inline frames be useful?
13. What is the advantage of using inline frames?
14. What are Web forms?
15. Which HTML tag pair is used to create Web forms?
16. How many forms can a Web page have?
17. Which form control provides an area that users can use to type in comments?
18. Which form attribute is used to specify the form-submission action?
19. Which HTTP method should be used when you want to transmit form data to the server without revealing the key-value pairs to the user?
20. What is the most widely used form control in a Web form?

Exercises

1. Write the HTML code for creating a two-column table that contains the words "Books" and "Publishers".
2. Write the HTML code for creating a table with three columns, three rows, no cellpadding, and no border.

3. Write the HTML code for creating a simple Web form with one input control and a Submit button.

4. Provide the HTML code for creating a four-column table as follows:

Caption: The caption should read "**Intro to HTML5**"
Row 1: Table headings contain the words **Images**, **Links**, **Tables**, **Videos**
Row 2: Contains the values 4, 7, 2, 3
Row 3: Contains the values 5, 5, 1, 6
Row 4: Table footer contains the total values of 9, 12, 3, 9

5. Create a Web page about your favorite books to include the following:
   a) A four-column table with the following headings:
      - **Title** – Place the book titles in this column
      - **Author** – List the author's name
      - **Year** – List the year the book was published
      - **Links** – List the links to sites about the book
   b) A Web form as follows:
      - Action = submit.php
      - Method = Post
      - Username field
      - Password field
      - Comment box
      - Submit button: submits the form
      - Clear button: clears the form

Web Application Overview

Up to this point, we've talked almost exclusively about HTML. Now that we have a foundation in place, and an understanding of how to use HTML to develop Web pages, it's time to move on to using Web pages in actual business applications. Development of business applications introduces new considerations and components.

Getting Familiar with Web Applications for Business

Traditional business applications typically use a single system and an emulator for access to that system. Web applications open up the use of your systems and software to more users and often involve multiple servers. These servers may be nearby, across the country, or even in another country. Users will be connecting and accessing the applications using Web browsers. The applications will serve up dynamic Web pages using one or more additional tools, such as Active Server Pages (ASP), PHP, or JavaServer Pages (JSP).

Before diving into some of these tools, let's take a closer look at the components of a Web application. Applications used only by internal staff will typically be less complex than those for use by the general Web community. In either case, a Web application may contain a number of confusing components. Remember, though, that a business application developer might only be responsible for part of the system. Especially within midsize and large organizations, there will probably be a separation of responsibility, with a webmaster or systems staff responsible for system configuration, security, and performance, another group responsible for developing applications, and possibly a design group.

For experienced business developers, this isn't anything new. It's similar to the separation of responsibilities in traditional applications. While a business developer might not need to be an expert on configuration, performance, or security, a basic understanding of each of these areas is helpful. A better understanding of the system components and requirements improves application design, resulting in better applications.

Components of a Web Application System

A business Web application system consists of hardware and software components, as shown in Figure 7.1. This diagram provides a basic understanding of the required components, but there might be additional components, depending on the complexity of an organization's specific environment. You probably already have an understanding of the basic components, but to fill in any blanks, we will review them.

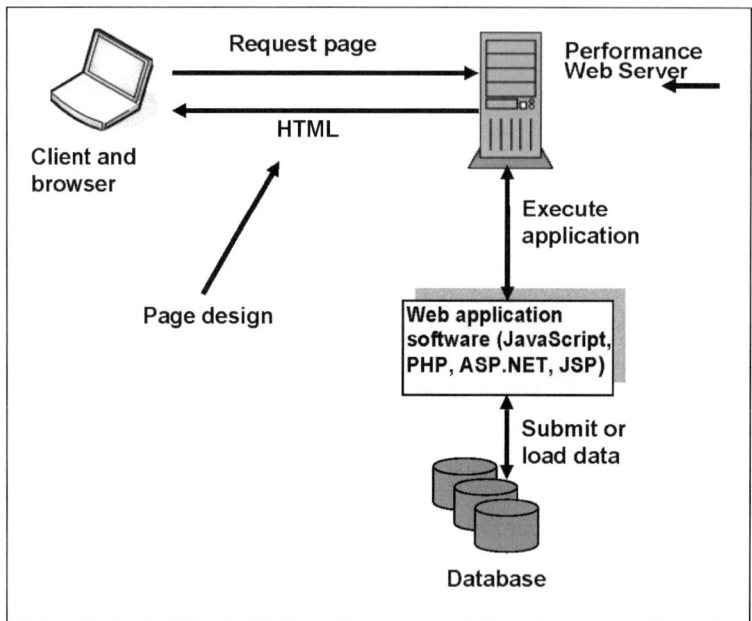

Figure 7.1: A Web application system

The Client

The client is the hardware device that will be used to access the Web application. It is probably a laptop or possibly a desktop computer, but it might be a handheld device such as a smartphone, tablet, iPad, or even a cell phone. Consider carefully what types of devices your application should support. This usually depends on who your application users are and what devices they use to access the Internet.

The client devices will probably use a variety of operating systems. The most common operating system, of course, is Microsoft Windows. Even if all your site visitors are using Windows on PCs, they might be using different screen sizes and resolutions. The screen size and resolution settings will affect the appearance of the site and applications.

All these factors can affect how applications are coded. For example, if your users access your site through handheld devices, your application might require special design and coding techniques to easily fit data on a smaller screen. If your application has many graphics, such as product pictures or logos, the need to consider performance and appearance will be even more important. Client device types, operating systems, screen sizes, and resolutions are discussed in more detail in chapter 12.

The Browser

A browser is software that acts as an interface between the client and the Web. The browser is also referred to as a **Web client**. The browser sends requests for information, receives the information, and displays it on the client. You are probably already familiar with the most popular available browsers: Chrome, Edge, Firefox, Internet Explorer, Safari, and Opera. Browsers are usually free to download. The popularity of individual browsers changes over time (remember Netscape?).

A browser can affect an application's appearance and may also impose other considerations for Web development. If your application is used by the general Web community, your site will very likely need to support many different browsers. Browsers are discussed in more detail in chapter 12.

HTML

As we've mentioned in previous chapters, HTML is the language of the Web, and if you are creating a Web application, HTML will almost certainly be used in that application. HTML has been around for quite a while and will likely be in use for a long time to come. It has changed, however, since its initial inception, to include functions and features that make it more flexible, current, and easier to use for developing Web applications. HTML has long been defined by specifications that greatly influence Web applications' compatibility and make it a universal standard for websites and Web applications.

An HTML document is *static*, meaning it exists in a constant state. To make a Web application dynamic, you can add client-side scripting to the HTML. Most often, the language used for client-side scripting is JavaScript. JavaScript code is embedded within the HTML. You'll learn about JavaScript and client-side scripting in chapter 8. Another option for adding interactivity to HTML is to use forms that incorporate Common Gateway Interface (CGI).

The Web Server

There are really two components of a Web server: hardware and software. So, the term **Web server** can mean either the hardware or the program that is responsible for communicating with client browsers. A Web server accepts HTTP requests from client Web browsers and serves HTTP responses, including data content, usually in the form of an HTML document and linked objects.

Writing Web applications doesn't necessarily mean that you'll need to purchase new hardware. Many platforms can be used to serve websites, although some are more compatible with and better suited to Web development than others. Your organization probably already has a system that can be used for serving a website and Web applications. However, additional hardware might be helpful to serve your site and Web applications, and as a means of including another layer of security. On the other hand, having additional hardware requires additional support and administration. Therefore, you might want to consider using a Web hosting service, discussed later in this chapter.

In terms of Web server software, many different products are available, but some are much more popular than others. Table 7.1 lists the top Web server software vendors, as published in a Netcraft survey in January 2016. (Netcraft is an Internet monitoring company based in England.)

Table 7.1: Netcraft Survey, January 2016—Top Web Server Software		
Vendor/Product	Percent	Websites Hosted
Apache/Apache	33.56%	304,271,061
Microsoft/IIS	28.95%	262,471,886
NGINX, Inc./nginx	15.60%	141,443,630
GWS/Google	2.29%	20,799,087

While Table 7.1 lists the top four Web server applications, inclusion of a particular server software product in the top four list does not mean that product will best fit your needs. Hundreds of Web server programs are available. Many have been created for specialized purposes. Following is a partial list of other available Web server software.

Abyss Web Server	Koala	Personal Web Server
Apache	LiteSpeed Web Server	PoorMan
Bad Blue	(Lighttpd)	SAP Web Application Server
Eagle	MacHTTP	Server2Go
Elemenope	Macromedia JRun	Stronghold
Google Web Server (GWS)	Merak Mail Server	Sun Java System Web Server
Httperf	Mod wsgi	Sun One Web Server
IBM Lotus Domino	NetDynamics Application	TV's server
IBM WebSphere Application	Server	UltiDev Cassini Web Server
Server	Netscape Enterprise Server	WebLogic
In-kernel Web Server	Oversee	WebSitePro
Jaminid	Oracle Application Server	Windows Personal Web Server
Kerio WebSTAR	Oracle HTTP Server	Zeus Web Server

How do you choose Web server software? Consider your needs and determine requirements. Research is the key. Consider and compare server software that meets your requirements and expectations. Here are some of the considerations that should be used for evaluation and comparison:

- Features provided
- Functionality provided
- Operating system support
- Cost
- Creator
- Open source or not
- Software license
- Dynamic content support
- Scripting languages supported
- Databases supported
- Platform compatibility
- Security provided
- Administration and support requirements
- Performance and response time
- Reliability

The Application Servers

Application servers are different from Web servers. A Web server provides client-side dynamic content and serving of the static components of a website. Application servers provide server-side dynamic content and integration with database engines. Usually, the application server is used for the business logic and data access of a Web application. Most Web servers can also be application servers.

Application server software is usually bundled with middleware to enable applications to communicate with dependent applications, including Web servers and database management systems. Some application servers also include an API, making them operating system independent. *Portals* are common application server mechanisms by which a single point of entry can be provided for multiple device types. Table 7.2 shows some of the reasons for incorporating an application server into your application design.

Table 7.2: Web Application Server Advantages	
Advantage	Description
Data and code integrity	By centralizing business logic on an individual or a small number of server machines, updates and upgrades to the application for all users can be guaranteed. There is no risk of old versions of the application accessing or manipulating data in an older, incompatible manner.
Security	Managing access to data and portions of the application through a central point provides a security benefit. Using an application server moves responsibility for authentication away from the potentially insecure client layer without exposing the database layer.
Centralized configuration	Changes to the application configuration, such as a move of the database server or new system settings, can be done centrally.
Performance	The client-server model improves the performance of large applications in heavy-usage environments.
Total cost of ownership	Using an application server can save an organization money through the benefits provided when developing business applications.

Business Web Application Software

Adding dynamic capability to a static website is what Web development is all about. The programming tools used to add that capability are very important. It is not just a matter of learning HTML. You'll be using a combination of tools to create your Web applications. Some form of HTML will be part of the framework for embedding and executing application logic, while the actual programming code may execute on the client or on the server side.

Client-side Programming and Scripting

On the client side, dynamic content is generated on the client system. The Web server retrieves HTML pages with code embedded and sends them to the client. The Web browser on the client then processes the code embedded in the page. Client-side code can be used for such things as changing content, input validation, identifying environmental conditions, or triggering action events. Often, the script language embedded in an HTML page is JavaScript.

Operations performed on the client side of a client-server relationship require access to information or functionality that is available on the client, but not the server. The client is a dedicated user resource, so client-side processing can provide quick response times when designed and coded properly. Completing processing on the client side may also reduce security risks.

Programmers have a variety of tools available for use in client-side coding. JavaScript (discussed in chapter 8) is the most common tool. Another option is Ajax, a combination of JavaScript and XML. Still other options include Python, VBScript, jQuery libraries used with JavaScript, and Perl.

Java is not a scripting language, but it can also be used for client-side applications. Java is an object-oriented, platform-independent language that has roots in C and C++. Any hardware that has a Java Virtual Machine (JVM) can be used with Java. Java, however, is more complex and has a longer learning curve than the true scripting languages. Java is a compiled language. The source is compiled into byte code, which is used for program execution. Java may also be used for server-side Web application development.

Most Web server software packages also have scripting gateways used to create dynamic content. Scripting gateways are used within Web applications to provide the gateway to connect the client and server. Consider two fields with a gated fence between them. The fields are the client and the server, and the gateway is the gate that connects them. CGI hooks are the most commonly used gateway to allow developers to create entire pages and graphics under program control. The CGI hooks are initiated within HTML pages on the client side.

Users' browser settings determine how client-side code embedded in HTML will be handled. Most, but not all, browsers and devices currently support JavaScript. However, users can disable this functionality. The argument might be made that mission-critical programming and scripting should reside on the server side for universal accessibility.

Server-side Programming and Scripting

Server-side programming and scripting provides another way to add dynamics to your website. Figure 7.2 provides a high-level summary of server-side application execution. As you can see, server-side scripts or programs are executed when called upon from the client via an HTTP request.

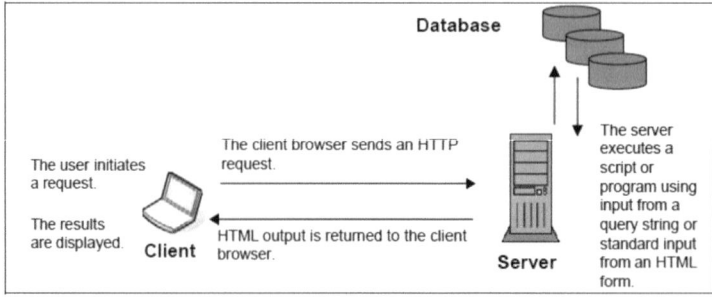

Figure 7.2: Server-side application execution

The HTTP protocol has been in use since 1990. Around 1993, the CGI specification was adopted, making possible server-side dynamic page creation. Shortly thereafter, Server-Side Includes (SSI) were introduced, providing a more direct way to include server-side scripting.

Some of the uses for server-side programming and scripting include the following:

- Processing user queries, retrieving and returning select data
- Adding, changing, or deleting Web page content
- Accessing data or databases to retrieve, add, change, or delete data
- Creating applications to process information
- Developing applications based on business logic
- Providing security and access control
- Validating data or input
- Tailoring output for different browser types
- Customizing Web pages to make them user-friendly
- Improving application performance
- Translating or transforming data formats
- Interfacing to other applications or systems

Basically, server-side development is used for all the same tasks that traditional programming languages are used for.

Unlike client-side scripts, server-side scripting does not allow the user to view the source code. Client-side scripts have greater access to information and functions on the user's computer. Server-side scripts require the language interpreter to be installed on the server and produce the same results regardless of the client browser or operating system used. Client-side scripts need to be written in a language that is supported by the browsers used by the majority of the site users.

Many application development tools are available for server-side Web application creation. In addition to SSI, some other tools include ASP, ASP.NET, APIs, CGI, Java, Java Servlets, JSP, Perl, PHP, Python, Ruby, Ruby on Rails, and Visual Basic. Choosing the right tools might seem like a daunting task, but learning about the tools available and how they work is the first step. You might already be familiar with some of the tools, or a decision on what tools fit within your existing standards might already have been made. Some of the tools are relatively quick to learn, like Visual Basic and PHP, while others, like Java, take longer to learn and master. Some of the most commonly used tools (ASP.NET, Java, JSP, and PHP) are discussed in later chapters.

Another option for server-side Web development is using *Rapid Application Development* **(RAD)** tools. RAD is a methodology that enables applications to be developed faster. Other potential benefits of RAD are that it enables developers of any skill level to create Web applications and offers developers a large body of support resources.

Many RAD tools are available for use with Web application development. RAD tools are purchased software. They come with support resources that developers may access as a part of the license agreement. Not all RAD tools are alike. Some are platform-specific, while others are portable or even platform-independent. Comparing RAD tools can be important to your success and satisfaction with a tool.

There is no single best tool for server-side application development. Many factors should be considered to determine what is best for your needs. These factors include the task at hand, security considerations, developer skill levels, organizational policies, procedures, and standards. To code Web applications, a developer should have a variety of tools available. With experience, a developer will learn how to choose the best tool for the task at hand.

Compatibility

Review the components of your system for compatibility. Research and test all the connection and interaction points within your system to be sure the components work well together and are compatible. For sites and applications where it is critical to have quick performance, or for sites that have heavy traffic, it is a good idea to retrieve and log environment information, including the browser used. This information can help you better understand what configurations your users have, for the purposes of analysis and testing.

Use Proven, Established Technology

Don't risk using unproven technology just for the sake of being on the cutting edge. Make sure the tools are stable and have a performance record that meets your requirements. Choose technology that has a support system in place. This support system can be a phone number you can call, a Web user community, or knowledgeable resources. If you choose common, well-established technology, and you have an issue related to that technology, others have probably already had the same experience and are willing to share a solution.

Often, errors are the result of improper coding techniques or using the technology in combination with incompatible components. Before using the tools in a production environment, be sure to learn about them and understand how they work. As with any technology, applications developed using Web development tools should be tested thoroughly.

Testing Devices, Browsers, Operating Systems, and Connections

When developing applications, it is easy to lose sight of the fact that end users will probably not have the same combination of device, browser, operating system, and connection you're using. For example, if you are using a high-speed connection, your response will not be the same as an end user who has a slower connection.

Applications should be tested using different browsers and different versions of browsers. The browser being used can have a noticeable impact on performance. Often, developers have newer devices that use a newer version of a common operating system. If your end users will potentially be using different devices with different operating systems, your application needs to address any differences.

A good Web application test plan will include testing using different combinations of devices, browsers, operating systems, and connections. Consider who your audience is and what the ultimate objective is for your application. This will help to determine what criteria to use for testing.

The Database

A database is a structured collection of information: an electronic filing system consisting of files, records, and fields. A *database management system* (**DBMS**) or *relational database management system* (**RDBMS**) is a software application used to manage, query, and update that data. The DBMS or RDBMS you are using for traditional applications can probably also be used for your Web applications, although some databases are better suited than others for Web applications.

When choosing programming tools, Web servers, and Web application servers, consider their compatibility with your existing database and DBMS or RDBMS. Alternatively, you might choose to have Web application data reside on a different system, for security purposes. If your data already resides in different locations, or more than one DBMS or RDBMS is being used, choosing the right tools for compatibility and security is important.

Accessing Data Using SQL

In the 1960s, database software required the use of complex mainframes that were difficult to maintain and run and often required tremendous resources to support. Each mainframe ran different software from different manufacturers. Structured Query Language (SQL) was created in the 1970s as a new standard for any database program. It quickly gained international popularity because it bridged the barriers between mainframes and allowed large corporations to network their efforts.

Today, SQL is both an ANSI and ISO standard. It is an interactive programming language for retrieving and updating data in RDBMSs. SQL forms the backbone of most modern database systems. It is compatible with most databases and database engines, including SQL Server, DB2, Oracle, Sybase, MySQL, dBase, UNIX, Linux, and Access. Many other products support SQL with proprietary extensions to the standard language.

SQL knowledge is invaluable for storing or retrieving data from a database. If you are not already familiar with SQL, you'll want to seriously consider developing SQL skills. Dynamic Web applications most likely will make use of some form of SQL.

Database Triggers

Database triggers are user-written programs that are activated by the DBMS when a data change is performed in a database. The change might be adding, changing, or deleting a record.

The main purpose of a trigger is to monitor database changes and provide a tool to initiate an action. Triggers are application independent, meaning a trigger is automatically activated regardless of the source of the database change. When a trigger is activated, the control shifts from the application program to the database system. The trigger program then performs the action you have designated to take place. Once the trigger action is completed, the control returns back to the application that initiated the trigger. The action performed may include executing a program. Figure 7.3 shows how a database trigger might be used within a Web application to reuse legacy code. (Reusing legacy code is discussed in more detail later in this chapter.)

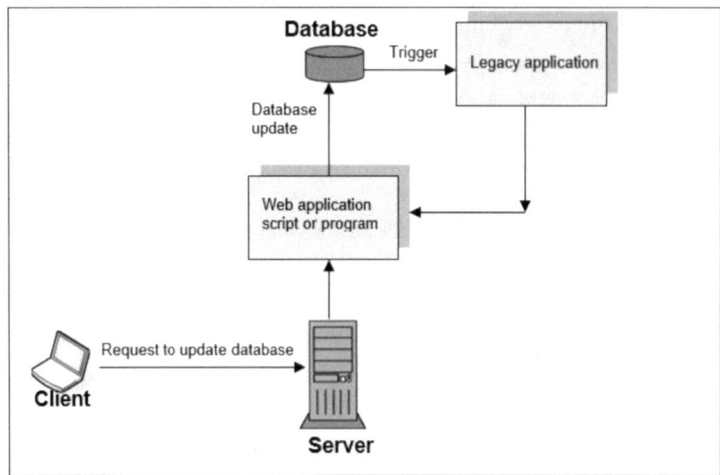

Figure 7.3: A database trigger making use of legacy code

Not all DBMS or RDBMS applications can use triggers. Those that do might have slightly different capabilities and will have different syntax and methods for creating the trigger. You'll need to investigate whether or not the DBMS or RDBMS you are using allows database trigger functionality. Most systems that use SQL as the backbone can use triggers.

Website Design

The focus of this book is not on a website's appearance, but rather on the business applications that must be created to fulfill system requirements. Sometimes a programmer will be responsible for graphics and appearance, but more often, a design or marketing group will be responsible for graphics and design. Even if you won't be responsible for website design, however, there are some site design considerations to keep in mind while developing a Web application, as listed in Table 7.3.

Table 7.3: Design Considerations	
Design Consideration	Description
Existing standards compliance	The design should be compatible with existing standards.
Development practices	Development practices currently used within the Web development community and industry best practices should be taken into consideration.
Device support	Device support and device independence should be considered.
Ease of use	Design and programming tools should be easy to use and avoid unnecessary complexity. Applications should be easy to use by developers, allow for effective usability and accessibility, and provide robust interoperability. The end result will be easy-to-use applications for end users.

Table 7.3: Design Considerations (continued)	
Design Consideration	Description
Security	Security should be considered. The design must incorporate security for end users as well as developers.
Internationalization and localization	Internationalization and localization guidelines should be followed, and current practical internationalization solutions should be considered.
Development space	Web application development space on both the client and server sides should be considered. Reducing fragmentation gives authors a common implementation framework, making it easier to develop, package, and deploy Web applications.
Web delivery	The design should focus on Web delivery and deployment.

Page Content

Providing too much information on a Web page negatively affects the user's experience. If you think a user will take the time to read every word on such a Web page, you're mistaken. To be sure a user reads particular text, make it the very first sentence or very close to the top of the page. If there is a lot you need to share with users, logically break up the content into multiple pages.

Sometimes less is more. Don't fill up pages with unnecessary text. The same applies to images. Sometimes images pack a lot of punch and can add great value to a page, but too many images are distracting for users. Also, when using graphics, consider performance. Loading images takes resources. How and when images are loaded should be considered. Simple and logically organized pages are most effective.

Search engines may also have a big impact on the content of your Web application page. Search engines are discussed later in this book.

Navigation

How users maneuver on a Web page is important. Keep it simple and logically organized. Try to create a common navigational structure for all the pages of an application. This will make the user's experience more intuitive.

Logically organize tasks and links to other pages. Keep the use of hyperlinks inside text paragraphs to a minimum. Having lots of hyperlinks inside text paragraphs destroys the feeling of a consistent navigational structure. Map out links and navigation to site pages, grouping like functions together. When hyperlinks to other pages are needed, add them to the bottom of a paragraph or to the navigational menus on your page.

Figures 7.4 and 7.5 are examples of sites that are simple, easy to understand, and easy to use. In these examples, the menu buttons are placed at the top of the page, and navigation capability is also provided through the menu list on the Web page. The verbiage used is simple, and the pages are not cluttered with too much information. The same visual look, menus, and buttons are used consistently throughout these websites to enhance the user's experience.

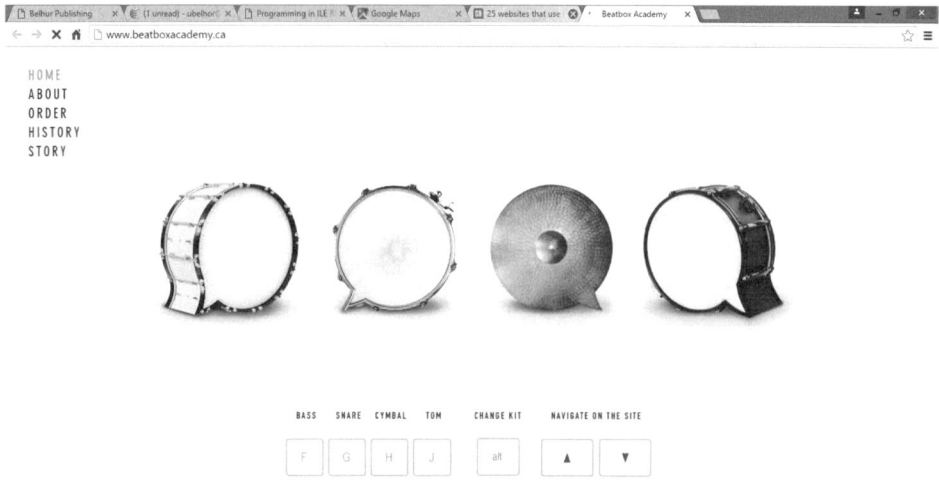

Figure 7.4: An example of an uncluttered Web page (Beatbox Academy)

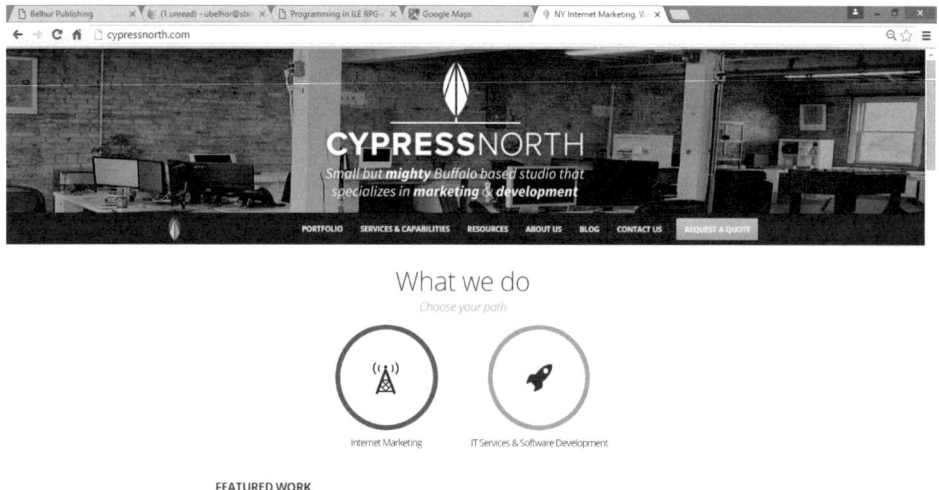

Figure 7.5: A Web page with simple, clear navigation tools (Cypress North)

Standards

Standards are an effective and useful mechanism for simplifying Web application development. Standards make it much easier for different developers to modify and support the Web application. In this respect, Web application development is no different from traditional application development.

Standards should include documentation, the location of code, technology used, website design, functions, features, and testing. Some developers might think that standards are restrictions, but they should understand that standards make the tasks of coding and debugging much easier. Coding errors, which are the most common source of application problems, can be minimized by using standards. Web standards also help ensure that all site users have access to the same information and have the same experience while using a Web application.

Choose your standard tools wisely. As mentioned earlier, many options are available for Web application programming. Be sure to choose tools that are stable, reliable, proven, and appropriate for the platform used for the website. In this book, we introduce several such tools. An understanding of the tools available and how they work will help you decide which ones to include in your standard toolset.

Other Considerations

Include in your site design a means for user feedback. Make the feedback mechanism easy to use to encourage users to provide feedback. Such feedback, whether positive or negative, can help improve your applications.

Unless the nature of your site dictates otherwise, make sure to provide appropriate contact information that is easy to find. There isn't anything more frustrating than visiting a website to get an organization's address, email address, phone number, or other contact information and not being able to easily find this information.

Consider who your audience is and what the ultimate objective is for your application. Doing so will help you to determine what types of devices, operating systems, and browsers should be used for testing.

Performance

Performance is a concern in developing any system or application, but it is especially important on the Web. Web servers are intended to receive and respond to user requests quickly. Slow applications quickly result in dissatisfied end users.

Many factors can affect performance. Depending on the site's purpose, some pages may have more activity or heavier traffic than others. On an informational or query page, you'll quickly lose users' interest if they have to wait for responses or for pages to load. If your site is intended to sell a product or service, this will probably result in a potential customer moving on to another site that responds faster. Within this section, we will review some of the opportunities to improve and control site performance.

Web Application Design

We've already discussed some of the factors to consider when designing a website and Web applications. The design will have an impact on performance. Jam-packed pages bogged down with too many images, in formats that make the files large, and with unnecessary content and poor design, all add up to slow loading. Design isn't limited to static content, but also includes a website's dynamic components. Unnecessary complexity or poor coding, such as multiple interactions with the database instead of just one interaction, can result in performance issues.

Offloading Tasks to the Client

The client is a dedicated resource for a user. The server, on the other hand, is a shared resource. Applications can be designed to offload some tasks, such as up-front validation or scripting logic, to minimize the server load. Client-side scripting isn't always the answer, but obviously as a dedicated user resource, it should be considered to minimize the performance impact of processing user requests and responses.

Configuration

A properly configured Web server and system will result in improved performance. Once a server has been sized and selected, the server's administrator should become thoroughly familiar with how the server works and how it should be configured. The same applies to other hardware, as well as the database being used.

Develop benchmark testing scripts to test server configuration. It is a good idea to test the configuration using real applications, taking into consideration the hardware devices and operating systems being used to access your website. Typically, a configuration has many settings that control how the system performs. Make sure you clearly understand the configuration impact of these settings.

Response Standards

Develop standards for your Web server and site's responsiveness. To start, estimate the potential maximum number of users who will access your site and applications concurrently. Take into consideration the code that will need to execute and whether the applications will be accessing, retrieving, and updating data. Based on this information, define an acceptable user response time. You should use these standards in coordination with application testing and for choosing hardware and software.

Web Server Performance

Key performance factors for the Web server include the following:

- Number of requests per second
- Throughput in bytes per second
- Concurrency level supported
- Latency response time in milliseconds for each new connection request

A Web server has defined load limits based on the number of concurrent client connections and a maximum number of requests it can serve per second. The load limits are determined by configuration, the HTTP request type, whether page content is static or dynamic, whether server content is cached, whether the application allows for multi-threaded processing, hardware limits, and the software limits of the operating system being used. When a server reaches its limits, it becomes overloaded and unresponsive.

A server can become overloaded for a number of reasons, including these:

- Too much user traffic
- Viruses
- Worms
- Distributed denial of service (DDoS) attacks
- Internet network slowdowns
- Server downtime

HTTP Traffic Managers

HTTP traffic managers are applications that monitor and classify bandwidth usage, providing system administrators live readings and long-term usage trends for their network devices. The most common usage is bandwidth management, but you can also monitor many other aspects of your network, such as memory and CPU utilization.

Traffic Load

Several options are available to control traffic load. You can use firewalls to block unwanted traffic coming in from select IP sources or to create specific patterns to reduce server traffic. HTTP traffic managers can drop, redirect, or rewrite requests by identifying undesirable traffic patterns. Traffic managers are also used to smooth peaks in network usage. Web caching techniques can also be used to reduce traffic.

Another possibility is using different domain names to serve static and dynamic content, or to separate large files from small and medium-sized files. The idea is to fully cache small and medium-sized files while efficiently serving large files by using a different configuration. Multiple servers may also be used to reduce traffic for a single server and to balance the server load. Of course, increasing RAM and processor capacity is an option. If the server isn't right-sized to your needs, this might be necessary.

Coding Techniques

Coding techniques should be used to minimize resource requirements and programming bugs. Establishing standards, as mentioned earlier, will help ensure applications are developed to perform well and are easier to support. When designing a Web application, as with a traditional application, keep it simple. Use coding techniques to avoid unnecessary code execution and unnecessary request and response interactions. Learning and understanding the language is the first step. Using caching and programming to prevent buffer overload are useful ways to improve performance.

Performance Monitoring and Logging Tools

Web server software often includes or has available for purchase performance monitoring and logging tools. These tools collect information for analysis to determine whether your system is operating at peak performance. They will also tell you whether the components you are using fall short of meeting users' needs. It is worth spending the time to learn what is available and to make use of these tools.

Reusing Legacy Code

Making the decision to include Web applications as part of your business systems doesn't mean you have to scrap the applications already in use. It might make sense to leave some of these applications as they are, and only deploy select applications on the Web. Many organizations already have applications in which they have invested considerable resources, time, and money. Many of these applications are stable and still well suited to the business requirements. There is no reason to rewrite all your applications unless a business need requires a change.

It's wise to consider whether legacy code can be reused. Doing so might well affect the design, choice of tools, and framework for Web application development. It isn't always feasible to rewrite legacy code or maintain two different versions of programs that do the same thing. If you have existing applications that include detailed and complicated logic, it is possible to include these applications without a complete rewrite. There are many ways you can reuse legacy code. We discuss a few options in the following pages.

APIs

An application program interface (API) enables one program to communicate with another. For example, an API can be used from within a PHP, JSP, or ASP.NET application program to execute and share data with a legacy application. APIs were developed in response to the need to exchange information between two or more different software applications. APIs have been around for a long time, and most systems can use them. Stored procedures and user-defined functions are two types of APIs.

Stored Procedures

A stored procedure is a subroutine available to applications that make use of a RDBMS. Stored procedures are typically used for data validation, access control, or to trigger execution of a legacy application. Stored procedures are used to consolidate and centralize logic that was originally implemented in applications. Stored procedures must be invoked using a call statement (unlike user-defined functions, which can be used like any other expression within SQL statements). Here is an example of a call statement:

```
CALL procedurename(parm1, parm2)
```

Stored procedures can be used to return data result sets or may be used as a method to initiate another application to execute. Stored procedures may also receive and return variables, making it possible to pass parameters between the Web application and the stored procedure. While the call to the stored procedure is quite simple, you need information specific to your platform and DBMS to create the stored procedure.

On most platforms, a stored procedure can only be used to execute SQL statements and directives. Stored procedures are cataloged in the SQL system catalog using the CREATE PROCEDURE statement. On an IBM i system, however, the rules for stored procedures are relatively relaxed; the stored procedure can be written in several languages, including RPG, COBOL, FORTRAN, PL/I, REXX, CL, and C. Stored procedures written in a language other than SQL are usually referred to as *external stored procedures*. External stored procedures do not necessarily have to include embedded SQL statements, and they do not need to be cataloged. Other platforms provide similar functionality. You will need to verify the platform that you are using provides this functionality.

One example of how a stored procedure can enable reuse legacy code is to create a stored procedure that executes a legacy application. You pass required parameters within the stored procedure call within the Web application. This enables you to access and use the complicated code or extensive business logic of the legacy application without a rewrite.

Figure 7.6 provides an example of creating a stored procedure using SQL on an IBM i to initiate running an RPGLE program. In this example, a stored procedure named MYSTRPRC is created in library MYLIB. The procedure created references the RPG program named MYRPGPGM in the library MYLIBRARY. In this example, no parameters are passed.

```
Step 1: Create the stored procedure on the IBM i

CREATE PROCEDURE MYLIB/MYSTRPRC ( )
              DYNAMIC RESULT SETS 1
              LANGUAGE RPGLE
              SPECIFIC MYLIB/MYSTRPRC
              NOT DETERMINISTIC
              MODIFIES SQL DATA
              CALLED ON NULL INPUT
              EXTERNAL NAME 'MYLIBRARY/MYRPGPGM'
              PARAMETER STYLE GENERAL;

Step 2: Call the stored procedure from a Web application

CallableStatement cstmt = connection.prepareCall("CALL
MYLIBRARY.MYSTOREDRPROC");
```

Figure 7.6: Using a stored procedure to call an IBM i RPGLE program

Figure 7.7 shows another example of creating a stored procedure using SQL on an IBM i to run a CL program. This example is very similar to the one in Figure 7.6, except it calls a CL program rather than an RPGLE program. Also, two parameters are passed: PARMIN and PARMOUT. The call statement is from a Java program.

```
Step 1: Create Stored Procedure

CREATE PROCEDURE LUBELHOR/HITACHICLP (IN PARMIN CHAR(120), PARMOUT CHAR(120))
LANGUAGE CL
SPECIFIC LUBELHOR/HITACHICLP
NOT DETERMINISTIC
MODIFIES SQL DATA
CALL ON NULL INPUT
EXTERNAL NAME LUBELHOR/HITACHICLP
PARAMETER STYLE GENERAL

Step 2: Call Stored Procedure

CallableStatement cstmt = connection.prepareCall("CALL LUBELHOR/HITACHICLP
(?, ?)");
```

Figure 7.7: Using a stored procedure to call an IBM i CL program.

User-defined Functions

User-defined functions (UDFs) are another possible option to reuse legacy code with minimal or no changes to the code. Most database management applications with SQL roots allow the use of UDFs. Calling legacy code is not the sole purpose of UDFs, but it is one of the possible uses.

Like a stored procedure, a UDF is executed by a call statement. The main difference between stored procedures and UDFs is that a stored procedure must be invoked using a call statement, while a UDF can be used like any other expression within a SQL statement.

Figure 7.8 is an example of how to create a DB2 UDF on an IBM i for referencing an RPGLE program. (The syntax for other database systems and platforms will vary slightly.) In the example, an integer variable is passed and will return a 15,0 decimal value. Once created, this function can be executed within PHP, JSP, or ASP.NET.

```
CREATE FUNCTION MYLIBRARY/MYFUNCTION(INTEGER)
 RETURNS DECIMAL(15,0)
 SPECIFIC MYUDFD1
 DETERMINISTIC
 LANGUAGE RPGLE
 NO SQL
 NO EXTERNAL ACTION
 RETURNS NULL ON NULL INPUT
 SCRATCHPAD
 FINAL CALL
 ALLOW PARALLEL
 EXTERNAL NAME 'MYLIBRARY/MYUDFPROGRAM(MYPARM)'
 PARAMETER STYLE DB2SQL;
```

Figure 7.8: Creating a UDF

While stored procedures can have input and output parameters, UDFs have only input parameters. An output parameter must be returned as a return value. However, just because UDFs return a single value does not mean they can't include applications with complex logic.

Some DBMSs with roots in SQL may allow use of user-defined table functions (UDTFs). A UDTF is a UDF that returns a virtual table instead of a single value. Using a UDTF, you can return a set of values. Like a stored procedure, a UDTF allows code reuse with minimal changes, enabling you to use legacy applications in coordination with Web applications.

The create function statement in Figure 7.9 identifies the function name in this example, MYFUNCTION, within the library MYLIBRARY. The external name keyword specifies the Integrated Language Environment (ILE) CL program the function calls. In this example, it is MYUDTFPGM, found in the library MYLIBRARY. The example uses two parameters: PARM1 is a character value, and PARM2 is a decimal value.

```
CREATE FUNCTION  MYLIBRARY/MYFUNCTION ()
RETURNS TABLE (
  PARM1      CHAR    (10)
, PARM2      DECIMAL (5, 0)
)
LANGUAGE CLLE
PARAMETER STYLE DB2SQL
NOT DETERMINISTIC
NO SQL
CALLED ON NULL INPUT
NO DBINFO
NO EXTERNAL ACTION
NOT FENCED
NO FINAL CALL
DISALLOW PARALLEL
SCRATCHPAD
EXTERNAL NAME MYLIBRARY/MYUDTFPGM
CARDINALITY 1
```

Figure 7.9: Creating a UDTF

If you want to reuse legacy code within Web applications, research the possibility of using a UDF or UDTF. The syntax is usually pretty similar from platform to platform. The answer to the question "how to" likely can be found within your DBMS documentation. Which one you use is best answered after thoroughly reviewing the documentation specific to your platform. The Web is another good resource for research. UDFs have been used in many organizations for legacy code reuse. If the DBMS you are using provides for UDFs or UDTFs, you'll easily be able to find examples of them on the Web.

Conversion Tools

Many platforms provide software applications that can be used to convert legacy programs from one language to another. Sometimes, the conversion tools are referred to as *migration tools*. On some platforms, the tools may be provided for free to encourage the use of newer technology. In other instances, the tools must be purchased. If you'd like to keep legacy code but don't want to rewrite applications, it is worth researching conversion tools. The work required to complete the conversion may be done by in-house staff or by an outside service provider. Conversion may also be used to move software from one platform to another in a format that can be used on the new platform.

Conversion likely will not be worthwhile if you only need to reuse a select few applications. If you need to reuse a large system or all your applications, however, a conversion tool might well be the right solution.

Security

Opening up your applications to the Web introduces new security considerations. If your site and applications will be used by a few users with controlled access, the security requirements will be far less complicated. On the other hand, if your site and applications will be used by a large number of users, security will be more complex. Both user carelessness and intentional attempts to damage or misuse your system create security risks that must be prevented or at least minimized. This book isn't focused on security, and we realize developers don't shoulder all the responsibility for this important function. However, developers do have an impact and should understand security considerations and prevention measures. Within this section, we review security and consider some of the opportunities to provide a secure Web application.

Table 7.4 lists some of the potential security risks you should take into account. This list is pretty intimidating, and it continues to grow as unethical users invent new ways to attack systems. But a well-thought-out security strategy and preventive action go a long way toward protecting your system from security threats.

Table 7.4: Potential Security Threats	
Security Threat	Description
Adware	Adware is software installed on your computer to show you advertisements. It can slow your system by using RAM and CPU cycles. It can also slow your Internet connection by using bandwidth to retrieve advertisements. In addition, adware can increase the instability of your system because many adware applications are not programmed well. Finally, adware can annoy you and waste huge amounts of your time by popping unwanted ads onto your screen, which require you to close them before you can get back to using your PC.
DDoS	In a distributed denial-of-service (DDoS) Internet attack, multiple external sources attack a single target system, with the goal of denying service for its users. DDoS attacks flood the target system with incoming messages at a rate much higher than it can process, slowing the system to where it is rendered useless.
Hacking	Hacking refers to attempts to gain unauthorized access to network and systems.
Interception of network data	Messages can be sent from the browser to the server or vice versa via network eavesdropping. Eavesdroppers can operate from any point on the pathway between the browser and the server.
Keystroke logging	Keystroke logging involves installing hardware on a computer that captures information typed into it. This is often used to capture personal details, including passwords.
Phishing	Phishing refers to an attempt to criminally and fraudulently acquire sensitive information by masquerading as an authorized entity. It is typically carried out by email or instant messaging, and often directs users to enter personal details at a website.
Smurf attack	The smurf attack is a way of generating a lot of computer network traffic to a victim site. That is, it is a type of DoS attack that floods a target system via spoofed broadcast ping messages.
Spam	Spam is flooding the Internet with many copies of the same message, in an attempt to force the message on people who would not otherwise choose to receive it. Most spam is commercial advertising, often for dubious products, get-rich-quick schemes, or quasi-legal services.
Spyware	Spyware is software that secretly gathers information about a user while the user navigates the Internet. This information is normally used for advertising purposes. Spyware can also gather information about email addresses and even passwords and credit card numbers.
Trinoo	Trinoo is a set of computer programs to conduct a DDoS attack. It is believed that trinoo networks have been set up on thousands of systems on the Internet that have been compromised by remote buffer overrun exploit. Trinoo is famous for allowing attackers to leave a message in a folder called "cry baby." The file is self-replicating and modified on a regular basis as long as port 80 is active.

Table 7.4: Potential Security Threats (continued)	
Security Threat	Description
Trojan horses	A Trojan horse is a program that disguises itself as another program. Similar to viruses, these programs are hidden and cause unwanted effects. They differ from viruses because they are normally not designed to replicate.
Unauthorized access	Unauthorized access is an attempt to steal confidential information, execute commands on a system to modify the system, gather information about a system, or launch a DoS attack to render the machine temporarily unusable.
Viruses	Computer viruses are small software programs that are designed to spread from one computer to another and to interfere with computer operation. A virus might corrupt or delete data on your computer, use your email program to spread itself to other computers, or even erase everything on your hard disk. Viruses are most easily spread by attachments in email messages or instant messaging (IM). That is why it is essential that you never open an email attachment unless you know who it's from and you are expecting it. Viruses can be disguised as attachments of funny images, greeting cards, or audio and video files. Viruses also spread through downloads from the Internet. They can be hidden in illicit software or other files or programs you might download.
Worms	A worm is a self-replicating virus that does not alter files, but resides in active memory and duplicates itself. Worms use parts of an operating system that are automatic and usually invisible to the user. It is common for worms to be noticed only when their uncontrolled replication consumes system resources, slowing or halting other tasks.

Security Practices

Here are some security practices that can help reduce risks:

- Limit the number of login accounts available on the machine. Delete inactive users.
- Make sure that people with login privileges choose good passwords. The Crack program will help you detect poorly chosen passwords.
- Turn off unused services. For example, if you don't need to run FTP on the Web server host, get rid of the software. The same applies to Sendmail, Gopher, Network Information Services (NIS) clients, Network File System (NFS), Finger, and Systat. Deactivate any services that you don't use.
- Remove shells and interpreters that you don't absolutely need. For example, if you don't run any Perl-based CGI scripts, remove the Perl interpreter.
- Check both the system and Web logs regularly for suspicious activity.
- Scan security logs for suspicious activity.
- Use Internet security-scanning software, and review the information provided.
- Make sure that permissions are set correctly on system files, to discourage tampering.
- Create and use firewalls. A *firewall* is a security scheme that prevents unauthorized users from gaining access to a computer network or that monitors transfers of information between the network and the client.
- Configure routers to provide additional security.
- Don't open all ports on your system.
- Use Secure Sockets Layer (SSL). SSL is a protocol that provides a high level of security for communication over the Internet.
- Use antispyware software. Antispyware software protects your client and server devices and helps keep personal details secure.
- Use antivirus software to detect viruses and prevent them from infecting your system.
- Use coding techniques to prevent injection. If an application does not consider injection, it may be possible to have security holes through SQL or other injection techniques.

Coding for Security

Developers have a lot of control over the security measures built into applications. Many of the same security concepts used within traditional application development apply to Web development. Table 7.5 lists some of the techniques you can use to reduce security risks.

Table 7.5: Security Coding Techniques	
Technique	**Description**
Avoid hard-coding	Avoid hard-coding user IDs and passwords, as well as sensitive information.
Use CGI scripts with care	CGI is not inherently insecure. However, CGI scripts must be written with just as much care as the server itself because CGI provides a gateway and connection between the client and the server.
Use SSI with care	SSI—snippets of server directives embedded in HTML documents—are another potential hole. A subset of the directives available in SSI instructs the server to execute arbitrary system commands and CGI scripts. Unless the author is aware of the potential problems, it's easy to introduce unintentional side effects. Unfortunately, HTML files containing dangerous SSI directives are easy to write.
Test the application	Within your application test plan, be sure to include security testing. Create and use a list of valid security risks for testing. The extra time spent identifying security holes during testing provides a high return on the resource investment. Security risks should be found during testing, not when the application is implemented and in production.
Limit updates	Build into the application limitations on the amount of data that can be updated within the appropriate logic for the application. Don't rely on defaults or ignore setting limits. Track how many update attempts are received per session, and don't allow users to add, change, or delete numerous records when it is not appropriate.
Require logins	Require a user login and password when it is appropriate.
Authenticate	Build in user authentication when appropriate.
Be aware of client-side information visibility	Do not use client-side scripting tools when the information should not be shared. Passed parameters and source code are easily viewed when embedded within HTML.
Validate input	Validate input from all untrusted data sources. Incorporating well-designed input validation can eliminate the majority of software vulnerabilities. Validate external data sources, including command-line arguments, network interfaces, environmental variables, and user-controlled files.
Keep it simple	Keep the design as simple and small as possible. Complex designs increase the likelihood that errors will occur during configuration, implementation, and ongoing use. The effort required to code and support an application will increase as the security design becomes more complex.
Define security requirements	Identify and document security requirements early in the development life cycle. Revisit the security requirements periodically to reflect environment and application changes. The security of a system cannot easily be evaluated if you don't have defined security requirements. Security requirements need to include the established organization requirements, such as those for ISO or Sarbanes-Oxley.
Model threats	Use threat modeling to anticipate the threats to which the application might be subjected. Threat modeling includes identifying key assets, decomposing the application, identifying and categorizing the threats to each asset or component, rating the threats based on a risk ranking, and then developing threat mitigation strategies that are implemented in designs, code, and test cases.
Default to deny	Base your access decisions on permission rather than exclusion. This means that, by default, access is denied, and the design identifies conditions under which access is permitted.

Table 7.5: Security Coding Techniques (continued)	
Technique	**Description**
Design for security policies	Create a software architecture that fits your security policies. Design your applications to implement and enforce security policies.
Use compiler warnings	Compile code using the highest warning level available for your compiler, and eliminate warnings by modifying the code. Ignoring warnings is risky.
Adopt a secure coding standard	Develop and use secure coding standards for the languages and platforms that will be used. Be sure to understand your system architecture's security capabilities and limitations.
Use the principle of least privilege	Processing should execute with the least level of authority necessary to complete the job. Any additional authority should be held for a minimum amount of time. This approach reduces the opportunities that an attacker has to execute arbitrary code and access your system with a higher level of authority.
Use effective quality assurance techniques	Using well-defined quality assurance (QA) techniques can be effective in identifying and eliminating security risks. QA should include penetration testing, fuzz testing, and source code audits. External testers will bring an independent perspective and should be able to complete quality testing without biases or assumptions.
Sanitize data sent to other systems	Sanitize data passed to complex subsystems such as command shells, relational databases, and commercial off-the-shelf components. Attackers may be able to invoke unused functionality in these components through the use of SQL, command, or other injection attacks.
Build in layers of defense	Build your security defense in layers. Don't rely on a single defensive strategy. Make sure to have additional layers to catch any breaches that slip through a layer.

Security Policy

If you are a webmaster, a system administrator, or are otherwise involved with administering a network, the single most important step you can take to increase your site's security is to create a written security policy. This security policy should clearly define your organization's rules with regard to the following:

- Determine who is allowed to use the system.
- Determine when they are allowed to use it.
- Determine what they are allowed to do. (Different groups may be granted different levels of access.)
- Define procedures for granting access to the system.
- Define procedures for revoking access, for example, when an employee changes position or leaves.
- Define what constitutes acceptable use of the system.
- Determine remote and local login methods.
- Define system monitoring procedures.
- Identify protocols for responding to suspected security breaches.
- Identify a course of action for a breach of security.

The policy needs to be clearly defined, communicated, implemented, and followed.

Security is vital to your system. Put together a security plan and incorporate it within your design, development, and testing standards. Revisit the plan periodically to include changes in the application environment and to address new security risks that arise. Evaluate the components of your Web application periodically and test how secure your system is. For more information about Web application security, visit the W3C Security page, *www.w3.org/Security/*.

Password Protection

Adding a prompt for a user ID and password is an easy way to allow only intended users access to a system, Web page, or Web application. Of course, users often aren't fond of being prompted for a user ID and password. (How often have you heard, "I've already logged on to the network. Why do I have to log on again?") However, user IDs and passwords are effective in reducing security risks.

Password protection should be thought out carefully. Static content doesn't usually require this kind of security (although it might, in some circumstances). A site that includes dynamic content is more likely to require a user ID and password. Similarly, there are probably pages on your site intended for the general public that can be unprotected, while other pages need password protection because they're intended for only specific users.

The password field type on an HTML form automatically makes the password unreadable by anyone who might be in sight of a user's screen. Examples of password field in use can be found later in this book.

Securing Data

If users will access data on your system, you will need to implement security measures to protect data from unauthorized access. Prompting for a user ID and password is one way to help protect data. If you deal with sensitive data such as bank account numbers, Social Security numbers, or financial information, you must make sure this information isn't shared with everyone on the Web. Encryption can help in securing sensitive data. Encryption transforms and stores plain-text data to make it unreadable to anyone except those who have the encryption key.

Your applications published on the Web should have layers of security to protect them from being accessed by unauthorized users and also from possible damage to data. For example, a malicious user might update your database with erroneous data, deleting data or adding large amounts of data to intentionally fill your server. Read-only access should be the default. Only provide the ability to update the database to authorized users. In your application design, where database update capability is provided, be sure to include data validation and logic to limit the size of transactions. All databases provide some measure of securing data. Be sure security is understood and implemented where needed. Don't leave your data unprotected.

Server Security

When choosing a server, know what security protection it provides, through its administration software. Servers usually come with server administration software that includes a complete range of password protection, authentication, and user-management solutions. Here are some of the security capabilities provided through server administration software:

- Password protection
- Authentication
- User management solutions
- Grant or deny any users/groups on a per-resource basis

- Capability to set user start and expiration dates
- User email authority control
- Audit logging
- Website file protection, including images, databases, HTML, scripts, and programs
- Directory security
- Concurrent user log-in protection
- Limits on user ID and password attempts
- Features to protect against hacking, worms, phishing, spam protection, viruses, Trojan horses, spyware, adware, keystroke logging, DDoS, smurf attack, trinoo, and other security risks
- Active Directory authentication
- Built-in firewall capabilities
- Built-in proxy capabilities
- Internal user access scheme
- LDAP authentication
- Other system authentication
- SSL hardware
- SSL software
- HIPAA and/or Sarbanes-Oxley compliance

As you can see, server administration software provides a means to secure your systems. Be sure to use the tools provided to protect your server(s).

Web Hosting

You might decide to forgo hosting your own website in favor of subscribing to a Web hosting or cloud service. Web hosting and cloud services provide a variety of solutions, from free, small-scale hosting, where files can be uploaded through FTP or a Web interface, to *colocation*, in which a host provides connectivity to the Internet for servers it does not own, but which are located in its data center. Table 7.6 shows some of the wide variety of services provided.

Table 7.6: Types of Web Hosting Services	
Service	Description
Free website hosting	Hosting is offered for free, with limited features and functionality, usually in return for allowing advertising on your site.
Shared Web hosting	Hosting is on a server shared with other sites, ranging from a few to many. The servers are configured to share server resources, including RAM and CPU.
Reseller Web hosting	This type of hosting allows clients to become Web hosts. The allotted hard drive space and bandwidth can be used to host third-party websites for a profit.
Virtual dedicated server	This hosting allows complete control over the server, similar to renting a server. The least expensive dedicated plans are usually those that are self-managed or unmanaged. In this case, the client has full administrative access to the server and is responsible for security and maintenance.
Managed hosting or cloud service	A dedicated server is provided, and you're allowed to manage data via FTP or other remote management tools. However, full control is not allowed because the hosting service guarantees the quality of service provided and assumes responsibility for modifications, configuration, and support.

Table 7.6: Types of Web Hosting Services (continued)	
Service	Description
Colocation Web hosting service	With this service, you own the server, and the hosting company physically houses and supports it. This is the most expensive option provided. Usually, with this service, you would have your own administrator who would visit the hosting center to complete hardware upgrades or changes.
Clustered hosting	Multiple servers are used for hosting the same content, for better resource utilization.
Grid hosting	The service provides a server cluster that acts like a grid and is composed of multiple nodes. The grid configuration makes this option very fault-tolerant and stable.
File hosting system	This service provides server space for files.
Image hosting service	This service provides server space for images.
Video hosting service	This service provides space for video.
Blog hosting service	This service provides space for blogs.
One-click hosting	This service allows Internet users to easily upload one or more files from their hard drives onto one-click host servers free of charge.
Shopping cart service	This service provides a secure and protected shopping-cart capability.

Hosting and cloud services are commonly used by larger organizations to outsource network infrastructure. How do you choose a hosting or cloud service? The best way is to consider your organization's website and Web application needs. You can easily find information about the many hosting and cloud service providers on the Web. Do your research, and keep in mind your goals and expectations. Here are some of the considerations to use when you evaluate and compare hosting and cloud service providers:

- Services provided
- Email services provided
- Scripting software supported
- Operating system support
- Compatibility
- Database support
- Application development options
- Security
- Interface provided
- Host's specialty
- E-commerce
- Length of time in business
- Pricing
- Hosting reliability and uptime
- Service-level agreements (SLAs)
- Network performance and response time

Summary

Since its inception, the Web has changed drastically. It's only relatively recently that developing business Web applications has become commonplace. The Web has evolved from displaying static content to including sites with dynamic content. There is a shift within organizations to create new applications as Web applications and to move existing applications to the Web. Doing so opens the applications to worldwide access. The browsers, Web servers, Web application servers, and programming technology available will continue to change.

Standards exist to guide Web application developers—for example, those developed by the Worldwide Web Consortium (W3C). These include standards for HTML. However, real Web applications require more than just HTML. While HTML is the foundation upon which Web application development is built, once you have mastered HTML, you need to start acquiring the other skills needed to develop Web applications. This chapter paints the big picture, showing you how HTML fits into that picture. To move forward, you'll need to know more about languages such as PHP, JavaScript, and ASP.NET. The following chapters introduce you to some of these languages and show you how they integrate with HTML to produce truly dynamic business Web applications.

As you go through the following chapters, keep in mind the big picture. Remember the many key areas discussed in this chapter, such as performance, security, database access, and integration with legacy applications. The information we've provided in this chapter will help shorten your learning curve and save you from some of the pitfalls we've encountered along the way.

Key Terms

application server	JVM	standards
APIs	navigation	stored procedures
browser	offloading tasks	SSI
client	password protection	standards
client-side	performance	static
client-side scripting	performance monitoring	traffic load
compatibility	RAD	triggers
coding techniques	RDBMS	UDF
configuration	response standards	Web client
conversion tools	securing data	Web hosting
DBMS	security	Web server
dynamic	security policy	Web server software
HTTP requests	server security	website design
HTTP responses	server-side scripting	
HTTP traffic managers	SQL	

Discussion Review/Questions

1. What are the components of a Web application system?
2. What is a client?
3. What is the difference between a Web server and an application server?
4. What is client-side programming and scripting?
5. What is server-side programming and scripting?

6. What is a RAD tool?
7. Why should you consider compatibility?
8. Should you consider using cutting-edge technology for Web applications? Why or why not?
9. What should be included within a good application testing plan?
10. What is a database?
11. Why might you use SQL within a Web application?
12. What design considerations are important for a business Web application?
13. Why should page content and navigation be considered in Web application design?
14. When should coding standards be used?
15. What impact does performance have on a Web application?
16. Should you consider reusing legacy code?
17. What is a stored procedure?
18. What are some security threats that can affect an application?
19. What coding techniques can be used to secure a Web application?
20. What is Web hosting, and should it be used for a Web business application?

Exercises

1. List several business Web application clients and give examples of how they might be used.
2. List six Web server products, where to find the products, and the potential advantages of each product.
3. Give an example of a client-side and a server-side programming or scripting language and explain how they might be used in a Web business application.
4. Research and provide examples of RDBMS and DBMS databases.
5. List five examples of websites that make good use of design techniques, and explain why they are examples of good website design.
6. In one paragraph, describe how performance can impact a Web application.
7. Research and provide a list of 10 Web application security threats and explain how to protect a website from the threats.
8. List five Web hosting providers, and for each provider briefly describe the services it provides and why a business might consider using the provider for hosting its website.

Incorporating JavaScript

Previous chapters have discussed how to create static documents using HTML. The next step is to incorporate automation to make Web pages dynamic. Many tools can be used to do this. This chapter introduces JavaScript, one of the most popular tools. JavaScript is a fairly simple but very powerful programming language, which is usually used along with other Web development tools to create dynamic Web applications.

In this chapter, you will learn the basics of JavaScript by example, to see how JavaScript is used within Web applications. The examples in this chapter are based on the most current version of JavaScript used in common browsers such as Chrome, Firefox, and Internet Explorer. This chapter assumes a basic understanding of HTML. If necessary, review the earlier chapters on HTML before proceeding.

Introduction to JavaScript

HTML and JavaScript are two different Web tools. HTML is used to create static Web page content, while JavaScript is designed for performing dynamic tasks. Java, JavaServer Pages (JSP), and JavaScript are not the same. They are completely different programming languages.

A JavaScript program consists of lines of executable computer code that can be embedded directly into HTML pages. JavaScript is an *interpreted* language, meaning the script will execute without preliminary compilation. JavaScript does not require a purchase or a license, nor does it require a special editor. To code in JavaScript, you can use anything from a simple text editor like Notepad or Notepad++ to a Web development integrated development environment (IDE) tool such as Eclipse, Microsoft Expression, Komodo IDE, NetBeans IDE, WebStorm, or Dreamweaver.

JavaScript is currently the most popular scripting language on the Web. It is the only language supported by all Web browsers that support client-side scripting. (Most browsers do.) Alternatives to JavaScript on the client side include VBScript and Perl. Other alternatives for some programming tasks are server-side languages like PHP, JSP, ASP.NET, or Java. Your decision of which language to use should be based on when you want the code to be run and what tasks are required. If your application requires the code to be run before the Web page loads, you will want to use a server-side language. If the code needs to run after the page is loaded, JavaScript is a good choice. Because JavaScript code runs on the client rather than on the server, it can respond to user actions quickly, making an application feel more responsive to users. JavaScript is not intended for stored data retrieval or update.

There are frameworks available to simplify using JavaScript on websites. Some JavaScript frameworks include AngularJS, Backbone.js, and React. There are also tools available to use with JavaScript. One of the most popular of these is the jQuery JavaScript library. jQuery takes many lines of code used for common tasks and wraps them into methods that can be executed with a single line of code.

Although JavaScript can be embedded directly into your HTML pages, if the code will be reused on multiple pages, you should put it into a separate file. The file's *.js* extension identifies it as JavaScript. The script file is linked with an HTML page by inserting a <script> tag.

For JavaScript to work properly, it must be enabled within the user's browser settings. On newer browsers, JavaScript scripts are run in a restricted "sandbox" environment that isolates them from the rest of the operating system. Scripts are permitted access only to data in the current document or documents from the same site. No access is granted to the local file system, the memory space of other programs running, or the operating system's networking layer. Containment of this kind is designed to prevent malfunctioning or malicious scripts from running in the user's environment.

JavaScript Compared to Other Tools

Since JavaScript is not the only language that can be used to make your Web applications more dynamic, how does it compare to other tools?

JavaScript Versus Server-side Scripting

Compared to using server-side scripting such Common Gateway Interface (CGI) to collect and validate data entered on a form, JavaScript is much easier to learn and to code. As you will soon see, JavaScript is not a difficult language to learn and can easily be placed within HTML pages. Use of a CGI script requires placing a hook for the CGI within the HTML, as well as writing the CGI script or program.

JavaScript provides quick response times because its validation takes place on the client side using a dedicated resource, rather than on the server. Using a server-side script, the information must be collected from a form entry, sent to the server, processed, and then returned to the browser as an HTML-based Web page. This must happen every time the user makes a change to an entry form. This results in slower response times for users.

JavaScript is compatible with any browser that supports client-side scripting; it is not platform-dependent like some server-side scripting languages. Therefore, JavaScript code can be written once and will work on any system using a browser that supports scripting. On the other hand, server-side scripting can be used to update databases, while JavaScript is not intended for data update.

JavaScript is a lightweight language intended for form processing and some other tasks to make a Web page more dynamic. Server-side scripting provides a gateway to access scripts and programs that may be used for incorporating intricate logic. You will probably find good uses for both JavaScript and server-side scripting languages within your Web applications.

JavaScript Versus VBScript

Like JavaScript, VBScript allows for embedding commands into an HTML document. VBScript is also an interpreted language that executes on the client side rather than on the server. In fact, JavaScript and VBScript are quite similar in functionality. VBScript, like JavaScript, is often used for collecting data from a form, validating it for completeness and correctness, and sending it off to a server-side application to update a database.

The most significant difference between JavaScript and VBScript is the language syntax. VBScript is a fast and flexible subset of the Microsoft Visual Basic language. JavaScript, on the other hand, is rooted in C, C++, and Java.

While VBScript may be an excellent choice if you are already familiar with Visual Basic, JavaScript is currently more widely used. More developers are familiar with JavaScript than with VBScript, and it appears this trend will not change soon. Those supporting the use of VBScript would argue this point, but it is easy to do the research to support this conclusion.

The preference for JavaScript over VBScript probably goes back to the roots of the languages. VBScript is rooted in Microsoft-specific tools and platforms, while JavaScript has roots that are not platform-specific. That's not to say using VBScript isn't a good fit for certain tasks. In fact, you could use both VBScript and JavaScript in the same HTML page, although this is uncommon. Choose the tools you are most comfortable with and that fit within your organization's standards.

JavaScript's Advantages and Disadvantages

Like any other tool, JavaScript has advantages and disadvantages. We will highlight some of each.

Here are some of the advantages of JavaScript:

- Easy to learn
- Interpreted language, resulting in a fast response time
- Uses client-side resources rather than server-side shared resources
- Runs on any browser that allows client-side scripting
- Most popular scripting language; many resources available
- Easily embedded within HTML
- No additional cost to use
- Platform independent
- Can easily be integrated for use with other languages

Here are some of JavaScript's disadvantages:

- Dependent on browser support
- Dependent on user's browser settings to allow scripts to run
- Source code viewable by users
- Does not allow for data update

What Can JavaScript Do?

JavaScript is a lightweight and very useful tool for a Web business application developer. Many developers know JavaScript, and there is a large community of JavaScript developers. You can do many things with JavaScript. Here are some of its common uses:

- *React to events*—JavaScript can be used to enable your HTML to react to events. Clicking the mouse, moving the mouse cursor over a hotspot, loading a page or image, selecting an input box on a form, submitting a form, or entering a keystroke can trigger some JavaScript code to be invoked.
- *Detect browser types*—JavaScript can be used to detect the type of browser being used by the client accessing the Web page. After determining the type of browser, JavaScript can be further used to determine what code should be executed. This enables you to accommodate browser differences, as described in chapter 12.
- *Make dynamic Web pages*—JavaScript can be used to make your Web pages dynamic. JavaScript can enhance static HTML pages through special effects, control of page behavior, animations, and inclusion of dynamic text.
- *Validate data*—JavaScript can be used to validate data. For example, suppose a user is required to fill out an online form. JavaScript checks the format and content of the data on the form before it is submitted. If the input is not valid, the JavaScript code prevents the form from being submitted and tells the user what needs to be corrected. Note that this validation is completed before the data is sent to the server. This eliminates the need for server-side validation processing, provides quick responses for application users, and reduces server-side processing activity.
- *Read and write HTML elements*—Because JavaScript is intended for client-side interaction, it can be used to read and change the content of an HTML element.
- *Display forms and pop-up windows*—JavaScript can be used to display forms and pop-up windows for data entry and validation. For example, it might be used to prompt for a user ID and password, then display a welcome window after the user enters the correct login information.
- *Create cookies*—JavaScript can be used to create **cookies**, which are used to retrieve and store information on the site visitor's computer.

Syntax

JavaScript was modeled on Java **syntax**. Java syntax, in turn, was modeled on C and C++ syntax. JavaScript was created to be easier for non-programmers to work with than C, C++, or Java. Programmers who have used C, C++, or Java will find that JavaScript syntax is comfortably familiar.

Case-sensitivity

JavaScript is a case-sensitive language. All **keywords** are in lower case. All variables, function names, and other identifiers must be typed with consistent capitalization.

Comments

JavaScript supports both C and C++ **comments**. Text on one or more lines between the special characters "/*" and "*/" is a comment and is ignored by JavaScript. Also, any text between "//" and the end of the current line is a single-line comment and is ignored by JavaScript.

Figure 8.1 shows examples of JavaScript comments. The first comment is a single-line, C++ style comment that begins with "//". The second comment is a multi-line, C-style comment the begins with "/*" and ends with "*/".

```
// Belhur Publishing - single-line comment

/* Date:   November 21, 2015
    Author:  Laura A. Ubelhor
    Purpose:  Script to prompt for User ID and password
    Multiple-line comment
*/
```

Figure 8.1: JavaScript comment styles

Identifiers

Variables, functions, and label names are JavaScript **identifiers**. Identifiers are made up of any number of letters and digits, along with the underscore character (_) and dollar sign ($). The first character of an identifier must not be a digit. Avoid creating variables that have the same names as global properties and methods. Figure 8.2 provides examples of legal identifiers.

```
x
X
Total_amount
total_amount
TotalAmount
Amount$
amount$
Amount123
amount123
```

Figure 8.2: Examples of legal identifiers

Reserved Words

Reserved words have special meanings to the JavaScript interpreter and cannot be used as identifiers, variables, labels, or function names. Following is a list of JavaScript reserved words.

abstract	char	do
arguments	class	double
boolean	const	else
break	continue	enum
byte	debugger	eval
case	default	export
catch	delete	extends

false	let	synchronized
final	long	this
finally	native	throw
float	new	throws
for	null	transient
function	package	true
goto	private	try
if	protected	typeof
implements	public	var
import	return	void
in	short	volatile
instanceof	static	while
int	super	with
interface	switch	yield

Additionally, there are other words you should avoid using, including JavaScript objects, properties, and methods; Java reserved words; Windows reserved words; and HTML **event handlers**.

Semicolons

A JavaScript statement is terminated by a **semicolon**. When a statement is followed by a new line, the terminating semicolon may be omitted. Note that this places a restriction on where you may legally break lines in your JavaScript programs. A statement may not be spread across two lines when the first line can be a complete, legal statement on its own. Although you can omit semicolons, there is an ongoing debate about the benefit of always incuding the semicolon.

With programming languages like Java and C++, each code statement must end with a semicolon. In JavaScript, on the other hand, the semicolon is generally optional. Still, many programmers use a semicolon as a standard to easily identify the end of a statement.

Whitespace

JavaScript ignores whitespace between tokens. Whitespace is empty space with no character representation. Whitespace characters include space characters, tabs, and line-break characters. You may use spaces, tabs, and new lines to format or indent your code to make it more readable. Therefore, all three of the following JavaScript statements will be interpreted the same way:

```
TotalAmount=Quantity*Price;
TotalAmount = Quantity * Price;
TotalAmount      =          Quantity        *       Price        ;
```

Because whitespace is ignored within JavaScript, you can make the code more readable and understandable.

How to Put JavaScript into an HTML Page

To insert JavaScript into an HTML page, use the <script> tag and the type attribute, as shown in Figure 8.3.

```
<html>
<body>
<script type="text/javascript">
// JS0804 - JavaScript Within HTML Example
document.write ("Welcome to Belhur Publishing Product Page")
</script>
</body>
</html>
```

Figure 8.3: Inserting JavaScript into an HTML page to display the message
"Welcome to Belhur Publishing Product Page" in the browser

The <script type="text/javascript"> tag tells where the JavaScript starts. The </script> tag tells where the JavaScript ends. The document.write command is a JavaScript command used for writing output to a page. Because document.write is between the start and end JavaScript tags, the browser recognizes the command as JavaScript and will execute the line of code.

JavaScript Code Placement

Because JavaScript is executed without any preliminary compilation, it will be executed while the page loads in the browser unless it is specially designed to be executed when an event occurs or the script is called. Scripts to be executed when a page loads go in the body section of the HTML. Scripts to be executed when explicitly called or triggered go in the head section of the HTML. Multiple scripts may be placed within the HTML, and scripts can be placed within both the head and body sections.

In the previous example, the JavaScript was in the body, so it executed as the page loaded. Figure 8.4 shows JavaScript in both the body and head sections of an HTML page. When the button in Figure 8.5 is clicked, the script in the head executes, resulting in the message, "Welcome to Belhur Publishing!"

```
<html>
<head>
<script type="text/javascript">
// JS0811 - JavaScript in HTML Head and Body Section Example
function welcome()
{
document.write ("Welcome to Belhur Publishinng!")
}
</script>
</head>
<body>
<input type="button" value="View Welcome Message" onClick="welcome()" />
                                                        Continued
```

```
<script type="text/javascript">
document.write ("The Ultimate Source for Technical Publications!")
</script>
</body>
</html>
```

Figure 8.4: JavaScript in the head and body of an HTML page

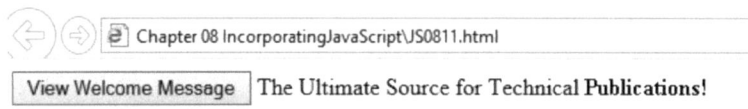

Figure 8.5: The initial results from Figure 8.4

Using an External JavaScript File

When a script will be used on multiple pages or multiple websites, it is practical to store it in an external file. The file is saved with a *.js* extension to indicate a JavaScript file type. To use an external JavaScript file, refer to it in the src attribute of the <script> tag. Be sure to use meaningful script filenames, to make it easy to identify the script files. (The examples provided in this book use names to make it easier for you to cross-reference code files.)

Figure 8.6 calls the script filename JS0815.js, in the js scripts folder. The file's code is shown in Figure 8.7. It is a good practice to place your script files in a separate folder to make them easier to find.

```
<html>
<body>
<script type="text/javascript" src="js scripts/JS0815.js">
// JS0814 - Using An External File Script Example
</script>
</body>
</html>
```

Figure 8.6: Calling an external JavaScript file from a Web page

```
// JS0815 - JavaScript in HTML Head and Body Section Example
// Author Laura A. Ubelhor November 21, 2015
document.write ("Welcome to Belhur Publishing Product Page!")
```

Figure 8.7: The JS0815.js file, which will display "Welcome to Belhur Publishing Product Page!"
in the browser

Breaking Up a Text String

A long **text string** in a code line can be broken up by using a backslash. A code line cannot be broken up outside of the text string's quotation marks, however. The backslash does not affect the output; it's just for readability in the code. For example, the output from Figure 8.8 would still display "Welcome to Belhur Publishing!" all on the same browser line, as in the previous examples.

```
document.write("Welcome to Belhur \
Publishing!")
```

Figure 8.8: Breaking up a text string with a backslash

Variables

Variables are used to store data. Variables are normally declared and initialized with the var statement. Although this is optional, it is a recommended practice to make it easier to identify variables quickly.

A variable must begin with a letter or with the underscore character (_). JavaScript is a case-sensitive language, so the variable employee is not the same as the variable EMPLOYEE.

Variables can contain values of any **data type**. The value of a variable can change during the script. By referring to the variable by name, the variable can be displayed or changed.

When you declare a variable within a function, it can only be accessed within that function. It no longer exists after you leave the function. This type of variable is called a *local variable*. The same variable names can be used in different functions because they are only recognized within the function they are declared in. Local variables are found within functions and are implemented as properties of the argument object for that function. Objects will be discussed later in this chapter.

If a variable is defined outside of a function, it is a *global variable* and can be accessed by all the functions on the page. Global variables in JavaScript are implemented as properties of a global object. Unlike C, C++, and Java, JavaScript does not have blocked-level scope. Variables declared within the curly braces of a **compound statement** are not restricted to that block and are visible outside of it.

The lifetime of a global variable starts when you open your page and ends when the page is closed. Here are some examples of variables:

```
var employeenumber = 105
employeenumber = 105
var employeelastname = "Ubelhor"
employeelastname = "Ubelhor"
```

The variable name is on the left side of the equal sign, and the value you want to assign to the variable is on the right. Multiple variables can be defined on the same line by using a comma to separate the variables, like this:

```
Var employeenumber = 105, employeelastname = "Ubelhor"
```

Data Types

JavaScript supports several value data types, including **Boolean**, number, and string, as shown in Table 8.1.

Table 8.1: JavaScript Value Data Types		
Type	Description	Example
String	A series of characters within quotation marks	"Welcome to Belhur Product Page"
Number	Any number not within quotation marks	7.13
Boolean	Logical true or false	True
Null	Devoid of any value	Null
Object	Collections of properties and methods	
Function	Function definition	
Array	A group of objects with the same attributes	
Undefined	A variable that has been declared but does not have a value assigned	var employee;

Boolean

The Boolean type has two possible values: true or false. The values are represented by the JavaScript keywords true and false. Boolean values include true or false, yes or no, on or off, and any other value that can be represented with one bit of information.

Numbers

Numbers in JavaScript are represented in 64-bit floating-point format. JavaScript makes no distinction between integers and floating-point numbers. Numeric literals appear in JavaScript programs using the syntax of a sequence of digits with an optional decimal point and an optional exponent. All of the following are valid numbers in JavaScript:

```
17
29.62
158.2345092
000013
5.02e23
```

Strings

A **string** is a sequence of letters, digits, and other characters from the 16-bit Unicode character set. String literals appear in JavaScript programs between single or double quotes. Single and double quotes can be nested within each other. Here are some examples of strings:

```
'books'
"9.99"
"Technical Publications"
```

Special escape characters can be used within a string to insert quotes, an apostrophe, a carriage return, or other special characters. As shown in Table 8.2, the backslash character begins the special escape sequence and can be placed anywhere within the string.

Table 8.2: JavaScript String Escape Characters	
Character	**Description**
\\	Single backslash (\)
\"	Double quote (")
\'	Single quote (')
\b	Backspace
\f	Form feed
\n	New line
\r	Carriage return
\t	Tab
\ddd	An octal number between 0 and 377 representing the Latin-1 character equivalent. For example, the octal code for the copyright symbol is \251.
\xXX	A hexadecimal number between 00 and FF representing the Latin-1 character equivalent. For example, the hexadecimal code for the copyright symbol is /xA9.
\uXXXX	A hexadecimal number between 00 and FF representing the Unicode character equivalent. For example, the hexadecimal code for the Unicode copyright symbol is \u00A9.

Figure 8.9 is an example of using the single-quote escape character to create the effect of an apostrophe in the message, "Welcome to Belhur Publishing What's New Page!"

```
<html>
<body>
<script type="text/javascript">
// JS0822 - String Escape Characters Example
document.write ("Welcome to Belhur Publishing What\'s New Page!")
</script>
</body>
</html>
```

Figure 8.9: Using a string escape character to produce a single quote

String values are *immutable* in JavaScript, which means their value cannot be modified. *Methods* may be used to operate on strings. A method is all about action related to an object like the string object. A method either does something to the object or with the object that affects other parts of a script or document. Methods can copy the value of a string and return the copied value, but cannot modify the value of a string. The string class includes many methods that can be used to manipulate strings.

Operators

Tables 8.3 through 8.6 list the **operators** supported by JavaScript. Arithmetic operators used within JavaScript are very similar to those used within other scripting and programming languages.

Table 8.3: Arithmetic Operators			
Operator	Description	Example	Result
+	Addition	x=5, y=7 x+y	12
-	Subtraction	x=3, y=1 x-y	2
*	Multiplication	x=2, y=4 x*y	8
/	Division	x=4, y=2 x/y	2
%	Modulus (division remainder)	x=5, y=2 x%y	1 (remainder of 5/2)
++	Increment	x=2 x++	3
--	Decrement	x=2 x--	1

In addition to arithmetic operatiors, assignment operators are also provided. An assignment operator assigns a value to its left operand based on the value of its right operand. The basic assignment operator is the equal sign, which assigns the value of its right operand to its left operand. That is, $x = y$ assigns the value of y to x. The other assignment operators are usually shorthand for standard operations.

Table 8.4: Assignment Operators				
Operator	Description	Example	Result	Is the Same As
=	Assignment	y=2, x=y	x=2	x=y
+=	Increment assignment	x=2, y=3 x+=y	x=5	x=x+y
-=	Decrement assignment	x=5, y=3 x-=y	x=2	x=x-y
*=	Multiplication assignment	x=5, y=3 x*=y	x=15	x=x*y
/=	Division assignment	x=6, y=2 x/=y	x=3	x=x/y
%=	Modulus assignment	x=6, y=5 x%=y	x=1	x=x%y

Comparison operators are used in logical statements to determine equality or difference between variables or values. The comparison operator is use to get a Boolean value indicating the result of the comparison.

Table 8.5: Comparison Operators			
Operator	Description	Example	Result
==	Is equal to	x=5, y=5, z=7 x==y x==z	True False

Table 8.5: Comparison Operators (continued)			
Operator	Description	Example	Result
!=	Is not equal to	x=5, y=5, z=7 x!=y x!=z	 False True
>	Is greater than	x=5, y=6, z=3 x>y x>z	 False True
<	Is less than	x=5, y=6, z=3 x<y x<z	 True False
>=	Is greater than or equal to	x=5, y=6, z=3 x>=y x>=z	 False True
<=	Is less than or equal to	x=5, y=6, z=3 x<=y x<=z	 True False

Logical operators are typically used with Boolean values. When logical operators are used with Boolean values, they return a Boolean value. However, the && and || operators actually return the value of one of the specified operands. If logical operators && and || are used with non-Boolean values, they may return a non-Boolean value.

Table 8.6: Logical Operators			
Operator	Description	Example	Result
&&	And	x=5 x==5 && x<3 x>3 && x==5	 False True
||	Or	x=5 x>3 || x>6 x==4 || x==3	 True False
!	Not	X=5 !(x==5) !(x==4)	 False True

Operator Precedence

Operator precedence determines the order in which operators are evaluated when combined within a statement. Operators with higher precedence are evaluated first. Associatively, left-to-right or right-to-left determines the order in which operators of the same precedence are processed. Table 8.7 is ordered from highest precedence (1) to lowest precedence (17).

Table 8.7: Operator Precedence				
Precedence	Associativity	Operator	Operator Type	Operation Peformed
1	left to right	[]	MemberExp Expression	Member
1	left to right	.	MemberExp Identifier	Member
1	right to left	New	MemberExp Arguments	New

	Table 8.7: Operator Precedence (continued)			
Precedence	Associativity	Operator	Operator Type	Operation Peformed
2	left to right	( )	CallExpression Arguments	Function call
2	left to right	[]	CallExpression Expression	Function call
2	left to right	.	CallExpression Identifier	Function call
3	n/a	++	LeftHandSideExp	Postfix increment
3	n/a	--	LeftHandSideExp	Postfix decrement
4	right to left	!	UnaryExp	Logical not
4	right to left	~	UnaryExp	Bitwise not
4	right to left	+	UnaryExp	Unary plus
4	right to left	-	UnaryExp	Unary minus
4	right to left	Typeof	UnaryExp	Return type of object
4	right to left	Void	UnaryExp	Eval and return undefined
4	right to left	delete	UnaryExp	Call delete method
5	left to right	*	MultExp UnaryExp	Multiplication
5	left to right	/	MultExp UnaryExp	Division
5	left to right	%	MultExp UnaryExp	Remainder
6	left to right	+	AddExp MultExp	Addition
6	left to right	-	AddExp MultExp	Subtraction
7	left to right	<<	ShiftExp AddExp	Bitwise left shift
7	left to right	>>	ShiftExp AddExp	Signed right shift
7	left to right	>>>	ShiftExp AddExp	Unsigned right shift
8	left to right	<	RelExp ShiftExp	Less than
8	left to right	<=	RelExp ShiftExp	Less than or equal to
8	left to right	>	RelExp ShiftExp	Greater than
8	left to right	>=	RelExp ShiftExp	Greater than or equal to
8	left to right	In	RelExp ShiftExp	Call has property method
8	left to right	instanceof	RelExp ShiftExp	Call has instance method
9	left to right	==	EqualExp RelExp	Is equal to
9	left to right	!=	EqualExp RelExp	Is not equal to
9	left to right	===	EqualExp RelExp	Is strictly equal to
9	left to right	!==	EqualExp RelExp	Is strictly not equal to
10	left to right	&	BitwiseAndExp EqualExp	Bitwise and
11	left to right	^	BitwiseOrExp EqualExp	Bitwise xor
12	left to right	|	BitwiseOrExp EqualExp	Bitwise or
13	left to right	&&	LogicalAndExp BitwiseOrExp	Logical and
14	left to right	||	LogicalOrExp LogicalAndExp	Logical or
15	right to left	?:	LogicalOrExp AssignExp	Conditional expression
16	right to left	=	LeftHandSideExp AssignExp	Assignment expression
16	right to left	+=	LeftHandSideExp AssignExp	Assignment with addition
16	right to left	-=	LeftHandSideExp AssignExp	Assignment with subtraction

Table 8.7: Operator Precedence (continued)				
Precedence	Associativity	Operator	Operator Type	Operation Peformed
16	right to left	*=	LeftHandSideExp AssignExp	Assignment with multiplication
16	right to left	/=	LeftHandSideExp AssignExp	Assignment with division
16	right to left	%=	LeftHandSideExp AssignExp	Assignment with remainder
16	right to left	<<=	LeftHandSideExp AssignExp	Assignment with bitwise left shift
16	right to left	>>=	LeftHandSideExp AssignExp	Assignment with bitwise right shift
16	right to left	>>>=	LeftHandSideExp AssignExp	Assignment with unsigned right shift
16	right to left	&=	LeftHandSideExp AssignExp	Assignment with bitwise and
16	right to left	^=	LeftHandSideExp AssignExp	Assignment with bitwise or
16	right to left	|=	LeftHandSideExp AssignExp	Assignment with logical not
17	left to right	,	Expression AssignExp	Sequential evaluation

Parentheses are used to alter precedence. The expression within the parenthesis is fully evaluated before the expression's value is used in the statement. An operator with higher precedence is evaluated before one with lower precedence. For example, consider the following:

```
OrderTotal$ = 9.99 * (2 + 3 + 4 - 1)
```

There are six operators in this expression: =, *, (), +, +, and -. Based on precedence, they are evaluated in this order: (), +, +, -, *, =. Evaluation of the expression in the parenthesis is from left to right, $2 + 3 + 4 - 1$, resulting in the value 8. Multiplication is next, so 9.99 multiplied by 8, resulting in the value 79.92. The assignment operator is last. The value 79.92 is assigned to OrderTotal$.

The equality operator, ==, can be used to compare two strings to determine if they include exactly the same sequence of characters, as shown in Figure 8.10.

```
var LastName = "UBELHOR"
LastName    ==  "Ubelhor"  // result is false because UBELHOR is not the
same as Ubelhor
```

Figure 8.10: JavaScript code using the equality operator

The inequality operator, !=, can be used to compare strings to determine if they are *not* exactly the same sequence of characters, as shown in Figure 8.11.

```
var LastName = "UBELHOR"
LastName    !=  "Ubelhor"  // result is true because UBELHOR is not the
same as Ubelhor
```

Figure 8.11: The inequality operator

The addition operator, +, can be used to concatenate strings and variables, as shown in Figure 8.12.

```
<html>
<body>
<script type="text/javascript">
// JS0827 - Addition Operator Used to Concatenate Data Example
var UserName = "Joe Walsh"
document.write ("Welcome to Belhur Publishing What\'s New Page! " +
UserName)
</script>
</body>
</html>
```

Figure 8.12: Code that displays "Welcome to Belhur Publishing What's New Page! Joe Walsh" in the browser

The relational operators (greater than, less than, greater than or equal to, and less than or equal to) can be used to compare strings using alphabetical order, as shown in Figure 8.13.

```
<html>
<body>
<script type="text/javascript">
// JS0829 - Relational Operator Compare Strings Using Alphabetical Order
Example
var City1 = "Ubly"
var City2 = "Lakeville"
if (City1 > City2)
{
document.write (City1 + " Comes After " + City2  + "Alphabetically")
}
</script>
</body>
</html>
```

Figure 8.13: The relational operators compare strings to produce "Ubly Comes After Lakeville Alphabetically" in the browser

Statements

JavaScript programs are made up of statements. Most of the statements used with JavaScript have the same syntax as C, C++, and Java statements.

Conditional Statements

Conditional statements perform actions based on whether a condition is true or false. When you want to perform different actions for different decisions, use a conditional statement. Conditional statements are case-sensitive and must be written in lower case, as shown in Table 8.8.

Table 8.8: Conditional Statements	
Statement	Description
if	Code is executed only if a specified condition is true.
if else	Code is executed if the condition is true and another group of code if the condition is false.
if else if else	One of multiple blocks of code is executed when the condition used in the block of code is true.
switch	One of multiple blocks of code is executed when the condition used in the block of code is true.

If Statements

The **if statement** is used when code is to be executed when a single condition is true.

```
if (condition) { code to execute if condition is true }
```

The code in Figure 8.14 displays a welcome message and prompts the site user for a password. If the password entered is "BelhurEmployee," the condition is true and an additional welcome greeting is displayed, as shown in Figure 8.15.

```
<html>
<body>
<script type language="javascript">
// JS0832 - If Statement Example
document.write("Welcome to Belhur Publishing Employee Page" + ".<BR>");
var passWord=prompt("Please enter your password:","")
if (passWord =="BelhurEmployee")
{
document.write("Welcome to the Employee Work Schedule Page" + ".<BR>");
}
</script>
</body>
</html>
```

Figure 8.14: An example of the if statement

> **Password entered "BelhurEmployee"**
>
> Welcome to Belhur Publishing Employee Page. Welcome to the Employee Work Schedule Page.

*Figure 8.15: The results when the **if** statement in Figure 8.14 is true*

The if else statement is used when code is to be executed when a single condition is false.

```
if (condition) { code to execute if condition is true } else
{
code to execute if condition is false
}
```

Figure 8.16 is very similar to Figure 8.14, but we have added code to include an else statement. With this change, if any value other than a valid user password is entered, a message will be displayed informing the site user the password is invalid, as shown in Figure 8.17.

```
<html>
<body>
<script type language="javascript">
// JS0835 - If Else Statement Example
document.write("Welcome to Belhur Publishing Employee Page" + ".<BR>");
var passWord=prompt("Please enter your password:","")
if (passWord=="BelhurEmployee")
{
document.write("Welcome to the Employee Work Schedule Page" + ".<BR>");
}
else
{
document.write("The password entered is invalid");
}
</script>
</body>
</html>
```

*Figure 8.16: An example of the **if else** statement*

> **Password entered is not = "BelhurEmployee"**
>
> Welcome to Belhur Publishing Employee Page. The password entered is invalid

*Figure 8.17: The results when the **if** statement in Figure 8.16 is false*

The if else if else statement is used when multiple conditions are tested and, when true, control execution of a block of code. The final else is used to execute code when all conditions are false.

```
if (condition1) { code to execute if condition is true } else if
    (condition2)
{
Code to execute if condition2 is true
}
else
{
Code to execute if condition1 and 2 are false }
```

The code in Figure 8.18 is very similar to Figure 8.16. However, another if else has been added.

```
<html>
<body>
<script type language="javascript">
// JS0838 - If Else If Else Statement Example
document.write("Welcome to Belhur Publishing Employee Page"  + ".<BR>");
var passWord=prompt("Please enter your password:","")
if (passWord=="BelhurEmployee")
{
document.write("Welcome to the Employee Work Schedule Page" +  ".<BR>");
}
else if (passWord=="BelhurManager")
{
document.write("Welcome to the Managers Work Schedule Page" +  ".<BR>");
}
else
{
document.write("The password entered is invalid");
}
</script>
</body>
</html>
```

*Figure 8.18: An example of the **if else if else** statement*

In this example, illustrated in Figure 8.19, if the user enters "BelhurEmployee" as the password, the message "Welcome to the Employee Schedule Page" will be displayed. If the user enters "BelhurManager," the message "Welcome to the Managers Work Schedule Page" will be displayed. If any other password is entered, a message stating the password is invalid will be displayed. Also notice the use of the break tag, <br>, ensuring that the next text displayed will be on a new line.

Password entered = "BelhurManager"

Welcome to Belhur Publishing Employee Page.
Welcome to the Managers Work Schedule Page.

Password entered = "BelhurEmployee"

Welcome to Belhur Publishing Employee Page.
Welcome to the Employee Work Schedule Page.

Password entered is anything other than "BelhurEmployee" or "BelhurManager"

Welcome to Belhur Publishing Employee Page.
The password entered is invalid

Figure 8.19: The results from the code in Figure 8.17

The Switch Statement

The **switch statement** is used to execute one of multiple blocks of code.

```
switch(expression)
{
case 1:
   execute code block 1
   break
case 2:
   execute code block 2
 default:
   execute code block when case 1 and case 2 are false
}
```

The case and default keywords are often used with the switch statement. These keywords are not JavaScript statements; rather, they are labels. The break keyword may be used to end execution of the statement when a condition is true.

The code in Figure 8.20 uses switch to evaluate the password entered by a user. The value of the password is compared with the values for each case. If "BelhurEmployee" is entered, there is a case match, and the alert "Welcome Employee!" is displayed. If "BelhurManager" is entered as the password, there is a case match, and the alert "Welcome Manager!" is displayed. If a case match is made, break terminates execution of the remaining code within the statement. If a case match is not made, the default statement executes the alert "Password is invalid," as shown in Figure 8.21.

```
html>
<body>
<script type language="javascript">
```
Continued

```
// JS0841 Switch Statement Example
document.write("Welcome to Belhur Publishing Employee Page"  + ".<BR>");
var passWord=prompt("Please enter your password:","");
switch (passWord){
case "BelhurEmployee":
alert("Welcome Employee!")
break;
case "BelhurManager":
alert("Welcome Manager")
break;
default :
alert("Password Is Invalid");
}
</script>
</body>
</html>
```

Figure 8.20: An example of the switch statement

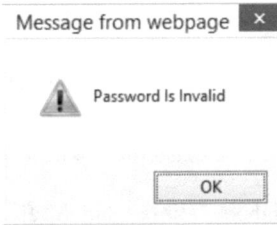

Figure 8.21: The result when an invalid password is entered

Expression Statements

Every expression used with JavaScript can stand alone as a JavaScript statement. Value assignments, math expressions, and method calls are all examples of JavaScript statements. Here are some examples of JavaScript expressions:

```
x++;
y--;
OrderTotal$ = LineTotal1$ + LineTotal2$ + LineTotal3$ +Tax$
Greeting = "Welcome to Belhur Publishing";
```

Compound Statements

When a sequence of JavaScript statements is enclosed within curly braces, { }, it counts as a single compound statement. Multiple statements enclosed with curly braces are considered compound statements. For example, the body of a while loop consists of a single statement. If you want the loop to execute more than one statement, a compound statement is needed. Compound statements are commonly used with if, if else, if else if else, for, and switch statements. Figure 8.22 is an example of a compound statement.

```
If (x == 1)
{
      If (y == 2)
            a = 5;
}
else
            a = 4;
```

Figure 8.22: A compound statement

The Empty Statement

The **empty statement** is simply a semicolon by itself. Although it does nothing, it might be used for coding empty loop bodies. Empty statements should be used cautiously, however. Some editors identify the empty statement with a warning.

Labeled Statements

A **labeled statement** provides an identifier that can be used with the break or the **continue statement**. In a labeled statement, break or continue must be followed with a label. Any type of statement can be used with a labeled statement. The labeled statement will be in the format *label: statement*.

The example in Figure 8.23 uses two labels, labelxy and labely. The script prompts for the value of x to be entered, asking for a number between zero and 10. It then prompts for the value of y to be entered, again between zero and 10. When the value of x is 10, the code found within labely will be executed. If the value of y is five, the code execution will break out of the code within labely and continue at the statement following the labely **loop**. The code to write a line will only be executed in this example when $x = 10$. Figure 8.24 shows the output for various inputs.

```
<html>
<body>
<script type="text/javascript">
// JS0845 Labeled Statement Example
var x=prompt("Enter a number value between 0 and 10 for x:","")
var y=prompt("Enter a number value between 0 and 10 for y:","")
labelxy :
        if (10==x) {
```
Continued

```
                document.write("You've entered " + x + ".<BR>");
            labely :
                if (5==y) {
                document.write("You've entered " + y + ".<BR>");
                break labely;
                    document.write("The sum is " + (x+y) + ".<BR>");
                        }
                document.write(x + "-" + y + "=" + (x-y) + ".<BR>");
                }
</script>
</body>
</html>
```

Figure 8.23: An example of labeled statements

```
You've entered 10.
10-4=6.

You've entered 10.
You've entered 5.
10-5=5.
```

Figure 8.24: The results when x=10 and y=4, and then when x = 10 and y = 5

The Break Statement

The **break statement** can be used in a while, for, or labeled statement. In a **while loop** or **for loop**, break will terminate the current loop and transfer control to the statement following the terminated loop. In a labeled statement, break will be followed by a label that identifies the statement and will transfer control to the statement following the terminated statement. Figure 8.25 is an example of break used in a labeled statement. The break and continue statements will only be used within a JavaScript loop.

```
<html>
<body>
<script type="text/javascript">
// JS0848 Break Statement Example
var x=0
for (x=0;x<=20;x++)
{
if (x==5){break}
```
Continued

```
document.write("Number " + x)
document.write("<br />")
}
</script>
</body>
</html>
```

Figure 8.25: An example of the break statement

In the example in Figure 8.25, break will execute when *x* is equal to 5. When break is encountered, control will be transferred and the loop will end. The result of the loop is shown in Figure 8.26.

```
Number 0
Number 1
Number 2
Number 3
Number 4
```

Figure 8.26: The results from the code in Figure 8.25

The Continue Statement

The continue statement can be used with a while, for, or labeled statement. It will break a current loop and continue with the next statement outside of the current loop. In a while or for loop, continue will terminate execution of the current loop with the next iteration of the loop. Unlike the break statement, continue does not terminate execution of the loop. In a while loop, execution will return to the increment expression. In a labeled statement, continue is followed by a label that identifies the labeled statement. The continue statement will terminate execution of the labeled statement and continue execution of the code within the labeled statement.

In the example in Figure 8.27, a prompt to enter the value of *y* is displayed. When the value of *y* is equal to three, the statements within the loop will be executed and execution will be returned to the next iteration of the labely loop. The results for *y*=3 and *y*=2 are shown in Figure 8.28.

```
<html>
<body>
<script type="text/javascript">
// JS0850 Continue Labeled Statement Example
var y=prompt("Enter a number value between 0 and 5 for y:","")
labely :
        while (y < 5) {
                y++
                                                    Continued
```

```
                    document.write("labely Loop y value is " + y + ".<BR>");
                        if (3==y) {
                                document.write("y is equal to 3!" + ".<BR>");
                                continue labely;
                                        }
                                }
</script>
</body>
</html>
```

Figure 8.27: An example of continue with a labeled statement

```
labely Loop y value is 4.
labely Loop y value is 5.

labely Loop y value is 3.
y is equal to 3!.
labely Loop y value is 4.
labely Loop y value is 5.
```

*Figure 8.28: The results from Figure 8.27 when the value 3 is entered for y,
and then when 2 is entered for y*

In Figure 8.29, the code will be executed until $x = 6$. When $x = 5$, the continue statement will direct execution to continue at the beginning of the loop, bypassing statements following continue. The results are shown in Figure 8.30.

```
<html>
<body>
<script type="text/javascript">
// JS0853 Continue Statement Example
var x=0
for (x=0;x<=6;x++)
{
if (x==5){continue}
document.write("Number " + x)
document.write("<br />")
}
</script>
</body>
</html>
```

Figure 8.29: A continue statement in a loop

```
Number 0
Number 1
Number 2
Number 3
Number 4
Number 6
```

Figure 8.30: The results of Figure 8.29

Loops

JavaScript has two kinds of loops: for and while.

While Loops

The **while loop** is used to repeat a block of code while a condition is true.

```
while(condition)
{
statement1;
statement2;
}
```

The while loop in Figure 8.31 defines a loop that will execute multiple statements under the condition that variable *x* is less than five, resulting in the output in Figure 8.32. The statement *x=x+1* increments the value of *x* by one each time the loop is executed.

```
<html>
<body>
<script type="text/javascript">
// FS0857 While Loop Example
var x=0
while (x<5)
{
document.write("Belhur Line " + x)
document.write("<br />")
x=x+1
}
</script>
</body>
</html>
```

Figure 8.31: An example of a while loop

```
Belhur Line 0
Belhur Line 1
Belhur Line 2
Belhur Line 3
Belhur Line 4
```

Figure 8.32: The results of executing the loop

The do while loop is a variation of the while loop in which the loop will always execute a block of code once, and then it will repeat the loop as long as the condition is true. The loop will always execute once because the loop statements are executed before the condition is tested.

```
do { statement1;
statement2;
} while (var<=endvalue)
```

Remember that the curly braces are used to execute multiple statements. They are not required if a single statement will be executed.

The do while loop in Figure 8.33 will execute at least once and will continue to execute while x is less than zero. The variable x is incremented by one each time the loop is executed. The result will be the single line "Belhur Line 0" because as soon as the condition is tested, it is found to be false.

```
<html>
<body>
<script type="text/javascript">
// JS0860 Do While Loop Example
var x=0
do
{
document.write("Belhur Line " + x)
document.write("<br />")
x=x+1
}
while (x<0)
</script>
</body>
</html>
```

Figure 8.33: An example of a do while loop

For Loops

The for loop repeats the specified condition until the condition is false. A for loop usually begins with an expression to initialize counters. Next, the condition of the expression is evaluated. If the condition is false, the loop terminates. If the condition is true, the loop statements execute. Multiple statements can be included using curly brackets and semicolons. After statement execution, there is usually an expression to increment the counters, and control returns to the condition of the expression.

```
var = value for condition; increment expression
{ statement1;
statement2;
}
```

The example in Figure 8.34 begins with variable x being initialized to zero. The loop will continue to run as long as x is less than or equal to four, producing the results in Figure 8.35.

```
<html>
<body>
<script type="text/javascript">
// JS0863 For Loop Example
var x=0
for (x=0;x<=4;x++)
{
document.write("Belhur Line " + x)
document.write("<br />")
}
</script>
</body>
</html>
```

Figure 8.34: An example of a for loop

```
Belhur Line 0
Belhur Line 1
Belhur Line 2
Belhur Line 3
Belhur Line 4
```

Figure 8.35: The results of executing the loop in Figure 8.34

The for in loop is a variation of the for loop. It is used to loop through elements of an **array**. The loop is executed once for each array.

```
for (variable in object)
{
statement1;
statement2;
}
```

The example in Figure 8.36 executes the document.write and <br> for each element within the array, resulting in Figure 8.37.

```
<html>
<body>
<script type="text/javascript">
// JS0866 For In Loop Example
var x
var BelhurBook = new Array()
BelhurBook[0] = "SQL Unleashed"
BelhurBook[1] = "Web Services for Everyone"
BelhurBook[2] = "PHP Hot Scripts"
BelhurBook[3] = "jQuery Uplifts Your Web Application"
BelhurBook[4] = "Modernize Your Applications with Ruby on Rails"
BelhurBook[5] = "Application Modernization"
for (x in BelhurBook)
{
document.write(BelhurBook[x] + "<br />")
}
</script>
</body>
</html></html>
```

*Figure 8.36: An example of a **for in** loop.*

SQL Unleashed
Web Services for Everyone
PHP Hot Scripts
jQuery Uplifts Your Web Application
Modernize Your Applications with Ruby on Rails
Application Modernization

Figure 8.37: The results of the loop in Figure 8.36

Functions

A JavaScript **function** is used to group and isolate code that will be executed by an event occurrence or by a call to the function, not simply executed when the page loads. A function can be called from anywhere within the page. If the function is saved in an external .js file, it can also be used from other pages.

Functions can be defined in the <head> or <body> section of an HTML document. If you would like a function to be loaded before being called, place it in the <head> section.

Defined Functions

Back in Figure 8.4, the JavaScript in the <head> section of the HTML document is actually an example of a **defined function**. The new function is named "welcome." Because it is placed in the <head> section, it will be loaded prior to being initiated when the button **View Welcome Message** is clicked.

```
function functionname(var1, var2, ... varx)
{
statement1;
statement2;
}
```

Parentheses are required within a defined function, even when variables are not used, so you can have a function like *functionname()*. The curly brackets define the start and the end of the function.

The JavaScript example in Figure 8.4 is triggered by the event onClick. A function may also be called, as in Figure 8.38. In this example, a new function named BelhurBooks is defined. The function is called, passing the Books array values as parameters. When the function is executed, the list of books is displayed, as shown in Figure 8.39.

```
<html>
<head>
<script language="javascript">
// JS0869 Called Function Example
function BelhurBooks(BelhurBook)
{
document.write("<UL>\n")
for (i = 0;i < BelhurBook.length;i++)
{
document.write("<LI>" + BelhurBook[i] + "\n")
}
document.write("</UL>\n")
```

Continued

```
}
</script>
</head>
<body>
<script language="javascript">
Books = new
Array("SQL Unleashed","Web Services for Everyone",
"PHP Hot Scripts","jQuery Uplifts Your Web Applicaiton","Modernize Your
Applications with Ruby on Rails",
"Application Modernization")
BelhurBooks(Books)
</script>
</body>
```

Figure 8.38: An example of a called function.

- SQL Unleashed
- Web Services for Everyone
- PHP Hot Scripts
- jQuery Uplifts Your Web Application
- Modernize Your Applications with Ruby on Rails
- Application Modernization

Figure 8.39: The results from the called function in Figure 8.38

Predefined Functions

JavaScript has a number of **predefined functions** available for use, listed in Table 8.9. The list provided here is not all-inclusive, but it gives you an idea of what predefined functions are available.

Table 8.9: JavaScript Predefined Functions

Function	Description	Use
eval(*expr*)	This function evaluates a string of JavaScript code without reference to a particular object.	*Expr* is a string to be evaluated. If the string represents an expression, eval evaluates the expression. If the argument represents one or more JavaScript statements, eval performs the statements. Do not call this function to evaluate an arithmetic expression; JavaScript evaluates arithmetic expressions automatically.

isFinite(*number*)	This function evaluates an argument to determine whether it is a finite number.	*Number* is the number to evaluate. If the argument is not a number, or is positive or negative infinity, this method returns false. Otherwise, it returns true. For example, the following code checks client input to determine whether it is a finite number:
		
		if(isFinite(ClientInput) == true)
		{
		  /* take specific steps */
		}

Table 8.9: JavaScript Predefined Functions (continued)		
Function	Description	Use

isNaN(*testValue*)	This function evaluates an argument to determine if it is not a number (NaN).	*TestValue* is the value you want to evaluate.
		
		 The parseFloat and parseInt functions return "NaN" when they evaluate a value that is not a number. The isNaN function returns true if passed "NaN," and false otherwise.
		
		 The following code evaluates the floatValue variable to determine if it is a number, and then calls a procedure accordingly:
		
		 `floatValue=parseFloat(toFloat)`
		 `if (isNaN(floatValue)) {`
		   `notFloat()`
		 `}`
		 `else`
		 `{`
		   `isFloat()`
		 `}`

parseInt(*str* [, *radix*])	These functions return a numeric value when given a string as an argument.	The parseInt function parses its first argument, the string *str*, and attempts to return an integer of the specified radix (base), indicated by the second, optional argument, *radix*. For example, a radix of 10 means to convert to a decimal number, eight means octal, 16 hexadecimal, and so on. For radixes above 10, the letters of the alphabet indicate numerals. For example, for hexadecimal numbers (base 16), A through F are used. If parseInt encounters a character that is not a numeral in the specified radix, it ignores it and all succeeding characters and returns the integer value parsed up to that point. If the first character cannot be converted to a number in the specified radix, it returns "NaN." The parseInt function truncates the string to integer values.
parseFloat(*str*)		The parseFloat function parses its argument, the string *str*, and attempts to return a floating-point number. If it encounters a character other than a sign (+ or -), a numeral (0-9), a decimal point, or an exponent, it returns the value up to that point and ignores that character and all succeeding characters. If the first character cannot be converted to a number, it returns "NaN" (not a number).
Number(*objRef*)	This function converts an object to a number.	*ObjRef* is an object reference.

String(*objRef*)	This function converts an object to a string.	*ObjRef* is an object reference.
		
		 The following example converts the Date object to a readable string:
		
		 `D = new Date (430054663215)`
		 `// The following returns`
		 `// "Thu Aug 18 04:37:43 GMT-0700 (Pacific Daylight Time) 1983"`
		 `x = String(D)`

escape(*string*)	This function returns the hexadecimal encoding of an argument in the ISO Latin character set.	These functions are used primarily with server-side JavaScript to encode and decode name/value pairs in URLs. The escape and unescape functions do not work properly for non-ASCII characters and have been deprecated.
unescape(*string*)	This function returns the ASCII string for the specified hexadecimal encoding value.	

In addition to the predefined functions in Table 8.9, there are also special message functions, including alert, confirm, and prompt. These functions provide a means of displaying user messages, alerts, and confirmation prompts in dialog boxes. How often have you needed this functionality within an application? With JavaScript's predefined functions, it takes very little code. There are endless possibilities for using the message functions in your applications.

alert(message)

The alert dialog box function displays an alert box with a message defined by the string *message*. For example, the function in Figure 8.40 displays the dialog box in Figure 8.41.

```html
<html>
<body>
<script language="javascript">
// JS0871 Alert Example
var Error1="Yes"
if (Error1="Yes") {
alert("An error occurred!  Press OK to continue.")
}
</script>
</body>
</html>
```

Figure 8.40: An example of the alert function

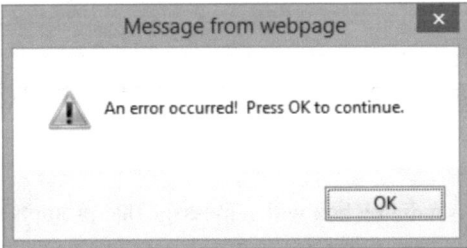

Figure 8.41: The dialog box displayed from the code in Figure 8.40

confirm(*message*)

The confirm function displays a message and two buttons, **OK** and **Cancel**. If the user clicks the **OK** button, a value of true is returned. If the user clicks **Cancel**, a value of false is returned. Figure 8.42 uses confirm to create the dialog box in Figure 8.43. If the user clicks **OK**, the message *OK Pressed - Continuing!* is displayed. If the user clicks **Cancel**, the message *Operation Cancelled!* is displayed.

```
<html>
<body>
<script language="javascript">
// JS0873 Confirm Example
if (confirm("Press OK to continue, or press cancel to cancel the
operation"))
{
  document.write("OK Pressed - Continuing!")
}
else
{
  document.write("Operation Cancelled!")
}
</script>
</body>
</html>
```

Figure 8.42: An example of the confirm function

Figure 8.43: The dialog box displayed from the code in Figure 8.42

prompt(*message*)

The prompt function displays a dialog box with a message that prompts the user to enter text in a field and click **OK** or **Cancel**. If the user clicks **Cancel**, a null value is returned. If the user clicks **OK**, the string value entered in the field is returned. The prompt function in Figure 8.44 creates the dialog box in Figure 8.45. It was also used in the examples earlier in this chapter in which the user was prompted for a password.

```
<html>
<html>
<body>
<script language="javascript">
// JS0876 Prompt Message Example
                                                  Continued
```

```
document.write("Welcome to Belhur Publishing Book Selection Page"  +
".<BR>");
var bookSelection=prompt("Please Enter Your Book Selection","")
if (bookSelection != null)
{
document.write("You have selected " + bookSelection);
}
</script>
</body>
</html>
```

Figure 8.44: An example of the prompt function

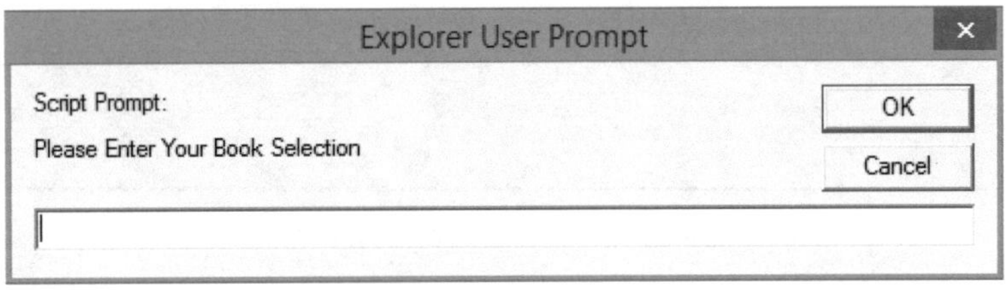

Figure 8.45: The dialog box displayed from the code in Figure 8.44

Figure 8.46 shows the message that is displayed if the user enters "SQL Unleashed" in the dialog box.

Welcome to Belhur Publishing Book Selection Page.
You have selected SQL Unleashed

Figure 8.46: The results from the prompt dialog box in Figure 8.45

The Return Statement

The **return statement** is used with a function to return a value from that function. Use a meaningful name with return so you can easily identify what the value is for. For example, the code in Figure 8.47 defines the function calculatePrice. When passed the quantity and unit price, the function calculates the extended price and returns the value extendedCost. Given the quantity and unit price in the sample HTML, the message *Extended Cost = 349.75* will be displayed when the function executes.

```
<html>
<head>
<script language="javascript">
// JSP0879 Function With Return Statement Example
function calculatePrice(quantity,unitPrice)
```
Continued

```
{
extendedCost=quantity*unitPrice
return extendedCost
}
</script>
</head>
<body>
<script language="javascript">
quantity = 5;
unitPrice = 69.95;
extendedCost = calculatePrice(quantity, unitPrice);
document.write("Extended Cost = " + extendedCost);
</script>
</body>
</html>
```

Figure 8.47: An example of a return statement

Catching Errors

When a browser encounters an error at a site, it will usually display an alert box stating the error and asking if the user wants to debug. To prevent errors from being handled this way, you can use special JavaScript statements to trap and react to them. Errors can be handled using **try catch throw** statements or the onerror event. The onerror event is described later in this chapter. Try catch throw is covered in this section.

```
try {
execute this block
} catch (error) {
execute this block if there is an error
}
```

The try and catch statements can be used without throw to test a block of code for errors. Try is used to identify errors, and catch contains code to be executed if an error occurs. The throw statement allows the creation of an exception. In combination, these statements can be used for data validation or capturing errors and controlling the response when errors occur.

Figure 8.48 is an example of using try and catch without throw. It has an intentional bug in the code (document.writ), so that clicking the Display Error Message button results in the dialog box in Figure 8.49. If you correct the error in the code from document.writ to document.write, the corrected page will display *Welcome to Belhur Publishing!*.

```
<html>
<head>
<script type="text/javascript">
// JS0882 Try Catch Example

var messageText=""
function message()
{
try
  {
  document.writ ("Welcome To Belhur Publishing!")
  }
catch(error)
  {
  messageText="An error was encountered on this page.\n\n"
  messageText+="Description: " + error.description + "\n\n"
  messageText+="Click OK to continue.\n\n"
  alert(messageText)
  }
}
</script>
</head>
<body>
<input type="button" value="Display Error Message" onclick="message()" />
</body>
</html>
```

Figure 8.48: An example of try catch

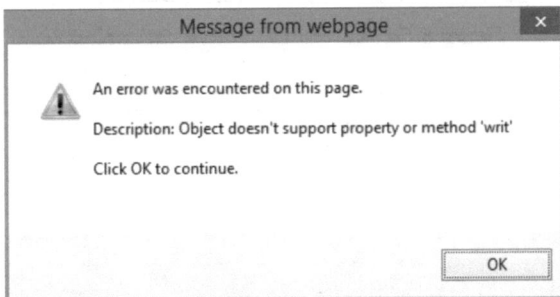

Figure 8.49: The dialog box displayed when an error occurs in the JavaScript code

The try catch throw statements can be used with if else statements to provide multiple criteria checks for errors. This enables you to display different messages when different error conditions are true. The code in Figure 8.50 prompts the user to enter an item number, using the dialog box in Figure 8.51. The item number is then evaluated. If it is greater than 10 or less than one, the throw statement is used to send the error to the catch statement, which displays the appropriate message.

```html
<html>
<body>
<script type="text/javascript">
// JS0885  Try Catch Throw Example
var item=prompt("Enter an item number between 1 and 10:","");
document.write("You entered item number " + item + ".<br>");
try
{
if(item>10)
throw "Error1"
else if(item<1)
throw "Error2"
}
catch(er)
{
if(er=="Error1")
alert("The item number entered is greater than 10.")
if(er == "Error2")
alert("The item number entered is less than 1.")
}
</script>
</body>
</html>
```

Figure 8.50: An example of try catch throw

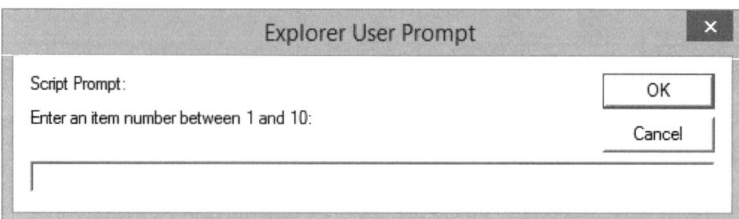

Figure 8.51: The dialog box created from the code in Figure 8.50

Suppose the user enters a zero. The error will be handled as shown in Figure 8.52. In this example, when the user enters a number less than one, a message will be displayed stating the item number entered is less than one. If, on the other hand, the user enters 11, the error message in Figure 8.53 is displayed.

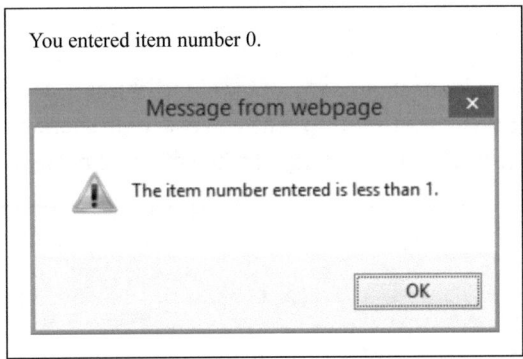

Figure 8.52: An error message for an item number less than one

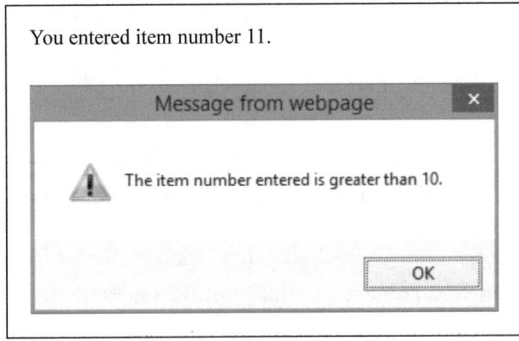

Figure 8.53: An error message for item numbers greater than 10

The try catch throw statements have very practical uses in business applications, to display more meaningful messages when errors are encountered.

Objects

JavaScript, like Java and C++, is an *object-oriented programming* (*OOP*) language. An OOP language allows you to define your own **objects** and also create variable types. (Object and variable-type creation is an advanced feature not be covered in this chapter.) Objects are a special kind of data. An object has *properties* and *methods*. Properties are the values associated with the object. Methods are the actions that can be performed on the object. This chapter shows you how some of the built-in objects provided in JavaScript can be used.

In JavaScript, everything you interact with is an object of some kind; from the strings, numbers, and arrays used in the script, to the functions that are executed. This is more than just a vague notion of objectness. In JavaScript, everything is an object. The JavaScript Object class is automatically inherited by every other object. This means that the methods and properties of the Object class are supported and implemented by all objects within JavaScript.

The first object to consider is the string object, which is used to manipulate a stored piece of text. It has two properties:

- The length property returns the number of characters in a string.
- The prototype property allows you to add properties and methods to an object.

In Figure 8.54, for example, the length property of the string object is used to determine the number of characters in the variable welcomeGreeting. The contents of the variable are "Welcome to Belhur Publishing!", so the message "29" will be displayed when the code runs.

```
<html>
<body>
<script type="text/javascript">
// JS0890 Length Properties String Object Example
var welcomeGreeting="Welcome to Belhur Publishing!";
document.write(welcomeGreeting.length)
</script>
</body>
<html>
```

Figure 8.54: An example of the length property

The predefined string objects listed in Table 8.10 extend the JavaScript language extensively. The format is the same for all predefined objects, so once you've understood the examples in the following pages, it will be easy for you to use any of the objects from the predefined list.

Table 8.10: Predefined Methods of String Objects		
Method	Description	String HTML Wrapper Methods (may not work the same in all browsers)
anchor()	Creates an HTML anchor	X
big()	Displays a string in a large font	X
blink()	Displays a blinking string	X
bold()	Displays a bold string	X
charAt()	Returns a character at a specified position	
charCodeAt()	Returns the Unicode value of a character at a specified position	
concat()	Joins multiple strings together	
fixed()	Displays a string as "teletype" text	X
fontcolor()	Displays a string in a designated font color	X
fontsize()	Displays a string in a designated font size	X
fromCharCode()	Translates a Unicode value into a string	
indexOf()	Returns the position of the first occurrence of a designated string value in a string	

Method	Description	String HTML Wrapper Methods (may not work the same in all browsers)
italics()	Displays a sting in italics	X
lastIndexOf()	Returns the position of the last occurrence of a designated string value, searching from left to right from the designated position	
link()	Displays a string as a hyperlink	X
match()	Searches for a designated value in a string	
replace()	Replaces some characters with other characters in a string	
search()	Searches a sting for a specified value	
slice()	Extracts part of a string and returns the extracted value in another string	
small()	Displays a string in a small font	X
split()	Splits a string into an array of strings	
strike()	Displays a string with a "strikethrough" effect	X
sub()	Displays a sting as a subscript	X
substr()	Extracts a specified number of characters in a string from a start index	
substring()	Extracts the characters in a string between a start and end position	
sup()	Displays a string in superscript	X
toLowerCase()	Displays a string in all lower case	
toUpperCase()	Displays a string in all upper case	

Table 8.10: Predefined Methods of String Objects (continued)

The format of the statement is *stringObject.property()* or *stringObject.method()*. The *stringObject* part of this reference can be any expression that evaluates to a string, including string literals, variables containing strings, or other object properties. The parentheses are used for any parameters. Parameters can include characters within quotes or one or more integers separated by commas, depending on what is appropriate. If no parameter is passed, the character being converted by default is the first character of the string. The list also includes string HTML wrapper methods. They are used to return a string wrapped inside an HTML tag and may not work the same in all browsers.

Figure 8.55 is an example of the **toUpperCase** method, which requires no parameters. This example will convert the string "welcome to belhur publishing!" to "WELCOME TO BELHUR PUBLISHING!"

```
<html>
<body>
<script type="text/javascript">
var WelcomeMessage ="welcome to belhur publishing!"
// JS0892  To Upper Case Example
document.write(WelcomeMessage.toUpperCase())</script>
</body>
</html>
```

Figure 8.55: An example of the toUpperCase method of the string object

Figure 8.56 is another example of a string method. In this case, the concat method does require a parameter in parentheses to concatenate with the rest of the string. The result will display "Laura Ubelhor."

```
<html>
<body>
<script type="text/javascript">
// JS0894 concat Method Example
var fullName="Laura ".concat("Ubelhor");
document.write(fullName);
</script>
</body>
</html>
```

Figure 8.56: An example of the concat method

Date Objects

A browser that supports scripts contains a **date object** that is always present and ready to be used. Date object methods, listed in Table 8.11, can be used to retrieve or set date and time values. There are additional date object methods available. The list represents some of the common date object methods.

Table 8.11: Date Object Methods		
Method	Value Range	Description
Date()		Today's data and time
getTime()	0-.....	Milliseconds since 1/1/70 00:00:00 GMT
getYear()	70-...	Specified year minus 1900; four-digit year for 2000+
getMonth()	0 – 11	Month within the year (January = 0)
getFullYear()		Four-digit year
getDate()	1 – 31	Date within the month
getDay()	0 – 6	Day of the week (Sunday = 0)
getHours()	0 – 23	Hour of the day, in 24-hour time
getMinutes()	0 – 59	Minute of the specified hour
getSeconds	0 – 59	Second within the specified minute
setTime()	0-.....	Milliseconds since 1/1/70 00:00:00 GMT
setYear()	70-...	Set specified year minus 1900; four-digit year for 2000+
setFullYear)		Set four-digit year; optionally, can set month and day
setMonth()	0 – 11	Set month within the year (January = 0)
setDate()	1 – 31	Set date within the month
setDay()	0 – 6	Set day of the week (Sunday = 0)
setHours()	0 – 23	Set hour of the day, in 24-hour time
setMinutes()	0 – 59	Set minute of the specified hour
setSeconds	0 – 59	Set second within the specified minute

A date object always returns the current date unless parameters are specified with the date object's method. The example in Figure 8.57 retrieves the current date, uses it with various date object methods, and displays the results in the browser, as shown in Figure 8.58.

```
<html>
<body>
<script type="text/javascript">
// JS0896 Date Object Examples
var today=new Date();
var time1=today.getTime();
var year1=today.getYear();
var month1=today.getMonth();
var date1=today.getDate();
var day1=today.getDay();
var hours1=today.getHours();
var minutes1=today.getMinutes();
var seconds1=today.getSeconds();
var time1=today.getTime();
document.write("The Date is " + today +  ".<BR>");
document.write("The Time is " + time1 +  ".<BR>");
document.write("The Year is " + year1 +  ".<BR>");
document.write("The Month is " + month1 +  ".<BR>");
document.write("The Date is " + date1 +  ".<BR>");
document.write("The Day is " + day1 +  ".<BR>");
document.write("The Hour is " + hours1 +  ".<BR>");
document.write("The Time is " + minutes1 +  ".<BR>");
</script>
</body>
</html>
```

Figure 8.57: Examples of date object "get" methods

The Date is Sun Jan 17 2016 10:37:27 GMT-0500 (Eastern Standard Time).
The Time is 1453045047772.
The Year is 116.
The Month is 0.
The Date is 17.
The Day is 0.
The Hour is 10.
The Time is 37.

Figure 8.58: The results from Figure 8.57

The code in Figure 8.57 uses the current date defined as the variable today. The values returned from using the "get" methods and the date object are stored in variables defined within the script. Figure 8.59 shows similar examples, using the "set" methods. The results are displayed in Figure 8.60.

```
<html>
<body>
<script type="text/javascript">
/* JS0898 Set Date Examples */

var today = new Date();
document.write("The current date is" + today + ".<br>");
var y = new Date();

var t = new Date();
t.setTime(9999999999999);
document.write("Example 9999999999999 since 1/1/70 00:00 GMT" + ".<br>")
document.write(t + ".<br>") ;

y.setYear(1891);
document.write("Example setting current date year to 1891" + ".<br>");
document.write(y + ".<br>") ;

var m = new Date();
m.setMonth(1);
document.write("Example setting current date month to 1" + ".<br>");
document.write(m + ".<br>");

var d = new Date();
d.setDate(1);
document.write("Example setting date within the month" + ".<br>");
document.write(d + ".<br>");

</script>
</body>
</html>
```

Figure 8.59: Examples of date object "get" methods

The current date is Sun Jan 17 2016 10:51:17 GMT-0500 (Eastern Standard Time).
Example 9999999999999 since 1/1/70 00:00 GMT.
Sat Nov 20 2286 12:46:39 GMT-0500 (Eastern Standard Time).
Example setting current date year to 1891.
Sat Jan 17 1891 10:51:17 GMT-0500 (Eastern Standard Time).
Example setting current date month to 1.
Wed Feb 17 2016 10:51:17 GMT-0500 (Eastern Standard Time).
Example setting date within the month.
Fri Jan 01 2016 10:51:17 GMT-0500 (Eastern Standard Time).

Figure 8.60: The results from Figure 8.59

The Date class is very useful for comparing dates, which is often necessary in business applications. For example, Figure 8.61 compares the ship date to the current date. If the ship date is less than or equal to the current date, the user is alerted that the order is on its way, as shown in Figure 8.62. If the ship date is greater than the current date, the user is given the date.

```
<html>
<body>
<script type="text/javascript">
/* JS08100 Comparing Dates Example */
var shipDate=new Date()
shipDate.setFullYear(2016,1,12)
var today = new Date()
if (shipDate>today)
  alert("Your Order will ship on " + shipDate) ;
else
  alert("Your Order shipped on " + shipDate +  "and is on its way") ;
</script>
</body>
</html>
```

Figure 8.61: Comparing dates in an application

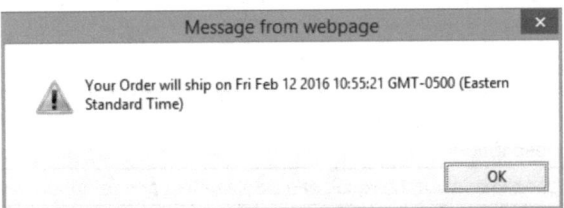

Figure 8.62: A dialog box produced from the code in Figure 8.61

In the example in Figure 8.63, the delivery date is calculated as four days from the ship date. The ship date is set as the current date. A message is displayed providing both the ship date and the arrival date, like this:

```
Your order is scheduled to ship on Sun Jan 17 2016 11:20:27 GMT-0500 (Eastern
Standard Time).
Your order will arrive by Thu Jan 21 2016 11:20:27 GMT-0500
(Eastern Standard Time).
```

```
<html>
<body>
<script type="text/javascript">
/* JS08102 Example To Calculate Delivery Date */
var shipDate=new Date();
var deliveryDate=new Date();
deliveryDate.setDate(shipDate.getDate()+4);
document.write("Your order is scheduled to ship on " +shipDate + ".<br>");
document.write("Your order will arrive by " +deliveryDate + ".<br>");
</script>
</body>
</html>
```

Figure 8.63: Calculating a delivery date

The Boolean Object

A **Boolean object** is useful in applications where you need the results of conditional tests. It has two possible values: true and false. These values can represent truth or falsehood, on or off, yes or no, or anything else that can be stored in one bit. The Boolean object is used to convert a non-Boolean value to a value of true or false. It is defined using the **Boolean()** keyword, like this:

```
var booleanTest=new Boolean()
```

If the Boolean object has no initial value, or if it is 0, -0, null, blank, false, undefined, or NaN (not a number), it is set to false. If it is not one of these values, it is true. Boolean objects have the methods shown in Table 8.12.

Table 8.12: Boolean Object Methods	
Method	Description
toString()	Used to convert the result of a Boolean test and return the result as a string
valueOf()	Used to return the primitive value of a Boolean object

Math Objects

The **Math object** enables you to perform common mathematical tasks. This object is most likely to be used when more than simple arithmetic is required for the coding solution. The Math object's properties, listed in Table 8.13, represent certain constant values needed in arithmetic.

Table 8.13: Math Object Properties	
Property	**Description**
Math.E	Euler's constant
Math.LN2	Natural log of 2
Math.LN10	Natural log of 10
Math.LOG2E	Log base-2 of E
Math.LOG10E	Log base-10 of E
Math.PI	Pi
Math.SQRT1_2	Square root of 0.5
Math.SQRT2	Square root of 2

These properties can be used in regular mathematical expressions. For example, the following statement obtains the circumference of a variable named diameter:

```
Circumference = diameter * Math.PI
```

The Math object also includes methods, listed in Table 8.14. With the exception of the Math.random() method, all Math object methods take one or more values as parameters.

Table 8.15: Math Object Methods	
Method(parms)	**Description**
Math.abs(n)	Absolute value of n
Math.acos(n)	Arc cosine in radians of n
Math.asin(n)	Arc sine in radians of n
Math.atan(n)	Arc tangent in radians of n
Math.atan2($n1,n2$)	Angle of polar coordinates $n1$ and $n2$
Math.ceil(n)	Next integer greater than or equal to n
Math.cos(n)	Cosine of n
Math.exp(n)	Euler's constant to the power of n
Math.floor(n)	Next integer less than or equal to n
Math.log(n)	Natural logarithm base E of n
Math.max($n1, n2$)	The greater of $n1$ or $n2$
Math.min($n1, n2$)	The lesser of $n1$ or $n2$
Math.pow($n1, n2$)	$n1$ to the $n2$ power
Math.random()	Random number between zero and one
Math.round(n)	Rounds to the next integer
Math.sin(n)	Sine in radians of n

Table 8.15: Math Object Methods (continued)	
Method(parms)	Description
Math.sqrt(*n*)	Square root of n
Math.tan(*n*)	Tangent in radians of n

The code in Figure 8.64 shows some uses of the Math object's methods. The results of this code are shown in Figure 8.65.

```
<html>
<body>
<script type="text/javascript">
// JS08106 Math Object Properties Examples
document.write("Absolute value of 133.17 is " + Math.abs(133.17) + "<br/>")
document.write("Absolute value of -133.17 is " +Math.abs(-133.17) +
"<br/>")
document.write("Absolute value of 133.17 minus 225.17 is " +Math.abs(133.17
- 225.17) + "<br/>")
document.write("Display a Random Number " + Math.random() + "<br/>")
document.write("Display Another Random Number " + Math.random() + "<br/>")
document.write("The Square Root of 10 is "+ Math.sqrt(10) + "<br/>")
document.write("The Square Root of 121 is "+ Math.sqrt(121) + "<br/>")
</script>
</body>
</html>
```

Figure 8.64: Using Math object methods

```
Absolute value of 133.17 is 133.17
Absolute value of -133.17 is 133.17
Absolute value of 133.17 minus 225.17 is 92
Display a Random Number 0.6953919309453365
Display Another Random Number 0.6771415344548015
The Square Root of 10 is 3.1622776601683795
The Square Root of 121 is 11
```

Figure 8.65: The results from the code in Figure 8.64

JavaScript Arrays

An array is a structure for storing and manipulating ordered collections of data. As a business application programmer, you are probably already familiar with arrays, but we will provide a brief review here.

An array can be visualized as a table, like a spreadsheet. In JavaScript, an array is limited to a one-column table, with as many rows as needed. Dimensional arrays can be created using an array of objects. That is beyond the scope of this chapter, but it is important to understand that the capability exists.

Previous code samples in this chapter have used arrays. For example, Figure 8.66 repeats the code from Figure 8.36, showing an example of a for loop. This example defines an array using the following statement:

```
Var Book = new Array()
```

```
<html>
<body>
<script type="text/javascript">
// JS08108 Simple Array Example
var x
var Book = new Array()
Book[0] = "SQL Unleashed"
Book[1] = "Web Services for Everyone"
Book[2] = "PHP Hot Scripts"
Book[3] = "jQuery Uplifts Your Web Application"
Book[4] = "Modernize Your Applications with Ruby on Rails"
Book[5] = "Application Modernization"
for (x in Book)
{
document.write(Book[x] + "<br />")
}
</script>
</body>
</html>
```

Figure 8.66: A simple array example

The array is defined as a new variable named Book. Values are *populated* (loaded) into the array using square brackets to designate the array index. The example array is populated with values as follows:

```
Book[1] = "Web Services for Everyone"
Book[2] = "PHP Hot Scripts"
Book[3] = "jQuery Uplifts Your Web Application"
Book[4] = "Modernize Your Applications with Ruby on Rails"
Book[5] = "Application Modernization"
```

Finally, the for loop cycles through the array elements and prints their contents, as shown in Figure 8.67.

SQL Unleashed
Web Services for Everyone
PHP Hot Scripts
jQuery Uplifts Your Web Application
Modernize Your Applications with Ruby on Rails
Application Modernization

Figure 8.67: The results from Figure 8.66

Array Methods

Table 8.16 lists JavaScript array object methods.

Table 8.16: JavaScript Array Object Methods	
Method	**Description**
array.concat()	Joins multiple arrays and returns the result
array.every()	Checks all array elements pass a test
array.filter()	Creates a new array with all elements that pass a test
array.indexOf()	Searches an array for an element and returns the elements position
array.join()	A string of entries from the array, delimited by the separatorString value. The join method is used to join all the elements of an array into a single string, separated by a specified string separator. If no separator is specified, the default is a comma.
array.lastIndexOf()	Searches an array for an element, starting at the end position of the array, and returns the position of the element
array.pop()	Removes and returns the last element of an array
array.push()	Adds one or more elements to the end of an array and returns the new length
array.reverse()	Returns an array of entries in the opposite order
array.shift([,])	Removes and returns the first element of an array
array.slice()	Returns selected elements from an existing array
array.some()	Checks an arrary to determine if any of the elements within the array pass a test
array.sort()	Sorts the elements of an array
array.splice()	Removes and adds new elements to an array
array.toString()	Converts an array to a string and returns the result
array.unshift()	Adds one or multiple elements to the beginning of an array and returns the new length
array.valueOf()	Returns the primitive value of the array object

The example in Figure 8.68 puts the array object method sort and reverse to use. Figure 8.68 uses the same array as the previous example, but the array is populated a little differently. The array's elements are all listed on the variable definition line, separated by commas. This example lists the array contents, sorts the array, writes the contents, reverses the order of the array and writes the contents. As shown in Figure 8.69, the contents of the array are displayed first in their original order, then in ascending order, and then in descending order.

```
<html>
<head>
<script type="text/javascript">
// JS08113 Array Object Method Sort Example
</script>
</head>
<body>
<script type="text/javascript">
var x
var Book = new Array("SQL Unleashed", "Web Services for Everyone", "PHP Hot
Scripts",
 "jQuery Uplifts Your Web Application", "Modernize Your Applications with
Ruby on Rails", "Application Modernization");

for (x in Book)
{
document.write(Book[x] + "<br />")
}

Book.sort();
document.write('Ascending : ' + Book + '<br />');
Book.reverse();
document.write('Descending : ' + Book + '<br />');

</script>
</body>
</html>
```

*Figure 8.68: An example of the **sort** array object method.*

> SQL Unleashed
> Web Services for Everyone
> PHP Hot Scripts
> jQuery Uplifts Your Web Application
> Modernize Your Applications with Ruby on Rails
> Application Modernization
> Ascending: Application Modernization,jQuery Uplifts Your Web Application,Modernize Your
> Applications with Ruby on Rails,PHP Hot Scripts,SQL Unleashed,Web Services for Everyone
> Descending: Web Services for Everyone,SQL Unleashed,PHP Hot Scripts,Modernize
> Your Applications with Ruby on Rails,jQuery Uplifts Your Web Application,Application
> Modernization

Figure 8.69: An array unsorted, sorted ascending, and sorted descending

At this point, you have seen several of the JavaScript objects available for use. This chapter does not include a complete list of objects available, but you have seen enough to know how powerful they are and how easy it is to use predefined objects.

Events

Events are actions that can be used within JavaScript. They are a significant component of JavaScript, providing a means to make use of the objects available, based on a user's action. Events enable you to create dynamic Web pages. Many Web-page elements have events associated with them that can trigger functions to execute an action.

Event Handlers

One way to embed client-side JavaScript into HTML documents is to use the event-handler attributes of HTML tags. Event handlers were a new addition to HTML in HTML 4.0. The current versions of the more popular browsers, including Chrome, Edge, Firefox, Internet Explorer, Opera, and Safari, all support event handlers. Table 8.17 lists some common event handlers that can be used in HTML tags.

Table 8.17: Some Common Event Handlers	
Handler	Event Triggered By
onabort	Image load aborted
onblur	Window or element loses keyboard focus
onchange	Displayed value changes
onclick	Mouse click and release
ondblclick	Mouse double-click
onerror	Image or document loading fails
onfocus	Window or element gets keyboard focus
onkeydown	Key pressed
onkeypress	Key pressed and released
onkeyup	Key released

Table 8.17: Some Common Event Handlers (continued)	
Handler	Event Triggered By
onload	Document, image, or object loaded
onmousedown	Mouse button pressed
onmousemove	Mouse moved
onmouseout	Mouse moves off element
onmouseover	Mouse moves over element
onmouseup	Mouse button released
onreset	Form reset requested
onresize	Window size changes
onselect	Text selected
onsubmit	Form submission requested
onunload	Document unloaded

Event handlers are quite easy to use, and their possibilities in connection with JavaScript functions are endless. For example, within a business application, a click of a button might display an order's status. A double-click on a product image might trigger the display of the product's details and price. A mouse-over on a location name might trigger the address of the location to be displayed. The following pages show examples of some common event handlers.

Onclick

The **onclick** event handler is triggered when the mouse button is pressed and released. The example in Figure 8.70 uses onclick to display an order's status when the button in Figure 8.71 is clicked.

```html
<html>
<head>
<script type="text/javascript">
/* JS08116 Event handler onclick Example */
function orderStatus()
{
/* Example to calculate delivery date */
var shipDate=new Date();
var deliveryDate=new Date();
deliveryDate.setDate(shipDate.getDate()+4);
document.write("Your order is scheduled to ship on " +shipDate + ".<br>");
document.write("Your order will arrive by " +deliveryDate + ".<br>");
}
</script>
</head>
```

Continued

```
<body>
<input type="button" value="Display Order Status" onclick="orderStatus()"
/>
</body>
</html>
```

Figure 8.70: An example of the onclick event handler

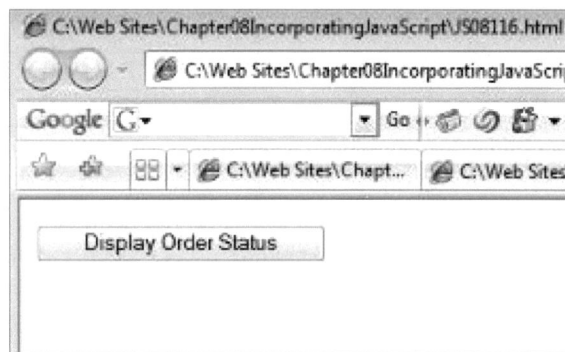

Figure 8.71: The button that will trigger the orderStatus function when clicked

The result of the event is the following messages:

```
Your order is scheduled to ship on Sun Jan 17 2016 21:15:47 GMT-0500 (Eastern
Standard Time).
Your order will arrive by Thu Jan 21 2016 21:15:47 GMT-0500 (Eastern Standard
Time).
```

Onmousedown

In the example in Figure 8.72, when the mouse button is pressed down while on the image in Figure 8.73, the "Belhur Publishing" address will be displayed. If you click anywhere else on the screen, no action is triggered. The **onmousedown** event does not gurantee that an onclick event will occur on the same target. For example, if you mouse over a link and then press and hold the click button, and then move off the link and release the button, the link will not be clicked.

```
<html>
<head>
<script type="text/javascript">
/* JS08118 Event handler onmousedown Example */
function displayAddress()
{
document.write("Belhur Publishing " + ".<br>");
```

Continued

```
document.write("123 Sunshine Drive "  + ".<br>");
document.write("Big Town, MI 97568 " + ".<br>");
document.write("(313) 264-3975 "  + ".<br>");
}
</script>
</head>
<body>
<img src="images/Belhur.JPG" width="276" height="200"
onmousedown="displayAddress()">
</body>
</html>
```

Figure 8.72: An example of the onmousedown event handler

Figure 8.73: This image is replaced with an address when the onmousedown event occurs

Onerror

Earlier in this chapter, you saw how try catch throw can be used to control responses when errors are encountered on a Web page. The onerror event can also be used to control errors. This event is triggered when an error is encountered on a page.

To use onerror, a function must be created to handle the errors. The function is called with the following arguments:

- msg—the error message
- url—the URL of the page that caused the error
- line—the line where the error occurred

The value returned by onerror determines the error message. If it returns false, the browser displays the standard error message in the JavaScript console. If it returns true, the browser does not display the standard error message.

In the example in Figure 8.74, a button is displayed (shown in Figure 8.75), prompting the user to display a welcome message. When the button is pressed, an error is encountered because within the code, adalert is spelled incorrectly as *aaaaaddddlert*. When the error is encountered, the onerror event is triggered. It calls a function to display a message with the error, URL address, and line number of the error, as shown in Figure 8.76. The error message prompts the user to click **OK** to continue.

```html
<html>
<head>
<script type="text/javascript">
/* JS08121 Event Handler onerror Example */
onerror=handleErr
var messageTxt=""
function handleErr(msg,url,l)
{
messageTxt="There was an error on this page.\n\n"
messageTxt+="Error: " + msg + "\n"
messageTxt+="URL: " + url + "\n"
messageTxt+="Line: " + l + "\n\n"
messageTxt+="Click OK to continue.\n\n"
alert(messageTxt)
return true
}
function message()
{
aaaaaddddlert("Welcome to Belhur Publishing!")
}
</script>
</head>
<body>
<input type="button" value="Display Welcome Message" onclick="message()" />
</body>
</html>
```

Figure 8.74: An example of the onerror event handler

Figure 8.75: The initial result of the code in Figure 8.74

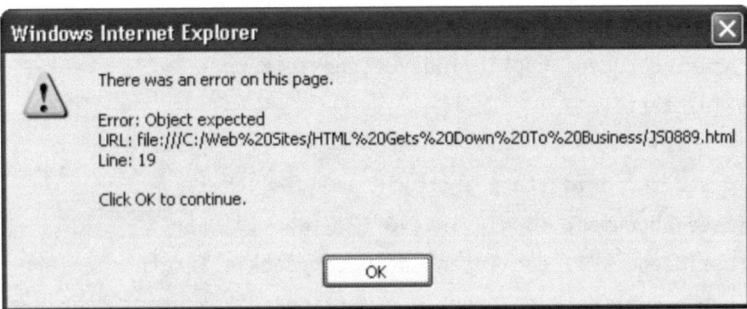

Figure 8.76: The error message displayed when the button is clicked

Events used to trigger actions make your Web application more dynamic and user-friendly.

Cookies

A cookie is a variable that is stored on the visitor's computer by a Web page. Each time the same computer requests the page with a browser, it sends the cookie, too. With JavaScript, you can both create and retrieve cookie values.

Cookies can be used for a variety of reasons. A cookie might be used to control the message displayed when the user visits a site, to retain a password so a returning user won't be required to enter it, or to store the date so the user can see the last time he or she visited the site.

In the cookie example in Figure 8.77, the first time a user visits the website, a prompt is displayed, requesting the user's name. The next time the user visits the site, he or she will not be prompted for a name. Instead, a "welcome back" message will be displayed.

To accomplish this, a cookie stores the user's name on the user's client computer. In this example, the cookie is set to expire after 30 days. When the cookie expires, the next time the user visits, he or she will again be prompted for a name, and that new name will be stored in the cookie. The cookie requires three functions: one to check to see if the cookie exists for this user, the second to store the name of the user if a cookie does not exist, and the third to display the user-name prompt or "welcome back" message.

```
<html>
<head>
<script type="text/javascript">
/* JS08124 Cookie Example
/* function to check to see if cookie exists for the user */
/* the cookies are stored in the document cookie object */
/* if a cookie is found the value will be returned, or if not found, */
/* an empty string will be returned */
function retreiveCookie(cookie_name)
{
if (document.cookie.length>0)
```

Continued

```
    {
    cookid_start=document.cookie.indexOf(cookie_name + "=")
    if (cookid_start!=-1)
      {
      cookid_start=cookid_start + cookie_name.length+1
      cookid_end=document.cookie.indexOf(";",cookid_start)
      if (cookid_end==-1) cookid_end=document.cookie.length
      return unescape(document.cookie.substring(cookid_start,cookid_end))
      }
    }
return ""
}
/* function that stores the name of a cookie in a variable*/
/* the parameters of the function hold the name of the cookie, the value */
/* of the cookie and the number of days until the cookie expires */

function storeCookie(cookie_name,value,expiredays)
{
var exdate=new Date()
exdate.setDate(exdate.getDate()+expiredays)
document.cookie=cookie_name+ "=" +escape(value)+
((expiredays==null) ? "" : ";expires="+exdate.toGMTString())
}
/* if the cookie user name exists, a welcome back message will be */
/* displayed; if not, the user will be prompted to enter their user */
/* name and the store cookie function will be called */
function checkCookie()
{
username=retreiveCookie('username')
if (username!=null && username!="")
  {alert('Welcome back to Belhur Publishing '+username+'!')}
else
  {
  username=prompt('Please enter your user name:',"")
  if (username!=null && username!="")
    {
    storeCookie('username',username,30)
    }
```

Continued

```
    }
}
</script>
</head>
<body onLoad="checkCookie()">
</body>
</html>
```

Figure 8.77: An example of creating and using a cookie

The first time the user runs the application, the screen shown in Figure 8.78 is displayed. The next time the same user accesses the application, the screen in Figure 8.79 is displayed (as long as the cookie hasn't expired).

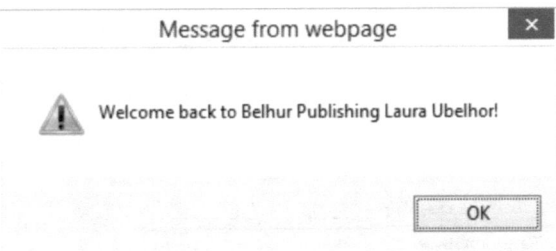

Figure 8.78: The cookie requesting the user's name the first time the page loads

Figure 8.79: The cookie displaying the welcome screen on subsequent page loads

Cookies can be used within business applications to display and use user-specific information, just like that information is used in traditional applications.

JavaScript Form Validation

Form validation is the process of checking that a form is filled out as expected. For example, an email address or phone number can be validated for the correct format, or required fields can be validated to ensure the user does not leave them blank. JavaScript can be used to validate data in an HTML form before sending that data to a server. Validation using JavaScript happens instantly because it takes place on the client rather than on the server.

Because form validation is one of the most valuable uses of JavaScript for the business application developer, the example in this section is a little more detailed and complex than most of the examples in this chapter. It uses a basic HTML form, shown in Figure 8.80, along with a number of functions to perform various form-validation tasks. The form requests a first name, last name, email address, phone number, message, and response. All the fields are required. The email address must be in a valid format, the phone number must be numeric, and the response field must be chosen from a pull-down list. Review the form before reviewing the code.

Figure 8.80: The customer service form to be validated

Defining the form is a pretty easy task using standard HTML tags. Figure 8.81 has the code for the page, as well as a reference to the JavaScript file JS08129.js, which contains the functions that will be used to validate the form data. (Coding forms in HTML is covered in more detail in chapter 9.)

```html
<html>
<head>
<script language="JavaScript" src="js scripts/JS08129.js" type="text/
javascript">
//JS08128 Form Validation Example
</script>
</head>
<body>
<p>Welcome to Belhur Publishing Customer Service Page.</p>
<p> Please enter your message and press the Submit button.
</p>
<form action="" name="myform" >
<table cellspacing="2" cellpadding="2" border="0">
<tr>
    <td align="right">First Name</td>
    <td><input type="text" name="FirstName"></td>
</tr>
<tr>
    <td align="right">Last Name</td>
    <td><input type="text" name="LastName"></td>
</tr>
<tr>
    <td align="right">Email Address</td>
    <td><input type="text" name="Email"></td>
</tr>
<tr>
    <td align="right">Phone #</td>
    <td><input type="text" name="Phone"></td>
</tr>
<tr>
    <td align="right">Message</td>
    <td><textarea cols="20" rows="5" name="Message"></textarea></td>
</tr>
<tr>
    <td align="right">Response</td>
    <td>
        <SELECT name="Response">
            <option value="" selected>[please choose]
```

Continued

```
                    <option value="001">No Response
                    <option value="002">Phone Call
                    <option value="003">Email Reply
            </SELECT>
            </td>
</tr>
<tr>
    <td align="right"></td>
    <td><input type="submit" value="Submit"></td>
</tr>
</table>
</form>
<script language="JavaScript" type="text/javascript">
  var frmvalidator  = new Validator("myform");
  frmvalidator.addValidation("FirstName","req","Please enter your First
Name");
  frmvalidator.addValidation("FirstName","maxlen=20",
      "Max length for FirstName is 20");
  frmvalidator.addValidation("FirstName","alpha");
  frmvalidator.addValidation("LastName","req");
  frmvalidator.addValidation("LastName","maxlen=20");
  frmvalidator.addValidation("Email","maxlen=50");
  frmvalidator.addValidation("Email","req");
  frmvalidator.addValidation("Email","email");
  frmvalidator.addValidation("Phone","maxlen=25");
  frmvalidator.addValidation("Phone","req");
  frmvalidator.addValidation("Message","maxlen=150");
  frmvalidator.addValidation("Message","req");
  frmvalidator.addValidation("Response","dontselect=0");
</script>
</body>
</html>
```

Figure 8.81: The code that creates the customer service form.

Validation can be done in many ways. This example uses a JavaScript class to make form validation easier. Figure 8.82 is the code for the JavaScript class, stored in the JS08129.js file. Functions have been created to complete various validation tasks, and a set of validation descriptors is associated with each of the form-field elements. The validation descriptors are strings specifying the type of validation to be performed. Each of the fields on the form has multiple validations.

```
/* JS08129 Form validation functions */
function Validator(frmname)
{   this.formobj=document.forms[frmname];
        if(this.formobj.onsubmit)
        {   this.formobj.old_onsubmit = this.formobj.onsubmit;
            this.formobj.onsubmit=null;
        }
        else
        {       this.formobj.old_onsubmit = null;
        }
                this.formobj.onsubmit=form_submit_handler;
                this.addValidation = add_validation;
                this.setAddnlValidationFunction=set_addnl_vfunction;
                this.clearAllValidations = clear_all_validations;
}

/* Additional Validation Function */
function set_addnl_vfunction(functionname)
{ this.formobj.addnlvalidation = functionname;
}
/* Clear all validations function */
function clear_all_validations()
{   for(var itr=0;itr < this.formobj.elements.length;itr++)
        {   this.formobj.elements[itr].validationset = null;
        }
}

/* form submit handler function */
function form_submit_handler()
{   for(var itr=0;itr < this.elements.length;itr++)
        {   if(this.elements[itr].validationset &&
            !this.elements[itr].validationset.validate())
                { return false;
                }
        }
        if(this.addnlvalidation)
        { str =" var ret = "+this.addnlvalidation+"()";
          eval(str);
    if(!ret) return ret;
```

Continued

```
        }
        return true;
}


/* add validation function */
function add_validation(itemname,descriptor,errstr)
{ if(!this.formobj)
        {
           alert("ERROR: the form object is not set properly");
                return;
        }// end if
        var itemobj = this.formobj[itemname];
  if(!itemobj)
        { alert("ERROR: Could not get the input object named: "+itemname);
                return;
        }
        if(!itemobj.validationset)
        { itemobj.validationset = new ValidationSet(itemobj);
        }
  itemobj.validationset.add(descriptor,errstr);
}
/* Validation descriptuon function */
function ValidationDesc(inputitem,desc,error)
{    this.desc=desc;
        this.error=error;
        this.itemobj = inputitem;
        this.validate=vdesc_validate;
}
/* Vdesc validate function  */
function vdesc_validate()
{ if(!V2validateData(this.desc,this.itemobj,this.error))
  {        this.itemobj.focus();
                return false;
  }
 return true;
}
/* Validation set function */
function ValidationSet(inputitem)
```

Continued

```
{   this.vSet=new Array();
      this.add= add_validationdesc;
      this.validate= vset_validate;
      this.itemobj = inputitem;
}
/* Add validation description */
function add_validationdesc(desc,error)
{     this.vSet[this.vSet.length]=
         new ValidationDesc(this.itemobj,desc,error);
}
/* Vset validate function */
function vset_validate()
{   for(var itr=0;itr<this.vSet.length;itr++)
      {    if(!this.vSet[itr].validate())
              {   return false;
              }
      }
      return true;
}
/* Email validation function */
function validateEmailv2(email)
{
    if(email.length <= 0)
      { return true;
      }
    var splitted = email.match("^(.+)@(.+)$");
    if(splitted == null) return false;
    if(splitted[1] != null )
    { var regexp_user=/^\"?[\w-_\.]*\"?$/;
      if(splitted[1].match(regexp_user) == null) return false;
    }
    if(splitted[2] != null)
    { var regexp_domain=/^[\w-\.]*\.[A-Za-z]{2,4}$/;
      if(splitted[2].match(regexp_domain) == null)
      { var regexp_ip =/^\[\d{1,3}\.\d{1,3}\.\d{1,3}\.\d{1,3}\]$/;
          if(splitted[2].match(regexp_ip) == null) return false;
      }// if
      return true;
```

Continued

```
        }
return false;
}
/* Validate data function  */
function V2validateData(strValidateStr,objValue,strError)
{   var epos = strValidateStr.search("=");
    var  command  = "";
    var  cmdvalue = "";
    if(epos >= 0)
    { command  = strValidateStr.substring(0,epos);
      cmdvalue = strValidateStr.substr(epos+1);
    }
    else
    { command = strValidateStr;
    }
    switch(command)
    { case "req":
        {
          if(eval(objValue.value.length) == 0)
          {
            if(!strError || strError.length ==0)
            {
              strError = objValue.name + " : Required Field";
            }//end if
            alert(strError);
            return false;
          }//end if
          break;
        }//case required
      case "maxlen":
        { if(eval(objValue.value.length) >  eval(cmdvalue))
            { if(!strError || strError.length ==0)
              {
                strError = objValue.name + " : "+cmdvalue+" characters
maximum ";
              }//end if
              alert(strError + "\n[Current length = " + objValue.value.
length + " ]");                    return false;
            }//end if
```

Continued

```
             break;
        }//case maxlen
     case "alpha":
        { var charpos = objValue.value.search("[^A-Za-z]");
          if(objValue.value.length > 0 &&  charpos >= 0)
          {    if(!strError || strError.length ==0)
            { strError = objValue.name+": Only alphabetic characters
allowed ";
            }
            alert(strError + "\n [Error: character pos " +
eval(charpos+1)+"]");
              return false;
          }
          break;
        }//alpha
     case "email":
        {    if(!validateEmailv2(objValue.value))
           { if(!strError || strError.length ==0)
             { strError = objValue.name+": Enter a valid email address
";
             }
             alert(strError);
             return false;
           }
        break;
        }//case email
     case "dontselect":
       {  if(objValue.selectedIndex == null)
          { alert("ERROR: dontselect command for non-select Item");
            return false;
          }
          if(objValue.selectedIndex == eval(cmdvalue))
          { if(!strError || strError.length ==0)
            {
            strError = objValue.name+": Please select a response ";
            }//end if
            alert(strError);
            return false;
          }
```

Continued

```
        break;
    }//case dontselect
}//switch
return true;
}
```

Figure 8.82: The JavaScript functions to validate the form

This example uses a lot of the JavaScript functionality described in this chapter. Let's look more closely at the application. The code in Figure 8.81 includes a reference to the external JavaScript file in Figure 8.82 with the following tag:

```
<script language="JavaScript" src="js scripts/JS08129.js"
type="text/javascript">
```

Referencing the external file is like including the additional code within the <head> section of the HTML page. Having the code in a separate file enables it to be reused by any application within the site. (In a real-world situation, a more meaningful name would be used for the file, such as formfieldvalidation.js.)

If no information is entered within the form and the user clicks the **Submit** button, the message in Figure 8.83 is displayed. The FirstName field is defined on the form within the HTML page with the code snippet in Figure 8.84.

Figure 8.83: The validation message for a missing first name

```
<tr>
    <td align="right">First Name</td>
    <td><input type="text" name="FirstName"></td>
</tr>
```

Figure 8.84: The FirstName form field definition

The action begins when the user clicks the **Submit** button, causing the script code in Figure 8.85 to be executed. This code first defines a variable named frmvalidator, which is the validator object that will be used for form-field validation. This variable is passed the name of the form, myform. Next, validations are added, such as the validations for the FirstName field shown in Figure 8.85.

```
var frmvalidator  = new Validator("myform");
  frmvalidator.addValidation("FirstName","req","Please enter your First Name");
  frmvalidator.addValidation("FirstName","maxlen=20",
      "Max length for FirstName is 20");
  frmvalidator.addValidation("FirstName","alpha");
```

Figure 8.85: The JavaScript to validate the first name

The first argument is the name of the field, FirstName. The second argument is the validation descriptor used to specify the type of validation to be performed. The third argument is the message that will be displayed if the field value does not pass validation. Using this technique requires that the validators be defined within the HTML page after the </form> end tag. The form-validation function code is executed. If the validation is false, the message will be displayed.

Suppose you entered a first name longer than the maximum allowed length of 20 characters. Because of the data validation, the message in Figure 8.86 would be displayed, indicating the maximum length allowed and the length of the value entered.

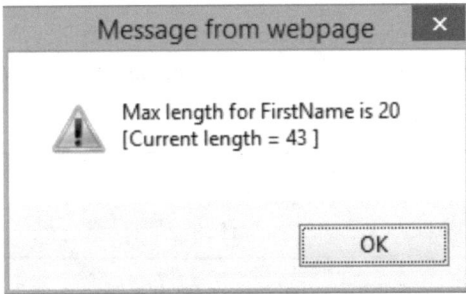

Figure 8.86: The validation message displayed when the first name exceeds the maximum length

As you continue testing each of the field validations on the form page, note that the "Response" form field has been defined as a list of values, as shown in Figure 8.87.

```
<SELECT name="Response">
            <option value="" selected>[please choose]
            <option value="001">No Response
            <option value="002">Phone Call
            <option value="003">Email Reply
    </SELECT>
```

Figure 8.87: The creation of the "Response" form field

When the user clicks the pull-down tab, the list of values for the response is displayed, as shown in Figure 8.88. The user would select a response from the list.

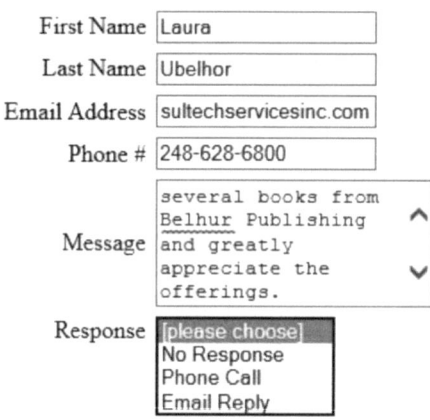

Figure 8.88: The pull-down list

Notice also the Message field, which is defined as a text area with 20 columns and 5 rows. The code in Figure 8.89 validates that the field is not left blank and doesn't exceed the maximum of 150 characters.

```
frmvalidator.addValidation("Message","maxlen=150");
frmvalidator.addValidation("Message","req");
```

Figure 8.89: The validators for the Message field

The data-validation example in this section uses just a few of the validation descriptors available. Table 8.18 provides a more complete list of the descriptors available.

Table 8.18: Validation Descriptors	
Descriptor	Description
alpha alphabetic	The value entered must be alphabetic data.
alnum alphanumeric	The value entered can only contain numbers and characters.
dontselect=99	This validator is used for input items in list boxes, when a selection is required. Usually, the index value 0 is associated with the default value of the list. The number referenced will correspond with the default value. In the example in Figure 8.81, the index is zero for the default value, *[please choose]*.
Email	The field value entered must be a valid email address.

Table 8.18: Validation Descriptors (continued)	
Descriptor	Description
gt=*999* greaterthan=*999*	The value entered is greater than the value passed. This validator is only for use with numeric fields.
lt=*999* lessthan=*999*	The value entered is less than the value passed. This validator is only for use with numeric fields.
num numeric	The value entered must be numeric data.
maxlen=*999* maxlength=*999*	The value entered is no longer in characters than the maximum value passed.
min=*999* minlength=*999*	The value entered is at least the same length in characters as the minimum value passed.
regexp=	The value is validated with a *regular expression*, which is a series of characters that defines a pattern. The value entered needs to match the pattern of the regular expression. For example, to validate for positive or negative number, you could use *regexp=^-{0,1}\d*\.{0,1}\d+$*. To ensure that a password was at least six symbols, you could use *regexp=^.{6,}$*
req required	The field value cannot be empty.

Summary

We have covered a lot of ground in this chapter, but even so, you have seen just a small amount of what can be done with JavaScript. Clearly, JavaScript is an essential tool for Web application development. It is easy to learn and browser-friendly. It can be used in coordination with other tools, including server-side programming languages.

JavaScript is often used for form validation. You will learn more about how forms are used in Web development in the PHP, ASP.NET, and JSP examples in chapters 9, 10, and 11.

After reading this chapter, you should understand the basic syntax of JavaScript, understand some of the tasks for which the language is suited, and have some experience working through the examples provided. After working through the examples, you will be ready to begin incorporating JavaScript into your Web business applications. When you are ready to go further, you can explore any of the many great websites that provide advanced code examples and forums for JavaScript developers to share ideas, experiences, and code.

Key Terms

array
array method
Boolean
Boolean object
break statement
case-sensitivity
catching errors
comments

compound statement
continue statement
cookies
data type
date object
defined function
empty statement
expression statement

events
event handlers
for loop
form validation
function
identifier
if statement
keyword

labeled statement	operator	syntax
loop	operator precedence	text string
math object	predefined function	try catch throw
number	return statement	variable
object	semicolon	while loop
onclick	string	
onmousedown	switch statement	

Discussion/Review Questions

1. Why would you use JavaScript for a Web application?
2. What can JavaScript do?
3. How can you add comments in JavaScript?
4. How are semicolons used in JavaScript?
5. What is a JavaScript variable?
6. What is a JavaScript data type?
7. What impact does operator precedence have in JavaScript?
8. What is an if statement?
9. How are switch statements used in JavaScript?
10. What is a compound statement?
11. How is a break statement used in JavaScript?
12. What is a while loop?
13. What is a function?
14. What two types of functions can be used in JavaScript?
15. What statement can be used to handle errors in JavaScript?
16. What is a JavaScript object?
17. What is the purpose of using arrays in JavaScript?
18. What are JavaScript events?
19. What is a cookie?

Exercises

1. Provide four examples of JavaScript operator precedence.
2. Provide a list of objects that can be used in JavaScript and an example of each.
3. Choose a JavaScript event and provide a code example (don't use an example provided within this chapter).
4. Write a script using if statements and an array.
5. Write a JavaScript function (don't use an example provided within this chapter).
6. Write a script to prompt for a username and password.

Web Development with PHP

Many languages can be used for server-side programming, including Java, JSP, ASP.NET, and PHP. This chapter introduces PHP, which stands for *PHP: Hypertext Preprocessor*. It is a scripting language embedded within HTML. Much of PHP's syntax is extracted from C, Java, and Perl, with some unique PHP-specific features. The goal of the language is to allow Web developers to write dynamically generated pages quickly. While PHP is mainly used for server-side scripting, it can also be used from a command-line interface or in standalone graphical user interface (GUI) applications. In this chapter, the focus is on server-side scripting with the business application developer in mind.

Introduction to PHP

PHP can be used to do anything any other Common Gateway Interface (**CGI**) programs can do, including retrieving and using input data, generating dynamic page content, and updating server-stored data. One of the most significant features of PHP is its support for a wide range of databases. Writing a **dynamic Web application**—one that can retrieve and store data—is very easy to do with PHP. Currently, PHP supports the following databases:

Access	FilePro (read only)	MSSql
Adabas D	Firebird	MSSqlPO
Ado	FilePro (read only)	MySQL
Ado_Access	FrontBase	MySQLi
Ado_MSSql	Hyperwave	MySQLt/MaxSql
dBase	iBase	Netzza
Direct MS-SQL	Informix	ODBC
DB2	Informix72	ODBC_MSSql
ODBC_DB2	Ingres	ODBC
Empress	Interbase	Oracle
FBSql	LDAP	ODBTP_Unicode

Oracle	Postgres (64 7 8 9)	Solid
OCI8	PostgreSQL	Sybase
OCI805	SAPDB	Velocis
OCI8Po	SQLAnywhere	UNIX dbm
Ovrimos	SQLite	Vfp
PDO	SQLitePO	

PHP's support of the Open Database Connectivity (**ODBC**) standard means it can be used to connect to any database that supports ODBC, including both Microsoft Access and SQL Server. Also, in addition to the databases listed, PHP can use a PDO extension, allowing use of any database supported by the PDO extension.

PHP may be used to solve business application needs, jazz up existing applications, create user interfaces, or make applications easily accessible for remote users without requiring additional software or hardware. You will learn the basics of PHP by reviewing examples in this chapter that show how to use it within Web business applications. Some knowledge of HTML will be helpful to understand these examples. If necessary, review the earlier chapters on HTML before proceeding.

PHP Compared with Other Tools

There are, of course, many tools that can be chosen for Web development. Choosing the best technologies for a development project is a complicated subject. How do you decide whether to learn PHP, and what would you use it for? Comparing PHP with other tools will help you decide whether or not to include it in your toolkit.

PHP Versus JavaScript

PHP and JavaScript are technically quite different languages. As discussed in chapter 8, JavaScript is intended for client-side computing; its code is executed locally at the browser on whatever device is being used. PHP, on the other hand, can be executed on the server. PHP is much more robust than JavaScript and is intended for tasks that cannot be done with JavaScript. For example, PHP easily interacts with a wide variety of databases and other server-side applications. JavaScript requires other tools to interact with a database.

Both PHP and JavaScript share roots in C and Java, so their syntax and statements are similar. Both languages are also embedded within HTML. Whether to use PHP or JavaScript will depend on your need for client-side versus server-side functionality. It might make sense to use PHP and JavaScript together in an application.

PHP Versus ASP.NET

ASP.NET is not really a language; rather, it is a Web-application framework, developed originally by Microsoft and now open source. (*Open source* refers to a program whose source code is available to the general public for use and/or modification from its original design, free of charge.) ASP is an acronym for *Active Server Pages*, and .NET refers to Microsoft's .NET Framework. ASP.NET supports several languages, including Visual Basic, C#, and J#. The biggest drawback of ASP.NET is that it is used primarily with Microsoft Internet Information Server (IIS), although efforts are under way to expand its portability and tools are available to use other servers.

Like ASP.NET, PHP is open source; it is also quite portable. PHP, like many other open source programs, has been created as a collaborative effort, in which programmers continue to improve upon the code and share the changes with the open source community.

PHP can run on almost any platform. Some developers consider PHP to be more stable and less resource-intensive than ASP.NET. ASP.NET is said by some developers to be slower and more cumbersome. ASP.NET, however, is easier to learn than PHP. While PHP isn't difficult, ASP.NET is very easy, especially if a developer has Visual Basic knowledge. Some developers also say PHP is more robust for adding advanced features like support for FTP servers, data parsing, and connectivity.

PHP Versus Java

Like JavaScript, PHP and Java are technically quite different, although the syntax of the languages is similar. Here is a brief overview of how PHP and Java differ:

- PHP supports fewer data types than Java. In addition to Boolean, integer, float, string, array, and object, Java supports char, byte, short, and long data types. (Data types are discussed later in this chapter.)
- PHP requires that variables start with a dollar sign ($), while Java doesn't. Both PHP and Java use case-sensitive variables. (Variables are discussed later in this chapter.) In PHP, a variable is declared when it is created, and the type is implied by the assigned value. Within PHP, a variable type can be changed by assigning a new value. In Java, variables must be declared with a specific data type before use.
- PHP includes libraries and Java imports libraries.
- Within PHP, constants are defined through **functions** (discussed later in this chapter). In Java, constants are defined like other variables.
- PHP passes method parameters by value and by reference. Java passes by value only.
- Both PHP and Java support function calls, but function calls are easier with PHP.
- Java supports polymorphism as a built in feature. PHP does not.
- PHP is considered a dynamic scripting langue, whereas Java is considered a **strongly typed language**. A strongly typed language means explicit statements of intent to function are required and required by a compiler.
- Some developers consider PHP to be better suited to smaller, Web-based applications, since its features are geared toward script coding and that Java is more general-purpose and suited for larger applications.
- PHP is an easier language to learn and grow into than Java. A new coder can begin writing Web applications more quickly with PHP and grow into functionality over time.
- Java is compiled; PHP is interpreted.
- PHP and Java are both *server-side languages*. Server-side means they run and execute from the hosting server through a browser. *Client-side languages* run and execute from the end user's computer through a browser.
- PHP code is executed on a server; Java is executed on the client. Java requires having Java Runtime Environment (JRE) on the client. PHP doesn't require having additional software loaded on the client.

- PHP is open source, whereas Java is not. Both PHP and Java are free.
- PHP and Java are both widely accepted and used for Web development. Java has a reputation of being more robust than PHP. PHP has changed significantly over the years and continues to add functionality. Java has been around a lot longer and has a large user community. PHP has not been around as long, but has grown rapidly in popularity because of its short learning curve and ease of use and also has a large user and support community and a larger set of support resources.

PHP is used for many businesses' websites. Java and JSP shine in large projects, where carefully developed objects can be reused and refined. Large projects imply in-house, dedicated servers to support the website, rather than a hosted site.

Both PHP and Java are well supported. PHP and Java technology may be used together in an application.

PHP's Advantages and Disadvantages

PHP is easily embedded in HTML and has the advantage of being executed on the server. One of the biggest advantages of PHP is that it is very easy for a programmer to learn and offers many advanced features to fulfill the development needs of a business application programmer. Table 9.1 reviews other advantages, as well as disadvantages, of using PHP. The review is relative to other Web development technologies.

Table 9.1: PHP's Advantages and Disadvantages	
Advantages	Explanation
Easy to learn	PHP has a very short learning curve. Programmers can learn the language and become productive quickly.
Easy to use	Scripting is easy to use; many programmers like PHP's ease of use.
Inexpensive	PHP is open source and free for both commercial and non-commercial use and development.
Extensive server support	PHP supports all common servers.
Extensive browser support	All popular browsers support PHP.
Extensive database access capability	PHP supports an extensive number of databases.
Widely used	Very popular, heavily used, and currently "in vogue," PHP has a large base of developers and users. It is easy to find programmers who are fluent in PHP.
Extensive user support	A massive body of information, examples, and blogs exist to support the large community of PHP users and developers. Several sites are dedicated to providing information and support for PHP, including *www.php.net* and *www.zend.com*.
Many extensions	PHP has many extensions with a wide variety of features, such as XML manipulation and encryption. There is also extensive source code available that can be used to quickly to put together advanced applications.
Transparent compilation	PHP is compiled before it is executed, using a special byte-code format. Compilation is transparent to programmers and users. Changes can be made to a PHP page, and the results can be seen immediately in a browser without an additional compile step like JSP.
Quick performance	PHP has been noted for its execution speed. When used for heavy database interaction, PHP performs well compared with other programming languages.

Table 9.1: PHP's Advantages and Disadvantages (continued)	
Disadvantages	Explanation
Relatively slow computation	PHP is probably not the best choice for applications requiring heavy computation or intense, detailed business logic. Java technologies or .NET may be better in these cases.
Open source	Most organizations are receptive to open source technologies, but some are not.
Viewable source code	PHP source code is frequently embedded in HTML, like other scripting languages, and can be easily viewed by users. For most applications, this is not an issue, but for applications that include sensitive information, it needs to be addressed.
Error-handling issues	PHP error-handling is currently not as robust as some of the other Web development languages. The PHP community is aware of this, and efforts are in progress to improve error-handling.

PHP is a good fit for many application requirements. PHP can be learned quickly, an advantage for an organization that has little or no in-house Web development skills. If the budget is limited, PHP may well be a good fit. If application requirements dictate accessing data from a variety of databases, PHP may also be the right choice. If the requirements include heavy computation and complicated business logic, however, other technologies may be a better fit—or you might consider using other languages in combination with PHP.

Introduction to PHP

PHP is a server-side, cross-platform scripting language. Like JavaScript, PHP code can be embedded into HTML. Unlike JavaScript, PHP executes on the Web server, not the client browser. *Cross-platform* means that PHP scripts can run on many different operating systems and Web servers, and supports the most popular configurations. PHP is currently available for the following operating systems:

- FreeBSD
- IBM i
- Linux
- Mac OS X
- NetBSD
- OpenBSD
- OpenSolaris
- UNIX
- Windows

As mentioned earlier, PHP is free. The main implementation is provided through the PHP Group and released under the PHP license. PHP requires software to be downloaded, installed, and configured. The installation of PHP produces a configuration file named php.ini that contains configuration values, controls the behaviors of PHP, and provides the capability to configure PHP to work with most platforms comfortably. PHP was created in 1994 and was released for use by the general public shortly thereafter. The language has evolved greatly over the years and continues to be enhanced to provide additional functionality and features.

PHP is easy to learn for someone with no Web programming experience, but offers advanced features for experienced programmers. The syntax is very similar to Perl and C. A PHP file may contain HTML tags, text, and scripts. PHP files have the extension *.php*, or *.phtml*. This chapter uses *.php* for examples.

What Can PHP Do?

PHP, like most server-side scripting languages, is an excellent tool for creating dynamic websites that incorporate database content. PHP uses external libraries and functions, making the language easy to use and providing extensive functionality. Functions make the language very robust and powerful. This chapter provides several examples of how functions can be used to incorporate PHP within business application websites.

Here are some example uses for PHP:

- Process an inquiry application requiring retrieval of data from a database, such as an inventory inquiry, an order inquiry, or an employee work-schedule inquiry.
- Read and process data.
- Connect to, read, and process database contents, as in an online-ordering or a customer-feedback application.
- Serve different content based on a user's ID and password, or characteristics of a user's environment (such as browser, IP address, and time). For example, based on a user's characteristics, display either a manager or an employee page.
- Provide a customer or employee feedback mechanism.
- Display images or text documents, such as a product catalog including detailed product pictures and product detail, or a contact list displaying employee pictures and contact information.
- Supply business-specific programming logic.

Preparing for PHP

To complete the examples in this chapter, you must have a PHP-capable server installed and configured; PHP needs to be downloaded, installed, and tested; and a compatible database needs to be made available. Also, check to make sure your browser is PHP-compatible. (Most recent versions of popular browsers are.)

You can download PHP from *www.php.net/downloads.php*. Download instructions are provided on the site. The site also provides details on which servers and databases are supported for use with PHP. (Server and database configuration is not covered in this chapter.) The examples in this chapter use the IBM i OS, DB2 for the database, and Apache for the Web server.

PHP code is often indented to make it easier to read. While there is not an official standard for indenting, unofficial conventions for indentation are often used. Some of the examples in this chapter do not include indentation, however, for the sake of formatting the code to fit within a text page. Keep in mind that indentation is not necessary, but can make code easier to read and work with.

Basic PHP Syntax

When PHP parses a file, it looks for opening and closing tags, which tell it to interpret the code between them. Parsing allows PHP to be embedded in all sorts of different documents, as everything outside of the opening and closing tags is ignored by the PHP parser.

Tags

A PHP block usually starts with the <?php tag and ends with the ?> tag. Everything in between is PHP program code rather than HTML. Alternatively, a <script> tag similar to that for JavaScript may be used. The tag <script language= "php"> tells PHP that everything that follows is PHP program code rather than HTML until the closing </script> tag is encountered, as shown in Figure 9.1.

```
<html>
<body>
<script language="php">
 </script>
</body>
</html>
```

Figure 9.1: PHP script tags

Figure 9.2 is a simple script that sends the text "Welcome to Belhur Publishing!" to be displayed. Any application text can be displayed this way. Rather than "Welcome to Belhur Publishing," for example, the text might be "XYZ Company Inventory Inquiry," "Mr. Widgets Purchase Order Inquiry Page," or whatever text is applicable to the business application being coded.

```
<html>
<body>
<?php
//  PHP0902.php
Echo "Welcome to Belhur Publishing";
?>
</body>
</html>
```

Figure 9.2: A simple PHP script

Statement Terminator

The semicolon is used as a **statement terminator** to indicate the end of a PHP command. The semicolon is not required, but it is good practice to always include it to show that a command is completed.

Comments

Comments can be included anywhere within the PHP script to document your code or make it more readable. Comments used in PHP are no less important than comments used in any other programming language. They often make ongoing support easier because they enable other developers to understand your code. As with any other language in a business environment, documentation standards for PHP should be defined, including standards for comments.

Two types of comments can be used in PHP:

- Two slashes (//) indicate a single-line comment. Everything to the end of the current line is considered a comment and ignored.
- The combination "/*" and "*/" indicates a single- or multiple-line comment. Everything between the /* and */ characters is considered a comment and ignored.

Figure 9.3 shows both kinds of comment lines included in a PHP script.

```
</html>
<head>
</head>
<body>
<?php
/*  PHP0903.php
    This script displays welcome text
*/
echo "Welcome to Belhur Publishing!"; // display welcome text
?>
</body>
</html>
```

Figure 9.3: PHP comments

Echo

The **echo** command is used to send text to the browser for display. The command is quite simple, starting with the word echo followed by a variable, or the text you would like displayed in quotation marks, and ending with a semicolon. Figure 9.3 uses echo to display *Welcome to Belhur Publishing!*

Variables

Variables are used for storing values, including text strings, numbers, or arrays. (Arrays are discussed later in this chapter.) A variable in PHP must start with a dollar sign. Once a variable is set in PHP, it can be used over and over again within a script.

Unlike some other Web programming languages, PHP is a **loosely typed language**, meaning you can assign a value to a new variable whenever you would like and start using the variable. Variables do not need to be declared before they are used. PHP will automatically convert variables to the correct data type depending on the values used to set the variables. In a *strongly typed* language, you need to declare or define the variable and the variable name and type before you are able to use it.

Here is a summary of the variable-naming rules for PHP:

- A variable must start with the dollar sign.
- A variable name must start with an underscore (_) or a letter.
- A variable cannot contain spaces. If a variable name contains more than one word, separate the words with underscores or use capitalization to distinguish them, as in *$variable_name* or *$variableName*.
- Variable names are case-sensitive ($books and $BOOKS are two different vairables).
- A variable name can contain only alphanumeric characters and underscores. Special characters cannot be used.

The syntax for setting a variable in PHP is as follows:

```
$variableName = value;
```

Figure 9.4 is an example of setting a variable value with a string and a variable with a number.

```
</html>
<head>
</head>
<body>
<?php
/* PHP0905 Defining Variables */
$text1 = "Welcome to Belhur Publishing ";
$number1 = 1017;
echo $text1;
echo $number1;
?>
</body>
</html>
```

Figure 9.4: Setting a variable string and number value

In this example, the text1 string is set to the value "Welcome to Belhur Publishing" and the number1 number is set to the value 1017, so the message *Welcome to Belhur Publishing 1017* would be displayed in the Web browser.

Expressions

The value of a variable assignment does not have to be a fixed value. It can be an expression. An **expression** is two or more values combined using an operator to produce a result, like this:

```
$sum = 16 + 30;
Echo $sum;
```

In this example, the variable $sum takes the value of the expression to the right of the equal sign. The value of 16 is added to 30, so the result would display the number 46 using the echo command.

Taking the example one step further, the same addition operation can be performed on two variables:

```
$qty1 = 16;
$qty2 = 30;
$totalqty = $qty1 + $qty2;
echo $totalqty;
```

The values of $qty1 and $qty2 are added together, and using echo, the number 46 would again be displayed.

Data Types

Every variable that holds a value also has a **data type** that defines what kind of value it is holding. The basic data types in PHP are listed in Table 9.2.

Table 9.2: Data Types		
Data Type	Description	Value
Boolean	A truth value	Either true or false
Integer	A numeric value	Either a positive or negative whole number
Double or float	A floating-point numeric value	Any decimal number
String	An alphanumeric value	Any number of ASCII characters
Array	Stores multiple values in one single variable	Any number of ASCII characters
Object	Stores data and information on how to process that data	Declared as a class of object. A class is a structure that can contain properties and methods.
NULL	Special data type which can only have the value NULL. NULL has no value assigned.	NULL
Resource	The storing of a reference to functions and resources external to PHP	A database call

The data type of a variable is set when a value is assigned. The data type is determined automatically based on the value assigned. The gettype function can be used to determine the PHP data type. Figure 9.5 is an example of using the gettype function. In this case, the result returned will be "double."

```
</html>
<head>
</head>
<body>
                                                              Continued
```

```
<?php
/* PHP0909 gettype Function Example */
$price = 9.999;
echo gettype($price);
?>
</body>
</html>
```

Figure 9.5: The gettype function

Operators

The standard **operators** used by most other scripting languages are also used within PHP. Tables 9.3 through 9.6 list the supported operators.

Table 9.3: Arithmetic Operators			
Operator	Description	Example	Result
+	Addition	x=5, y=7 x+y	12
-	Subtraction	x=3, y=1 x-y	2
*	Multiplication	x=2, y=4 x*y	8
/	Division	x=4, y=2 x/y	2
%	Modulus (division remainder)	x=5, y=2 x%y	1 (remainder of 5/2)
++	Increment	x=2 x++	3
--	Decrement	x=2 x--	1

The basic **assignment operator** is the equal sign (=). It doesn't mean "equal to"; rather, it means that the left operand is set to the value of the expression on the right. In addition to this basic assignment operator, there are "combined operators" for all the binary arithmetic and string operators that allow you to use a value in an expression and then set its value to the result of that expression.

Table 9.4: Assignment Operators				
Operator	Description	Example	Result	Is the Same as
=	Assignment	y=2 x=y	x=2	x=y
+=	Increment assignment	x=2, y=3 x+=y	x=5	x=x+y

Table 9.4: Assignment Operators (continued)				
Operator	Description	Example	Result	Is the Same as
-=	Decrement assignment	x=5, y=3 x-=y	x=2	x=x-y
*=	Multiplication assignment	x=5, y=3 x*=y	x=15	x=x*y
/=	Division assignment	x=6, y=2 x/=y	x=3	x=x/y
%=	Modulus assignment	x=6, y=5 x%=y	x=1	x=x%y

Comparison operators, as the name implies, allow you to compare two values.

Table 9.5: Comparison Operators			
Operator	Description	Example	Result
==	Is equal to	x=5, y=5, z=7 x==y x==z	 True False
!=	Is not equal to	x=5, y=5, z=7 x!=y x!=z	 False True
>	Is greater than	x=5, y=6, z=3 x>y x>z	 False True
<	Is less than	x=5, y=6, z=3 x<y x<z	 True False
>=	Is greater than or equal to	x=5, y=6, z=3 x>=y x>=z	 False True
<=	Is less than or equal to	x=5, y=6, z=3 x<=y x<=z	 True False

In addition to comparison operators, PHP also uses **logical operators**. Logical operators are typically used when you want to test more than one condition at a time.

Table 9.6: Logical Operators			
Operator	Description	Example	Result
&&	And	x=5 x==5 && x<3 x>3 && x==5	 False True
||	Or	x=5 x>3 || x>6 x==4 || x==3	 True False
!	Not	x=5 !(x==5) !(x==4)	 False True

Conditional Statements

A **conditional statement** is used to perform actions based on whether a condition is true or false. They provide the ability to perform different actions for different decisions. Conditional statements are case-sensitive and must be written in lower case, as shown in Table 9.7.

Table 9.7: Conditional Statements	
Statement	**Description**
if	Code is executed only if a specified condition is true.
if else	One block of code is executed if the condition is true, and another block of code is executed if the condition is false.
elseif	One of multiple blocks of code is executed when the condition used in the block of code is true.
switch	This statement is similar to a series of *if* statements on the same expression. It is useful when you want to compare the same variable or expression with many different values, and execute a different block of code depending on which value it is equal to.

If Statements

The **if statement** is used when code is to be executed when a single condition is true.

```
if (condition)
code to execute if condition is true;
```

In the example in Figure 9.6, an initial welcome message, *Welcome to Belhur Publishing Employee Page*, is displayed. Then, the password is set to BelhurEmployee. The if condition is now true, so another welcome greeting, *Welcome to the Employee Work Schedule Page*, is displayed. Note that the <br> tags result in the messages being on separate lines.

```
<html>
<body>
<?php
/* PHP0911 - Example if statement */
echo("Welcome to Belhur Publishing Employee Page" . "<br>");
$password = "BelhurEmployee";
if ($password=="BelhurEmployee")
        echo ("Welcome to the Employee Work Schedule Page" .  "<br>");
?>
</body>
</html>
```

Figure 9.6: An example of the if statement

The **if else statement** is used when code is to be executed when a single condition is false.

```
if (condition)
code to execute if condition is true;
else
code to execute if condition is false;
```

The example in Figure 9.7 is very similar to Figure 9.6, but we have added code to include an else.

```
<html>
<body>
<?php
/* PHP0914 - Example if else statement */
echo("Welcome to Belhur Publishing Employee Page" . "<br>");
$password = "BelhurManager";
if ($password=="BelhurEmployee")
        echo ("Welcome to the Employee Work Schedule Page" .  "<br>");
else
        echo ("The Password is invalid." .  "<br>");
?>
</body>
</html>
```

Figure 9.7: An example of if else

Making this change, if the password value is anything other than "BelhurEmployee," a message will be displayed informing the site user that the password is invalid, as shown in Figure 9.8.

Password entered is not = "BelhurEmployee"

Welcome to Belhur Publishing Employee Page.
The Password is Invalid

Figure 9.8: The results from Figure 9.7 for an invalid password

The **if elseif else statement** is used when multiple conditions are tested. When the if condition is true, the block of code associated with that statement will be executed. When it is not true, the elseif condition will be tested, and if true, the associated block of code will be executed. The statement might contain multiple elseif statements. Finally, when the if and all the elseif conditions are not true, the final else is used to associate a block of code to execute.

```
if (condition1)
code to execute if condition is true;
elseif (condition2);
code to execute if condition2 is true;
```

```
else
    code to execute if condition1 and 2 are false;
```

The if elseif else example will use forms and two documents, PHP0917.html and PHP0917.php, shown in Figure 9.9. Any form element in an HTML page will automatically be made available to your PHP scripts. The HTML page includes a form to prompt the user for a password. When the user enters a password and clicks **Submit**, the form data is sent to the PHP0917.php file. The password is then used for conditional logic.

```
HTML document PHP0917.html:

<html>
<body>
Welcome to Belhur Publishing!
<form action="PHP0917.php" method="post">
Password: <input type="text" name="password"/>
<input type="submit" />
</form>
</body>
</html>


PHP document PHP0917.php:

<html>
<body>
<?php
/* PHP0917 - Example elseif statement */
if ($_POST["password"] == "BelhurEmployee")
        echo ("Welcome to the Employee Work Schedule Page" .  "<br>");
elseif ($_POST["password"] == "BelhurManager")
        echo ("Welcome to the Manager Work Schedule Page" .  "<br>");
else
        echo ("The Password Entered is Invalid" .  "<br>");
?>
</body>
</html>
```

Figure 9.9: The if elseif else statement

The conditional logic of the if elseif else statement controls the actions performed. As shown in Figure 9.10, if the user enters the password "BelhurEmployee", the message *Welcome to the Employee Work Schedule* is displayed. If the user enters the password "BelhurManager", *Welcome to the Manager Work Schedule Page* is displayed. Otherwise, the message *The Password Entered is Invalid* is displayed.

Password entered = "BelhurEmployee"

Welcome to the Employee Work Schedule Page

Password entered = "BelhurManager:

Welcome to the Manager Work Schedule Page

Any other Password entered:

The Password Entered is Invalid

Figure 9.10: The results from the code in Figure 9.9

The Switch Statement

The **switchstatement** is used to execute one of multiple blocks of code. It is often used in place of a long if elseif else statement to execute one of multiple blocks of code. The **case**, **default**, and **break** keywords are often used with switch. The break keyword will end execution of the switch when the case condition is true.

```
switch(expression)
case 1:
   execute code block 1;
   break;
case 2:
   execute code block 2;
 default:
   execute code block when case 1 and case 2 are false;
```

The example in Figure 9.11 is very similar to the one in Figure 9.9. In fact, the prompt screen is exactly the same. Again, the password is passed, but this time, the code uses switch, case, break, and default to handle the different conditions. The results will be the same as Figure 9.9.

```
HTML Document PHP0921.html:

<body>
Welcome to Bellhur Publishing!
<form action="PHP0921.php" method="post">
Password:
  <input type="text" name="password"/>
<input type="submit" />
</form>
</body>
</html>
                                              Continued
```

```
PHP Document PHP0921.php:
<html>
<body>
<?php
/* PHP0921 - Example switch statement */

switch ($_POST["password"])
{
case "BelhurEmployee":
        echo ("Welcome to the Employee Work Schedule Page" .  "<br>");
        break;
case "BelhurManager":
        echo ("Welcome to the Manager Work Schedule Page" .  "<br>");
        break;
default:
        echo ("The Password Entered is Invalid" .  "<br>");
}
?>
</body>
</html>
```

Figure 9.11: The switch statement

Notice the syntax of case in Figure 9.11: curly braces enclose the statements, and break is used when a match is found so that the remaining case statements are not executed. The default statement provides the action when none of the criteria are true. The same example could be used for many other applications, including customer and vendor inquiries.

Loops

PHP has two types of **loops**, the **while loop** and the **for loop**. The for loop executes the same block of code a specified number of times. The while loop executes a block of code when a condition is true.

While Loops

The syntax for a while loop is quite simple:

```
while(condition)
statement
```

The loop will repeat until the condition is no longer true. Figure 9.12 defines a loop that displays the line count when the condition variable $count is less than five. The variable $count is initialized to one before the loop begins and is incremented by one each time the loop is executed, resulting in the following:

```
Belhur Line 1
Belhur Line 2
Belhur Line 3
Belhur Line 4
```

```
<html>
<body>
<?php
/* PHP0923 - Example of while loop */
$count=1;
while($count<5)
  {
  echo "Belhur Line " . $count . "<br />";
  $count++;
  }
?>
</body>
</html>
```

Figure 9.12: The while loop

The **do while loop** is a variation on the while loop. This loop always executes a block of code once, and then repeats the loop as long as the condition is true. The condition is tested after the loop statement(s) are executed.

```
do
{
statement;
statement;
}
while (condition);
```

Figure 9.13 defines a loop that will execute at least once and will execute while the condition variable $count is less than zero. The variable $count is incremented by one each time the loop is executed. The statement is true until $count is no longer less than zero. This loop always executes at least once, as shown in the results in Figure 9.14.

```
<html>
<body>
<?php
/* PHP0926 - Example of do while loop */
$count=0;
```
                                                                    Continued

```
do
{
 echo "Belhur Line " . $count . "<br />";
 $count++;
 }
while ($count<0);
?>
</body>
</html>
```

Figure 9.13: The *do while* loop

Belhur Line 0

Same Example Change line of code while ($count<0) to while ($count<=5).

Belhur Line 0
Belhur Line 1
Belhur Line 2
Belhur Line 3
Belhur Line 4

Figure 9.14: The results from executing the code in Figure 9.13

For Loops

The for loop repeats the specified condition until the condition is false. A for loop begins with an expression to initialize counters. Next, the condition of the expression is evaluated and followed by an expression to increment the counter. If the condition is false, the loop terminates. If the condition is true, the loop's statements execute. Multiple statements can be included using curly braces and semicolons.

```
for (initialization; condition; increment)
{
statement;
statement;
}
```

The example in Figure 9.15 begins with variable **$count** being initialized to one. The loop will continue to run as long as $count is less than or equal to four, resulting in the following:

```
Belhur Line 1
Belhur Line 2
Belhur Line 3
Belhur Line 4
```

```
<html>
<body>
<?php
/* PHP0929 - Example for loop */
for ($count=1; $count<=4; $count++)
{
echo "Belhur Line " . $count . "<br />";
}
?>
</body>
</html>
```

Figure 9.15: The for loop

The foreach loop is used to loop through arrays. For each loop, the value of the current array element is assigned to a variable. The array index is incremented by one, and the next cycle through the loop will look at the next element in the array.

```
foreach (array as value)
{
statement;
statement;
}
```

The example in Figure 9.16 executes the echo statement for each element in the Belhur Publishing book array, as shown in Figure 9.17.

```
<html>
<body>
<?php
/* PHP0932 - Example foreach loop */
$belhurpublishingbookarray=array("Web Services for Everyone", "PHP
Hot Scripts", "jQuery Uplifts Your Web Application", "Modernize Your
Applications with  Ruby on Rails", "Application Modernization",
"Integrating Legacy Code on the Web");
foreach ($belhurpublishingbookarray as $value)
{
echo $value . "<br />";
}
?>
</body>
</html>
```

Figure 9.16: The foreach loop.

Web Services for Everyone
PHP Hot Scripts
jQuery Uplifts Your Web Application
Modernize Your Applications with Ruby on Rails
Application Modernization
Integrating Legacy Code on the Web

Figure 9.17: The results from the code in Figure 9.16

Arrays

An **array** is a variable type that can store and index a set of values. Arrays are useful for data that has something in common or is logically grouped, like the array that contains Belhur Publishing books in Figure 9.16. An array can be visualized as a table, like a spreadsheet. Like most other programming languages, PHP is capable of using arrays, although its syntax may be a little different than you are used to.

Arrays are stored with a unique key, usually referred to as an *index*. The index provides each element of data an ID so that it can be easily accessed. Array indexes are usually numeric, but can also be another assigned value. Array indexing, if not specified, begins with the numeric index 0. In the example in Figure 9.18, the index is automatically assigned. In the example in Figure 9.19, the index is manually assigned.

```
$bookarray[ ] = "Web Services for Everyone";

$bookarray[ ] = "PHP Hot Scripts";

$bookarray[ ] = "jQuery Uplifts Your Web Application";

$bookarray[ ] = "Modernize Your Applications with Ruby on Rails";

$bookarray[ ] = "Application Modernization";

$bookarray[ ] = "Integrating Legacy Code on the Web";
```

Figure 9.18: An array with an index automatically assigned

```
$bookarray[0] = "Web Services for Everyone";

$bookarray[1] = "PHP Hot Scripts";

$bookarray[2] = "jQuery Uplifts Your Web Application";

$bookarray[3] = "Modernize Your Applications with Ruby on Rails";

$bookarray[4] = "Application Modernization";

$bookarray[5] = "Integrating Legacy Code on the Web";
```

Figure 9.19: An array with an index manually assigned

Once an array is defined and populated, it is ready to be used. An *associative array* uses a textual key for the index to make the index more descriptive. The examples in Figures 9.20 and 9.21 define arrays using associative indexes. The syntax is a little different for each. In Figure 9.20, the index is defined within single quotes, and the elements are within double quotes. In Figure 9.21, the index is in double quotes, and the symbol => is used to show the relationship between the index and the element value. Note that the array index must be unique.

```
$book['Web Services for Everyone'] = "69.95";
$book['PHP Hot Scripts']= "79.95";
$book['jQuery Uplifts Your Web Application'] = "59.95'";
$book['Modernize Your Applications with Ruby on Rails'] = "61.95";
$book['Application Modernization'] = "89.95";
$book['Integrating Legacy Code on the Web'] = "75.95";
```

Figure 9.20: One way to define an array with an associative index

```
$book = array("Web Services for Everyone" => 69.95, "PHP Hot Scripts" =>
79.95, "jQuery Uplifts Your Web Application" => 59.95, "Modernize Your
Applications with Ruby on Rails" => 61.95, "Application Modernization" =>
89.95, "Integrating Legacy Code on the Web" => 75.95);
```

Figure 9.21: An alternative way to define an array with an associative index

Arrays can be very useful, and there are limitless possibilities for using them within business applications. In the example in Figure 9.22, the bookarray is used to sort and display the list of books ordered by price, as shown in Figure 9.23. (This code also uses assort, a predefined function that can be used with arrays. Functions are explained later in this chapter.)

```
<html>
<body>
<?php
/* PHP0939 - Example sorted associative array */
$bookprice['Web Services for Everyone'] = "65.95";
$bookprice['PHP Hot Scripts'] = "72.95";
$bookprice['jQuery Uplifts Your Web Application'] = "64.95";
$bookprice['Modernize Your Applications with Ruby on Rails'] = "71.95";
$bookprice['Application Modernization'] = "82.95";
$bookprice['Integrating Legacy Code on the Web'] = "59.95";
asort($bookprice);
foreach ($bookprice as $book => $price)
{
echo "$book: $price <br />";
}
?>

                                                            Continued
```

```
</body>

</html>
```

Figure 9.22: An array with an associative index, sorted and displayed

Integrating Legacy Code on the Web: 59.95
jQuery Uplifts Your Web Application: 64.95
Web Services for Everyone: 65.95
Modernize Your Applications with Ruby on Rails: 71.95
PHP Hot Scripts: 72.95
Application Modernization: 82.95

Figure 9.23: The results from Figure 9.22

Multidimensional Arrays

PHP can also use multidimensional arrays. A **multidimensional array** is an array that contains more arrays. Think of it like a spreadsheet that has multiple rows and multiple columns. The multidimensional array is very similar to a regular array in how it is defined and used. The example in Figure 9.24 uses a multidimensional sales array. Within the sales array are the arrays Web Services and PHP Hot Scripts. The contents within the arrays represent the sales quantities by month; thus, there are 12 entries in each array.

```
<html>
<body>
<?php
/* PHP0941 Multidimensional array example sales by month for books*/
$sales = array
(
"Web Services"=>array
(
"5,000", "4,500", "4,750", "5,200", "5,000", "4,200",
"5,200", "4,960", "5,010", "4,325", "6,300", "7,200"
),
"PHP Hot Scripts"=>array
(
"3,000", "2,500", "3,750", "3,300", "3,000", "5,200",
"6,200", "3,020", "5,010", "3,325", "4,300", "5,300"
)
);
```

Continued

```
print_r ($sales);
echo "<br />";
echo "<br />";
echo "Sales for Web Services in January were ", $sales["Web Services"][0],
"<br />";
?>
</body>
</html>
```

Figure 9.24: A multidimensional array

This code prints out the value of the array using the print_r statement, as shown in Figure 9.25.

Array ([Web Services] => Array ([0] => 5,000 [1] => 4,500 [2] => 4,750 [3] => 5,200 [4] => 5,000 [5] => 4,200 [6] => 5,200 [7] => 4,960 [8] => 5,010 [9] => 4,325 [10] => 6,300 [11] => 7,200) [Hot and Spicy] => Array ([0] => 3,000 [1] => 2,500 [2] => 3,750 [3] => 3,300 [4] => 3,000 [5] => 5,200 [6] => 6,200 [7] => 3,020 [8] => 5,010 [9] => 3,325 [10] => 4,300 [11] => 5,300))

Sales for Web Services in January were 5,000

Figure 9.25: The results from Figure 9.24

Functions

Functions make the PHP scripting language very powerful. A function is used to define a task that may consist of many lines of code. Once defined, the function can be called using a single instruction. PHP has hundreds of predefined functions that perform a wide range of tasks. Some of the functions are built into the PHP language, and others are available only after specific extensions are installed and activated within PHP.

In this chapter, we will review some of the predefined functions. Appendix C (which you can download at *https://goo.gl/2uYjHb*) provides a more complete reference to these functions, but the list is still not all-inclusive. For a complete list, visit the official PHP website, *www.php.net*. This website provides extensive information about the PHP language and is a very useful reference.

Following is a list of some of the available PHP built-in functions. These functions are part of the PHP core language and require no special installation, except that the Linux platform requires a special update to the php.ini file for the calendar, FTP, and **MySQL** functions. You can find details on the configuration and update of php.ini at *www.php.net*.

- *Array functions*—allow you to manipulate arrays. There are also specific functions for populating arrays from database queries.
- *Calendar functions*—are useful when working with different calendar formats.
- **Date/time functions**—allow you to extract and format the date and time on the server. These functions depend on the local settings on the server. Date/time functions require runtime configuration through settings in the php.ini file.

- *DB2 functions*—enable access to IBM's DB2 Universal Database, IBM Cloudscape, and the Apache Derby databases using the DB2 Call Level Interface (DB2 CLI).
- *dBase functions*—let you access records stored in dBase-format (.dbf) databases.
- *Directory functions*—allow you to retrieve information about directories and their contents.
- *Error functions*—allow error-handling and logging. The error functions let users define error-handling rules and modify the way the errors can be logged. The logging functions let users log applications and send log messages to email, system logs, or other machines.
- *Filesystem functions*—allow you to access and manipulate the file system.
- *Filter functions*—validate and filter data coming from insecure sources, like user input.
- *FTP functions*—give client access to file servers through the File Transfer Protocol (FTP). The FTP functions are used to open, log in, and close connections, as well as upload, download, rename, delete, and get information on files from file servers. Not all the FTP functions work with every server or return the same results. These functions are meant for detailed access to an FTP server. If you only want to read from or write to a file on an FTP server, consider using the *ftp://* wrapper with the filesystem functions.
- *HTTP functions*—let you manipulate information sent to the browser by the Web server, before any other output has been sent.
- *Mail functions*—allow you to send emails directly from a script. For the **mail functions** to be available, you must have an installed and working email system. The program to be used is defined by the configuration settings in the php.ini file.
- *Math functions*—can handle values within the range of integer and float types.
- *Miscellaneous functions*—functions that do not fit within the other categories.
- *MySQL functions*—allow you to access MySQL database servers.
- *SimpleXML functions*—let you convert XML to an object. This object can be processed like any other object, with normal property selectors and array iterators. Some of these functions require the newest PHP build.
- *String functions*—allow you to manipulate strings.
- *XML parser functions*—let you parse, but not validate, XML documents.

As mentioned earlier, there are many more functions available through PHP, specific to particular databases, operating systems, FTP, Java, .NET, and many more. When coding business applications, you will use functions. These are the tools that make it easy to incorporate extended functionality within an application with very little coding.

Functions can be very useful, especially for code that is reused. Use a modular coding approach by grouping tasks into functions to help keep code more manageable. In addition to predefined, built-in functions, PHP functions can be user-defined. Every function has a prototype that defines how many arguments it takes, the arguments' data types, and what value is returned by the function. Optional arguments are shown in square braces ([ ]). This applies to both predefined and user-defined functions.

A function begins with the word *function*, followed by a function name that should identify what it does and parentheses that will hold any parameters. The name can start with a letter or an underscore, but not a number. The code executed when the function is called is contained within curly braces. Figure 9.26 is an example of creating a user-defined function that will display the welcome message *Welcome to Belhur Publishing!*.

```
<html>
<body>
<?php
/* PHP0943 User-defined function to display welcome message */
function display_welcome()
 {
echo "Welcome to Belhur Publishing!" . "<br />";
}
display_welcome();
?>
</body>
</html>
```

Figure 9.26: The display_welcome() user-defined function

The example in Figure 9.27 uses another user-defined function to calculate sales tax. This example involves a parameter contained within the function's parentheses and is used just like a variable.

```
<html>
<body>
<?php
/* PHP0945 User-defined function to calculate sales tax */
function salestax($amount)
{
$total = $amount * .06;
return $total;
}
$price = 65.95;
$taxamount = salestax($price);
$total = $taxamount + $price;
echo "Unit Price : " . $price . "<br />";
echo "Tax Amount : " . salestax($price) . "<br />";
echo "Total : " . $total;
?>
</body>
</html>
```

Figure 9.27: A user-defined function with a parameter

When the salestax() function is called in Figure 9.27, the block of code defined within the function will execute, using the argument stored in the variable $amount. In this example, salestax() is called once to calculate the value of the variable $taxamount. Next, the total is calculated by adding $price and $taxamount, and the value is returned from the function. The example then displays the unit price, tax amount, and total, as shown:

```
Unit Price : 65.95
Tax Amount : 3.957
Total : 69.907
```

The next example uses a function stored in a separate PHP file, shown in Figure 9.28. A separate file can contain common created functions for use on multiple site pages. The file is included within the current page using the include statement, as shown in Figure 9.29. The function in this example calculates an extended price using two parameters, the quantity and the price, passed to the function. After calling the function, the quantity, price, and extended price are displayed. Having a common function file enables you to make changes in one place to change the way a function works on many pages.

```
<html>
<body>
<?php
/* PHP0947 User-defined functions  */
function ext_price($price, $quantity)
{
$extprice = $price * $quantity;
return $extprice;
}
?>
</body>
</html>
```

Figure 9.28: A function included from a separate file

```
<html>
<body>
<?php
/* PHP0948 Calculate extended price */
include ("PHP0947.php");
$quantity = 5;
$price = 65.95;
echo "quantity " . $quantity . "<br />";
```
                                                                    Continued

```
echo "price " . $price . "<br />";
echo "extended price " . ext_price($quantity, $price);
?>
</body>
</html>
```

Figure 9.29: Calculating an extended price with a function from a separate file

With these examples, you can see how easy it is to define and use functions in PHP. Predefined functions work the same way.

Getting Down to Business with PHP

Now the fun begins. We'll introduce, discuss, and work through examples that can be used to provide PHP functionality within business Web applications.

Cookies

A **cookie** is a small file that is stored on the visitor's computer. Each time the same computer requests a page with a browser, it will send the cookie, too. PHP provides the ability to create and retrieve cookie values. Most current versions of popular browsers are capable of supporting cookies. A form may also be used to retain and pass data. Use of cookies allows functionality that may be similar to what has been used for other business applications that display a name, ID, or other information specific to an application user. Is this critical to a business application? It might be, depending on the specifics of an application. It is common to provide user-specific information or to use environment details to control application logic or for informational purposes.

Cookies can be used for a variety of reasons. A cookie might be used to control the message displayed when the user visits a site, retain a password so a returning user won't be required to enter it, or store the date so that the next time a visitor returns to the site, the date of the last visit is displayed. For example, a purchasing-department inquiry application might display the last date the user accessed the page, to make it easier for the user to identify new entries.

The predefined setcookie() function is used to create a cookie. This function must appear before the <html> tag. The instruction to create a cookie is sent as an HTTP header before a Web page is transmitted. A cookie has an expiration date. Some cookies only last as long as the Web browser is open and are kept in the client computer's memory. A cookie can also have a fixed expiration date and can be saved on the client's hard drive. The cookie will be removed when the browser is closed if the expires attribute is not sent in the setcookie() function.

In the example in Figure 9.30, the visitor's name will be retained in the cookie visitor_name. The cookie is set to expire 60 days from the last visit, using the time() function (60 seconds × 60 hours × 24 hours × 60 days = 5,184,000 seconds). In this example, the cookie is retained on the logout page. This is so we don't display the "welcome back" message the first time a user visits the page.

```
<?php
// PHP0949 Logout page retain visitor name
// information will be retained for 60 days
setcookie(visitor_name, "Joe Walsh", time()+5184000);
?>
<html>
<head>
</head>
<body>
Thank you for visiting Belhur Publishing!
</body>
</html></html>
```

Figure 9.30: Creating a cookie

In Figure 9.31, there is a check to determine whether the cookie exists. If it does, the name is used to format the "welcome back" message.

```
html>
<body>
<?php
/* PHP0950 check for cookie display welcome message */
if(isset($_COOKIE['visitor_name']))
{
$name = $_COOKIE['visitor_name'];
echo "Welcome back to Belhur Publishing! " .  $name;
}
else
{
echo "Welcome to Belhur Publishing!";
}
?>
</body>
</html>
```

Figure 9.31: Checking for a cookie and retrieving its value

This example will welcome back a site user who has visited within 60 days, as shown in Figure 9.32.

> **First time user visits site:**
>
> Welcome to Belhur Publishing!
>
> **On user's return visit within 60 days of last visit:**
>
> Welcome back to Belhur Publishing! Joe Walsh

Figure 9.32: The results from the cookie created and used in Figures 9.30 and 9.31

To delete a cookie, set the expiration date to a date in the past, as shown in Figure 9.33. The cookie will be removed.

```php
<?php
// PHP0951 Delete Cookie
setcookie(visitor_name, " ", time()-5184600);
?>
<html>
<head>
</head>
<body>
</body>
</html>
```

Figure 9.33: Deleting a cookie

The same cookie example may be used within many business applications, including a customer, vendor, or employee inquiry page, or any other place where this user-specific information would be useful.

Date/Time

Dates are an important part of business applications and are often used in programming logic. PHP does not have a native date data type, but it does have the date() function, which formats a timestamp to a readable date and time. A *timestamp* is the number of seconds since midnight on January 1, 1970. This is also known as the *UNIX timestamp*. The maximum value of a UNIX timestamp depends on the system's architecture. Most systems use a 32-bit integer to store a timestamp, in which case the latest time that can be represented is 3:14 a.m. on January 19, 2038.

To find the current timestamp, use the time() function. To provide the date in a particular format, use the date() function with a format code included as a parameter. Figure 9.34 uses time(), followed by date() with various format codes for different types of date formatting.

```
<html>
<body>
<?php
/* PHP0953 Date and Time function example  */
echo "Time function: " . time() . "<br />";
echo "Date function Format Codes:" . "<br />";
echo "a---Lowercase am or pm------------------------: " . date(a) . "<br />";
echo "A---Uppercase AM or PM------------------------: " . date(A) . "<br />";
echo "d---Two-digit day of month 01 - 31-------------: " . date(d) . "<br />";
echo "D---Three-letter day name Mon - Sun------------: " .date(D) . "<br />";
echo "F---Full month name January - December---------: " . date(F) . "<br />";
echo "g---12-hour hour with no leading zero 0 - 23---: " . date(g) . "<br />";
echo "G---24-hour hour with no leading zero 0 - 23---: " . date(G) . "<br />";
echo "h---12-hour hour with leading zero 01 - 12-----: " . date(h) . "<br />";
echo "H---24-hour hour with leading zero 00 - 23-----: " . date(H) . "<br />";
echo "I---Minutes with leading zero 00 - 59----------: " . date(I) . "<br />";
echo "j---Day of month with no leading zero 1 - 31---:  " . date(j) . "<br />";
echo "l---Full day name Monday - Sunday--------------:  " . date(l) . "<br />";
echo "m---Month number with leading zeros 01 - 12----:  " . date(m) . "<br />";
echo "M---Three-letter month name Jan - Dec----------:  " . date(M) . "<br />";
echo "n---Month number with no leading zeros 1 - 12--: " . date(n) . "<br />";
echo "s---Seconds with leading zero 00 - 59----------: " .date(s) . "<br />";
echo "S---Ordinal suffix for day of mo st,nd,rd or th: " .date(S) . "<br />";
echo "w---Number of day of week 0 - 6, 0 is Sunday---: " . date(w) . "<br />";
echo "W---Week number 0 - 53-------------------------: " . date(W) . "<br />";
echo "y---Two-digit year number----------------------: " . date(y) . "<br />";
echo "Y---Four-digit year number---------------------: " . date(Y) . "<br />";
echo "z---Day of year 0 - 365------------------------: " . date(z) . "<br />";
?>
</body>
</html>
```

Figure 9.34: The time() and date() functions

Figure 9.35 shows the results from running the code in Figure 9.34 for Tuesday, January 23, 2016, at 11:50 p.m.

```
← → C ⌂  ⌕ Laura/MCPRESS/PHP0953.PHP

Time function: 1468688360
Date function Format Codes:
a---Lowercase am or pm------------------------- pm
A---Upper case AM or PM----------------------- PM
d---Two digit day of month 01 - 31------------- 16
D---Three letter day name Mon - Sun------------ Sat
F---Full month name January - December--------- July
g---12 hour hour with no leading zero 0 - 23--- 4
G---24 hour hour with no leading zero 0 - 23--- 16
h---12 hour hour with leading zero 01 - 12----- 04
H---24 hour hour with leading zero 00 - 23----- 16
i---Minutes with leading zero 00 - 59---------- 0
j---Day of month with no leading zero 1 - 31--- 16
l---Full day name Monday - Sunday-------------- Saturday
m---Month number with leading zeros 01 - 12---- 07
M---Three letter month name Jan - Dec---------- Jul
n---Month number with no leading zeros 1 - 12-- 7
s---Seconds with leading zero 00 - 59---------- 20
S---Ordinal suffix for day of mo st,nd,rd or th th
w---Number of day of week 0 - 6, 0 is Sunday--- 6
W---Week number 0 - 53------------------------ 28
y---Two digit year number--------------------- 16
Y---Four digit year number-------------------- 2016
z---Day of year 0 - 365----------------------- 197
```

Figure 9.35: The results from the time() and date() functions

Characters like dashes, slashes, and periods, can be inserted in the date() parameter to provide additional formatting. For example, the code in Figure 9.36 would produce the results like this:

```
The current date is: Sunday February 14, 2016 05:0:31

The current date in YYYY/MM/DD format:2016/02/14
```

```
<html>
<body>
<?php
/* PHP0955 Formatted date function examples  */
echo "The current date is: " . date("l F d, Y H:I:s") . "<br />";
echo "<br />";
echo "The current date in YYYY/MM/DD format:" . date("Y/m/d");
?>
</body>
</html>
```

Figure 9.36: Adding additional formatting to date() examples

The date() function actually allows two parameters:

```
date(format, timestamp)
```

The previous examples used the format parameter. The timestamp parameter is optional. If it is not provided, the current time will be used.

The "make time" function, mktime(), can be used for date calculations. Its format is as follows:

```
mktime(hour,minute,second,month,day,year, is_dst)
```

The example in Figure 9.37 uses mktime() to calculate a date that is one year, one month, and one day in the future, to determine the account expiration date. If today's date was 01/24/2016, this example would display the following:

```
Today's date is: 01/24/2016
Your account will expire on: 02/25/2017
```

```
<html>
<body>
<?php
/* PHP0958 Make time function calculate date 1 year, 1 month and 1 day from
the current date example  */
$expire_date = mktime(0,0,0,date("m")+1, date("d")+1,date("Y")+1);
echo "Today's date is: " . date("m/d/Y") . "<br />";
echo "<br />";
echo "Your account will expire on: " . date("m/d/Y", $expire_date);
?>
</body>
</html>
```

Figure 9.37: The mktime() function

This section has only scratched the surface of date and time functionality, but the examples show how easy it is to work with dates in PHP and how powerful the predefined **date functions** are.

Email

Email is a commonplace form of communication that can be incorporated into a business application for internal or external communication. For example, when an order is placed, an order-entry application might email the department responsible for processing orders with the message that activity to process the order should begin. An email could also be sent to the customer, with details about the order, including the expected delivery schedule.

While some traditional application-development languages do not provide functionality for easily sending email, email can be easily sent through PHP using the mail() function. All that is needed is an installed and working email system, and for the email server to be identified in the php.ini file. The authentication and authorization for your email server might need to be reviewed to determine the settings. In Figure 9.38, the default settings are used with the sendmail_from address changed.

```
[mail function]
; For Win32 only.
;SMTP = localhost
smtp_port = 25

; For Win32 only.
sendmail_from = myemail@sbcglobal.net
```

Figure 9.38: The php.ini email settings

The format for the mail() function is as follows:

```
mail(to,subject,message,headers,parameters)
```

Sending a text message is the simplest way to send email using PHP. In Figure 9.39, a simple email message is sent to thank the customer for placing an order. In this example, the ini_set() function is used to set the value of the SMTP configuration.

```
<html>
<body>
<?php
/* PHP0962 Sending a text email example  */
ini_set('SMTP', 'mail.sbcglobal.net');
$to = "toemail@sbcglobal.net";
$subject = "Thank You";
$message = "Thank you for placing an order at Belhur Publishing!";
$from = "myemail@sbcglobal.net";
$headers = "From: $from";
mail($to,$subject,$message,$headers);
echo "Mail Sent.";
?>
</body>
</html>
```

Figure 9.39: A simple email example

The message "mail sent" will be displayed on the site page. Figure 9.40 is the resulting email sent.

Figure 9.40: The email sent as a result of the code in Figure 9.39

Email functions can also be used with forms. For example, you could use a feedback form to trigger an email. Figure 9.41 is such an HTML form, and Figure 9.42 is the PHP file used to send the email.

```
<html>
<head>
<!** PHP0965 Customer service email form example **>
<br>
<form method="post" action="PHP0966.php">
  Email: <input name="email" type="text" /><br />
  Customer Service Message:<br />
  <textarea name="message" rows="15" cols="40">
  </textarea><br />
  <input type="submit" />
</form>
</head>
</html>
```

Figure 9.41: The HTML to create a customer-service feedback form

```
<head>
<?php
/* PHP0966 Email form example */
ini_set('SMTP', 'mail.sbcglobal.net');
  $to = "myemail@sbcglobal.net";
  $email = $_REQUEST['email'] ;
  $message = $_REQUEST['message'] ;
  mail( $to, "Customer Service Feedback",$message, $email );
  echo "Email sent";
?>
</head>
</html>
```

Figure 9.42: The PHP to send an email based on the form in Figure 9.41

In this example, the form displayed in Figure 9.43 prompts for an email address and a customer-service message. When **Submit** is clicked, the PHP0966.php file is accessed to send the email. The $to variable is the email address that will receive the customer-service message.

Figure 9.43: The form created from Figure 9.41

The site user fills in the email address, enters a message, and clicks the **Submit** button. PHP0966.php is executed and displays the message *Email sent*. The resulting email is shown in Figure 9.44.

Figure 9.44: A customer-service email

Email Injection Attacks

The previous email examples have used hard-coded email addresses. PHP, like any language that uses the MIME and SMTP standards for sending email, has the potential problem of email injection. An *injection* is content inserted into the header level of an email. MIME and SMTP allow for multiple headers with the same name, enabling attackers to define additional recipients for a message or adding "bcc:" and "cc:". In addition, a message is open to attack. To prevent injections, input data should be validated or filtered when scripts are used for creating email.

The preg_match() function might be used to check for injections. This function performs a regular expression match, looking for a pattern, as shown in Figure 9.45. Alternatively, you might use the strpos() or strstr() function to check for the "at" sign (@) in an email address.

```
$email_address = '/^[^@\s]+@([-a-z0-9]+\.)+[a-z]{2,}$/i';
  if (!preg_match($email_address, $to_email))
  {
  echo "Email address entered is invalid.";
  }
```

Figure 9.45: Checking for multiple email addresses using preg_match()

Figure 9.46 shows an example use of this function.

```
<html>
<body>
<?php
/* PHP0971 email form example with email injection check */
function injectcheck($field)
  {
//preg_match function used to perform case-insensitive match on to: and
cc:.
// using cc:  will also catch bcc:.

  if(preg_match("to:",$field) || eregi("cc:",$field))
    {
    return TRUE;
    }
  else
    {
    return FALSE;
    }
  }

//check to verify email field has been entered
echo $_REQUEST['email'];

if (isset($_REQUEST['email']))
  {
  //check email address for injection
  $emailcheck = injectcheck($_REQUEST['email']);
  echo $email;
  if ($emailcheck==TRUE)
    {
```

                                                                    Continued

```
        echo "Email entered is invalid. Please correct and try again.";
      }
    else
      {
      //send email
      $email = $_REQUEST['email'] ;
      $message = $_REQUEST['message'] ;
      mail("To: $email", "Subject: $subject",
      $message, "ubelhor@sbcglobal.net" );


        echo "Email sent to" . $email;
      }
    }
  else
  //if the email address hasn't been entered, display the form
   {
     echo "<form method='post' action='PHP0972.php'>
     Email: <input name='email' type='text' /><br />
     Subject: <input name='subject' type='text' /><br />
     Customer Service Message:<br />
     <textarea name='message' rows='15' cols='40'>
     </textarea><br />
     <input type='submit' />
     </form>";
     }
  ?>
  </body>
  </html>
```

Figure 9.46: An email form with an email injection check

Figure 9.47 is an email form that can be used as a template to send an email. The message, subject, and email address will need to be changed to valid values for the application.

```
<html>
<head>
<?php
/* PHP0972 Email form example */
ini_set('SMTP', 'mail.sbcglobal.net');
  $to = $_REQUEST['email'];
```

Continued

```
    $email = "email@sbcglobal.net";
    $message = $_REQUEST['message'] ;
    $subject = $_REQUEST['subject'] ;
    mail( $to, $subject,$message, $email );
    echo "Email sent";
?>
</head>
</html>
```

Figure 9.47: A template for an email form

PHP Error Handling

PHP has a configurable error-reporting system that provides for a variety of error-reporting levels. The level can be changed through the error-reporting function with the error-reporting constants. Appendix C (which you can download at *https://goo.gl/2uYjHb*) lists error-logging constants. To set the error-reporting level so that all warnings and notices are displayed, use the error_reporting(E_ALL); setting.

The type of notices that are not displayed by default are not usually threatening and normally would not affect the execution of script. You may find it helpful to use a different error level for development than for a production website. Displaying errors on the screen on a production website might pose a security risk, by exposing information that is not intended to be shared with site visitors, especially not potential intruders or competitors. The log_errors and display_errors configuration directives let you choose to have warnings displayed on the screen or written to a log file. The display_errors directive can be set to off in the php.ini file to prevent any errors from being displayed on screen.

Figure 9.48 is a snippet of the php.ini default settings. The semicolon indicates a comment line in the file. By default, display_errors is turned on. To turn it off, uncomment the line within the php.ini file designating display_errors = Off by removing the semicolon at the beginning of the line.

```
; - display_errors = Off            [Security]
;     With this directive set to off, errors that occur during the
execution of
;     scripts will no longer be displayed as a part of the script output,
and thus,
;     will no longer be exposed to remote users.  With some errors, the
error message
;     content may expose information about your script, Web server, or
database
;     server that may be exploitable for hacking.  Production sites should
have this
;     directive set to off.
; - log_errors = On                 [Security]
                                                    Continued
```

```
;      This directive complements the above one.  Any errors that occur
during the
;      execution of your script will be logged (typically, to your server's
error log,
;      but can be configured in several ways).  Along with setting
display_errors to off,
;      this setup gives you the ability to fully understand what may have
gone wrong,
;      without exposing any sensitive information to remote users.
```

Figure 9.48: The php.ini error settings

Logging Errors

The error_log() function can be used to write an error message to the Web server log file or another local file, or to send the error message by email. When log_errors is turned on in the php.ini file, errors will be logged. The default is to write the errors to the PHP log file on the Web server. Sending errors to the site administrator is also an option and can be coded to send only selected error messages. Figure 9.49 is an example of sending an email to the site administrator when a particular error occurs.

```php
<html>
<head>
<?php
// PHP0974 - Send an email error message example
// Error handler function
function customError($errno, $errstr)
 {
 echo "<b>Error:</b> [$errno] $errstr<br />";
 echo "Error has been sent to the Webmaster";
 error_log("Error: [$errno] $errstr",1,
 "toemail@sbcglobal.net","From: fromemail@sbcglobal.net");
}
set_error_handler("customError",E_USER_WARNING);
//Check for and trigger error
$orderquantity=99;
if ($orderquantity>25)
 {
 trigger_error("Order quantity must be less than 25",E_USER_WARNING);
 }
?>
</head>
</html>
```

Figure 9.49: Logging errors via email

In this example, a custom error-handler function is created to send an email with the following error message to the webmaster:

```
Error: [512] Order quantity must be less than 25
```

This **error handler** could be added to a common function file, to be used by all the pages on a site. In this example, note that the error_log is passed parameters. The message type 1 is used to direct that the message to be sent via email. Note also that the to and from addresses will need to be changed to valid site email addresses.

Error-handling Components

Error handling is an important part of creating PHP scripts. Not handling errors can leave the site open to potential security risks, provide hackers or competitors the ability to access site information, or leave site visitors with the impression that the site is not friendly or professional. The previous examples cover some of the functionality of error handling. Now, let's look at the components more closely.

In Figure 9.50, the script tries to open a file that does not exist, so the following warning is displayed:

```
Warning: fopen(belhur.txt) [function.fopen]: failed to open
stream: No such file or directory in
C:\Inetpub\wwwroot\Belhur\PHP0976.php on line 5
```

This message provides a lot of information about the site that should not be shared.

```
<html>
<head>
<?php
// PHP0976 Example error handling open a file
$file = fopen("belhur.txt", "r")
?>
</head>
Warning: fopen(belhur.txt) [<A href="function.fopen">function.fopen</A>]:
failed to open stream: No such file or directory in
C:\Inetpub\wwwroot\Belhur\PHP0976.php on line 5
</html>
```

Figure 9.50: A script to open a file, with inappropriate error handling

To avoid this and handle the error, combine a check for the existence of the file with the die() function, as shown in Figure 9.51. This time, the results are much friendlier. If the file does not exist, the following message will be displayed:

```
File belhur.txt not found
```

```
<html>
<head>
<?php
// PHP0978 Example error handling. Open a file
// with a check the file exists and using the die
// function to exit the script.
if(!file_exists("belhur.txt"))
{
die("File belhur.txt not found");
}
else
{
$file = fopen("belhur.txt", "r");
}
?>
</head>
</html>
```

Figure 9.51: Error handling with die()

This example shows that when errors are handled properly, the results are much more secure and professional. Note that in this case, it works well to end the script and display a message, but ending the script might not always fit the application's needs.

A Custom Error-handler

The earlier example of sending an email to the webmaster used a custom error-handler. Now, let's look at this component more closely. Creating an error handler is quite simple. Custom functions can be defined and saved in a common function file to be shared by site pages and Web applications, eliminating the need for the same code in multiple pages. Here is an example of a custom error function:

```
error_function(error_level,error_message,
error_file,
error_line,error_context)
```

The first two parameters, error_level and error_message, are required; the others are optional. The error_level parameter refers to the error report level. For example, a value of 2 corresponds to E_WARNING. (Refer to Appendix C, which you can download at *https://goo.gl/2uYjHb*, for error-value constants and more information about the parameters.)

The example from Figure 9.49 will be used for a custom error function. Figure 9.52 is the function definition. This custom function uses the error_level and error_mesage parameters. When the function is triggered, it receives the error level and an error message. It then sends an email.

```
// PHP0974 - Send an email error message example
// Error handler function
function customError($errno, $errstr)
 {
 echo "<b>Error:</b> [$errno] $errstr<br />";
 echo "Error has been sent to the webmaster";
 error_log("Error: [$errno] $errstr",1,
 "toemail@sbcglobal.net","From: fromemail@sbcglobal.net");
 }
```

Figure 9.52: Creating a custom error function

To trigger the customError() function, we first need to set the error handler to point to the function:

```
set_error_handler("customError",E_USER_WARNING);
```

Next, we check for an error and trigger the error function. In Figure 9.53, an order quantity greater than 25 triggers the error. The actual value of the order in this example is 99, so the error function will be triggered.

```
//Check for and trigger error
$orderquantity=99;
if ($orderquantity>25)
 {
 trigger_error("Order quantity must be less than 25",E_USER_WARNING);
 }
```

Figure 9.53: Triggering the error function

When the error is triggered, the warning "Order quantity must be less than 25" is displayed. Then, the custom error function sends an email and causes the message "Error has been sent to the webmaster" to be displayed.

More advanced error management can be done with exception handling, to change the normal flow of script execution when an error is encountered. This works through a check or validation, or when a specific condition is encountered. Combinations of try, throw, and catch can be used for more advanced error handling.

Filters

Filters are used to make sure applications receive correct input. A number of predefined filter functions are provided with PHP to validate or sanitize input. (Appendix C, which you can download at *https://goo.gl/2uYjHb*, lists some of them.) A custom filter can also be created.

Filters are used when a site requires external data input. Using external input on a website raises security considerations, but it also makes the site much more dynamic. Filtering can minimize the security risks and also improve and control data integrity. These are important factors for business applications.

Figure 9.54 uses the filter_var() filter function to validate that the integer value is a valid integer. The filter checks the variable input for the order quantity to determine if it is a valid integer. In this example, the results will be true, so the message *Order Quantity = 1* will be displayed. If you change the order quantity's value to *x*, which is not a valid integer, the message *Order Quantity is invalid* will be displayed.

```
<html>
<head>
<?php
// PHP0985 Filer validation example
$orderquantity = 1;
if(!filter_var($orderquantity, FILTER_VALIDATE_INT))
 {
  echo("Order Quantity is invalid");
 }
else
 {
  echo("Order Quantity = " . $orderquantity);
 }
?>
</head>
</html>
```

Figure 9.54: Filter validation

Similar validate functions can be used for Boolean, float, regular expression, URL, email, and IP address entries.

Sanitize filter functions clean up data. The same example of order quantity will be used to demonstrate sanitization. In Figure 9.55, the input for the order quantity variable is abcdefg12. The filter_sanitize_number_int() function cleans up the order quantity value by removing invalid characters. The result in this example is 12.

```
<html>
<head>
<?php
// PHP0988 Filter sanitization example
$orderquantity = "abcdefg12";
echo filter_var($orderquantity, FILTER_SANITIZE_NUMBER_INT);
?>
  </head>
</p>
</html>
```

Figure 9.55: Filter sanitization

Similar prebuilt sanitization functions can be used for string, email, URL, and float entries.

In addition to predefined filter functions, custom functions can also be created. Figure 9.56 creates a custom function to replace all dashes in a phone number with spaces.

```
<html>
<head>
<?php
// PHP0990 Custom function with filter callback
function convert_phone_number($phone_number)
{
return str_replace("-", " ", $phone_number);
}
$phone_number = "248-701-9999";
echo filter_var($phone_number, FILTER_CALLBACK,
array("options"=>"convert_phone_number"));
?>
  </head>
</p>
</html>
```

Figure 9.56: A custom filter function

This example uses the filter_callback() function and an array containing the custom function. The results will return the phone number 248-701-9999 as 248 701 9999.

Forms

Forms are often used for user input on websites. User input should always be validated. Input data might be validated using JavaScript on the client side. Client-side validation is faster and reduces the load on the server. A site with a lot of activity or a site that uses databases, however, poses concerns regarding site security. Server-side validation with PHP can be used when a form accesses a database.

Forms in HTML are simple and useful for submitting data, as shown in previous examples in this book. A good way to validate a form is to have the form and processing script in the same file, rather than within separate files, and have the form post to itself. By using this technique, any errors can be displayed on the same page as the form, and the previously entered data will be defaulted and automatically displayed on the form. Using this approach will make it easier to determine the error and the data entered resulting in the error.

All form elements are automatically available to PHP scripts. The $_GET, $_POST, and $_REQUEST variable submission methods are used in PHP to retrieve input from forms. The **$_GET variable** collects input values from a form that uses the HTML form method get. The data collected using $_GET is visible to everyone and will be displayed in the browser's address bar. The $_GET variable can send only a maximum of 100 characters. It should not be used for data that should not be seen when sending information, such as a password. Because the data can be seen in the URL, $_GET allows for bookmarking by saving the URL information. This may be helpful for repetitive tasks, such as looking at an employee's work schedule.

Figure 9.57 is an example of using $_GET with a form. The example prompts the user for first and last name, validates the data input, and if a valid name is entered, displays an employee's work schedule.

```
HTML Document PHP0992.html:
<html>
<head>
<!-- PHP0992.html $_GET variable example  -->
Welcome to Belhur Publishing Employee Page!
<br>
Please enter your first and last name and press submit to view your
schedule.
<form action="PHP0992.php" method="get">
First Name: <input type="text" name="first_name" />
Last Name: <input type="text" name="last_name" />
<br>
<input type="submit" />
</form>
</head>
</html>
```

Continued

```
PHP Document PHP0992.php:
<html>
<body>
<?php
/* PHP0992 - $_GET variable example */
if (! preg_match( "/^[A-Za-z]+$/", trim($_GET["first_name"]) ))
        echo ("Please enter your first name." . "<br>");
elseif (! preg_match( "/^[A-Za-z]+$/", trim($_GET["last_name"]) ))
        echo ("Please enter your last name." . "<br>");
else
        echo ("Employee Work Schedule Page." . "<br>");
        echo ("Welcome " . $_GET["first_name"] . " " . $_GET["last_name"] .
"<br>");
?>
</body>
</html>
```

Figure 9.57: Using the $_GET variable

The HTML in Figure 9.57 causes the page in Figure 9.58 to be displayed. In this example, the first and last name have been entered on the page's form.

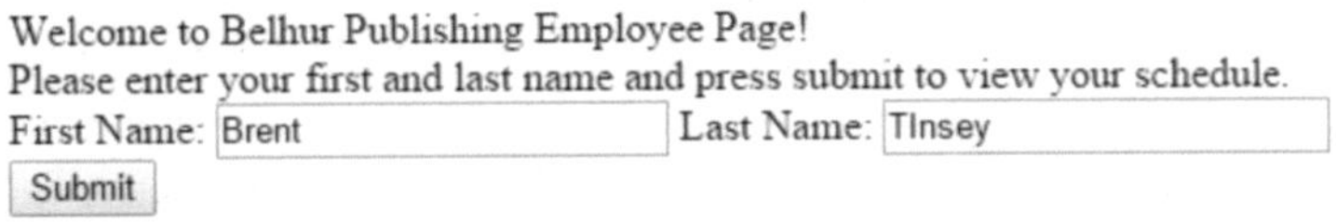

Welcome to Belhur Publishing Employee Page!
Please enter your first and last name and press submit to view your schedule.
First Name: Brent   Last Name: Tinsey
Submit

Figure 9.58: The Web page created from the HTML in Figure 9.57

When the form is submitted, the file PHP0992.php is initiated. This document validates the data, checking that valid first and last names have been entered. If the first or last name is invalid, a message is displayed prompting for a valid entry. If the data is valid, the employee's work schedule is displayed. The work schedule page displays a welcome message and will also contain the values entered on the form for the first and last name in the browser's URL line, like this:

```
http://localhost/BelhurPublishing/PHP0992.php?first_name=Brent&last_name=Tinsey
```

Notice that the first and last name values are clearly visible, along with the website's path.

The PHP $_REQUEST variable contains the contents of $_GET, $_POST, and $_COOKIE. The $_REQUEST variable can be used to get the result from form data sent with either the get or post method. An application that uses both get and post for the same variable name may be a case where the $_REQUEST variable would be used. It might be argued that it is better to know where the data comes from and avoid using the $_REQUEST variable. It may also be argued that having two or more inputs to a script having the same name, for example, one each from a $_GET, $_POST, and $_COOKIE variable, is a pretty confusing design. This may also open up some security issues. Regardless, the variable is available for use in PHP. Here is an example of using the $_REQUEST variable:

```
echo ("Welcome " . $_REQUEST["first_name"] . " " .
$_REQUEST["last_name"] . "<br>");
```

The $_POST variable is an array of variable names and values sent by the HTTP post method. The $_POST variable is used to collect values from a form with the HTML method post. Information collected and sent using this method is invisible to others and has no limit on the amount of information that is sent. When the post method is used in an HTML form, the $_POST variable can be used in a PHP script to catch the entered form data. $_POST has been used in previous examples in this chapter. Refer back, for example, to Figure 9.9.

The importance of form validation is obvious. The PHP language provides many options and flexibility for the application programmer. Care should be taken to make the application user-friendly and well-designed, just like applications in any other programming language. A well thought-out design will result in an improved application. When an error is identified through filtering or validation, the error should be clearly identified and information returned so the user can correct the error.

Sessions

When a user visits a dynamic website, an application is initiated, some activity occurs, and then the application is closed. This is very similar to a traditional computer session. The computer knows who the user is, when an application is started, and when it is ended. On the Internet, this information is not automatically retained on the Web server. A PHP session can be used to store the information on the server for later use. The information is only retained while the session is active and deleted when the session ends. If it must be kept, a permanent record of the data can be stored in a database.

Sessions work by creating a UID, a unique ID for each visitor. The UID is used to uniquely identify and store variables. The PHP session will be started, and then session information will be stored. Session information can also be deleted.

To start a session, use the session_start() function. As shown in Figure 9.59, this function must be placed before the <html> tag. Once started, a user's session is registered on the server, and user information can be saved using the assigned UID for the session.

```php
<?php
// PHP0997 PHP session example.
session_start();
if ($SESSION["last_visit"])
{
echo "Date of your last visit is: ";
                                              Continued
```

```
echo date ("j F Y, H:i:s", $SESSION["last_visit"]);
echo "<br>";
echo "Total number of visits: "  . $_SESSION["number_visits"];
}
else
echo "This is your first visit.";
$_SESSION["last_visit"] = time();
$_SESSION["number_visits"]++;
?>
<html>
<body>
Welcome to Belhur Publishing!
</body>
</html>
```

Figure 9.59: Starting a PHP session

The PHP $_SESSION variable is used to store and retrieve session variables. In this example, we store the last visit information. The first time the user visits the site, the following message will be displayed:

```
This is your first visit. Welcome to Belhur Publishing!
```

Each time the page is visited during the session, the values will be saved. If other website pages are visited and the user then returns to this page, the values will be remembered. If the browser is closed, the values will be reset. Each time the user returns to this page during a session, a message will be displayed with the date of the last visit and the number of times the page has been visited.

As mentioned earlier, a session may also be deleted. The unset() or session_destroy() function can be used for this purpose. The unset() function is used to reset a specific session variable.

```
<?php
unset($SESSION[number_visits];
?>
```

The session_destroy() function will be used to destroy and reset the session. The stored session data will be deleted.

```
<?php
session_destroy();
?>
```

Working with Data

Web business applications often need to retrieve data from and store data in a database table or file on the server. PHP can be used for these tasks.

DB2 is the database used on an IBM i and will be used for the remaining examples in this chapter. In the examples that follow, you will learn how to connect to a DB2 database and input and output data. Some knowledge of **SQL** is helpful to better understand these examples, but it is not required. These examples could easily be used to access other databases by making slight changes. You can find examples on the *www.php.net* website.

The code in Figure 9.60 connects to a DB2 server and retrieves data from the UBELHOR database, in a table named CUSTOMERS. The retrieved data is displayed on a Web page.

```
<html>
<head>
<img src="images/BP.JPG">
<br>
Welcome to Belhur Publishing!
<br><br>
<body>
<?php
//  PHP09101 - Working with Data Example
// Connect to data source
$conn_resource = db2_connect("*LOCAL", "", "");

if (!$conn_resource) {
        echo "Connection failed. SQL Err:";
        echo db2_conn_error();
        echo "<br>";
        echo db2_conn_errormsg();
exit();
}
echo "List of Customers WHERE CUST_ID > 1220"."<br>", "<br>";
// Select database
/* Construct the SQL statement */
$sql = "SELECT * FROM UBELHOR.CUSTOMERS WHERE CUST_ID > ?  order by CUST_ID
FOR FETCH ONLY";
/* Prepare, bind and execute the DB2 SQL statement */
$stmt= db2_prepare($conn_resource, $sql);
$lower_limit = 1220; //from the CUST_ID value
$flds = db2_num_fields($stmt);
if($flds > 0 )
{
//show Table Header (analyze result set)
```

Continued

```
        echo "<table border=1>";
        echo "<tr>";
        for($i=0; $i<$flds; $i++)
        {
                echo '<td width="20%">';
                $name = db2_field_name($stmt, $i);
                echo $name;
                echo "</td>";
        }
        echo "</tr>";
//Execute statement , uses a binding of parameters
db2_bind_param($stmt, 1, "lower_limit", DB2_PARAM_IN);
$result = db2_execute($stmt);
        if (!$result) {
            echo 'The db2 execute failed. ';
            echo 'SQLSTATE value: ' . db2_stmt_error();
            echo ' Message: ' .  db2_stmt_errormsg();
        }
        else
        {
          while ($row = db2_fetch_array($stmt))
          {
              echo "<tr>";
              for($i=0; $i<$flds; $i++){
              echo '<td width="20%">';
              echo $row[$i] . ' ';
              echo "</td>";
              }
            echo "</tr>";
          }
        }
     echo  "</table>";
}
?>
</body>
</head>
</html>
```

Figure 9.60: Retrieving data from a DB2 database

There isn't much code here, but it produces big results, as shown in Figure 9.61. It's really that simple.

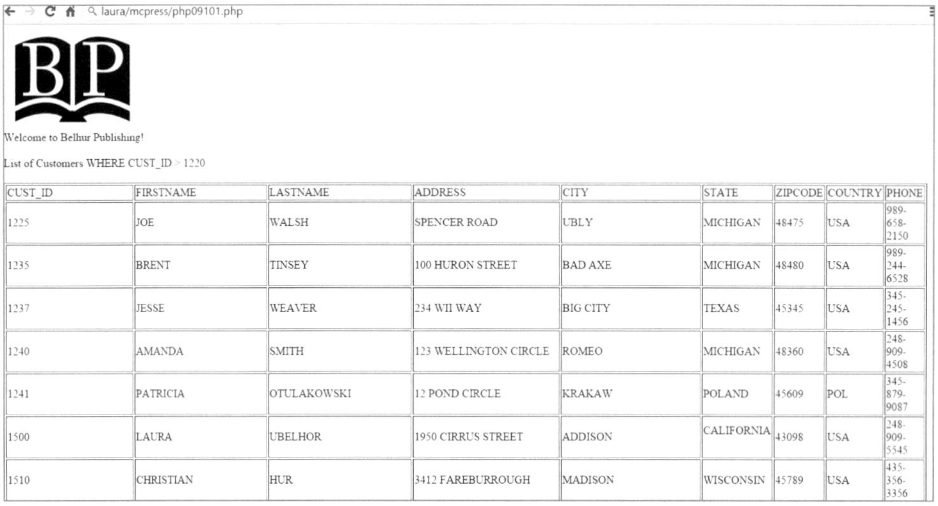

CUST_ID	FIRSTNAME	LASTNAME	ADDRESS	CITY	STATE	ZIPCODE	COUNTRY	PHONE
1225	JOE	WALSH	SPENCER ROAD	UBLY	MICHIGAN	48475	USA	989-658-2150
1235	BRENT	TINSEY	100 HURON STREET	BAD AXE	MICHIGAN	48480	USA	989-244-6528
1237	JESSE	WEAVER	234 WII WAY	BIG CITY	TEXAS	45345	USA	345-245-1456
1240	AMANDA	SMITH	123 WELLINGTON CIRCLE	ROMEO	MICHIGAN	48360	USA	248-909-4508
1241	PATRICIA	OTULAKOWSKI	12 POND CIRCLE	KRAKAW	POLAND	45609	POL	345-879-9087
1500	LAURA	UBELHOR	1950 CIRRUS STREET	ADDISON	CALIFORNIA	43098	USA	248-909-5545
1510	CHRISTIAN	HUR	3412 FAREBURROUGH	MADISON	WISCONSIN	45789	USA	435-356-3356

Figure 9.61: Data retrieved from a DB2 database

In this example, we are connecting to a DB2 database, so the connection type is **db2_connect**:

```
// Connect to data source
$conn_resource = db2_connect("*LOCAL", "", "");
```

The connection has three parameters: the connection, the user ID, and the password. The connection is the DSN where the data resides. In this example, *LOCAL is the location, but it could be a DNS server name or an IP address. The user ID and password parameters are the IDs required to connect to the DB2 database.

There is also a check to make sure the connection doesn't fail:

```
if (!$conn_resource) {
        echo "Connection failed. SQL Err:";
        echo db2_conn_error();
        echo "<br>";
        echo db2_conn_errormsg();
exit();
}
```

The DB2 database name is UBELHOR, and the table name is CUSTOMERS.

```
// Retrieve data
$sql = "SELECT * FROM UBELHOR.CUSTOMERS WHERE CUST_ID > ?  order by CUST_ID FOR
FETCH ONLY";
```

All fields and records with a customer ID greater than 1220 are selected from the table CUSTOMERS.

```
$stmt= db2_prepare($conn_resource, $sql);
$lower_limit = 1220; //from the CUST_ID value
$flds = db2_num_fields($stmt);
```

The data is accessed using the db2_fetch_array statement. The data is put into the variable $row. The while statement continues to fetch data until no more exists. Finally, the contents are printed, listing all the fields from the CUSTOMERS table.

```
while ($row = db2_fetch_array($stmt))
        {
            echo "<tr>";
            for($i=0; $i<$flds; $i++){
            echo '<td width="20%">';
            echo $row[$i] . ' ';
            echo "</td>";
            }
```

The example in Figure 9.62 adds a few more pieces to further show how data can be used within an application. Some of the code is slightly different to show different techniques of retrieving and displaying data. This example begins with a form prompting the user to enter a state name, as shown in Figure 9.63. When a valid state is entered and the **Submit** button is clicked, a list of customers for the state will be retrieved from the database and displayed. This application uses the same database and table as the previous example.

```
HTML Document PHP09107.html:
<html>
<head>
<!-- PHP09107.html Customers in Entered State example  -->
Welcome to Belhur Publishing Customer Master Page!
<br>
This page is used to retrieve and display a list of customers from a state.
<br>
Enter the state name and press Submit to view a list of customers from that
state.
<form action="PHP09107.php" method="get">
State: <input type="text" name="State" />
<br>
<input type="submit" />
</form>
```

Continued

```
</head>
</html>

PHP Document PHP09107.php:
<html>
<head>
<img src="images/BP.JPG">
<br>
Belhur Publishing Customer List Page!
<br>
<body>
<?php
// PHP09107 Customers in Entered State example
// Edit check to confirm a state has been entered
if (! preg_match( "/^[A-Za-z]+$/", trim($_GET["State"]) ))
{
        echo ("Please enter a state." . "<br>");
        die;
}
else
        echo ($_GET["State"] . " " . " Based Customers." . "<br>");

$State = $_GET['State'];

//connect to db, not good practice to use blank user/pass best to pass as
parms or prompt for ID and password
$conn = db2_connect("","","");

//if not connected, display error message
if(!$conn) echo 'Connection failed:'.db2_stmt_error().':'.
                db2_stmt_errormsg();
// format SQL statement
$sql = "SELECT * FROM UBELHOR.CUSTOMERS WHERE STATE='$State'"; //select all
$stmt = db2_exec($conn,$sql);
$stmt = db2_exec($conn,$sql);

//if execution failed, display error msg
if (!$stmt) echo 'Failed query:'.db2_stmt_error().':'.
```

Continued

```
                db2_stmt_errormsg();
?>
<!-- html outside of php to format table headers -->
<h1>Customer List</h1>
<table border=2>
<tr>
<td>Customer Id</td><td>First Name</td>
<td>Last Name </td><td>Address</td><td>City</td>
<td>State</td><td>Zip</td><td>Country</td></tr>
</tr>
</tr>
<?php
 while($row = db2_fetch_array($stmt)){
  list($CUST_ID,$FIRSTNAME,$LASTNAME,$ADDRESS,
  $CITY,$STATE,$ZIP,$COUNTRY)=$row;


  //html in php to display retrieved table records
  echo("<tr><td>$CUST_ID</td>
        <td>$FIRSTNAME</td><td>$LASTNAME</td>
        <td>$ADDRESS</td>
        <td>$CITY</td><td>$STATE</td>
        <td>$ZIP</td><td>$COUNTRY</td></tr>");
 }
 echo "</table>";
 ?>
</body>
</head>
</html>
```

Figure 9.62: Creating an application to retrieve customer records for a specified state

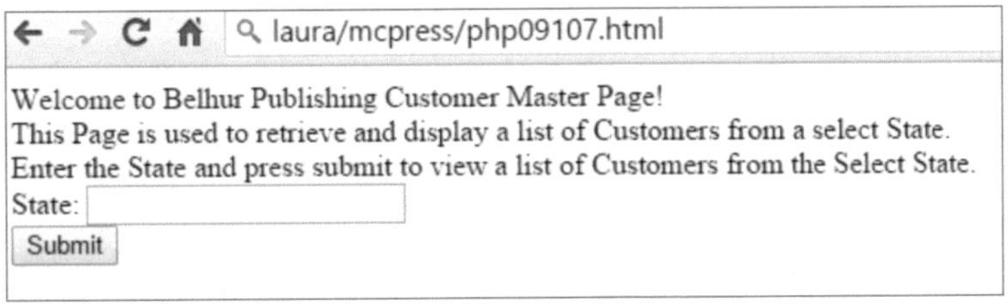

Figure 9.63: The HTML form created by PHP09107.html

The user is prompted for the state the form in file PHP09107.html. When the user clicks **Submit**, PHP09107.php is initiated. The code starts by validating the state name entered. If the name is valid, the connection is made and data is retrieved using SQL. To format the SQL statement, the state entered by the user is used for selection. The example first retrieves the fields using $_GET, then formats the names within single quotes to follow correct syntax for the SQL statement:

```
$State = $_GET['State'];
```

With MICHIGAN entered for the state, the SQL statement would look like this:

```
$sql = "SELECT * FROM UBELHOR.CUSTOMERS WHERE STATE='MICHIGAN'";
```

The SQL statement selects all records from the CUSTOMERS table where the state is MICHIGAN. The db2_fetch_array function is used to retrun an array, indexed by column position, representing a row of the SQL result set.

```
$sql = "SELECT * FROM UBELHOR.CUSTOMERS WHERE STATE='$State'"; //select all
$stmt = db2_exec($conn,$sql);
$stmt = db2_exec($conn,$sql);

while($row = db2_fetch_array($stmt)){
  list($CUST_ID,$FIRSTNAME,$LASTNAME,$ADDRESS,
  $CITY,$STATE,$ZIP,$COUNTRY)=$row;
```

The $state variable allows for passing the selection information using the user form displayed in PHP09107.html. The variable also formats the selection criteria within single quotes to accommodate appropriate statement syntax.

Figure 9.64 shows the list of customers displayed for MICHIGAN, with customer ID, first name, last name, address, city, state, zip, and country. This technique will work just as well with many other business inquiries.

Figure 9.64: The results of the customer inquiry

A dynamic application may require a database table to be updated. We will use a customer-service feedback application to show how this can be done. The code in Figure 9.65 prompts the user to enter feedback information in a form, validates the data, and updates the customer service database. Although the example is simple, it provides the techniques to complete the very important task of updating and storing data. You could use the same method to place online orders or update other data.

```html
HTML file - PHP09113.html:
<html>
<head>
<!** PHP09113 Customer service feedback form example **>
Belhur Publishing Customer Service Feedback Page
<br>
<form method="post" action="PHP09113.php">
<br>
  Email: <input name="email" type="text" /><br />
<br>
  First Name: <input name="firstname" type="text" /><br />
<br>
  Last Name: <input name="lastname" type="text" /><br />
<br>
  Phone Number: <input name="phonenbr" type="text" /><br />
<br>
  Follow Up (Yes or No): <input name="followup" type="text" /><br />
<br>
  Customer Service Message:<br />
  <textarea name="message" rows="5" cols="40">
  </textarea>
  <br />
  <input type="submit" />
</form>
</head>
</html>


PHP file - PHP09113.php:
<html>
<head>
<img src="images/BP.JPG">
<br>
Belhur Publishing Customer Feedback Page!
```

Continued

```php
<br>
Your Customer Service Message Has Been Sent.
<body>
<?php
// PHP09113 Customer Service Feedback Form Example
// perform entry edit checks
$email_address = '/^[^@\s]+@([-a-z0-9]+\.)+[a-z]{2,}$/i';
$message=$_POST["message"];
$phonenbr=$_POST["phonenbr"];
$followup=$_POST["followup"];
if (!preg_match($email_address, trim($_POST["email"])))
  {
  echo "Email address entered is invalid.";
  die;
 }
elseif (! preg_match( "/^[A-Za-z]+$/", trim($_POST["firstname"]) ))
{
      echo ("Please enter your first name." . "<br>");
   die;
}
elseif (! preg_match( "/^[A-Za-z]+$/", trim($_POST["lastname"]) ))
{
      echo ("Please enter your last name." . "<br>");
   die;
}
elseif (strlen($phonenbr)<1)
{
      echo ("Please enter your phone number." . "<br>");
   die;
}
elseif ($followup !== 'Yes' and $followup !== 'No')
{
      echo ("Please enter Yes or No for Follow Up." . "<br>");
   die;
}
elseif (strlen($message)<1)

{
```

Continued

```
        echo ("Please enter your message." . "<br>");
    die;
}
?>
<?php
// Format Fields
$email="'" . $_POST["email"] . "'";
$lname="'" . $_POST["lastname"] . "'";
$fname="'" . $_POST["firstname"] . "'";
$phonenbr="'" . $_POST["phonenbr"] . "'";
$message="'" . $_POST["message"] . "'";
$followup="'" . $_POST["followup"] . "'";
//connect to db, not good practice to use blank user/pass best to pass as
parms or prompt for id and password
$host = "hostname";
$user = 'ueserid';
$pass = 'password';
$conn = db2_connect ($host,$user,$pass);
//if not connected, display error message
if(!$conn) echo 'Connection failed:'.db2_stmt_error().':'.
            db2_stmt_errormsg();
// format SQL statement
$sql = "INSERT INTO UBELHOR.FEEDBACK(DateRecvd, Emailaddr, FirstName,
LastName, PhoneNbr, Message, FollowUp, Status) VALUES(CURDATE(), $email,
$fname, $lname, $phonenbr, $message, $followup, 'Open')";
$stmt = db2_exec($conn,$sql);
//if execution failed display error msg
if (!$stmt) echo 'Failed query:'.db2_stmt_error().':'.
            db2_stmt_errormsg();
?>
</body>
</head>
</html>
```

Figure 9.65: Updating a customer service database

The code in PHP09113.html displays the customer service form in Figure 9.66. Once data is entered in the form and the **Submit** button is clicked, the PHP09113.php document is initiated. The data is retrieved using $_POST and then validated. If the data is valid, the DB2 connection is made and the database table is updated, using the INSERT INTO DB2 SQL syntax. The fields to be updated are listed, and the values are populated using the data retrieved from the form.

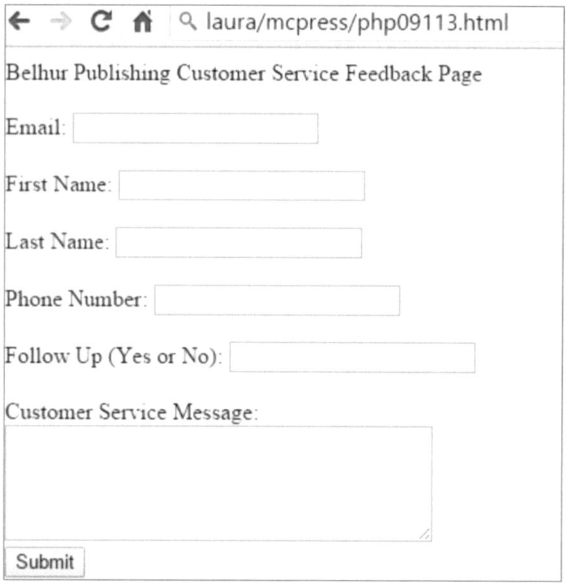

Figure 9.66: The customer service feedback form

Note in Figure 9.65 that the status is defaulted to the value 'Open' and the date received is defaulted to the current date. Once the update is complete, the message in Figure 9.67 is displayed, letting the user know the data has been sent.

Figure 9.67: Notifying the user of the result of the data update

PHP may also be used to work with a text file. The file must first be opened using the fopen() function (**file open function**). The function uses two parameters. The first is for the filename, and the second is for the mode. The example in Figure 9.68 opens the file in read-only mode. Table 9.8 lists valid modes that can be used with fopen().

```
$file=fopen("PHP09119.txt","r");
```

Figure 9.68: The file open function

Table 9.8: Valid Modes for the File Open Function	
Mode	Description
r	Read-only; starts at the beginning of the file.
r+	Read/write; starts at the beginning of the file.
w	Write-only; opens and clears the contents of the file or creates a new file if the file referenced does not exist.
w+	Read/write; opens and clears the contents of the file or creates a new file if the file referenced does not exist.
a	Append; opens and writes to the end of the file or creates a new file if the file referenced does not exist.
a+	Read/append; preserves file's contents and writes to the end of the file.
x	Write-only; creates a new file and returns false and an error if the file already exists.
x+	Read/write; creates a new file and returns false and an error if the file already exists.

The example in Figure 9.69 reads the text file PHP09119.txt to display the offers from Belhur Publishing for the month of May. The text file is read and displayed using the fopen() and fclose() functions. To access a file, it must be opened. It is also important to close the file.

The while loop uses the end-of-file function, feof(), to read through the file line by line and display the contents using echo. The loop will complete when the end of the file is reached, and the contents of the text file will be displayed to the screen, as shown in Figure 9.70.

```
Text File - PHP09119.txt:

Belhur Publishing May Special Offers!
***************************************************

10% off all merchanidise ordered online
reference offer belhur0216
***************************************************

20% your entire order when 2 or more books are
ordered
reference offer belhur20
***************************************************

Offers valid May 1st through May 31st
***************************************************


PHP File - PHP09119.php:

<html>
<head>
<img src="images/BP.JPG">
```

Continued

```
<br>
Belhur Publishing Special Offers Page!
<br>
<body>
<?php
// PHP09119 - Read and display text file example
$file = fopen("PHP09119.txt", "r") or exit("Unable to open file!");
// Display the file line until the end of the file is reached
while(!feof($file))
  {
  echo fgets($file). "<br />";
  }
fclose($file);
?>
</body>
</head>
</html>
```

Figure 9.69: The code to read and display a text file

The list of monthly specials for Belhur Publishing is a good example of this kind of application. The promotions can be easily changed by replacing the contents of the text document, without having to make changes to the website application. This same technique could be used for product-specific information, employee procedures, or order comments.

Figure 9.70: Displaying a text file on a Web page

Although the examples in this chapter use DB2, you can use connections to other databases as well. Figures 9.71 through 9.73 show examples of a few other **database connections**.

```php
<?php

$db_host      = "server.mynetwork";
$db_user      = "dbuser";
$db_pass      = "dbpass";

odbc_connect($db_host, $db_user, $db_pass, "SQL_CUR_USE_ODBC");

@odbc_setoption($this->db_connectid, 1, SQL_ATTR_COMMIT, SQL_TXN_NO_COMMIT)
   or die('Failed setoption: ' . odbc_error() . ":" . odbc_errormsg());
                                                              Continued


@odbc_setoption($this->db_connectid, 1, SQL_ATTR_DBC_DEFAULT_LIB, $this->dbname)
   or die('Failed select: ' . odbc_error() . ":" . odbc_errormsg());

?>
```

Figure 9.71: Making an ODBC connection

```php
<?php

mysql_connect("localhost", "userid", "password") or die(mysql_error());

// Select database
mysql_select_db("Belhur") or die(mysql_error());

// Add data
$data = mysql_query("INSERT INTO CustomerService (DateReceived,
TimeReceived, EmailAddress, FirstName, LastName, PhoneNumber, Message,
FollowUp, Status) VALUES(CURDATE(), CURTIME(), $email, $fname, $lname,
$phonenumber, $message, $followup, 'Open')")
or die(mysql_error());
?>
```

Figure 9.72: Making a MySQL connection

```
INSERT INTO table VALUES(val1, val2, ... valn);
//MySQL Insert Statement


INSERT INTO table VALUES(val1, val2, ... valn);
INSERT INTO schema.table VALUES(val1, val2, ... valn);
//DB2 Insert Statements
```

Figure 9.73: Using a DB2 table reference

Summary

This chapter has covered a lot of ground to introduce you to PHP programming. We've provided a starting point from which you can further explore PHP's capability and functionality. PHP can be used for advanced validation, XML processing, FTP, file uploads, and much more.

PHP can bring dynamic capability to a business Web application. If your goal is to get to the Web fast, consider including PHP in your Web application development efforts. PHP's user base continues to grow, and the language continues to evolve, thanks to the efforts of the PHP community.

Key Terms

arithmetic operator	email functions	loops
array	email injection attacks	loosely typed language
assignment operator	error handler	mail functions
break keyword	error handling	multidimensional array
case keyword	expression	MySQL
CGI	filter	ODBC
comparison operators	file open function	operators
conditional statement	for loop	php.ini
cookie	forms	server-side
database connection	functions	SQL
data type	GET variable	statement terminator
date functions	if else statement	strongly typed language
default keyword	if elseif else statement	switch statement
do while loop	if statement	time functions
dynamic Web application	logging errors	variables
echo	logical operators	while loop

Discussion/Review Questions

1. What are some reasons to use PHP for Web development?
2. What can PHP be used for in business application Web development?
3. What databases can be used with PHP?

4. What significance does a statement terminator have when coding a PHP script?
5. How do you include comments within PHP code?
6. What is a PHP echo command?
7. How do you define a variable in PHP?
8. How is an expression used in PHP?
9. What are operators in PHP, and how can they be used?
10. How are conditional statements used in PHP?
11. What is a loop in PHP?
12. What is a PHP function?
13. How can date and time be used in PHP?
14. How can an email be sent using PHP?
15. What is injection?
16. How can errors be addressed using PHP?
17. How are forms used in PHP?
18. What is a session?
19. How can you retrieve data using PHP?
20. How can a database be updated in PHP?

Exercises

1. Create a PHP script using HTML, JavaScript, and PHP.
2. Write a PHP script using arithmetic operators.
3. Create a PHP script that displays an image and uses the switch statement and a for loop.
4. Write a PHP script using an array to include some of your areas of interest.
5. Code a PHP script using three predefined PHP functions.
6. Create a PHP script that makes use of cookies, sends an email, and includes code to prevent email injection.
7. Write a PHP script that includes error handling.
8. Create a PHP script that uses a form and displays data from a database.
9. Code a PHP script that uses sessions, displays an image, and updates a database.

CHAPTER 10

Web Development with ASP.NET

> In this chapter, you'll explore Microsoft's Active Server Pages, also known as *ASP*. The latest version of ASP is included within Microsoft's .NET Framework, and is referred to as ASP.NET. This chapter goes into detail on what ASP.NET is, what tools you need to work with it, how it integrates with HTML, and how it integrates with your database.

ASP.NET Compared with Other Tools

As you might guess from the word "Server" in "**Active Server Pages**," the processing for **ASP.NET** takes place primarily on the server itself. Be aware, however, that there are differences between ASP .NET and the older version of ASP. ASP.NET is compiled, whereas its predecessor was not. This gives ASP.NET a distinct performance advantage. There are also numerous additional controls available for ASP.NET.

Because ASP.NET is built on Microsoft's .NET Framework, it interacts with the Common Language Runtime (CLR). Therefore, developers can code in any of the .NET languages. Most commonly, this would be either VB.NET or C# (pronounced *C sharp*). This book uses VB.NET because it provides a distinct alternative to some of the other languages discussed in this book. VB.NET is also a popular programming language, so examples in that language will be valuable to many readers.

ASP.NET Is Now Open Source

The notion of an open source platform isn't new. A prime example of an open source platform that's been used freely by companies and individuals around the world for the last 25 years is the highly acclaimed operating system (OS) kernel called *Linux*. Linux was created in 1991 and was made available to the (at the time) small open source community. The huge success of Linux helped pave the way for the large and growing open source communities of today.

As the successor to the legacy Active Server Pages (ASP) technology since the early 2000s, ASP.NET remained Microsoft's proprietary technology for many years despite the rapid growth and popularity of the open source communities. Surprisingly, in late 2014 Microsoft made ASP.NET and its popular

.NET Core cross-platform framework open source. Since ASP.NET has joined the families of open source programming languages (such as PHP, Java, and Python), developers can now start using the ASP.NET platform in production environments. Microsoft continues to support ASP.NET and has continued its commitment to open source.

ASP.NET Versus PHP

As you learned in the previous chapter, PHP is open source and portable, because it can be run on almost any platform. PHP is commonly said to be more stable and less intensive on resource requirements than ASP.NET. For some programmers who are already familiar with Visual Basic, however, ASP.NET might be easier to learn than PHP.

Some people say that PHP is more robust because of its advanced features—like working with FTP servers, parsing data, and connectivity. Others, however, contend that the available controls within ASP.NET make many programming jobs dramatically easier.

ASP.NET Versus Java

Although both languages are open source, ASP.NET and Java differ in many ways. For one thing, the languages' syntax is different. For another, ASP.NET is still new to the open source communities, and thus many of its components are still being provided and supported by Microsoft. To find similar components for Java, you might need to include additional open source material from a third party, or develop the tools yourself. Another major difference is that Java is platform independent both at the source and binary levels, which makes Java very portable and capable of being integrated to work with virtually any device.

ASP.NET Versus CGI

Common Gateway Interface (CGI) is at its best when you have large amounts of existing useful code that perform the tasks necessary for your Web application. With CGI, you can easily interact with these existing applications without needing to learn many new programming languages.

When you're creating truly sophisticated Web pages that perform important tasks such as validating input data, however, CGI can become labor intensive, depending on what platform you are working with, what languages you use, and the available toolset. ASP.NET may be better suited than CGI for businesses that are developing new applications where there is little legacy code to reuse, or when the legacy code can be accessed via stored procedures. Whereas the exact nature of the server side of a CGI application changes from server to server, the ASP.NET server-side coding is always consistent.

ASP.NET's Advantages and Disadvantages

Like any other tool, ASP.NET has advantages and disadvantages. Here are a few of its advantages:

- Object-oriented
- Requires less code

- Has powerful prebuilt controls available
- Can be used with any .NET programming language
- Server-compiled pages for faster performance on subsequent calls
- Better security; code is never sent to a remote browser

Here are ASP.NET's main disadvantages:

- Microsoft-specific
- Windows-based
- Fairly complex
- Difficult to control much of the HTML code

ASP.NET Processing

Like its counterparts PHP and JSP, ASP.NET is a server-side language. While it is possible to incorporate client-side ASP.NET processing through scripting languages such as VBScript or JavaScript, the focus of ASP.NET coding remains on the server. ASP.NET source files end with a suffix of *.aspx* rather than *.htm* or *.html*, as would normally be the case for Web pages. This suffix signals the server that the document contains HTML code as well as special ASP.NET code that must be processed before the contents of the document are sent to the remote user. Figure 10.1 illustrates this process, and shows how the ASP.NET server-side code is replaced at run time with dynamic HTML content.

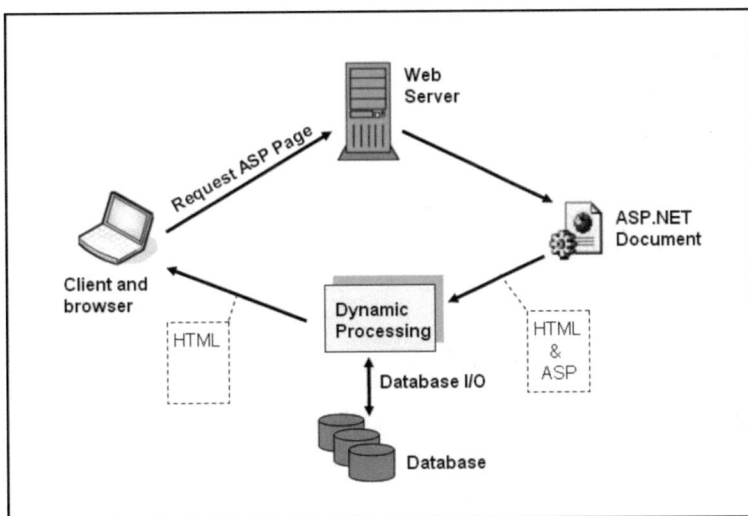

Figure 10.1: Processing an ASP.NET document

Figure 10.2 shows ASP.NET code inserted inside HTML. This code creates the Web page shown in Figure 10.3.

```
<%@ Page Language="VB" AutoEventWireup="false" CodeFile="Default.aspx.vb"
Inherits="_Default" %>


<!DOCTYPE html>
<html>
<head>
  <meta charset="utf-8"/>
  <title>VB Script Heading</title>
</head>
<body>
  <%Response.Write("<p>Paragraph One")%>
  <%Response.Write("<p>Paragraph Two")%>
  <%Response.Write("<p>Paragraph Three")%>
</body>
</html>
```

Figure 10.2: The ASP.NET code to create three paragraphs

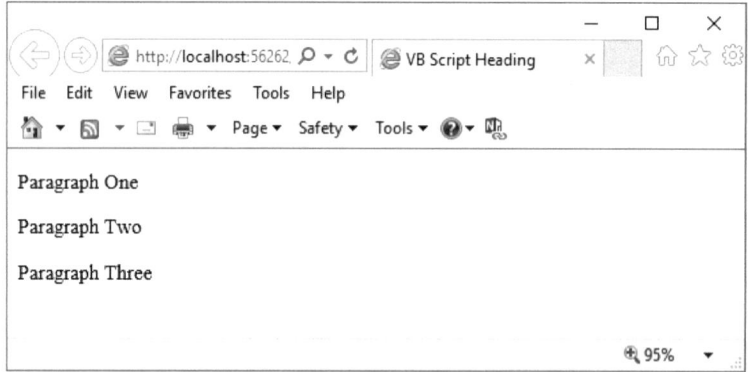

Figure 10.3: An ASP.NET page with three paragraphs

The code contains very familiar-looking HTML, but there are three lines containing a new type of code in the middle of the document. Anywhere in an HTML page that you need to execute server-side logic, insert ASP.NET code delimited by <% and %>.

This example uses the **Response.Write** method, which simply inserts the given string into the HTML page. The string can contain HTML tags, plain text, or a combination of the two, as in Figure 10.2.

```
Response.Write("..")
```

Processing the ASP.NET document and properly handling the code within it requires a special server, such as Microsoft's Internet Information Server (IIS). This server is an optional component of Windows that can be installed using the *Add or Remove Program* wizard in the Windows Control Panel. You might need the Install CD to complete the installation.

What Tools to Use

To develop pages using ASP.NET, you may want to install a tool that will assist in creating the Web pages. Microsoft provides a powerful integrated development environment (IDE) tool, Microsoft Visual Studio. Visual Studio comes in several versions and editions. At the time of this writing, however, we were using the 2013 edition, not 2015, which was released in Q3 2015. Each version includes several editions, from the free Express and Community editions to the Enterprise edition. Table 10.1 shows a list of Visual Studio versions and their editions. You can download the tools and get more information from the Visual Studio website, *www.visualstudio.com*.

Table 10.1: Microsoft Visual Studio Editions			
Edition Name	2012	2013	2015
Express (*Free*)	✓		
Community (*Free*)		✓	✓
Professional	✓	✓	✓
Premium	✓	✓	
Ultimate	✓	✓	
Enterprise	✓	✓	✓
Test Professional	✓	✓	✓

Once installed, this tool will help you to edit and manage pages that incorporate ASP.NET. To get started, open Visual Studio and create a new website using the wizard in the **File** pull-down menu, shown in Figure 10.4.

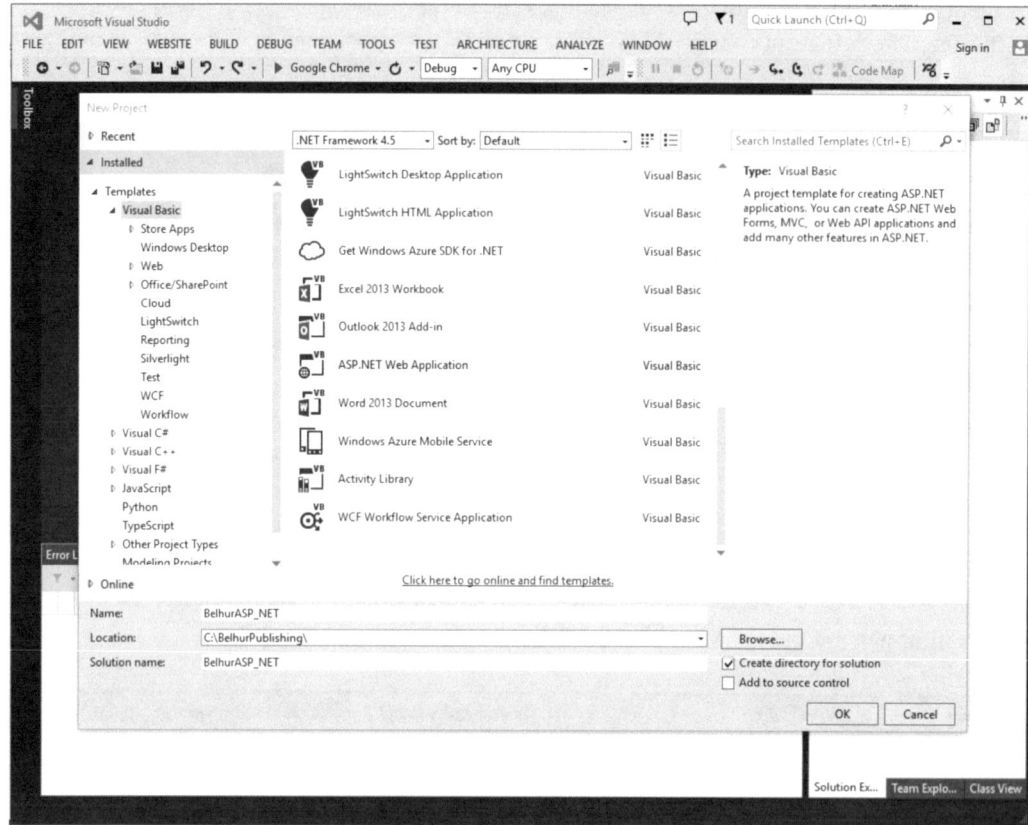

Figure 10.4: The ASP.NET wizard

This wizard creates the space for a website, as shown in Figure 10.5. To start creating a new ASP page, click **FILE** > **New** > **File…** (or press Ctrl + N), then select **Web Form**. The wizard creates the shell of an ASP page, as shown in Figure 10.5.

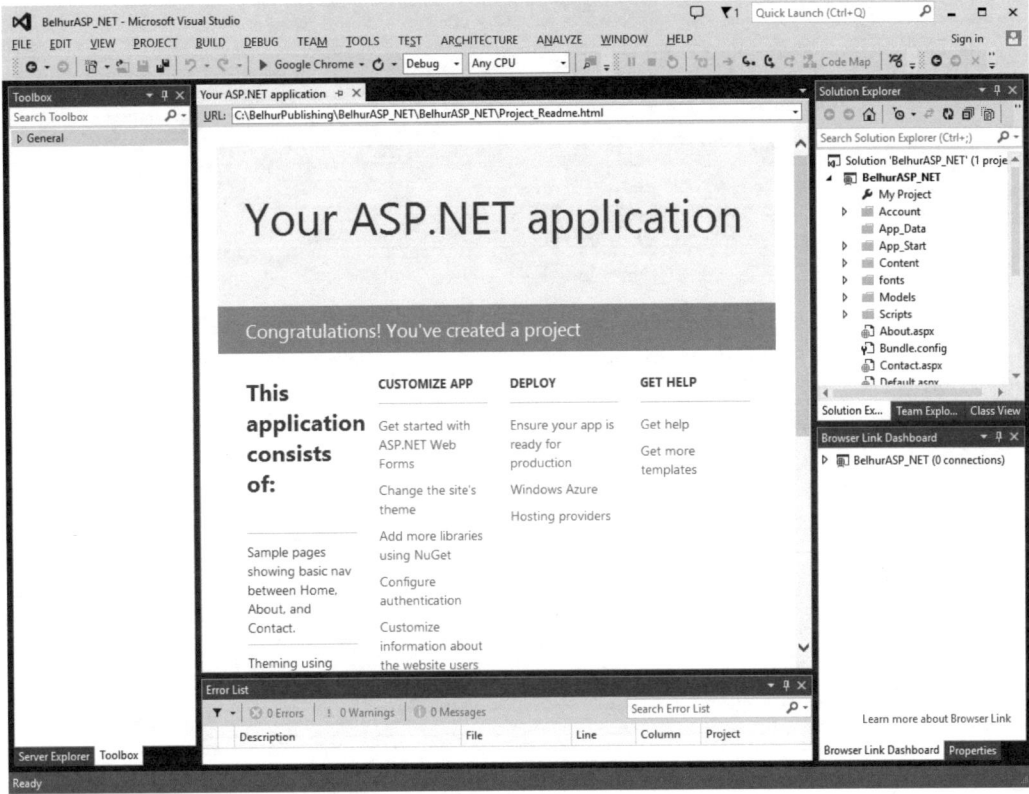

Figure 10.5: The Default Website Project generated by the Visual Studio 2013 wizard

The default project comes with a preset master template that already includes the header, main body, and footer sections of the site. You can use the default and tweak things, or you can start by creating a brand new ASP form page. Let's create a new ASP page. On the menu bar, click **PROJECT** > **Add New Item**… > **Web Form**, and name it index.aspx, as shown in Figure 10.6.

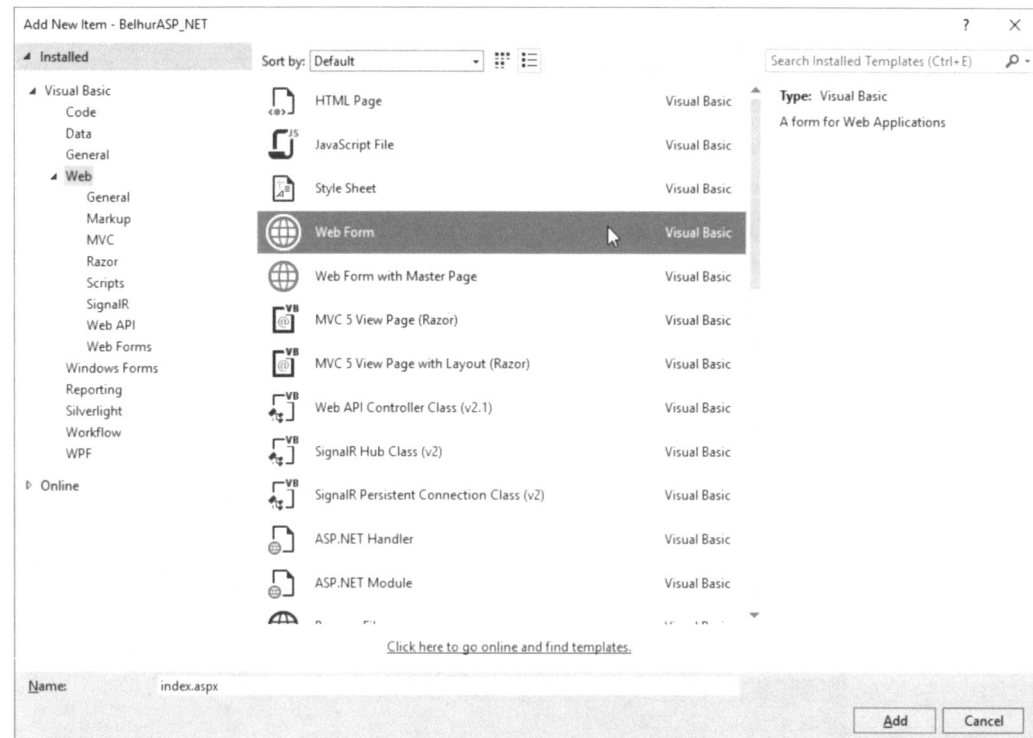

Figure 10.6: Creating a new ASP file

Next, you should see the source view of our newly created ASP file, which is shown in Figure 10.7. You can toggle between three different views by clicking the **Design**, **Split**, or **Source** buttons located at the bottom of the main window. The IDE works similarly to Visual Basic. In Design view (or GUI mode), you can simply drag and drop objects from the Tools box to the **Web form** to begin designing your Web page. In Source view (or Code view), simply insert HTML and ASP code into this document as needed.

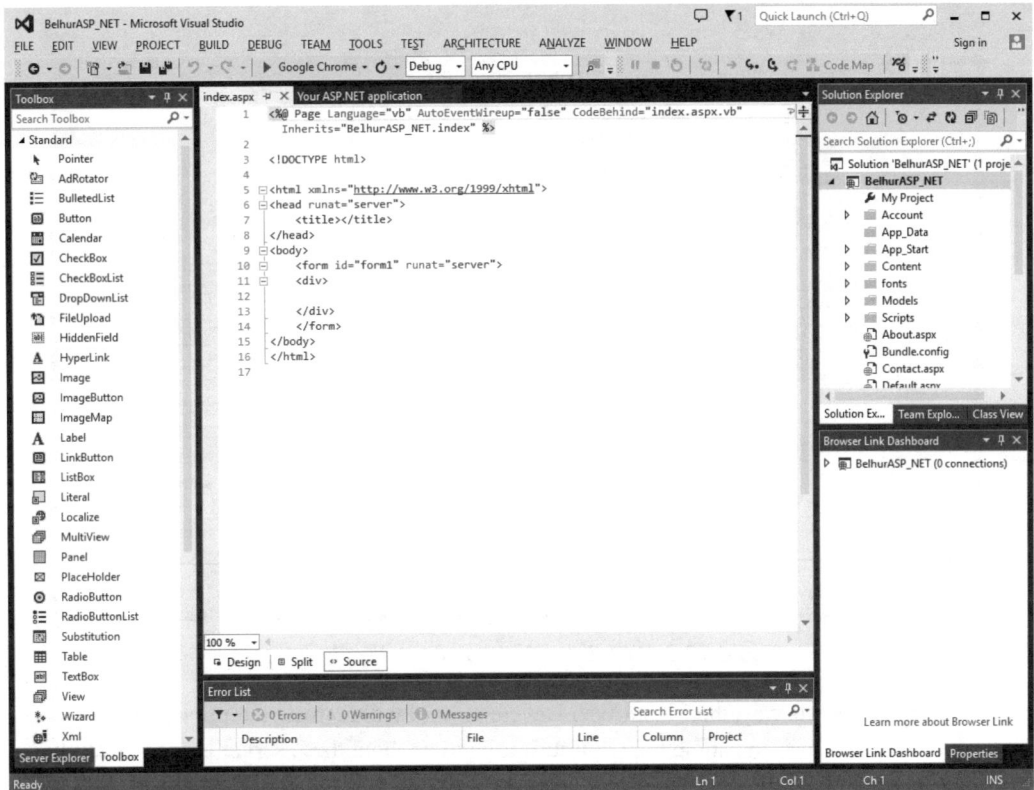

Figure 10.7: Default HTML/ASP code generated by the wizard

In the code created by the wizard, you'll see lines that are not absolutely required or lines that are missing (such as `<meta charset="utf-8"/>`). The examples in this chapter may omit some or all of this default code, allowing us to better focus on the samples being discussed. Until you are sure you understand the implications of changing the default code, however, it's best to leave it as-is in your own development efforts. Initially, focus on adding new code within the <body> and </body> tags (between lines 9 and 15).

To view the rendered output from this or any other ASP.NET page, simply right-click on the page and select the option **View in Browser**. Alternatively, you can click the Play icon (green arrow) and select a default browser to view the page, as shown in Figure 10.8. If the current page has unsaved changes, you will be prompted to save them before the page is rendered. However, if this page links to other pages that have changes, those changes will be ignored, and the last saved version of those pages will be used.

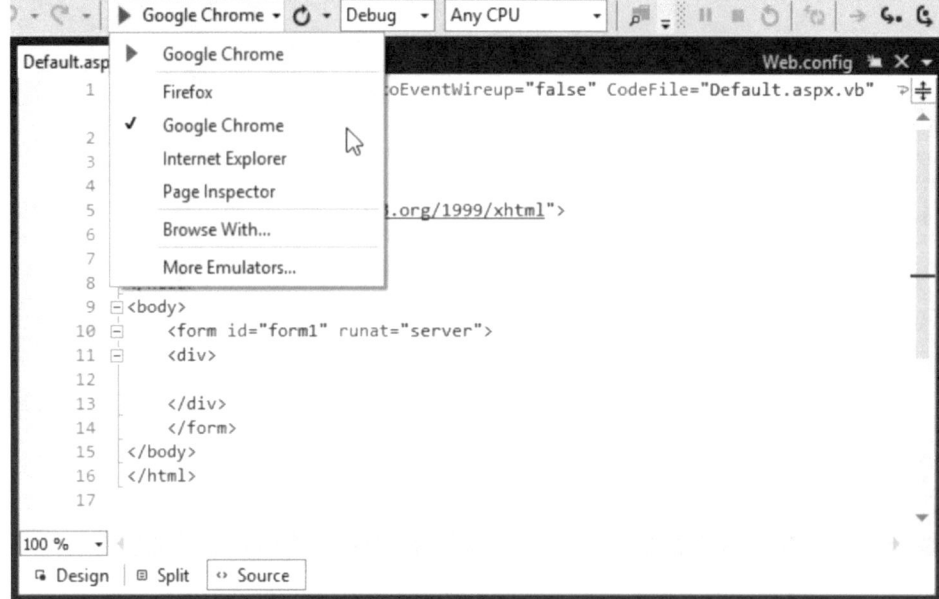

Figure 10.8: View the ASP page on a Web browser

When viewing pages this way, the Visual Web Developer tool will activate temporary server processes on specific ports to handle the request. Information about these server processes can be found in the system tray.

Server Information

If you want to use IIS to present and test your Web page, first make sure that you've installed the IIS Windows component, as discussed earlier in the chapter. Once that is installed, direct your browser to the URL http://localhost. Doing so presents the default page shown in Figure 10.9. This default page is from a Windows 10 system. If you're using a different Windows OS, the default page might look slightly or completely different. However, if you're seeing a default page and not a broken page, then your local **IIS server** is working and running properly.

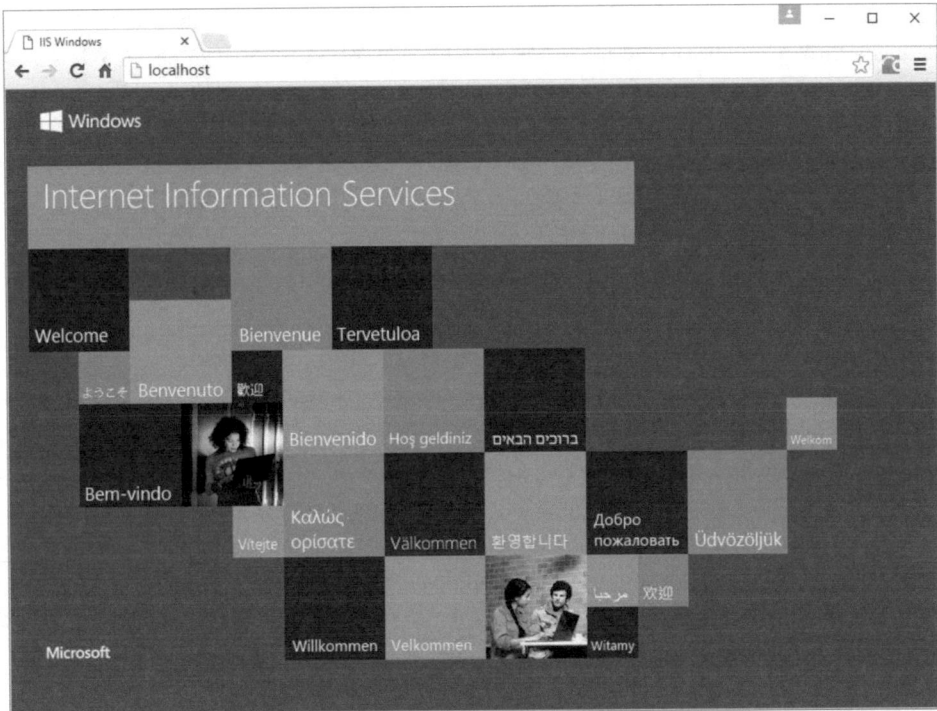

Figure 10.9: The IIS default page on Windows 10

As this page explains, you do not yet have a default website configured for users attempting to connect to your server. Anyone who does attempt to connect will receive a notice that your page is under construction. To define a default page for the IIS server, load the files for your website into the folder c:\inetpub\wwwroot\, as indicated in Figure 11.8. Set the initial page to default.aspx or default.htm. Also, make sure that you have the latest version of the .NET Framework installed, which you can verify though the administrative tools in the Windows Control Panel.

The default.aspx page can be accessed by simply typing the URL http://localhost into the URL input box of your Web browser. To access other documents in the c:\inetpub\wwwroot\ folder, simply reference them in the localhost directory, such as http://localhost/default.aspx or http://localhost/shop/default.aspx.

The IIS server is fine for hosting a single website or an FTP site. For more sophisticated implementations that involve multiple sites, however, consider upgrading to Windows Server.

Writing VBScript in Your Web Pages

VBScript is a scripting language based in part on Microsoft's Visual Basic (VB) programming language. It can be used as both a client-side and a server-side scripting language. VBScript is the default scripting language in ASP.NET on the server side. Since VBScript bears a strong resemblance to ASP.NET code, ASP.NET developers who need to include client-side logic within their Web pages often choose VBScript rather than JavaScript.

More advanced ASP.NET controls provide much of the capability that developers have often had to code manually through client-side scripts using such tools as VBScript or JavaScript. While you can certainly continue to perform such functions with client-side scripts, you might find that using some of the newer ASP.NET controls will improve your capability and productivity. As with all things, there will likely be a learning curve as you begin working with these new controls. In the long run, however, an investment in developing those skills should more than pay for itself.

Learning to use client-side VBScript is also good preparation for getting started with ASP.NET programming. You'll be familiarizing yourself with the VB language syntax and also learning to do manually what ASP.NET will later automate. The scripts can include procedures, functions, and a variety of logical operations, allowing you to create Web pages with dynamic client-side processing. Client-side processing often provides far better performance and responsiveness than server-based logic. The downside is that since VBScript is a Microsoft technology, only Internet Explorer (IE) can interpret VBScript when it's used for client-side scripting. In addition, at the time this book was written, VBScript was considered deprecated and no longer supported in IE 11 Edge mode. Therefore, programmers should discontinue using VBScript as a client-side scripting language for IE 11. However, VBScript is the default setting for ASP.NET on the server side. Although we think it's likely a considerable number of users still use IE 10 or earlier to view Web pages, this chapter is tailored to learning VBScript running primarily on the server side.

Where to Place VBScript Code

VBScript code can be inserted directly within the body of the HTML document. This causes the VBScript code to execute as the page contents are loaded. Typically, this is done if the VBScript code is controlling the content included on the page.

VBScript code can also be included within the heading section of the HTML document. This code is loaded before the page is displayed; this usage is very popular for coding functions and procedures that are called from elsewhere on the page. The code in Figure 10.10 illustrates how VBScript code can be written in both the body and heading sections of an HTML document.

```
<%@ Page Language="VB" AutoEventWireup="false" CodeFile="Default.aspx.vb"
Inherits="_Default" %>

<!DOCTYPE html>
<html>
<head runat="server">
    <meta charset="utf-8"/>
    <%Response.Write("<title>VBScript Heading</title>")%>
</head>
<body>

    <%Response.Write("<h1>VBSCRIPT HEADING</h1>")%>
```

Continued

```
</body>
</html>
```

Figure 10.10: Placing code in the header and body HTML sections

ASP.NET Page Directives

Let's briefly review some very important components in ASP.NET pages. On every ASP.NET page, you'll see the ASP.NET directives. Table 10.2 shows a list of some common ASP.NET **page directives**. These are special directives that the compiler uses to control the behavior of ASP.NET pages, such as their settings and properties. The most common and frequently used directives are the **@Page** directives shown in line 1 in Figure 10.10. They are generated automatically for you if you use the wizard to create a blank ASP.NET page. Otherwise, you have to manually code them in order for ASP.NET to recognize and parse any VBScript codes on the page.

Table 10.2: ASP.NET Page Directives	
Directive	Description
@Assembly	Links an assembly to the current page or user control
@Control	Defines control-specific attributes used by ASP.NET page parser and compiler
@Implement	Implements a specified .NET Framework interface declaratively
@Import	Explicitly imports a namespace into a page or user control
@Master	Identifies an ASP.NET page as a master page and defines any attributes used by the page parser and compiler; can be included only in master files
@MasterType	Specifies the class or virtual path used to type the Master property of an ASP.NET page
@OutputCache	Controls the output of caching policies of a page or user control
@Page	Defines page-specific attributes used by the page parser and compiler; can be included only in .aspx files
@PreviousPageType	Creates a reference to the source page from the target of another page
@Reference	Links a page or user control to the current page or user control
@Register	Associates aliases with namespaces or classes

We will not cover all the directives, as they are beyond the scope of this book. However, it is important that we cover two important attributes of the @Page directive: Language and CodeFile. The Language attribute specifies the type of language being used in the ASP.NET page. Certainly, we're interested in VBScript (or VB). However, if you want to use C# instead of Visual Basic, then you just set the Language attribute to Language="C#".

The CodeFile attribute specifies the **code-behind file** the ASP.NET page is associated with. This is where you can put all your custom subprocedures, functions, and classes. Subprocedure or function declarations can be declared within the ASP.NET page by enclosing them within the **<script runat="server">** and **</script>** tags. As indicated in line 1 in Figure 10.11, any user-defined subprocedures and functions declared in the code-behind file called Default.aspx.vb as specified by the CodeFile attribute can be accessed directly from the ASP.NET page.

```
<%
...
%>
```

ASP.NET codes are encapsulated within the <% and %> tags, which act as delimiters for the code. Let's look at an example. The Response.Write method is perhaps the most important command in ASP.NET. It is similar to the PHP constructs echo and print or JavaScript method document.write discussed in earlier chapters. It allows you to write text that is then rendered by the .NET Framework as plain text into the HTML document. This text can include HTML tags or be just plain text. The sample code in Figure 10.11 shows how to use the Response.Write method to print text on a Web page, shown in Figure 10.12.

```
<%@ Page Language="VB" AutoEventWireup="false" CodeFile="Default.aspx.vb"
Inherits="_Default" %>


<!DOCTYPE html>
<html>
<head runat="server">
   <meta charset="utf-8"/>
   <%Response.Write("<title>VBScript Heading</title>")%>
</head>
<body>    <%Response.Write("<h1>VBSCRIPT HEADING</h1>")%>
  <%Response.Write("<p>Paragraph One")%>
  <%Response.Write("<p>Paragraph Two")%>
  <%Response.Write("<p>Paragraph Three")%>
</body>
</html>
```

Figure 10.11: ASP.NET code with server-side VBScript

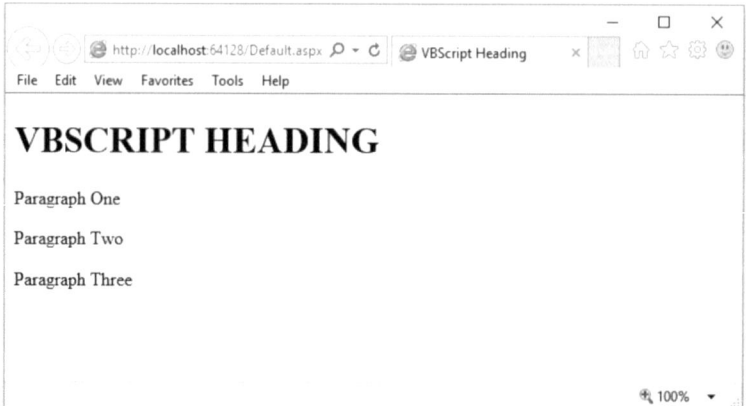

Figure 10.12: A heading created with Response.Write

In Figure 10.11 you see that each of the four ASP.NET statements is enclosed within its own pair of <% and %> tags. Since there are no other non-ASP.NET codes between them, they could also be enclosed with a single pair of ASP.NET delimiters, as shown in Figure 10.13.

```
<%@ Page Language="VB" AutoEventWireup="false" CodeFile="Default.aspx.vb"
Inherits="_Default" %>


<!DOCTYPE html>
<html>
<head runat="server">
    <meta charset="utf-8"/>
    <%Response.Write("<title>VBScript Heading</title>")%>
</head>
<body>
  <%
    Response.Write("<h1>VBSCRIPT HEADING</h1>")
    Response.Write("<p>Paragraph One")
    Response.Write("<p>Paragraph Two")
    Response.Write("<p>Paragraph Three")
  %>
</body>
</html>
```

Figure 10.13: ASP.NET code using a single set of <% and %> delimiters

```
MsgBox(text,options,title)
```

Another popular tool in VBScript is the message box, which displays the specified text to the user. There are many message-box options relating to what buttons are available and what icon is displayed for the message box. The third parameter is the title for the message box. There are additional parameters beyond the ones discussed here; these parameters deal with option help-text documents, which are beyond the scope of this topic.

The code in Figure 10.14 creates the sample message box shown in Figure 10.15.

```
<%@ Page Language="VB" AutoEventWireup="false" CodeFile="Default.aspx.vb"
Inherits="_Default" %>


<!DOCTYPE html>
```
Continued

```
<html>
<head runat="server">
    <meta charset="utf-8"/>
    <%Response.Write("<title>VBScript Heading</title>")%>
</head>
<body>
<%
  Response.Write("<h1>VBSCRIPT HEADING</h1>")
  Response.Write("<p>Paragraph One")
  Response.Write("<p>Paragraph Two")
  Response.Write("<p>Paragraph Three")
  Dim message As String
  message=MsgBox("This is a test message",16,"Sample Message Box")

%>
</body>
</html>
```

Figure 10.14: Using the *MsgBox* function

Figure 10.15: A sample message box from VBScript

The value returned by the **MsgBox** function indicates what option the user took. The possible values are:

- 1 = OK button clicked
- 2 = Cancel button clicked
- 3 = Abort button clicked
- 4 = Retry button clicked

- 5 = Ignore button clicked
- 6 = Yes button clicked
- 7 = No button clicked

As you can see in Figure 10.15, not all the possible buttons are displayed in every message box. The available buttons are controlled by the numeric value in the function's second parameter. Four different options are controlled by this number; simply add up the numeric value of one option in each set to determine what value to place in the second parameter.

The first option controls the buttons displayed:

- 0 = OK button
- 1 = OK and Cancel buttons
- 2 = Abort, Retry, and Ignore buttons
- 3 = Yes, No, and Cancel buttons
- 4 = Yes and No buttons
- 5 = Retry and Cancel buttons

For example, if you want to show the **Retry** and **Cancel** buttons on a message box, you would use 5 as your numeric value in the second parameter. This could change as other options are selected.

The second option controls the icon:

- 0 = No icon
- 16 = Critical icon (X)
- 32 = Query icon (?)
- 48 = Message icon (!)
- 64 = Information icon (i)

To add an exclamation icon to a message box, you would add 48 to the previous value of 5, for a total of 53.

The third option indicates which button is the default in case the user presses the **Enter** key rather than clicking on a button:

- 0 = First button
- 256 = Second button
- 512 = Third button
- 768 = Fourth button

To define the **Cancel** button as the default, you would add 256 to the numeric value of 53, for a total of 309.

The fourth option indicates the modal nature of the message box. This controls whether or not the user can switch from the message box to another application:

- 0 = Application modal
- 4096 = System modal

A value of 0 makes the message box modal for the application. This essentially means the Web page is locked until the user clicks a button in the message box. A value of 4096 defines the message box as modal for the entire system, meaning the user cannot perform any work on the computer until the message box is responded to. To define the message box as modal just for the application, you would add zero to the numeric value, so it would remain 309. If possible, avoid system-modal message boxes, as they can be very frustrating for users.

You can do far more with VBScript than we've discussed here. Throughout the remainder of this chapter, we'll continue to explore the capabilities of VBScript, but understand that there is no way to fully explore them in a single chapter of a book.

Defining Variables

Variables are temporary memory locations that can be used to store information, primarily data. In the example in Figure 10.16, you can see how the variable message is defined using the **Dim** statement. Variables in ASP.NET are declared with the keyword Dim (dimension) follow by the variable name. However, variables in VBScript are not given explicit data types; they can hold either text or numeric data. To display the content of a variable in the Web page, use the Response.Write method, which was mentioned earlier. Figure 10.17 shows an example of using Response.Write for displaying a variable.

```
<%
    Response.Write("<h1>VBSCRIPT HEADING</h1>")
    Dim message
    message = "This is a test message."
    Response.Write(message)
%>
```

Figure 10.16: Displaying a variable

Figure 10.17: Displaying a variable

Variables created in an ASP.NET page have **procedure-level** (or **local-level**) scope. They are often referred to as just "local" variables. To declare a variable with **class-level** (or **global**) scope, you must declare it within the Class namespace in the code-behind file.

Using Arrays

An **array** is defined using the Dim statement by simply following the variable name with parentheses containing a numeric value. Like many of its counterparts, VB is known as a *zero-based language*. Thus, arrays are zero-based, so the number of elements in an array is one more than the number in parentheses (called an array's *index*). For example, in Figure 10.18, the Dim msgArray(4) statement defines an array with five elements. The first element is loaded with the string "Number One"; Figure 10.19 shows the result.

```
<%
   Response.Write("<h1>VBSCRIPT HEADING</h1>")
   Dim msgArray(4)
   msgArray(0)= "Number One"
   Response.Write("Message = " & msgArray(0))
%>
```

Figure 10.18: Using an array

Figure 10.19: Displaying an array element

Arrays are useful when you have a number of similar values that you need to work with. We'll continue to discuss arrays throughout the remainder of this chapter.

Defining Subprocedures

Subprocedures are sections of VBScript that are identified by a name and can be executed as needed from anywhere within the HTML document. As discussed earlier, subprocedures can be declared within the code-behind file that is specified by the CodeFile attribute in the @Page directive or placed directly on the ASP.NET page by enclosing them inside the <script run="server"> and </script> tags.

```
[Access modifier] Sub ProcedureName( [arg1,...] )
   VBScript code
End Sub
Call ProcedureName( [arg1,...] )
```

Subprocedures are particularly useful when you have a task that must be repeated in more than one place. In such situations, subprocedures provide a single point of control, making the code easier to write and maintain. You can pass no argument or multiple arguments (parameters) into the subprocedure, if needed. These parameters are listed in the parentheses after the subprocedure name, separated by commas. The *access modifiers* are special keywords that set the level of access privileges to other objects or classes. Some common access modifiers in VB include Public, Private, Protected, Partial, and Friend. Subprocedures and functions are set to Public by default if they're not explicitly specified.

To run the code in a subprocedure, a subprocedure call is required. You call the subprocedure by its name, including any necessary arguments. You can also use the optional Call keyword to call the subprocedure—for example, Call YourSub(). The code in Figure 10.20 shows an example of a subprocedure and how it might be called. Figure 10.21 shows the resulting Web page.

```
<%@ Page Language="VB" AutoEventWireup="false" CodeFile="Default.aspx.vb"
Inherits="_Default" %>


<script runat="server">
  Sub AskImages(answer)
    answer = MsgBox("Show Images?", 36, "Image Question")
  End Sub
</script>


<!DOCTYPE html>
<html>
<head runat="server">
   <meta charset="utf-8"/>
   <%Response.Write("<title>VB Script Heading</title>")%>
</head>
<body>
<%
  Response.Write("<H1>VB SCRIPT HEADING</H1>")
  Dim showImg
  Call AskImages(showImg)

  Response.Write("<p>Paragraph One")
  Response.Write("<p>Paragraph Two")
  Response.Write("<p>Paragraph Three")
```

Continued

```
%>
</body>
</html>
```

Figure 10.20: Calling a subprocedure declared in Figure 10.18

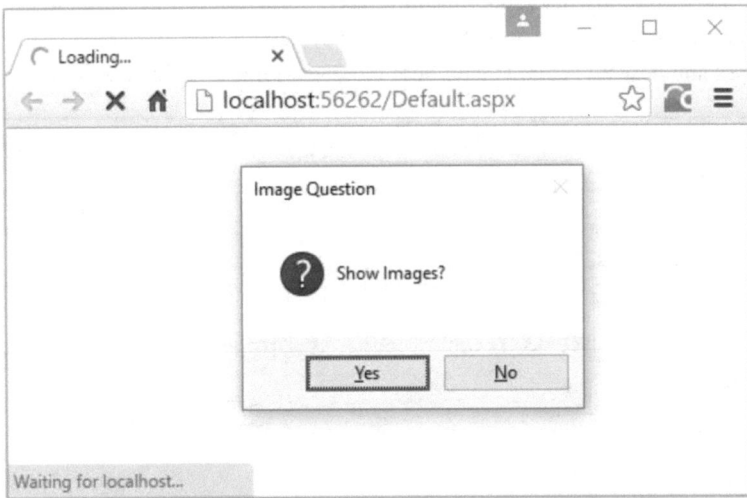

Figure 10.21: A message box created using a subprocedure

In the code in Figure 10.20, the variable showImg is defined and then passed to the AskImages subprocedure. At this point, the variable has not been assigned a value. We are passing it to the subprocedure so that we can receive the updated value after the subprocedure executes. Within the subprocedure, we have defined the argument as answer. The answer variable is local to the subprocedure, meaning it cannot be used anywhere except inside AskImages. The subprocedure displays a message box, and then loads the answer variable with the return information, which indicates which button was pressed. This value is then returned into the showImg variable as the subprocedure ends.

Obviously, this code is somewhat simplistic. We are not yet doing very much with the information received from the user. As you become more familiar with VBScript throughout the chapter, we'll make the sample code more and more useful.

Defining Functions

Functions are similar to subprocedures, but they are more specialized. They are procedures that must return one and only one value.

```
[Access modifier] Function FunctionName( [arg1,...] ) As data type
    VBScript code
    Return value
End Function
```

```
Dim result = FunctionName( [arg1,...] )
```

Functions may have parameters passed to them or no parameters, just as subprocedures do. In addition, a single value must be loaded into a variable with the same data type as the function specified by the "*As data type*" clause. This value is the return value of the function.

Functions are called differently than subprocedures are. A function can be called in two ways: to the right of the assignment (=) operator or within an expression. The code in Figure 10.22 shows how a function is created and how it is called using both methods. Figure 10.23 shows the result.

```
<%@ Page Language="VB" AutoEventWireup="false" CodeFile="Default.aspx.vb"
Inherits="_Default" %>


<script runat="server">


Function GetLarger(num1 As Integer, num2 As Integer) As Integer
    If (num1 > num2) Then
        Return num1
    Else
        Return num2
    End If
End Function
</script>


<!DOCTYPE html>
<html>
<head runat="server">
    <meta charset="utf-8"/>
    <%Response.Write("<title>VBScript Heading</title>")%>
</head>
<body>
<%
    Response.Write<H1>VBSCRIPT HEADING</H1>")
    Dim num1 = 5, num2 = 7


    Dim result = GetLarger(num1, num2)
    Response.Write("<p>" & result & " is greater!")
```

Continued

```
        Response.Write("<p>" & GetLarger(num1, num2) & " is greater!")

%>
</body>
</html>
```

Figure 10.22: Two methods for calling a function

Figure 10.23: Result of two function calls

In the first **function call**, Dim result = GetLarger(num1, num2) in Figure 10.22, the function is invoked on the right side of the assignment operator. Two arguments (num1 and num2) of type Integer are passed to the function GetLarger. The function accepts the two integer values, compares them, and returns the larger of the two to the caller. The second function call is inside the expression of the Response.Write method: Response.Write("<p>" & GetLarger(num1, num2) & " is greater!"). Instead of returning the result to a **local variable**, the result is returned as a part of the argument for the Response.Write method.

Built-in Functions

Writing your own functions, as shown in the previous example, is a powerful way to extend the capabilities of the language in which you are coding. Most languages include some built-in functions. These functions typically perform common tasks, such as date and time manipulation, data type conversions, string manipulation, and basic arithmetic. VBScript has many built-in functions. We've already discussed some of these functions, such as MsgBox. Reviewing each of these functions is beyond the scope of this book, but to help you get started with VBScript, you can review the lists of built-in functions in Tables 10.3 through 10.8.

Table 10.3 shows the VBScript functions for working with dates and times. Use the Date function to return the current system time. The Time function returns the current system time. To return both the current date and time, use the Now function.

Table 10.3: Date and Time Functions	
Function	Description
Date	Returns the current system date
DateAdd	Returns a date after adding a specified time interval
DateDiff	Returns the difference between two dates
DatePart	Returns the specified part of a date
DateSerial	Returns the date for a specified year, month, and day
DateValue	Returns a date
Day	Returns the day of the month (between 1 and 31)
FormatDateTime	Returns a formatted date or time
Hour	Returns the hour of the day (between 0 and 23)
IsDate	Returns a Boolean value that indicates if a specified value can be converted to a date
Minute	Returns the minute of the hour (between 0 and 59)
Month	Returns the month of the year (between 1 and 12)
MonthName	Returns the name of a month
Now	Returns the current system date and time
Second	Returns the second of the minute (between 0 and 59)
Time	Returns the current system time
Timer	Returns the number of seconds since 12:00 a.m.
TimeSerial	Returns the time for a specific hour, minute, and second
TimeValue	Returns a time
Weekday	Returns the day of the week (between 1 and 7)
WeekdayName	Returns the name of a specified day of the week
Year	Returns the year

Table 10.4 lists functions for conversion and formatting. To convert a value into a currency amount, use the FormatCurrency function. Use the FormatPercent function to convert a value into a percent.

Table 10.4: Conversion and Formatting Functions	
Function	Description
Asc	Converts the first letter in a string to ANSI code
CBool	Converts an expression to a variant of subtype Boolean
CByte	Converts an expression to a variant of subtype Byte
CCur	Converts an expression to a variant of subtype Currency
CDate	Converts a valid date and time expression to the variant of subtype Date
CDbl	Converts an expression to a variant of subtype Double
Chr	Converts the specified ANSI code to a character
CInt	Converts an expression to a variant of subtype Integer
CLng	Converts an expression to a variant of subtype Long
CSng	Converts an expression to a variant of subtype Single
CStr	Converts an expression to a variant of subtype String

Table 10.4: Conversion and Formatting Functions (continued)	
Function	**Description**
FormatCurrency	Returns an expression formatted as currency
FormatDateTime	Returns an expression formatted as a date or time
FormatNumber	Returns an expression formatted as a number
FormatPercent	Returns an expression formatted as a percentage
Hex	Returns the hexadecimal value of a specified number
Oct number	Returns the octal value of a specified number

Table 10.5 lists common math functions in VBScript. Use the Int function to return the integer portion of a number. The Fix function does the same thing as Int, but behaves differently if used with negative numbers. For a negative value, Int returns the next lowest integer, and Fix returns the next greater integer.

Table 10.5: Math Functions	
Function	**Description**
Abs	Returns the absolute value of a specified number
Atn	Returns the arctangent of a specified number
Cos	Returns the cosine of a specified number (angle)
Exp	Returns *e* raised to a power
Hex	Returns the hexadecimal value of a specified number
Int	Returns the integer part of a specified number
Fix	Returns the integer part of a specified number
Log	Returns the natural logarithm of a specified number
Oct	Returns the octal value of a specified number
Rnd	Returns a random number less than one but greater or equal to zero
Sgn	Returns an integer that indicates the sign of a specified number
Sin	Returns the sine of a specified number (angle)
Sqr	Returns the square root of a specified number
Tan	Returns the tangent of a specified number (angle)

Table 10.6 contains a list of functions for manipulating arrays. Use the UBound function to return the highest used subscript for an array. The LBound function returns the lowest subscript used for an array.

Table 10.6: Array Functions	
Function	**Description**
Array	Returns a variant containing an array
Filter	Returns a zero-based array that contains a subset of a string array based on filter criteria
IsArray	Returns a Boolean value that indicates whether a specified variable is an array
Join	Returns a string that consists of a number of substrings in an array

Table 10.6: Array Functions (continued)	
Function	Description
LBound	Returns the smallest subscript for the indicated dimension of an array
Split	Returns a zero-based, one-dimensional array that contains a specified number of substrings
UBound	Returns the largest subscript for the indicated dimension of an array

Table 10.7 lists VBScript's string-manipulation functions. The UCase function converts a string into upper case, while LCase converts it into lower case. Use the Mid function to extract a portion of a string.

Table 10.7: String Functions	
Function	Description
InStr	Starting at the first character of the string, returns the position of the first occurrence of one string within another
InStrRev	Starting at the last character of the string, returns the position of the first occurrence of one string within another
LCase	Converts a specified string to lower case
Left	Returns a specified number of characters from the left side of a string
Len	Returns the number of characters in a string
LTrim	Removes spaces on the left side of a string
RTrim	Removes spaces on the right side of a string
Trim	Removes spaces on both the left and right sides of a string
Mid	Returns a specified number of characters from a string
Replace	Replaces a specified part of a string with another string a specified number of times
Right	Returns a specified number of characters from the right side of a string
Space	Returns a string that consists of a specified number of spaces
StrComp	Compares two strings and returns a value that represents the result of the comparison
String	Returns a string that contains a repeating character of a specified length
StrReverse	Reverses a string
UCase	Converts a specified string to upper case

Table 10.8 contains other miscellaneous VBScript functions. Use the MsgBox function to display a pop-up message box. The InputBox function is similar to the message box, but it also allows for the input of a value.

Table 10.8: Miscellaneous Functions	
Function	Description
CreateObject	Creates an object of a specified type
Eval	Evaluates an expression and returns the result
GetLocale	Returns the current locale ID
GetObject	Returns a reference to an automation object from a file

Table 10.8: Miscellaneous Functions (continued)	
Function	Description
GetRef	Allows you to connect a VBScript procedure to a DHTML event on your pages
InputBox	Displays a dialog box where the user can write some input and/or click a button, and returns the contents
IsEmpty	Returns a Boolean value that indicates whether a specified variable has been initialized or not
IsNull	Returns a Boolean value that indicates whether a specified expression contains no valid data (null)
IsNumeric	Returns a Boolean value that indicates whether a specified expression can be evaluated as a number
IsObject	Returns a Boolean value that indicates whether the specified expression is an automation object
LoadPicture	Returns a picture object; available only on 32-bit platforms
MsgBox	Displays a message box, waits for the user to click a button, and returns a value that indicates which button the user clicked
RGB	Returns a number that represents an RGB color value
Round	Rounds a number
ScriptEngine	Returns the scripting language in use
ScriptEngineBuildVersion	Returns the build version number of the scripting engine in use
ScriptEngineMajorVersion	Returns the major version number of the scripting engine in use
ScriptEngineMinorVersion	Returns the minor version number of the scripting engine in use
SetLocale	Sets the locale ID and returns the previous locale ID
TypeName	Returns the subtype of a specified variable
VarType	Returns a value that indicates the subtype of a specified variable

If Statements

The If statement is an important feature of VBScript. This statement allows us to make decisions and dynamically control the behavior of the Web page as it's processed. There are several different formats for the If statement. It can be a single line of code where some condition causes a single statement to execute.

```
If condition Then VBScript code
```

It can also be coded with an End If that marks the end of an entire block of code that executes when the condition is true.

```
If condition Then
    VBScript code
End If
```

You can add an Else statement to define a block of code that executes if the given condition is false.

```
If condition Then
  VBScript code
Else
  VBScript code
End If
```

The condition is a logical operation that compares two or more values, for example, showImg = 6. In earlier examples in this chapter, showImg holds the return value from a message box. A value of 6 from a message box indicates that its **Yes** button has been clicked. We could add an If statement that adds an image to the Web page when the user clicks the **Yes** button. Figure 10.24 shows the code that does this.

```
<%
  Dim showImg As Integer


  WriteHeadings()
  showImg = AskImages()
  If (showImg = 6) Then
      Response.Write("<img src=" & Chr(34) & "html_book.jpg" & Chr(34) & ">")
  End If
%>
```

Figure 10.24: Using an If statement

If the showImg variable is equal to 6, then the image of the HTML book is displayed. This is not the most efficient way to code this particular If statement, however. We can eliminate the showImg variable and call the AskImages function directly from the If. Note, though, that this is only more efficient if the user's response to the question is needed just once. If the response is needed in more than one place in the code, it's probably better to define a variable to hold the value rather than executing the code twice. The alternative code is shown in Figure 10.25.

```
<%
  WriteHeadings()
  If (AskImages() = 6) Then
      Response.Write("<img src=" & Chr(34) & "html_book.jpg" & Chr(34) & ">")
  End If
%>
```

Figure 10.25: Invoking a function in an If statement

In both If examples, you can see how the chr(34) function is used to insert double quotes into the HTML tag. The src attribute of the <img> tag is typically enclosed in double quotes. Coding those within the

Response.Write method, however, would conflict with the double quotes being used to delimit the text written into the Web page. To avoid that conflict, we use the chr(34) function, which inserts the double quotes into the HTML document without conflicting with the double quotes used in the VBScript.

To create a list of mutually exclusive conditions, we can add Elseif to the If statement.

```
If condition1 Then
  VBScript code
Elseif condition2 Then
  VBScript code
End If
```

For example, to test a variable for a series of different values, we could use Elseif, as shown in Figure 10.26. This example shows the showImg variable being tested for a 6, meaning that the **Yes** button was clicked, or a 7, indicating that the **No** button was clicked, or anything else, which would have to be the **Cancel** button. Because the same value is being tested more than once, we use the showImg variable to hold the return value from the AskImages function.

```
<%
  Dim showImg
  showImg = AskImages()
  WriteHeadings()
  If (showImg = 6) Then
    Response.Write("<img src=" & chr(34) & " html_book.jpg" &
    chr(34) & ">")
  Elseif (showImg = 7) Then
    Response.Write("They said No Images")
  Else
    Response.Write("They Canceled")
  End If
%>
```

Figure 10.26: Using Elseif

And/Or/Not Logical Operators

We can make the conditions in our statements increasingly complex using "and/or/not" logic. This allows us to define multiple conditions that must be true before a section of code is executed, and to define optional conditions that can cause the code to execute.

```
If (a = b) Or (a = c) And Not (b = 0) Then VBScript code
```

The And and Or operators are used to combine two or more conditions into a compound conditional statement. If And is used, the conditions on both sides of the And must be evaluated to true for the code to execute. When an Or is used, if the condition on either side of it is evaluated to true, the code executes. Each Or represents a completely new condition. An And listed on one side of the Or has no impact on the tests being performed on the other side. The Not operator negates the expression. If the expression is evaluated to true, then the Not operator will reverse the result to false. Figure 10.27 shows some examples of these **logical operators**.

```
Dim num1 As Integer = 7, num2 As Integer = 5
Dim found As Boolean = false

If ((num1 = num2) And (found = false)) Then
    MsgBox("Result is false")
End If

If ((num1 > num2) Or (found = true)) Then
    MsgBox("Result is true")
End If

If Not (found = true) Then
   MsgBox("Result is true")
End If
```

Figure 10.27: Using And, Or, and Not

Short-Circuit Logical Operators

In addition to the logical operators And and Or, there are two additional logical operators: AndAlso and OrElse. They are sometimes referred to as **short-circuit logical operators** because of the manner in which the conditions are evaluated.

```
If (a = b) OrElse (a = c) AndAlso (b = 0) Then VBScript code
```

In a compound conditional statement that uses either the And or Or logical operator, both conditions of the operator must be evaluated. In contrast, if the first condition of an AndAlso or OrElse is satisfied, then the second and any subsequent conditions are completely ignored. The code shown in Figure 10.28 illustrates these examples.

```
Dim num1 As Integer = 7, num2 As Integer = 5
Dim found As Boolean = false

If ((num1 = num2) AndAlso (found = false)) Then
    MsgBox("First condition is false, ignore second condition")
End If
```

Continued

```
If ((num1 > num2) OrElse (found = true)) Then
    MsgBox("First condition is true, ignore second condition")
End If


If ((num1 > num2) AndAlso (found = true)) Then
   MsgBox("First condition is true, second condition must also be evaluated")
End If
```

Figure 10.28: Using AndAlso and OrElse

Select Case Statements

Another way to handle mutually exclusive sets of tests is with the Select Case statement.

```
Select Case selector
 Case value1
    VBScript code
 Case value2
    VBScript code
 Case Else
    VBScript code
End Select
```

This statement defines a single value that is tested (the selector), then defines what it is tested for (the case) and what code runs when one of those tests is true. The value of the selector and the values to be evaluated in each Case statement must be of the same data type. The value list in the Case statement can contain one or more of the following: a literal, a variable, an expression, an equality sign, and a range of items.

All the Case statements are mutually exclusive. As soon as one is found to be true and its associated code is executed, processing continues after the End Select. The Case Else statement is optional and is only executed when all the preceding Case statements are false. If the Case Else statement is used, it must be the last Case statement in the **Select Case block**. The code in Figure 10.29 shows how we could rewrite the previous If ... Elseif example earlier using Select Case instead.

```
<%
  WriteHeadings()
  Select Case AskImages()
    Case 6
       Response.Write("<img src=" & chr(34) & "html_book.jpg" & chr(34) & ">")
    Case 7
       Response.Write("They said No Images")
                                                          Continued
```

```
      Case Else
         Response.Write("They Canceled")
   End Select
%>
```

Figure 10.29: Using the Select Case statement

The code shown in Figure 10.30 shows how multiple values are used in each Case statements.

```
<%
   Dim randNum As New Random
   Select Case randNum.Next(1,100)
     Case 1,3,5,10
        Response.Write("It's either 1, 3, 5, or 10")
     Case 11 To 20
        Response.Write("It's between 11 and 20")
     Case Is = 50
        Response.Write("It's 50")
     Case > 50
        Response.Write("It's between 51 and 100")
     Case Else
        Response.Write("No match")
   End Select
%>
```

Figure 10.30: Using multiple values in the Case statement

For Next/Each Loops

Sometimes, we need to loop through a section of code a certain number of times. In these cases, the **For Next loop** is useful.

```
For x = start To limit [Step y]
  VBScript code
  [ Exit For ]
Next
```

This loop defines an index variable that is loaded with the starting numeric value before the VBScript code within the loop is executed. After it executes the code the first time, the index is increased by one, and the code repeats. This continues until the limit value is reached. To increment the index by a value other than one (default), use the optional Step parameter. To exit the loop before the limit is reached, use the Exit For statement. This loop can be very useful in handling arrays.

Figure 10.31 shows how the For Next loop can be used to display images on a page. This example shows additional code in the WriteHeadings procedure that loads the URLs of a series of images into the imgArray array. The imgArray is declared with global scope and uses the Public access modifier instead of the Dim. The script in the body of the page uses a For Next loop to cycle through the array, displaying each image on the page as shown in Figure 10.32.

```vb
<%@ Page Language="VB" AutoEventWireup="false" CodeFile="Default.aspx.vb"
Inherits="_Default" %>

<script runat="server">
  Dim imgArray(3) As String
  Sub ShowImage(i As Integer)
     Response.Write("<img src=" & Chr(34) & imgArray(i) & Chr(34) & ">
 ")
  End Sub

  Sub WriteHeadings()
     Response.Write("<H1>VBSCRIPT HEADING</H1>")
     imgArray(0) = "html_book.jpg"
     imgArray(1) = "ibmi_php.jpg"
     imgArray(2) = "mastering_ibmi.jpg"
     imgArray(3) = "websphere.jpg"
  End Sub
</script>

<!DOCTYPE html>

<html>
<head runat="server">
   <meta charset="utf-8"/>
   <% Response.Write("<title>VBScript Heading</title>")%>
</head>
<body>
 <%
    WriteHeadings()
    For counter As Integer = 0 To imgArray.GetUpperBound(0)
      ShowImage(counter)
    Next
%>
```

Continued

```
</body>
</html>
```

Figure 10.31: A For Next loop

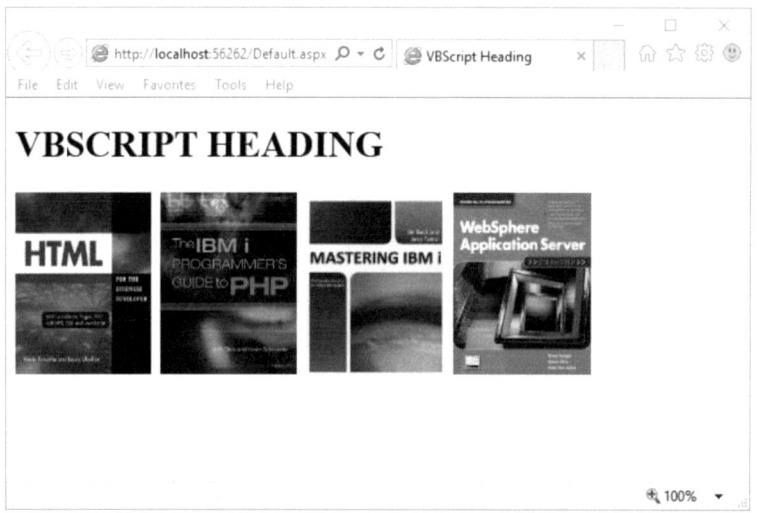

Figure 10.32: Resulting page for a For Next loop

A variation on the For Next loop is the **For Each loop**.

```
For Each element In array
  VBScript code
  [ Exit For ]
Next
```

This loop is designed to work with arrays. It loops through each element in an array, incrementing the index by one. The value of each element of the array is stored in the variable element. You can break out of the loop with the Exit For statement. We could rewrite the For Next loop in Figure 10.31 as a For Each loop, as shown in Figure 10.33.

```
For Each image in imgArray
    Response.Write("<img src=" & Chr(34) & image & Chr(34) & ">  ")
Next
```

Figure 10.33: A For Each loop

While/Do While/Until Loops

Two other forms of loop are the While and Do While, which loop as long as the given condition is true. The **While loop** always tests the condition at the top and will continue executing the code until the condition is false. There are two different formats for coding the Do While: one that tests the condition before executing the code in the loop (pre-test loop) similarly to the While loop, and another that tests the condition after the loop has processed at least once (post-test loop).

```
While condition
   VBScript code
   [ Exit While ]
End While

Do While condition
   VBScript code
   [ Exit Do ]
Loop

Do
   VBScript code
   [ Exit Do ]
Loop While condition
```

To exit the loop before the condition is not true, you can use the Exit While statement for the While loop or Exit Do statement for the **Do While loop**, which is very similar to the Exit For statement. The same loop coded with For in the previous examples could be coded with While and Do While loops, as shown in Figures 10.34. 10.35, and 10.36.

```
n = 0
While (n < 5)
    ShowImage(n)
   n = n + 1
End While
```

Figure 10.34: A While loop

```
n = 0
Do While (n < 5)
    ShowImage(n)
   n = n + 1
loop
```

Figure 10.35: A Do While loop (pre-test)

```
n = 0
Do
    ShowImage(n)
    n = n + 1
Loop While (n < 5)
```

Figure 10.36: An alternative Do While loop (post-test)

Another form of loop is the **Do Until loop**. In contrast to the Do While loop, the Do Until loop performs a negative test on the condition until it's true.

```
Do Until condition
  VBScript code
  [ Exit Do ]
Loop

Do
  VBScript code
  [ Exit Do ]
Loop Until condition
```

This statement is very similar to the Do While, but it stops looping when the given condition is true. It can also be coded in two forms, one that tests the condition before the code executes (pre-test), and the other that tests after it has executed at least once (post-test).

The Do Until loops could also be used in the previous examples. Figures 10.37 and 10.38 show how each version of the Do Until loop would work.

```
n = 0
Do Until (n = 5)
    ShowImage(n)
    n = n + 1
Loop
```

Figure 10.37: A Do Until loop (pre-test)

```
n = 0
Do
    ShowImage(n)
    n = n + 1
Loop Until (n = 5)
```

Figure 10.38: An alternative Do Until loop (post-test)

ASP.NET Code to Create a Simple Table

Now that you have learned the basics of VBScript, it's time to take a closer look at some of the other server-side code for ASP.NET. Since this chapter is just a brief introduction to the topic, we'll avoid a lengthy discussion of all the possible things you could do with ASP.NET. That could fill multiple books. Instead, we'll focus on a few practical examples that show typical uses for ASP.NET in business applications.

Tables 10.9 through 10.13 contain lists of common ASP.NET controls for manipulating Web pages. Table 10.9 focuses on HTML controls, which are ASP.NET tools used to replicate the function of common HTML tags. For example, to create a table in the Web page, you would use the HtmlTable control.

Table 10.9: HTML Controls in ASP.NET	
HTML Server Control	**Description**
HtmlAnchor	Controls the <a> tag
HtmlButton	Controls the <button> tag
HtmlForm	Controls the <form> tag
HtmlGeneric	Controls a generic HTML element, such as <body>, <div>, <span>, <p>, or <font>
HtmlImage	Controls the <image> tag
HtmlInputButton	Controls the <input type="button">, <input type="submit">, or <input type="reset"> buttons
HtmlInputCheckBox	Controls the <input type="checkbox"> tag
HtmlInputFile	Controls the <input type="file"> tag
HtmlInputHidden	Controls the <input type="hidden"> tag
HtmlInputImage	Controls the <input type="image"> tag
HtmlInputRadioButton	Controls the <input type="radio"> button
HtmlInputText	Controls the <input type="text"> or <input type="password"> tags
HtmlSelect	Controls the <select> tag
HtmlTable	Controls the <table> tag
HtmlTableCell	Controls the <td> and <th> tags
HtmlTableRow	Controls the <tr> tag
HtmlTextArea	Controls the <textarea> tag

Table 10.10 lists standard controls in ASP.NET. These controls provide the ability to create specialized objects such as buttons, datagrids, and calendars. This set of controls also includes tools for connecting to **databases**, such as **AccessDataSource** and **SqlDataSource**.

Table 10.10: Standard Controls in ASP.NET	
Control	Description
AccessDataSource	Defines a connection to a Microsoft Access database
AdRotator	Displays a sequence of images
Button	Displays a push button
Calendar	Displays a calendar
CalendarDay	Controls a day in a calendar control
CheckBox	Displays a check box
CheckBoxList	Creates a multi-selection check box group
DataGrid	Displays the fields of a data source in a grid
DataList	Displays items from a data source by using templates
DetailsView	Presents a single row from a data source with navigation buttons
DropDownList	Creates a drop-down list
FormView	Presents a single row from a data source
GridView	Controls an enhanced data grid
HyperLink	Creates a hyperlink
Image	Displays an image
ImageButton	Displays a clickable image
Label	Displays static content which is programmable (can apply styles to its content)
LinkButton	Creates a hyperlink button
ListBox	Creates a single- or multi-selection drop-down list
ListItem	Creates an item in a list
Literal	Displays static content which is programmable (cannot apply styles to its content)
ObjectDataSource	Defines a database connection
Panel	Provides a container for other controls
PlaceHolder	Reserves space for controls added by code
RadioButton	Creates a radio button
RadioButtonList	Creates a group of radio buttons
BulletedList	Creates a list in bullet format
Repeater	Displays a repeated list of items bound to the control
SqlDataSource	Defines an ADO.NET SQL connection
Style	Sets the style of controls
Table	Creates a table
TableCell	Creates a table cell
TableRow	Creates a table row
TextBox	Creates a text box
Xml	Displays an XML file or the results of an XSL transform
XmlDataSource	Defines an XML data source

Table 10.11 lists ASP.NET validation controls. These unique controls provide client-side editing of user input on the Web page. For example, RangeValidator provides the ability to assign a specific range to another control. Entries that are outside that range will be caught before the page is transmitted to the server.

Table 10. 11: Validation Controls in ASP.NET	
Validation Server Control	**Description**
CompareValidator	Compares the value of one control to another control or value
CustomValidator	A custom method to validate input
RangeValidator	Verifies that a value is within a range
RegularExpressionValidator	Verifies that input matches a specified pattern
RequiredFieldValidator	Makes an input control a required field
ValidationSummary	Displays a report of all validation errors in a Web page

Table 10.12 lists controls used to navigate between pages. These specialized controls allow the user to navigate between pages in the website. Use the Menu control to create pop-up menus.

Table 10.12: Navigation Controls in ASP.NET	
Control	**Description**
Menu	Displays static and pop-up navigation options
SiteMapPath Web	Displays a hierarchical path back to the main page
TreeView	Displays static, dynamic, or data-bound trees

Table 10.13 contains ASP.NET controls for managing user logins. The Login control allows users to log in. The LoginName control displays the name of the currently logged-in user.

Table 10.13: Login Controls in ASP.NET	
Control	**Description**
Login	Controls user login interface
PasswordRecovery	Retrieves or resets passwords
LoginName	Displays user's name
ChangePassword	Controls updating passwords
LoginView	Displays templates based on login status
LoginStatus	Detects status and displays login options
CreateUserWizard	Creates a new user

The first example is a simple Web page that lists all the authors in a books table stored in a Microsoft Access database. The ASP.NET code, shown in Figure 10.39, produces the example shown in Figure 10.40.

```
<%@ Import Namespace="System.Data.OleDb" %>


<script  runat="server">
Sub Page_Load
  dim dbconn,sql,dbcomm,dbread
  dbconn = New OleDbConnection("Provider=Microsoft.ACE.OLEDB.12.0;Data
Source=" & Server.MapPath("App_Data\BookData.accdb;Persist Security
Info=True"))
  dbconn.Open()
  sql = "SELECT * FROM Books"
  dbcomm=New OleDbCommand(sql,dbconn)
  dbread=dbcomm.ExecuteReader()
  books.DataSource = dbread
  books.DataBind()
  dbread.Close()
  dbconn.Close()
End Sub
</script>


<!DOCTYPE html>
<html>
<head>
<link href="asp.css" rel="stylesheet" type="text/css">
</head>
<body>


<form id="Form1" runat="server">
<asp:DataList
id="books"
runat="server">


<HeaderTemplate>
<asp:Table ID="Table1" runat=server>
<asp:TableHeaderRow>
```

Continued

```
<asp:TableHeaderCell Width="40" BackColor=#CCCCCC>Book ID</
asp:TableHeaderCell>

<asp:TableHeaderCell Width="100" BackColor=#CCCCCC>Author</
asp:TableHeaderCell>

<asp:TableHeaderCell Width="100" BackColor=#CCCCCC>Title</
asp:TableHeaderCell>

</asp:TableHeaderRow>

</asp:Table>

</HeaderTemplate>


<ItemTemplate>

<asp:Table ID="Table2" runat=server>

<asp:tablerow ID="Tablerow1" runat=server>

<asp:tablecell ID="Number" runat=server CssClass=Number>

<%#Container.DataItem("BookNumber")%>

</asp:tablecell>

<asp:tablecell ID="Author" runat=server cssclass=Name>

<%#Container.DataItem("AuthorName")%>

</asp:tablecell>

<asp:tablecell ID="Title" runat=server cssclass=Title>

<%#Container.DataItem("BookTitle")%>

</asp:tablecell>

</asp:tablerow>

</asp:Table>

</ItemTemplate>

<FooterTemplate>

Source: BookData Database

</FooterTemplate>


</asp:DataList>

</form>


</body>

</html>
```

Figure 10.39: ASP.NET code to list books

BookID	AuthorName	BookTitle
1	Laura Ubelhor	HTML for the Business Developer
2	Jeff Olen	The IBM I programmer's Guide to PHP
3	Jim Buck	Mastering IBM I
4	Rama Turaga	WebSphere Application Server: Step by Step
5	Kevin Schroeder	Advanced Guide to PHP on IBM I
6	Jane Fung	An Introduction to IBM Rational Application Developer
7	Ted Holt	Complete CL
8	James Cooper	Database Design and SQL for DB2
9	Dauve Beulke	DB2 10 for z/OS
10	Roger E. Sanders	DB2 9 Fundamentals
11	Joe Pluta	Developing Web 2.0 Applications with EGL for IBM I
12	Colette Burrus	Developing Web Services for Web Applications
13	Ken Milberg	Driving the Power of AIX
14	Ben Margolis	Enterprise Web 2.0 with EGL
Source: BookData Database		

Figure 10.40: A simple table created from the ASP.NET in Figure 10.39

You can use this example as a simple template to display data from any table in your database. Similar code could be used in your business applications to list such things as current production orders, a shipping schedule, a contact list, or a daily sales activity log. While there are certainly many other ways to list data, this one is reasonably easy.

In the pages that follow, the code in Figure 10.39 is broken into smaller sections and discussed piece by piece.

Section 1 of 3

The section of code in Figure 10.41 defines the OLEDB connection to the Access database.

```
<%@ Import Namespace="System.Data.OleDb" %>


<script  runat="server">
Sub Page_Load
Dim dbconn,sql,dbcomm,dbread
        dbconn = New OleDbConnection("Provider=Microsoft.ACE.
OLEDB.12.0;Data Source=" & Server.MapPath("App_Data\BookData.accdb;Persist
Security Info=True"))
dbconn.Open()
        sql = "SELECT * FROM Books"
dbcomm=New OleDbCommand(sql,dbconn)

                                                       Continued
```

```
dbread=dbcomm.ExecuteReader()
        books.DataSource = dbread
        books.DataBind()
dbread.Close()
dbconn.Close()
End Sub
</script>
```

Figure 10.41: Section 1 of the ASP.NET code for Figure 10.39

This example uses Access rather than SQL Server because it is easier for you to recreate an Access database for testing purposes. The script is defined as a server-side script by the statement <script runat="server">. The Page_Load subprocedure is automatically executed as the page loads. The Dim statement defines a number of loosely typed variables. The dbconn statement defines the connection to the Access database BookData.accdb, located in the APP_Data folder. The Server.MapPath function returns the name and path of the Access database. Its path is relative to the ASP file. In this case, both the ASP file and the database reside in the same folder.

The sql variable contains the SELECT statement, which selects all the columns from the table Books. In the sample database, this table includes the book number, author, and book title. Just because we selected all the data doesn't mean we need to use it, but it is available if needed. The emps datalist contains the result of the SELECT statement and is loaded by binding the datalist to the data reader. Once the datalist is loaded, the reader and database connection are closed.

Section 2 of 3

The section of the ASP.NET file shown in Figure 10.41 begins the HTML code.

```
<!DOCTYPE html>
<html>
<head>
<link href="asp.css" rel="stylesheet" type="text/css">
</head>
<body>

<form id="Form1" runat="server">
<asp:DataList id="books" runat="server">

<HeaderTemplate>
<asp:Table ID="Table1" runat=server>
<asp:TableHeaderRow>
                                              Continued
```

```
<asp:TableHeaderCell Width="40" BackColor="#FFFFFF">BookID</
asp:TableHeaderCell>

<asp:TableHeaderCell width="100" BackColor="#FFFFFF">Author</
asp:TableHeaderCell>

<asp:TableHeaderCell Width="100" BackColor="#FFFFFF">Title</
asp:TableHeaderCell>

</asp:TableHeaderRow>

</asp:Table>

</HeaderTemplate>
```

Figure 10.41: Section 2 of the ASP.NET code for Figure 10.39

The header section contains a link to a Cascading Style Sheet, also stored in the same folder as the ASP file. The body section contains a simple form named Form1. (Forms are discussed in chapter 9.) It also defines the books datalist. The ASP page will automatically produce a table that holds the information from the datalist. This table is built using properties set by three specialized controls: **HeaderTemplate**, **ItemTemplate**, and **FooterTemplate**. In this section, HeaderTemplate defines a table and a table header row containing header cells for each column in the table. Although the width and background color of these cells are set here, this method of styling is deprecated and should not be used. In the next section, you'll see that the cell properties are set through the style sheet.

Section 3 of 3

The ItemTemplate control defines the formatting of each record read from the datalist, as shown in Figure 10.42.

```
<ItemTemplate>
<asp:Table ID="Table2" runat=server>
<asp:tablerow ID="Tablerow1" runat=server>
<asp:tablecell ID="Number" runat=server CssClass=Number>
<%#Container.DataItem("BookID")%>
</asp:tablecell>
<asp:tablecell ID="Name" runat=server cssclass=Name>
<%#Container.DataItem("AuthorName")%>
</asp:tablecell>
<asp:tablecell ID="Title" runat=server cssclass=Title>
<%#Container.DataItem("BookTitle")%>
</asp:tablecell>
</asp:tablerow>
</asp:Table>
</ItemTemplate>

                                                    Continued
```

```
<FooterTemplate>
Source: BookData Database
</FooterTemplate>

</asp:DataList>
</form>

</body>
</html>
```

Figure 10.42: Section 3 of the ASP.NET code for Figure 10.39

In this case, each record is defined as being a table with one row and three cells. The width, color, and other properties are defined in the style sheet linked to in the header section. The cells are each defined with their own class name using the cssclass property. Each cell is associated with a data item from the datalist using the Container.DataItem function, which identifies the desired column from the datalist. The names of the data items correspond to the column names from the table read in the SELECT statement. A FooterTemplate defines the text displayed at the bottom of the table, and then the datalist, form, and Web page are all closed.

The code for the CSS associated with this ASP.NET example is shown in Figure 10.43. The table and table row elements have their width set to 300 pixels. The background color of the table is set to gray. The style sheet contains several subclasses for the table data element. Each of the columns has its own class with a specific width and color. Some of the classes shown here are used in later examples.

```
.data {width:20%; position:absolute; top:10px; left:20px;
}
.TblTitle {background-color:#CCC;
}
table {width:300px; background-color:#CCC;
}
tr {width:300px; background-color: #FFF;
}
td.number {width:40px;
}
td.name {width:100px;
}
td.title {width:100px; text-align: left;
}
td.date {width:90px; background-color:#FFF;
}
```

Figure 10.43: The code for a CSS style sheet

Creating a More Advanced Table

The previous example showed how to use ASP.NET to create a simple list. That is fine for many business functions; it's possible that all you need to do is present a list of current orders, inventory, scheduling information, or similar information. However, this is not always sufficient. You might have layers of pages where, for example, the first page presents a list of books whose titles are hypertext links. Clicking a book's title displays a second page with the book information for that book. Figure 10.44 shows the code for building the initial list of books, shown in Figure 10.45.

```
<%@ Page Language="VB" Debug="true" %>
<%@ Import Namespace="System.Data.OleDb" %>


<script  runat="server">
Sub Page_Load
        Dim dbconn, sql, dbcomm, dbread
        dbconn = New OleDbConnection("Provider=Microsoft.ACE.
OLEDB.12.0;Data Source=" & Server.MapPath("App_Data\BookData.accdb;Persist
Security Info=True"))
dbconn.Open()
        sql = "SELECT * FROM Books"
dbcomm=New OleDbCommand(sql,dbconn)
dbread=dbcomm.ExecuteReader()
        books.DataSource = dbread
        books.DataBind()
dbread.Close()
dbconn.Close()
End Sub


</script>
<!DOCTYPE html>
<html>
<head>
<link href="asp.css" rel="stylesheet" type="text/css">
</head>
<body>
<div class="data">
<form id="Form1" runat="server">
<asp:DataList id="books" runat="server">
```

Continued

```
<HeaderTemplate>
<asp:Table ID="Table1" runat=server>
<asp:TableHeaderRow>
<asp:TableHeaderCell>BookID</asp:TableHeaderCell>
<asp:TableHeaderCell>Author</asp:TableHeaderCell>
<asp:TableHeaderCell>Title</asp:TableHeaderCell>
</asp:TableHeaderRow>
</asp:Table>
</HeaderTemplate>


<ItemTemplate>
<asp:Table runat=server>
<asp:tablerow runat=server>
<asp:tablecell ID="Number" runat=server CssClass=Number>
<%#Container.DataItem("BookID")%>
</asp:tablecell>
<asp:tablecell ID="Name" runat=server CssClass=Name>
<%#Container.DataItem("AuthorName")%>
</asp:tablecell>
<asp:tablecell ID="Title" runat=server CssClass=Title>
<a href="details.aspx?ID=<%#Container.DataItem("BookNumber")%>&Title=<%#Con
tainer.DataItem("BookTitle")%>"><%#Container.DataItem("BookTitle")%></a>

</asp:tablecell>
</asp:tablerow>
</asp:Table>
</ItemTemplate>
<FooterTemplate>
Source: BookData Database
</FooterTemplate>


</asp:DataList>
</form>
</div>
</body>
</html>
```

Figure 10.44: The ASP.NET code that creates the page in Figure 10.45

BookID	AuthorName	BookTitle
1	Laura Ubelhor	HTML for the Business Developer
2	Jeff Olen	The IBM I programmer's Guide to PHP
3	Jim Buck	Mastering IBM I
4	Rama Turaga	WebSphere Application Server: Step by Step
5	Kevin Schroeder	Advanced Guide to PHP on IBM I
6	Jane Fung	An Introduction to IBM Rational Application Developer
7	Ted Holt	Complete CL
8	James Cooper	Database Design and SQL for DB2
9	Dauve Beulke	DB2 10 for z/OS
10	Roger E. Sanders	DB2 9 Fundamentals
11	Joe Pluta	Developing Web 2.0 Applications with EGL for IBM I
12	Colette Burrus	Developing Web Services for Web Applications
13	Ken Milberg	Driving the Power of AIX
14	Ben Margolis	Enterprise Web 2.0 with EGL
Source: BookData Database		

Figure 10.45: A table with linked items

The lines in Figure 10.44 that create the hypertext link are shown again in Figure 10.46.

```
<asp:tablecell ID="Title" runat=server CssClass=Title>
<a href="details.aspx?ID=<%#Container.DataItem("BookNumber")%>&Title=<%#Con
tainer.DataItem("BookTitle")%>"><%#Container.DataItem("BookTitle")%></a>
</asp:tablecell>
```

Figure 10.46: The code to create a hypertext link

In this case, we use a simple anchor tag and assemble the href property. It begins with the name of the next ASP page to open. Then, additional information is added to the URL to pass the book ID and title as parameters to the next page. The list of parameters starts with a question mark. Each parameter begins with the parameter name followed by an equal sign, and then the value for the parameter. Ampersands separate the parameters. The data passed in this manner is referred to as the *query string*. For example, the query string for "The IBM i Programmer's Guide to PHP" in the second row of the table would look like this:

```
details.aspx?ID=2&Title=The%20IBM%20i%20Programmer's%20Guide%20to%20PHP
```

Notice how the data items are rendered into the page without requiring any kind of concatenation. The characters %20 represent a white space character encode, which is rendered automatically by the Web browser if a white space is included as a part of the URL.

The code for the schedule data page is shown in Figure 10.47, and the results for the book *The IBM i Programmer's Guide to PHP* are shown in Figure 10.48.

```
<%@ Page Language="VB" Debug="true" %>
<%@ Import Namespace="System.Data.OleDb" %>

<script  runat="server">
Sub Page_Load

        Dim dbconn, sql, dbcomm, dbread, bookID
        bookID = Request.QueryString("ID")

        dbconn = New OleDbConnection("Provider=Microsoft.ACE.
OLEDB.12.0;Data Source=" & Server.MapPath("App_Data\BookData.accdb;Persist
Security Info=True"))
        dbconn.Open()

       sql = "SELECT BookID, Qty, FORMAT(Price, 'C') as Price FROM
BookDetails WHERE BookID = " & bookID
        dbcomm = New OleDbCommand(sql, dbconn)
        dbread = dbcomm.ExecuteReader()
        books.DataSource = dbread
        books.DataBind()
        dbread.Close()
        dbconn.Close()
End Sub

</script>

<!DOCTYPE html>
<html>
<head>
<link href="asp.css" rel="stylesheet" type="text/css">
</head>
<body>

<form id="Form1" runat="server">
<asp:DataList id="books" runat="server">

<HeaderTemplate>
<asp:Table ID="Table1" runat=server>
<asp:TableHeaderRow>
```

Continued

```
<asp:TableHeaderCell colspan="3"><%  Response.Write(Request.
QueryString("Title"))%></asp:TableHeaderCell>
</asp:TableHeaderRow>
<asp:TableHeaderRow>
<asp:TableHeaderCell>BookID</asp:TableHeaderCell>
<asp:TableHeaderCell >Qty</asp:TableHeaderCell>
<asp:TableHeaderCell>Price</asp:TableHeaderCell>
</asp:TableHeaderRow>
</asp:Table>
</HeaderTemplate>

<ItemTemplate>
<asp:Table runat=server >
<asp:tablerow runat=server>
<asp:tablecell ID="Number" runat=server CssClass=Number>
<%#Container.DataItem("BookID")%>
</asp:tablecell>
<asp:tablecell ID="Qty" runat=server cssclass=Qty>
  <%#Container.DataItem("Qty")%>
</asp:tablecell>
<asp:tablecell ID="Price" runat=server cssclass=Price>
<%#Container.DataItem("Price")%>
</asp:tablecell>
</asp:tablerow>
</asp:Table>
</ItemTemplate>
<FooterTemplate>
Source: BookData Database
</FooterTemplate>

</asp:DataList>
</form>

</body>
</html>
```

Figure 10.47: The ASP.NET code to create the page in Figure 10.48

The IBM i Programmer's Guide to PHP		
BookID	**Qty**	**Price**
2	150	$41.95
Source: BookData Database		

Figure 10.48: Selected book data

This code is very similar to that shown in Figure 10.44, except that it has input parameters to read from the query string. The book ID is read with the following statement:

```
bookID = Request.QueryString("ID")
```

This statement loads the value of the ID parameter into the bookID variable. This variable is then used in assembling the SELECT statement. For this page to work correctly, the SELECT statement needs to limit the data displayed to only the book entries for one book—*The IBM i Programmer's Guide to PHP*, in this case. The code sample in Figure 10.49 shows how the SELECT statement was assembled. At the end of this statement, you can see how the bookID variable is concatenated into the WHERE clause.

```
sql = "SELECT BookID, Qty, FORMAT(Price, 'C') AS Price FROM BookDetails
WHERE BookID = " & bookID
```

Figure 10.49: The code to build a precise SELECT statement

The Format function modifies the date variable from the Access database to display the appropriate information. The book title from the query string is displayed in the table headings using this simple statement:

```
<%Response.Write(Request.QueryString("Title"))%>
```

The Response.Write method was discussed earlier in this chapter.

Updating Data in a Database

Suppose we want to create a page to update the book details data in the Access database discussed in the previous examples. There are a number of ways we can accomplish that. One of the standard data controls included in ASP.NET is **FormView**. This control is designed to manage a connection to a database, allowing an application user to navigate through all the rows in a table. As the user moves through the database, he or she can edit, delete, or insert records. Of course, those are configurable options, so if you don't want to allow them, you can disable them.

The code in Figure 10.50 creates the FormView control shown in Figure 10.51.

```
<%@ Page Language="VB" Debug="true" %>
<%@ Import Namespace="System.Data.OleDb" %>
<%@ Import Namespace="System.Web.UI.WebControls" %>

<!DOCTYPE html>
<html>
<body>

<form id="Form1" runat="server">
<asp:FormView
        datasourceid="BookDetailsSource"
        allowpaging="True"
        datakeynames="BookID,PubDate"
        id="bookdetails"
        runat="server"
        BackColor=lightgray
        BorderWidth=3
        borderstyle=Inset>

<edititemtemplate>
    BookID:
    <asp:Label ID="BookIDLabel1" runat="server" Text='<%# Eval("BookID")
%>'></asp:Label><br />
    PubDate:
    <asp:Label ID="PubDateLabel1" runat="server" Text='<%# Eval("PubDate")
%>'></asp:Label><br />
    Qty:
    <asp:TextBox ID="QtyTextBox" runat="server" Text='<%# Eval("Qty")
%>'></asp:TextBox><br />
    Price:
    <asp:TextBox ID="PriceTextBox" runat="server" Text='<%# Bind("Price")
%>'></asp:TextBox><br />

    <asp:LinkButton ID="UpdateButton" runat="server"
CausesValidation="True" CommandName="Update"
        Text="Update">
    </asp:LinkButton>
    <asp:LinkButton ID="UpdateCancelButton" runat="server"
CausesValidation="False" CommandName="Cancel"
        Text="Cancel">
    </asp:LinkButton>
```

Continued

```
</edititemtemplate>
    <InsertItemTemplate>
        BookID:
        <asp:TextBox ID="BookIDTextBox" runat="server" Text='<%#
Bind("BookID") %>'>
        </asp:TextBox><br />
        PubDate:
        <asp:TextBox ID="PubDateTextBox" runat="server" Text='<%#
Bind("PubDate") %>'>
        </asp:TextBox><br />
        Qty:
        <asp:TextBox ID="QtyTextBox" runat="server" Text='<%# Bind("Qty")
%>'>
        </asp:TextBox><br />
        Price:
        <asp:TextBox ID="PriceTextBox" runat="server" Text='<%#
Bind("Price") %>'>
        </asp:TextBox><br />

        <asp:LinkButton ID="InsertButton" runat="server"
CausesValidation="True" CommandName="Insert"
            Text="Insert">
        </asp:LinkButton>
        <asp:LinkButton ID="InsertCancelButton" runat="server"
CausesValidation="False" CommandName="Cancel"
            Text="Cancel">
        </asp:LinkButton>
    </InsertItemTemplate>
    <ItemTemplate>
        BookID:
        <asp:Label ID="BookIDLabel" runat="server" Text='<%# Eval("BookID")
%>'></asp:Label><br />
        PubDate:
        <asp:Label ID="PubDateLabel" runat="server" Text='<%#
Eval("PubDate") %>'></asp:Label><br />
        Qty:
        <asp:Label ID="QtyLabel" runat="server" Text='<%# Eval("Qty")
%>'></asp:Label><br />
        Price:
        <asp:Label ID="PriceLabel" runat="server" Text='<%# Bind("Price")
%>'></asp:Label><br />
```

Continued

```
        <asp:LinkButton ID="EditButton" runat="server"
CausesValidation="False" CommandName="Edit"
            Text="Edit">
        </asp:LinkButton>
        <asp:LinkButton ID="DeleteButton" runat="server"
CausesValidation="False" CommandName="Delete"
            Text="Delete">
        </asp:LinkButton>
        <asp:LinkButton ID="NewButton" runat="server"
CausesValidation="False" CommandName="New"
            Text="New">
        </asp:LinkButton>
    </ItemTemplate>
</asp:FormView>

    <asp:AccessDataSource ID="schedsource" runat="server" DataFile="~/App_
Data/BookData.accdb"
        selectcommand="SELECT BookID, FORMAT(PubDate, 'Short Date')
as PDate, Qty, FORMAT(Price, 'C') as Price FROM [BookDetails] ORDER
BY [BookID], [PubDate] " DeleteCommand="DELETE FROM [BookDetails]
WHERE [BookNumber] = ? AND [PubDate] = ? " InsertCommand="INSERT INTO
[BookDetails] ([BookNumber], [PubDate], [Qty], [Price]) VALUES (?, ?, ?,
?)" UpdateCommand="UPDATE [BookDetails] SET [Qty] = ?, [Price] = ? WHERE
[BookID] = ? ">
        <DeleteParameters>
            <asp:Parameter Name=" BookID" Type="Int32" />
            <asp:Parameter Name="PubDate" Type="DateTime" />
        </DeleteParameters>
        <UpdateParameters>
            <asp:Parameter Name="Qty" Type="Int32" />
            <asp:Parameter Name="Price" Type="Decimal" />
        </UpdateParameters>
        <InsertParameters>
            <asp:Parameter Name="BookID" Type="Int32" />
            <asp:Parameter Name="PubDate" Type="DateTime" />
            <asp:Parameter Name="Qty" Type="Int32" />
            <asp:Parameter Name="Price" Type="Decimal" />
        </InsertParameters>

    </asp:AccessDataSource>
</form>
```

Continued

```
</body>
</html>
```

Figure 10.50: The code to update a database

BookID: 1
PubDate: 8/1/2008
Qty: 200
Price: 23.95
Edit Delete New
1 2 3 4 5 6 7 8 9 10 ...

Figure 10.51: A form for updating data in a database

This simple form lists each of the columns in the table, and presents a navigation tool at the bottom so that the user can move through all the records. It also provides options to edit or delete the current record, or even insert a new record.

All of this is done with very little coding on your part if you use the tools in the Visual Web Developer. Simply open a new file within your website, and select the **Web Form** option. When the new file is opened in edit mode, select the **Desig**n option in the lower left corner of the page. This switches you from views of the code to looking at the palette. Using the toolbox typically located on the left side of the screen, drag a **FormView** control from the data controls onto the page. Then drag an **AccessDataSource** control onto the page. Figure 10.52 shows the page with these two controls added.

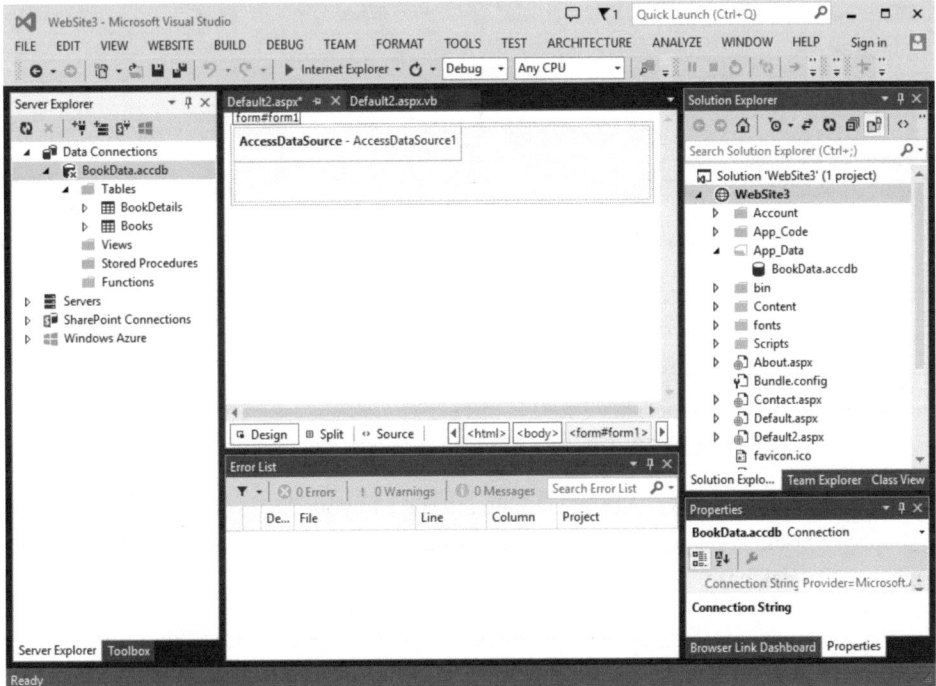

Figure 10.52: A new page in design mode

Once these controls are located on the screen, you can right-click the **AccessDataSource** control and select the **Configure Data Source** option. This walks you through a series of prompts asking you the location of the database you want to connect to, what table in the database you want to connect to, and what columns within the table you want to use. You also have the option to have this wizard generate the appropriate SELECT, INSERT, UPDATE, and DELETE commands for you.

Right-click the **FormView** control and select the **AutoFormat** option; you can select from one of several preconfigured layout options. For this example, select **Black & Blue 2**. Then, select the properties of the FormView control and update the data source to point at the **AccessDataSource** control you've already placed on the page. They are not automatically associated because, in more sophisticated applications, you might have multiple data sources in use on the same page. If you used the data in the Books table, your control would look like the example in Figure 10.53.

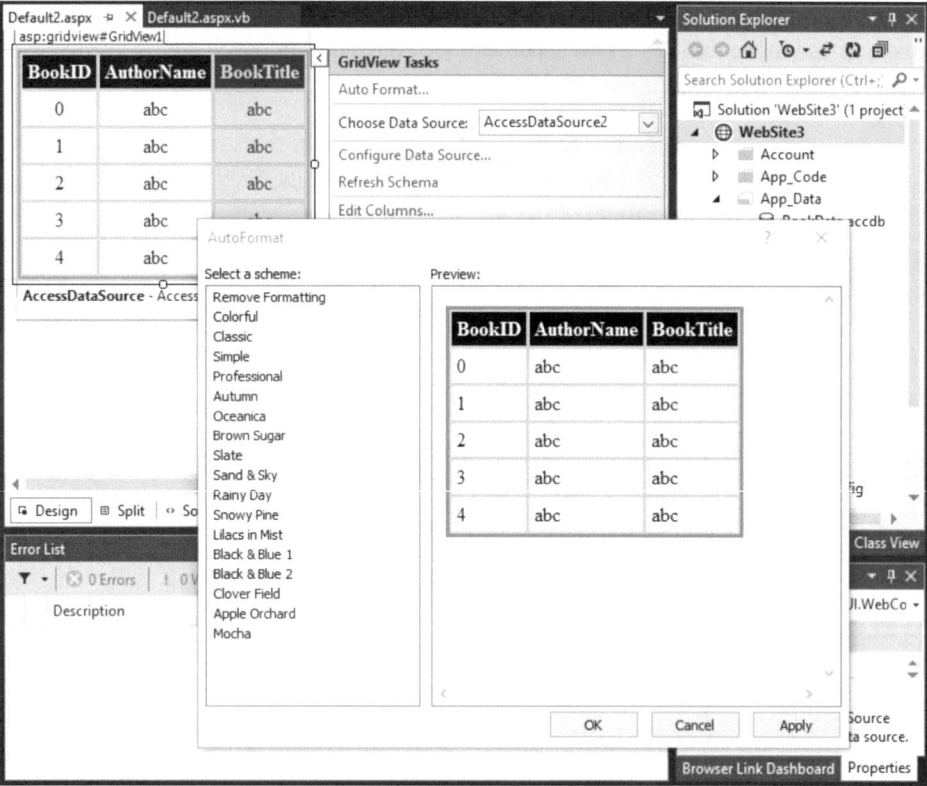

Figure 10.53: The new page after configuring the options

That is essentially all it takes to create an editable interface to your Access database. To see it in action, simply right-click the page and select **View in Browser**. This launches the page and allows you to update your database.

With the control completed, let's go back to reviewing some of the code from Figure 10.50. The snippet shown in Figure 10.54 shows the definition of the FormView control. In this case, we define the keys to the table as the employee number and schedule data. The background color, style, and width are also set here.

```
<form id="Form1" runat="server">
<asp:FormView
        datasourceid="BookDetailsSource"
        allowpaging="True"
        datakeynames="BookID,PubDate"
        id="bookdetails"
        runat="server"
        BackColor=lightgray
        BorderWidth=3
        borderstyle=Inset>
```

Figure 10.54: The FormView definition from the application in Figure 10.50

The code snippet in Figure 10.55 shows only EditTemplate. This controls the look and behavior of the form while in edit mode. As you can see, the two key fields, BookID and PubDate, are displayed in Label controls. These are read-only, so no updating of these columns is allowed. The other fields are all shown in text boxes, which allow for easy updating. This section is completed by the **Update** and **Cancel** buttons.

```
<edititemtemplate>
    BookID:
    <asp:Label ID="BookIDLabel1" runat="server" Text='<%# Eval("BookID")
%>'></asp:Label><br />
    PubDate:
    <asp:Label ID="PuDateLabel1" runat="server" Text='<%# Eval("PubDate")
%>'></asp:Label><br />
    Qty:
    <asp:TextBox ID="QtyTextBox" runat="server" Text='<%# Eval("Qty")
%>'></asp:TextBox><br />
    Price:
    <asp:TextBox ID="PriceTextBox" runat="server" Text='<%# Bind("Price")
%>'>
    </asp:TextBox><br />


    <asp:LinkButton ID="UpdateButton" runat="server"
CausesValidation="True" CommandName="Update"
        Text="Update">
                                                      Continued
```

```
    </asp:LinkButton>
    <asp:LinkButton ID="UpdateCancelButton" runat="server"
CausesValidation="False" CommandName="Cancel"
        Text="Cancel">
    </asp:LinkButton>
</edititemtemplate>
```

Figure 10.55: The EditTemplate code

The code snippet in Figure 10.56 shows InsertTemplate. In this case, all the columns are editable, since even the key fields need to be provided here.

```
    <InsertItemTemplate>
        BookID:
        <asp:TextBox ID="BookIDTextBox" runat="server" Text='<%#
Bind("BookID") %>'>
        </asp:TextBox><br />
        PubDate:
        <asp:TextBox ID="PubDateTextBox" runat="server" Text='<%#
Bind("PubDate") %>'>
        </asp:TextBox><br />
        Qty:
        <asp:TextBox ID="QtyTextBox" runat="server" Text='<%# Bind("Qty")
%>'>
        </asp:TextBox><br />
        Price:
        <asp:TextBox ID="PriceTextBox" runat="server" Text='<%#
Bind("Price") %>'>
        </asp:TextBox><br />


        <asp:LinkButton ID="InsertButton" runat="server"
CausesValidation="True" CommandName="Insert"
            Text="Insert">
        </asp:LinkButton>
        <asp:LinkButton ID="InsertCancelButton" runat="server"
CausesValidation="False" CommandName="Cancel"
            Text="Cancel">
        </asp:LinkButton>
    </InsertItemTemplate>
```

Figure 10.56: The InsertTemplate code

The code snippet in Figure 10.57 shows ItemTemplate, which defines the look and behavior of the form while the user is simply browsing data, not editing or inserting. As you can see in this example, all the columns are displayed as read-only Label controls. Buttons for switching to edit or delete mode complete the template.

```
    <ItemTemplate>
        BookID:
        <asp:Label ID="BookIDLabel" runat="server" Text='<%# Eval("BookID")
%>'></asp:Label><br />
        PubDate:
        <asp:Label ID="PubDateLabel" runat="server" Text='<%#
Eval("PubDate") %>'></asp:Label><br />
        Qty:
        <asp:Label ID="QtyLabel" runat="server" Text='<%# Eval("Qty")
%>'></asp:Label><br />
        Price:
        <asp:Label ID="PriceLabel" runat="server" Text='<%# Bind("Price")
%>'></asp:Label><br />

        <asp:LinkButton ID="EditButton" runat="server"
CausesValidation="False" CommandName="Edit"
            Text="Edit">
        </asp:LinkButton>
        <asp:LinkButton ID="DeleteButton" runat="server"
CausesValidation="False" CommandName="Delete"
            Text="Delete">
        </asp:LinkButton>
        <asp:LinkButton ID="NewButton" runat="server"
CausesValidation="False" CommandName="New"
            Text="New">
        </asp:LinkButton>
    </ItemTemplate>
```

Figure 10.57: The ItemTemplate code

The last code snippet, in Figure 10.58, shows AccessDataSource. You'll see that we added the same Format() function to the SELECT statement that we used in an earlier example. Again, this formats the data and time fields from the Access database correctly for our needs. After the SELECT statement, the DELETE, INSERT, and UPDATE commands are all listed. Whenever a field from the FormView is referenced, parameter markers (question marks) are used in the code. Then, the parameters are defined below.

```
</asp:FormView>

    <asp:AccessDataSource ID="schedsource" runat="server" DataFile="~/App_
Data/BookData.accdb"


        SelectCommand = "SELECT BookID, FORMAT(PubDate, 'Short Date')
AS Pdate, Qty, FORMAT[Price, 'C'] AS Price FROM [BookDetails] ORDER BY
[BookID], [PubDate]"
        DeleteCommand = "DELETE FROM [BookDetails] WHERE [BookNumber] = ?
AND [PubDate] = ?"
        InsertCommand = "INSERT INTO [BookDetails] ([BookID],[PubDate],[Qty]
,[Price]) VALUES (?, ?, ?, ?)"
        UpdateCommand = "UPDATE [BookDetails] SET [Qty]=?, [Price]=? WHERE
[BookID] = ? AND [PubDate] = ?">


        <DeleteParameters>
            <asp:Parameter Name="BookID" Type="Int32" />
            <asp:Parameter Name="PubDate" Type="DateTime" />
        </DeleteParameters>
        <UpdateParameters>
            <asp:Parameter Name="Qty" Type="Int32" />
            <asp:Parameter Name="Price" Type="Decimal" />

        </UpdateParameters>
        <InsertParameters>
            <asp:Parameter Name="BookID" Type="Int32" />
            <asp:Parameter Name="PubDate" Type="DateTime" />
            <asp:Parameter Name="Qty" Type="Int32" />
            <asp:Parameter Name="Price" Type="Decimal" />
        </InsertParameters>

    </asp:AccessDataSource>
</form>
</body>
</html>
```

Figure 10.58: The AccessDataSource code

Connecting to SQL Server

All the examples in this chapter have involved an Access database. One of the reasons for this is because it is somewhat simpler to distribute an Access database than a SQL Server database, so we can make the database available to our readers through this book's page in the MC Press Bookstore, *https://goo.gl/2uYjHb*.

If you want to use a SQL Server database instead, however, it is an easy change to make. Simply go to the **Data Controls** in the toolbox, drag the **SQLDataSource** onto the page, and configure it in much the same fashion as the **AccessDataSource** discussed earlier. Once it is configured, simply attach the appropriate data controls to the data source by changing their **Datasource** property, and you're connected.

Summary

The large number of specialized controls combined with a robust programming language makes ASP .NET an extremely diverse development environment. We've only touched the basics of programming with it in this chapter. To truly master ASP.NET takes considerable effort, but we hope the examples here have helped you see that you can create productive and effective Web pages fairly easily, once you get the basics figured out.

Key Terms

@Import
@Page
<FooterTemplate>
<HeaderTemplate>
<ItemTemplate>
<script runat="server">
AccessDataSource
Active Server Pages (ASP)
array
ASP.NET
class-level variable
code-behind file
database
Dim

Do Until loop
Do While loop
For Each loop
For Next loop
FormView
function
function call
global variable
If statements
IIS server
local variable
logical operators
MsgBox
page directives

post-test loop
pre-test loop
procedure-level variable
Response.Write
Select Case Statements
short-circuit logical operators
SqlDataSource
subprocedures
subprocedure call
VBScript
Web form
While loop

Discussion/Review Questions

1. What are three differences between ASP.NET and Java?
2. What languages can developers use to code in ASP.NET?
3. What is the file extension for ASP.NET source files?
4. Which integrated development environment (IDE) is best suited for ASP.NET development?
5. In Visual Studio, how do you toggle between the three different views of an ASP file?

6. What is VBScript?
7. Where do you place VBScript code in an ASP file?
8. What are ASP.NET page directives?
9. The code-behind file of an ASP.NET page is specified in which @Page attribute?
10. Which tags are used to encapsulate ASP.NET codes?
11. What is the .NET Framework?
12. What is the most common and frequently used directive in an ASP file?
13. If a variable is declared within the Class namespace in the code-behind file, what level of scope does the variable have?
14. What are two major differences between a subprocedure and a function?
15. How do you call subprocedures and functions?
16. What are the differences between the logical operators And/Or and short-circuit logical operators AndAlso/OrElse?
17. How do you connect to a Microsoft Access database in ASP.NET?
18. What is a query string, and how do you access its data within an ASP file?
19. What are the three specialized table controls used to set and build advanced data tables in ASP .NET?
20. What is the standard data control in ASP.NET that allows you to quickly and easily modify data in your database?

Exercises

1. Create a new website project in Visual Studio.
2. In the website project you created in Exercise 1, create a new Web form called MyPage.aspx. Open MyPage.aspx in code view and write the VBScript code to display an image and a paragraph to the Web page using the Response.Write method.
3. Provide the VBScript code to generate the following information message box:

4. Provide the VBScript code to declare the following variables and store their corresponding data:

Variables	Data Types	Values
Age	Integer	23
City	String	Racine
Salary	Decimal	$100,000.00

Found	Boolean	True
Book	String array of 3 elements	HTML5 PHP ASP.NET

5. Write the VBScript code for a function to perform the following task:

   Function Name: GetUrl
   Parameter: url (String)
   Return: String
   Task: Returns the string of an anchor tag that links to the url parameter

6. Write a For Next loop to print the content of the following array to a Web page:

   ```
   Dim books() As String = {"HTML5","IBM
   i","PHP","Java","JavaSscript","DB2"}
   ```

7. Provide the code to connect a Microsoft Access file called BookAuthors.accdb located in the App_Data folder of an ASP.NET project.

8. BookAuthors.accdb has a table called authors with the following fields: id, first_name, last_name, city, state, zip. Write the SQL statement to select the id, first_name, last_name, and city fields and sort the result by last_name.

9. Assume that the query from Exercise 8 results in the following:

ID	First_name	Last_name	City
3	Buck	Jim	Madison
1	Hur	Christian	Fresno
2	Ubelhor	Laura	Columbus
5	Williams	Christine	London
4	Young	Bruce	Denver

   Provide the code to populate these data to a table using HeaderTemplate, ItemTemplate, and FooterTemplate controls. The result should look identical to the table shown above.

11

JavaServer Pages

First Java, then JavaScript, and now JavaServer Pages (JSP). They have similar names, but are different programming tools. Yes, it is confusing! Chapter 8 introduced JavaScript, the client-side scripting language that can be embedded in HTML to make Web pages more dynamic. This chapter introduces JavaServer Pages (JSP). Like JavaScript, JSP makes Web pages more dynamic. Like PHP and ASP.NET, JSP is a server-side programming tool.

In this chapter, you will be introduced to the JSP used in HTML, learn the basics of JSP syntax, and learn by example how to use JSP within Web applications. Learning JSP does not require Java knowledge or experience, but if you are already familiar with Java, JSP programming will be easy.

JSP Overview

JSP technology provides a simple, fast way to create dynamic Web-page content. The JSP specifications are developed through an industry-wide initiative led by Oracle. The specifications define the interaction between the server and JSP and describe the format and syntax of JSP. JSP can be viewed as a high-level abstraction of servlets and is implemented as an extension of the **Servlet API**.

JSP is a Java technology that allows programmers to dynamically generate HTML in response to a Web client's request. The technology allows Java code and certain predefined actions to be embedded in static Web content.

The JSP syntax adds additional **tags**, called **JSP actions**, to be used to invoke built-in functionality. These tags allow for the creation of JSP **tag libraries** that act as extensions to the standard HTML and **XML tags**. Tag libraries provide a platform-independent way of extending the capabilities of a Web server. JSP pages are platform- and Web-server independent.

JSP pages use XML tags and **scriptlets** written in the Java programming language to encapsulate the logic that generates the content for a Web page. A JSP page usually has the extension **.jsp**, or it may use the extension *.jspx* for XML deployment. This chapter works with the *.jsp* extension. Any formatting tags (HTML or XML) are passed directly back to the response page. In this way, JSP separates the page logic from the design and display.

JSP pages are compiled into **Java servlets** by a JSP compiler. A servlet is a program written in the Java programming language that runs on the server. A JSP compiler may generate a servlet in Java code that is then compiled by the Java compiler, or it may generate byte code for the servlet directly. A servlet may call *JavaBeans* to perform processing on the server. JavaBeans are classes written in Java. They are used to encapsulate many objects into a single **bean** object. The bean can be passed around and shared, rather than having many individual objects.

In the real world, you'll often find many individual objects all of the same kind. Similarly, there are many cars of the same make and model. Each one was built from the same set of blueprints, and therefore contains the same components. In object-oriented terms, an individual car is an *instance* of the class of objects known as "cars." A *class* is the blueprint from which individual objects are created. A **superclass** is a class that is inherited. **Inheritance** is the process by which one object acquires the properties of another object.

JSP technology is designed to simplify the process of creating pages by separating Web presentation from Web content. In a dynamic website, there will probably be a combination of static data and dynamically generated data. The data will be sent in response to a client request, through the browser. A JSP engine interprets tags and generates the content required by, for example, calling a bean, accessing a database with the JDBC API, or including a file. It then sends the results back to the browser in the form of an HTML or XML page. The logic that generates the content is encapsulated in tags and beans processed on the server.

It is much easier to work with JSP pages than to do everything with servlets. Servlets are the counterpart to non-Java dynamic Web-content technologies such as PHP, CGI, and ASP.NET. Servlets are programs that run on a Web server and build Web pages on the fly. JSP technology is a key component in a highly scalable architecture for Web-based applications.

What JSP Is Used for

JSP can be used for many applications. Here are just a few examples:

- Web pages that use data from business databases—for example, an application that displays inventory stock or current product prices for an online order system.
- Web pages based on data submitted by a user—for example, an online customer-service application or an online ordering application. Other examples are an online work schedule for employees or a search engine.
- Web pages with data that changes often—for example, a special events page that is updated frequently. The events may change, requiring a new page, or a previously built page might be returned if the information is still up to date.

Why use JSP instead of other tools? Here are some of the most common reasons.

- **JSP servlets** are efficient, easy to use, portable, platform-independent, and inexpensive.
- JSP makes it easy and convenient to add dynamic content to an otherwise static HTML page.
- Comparing JSP to JavaScript, JavaScript is limited to the client environment. It can generate HTML dynamically on the client, which is a useful capability, but with the exception of cookies, HTTP and form-submission data is not available to JavaScript. JavaScript can't access server-side resources like databases. Often, JSP will be used with JavaScript.
- Comparing JSP to pure servlets, JSP is more convenient to write and modify and provides the same functionality. JSP separates the look from the content. This might be an important consideration, especially for a large organization that has some staff members who work on page design and others who work on the dynamic content of the site.
- Comparing JSP to traditional CGI, JSP's servlets allow you to do several things that are difficult or impossible with CGI. For example, servlets can talk directly to the Web server. A CGI program cannot. Also, with traditional CGI, a new process is started for each HTTP request. With JSP servlets, the Java Virtual Machine (**JVM**) stays up, and each request is handled by a lightweight Java thread, not a heavyweight operating system process. Traditional CGI loads the request in memory for each CGI program request. Servlets have multiple threads, but only a single copy of the servlet class.
- JSP is a similar technology to .NET, discussed in chapter 10. However, the dynamic part of JSP is written in Java, not Visual Basic or another Microsoft-specific language, so JSP is portable and can be used with non-Microsoft operating systems and servers, unlike .NET. In an environment that uses non-Microsoft technology or requires multiple platforms, JSP would be the likely choice. JSP can also be used on a Microsoft server. Over 3 billion devices run Java.
- PHP is portable like JSP, and arguably easier to learn. However, PHP has not been around as long as JSP. There is a large body of readily available information on Java technologies. PHP has become very popular and also has a lot of information readily available. JSP is sponsored by Oracle, and PHP is sponsored by Zend. Oracle has been around a lot longer and is a much larger organization. Does this matter? Big names are sometimes important when choosing technology. For example, company policy might consider it important in regard to the possible support available for the technology. Also, PHP is open source. Some organizations are comfortable with using open source technologies, while others are not.

JSP has been around a while and has been incorporated for dynamic Web development, within many environments, large and small. However, all the alternatives to JSP have their own advantages. When making your choice, keep in mind the expertise of your development resources and your organization's goals, including longer-term goals. Of course, don't lose sight of the purpose of your Web application! Ultimately, you may decide to use a combination of tools, including JSP.

JSP's Advantages and Disadvantages

Like all other Web development tools, JSP has advantages and disadvantages. Here are some of its advantages:

- Portability: JSP is available on any JVM machine.
- Java is a very popular language, with extensive support and resource knowledge.
- Java is a robust and very functional language.

- You can easily incorporate extensive functionality through JSP without completely mastering Java.
- JSP provides full security functionality.
- Performance is strong.
- JSP separates content from presentation, and thus the designer role from the developer role.
- JSP allows for multi-threading and multi-tasking to accommodate resources.
- JSP is easily incorporated for use with other languages and tools.
- Strong error-identification and error-handling are included.

Here are JSP's perceived disadvantages:

- It's a little harder to learn than some other server-side languages.
- It is a compiled language. The extra step of compiling is required prior to executing code.
- It can be difficult to debug.

What You Need to Use JavaServer Pages

Here's what you need to get started with JSP:

- You'll need a development environment, in which you will develop your JSP programs, test them, and finally run them.
- JSP pages are usually compiled into Java servlet classes. Therefore, to use JSP, you need a JVM that supports the Java platform servlet specifications. Most platforms support JVM.
- Obtain, install, and set up the **Java Development Kit** (JDK). You can download the JDK from Oracle's Java site: Java SE Downloads, at *www.oracle.com/technetwork/java/javase/downloads/ index.html*. Directions on how to download, install, and configure the tools are provided on the site.
- Install a JSP-capable Web server. You will find a list of these servers on the Oracle website. The server will need to be downloaded, installed, and configured. The most common server used is Apache Tomcat. The examples provided within this chapter use Apache Tomcat.
- Choose an **editor**. JSP can be coded using a simple text editor like Notepad or TextPad, or a more full-featured editor like UltraEdit, SlickEdit, or ConTEXT that provides functions like syntax-checking. Another option is to use an integrated development environment (IDE), which provides additional functionality—for example, Adobe Dreamweaver, Eclipse, NetBeans, JBuilder, and IBM Rational Application Developer for WebSphere Software are full-featured editors that support JSP.

A Simple JSP Script

Pages built using JSP technology are typically implemented using a one-time translation phase that is performed the first time the page is called. The page is compiled into a Java servlet class and remains in sever memory, providing quick response time for subsequent calls.

JSP simply puts Java inside HTML pages. To turn any existing HTML page into JSP, you can just change its extension from *.htm* or *.html* to *.jsp*. For example, consider the simple HTML page in Figure 11.1.

```
<html>
<body>
<!--  JSP1101 - Simple JSP Example -->
Welcome to Belhur Publishing
</body>
</html>
```

Figure 11.1: A simple JSP script

Just give that file the extension *.jsp* and load it in your browser. The same message will be displayed in the browser as if this were an HTML file:

Welcome to Belhur Publishing

The first time the page loads, it will take a little longer. The JSP file will be turned into a Java file in the form of a compiled and loaded Java servlet class. The compile only takes place once and will load quickly the next time it's run. If the JSP file is changed, it will be compiled again the first time the changed file is loaded.

JSP Syntax Summary

A JSP page is a text document that contains two basic elements: static data, which can be expressed in any text-based format like HTML, and JSP code, which constructs dynamic content.

Tags are used within JSP code. All **JSP tags** are case-sensitive. In JSP, a pair of single quotes ('..') is equivalent to a pair of double quotes (".."). Either single or double quotes can be used. Also, spaces are not allowed between an equal sign and an attribute value. The basic JSP elements are listed in Table 11.1.

Table 11.1: JSP Syntax		
Element	Syntax	Description
jsp:forward action	<%jsp:forward page="relative URL"/>	Forwards a client request to an HTML file, a JSP file, or a servlet for processing.
jsp:getProperty action	<%jsp:getProperty name="propertyName" value="val"/>	Gets the value of a bean property so that you can display it in a JSP page.
jsp:include action	<jsp:include page="relative URL" flush="true"/>	Sends a request to an object and includes the result in a dynamic JSP file.

Table 11.1: JSP Syntax (continued)

Element	Syntax	Description
jsp:plugin action	<jsp:plugin type="type" atrribute="value"*> .... </jsp:plugin> Type values: bean applet Attribute values: code="classFileName" codebase="classFileDirectoryName" name="instanceName" archive="URIToArchive,…" align="value" (valid values bottom, top, middle, left or right) height=displayPixels" width="displayPixels" hspace="leftRightPixels" vspace="topBottomPixels" jreversion="value" (valid values JREVersionNumber or 1.1" nspluginurl="URLToPlugin" iepluginurl="URLToPlugin"	Downloads a Java plug-in to the client Web browser to execute a Java applet or bean.
jsp:setProperty action	<jsp:setProperty att=val*/>	Sets a property value or values in a bean.
jsp.useBean action	<jsp:useBean att=val*/> or jsp:useBean att=val*> .... </jsp:useBean>	Finds or builds a Java bean.
Hidden comment	<%-- comment --%>	Used to document the JSP file. Hidden comments are not sent to the client.
HTML comment	<!-- comment -->	Creates a comment. HTML comments are sent to the client in the viewable page source.
HTML comment with an expression	<!-- comment [<%= expression %>] -->	Comment with expression. The expression is dynamic and is evaluated when the page is loaded in the Web browser.
Declaration	<%! declaration %>	Declares a variable or method valid in the page scripting language. The declaration can be referenced by other declarations, scriptlets, or expressions within the page.
Expression	<%= expression %>	Defines a Java expression that is evaluated at page request time, converted to a string, and sent inline to the output stream of the JSP response.
Include directive	<%@ include file="URL" %>	Includes a static file, parsing the file's JSP elements.

Table 11.1: JSP Syntax (continued)		
Element	Syntax	Description
Page directive	<%@ page attribute="value" %> Legal attributes with default values in **bold**: autoflush="**true**|false" buffer="sizekb|none" contentType="MIME-Type" errorPage="url" extends="package.class" import="package.class" info="text" isErrorPage="true|**false**" isThreadSafe="**true**|false" language="java" session="**true**|false"	Gives directions to the servlet engine about general setup. This defines attributes that apply to an entire JSP page.
Taglib directive	<%@ taglib uri="URIToTagLibrary" prefix="tagPrefix" %>	Defines a tag library and prefix for the custom tags used in the JSP page.
Scriptlet	<% code %>	Contains a code fragment valid in the page scripting language. This tag embeds a Java source code scriptlet in HTML page. The Java code is executed, and the output is inserted in sequence with the rest of the HTML page.

Four main types of JSP constructs can be embedded in a Web page. These constructs are listed in Table 11.2.

Table 11.2: JSP Constructs	
Construct	Description
Template text	Regular HTML.
Scripting elements, objects, and variables	Used to specify Java code that will become part of a servlet. There are many predefined variables that can be accessed and used.
Directives	Used to control the structure of a servlet.
Actions	Used to specify existing components to be used and to control the behavior of the JSP engine.

Template Text

Most of a JSP page usually consists of static HTML known as *template text*. The HTML looks just like normal HTML. It follows the same syntax rules as and is passed through to the client. Figure 11.1 is an example of using all template text for a JSP page.

Scripting Elements

JSP **scripting elements** are used to insert Java code into the servlet that will be generated from the JSP page. There are three basic kinds of scripting elements: the declaration tag, the expression tag, and the scriptlet tag.

Declaration Tag

A **declaration** tag is used to declare one or more variables or methods. The variable or method is placed inside the body of the Java servlet class and outside of existing methods. Declarations do not create output and are usually used with expressions and scriptlets.

A variable or method must be declared before it can be used in the JSP file. To declare more than one variable or method within a declaration element, separate them with semicolons. Variables and methods declared in an imported package may also be used. A *package* is a namespace that organizes a set of related classes and interfaces. Conceptually, packages are similar to folders on your computer. You might keep images in one folder, HTML in another, and scripts in another. Because software written in the Java programming language can be composed of hundreds of individual classes, it makes sense to keep things organized by placing related classes and interfaces in packages. Figure 11.2 gives some examples of declaration tag syntax.

```
<%! Declaration; Declaration;  %>

<%! int price = 0; %> <%!
int price = 0; quantity = 0;
string greeting= "Welcome"; %>
```

Figure 11.2: Declaration tag syntax

To simplify code in JSP expressions and scriptlets, use the **predefined variables** listed in Table 11.3. Predefined variables are also referred to as **implicit objects**.

Table 11.3: Predefined Variables			
Predefined Variable/ Implicit Object	Scope	Description	Commonly Used Methods
Application	Application	HttpServletRequest associated with the request. Allows access to content of request parameters through getParameter, the request type, and incoming HTTP headers.	getMimeType, getRealPath
Config	Page	ServletConfig object for the page.	getInitParameter, getInitParameterNames
Exception	Page	Exceptions not caught by application code.	getMessage, getLocalizedMessage, printStackTrace,toString
Out	Page	The PrintWriter used to send output to the client. To make the response object useful, there is a buffered version of PrintWriter called JspWriter. The buffer size can be adjusted or turned off through the buffer attribute of the page directive. JSP expressions are placed in the output stream and usually do not need to refer to out. It is usually used in scriptlets.	clear, clearBuffer, flush, getBufferSize, getRemaining

Table 11.3: Predefined Variables (continued)			
Predefined Variable/ Implicit Object	**Scope**	**Description**	**Commonly Used Methods**
Page	Page	The servlet itself.	Not typically used by JSP page authors
pageContext	Page	An instance that contains data associated with the whole page. A given HTML page may be passed among multiple JSPs.	findAttribute, getAttribute, getAttributesScope, getAtributeNamesInScope
Response	Page	HttpServletResponse associated with the response to the client. Since the output stream is buffered, it is legal to set HTTP status codes and response headers. It is not legal to set HTTP status codes and response headers in regular servlets once output has been sent to the client.	Not typically used by JSP page authors
Request	Request	HttpServletRequest associated with a request. Allows access to content, including parameters through getParameter, request type, and incoming HTTP headers.	getAttribute, getParameter, getParameterNames, getParameterValues
Session	Session	HttpSession object associated with the request. Session are created automatically. If the session attribute is turned off through the session attribute of a page directive, an error will occur when trying to use session when the JSP page is compiled into a servlet.	getId, getValue, getValueNames, putValue

Expression Tag

An expression tag is used to define an **expression**. The expression is evaluated, converted to a string, and inserted where the expression appears in the JSP file. The conversion to a string allows the use of an expression within a line of text with or without an HTML tag in the JSP file. The expression is used to insert Java values directly into the page output. A semicolon cannot be used to end an expression, unlike a scriptlet, which requires a semicolon. Expressions can be simple or complex and can be composed of multiple expressions. An expression is evaluated from left to right.

Any valid Java expression can be used within the expression tag. There are also predefined variables that can be used within the expression tag. These variables are referred to as *expression objects* and can be used for a request, a response, session information, and output. The expression objects are also referred to as implicit objects.

Figure 11.3 gives some examples of expression tag syntax. In this figure, an expression is used to get the remote host name, and the import **directive** is used to display the current date. The example is being served on the localhost. The example of **getRemoteHost()** returns the IP address (in IPv6 format) of the browser host. (This is the same as 127.0.01 in IPv4.) The result of the code is shown in Figure 11.4.

```
<html>
<body>
```
Continued

```
<!-- JSP1104 - Expression and Directive Tag Example -->
<font size=4>
<ul> <b> Example of Expression and Directives:</b> </ul>
<li> <b> Expression: </b><br>
Belhur Publishing Host Name: <%= request.getRemoteHost() %>
<br>
<li> <b> Expression and Directive: </b><br>
Current System Time: <br>
<%= new java.util.Date()  %>
</body>
</html>
```

Figure 11.3: Expression tag syntax

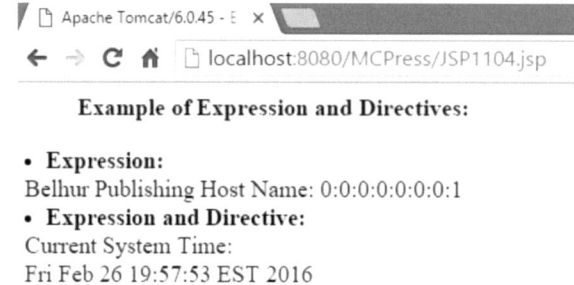

Example of Expression and Directives:

- **Expression:**
Belhur Publishing Host Name: 0:0:0:0:0:0:0:1
- **Expression and Directive:**
Current System Time:
Fri Feb 26 19:57:53 EST 2016

Figure 11.4: The page displayed from the code in Figure 11.3

Scriptlet Tag

A scriptlet tag is used to insert code into the servlet method that will be built to generate the JSP page. The tag places the code statements inside the service method JSPService() of the Java servlet class. Scriptlets are often used to perform more complex tasks than those performed by expressions. Scriptlets have the same access to the predefined variables as expressions. Scriptlets are executed when the client request is processed. When output is generated from the scriptlet, it is stored in the out object. Text, HTML tags, and JSP elements must be outside of the scriptlet.

A scriptlet can contain variable or method declarations, language statements, and/or expressions that are valid in the page scripting language. A scriptlet can be used for many tasks, including writing valid scripting language statements, writing expressions, declaring variables or methods, and using objects declared with the jsp:useBean element. The beginning scriptlet tag is <%, and the ending tag is %>. A semicolon is required to end a scriptlet statement.

In Figure 11.5, two scriptlets are used. Notice the scriptlets start with <% and end with %>. The first one declares and initializes the date value. The second one generates the date output using the out variable. The scriptlet does not generate HTML. The HTML output is created by using the out variable. This variable does not need to be declared because it is already predefined for a scriptlet to use.

```
<HTML>
<HEAD>
<TITLE>Belhur Publishing</TITLE>
</HEAD>
<%

      // JSP1106 - Scriptlet Example
    // This scriptlet declares and initializes the date
    java.util.Date date = new java.util.Date();
%>
Welcome to Belhur Publishing!  <BR>
Today is:
<%
    // This scriptlet generates HTML date output
    out.println( String.valueOf( date ));
%>
</BODY>
</HTML>
```

Figure 11.5: Scriptlet syntax

JSP Directives

JSP directives, listed in Table 11.4, control how the JSP compiler generates the servlet. A directive affects the overall structure of a servlet class. There are three types of directives: include, page, and taglib. The include directive inserts a file into the servlet class at the time the JSP is compiled into a servlet. The page directive provides such capabilities as importing classes, allowing multiple pages to execute at the same time, and allowing the JSP page to participate in a session. The taglib directive is used to define a tag library with a prefix that can be used in a JSP page.

Table 11.4 JSP Directives	
Directive	Description
<%@include file="path" %>	Includes a file path on the local system to be included when the JSP page is compiled into a servlet.
<%@ page autoFlush="true" %>	Indicates whether JSP should automatically flush the page buffer when it is full. The default is true. When the buffer is set to none, the autoFlush directive cannot be set to false. When autoFlush is set to false, an exception will be encountered when the buffer is full and overflows.
<%@ page buffer=sizkb %>	Gives the size of the page buffer in KB, or *none* for no buffer. The default is 8KB. If a size is designated, the output is buffered with the size specified. For pages with a lot of output activity, it might be desirable to control the buffer size.

Table 11.4 JSP Directives (continued)

Directive	Description
<%@ page contentType="description" %>	Sets the MIME content type and character encoding of the page used by the JSP file for the response it sends to the client. Any MIME type or character set that is valid for the JSP container can be used. The default value is MIME type text/html, and the default character set is ISO-8859-1.
<%@ page errorPage="path" %>	Defines a page to display if an unhandled error occurs while running the JSP page. When a slash (/) is used to start the path, the path will be relative to the JSP file's root directory.
<%@ page extends="Java class" %>	Changes the generated servlet's class. The extends attribute should be used with caution, as it might affect quality and performance. It will also result in errors when a superclass is already being used by the server.
<%@ page import="package" %>	Provides a means to extend page functionality by importing packages or classes beyond the default list of imported classes and packages for JSP pages. The classes and packages can include java.lang.*, javax.servlet.*, javax.servlet.jsp.*, and javax.servlet.http.*. You can list multiple classes by separating them with commas. This page directive must be designated before the element that calls the imported class. It is the only attribute that can appear multiple times on the same page.
<%@ page info="description" %>	Gives a brief description of the JSP page in the form of a string that can be retrieved using the Servlet.getServletInfo() method.
<%@ page isErrorPage="true" %>	Indicates whether to give an error page access to the exception implicit variable. When set to true, the page can be used for the exception object in a JSP file. The default is false.
<%@ page isThreadSafe="true" %>	Controls whether or not the JSP page is *thread safe*, meaning it will function correctly during simultaneous execution of multiple threads (program parts). Thread safe also means the application will satisfy the need for multiple threads to access the same shared data and the need for a shared piece of data to be accessed by only one thread at a given time. The default value is true. When true, the JSP container can send multiple concurrent client requests to the JSP page. In that case, code should be included to synchronize access to instance variables and the multiple client threads.
<%@ page language="language" %>	Designates the language used for writing the script, declarations, expressions, and any files included within the JSP page. Currently, *java* is the default and only legal language choice.
<%@ page session="true" %>	Tells JSP whether the page participates in a session. The default is true, making session data available to the page. When the value is false, the session object cannot be used.
<%@ taglib prefix="x" uri="libraryname" %>	Configures tags with the prefix *x* to use the tag library. Tag libraries are discussed later in this chapter.

The start tag for a directive is <%@, and the end tag is %>. The statement consists of the directive, attribute, and value in the form <%@ *directive, attribute*="*value*"%>. Multiple attribute settings can be used within a single directive, as shown in Figure 11.6.

```
Syntax:

<%@ directive attribute="value"
               attribute="value"
                attribute="value"
             attribute="value" %>


Code example:

%@page language="java" import="java.sql.*,java.util.*" session="true"
errorPage="ErrorPage.jsp" %
```

Figure 11.6: The syntax for a directive with multiple attribute settings

Include Directive

The include directive is used to bring a file's content into the current file. The file is included at the time the JSP page is compiled into a servlet. The contents of the file are included as a part of the servlet object. In the example in Figure 11.7, the JSP file JSP1109date.jsp, containing code to retrieve the current date, will be included within the file JSP1108.jsp. The code for file JSP1109date.jsp is shown in Figure 11.8.

```
<html>
<body>
<!-- JSP1108 - JSP Include Directive Example -->
Welcome to Belhur Publishing!  <BR>
              The current date and time is:
<%@ include file="JSP1109date.jsp" %>
</body>
</head>
</html>
```

Figure 11.7: An example of the JSP include directive

```
<!-- JSP1109date - JSP include directive example current date -->

<%= (new java.util.Date() ).toLocaleString() %>
```

Figure 11.8: The JSP file included with the include directive

The message displayed when this file is run is as follows:

Welcome to Belhur Publishing!
The current date and time is: Feb 26, 2016 8:23:18 PM

This simple example shows how easily additional code can be incorporated into a JSP file. If the included JSP file is changed, the JSP files that include this file must be recompiled.

Page Directive

The page directive applies to the current JSP file and any static files included within the JSP page. This directive can be used more than once on a JSP page, but can only use each attribute once within the page, with the exception of the import attribute. Usually, page directives are placed together at the top of the JSP file. Consistently grouping directives together at the top is a standard that makes it easier for the developer, but they can be placed anywhere.

Figure 11.9 uses some of the page directive's attributes. In this example, the errorPage attribute references a page named JSP1113errorpage.jsp. The code for that page is shown in Figure 11.10.

```
<html>
<body>
<!-- JSP1111 - JSP Page Directives Example -->
Welcome to Belhur Publishing <BR>
<%@ page autoFlush="true" %>
<%@ page buffer="8kb"  %>
<%@ page contentType="text/html" %>
<%@ page errorPage="JSP1113errorpage.jsp" %>
<%@ page import = "java.util.*" %>
<%@ page info="JSP Page Directives Example"  %>
<%@ page isErrorPage="false"  %>
<%@ page isThreadSafe="true"  %>
<%@ page language="java"  %>
<%@ page session="true"  %>
          Current Date: <%= new Date() %>
</body>
</html>
```

Figure 11.9: Using the JSP page directive

```
<html>
<body>
<!-- JSP1113errorpage - JSP Page Directives Example Error Page -->
<%@ page isErrorPage="true" %>
Welcome to Belhur Publishing <BR>
An Error Has Been Encountered!!

                                              Continued
```

```
</body>
</html>
```

Figure 11.10: An errorPage file

This page will only be called when an unhandled error is encountered on the page. In that case, the following message will be displayed:

```
Welcome to Belhur Publishing
An Error Has Been Encountered!!
```

The page may contain text to be displayed or additional application code.

JSP Actions

JSP **actions** are executed at run time and provide built-in Web server functionality. JSP actions are used to modify, use, or create objects that are represented by JavaBeans. Actions use XML syntax. Several standard actions are provided for use with JSP, listed in Table 11.5. Custom actions can be developed using the Java language.

Table 11.5: JSP Actions		
Action	Use	Description
jsp:fallback	Show content.	Content to show if a browser supports applets.
jsp:forward	Forward requester to a new page.	Used to hand off a request and response to a JSP or servlet. Once handed off, the control will not return the current page.
jsp:getProperty	Insert the property of a JavaBean into output.	Used to get a property from a designated JavaBean.
jsp:include	Include a file when a page is requested.	Comparable to a subroutine. The servlet will temporarily hand the request and response off to a specified JSP. Control will return to the current JSP once the other has completed. This action allows code to be shared by multiple other JSPs.
jsp:param	Designate an additional parameter.	May be used inside a jsp:forward, jsp:include, or jsp:params action. This action designates a parameter to be included in addition to the request's current parameters.
jsp:plugin	Generate browser code that makes an <object> or <embed> tag for a Java plug-in.	Generates a browser-specific tag to include an applet.
jsp:setProperty	Set the property of a JavaBean.	Sets a property in a designated JavaBean.
jsp:useBean	Find or instantiate a JavaBean.	Creates or allows reuse of a JavaBean available to the current JSP page.

jsp:fallback

The <jsp:fallback> tag enables you to substitute HTML for browsers that are not supported by the <jsp:plugin> action, or when the plug-in fails. The HMTL found between the <fallback> and

<jsp:fallback> tags is the content that will be shown if the browser doesn't support applets. Most current browsers, however, support the <jsp:plugin> action.

For example, if the plug-in in Figure 11.11 fails, the following content will be displayed:

Welcome to Belhur Publishing
The Java applet cannot be run!!

```
<html>
<body>
<!-- JSP1115 - jsp:fallback Action Example -->
Welcome to Belhur Publishing <BR>
<jsp:plugin type="applet" code="BelhurPublishing"
  codebase="/belhur/" height="800" width="500">
<jsp:params>
<jsp:param name="author" value="Laura"/>
</jsp:params>
<jsp:fallback>
<font color=#FF0000 > The Java applet cannot be run!!</font>
</jsp:fallback>
</jsp:plugin>
</body>
</html>
```

Figure 11.11: Using the <jsp:fallback> action

In this case, the plug-in will fail because it does not exist.

jsp:forward

The <jsp:forward> tag is used to hand off the request and response to another JSP or servlet. The control will not return to the current JSP page. In the example in Figure 11.12, JSP1117.jsp uses the <jsp:forward> action tag to direct the page to JSP1118.jsp, shown in Figure 11.13. The control remains with JSP1118.jsp and does not return. The parameter forwardedFrom is set in the request before the hand off. The result will be the following:

Welcome to Belhur Publishing
We have been forwarded from JSP1117.jsp!

```
<html>
<body>
<!-- JSP1117 - JSP Actions jsp:forward Example -->
<jsp:forward page="JSP1118.jsp" >
<jsp:param name="forwardedFrom" value="JSP1117.jsp" />
</jsp:forward>
</body>
</html>
```

Figure 11.12: The JSP file forward from using <jsp:forward>

```
<html>
<body>
<!-- JSP1118 - JSP Actions jsp:forward Example -->
Welcome to Belhur Publishing <BR>
We have been forwarded from JSP1117.jsp!
</body>
</html>
```

Figure 11.13: The JSP file forwarded to

jsp:getProperty

The <jsp:getProperty> tag gets the property from the specified JavaBean. In the example in Figure 11.14, the month, day, year, hours, and minutes are retrieved from the JavaBean named "clock". The bean is referenced with the parameter name in the <jsp:getProperty> statements, and the property identifies the property being retrieved.

In the results shown in Figure 11.15, the month is actually February. This is because the java.util. Date class uses the numbers for months from 0 to 11: 0 is January, 1 is February, and 11 is December. The year is the current year minus 1900.

```
<%@ page language="java" contentType="text/html" %>
<html>
<body>
<!-- JSP1120 - JSP Actions jsp:getProperty Example -->
Welcome to Belhur Publishing <BR>
<jsp:useBean id="clock" class="java.util.Date" />
The current date and time is:
<ul>
```
Continued

```
<li>Month: <jsp:getProperty name="clock" property="month" />
<li>Day: <jsp:getProperty name="clock" property="date" />
<li>Year: <jsp:getProperty name="clock" property="year" />
<li>Hours: <jsp:getProperty name="clock" property="hours" />
<li>Minutes: <jsp:getProperty name="clock" property="minutes" />
</ul>
</body>
</html>
```

Figure 11.14: Using the <jsp:getProperty> action

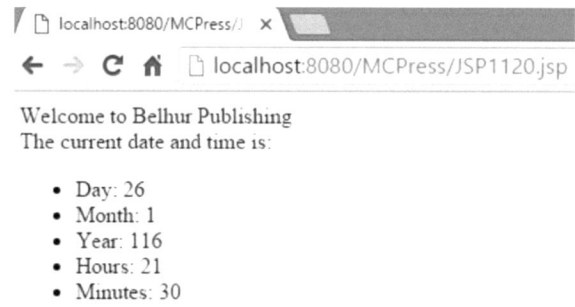

Figure 11.15: The results from Figure 11.14

There are other ways to display a date, but for the purposes of this example, this is a simple way to show how jsp:getProperty works.

jsp:include

The <jsp:include> action tag is similar to the concept of a subroutine, which is used in many application development languages, including RPG on the IBM i. The Java servlet temporarily hands the request and response off to the specified JSP. Control will then return to the current JSP page, once the other JSP page finishes. The <jsp:include> tag allows JSP code to be shared among multiple JSPs rather than duplicated.

The example in Figure 11.16 includes the page JSP1123.jsp, shown in Figure 11.17. The include allows for reuse of code. Notice the flush parameter. Usually this will be set to true. However, there might be instances when it should be set to false, such as when multiple actions, directives, or parameter values need to be retained.

```
<html>
<body>
<!-- JSP1122 - JSP Actions jsp:include Example -->
<p>Welcome to Belhur Publishing</p>
```
                                                          Continued

```
<jsp:include page="JSP1123.jsp" flush="true"/>
</body>
</html>
```

Figure 11.16: Using the <jsp:include> action

```
<!-- JSP1123 - JSP Actions jsp:include Example -->
<%@ page import = "java.util.*" %>
<%
Date todaysdate = new Date();
out.print("<p>Current Date:" + todaysdate + ".</p>");
%>
```

Figure 11.17: The JSP page included in Figure 11.16

In this example, the first JSP displays "Welcome to Belhur Publishing," and the second JSP displays the current date. There are two include mechanisms here: the include directive and the include action. The include directive includes the content of the file during the translation phase. The include action includes the content of the file during the execution of the request-processing phase. For the include directive, the JSP engine adds the content of the inserted page during the translation phase, so it does not affect performance. For the include action, the JSP engine adds the content of the inserted page at run time, which adds extra overhead to the application.

Take care when including large pages in instances when performance can noticeably be affected. Generally, though, the include action has a small negative impact on performance but greatly improves flexibility.

jsp:param

The <jsp:param> tag can be used inside of a <jsp:forward>, <jsp:include>, or <jsp:plugin> block. The tag specifies a parameter that will be available for use by the forward, include, or plug-in code.

The example in Figure 11.18 uses <jsp:param> in coordination with <jsp:forward>. This example is very similar to the forward example in figures 11.11 and 11.13. In this case, the parameter is passed to the forward page, JSP1126.jsp, which retrieves the parameter using the getParameter request. The forwardedFrom parameter is then printed. The result would be the following message:

Welcome to Belhur Publishing
Forwarded From: JSP1125.jsp.

```
<html>
<body>
<!-- JSP1125 - JSP Actions jsp:param Example -->
                                              Continued
```

```
<jsp:forward page="JSP1126.jsp" >
<jsp:param name="forwardedFrom" value="JSP1125.jsp" />
</jsp:forward>
</body>
</html>
```

Figure 11.18: Using the <jsp:param> action

```
<html>
<body>
<!-- JSP1126 - JSP Actions jsp:param Example -->
Welcome to Belhur Publishing <BR>
<%
String forwardedFrom = request.getParameter("forwardedFrom");
out.print("<p>Forwarded From: " + forwardedFrom + ".</p>");
%>
</body>
</html>
```

Figure 11.19: The JSP file forwarded to

Not only does the application forward the user to a new page, but it also passes a parameter to be used within the page. Although this example is simple, it should give you an idea of how powerful and useful the <jsp:param> action is.

jsp:plugin

The <jsp:plugin> action is used to include the Java plug-in applets on a Web page. The Java plug-in allows you to use a Java Runtime Environment (JRE) supplied by Oracle, instead of using the JVM implemented through the client Web browser. Java plug-in technology is part of the JRE standard edition and establishes a connection between popular browsers and the Java platform. The connection enables website applets to be run within a browser on a user's desktop.

A plug-in can be used to avoid problems between applets and specific types of Web browsers. The syntax used for Internet Explorer and Chrome, for example, is different. The servlet code generated when using <jsp:plugin> dynamically senses the type of browser and sends <object> and <embed> elements for that browser. The plug-in serves as a bridge between the browser and JRE.

A plug-in is executable code that is stored in a library file. A developer "tells" the browser to use this external JRE by placing special HTML tags on a Web page. Once this is done, a browser can run Java applets or JavaBean components that have access to the features of this external JRE.

To use a plug-in, you will need to download and possibly also configure it. Oracle provides detailed information about plug-ins that can be downloaded for a variety of uses at *www.oracle.com/ technetwork/java/index-jsp-141438.html*. There are many sources on the Web to download plug-ins. Some sources provide plug-ins for a fee, while many provide plug-ins for free. In addition, a developer can create a new plug-in.

In the example in Figure 11.20, the applet code referenced is com.example.MyApplet. This example shows a uniform way of embedding applets in a Web page. The <object> tag provides a common way of embedding applets. Currently, <jsp:plugin> does not allow for dynamically called applets. Parameters can be passed as constants, but not as variable values.

```
<jsp:plugin type=applet height="100%" width="100%"
archive="myjarfile.jar,myotherjar.jar"
codebase="/jspapplets"
code="com.example.MyApplet" >
<jsp:params>
<jsp:param name="enableDebug" value="true" />
</jsp:params>
<jsp:fallback>
Your browser does not support applets.
</jsp:fallback>
</jsp:plugin>
```

Figure 11.20: Using the <jsp:plugin> action

jsp:setProperty

The <jsp:setProperty> action sets the property in the specified JavaBean. Four possible attributes can be used for the jsp:setProperty action, listed in Table 11.6.

Table 11.6: Attributes for <jsp:setProperty>	
Attribute	Description
Name	This attribute is required and designates the bean the property will be set for. The <jsp:useBean> action must appear before the <jsp:setProperty> action.
property	This attribute is required and designates the property to be set. When a value of "*" is used, all request parameters with names that match the bean property names will be passed to the setter methods.
value	This attribute is optional and designates the value for the property. You cannot use both the value and param attributes for a single <jsp:setProperty> action. One or the other may be used, although neither is required. String values are automatically converted to numbers, Boolean, byte, and character through the standard valueOf method in the target wrapper class. For example, a value of "17" of an integer property will be converted through the Integer.valueOf method.

Table 11.6: Attributes for <jsp:setProperty> (continued)	
Attribute	Description
param	This attribute is optional and designates the request parameter used to retrieve the property. If the request does not have a parameter, nothing will be done. In other words, a null value will not be passed to the setter method of the property. The bean can supply default values. The param attribute can be used to override the property values.
	The bean itself can be used to supply default values, or the request parameters can be used to provide values.
	The following code is used to set the numberOfFields property to the value provided from the value of the numFields request parameter:
	<jsp:setProperty name="promptBean" property="numberOfFields" param="numFields" />
	If the numFields request parameter does not exist, nothing will be done.
	When both the value and param attributes are not used, it is the same as using a param name that matches the property name. When both the value and param attributes are not used, "*" can be used to iterate through available properties and request parameters matching those with identical names:
	<jsp:setProperty name="promptBean" property="*" />

jsp:useBean

The <jsp:useBean> action is used to instantiate Java objects that comply with the JavaBean specification and refer to the beans from JSP pages. In other words, it creates or reuses a JavaBean available to the JSP page. Several attributes can be used with <jsp:useBean>, listed in Table 11.7.

Table 11.7: Attributes for <jsp:UseBean>	
Attibute	Description
BeanName	The name of the bean provided to instantiate the method of Beans. The type and beanName can be provided and the class attribute omitted.
Class	The full package name of the bean.
Id	The name of the variable that will reference the bean. If the id and scope are the same as a previously used bean object, it will be used instead of instantiating a new bean.
Scope	The context in which the bean should be made available to the application. There are four possible values: application, page, request, and session. A <jsp:useBean> entry will only result in a new object being instantiated if there is no previous object with the same id and scope.
Type	The type of the variable that will refer to the object. The name of the variable is designated through the id attribute. The type must match the classname or be a superclass or an interface that the class implements.

The example in Figure 11.21 shows the use of the <jsp:useBean> and <jsp:setProperty> actions and also the use of a user-created JavaBean. The user is prompted to enter his or her name. Once the name is entered and submitted, a "hello" message is displayed. The example uses the Bean Manager to instantiate an instance of the class JavaSource.NameBean and store the class in the attribute promptBean. The attribute will be available for use throughout the current runtime of the request because the scope attribute value is request. The attribute can be shared within all JSPs included or forwarded from the main JSP that first received the request. The scope attribute can be one of four values, listed in Table 11.8.

```
<%@ page import="JavaSource.*"  %>
<jsp:useBean id="promptBean" class="JavaSource.NameBean" scope="request"></
jsp:useBean>
<jsp:setProperty name="promptBean" property="*" />
<HTML>
<!-- JSP1130 - JSP Actions jsp:useBean and jsp:setProperty Example -->
<H3>Welcome to Belhur Publishing Inquiry Page!</H3>
<% if (promptBean.getNewName().equals("")) { %>
User Unknown.
<% } else { %>
Welcome
<%= promptBean.getNewName() %>
!
<%  } %>
<P>Please Enter Your Name
<FORM METHOD=get><INPUT TYPE=TEXT name=newName size=20> <INPUT
      TYPE=SUBMIT VALUE="Submit Your Name"></FORM>
</BODY>
</HTML>
```

Figure 11.21: Using the <jsp:useBean> and <jsp:setProperty> actions

Table 11.8: Values for the Scope Attribute	
Value	Description
Application	This is the same as using a global variable. The attribute is available to every instance and is never de-referenced.
Page	The attribute is available to the current JSP page only.
Request	The attribute is available for the lifetime of the request. Once the request has been processed by all of the JSPs, the attribute will be de-referenced.
Session	The attribute is available for the lifetime of the user's current session.

Figure 11.21 references the user-defined bean **NameBean**. Although the focus of this chapter is JSP, the Java source code for this user-defined JavaBean is given in Figure 11.22. You will often see JSP and Java used together within applications. This example helps you understand how this is done. This does not mean that to use JSP, you must know how to code Java. There are many existing JavaBeans, available on the Web, which can easily be included in an application.

```
/*JSP1131 Java NameBean Example */
0.06 in
```

Continued

```
public class NameBean {

  String newName="";

  public void NameBean() {  }

  public String getNewName() {
      return newName;
  }
  public void setNewName(String newName) {
      this.newName = newName;
  }

}
```

Figure 11.22: The Java code for a user-defined bean

The components in this example include the JSP file JSP1130.jsp and the user-defined bean in NameBean.java. Figure 11.23 is the screen that will be displayed when the application is run.

Welcome to Belhur Publishing Inquiry Page!

User Unknown

Please Enter Your Name

[   ] [Submit Your Name]

Figure 11.23: The screen displayed from the code in Figure 11.21

The first time the page is displayed upon initiation of the application, the user is prompted to enter his or her name. Also, the text "User Unknown" is displayed. This is because the following code checks for the value of promptBean.getNewName:

<% if (promptBean.getNewName().equals("")) { %>

Once the user enters a name and clicks **Submit**, the page will be redisplayed with the entered name and a new message, as shown in Figure 11.24.

Welcome To Belhur Publishing Inquiry Page!

Welcome Joe Walsh !

Please Enter Your Name

[   ] [Submit Your Name]

Figure 11.24: The screen after entering a name

This example is not a complete application, but it should give you an idea of the possibilities for <jsp:useBean> and <jsp:setProperty> in business applications. The bean incorporates use of an HTML form to prompt for the name value, use the entered value within the JSP code, and then display the value. These are activities very familiar to a business developer.

The <jsp:useBean> action lets you load a JavaBean to a JSP page. This is a very useful capability, allowing the reusability of Java classes without sacrificing the convenience that JSP adds over servlets alone. The beans should be stored in a directory included in the site's class path.

JSP Implicit Objects

Implicit objects in JSP are objects that are automatically available within JSP. They are Java objects that the JSP container provides to a developer to access in expressions and scriptlets. They are called "implicit" because they are automatically instantiated. The implicit object is created by the JSP environment, so you do not need to initialize it. The JSP implicit objects in Table 11.9 are exposed by the JSP container and can be referenced by the application developer. The implicit objects act as wrappers around underlying Java classes or interfaces that are typically defined with the servlet API.

Implicit objects are provided as a convenience for programmers and are commonly used by developers. They are introduced in this section and included in code examples throughout this chapter. Implicit objects are only visible within the system-generated _jspService() method. They are not visible within user-defined methods created in declarations.

Table 11.9: JSP Implicit Objects	
Implicit Object	**Description**
Application	Represents the ServletContext obtained from the servlet configuration object. It is used to find information about the servlet engine and environment. The information is shared by all JSPs and servlets in the application.
Config	Represents ServletConfig for the JSP. It provides access to the servlet instance initialization parameters. In other words, it is the servlet configuration data.
Exception	Provides the uncaught throwable object that results in an error page being invoked. It is used for exceptions not caught by application code.
Out	This JSPWriter object is used to write the data to the response output stream.
Page	Represents the servlet instance generated from the JSP page as an HTTPJSPPage. It is the same as using the Java keyword *this* in scriptlet code.
PageContext	Represents a PageContext instance that contains data associated with the whole page. An HTML page may be passed to multiple JSPs. It is a convenient API for accessing scoped namespaces and servlet-related objects. The pageContext object provides wrapper methods for common servlet-related functionality.
Request	This HttpServletRequest object provides HTTP request information, including methods for getting cookie, header, and session data. It represents the client request.
Response	The HTTPServlet response object provides HTTP response information, including cookies and other header information. It represents the page response.
Session	This HTTPSession object can be used to track information about a user from one request to another. The session directive is set to true by default, so the session is valid by default.

A request-and-response cycle consists of a request where the client asks for data from the server, and a response where the server sends the data to the client. This cycle is represented by the request and response implicit objects, as shown in Figure 11.25. The request object handles the information sent from the client, and the response object handles the information sent to the client. Table 11.10 lists **request methods**, and Table 11.11 lists **response methods**.

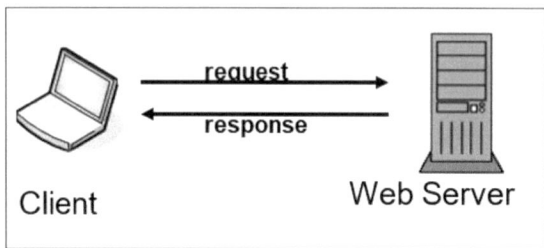

Figure 11.25: The request and response cycle

Table 11.10: Request Methods		
Return Type	Method	Description
HttpSession	getSession()	Returns the session associated with the request
String	getHeader(String headerName)	Returns the value associated with the header name of the request
Enumeration	getHeaderNames()	Returns all of the header names associated with a request
Cookie[]	getCookies()	Returns the cookies associated with a request
Object	getAttribute(String attributeName)	Returns the object that is paired with an attribute's name
void	setAttribute(String nameOfTheAttribute, Object valueOfTheAttribute)	Sets an attribute named nameOfTheAttribute to the value of valueOfTheAttribute

Table 11.11: Response Methods		
Return Type	Method	Description
Void	addCookie(Cookie cookie)	Adds the specified cookie to the response
Void	addHeader(String headerName, String value)	Adds the header to the response
Void	sendError(int statusCode) throws IOException	Sends a predefined error message back to the client
Void	sendRedirect(String newURL) throws IOException	Redirects the client browser to a different URL

Web application information can be stored in the application, session, and page scope. The *page scope* refers to the information that pertains to a specific instance of a given page. The server keeps the page-specific information as long as the page exists. The *session scope* contains information pertaining to a session instance. The server keeps session-specific information until the session has been ended. The *application scope* contains information that is available to all sessions in an application, as long as the application is running.

You can access information stored in the application, page, and session scopes using the application, pageContext, and session implicit objects. The methods for these objects are listed in Tables 11.12, 11.13, and 11.14, respectively.

Table 11.12: Application Methods		
Return Type	**Method**	**Description**
Object	getAttribute(String attributeName)	Returns the object that is paired with an attribute's name.
Void	setAttribute(String nameOfTheAttribute, Object valueOfTheAttribute)	Sets an attribute named nameOfTheAttribute to the value of valueOfTheAttribute.
Enumeration	getAttributeNames()	Returns an array of the names of the attributes for a given application.

Table 11.13: pageContext Methods		
Return Type	**Method**	**Description**
Object	findAttribute(String attributeName)	Searches the page, session, application, and request scopes for an attribute named attributeName and returns the attribute or null if the attribute does not exist.
Object	getAttribute(String attributeName)	Returns the object that is paired with an attribute's name.
Void	setAttribute(String nameOfTheAttribute, Object valueOfTheAttribute)	Sets an attribute named nameOfTheAttribute to the value of valueOfTheAttribute.
HttpServletRequest	getRequest()	Returns the request object associated with the page.
HttpServletResponse	getResponse()	Returns the response object associated with the page.

Table 11.14: Session Methods		
Return Type	**Method**	**Description**
Object	getAttribute(String attributeName)	Returns the object that is paired with an attribute named attributeName.
Void	setAttribute(String nameOfTheAttribute, Object valueOfTheAttribute)	Sets an attribute named nameOfTheAttribute to the value of valueOfTheAttribute.
String	getAttributeNames()	Gets the name of all attributes.

JSP Standard Tag Libraries

In addition to using the predefined JSP actions, you can create custom actions using the JSP Tag Extension API. Custom actions are created by writing a Java class that implements one of the tag interfaces and providing a tag-library XML description file that specifies the tags and the Java classes that implement the tags. JSP tag libraries define declarative, modular functionality that can be reused by any JSP page. The tag libraries reduce the requirement to embed large amounts of Java code in JSP pages by moving the functionality of the tags into tag implementation classes.

JSP standard tag libraries (**JSTL**) encapsulate, as simple tags, the core functionality common to many Web applications. JSTL has support for common structural tasks such as iteration, conditions, control flow, and text inclusion; tags for manipulating XML documents; internationalization tags; and SQL tags. For example, with JSTL, <forEach> can be used to standardize iteration. This standardization lets you learn a single tag and use it on multiple JSP containers.

The expression language that JSTL defines is an integral part of the JSP 2.0 specification. You might also be interested in JSTL's current extensibility mechanisms. JSTL provides a framework for integrating custom tags with JSTL tags. You can find all the information you need to dive in to JSTL at *www.oracle.com/technetwork/java/index-jsp-135995.html* and other websites. Oracle's JavaServer Pages Standard Tag Library page includes downloads, API specifications, documentation, and forums specific to JSTL. Table 11.15 lists the standard JSTL libraries.

Table 11.15: JSP Standard Tag Libraries		
Library	Description	Prefix
JSTL core	The core group of tags are the most frequently used JSTL tags.	c
JSTL fmt	The JSTL formatting tags are used to format and display text, the date, the time, and numbers for internationalized websites.	fmt
JSTL sql	The JSTL SQL tag library provides tags for interacting with relational databases (RDBMSs) such as Oracle, mySQL, DB2, or Microsoft SQL Server.	sql
JSTL xml	The JSTL XML tags provide a JSP-centric way of creating and manipulating XML documents.	xml
JSTL functions	JSTL includes a number of standard functions, most of which are common string manipulation functions.	fn

The standard tag libraries provide many standard tags and functions. Table 11.16 lists many of the **JSTL standard tags**, and Table 11.17 lists many of the **JSTL standard functions**.

Table 11.16: JSTL Standard Tags

Library	Tag	Description
core	catch	Catches any throwable error that occurs in its body and optionally exposes it.
	choose	A simple conditional tag that establishes a context for mutually exclusive conditional operations, marked by <when> and <otherwise>.
	If	A simple conditional tag that evaluates its body if the supplied condition is true and optionally exposes a Boolean scripting variable representing the evaluation of this condition.
	import	Retrieves an absolute or relative URL and exposes its contents to either the page, a string in "var", or a Reader in 'varReader'.
	forEach	The basic iteration tag, accepting many different collection types and supporting subsetting and other functionality.
	forTokens	Iterates over tokens, separated by the supplied delimiters.
	out	Like <%= ... >, but for expressions.
	otherwise	A subtag of <choose> that follows <when> tags and runs only if all of the prior conditions evaluated to false.
	param	Adds a parameter to a containing <import> tag's URL.
	redirect	Redirects to a new URL.
	remove	Removes a scoped variable (from a particular scope, if specified).
	set	Sets the result of an expression evaluation in a scope.
	url	Creates a URL with optional query parameters.
	when	A subtag of <choose> that includes its body if its condition evaluates to true.
fmt	requestEncoding	Sets the request character encoding.
	setLocale	Stores the given locale in the locale configuration variable.
	timeZone	Specifies the time zone for any time formatting or parsing actions nested in its body.
	setTimeZone	Stores the given time zone in the time zone configuration variable.
	bundle	Loads a resource bundle to be used by its tag body.
	setBundle	Loads a resource bundle and stores it in the named scoped variable or the bundle configuration variable.
	message	Maps key to localized message and performs parametric replacement.
	param	Supplies an argument for parametric replacement to a containing <message> tag.
	formatNumber	Formats a numeric value as number, currency, or percentage.
	parseNumber	Parses the string representation of a number, currency value, or percentage.
	formatDate	Formats a date and/or time using the supplied styles and pattern.
	parseDate	Parses the string representation of a date and/or time.
sql	transaction	Provides nested database action elements with a shared connection, set up to execute all statements as one transaction.
	query	Executes the SQL query defined in its body or through the sql attribute.
	update	Executes the SQL update defined in its body or through the sql attribute.
	param	Sets a parameter in an SQL statement to the specified value.
	dateParam	Sets a parameter in an SQL statement to the specified java.util.Date value.
	setDataSource	Creates a simple DataSource suitable only for prototyping.

Table 11.16: JSTL Standard Tags (continued)

Library	Tag	Description
xml	choose	A simple conditional tag that establishes a context for mutually exclusive conditional operations, marked by <when> and <otherwise>.
	out	Like <%= ... >, but for XPath expressions.
	If	An XML conditional tag, which evaluates its body if the supplied XPath expression evaluates to true.
	forEach	The XML iteration tag
	otherwise	A subtag of <choose> that follows <when> tags and runs only if all of the prior conditions evaluated to false.
	param	Adds a parameter to a containing <transform> tag's Transformer.
	parse	Parses XML content from a "source" attribute or 'body'.
	set	Saves the result of an XPath expression evaluation in a "scope".
	transform	Conducts a transformation given a source XML document and an XSLT style sheet.
	when	A subtag of <choose> that includes its body if its expression evaluates to true.

Table 11.17: JSTL Standard Functions

Type	Function Tag	Description
Boolean	contains(java.lang.String, java.lang.String	Tests whether an input string contains the specified substring.
Boolean	containsIgnoreCase (java.lang.String, java.lang.String)	Tests whether an input string contains the specified substring in a case-insensitive way.
Boolean	endsWith (java.lang.String, java.lang.String)	Tests whether an input string ends with the specified suffix.
Boolean	startsWith (java.lang.String, java.lang.String	Tests if an input string starts with the specified prefix.
Int	indexOf (java.lang.String, java.lang.String)	Returns the index within a string of the first occurrence of a specified substring.
Int	Length (java.lang.Object)	Returns the number of items in a collection, or the number of characters in a string.
java.lang.String	escapeXml (java.lang.String)	Escapes characters that could be interpreted as XML markup.
java.lang.String	join (java.lang.String[], java.langString	Joins all elements of an array into a string.
java.lang.String	replace (java.lang.String, java.lang.String, java.lang.String)	Returns a string resulting from replacing an input string in all occurrences of a "before" and "after" substring.
java.lang.String	split (java.lang.String, java.lang.String)	Splits a string into an array of substrings.
java.lang.String	substring (java.lang.Stirng, int, int)	Returns a subset of a string.
java.lang.String	substringAfter (java.lang.String, java.lang.String)	Returns a subset of a string following a specific substring.
java.lang.String	substringBefore (java.lang.String, java.lang.String)	Returns a subset of a string before a specific substring.
java.lang.String	toLowerCase (java.lang.String)	Converts all the characters of a string to lower case.

Table 11.17: JSTL Standard Functions (continued)		
Type	Function Tag	Description
java.lang.String	toUpperCase (java.lang.String)	Converts all the characters of a string to upper case.
java.lang.String	trim (java.lang.String)	Removes white space from both ends of a string.

Sessions

On a typical visit to a website, a user will probably view several pages. The session object allows an application developer to associate data specific to an individual site visitor. Data can be stored in and retrieved from a session. The three Web pages in Figures 11.26, 11.27, and 11.28 show an application using sessions to store and retrieve the user name. Figure 11.26 is an HTML file that prompts for the site user's name. Figure 11.27 is a JSP page that stores the name and provides a link to another site page. Figure 11.28 is the page referenced in the link provided.

```
<HTML>
<BODY>
<!-- JSP1137.html Session Example -->
Welcome to Belhur Publishing Home Page!  <BR>
<FORM METHOD=POST ACTION="JSP1138.jsp">
Please Enter Your Name and Press the Submit Button. <INPUT TYPE=TEXT
NAME=siteusername SIZE=30>
<P><INPUT TYPE=Submit>
</FORM>
</BODY>
</HTML>
```

Figure 11.26: The HTML page of the sessions example

```
<%--JSP1138.jsp Session Example --%>
<%
    String name = request.getParameter( "siteusername" );
    session.setAttribute( "theUserName", name );
%>
<HTML>
<BODY>
<A HREF="JSP1139.jsp">Link to Belhur Publishing Inventory Inquiry Page.</A>
</BODY>
</HTML>
```

Figure 11.27: The first JSP page of the sessions example

```
<%--JSP1139.jsp Session Example --%>
<HTML>
<BODY>
Belhur Publishing Product Inventory Inquiry Page! <BR> <BR>
Welcome <%= session.getAttribute( "theUserName" ) %> !
</BODY>
</HTML>
```

Figure 11.28: The second JSP page of the sessions example

The page JSP1137.html is displayed first, as shown in Figure 11.29. It prompts for and retains the user's name in the session. The name retained using the session.setAttribute is theUserName.

Figure 11.29: The page displayed from the HTML in Figure 11.27

Once the user has entered a name and clicked **Submit**, the user is directed to the JSP1138.jsp page through this message:

Link to Belhur Publishing Inventory Inquiry Page.

This page uses the request getParameter to retrieve the name entered and the session setAttribute to retain the name entered. When the site user clicks the link provided, he or she will be routed to the JSP1139.jsp page, and a message like this will be displayed:

Belhur Publishing Product Inventory Inquiry Page! Welcome Brent Tinsey !

The session value is retrieved using the session getAttribute and is used to display a "Welcome" message.

This example shows how useful sessions can be within JSP. Additional data can be retained by adding another attribute. Sessions provide many practical uses for business application developers.

Sessions are enabled by default. The session object is stored on the server side, so each session object will use a little bit of the system resources. Using sessions also increases the server traffic, as the session ID is sent from the server to the client. The client will send the session ID along with each request made. If a site has heavy traffic and the stored session data is not really required, you might consider disabling the session in a JSP page by setting the page directive to false, like this:

<%@ page session="false" %>

Cookies

Cookies are small bits of information sent to and saved by a browser. Cookies can be retrieved and reused when a visitor returns to a site, providing the visitor with conveniences that enhance the user experience. Here are a few ways a cookie may be used:

● Identify a user during a website session, as in the previous example that retains the user's name to display a greeting.
● Enable the user to bypass entering a username and password on a return visit to a site.
● Customize a site by incorporating cookie information into site application logic. For example, a page with instructions on how to use the site would not be displayed on a return visit.

The javax.servlet.http.Cookie class is used to create a JSP cookie. The information contained within a cookie can uniquely identify a client. A cookie consists of a cookie name, a cookie value, and optional attributes. The request method getCookies() is used to retrieve cookie information and return the values in an array of cookie objects. The cookie is added to the Set-Cookie response header by using the addCookie method of HttpServletResponse. Figure 11.30 shows the code to add a cookie.

```
Cookie userCookie = new Cookie("username", "siteusername");
response.addCookie(userCookie);
```

Figure 11.30: Adding a cookie

Cookie objects have the methods listed in Table 11.18.

Table 11.18: Methods for Getting and Setting Cookie Attributes	
Cookie Object Method	**Description**
getComment() setComment()	Gets or sets the comment describing the purpose of the cookie, or returns null if a comment has not been defined.
getDomain() setDomain()	Gets or sets the domain to which the cookie applies. Cookies normally are returned to the exact hostname that sent them. This method can be used to instruct the browser to return the user to other hosts within the same domain.
getMaxAge() setMaxAge()	Gets or sets the maximum allowed age of the cookie. The value is stored in seconds that will elapse before a cookie expires. When the maximum age is not set, the cookie will only be retained for the current session and will not be stored on the client.
getName() setName()	Gets or sets the name of the cookie.
getPath() setPath()	Gets or sets the path to which the cookie applies.
getSecure() setSecure()	Gets or sets the Boolean value indicating whether a cookie should only be sent over an encrypted connection like SSL.
getValue() setValue()	Gets or returns the value of a cookie.

A cookie may be used to prompt for a value and can store and retain that value for a designated period of time to use when a site visitor returns to the site. The cookie is dependent upon the specific client connecting. Figure 11.31 is an example of JSP to request a cookie.

```
<%--JSP1145.jsp Cookie Example --%>
<%@ page language="java" %>
<%
String cookieName = "siteusername";
Cookie cookies [] = request.getCookies ();
Cookie myCookie = null;
if (cookies != null)
{
for (int i = 0; i < cookies.length; i++)
{
if (cookies [i].getName().equals (cookieName))
{
myCookie = cookies[i];
break;
}
}
}
%>
<html>
<body>
<%
if (myCookie == null) {
%>
No Cookie found with the name <%=cookieName%> <BR>
Welcome to Belhur Publishing! <BR>
<form method="post" action="JSP1146.jsp">
<p><b>Please Enter Your Name: </b><input type="text"
name="siteusername"><BR>
<input type="submit" value="Submit">
</form>
<%
} else {
%>
<p>
Welcome <%=myCookie.getValue()%> to Belhur Publishing!
<%
}
%>
</body>
```

Figure 11.31: Requesting a cookie

In this example, request.getCookies() is used to determine if the siteusername cookie exists. If it doesn't exist, the user is prompted to "Please Enter Your Name" using an HTML form. When the user clicks **Submit**, the browser is directed to the JSP1146.jsp page, shown in Figure 11.32.

```
<%--JSP1146.jsp Cookie Example Set Cookie Provide Link --%>
<%@ page language="java" import="java.util.*"%>
<%
String siteusername=request.getParameter("siteusername");
if(siteusername==null) siteusername="";
Date now = new Date();
String timestamp = now.toString();
Cookie cookie = new Cookie ("siteusername",siteusername);
cookie.setMaxAge(90 * 24 * 60 * 60);
response.addCookie(cookie);
%>
<html>
<head>
<title>Cookie Saved</title>
</head>
<body>
<p><a href="JSP1145.jsp">Next Page to view the cookie value</a><p>
</body>
```

Figure 11.32: Creating a cookie

This page creates the cookie, retains the value for siteusername, and provides a link to return back to the Welcome page. If the cookie value exists for siteusername, its value is retrieved using getValue() and displayed on the Welcome page. The Welcome page will be displayed when the client returns to the site or after the cookie has been created and the user clicks the link to return to the Welcome page. In this example, note that the cookie will not expire for 90 days, because cookie.setMaxAge(90 * 24 * 60 * 60) multiplies 90 days, 24 hours, 60 minutes, and 60 seconds.

The Welcome page displayed if no cookie is found is shown in Figure 11.33. After the user's name is entered and retained in siteusername, a message containing a link to return back to the home page will be displayed, like this:

Next Page to view the cookie value

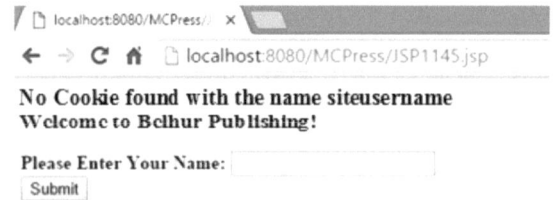

Figure 11.33: The Welcome page prompting for a username

Once the username has been entered, the following text will be displayed:

Welcome *username* to Belhur Publishing!

This example should inspire some thought as to how cookies can be used in business applications. On sites requiring an ID and password, a cookie can even be compared to a database value to determine whether the user is still valid.

Accessing a Database

As a business application developer, you must be able to access stored data. JSP can be used to connect to and retrieve data from most databases, including SQL Server, MySQL, DB2, and Oracle. The examples in this chapter use MySQL on a local system. The examples can be used with other databases with minor changes, including the appropriate database connection type.

Displaying Database Records

In the first example, an employee table will be displayed containing an automatically assigned employee ID, last name, first name, and position. To prepare for this example, you will need to load MySQL on your PC and configure it as a local source. This chapter isn't intended to teach MySQL, but we will briefly walk through the creation of a MySQL database to be used with the examples. Here is the MySQL statement to create the Belhur database:

```
CREATE DATABASE Belhur;
```

Here is the MySQL statement to create an employee table:

```
CREATE TABLE employee (id INT NOT NULL AUTO_INCREMENT ,
LastName VARCHAR( 30 )  ,FirstName VARCHAR( 30 )  , Position VARCHAR(30),
PRIMARY KEY (id));
```

Next, you need to add a few records to the table, to have something to display from it, like this:

```
INSERT INTO employee (LastName, FirstName, Position) VALUES('Ubelhor',
'Laura', 'Author');
```

The id field is defined as an auto-increment field, so its numeric value will automatically be assigned when a record is added. Add a few more records in the table, changing the values of the last name, first name, and position.

This example uses a single JSP file, shown in Figure 11.34, to provide a display screen listing employees in order by last name and then first name.

```jsp
<%--JSP1153.jsp Accessing a Database Displaying Data Example--%>
<%@ page language="java" import="java.sql.*" %>
  <%

      Class.forName("com.mysql.jdbc.Driver");
      java.sql.Connection con = null;
      Statement stmt=null;
      ResultSet rst=null;

      try{
              String url="jdbc:mysql://localhost/Belhur?user=userid&passwo
rd=pw";
              con=DriverManager.getConnection(url);
              stmt=con.createStatement();
      }catch(Exception e){
                  System.out.println(e.getMessage());
              }
              rst=stmt.executeQuery("select * from employee order by
LastName, FirstName");
      %>
<html>
    <body>
    <center><h2>Employee List</h2>
    <table border="1" cellspacing="0" cellpadding="0">
        <tr><td><b>Employee No</b></td><td><b>Last Name</
b><td><b>FirstName</b></td><td><b>Position</b></td></tr>
        <%
              while(rst.next()){
```
Continued

```
        %>
                <tr><td><%=rst.getInt("Id")%></td>
                <td><%=rst.getString("LastName")%></td>
                <td><%=rst.getString("FirstName")%></td>
                <td><%=rst.getString("Position")%></td>
                </tr>
            <%

                            }

            rst.close();
                    stmt.close();
                    con.close();
            %>
                <tr>
    </table>
    </center>
    <body>
<html>
```

Figure 11.34: Accessing data with JSP

The example begins with the following directive:

```
<%@ page language="java" import="java.sql.*" %>
```

Java, of course, is identified as the language for the JSP file. The directive is important because the java.sql* classes are imported and can be used throughout the JSP code. The import statement provides access to the java.sql classes required to access the data and run MySQL statements. Other classes can be imported to access a variety of databases.

A connection is needed when accessing a database. As discussed earlier in this chapter, a variable or method must be declared before it can be used in the JSP file. We declare variables and make a connection to the database using the code in Figure 11.35.

```
        Class.forName("com.mysql.jdbc.Driver");
        java.sql.Connection con = null;
        Statement stmt=null;
        ResultSet rst=null;
```

Figure 11.35: The code to declare variables and load the database driver

In this example, the variable con is the connection type, rst is the object that will hold the result set from the database **query**, and stmt is the object that will be used to execute the query.

To connect to the database, we need to load the database driver. In this case, a MySQL driver is loaded. Calling Class.forName(driver) results in the driver class being loaded. JSP can access many databases, as mentioned early. Here are some additional drivers that can be used:

com.mysql.jdbc.Driver
com.ibm.as400.access.as400jdbcdriver
com.ibm.db2.jcc.db2driver
oracle.jdbc.driver

After the driver is loaded, the next step is to make the connection. Figure 11.36 shows the code to do this.

```
url="jdbc:mysql://localhost/Belhur?user=userid&password=password";

con=DriverManager.getConnection(url);
```

Figure 11.36: Making the connection

The URL path is first defined, so it can be used by the connection. The JDBC URL for MySQL consists of *jdbc:mysql://* followed by the name of the MySQL server, in this example *localhost*, followed by the database, *Belhur*, followed by the user ID and password. The ID and password need to be valid, with authority to access the database. When the URL is passed to the getConnection() method of the DriverManager class, the connection object is returned, which completes the connection to the database.

The connection could be defined a little differently, passing the URL, user ID, and password as separate parameters, like this:

con = DriverManager.getConnection (url, userName, password);

You might opt to do this for security purposes. The ID and password will be provided through a prompted parameter.

With the connection made, we are ready to run the query using the database specified in the connection and a designated table. A statement object is created by calling the createStatement() method. After creating the statement object, we are ready to execute the query. The statement variable name is stmt, and the recordset variable is rst. The query is executed on the statement object, as shown in Figure 11.37. The executeQuery() method runs the SQL statement and returns a single **result object** in rst. The method also returns the number of records from the table included in the query, based on the selection criteria.

```
rst=stmt.executeQuery("select * from employee order by LastName,
FirstName");
```

Figure 11.37: Query execution

In summary, the statement is created, the executeQuery() method is called on the stmt object, and the SQL query string is passed in method executeQuery() to the rst result set. Using an asterisk in the statement means all the fields within the table are included in the result. All records in the table will be retrieved in order by last name and first name.

The example also includes code to address any errors encountered, shown in Figure 11.38. In this example, try and catch are used. These are one construct, and must be included in the same block of code. If an exception is encountered, a message will be displayed. Errors will be discussed in more detail later in this chapter.

```
try{
    }catch(Exception e){
                System.out.println(e.getMessage());
        }
                }
```

Figure 11.38: Catching errors

Once the query is executed and the result set is returned, the results are available for use in the application. The result set represents a table including the fields designated in the query statement. The table cursor initially is positioned before the first row selected. To access the first row in a result set, the next() method is used, as shown in Figure 11.39. This method moves the cursor to the next record. It returns a value of true if the next row is valid, or false if there are no more records within the result set.

```
while(rst.next()){
%>
        <tr><td><%=rst.getInt("Id")%></td>
        <td><%=rst.getString("LastName")%></td>
        <td><%=rst.getString("FirstName")%></td>
        <td><%=rst.getString("Position")%></td>
        </tr>
    <%
}
```

Figure 11.39: Reading rows from the result set

The getString() method retrieves a string value from the current row. In this example, the ID, last name, first name, and position values are retrieved. The getInt() or getDate() methods would be used to retrieve integer or date values. (Refer to Appendix D, which you can download at *https://goo .gl/2uYjHb*, for a list of JDBC types, for other data type methods that may be used.)

The values are retrieved and displayed. We loop through the record set until we have reached the end of the record set. We finish by closing the table and connection, as shown in Figure 11.40.

```
                    rst.close();
                stmt.close();
                con.close();
```

Figure 11.40: Closing the connection

Figure 11.41 shows the result that will be displayed to the user. Notice that the employee ID, last name, first name, and position are displayed in order by last name, followed by first name.

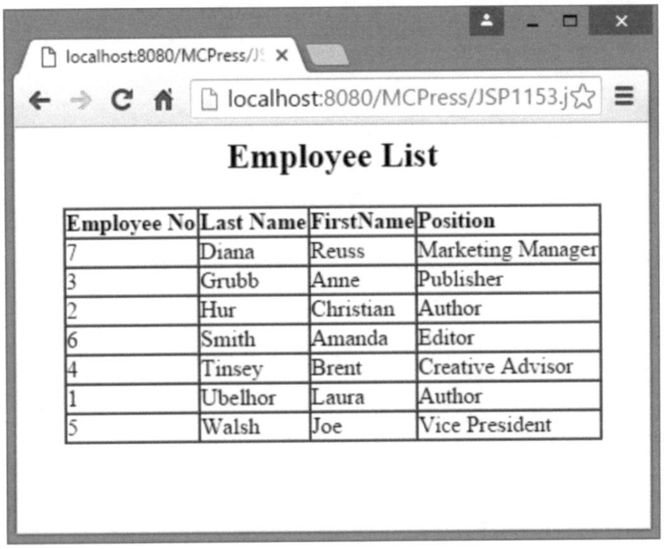

Employee No	Last Name	FirstName	Position
7	Diana	Reuss	Marketing Manager
3	Grubb	Anne	Publisher
2	Hur	Christian	Author
6	Smith	Amanda	Editor
4	Tinsey	Brent	Creative Advisor
1	Ubelhor	Laura	Author
5	Walsh	Joe	Vice President

Figure 11.41: The results from accessing a database with JSP

Adding Data to a Database

In the next example, a record will be added to a table, and the table will be displayed after the record is added. The executeUpdate() method is used to insert a record in the table. As in the previous example, we will work with the employee table. Figure 11.42 shows the single JSP file that provides an entry form, adds records to the employee table, and displays the contents of the employee table.

```
<%--JSP1166.jsp Accessing a Database Example--%>
<%@ page language="java" import="java.sql.*" %>
  <%
       Class.forName("com.mysql.jdbc.Driver");
       java.sql.Connection con = null;
       Statement stmt=null;
       ResultSet rst=null;
try{
                                                    Continued
```

```
                String
url="jdbc:mysql://localhost/Belhur?user=ubelhor&password=Duke0704";
                con=DriverManager.getConnection(url);
                stmt=con.createStatement();
        }catch(Exception e){
                        System.out.println(e.getMessage());
                }
    if(request.getParameter("action") != null){
            String lastname=request.getParameter("lastname");
        String firstname=request.getParameter("firstname");
        String position=request.getParameter("position");
            stmt.executeUpdate("insert into
employee(LastName,FirstName,Position)
values('"+lastname+"','"+firstname+"','"+position+"')");

            rst=stmt.executeQuery("select * from employee order by position");
        %>
<html>
    <body>
    <center><h2>Employee List</h2>
    <table border="1" cellspacing="0" cellpadding="0">
            <tr><td><b>Number</b></td><td><b>Employee
Number</b></td><td><b>Last
Name</b></td><td><b>FirstName</b></td><td><b>Position</b></td></tr>
            <%
            int no=1;
                    while(rst.next()){
        %>
            <tr><td><%=no%></td>
            <td><%=rst.getInt("Id")%></td>
            <td><%=rst.getString("LastName")%></td>
            <td><%=rst.getString("FirstName")%></td>
            <td><%=rst.getString("Position")%></td>
            </tr>
        <%
                no++;
                    }

            rst.close();
                    stmt.close();
                    con.close();
```

Continued

```
              %>
                <tr>
    </table>
    Total Number of Employees: <%=no - 1%>  <br>
          <A HREF="JSP1266.jsp">Add Another Employee.</A>
    </center>
    <body>
<html>
<%}else{%>

<html>

                <head>
                <title>Employee Entry FormDocument</title>
          <script language="javascript">
                    function validate(objForm){
                          if(objForm.lastname.value.length==0){
                                alert("Please enter Last Name!");
                                objForm.lastname.focus();
                                return false;
                          }
                          if(objForm.firstname.value.length==0){
                                alert("Please enter First Name!");
                                objForm.firstname.focus();
                                return false;
                          }
                          if(objForm.position.value.length==0){
                                alert("Please enter Position!");
                                objForm.position.focus();
                                return false;
                          }
                          return true;
                    }
          </script>
                </head>
                <body><center>
                <form action="JSP1166.jsp" method="post" name="entry"
onSubmit="return validate(this)">
                <input type="hidden" value="list" name="action">
                <table border="1" cellpadding="0" cellspacing="0">
```
Continued

```
                        <tr>
                              <td>
                                    <table>
                                          <tr><td colspan="2"
align="center"><h2>Employee Entry Form</h2></td></tr>
                                          <tr><td colspan="2"> </td></tr>
                                          <tr><td>Last
Name:</td><td><input name="lastname" type="text" size="30"></td></tr>
                                          <tr><td>First
Name:</td><td><input name="firstname" type="text" size="30"></td></tr>
                  <tr><td>Position:</td><td><input name="position" type="text"
size="30"></td></tr>
                                          <tr><td colspan="2"
align="center"><input type="submit" value="Submit"></td></tr>
                                    </table>
                              </td>
                        </tr>
                  </table>
                  </form>
                  </center>
                  </body>
      </html>
<%}%>
```

Figure 11.42: Adding and displaying data

When the JSP file is run, the entry screen in Figure 11.43 will be displayed. The screen prompts for the employee information to be entered.

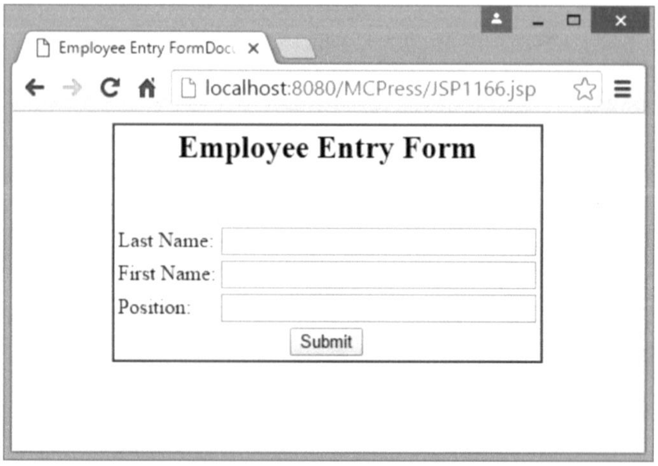

Figure 11.43: The employee entry form

The code includes JavaScript edit checks requiring the last name, first name, and position to be entered, shown in Figure 11.44. JavaScript, introduced in chapter 8, is often used with JSP for such things as client-side validation.

```
script language="javascript">
                function validate(objForm){
                        if(objForm.lastname.value.length==0){
                                alert("Please enter Last Name!");
                                objForm.lastname.focus();
                                return false;
                        }
                        if(objForm.firstname.value.length==0){
                                alert("Please enter First Name!");
                                objForm.firstname.focus();
                                return false;
                        }
                        if(objForm.position.value.length==0){
                                alert("Please enter Position!");
                                objForm.position.focus();
                                return false;
                        }
                        return true;
                }
        </script>
```

Figure 11.44: JavaScript data validation

If the last name, first name, or position is missing when the user clicks **Submit**, a message like the one in Figure 11.45 will be displayed.

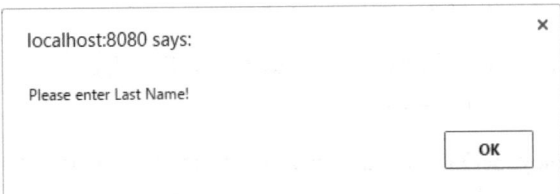

Figure 11.45: A JavaScript validation message

When all required data is entered and the user clicks **Submit**, we loop back again through the code. This time the "action" is not null, so the code in Figure 11.46 is executed. This code constructs MySQL statements to insert the new data into the employee table and display all the records in the table, in order of position.

```
if(request.getParameter("action") != null){
       String lastname=request.getParameter("lastname");
      String firstname=request.getParameter("firstname");
      String position=request.getParameter("position");
         stmt.executeUpdate("insert into
employee(LastName,FirstName,Position)
values('"+lastname+"','"+firstname+"','"+position+"')");

         rst=stmt.executeQuery("select * from employee order by
position"));
```

Figure 11.46: Code to execute MySQL insert *and* select *statements*

In our example, the database already contained five employees. We added employee 8, Jesse Weaver, Director. Figure 11.47 shows the resulting display.

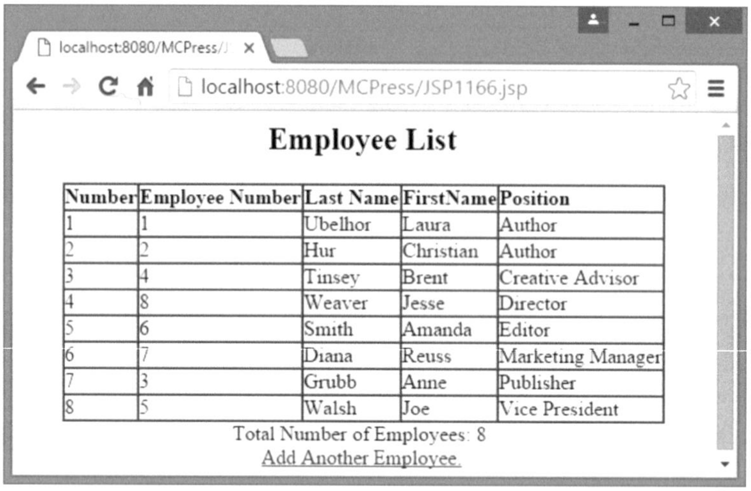

Number	Employee Number	Last Name	FirstName	Position
1	1	Ubelhor	Laura	Author
2	2	Hur	Christian	Author
3	4	Tinsey	Brent	Creative Advisor
4	8	Weaver	Jesse	Director
5	6	Smith	Amanda	Editor
6	7	Diana	Reuss	Marketing Manager
7	3	Grubb	Anne	Publisher
8	5	Walsh	Joe	Vice President

Figure 11.47: The results of adding a new employee

Notice the **Add Another Employee** link. When that link is clicked, the application runs again, and the employee entry form will be redisplayed.

In this example, the employee ID is automatically assigned without entry because that field is defined to auto-increment in the MySQL table definition. The integer no, used to increment the record count and assign a number to the entries, is not the same as the employee ID. This example adds a line of code to display the total employee count, using the accumulated value of no. Because this integer is incremented each time the loop is executed, and the loop is executed until a value of false is returned for the result set, the integer count is one more than the record count. The code in Figure 11.48 handles this task.

```
Total Number of Employees: <%=no - 1%>   <br>
```

Figure 11.48: Displaying the total number of employees

Updating a Database

The next example takes access to a database further, providing capabilities to add, update, and delete rows in a table. Again, the employee table of the Belhur database will be used. The table includes the fields employee number, last name, first name, and position.

This application consists of four JSP files:

- The employee list page (the main application page), JSP1175EEDisplay.jsp
- The employee add page, JSP1175Add.jsp
- The employee update page, JSP1175Update.jsp
- The employee delete page, JSP1175Delete.jsp

The main application page, shown in Figure 11.49, displays a list of the employee table entries and provides options to add, update, or delete an employee. The rows of the employee table are displayed in order by last name, followed by first name. The employee list page also provides a total number of employees.

```
<%--JSP1175EEDisplay.jsp Employee Modification Example--%>
<%@ page language="java" import="java.sql.*" %>
  <%

Class.forName("com.mysql.jdbc.Driver");
      Connection con=null;
      ResultSet rst=null;
      Statement stmt=null;
    try{
            String url="jdbc:mysql://localhost/Belhur?user=youruserid&pas
sword=yourpassword";
            con=DriverManager.getConnection(url);
            stmt=con.createStatement();
      }catch(Exception e){
                  System.out.println(e.getMessage());
            }
            rst=stmt.executeQuery("select * from employee order by
LastName, FirstName");
      %>
<html>
                                                        Continued
```

```
   <body>
   <center><h2>Employee List</h2>
   <table border="1" cellspacing="0" cellpadding="0">
        <tr><td><b>Employee No</b></td>
        <td><b>Last Name</b></td>
        <td><b>FirstName</b></td>
        <td><b>Position</b></td>
        <td><b>Update</b></td>
        <td><b>Delete</b></td>
        </tr>
        <%
            int no=1;
              while(rst.next()){
        %>
            <tr><td><%=rst.getInt("Id")%></td>
            <td><%=rst.getString("LastName")%></td>
            <td><%=rst.getString("FirstName")%></td>
            <td><%=rst.getString("Position")%></td>
                    <td><a href="JSP1175EEUpdate.jsp?id=<%=rst.
getInt("Id")%>">Update</a></b>
                    <td><a href="JSP1175EEDelete.jsp?id=<%=rst.
getInt("Id")%>">Delete</a></b>
            </tr>
        <%
                    no++;
                        }

            rst.close();
                    stmt.close();
                    con.close();
            %>
            <tr>
   </table>
       Total Number of Employees: <%=no - 1%>  <br>
        <A HREF="JSP1175EEAdd.jsp">Add An Employee.</A>
   </center>
   <body>
<html>
```

Figure 11.49: The main JSP page for updating employee data

The file in Figure 11.49 creates and makes the connection, displays all the entries in the employee table, and displays the accumulated count, as shown in Figure 11.50.

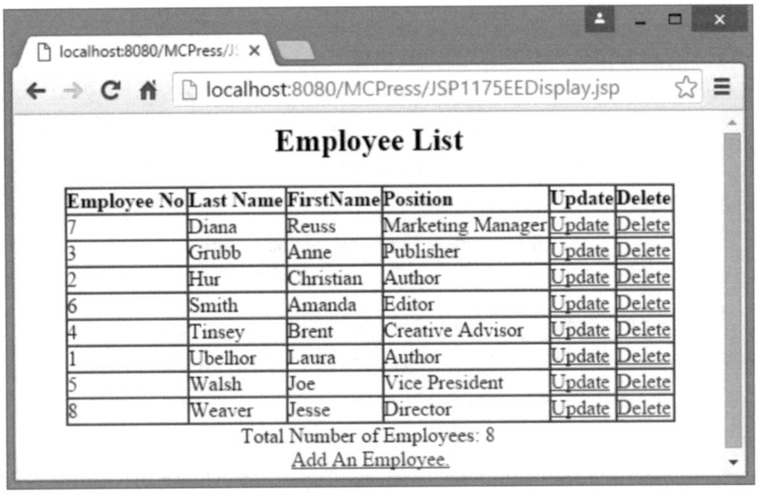

Figure 11.50: The initial screen for the application to update employee data

Notice there are additional columns for updating and deleting records. A link to add an employee is also displayed. When the user clicks a link, the application is directed to the add, change, or delete a page to complete the appropriate action, as shown in Figure 11.51. The employee number is the key to accessing the employee record.

```
<td><a href="JSP1175EEUpdate.jsp?id=<%=rst.getInt("Id")%>">Update</a></b>
<td><a href="JSP1175EEDelete.jsp?id=<%=rst.getInt("Id")%>">Delete</a></b>

<A HREF="JSP1175EEAdd.jsp">Add An Employee.</A>
```

Figure 11.51: Links for updating, deleting, and adding employee records

For the update and delete functions, the parameter Id will be passed by using the record set type variable to retrieve the Id value. Notice the <%= %> tags used, to allow use of the getint() method.

The add function is very similar to the earlier example of adding records to a table. However, in this example, the add page is accessed through an HTML link. When the user clicks the link on the main page, the JSP file in Figure 11.52 will be executed, and the screen in Figure 11.53 will be displayed.

```
<%--JSP1175EEAdd.jsp Add an Employee Example--%>
<%@ page language="java" import="java.sql.*" %>
  <%
Class.forName("com.mysql.jdbc.Driver");
      Connection con=null;
                                                        Continued
```

```
        ResultSet rst=null;
        Statement stmt=null;
    try{
            String
url="jdbc:mysql://localhost/Belhur?user=youruserid&password=yourpassword";
            con=DriverManager.getConnection(url);
            stmt=con.createStatement();
        }catch(Exception e){
                    System.out.println(e.getMessage());
            }
    if(request.getParameter("action") != null){
        String lastname=request.getParameter("lastname");
      String firstname=request.getParameter("firstname");
      String position=request.getParameter("position");
      stmt.executeUpdate("insert into employee(LastName,FirstName,Position)
values('"+lastname+"','"+firstname+"','"+position+"')");
      %>
 <html>
Employee Record Successfully Added! <br> <br>
<A HREF="JSP1175EEDisplay.jsp">Return to Employee Display.</A>
</hmtl>
<%}else{%>
<html>
            <head>
            <title>Employee Entry FormDocument</title>
        <script language="javascript">
                function validate(objForm){
                    if(objForm.lastname.value.length==0){
                        alert("Please enter Last Name!");
                        objForm.lastname.focus();
                        return false;
                    }
                    if(objForm.firstname.value.length==0){
                        alert("Please enter First Name!");
                        objForm.firstname.focus();
                        return false;
                    }
                    if(objForm.position.value.length==0){
                        alert("Please enter Position!");
```

Continued

```
                                    objForm.position.focus();
                                    return false;
                    }
                    return true;
            }
        </script>
    </head>
    <body><center>
    <form action="JSP1175EEAdd.jsp" method="post" name="entry"
onSubmit="return validate(this)">
    <input type="hidden" value="list" name="action">
    <table border="1" cellpadding="0" cellspacing="0">
<tr>
<td>
<table>
<tr><td colspan="2" align="center"><h2>Employee Entry Form</h2></td></tr>
<tr><td colspan="2"> </td></tr>
<tr><td>Last Name:</td><td><input name="lastname" type="text" size="30"></
td></tr>
<tr><td>First Name:</td><td><input name="firstname" type="text"
size="30"></td></tr>
<tr><td>Position:</td><td><input name="position" type="text" size="30"></
td></tr>
<tr><td colspan="2" align="center"><input type="submit" value="Add
Employee"></td></tr>
                                    </table>
                            </td>
                    </tr>
            </table>
<A HREF="JSP1175EEDisplay.jsp">Return to Employee Display Page Without
Adding an Employee.</A>
                    </form>
                    </center>
                    </body>
    </html>
<%}%>
```

Figure 11.52: Adding an employee

JavaScript code is used for field validation on the client side. Like the example earlier in this chapter, the validation checks to make sure a last name, first name, and position are entered. When the user clicks the **Add Employee** button and there are no field validation errors, the action parameter value is set to "Add Employee". The value is not null, so the SQL statement is executed to insert a record. The user also has the option to return to the main application page without adding an employee through the use of an HTML link.

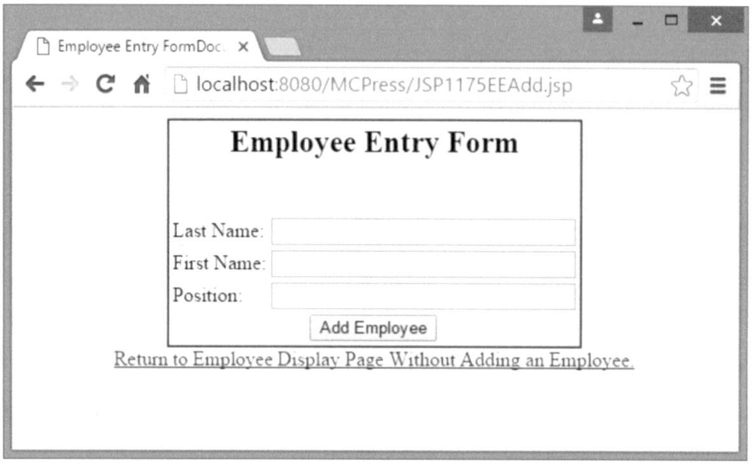

Figure 11.53: The screen to add an employee

When the action parameter is set to "Add Employee", the following message is displayed:

Employee Record Successfully Added!
Return to Employee Display.

The user clicks the **Return to Employee Display** link to return to the main application page. In this example, employee 9 has been added, as shown in Figure 11.54. Notice the employee count has been incremented. The new entry is displayed at the top of the page because the records are displayed by last name and first name.

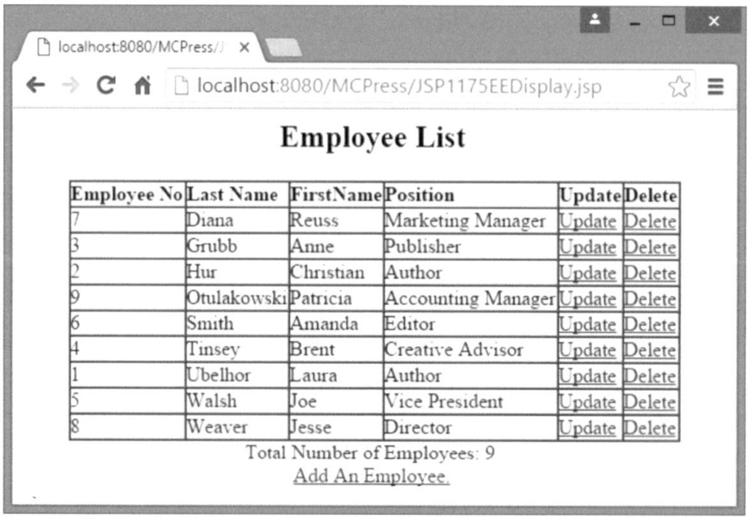

Figure 11.54: The main application page after employee 9 has been added

The update feature is initiated by clicking an **Update** link reference. It will execute the JSP in Figure 11.55, passing the id parameter with the value of the employee number.

```
<%--JSP1175EEUpdate.jsp Update an Employee Example--%><%@ page
language="java" import="java.sql.*" %>
  <%
      Class.forName("com.mysql.jdbc.Driver");
      Connection con=null;
      ResultSet rst=null;
      Statement stmt=null;
    try{
          String
url="jdbc:mysql://localhost/Belhur?user=youruserid&password=yourpassword";
          con=DriverManager.getConnection(url);
          stmt=con.createStatement();
      }catch(Exception e){
              System.out.println(e.getMessage());
          }
    if(request.getParameter("action") != null){
    int selectionId = Integer.parseInt(request.getParameter("id"));
    String lastname=request.getParameter("lastname");
    String firstname=request.getParameter("firstname");
    String position=request.getParameter("position");
      stmt.executeUpdate("UPDATE employee SET LastName=' "+ lastname +" ',
FirstName=' "+ firstname +" ', Position=' "+ position +" ' where Id =11");

    %>
  <html>
Employee Id <%= request.getParameter ("id") %> Successfully Updated!  <br>
<br>
<A HREF="JSP1175EEDisplay.jsp">Return to Employee Display.</A>
</html>
<%}else{%>
<%
int selectionId = Integer.parseInt(request.getParameter("id"));
String lastname=null;
String firstname=null;
String position=null;
rst=stmt.executeQuery("select * from employee where Id = " + selectionId +
"");
                                                          Continued
```

```
        if (rst.next())
        {
    lastname = rst.getString("LastName");
    firstname = rst.getString("FirstName");
    position = rst.getString("Position");

        }
        else
        {
            lastname = "Unknown.";
            firstname = "Unknown.";
            position = "Unknown.";
        }
%>
<html>
        <head>
                <script language="javascript">
                function validate(objForm){
                        if(objForm.lastname.value.length==0){
                                alert("Please enter Last Name!");
                                objForm.lastname.focus();
                                return false;
                        }
                        if(objForm.firstname.value.length==0){
                                alert("Please enter First Name!");
                                objForm.firstname.focus();
                                return false;
                        }
                        if(objForm.position.value.length==0){
                                alert("Please enter Position!");
                                objForm.position.focus();
                                return false;
                        }
                        return true;
                }
        </script>
</head>
<body><center>
<form action="JSP1175EEUpdate.jsp" method="post" name="update"
onSubmit="return validate(this)">
```

Continued

```
<input type="hidden" value="list" name="action">
<input type="hidden" value=<%= request.getParameter ("id")%>  name="id"">
<table border="1" cellspacing="0" cellpadding="0">
          <tr><td colspan="4" align="center"><h2>Employee Update Form</
h2></td></tr>
          <tr><td><b>Employee No</b></td>
          <td><b>Last Name</b></td>
          <td><b>FirstName</b></td>
          <td><b>Position</b></td>
          </tr>
          <tr><td><%=selectionId%></td>
          <td><input name="lastname" type="text" size="30"
value="<%=lastname%>"></td>
          <td><input name="firstname" type="text" size="30"
value="<%=firstname%>"></td>
          <td><input name="position" type="text" size="30"
value="<%=position%>"></td>
</tr>
<tr><td colspan="4" align="center"><input type="submit" value="Update
Employee <%= request.getParameter ("id") %>"></td></tr>
          </table>
<A HREF="JSP1175EEDisplay.jsp">Return to Employee Display Page Without
Updating Employee.</A>
          </form>

          </center>
          </body>
   </html>
<%}%>
```

Figure 11.55: Updating an employee

When the update page is initially displayed, the action value is null. Using the id parameter passed, a query is executed, as shown in Figure 11.56, retrieving the matching employee record.

```
rst=stmt.executeQuery("select * from employee where Id = " + selectionId +
"");
```

Figure 11.56: The query to select an employee record by ID

Before the query is executed, the selectionId integer is defined, and the value is set to the passed id parameter using the getParameter() method. The update form is displayed using the retrieved table row values from the query for the matching selection. The row values are displayed within the form table by inserting JSP code to set the value of the display field, as shown in Figure 11.57.

```
<td><input name="lastname" type="text" size="30" value="<%=lastname%>"></
td>
```

Figure 11.57: Setting HTML form field values

The update also has a validation check to ensure the fields are not blank. If the last name, first name, or position is blank, a message will be displayed prompting the user to enter the missing value.

Figure 11.57 shows the update function if the **Update** link for employee 8 is clicked on the main application page. After making corrections to the position from Director to President, the user clicks the **Update Employee 8** button. Alternatively, the user can click the **Return to Employee Display Page Without Updating Employee** link. This HTML link will return the user to the main application page without completing the update.

The **Update Employee 8** button shown in Figure 11.58 displays the employee number using JSP code embedded within the JSP tags, as shown in Figure 11.59.

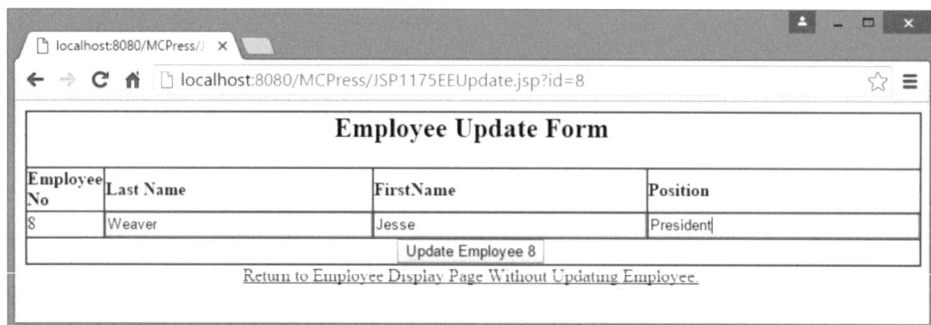

Figure 11.58: An employee update form

```
<%= request.getParameter ("id") %>
```

Figure 11.59: Displaying the employee number on a button

When the **Update Employee 8** button is clicked, hidden field values will be available for use on the post action, as shown in Figure 11.60. The id field will be used for the MySQL update statement's selection criteria. On submit, the action value is set to "Update Employee", and the value will no longer be null, triggering executeUpdate to be run.

```
<input type="hidden" value="list" name="action">
<input type="hidden" value=<%= request.getParameter ("id")%>  name="id"">
```

Figure 11.60: Hidden form values

The form field values for last name, first name, and position will be used to update the table row with an employee ID matching the id field value. After the update is complete, an HTML page with the following message is displayed:

Employee Id 8 Successfully Updated!
Return to Employee Display.

When the user clicks the **Return to Employee Display** link, the main application page will again display the employee list, as shown in Figure 11.61.

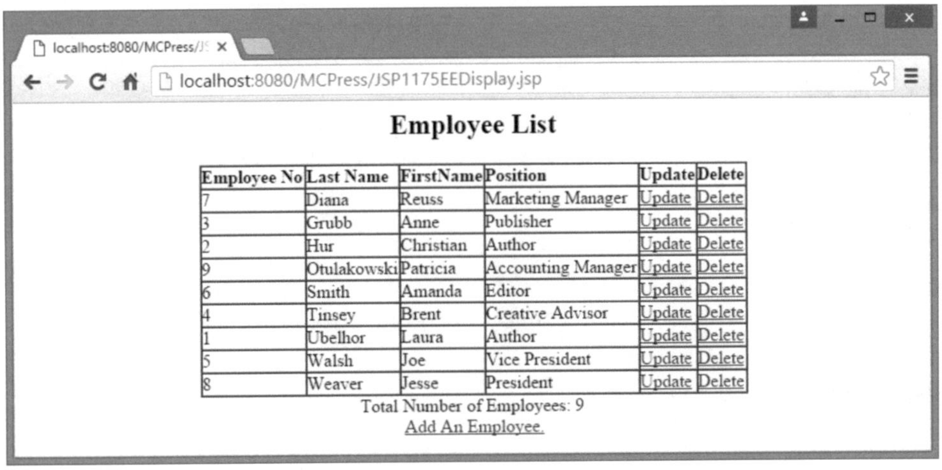

Employee No	Last Name	FirstName	Position	Update	Delete
7	Diana	Reuss	Marketing Manager	Update	Delete
3	Grubb	Anne	Publisher	Update	Delete
2	Hur	Christian	Author	Update	Delete
9	Otulakowski	Patricia	Accounting Manager	Update	Delete
6	Smith	Amanda	Editor	Update	Delete
4	Tinsey	Brent	Creative Advisor	Update	Delete
1	Ubelhor	Laura	Author	Update	Delete
5	Walsh	Joe	Vice President	Update	Delete
8	Weaver	Jesse	President	Update	Delete

Total Number of Employees: 9
Add An Employee.

Figure 11.61: The updated employee list

Notice employee 8's position in the list has changed to reflect the updated position to President.

The final function in this application is deleting a record. When the **Delete** link is clicked, the JSP file in Figure 11.62 will be loaded. Again, the id value for the selected row is passed as a parameter using JSP code embedded in the HTML link reference and the getint() method.

```
<%--JSP1175EEDelete.jsp Delete an Employee Example--%>
<%@ page language="java" import="java.sql.*" %>
  <%
        Class.forName("com.mysql.jdbc.Driver");
        Connection con=null;
        ResultSet rst=null;
        Statement stmt=null;
    try{
              String url="jdbc:mysql://localhost/Belhur?user=youruserid&pas
sword=yourpassword";
              con=DriverManager.getConnection(url);
              stmt=con.createStatement();
                                                               Continued
```

```
            }catch(Exception e){
                        System.out.println(e.getMessage());
                }
    if(request.getParameter("action") != null){
    int selectionId = Integer.parseInt(request.getParameter("id"));
        stmt.executeUpdate("delete from employee where Id ="+ selectionId );


            %>
 <html>
Employee Id <%= request.getParameter ("id") %> Successfully Deleted!   <br>
<br>
<A HREF="JSP1175EEDisplay.jsp">Return to Employee Display.</A>
</html>
<%}else{%>
<%
int selectionId = Integer.parseInt(request.getParameter("id"));
String lastname=null;
String firstname=null;
String position=null;
rst=stmt.executeQuery("select * from employee where Id = " + selectionId +
"");
        if (rst.next())
        {
        lastname = rst.getString("LastName");
        firstname = rst.getString("FirstName");
        position = rst.getString("Position");

        }
        else
        {
                lastname = "Unknown.";
                firstname = "Unknown.";
                position = "Unknown.";
        }
%>
<html>
                <head>
                </head>
```

Continued

```
                    <body><center>
                    <form action="JSP1175EEDelete.jsp" method="post"
name="delete"">
                                <input type="hidden" value="list" name="action">
                                <input type="hidden" value=<%= request.
getParameter ("id")%>  name="id"">
                                <table border="1" cellspacing="0"
cellpadding="0">
                    <tr><td colspan="4" align="center"><h2>Employee Delete Form</
h2></td></tr>
                    <tr><td><b>Employee No</b></td>
                    <td><b>Last Name</b></td>
                    <td><b>FirstName</b></td>
                    <td><b>Position</b></td>
                    </tr>
                    <tr><td><%=selectionId%></td>
                    <td><%=lastname%></td>
                    <td><%=firstname%></td>
                    <td><%=position%></td></tr>
                    <tr><td colspan="4" align="center"><input type="submit"
value="Delete Employee <%= request.getParameter ("id") %>"></td></tr>
                    </table>
            <A HREF="JSP1175EEDisplay.jsp">Return to Employee Display Page
Without Deleting Employee.</A>
                    </form>


                    </center>
                    </body>
    </html>
<%}%>
```

Figure 11.62: Deleting an employee

The delete JSP file is very similar to the update JSP file. The biggest difference is that the page retrieves the employee row and displays the fields within an HTML form as display values, instead of form input fields. Also, the executeQuery statement uses a delete SQL statement. No field edit checks are required because the application will not be changing the values of the fields. The application again provides the capability to return to the main employee page without deleting the employee through an HTML link.

The HTML page in Figure 11.63 is displayed after the user clicks the **Delete** link next to employee 9.

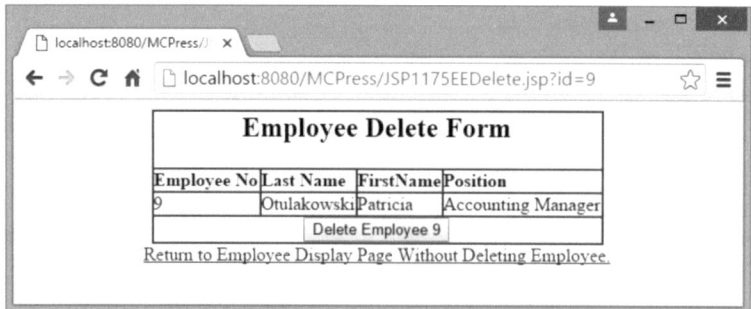

Figure 11.63: An employee delete page

When the user clicks the Delete Employee 9 button, the action value will be set to "Delete Employee", initiating executeUpdate and using the passed id value to select the row to be deleted from the employee table, as shown in Figure 11.64.

```
Execute Update:

if(request.getParameter("action") != null){
    int selectionId = Integer.parseInt(request.getParameter("id"));
        stmt.executeUpdate("delete from employee where Id ="+ selectionId );


Retrieve Id:

<html>
Employee Id <%= request.getParameter ("id") %> Successfully Deleted!  <br>
<br>
<A HREF="JSP1175EEDisplay.jsp">Return to Employee Display.</A>
</html>
```

Figure 11.64: Initiating executeUpdate for deletion

When the deletion is complete, the page shown in Figure 11.65 will be displayed. The HTML code includes embedded JSP code to use the getParameter() function to retrieve the employee ID to display.

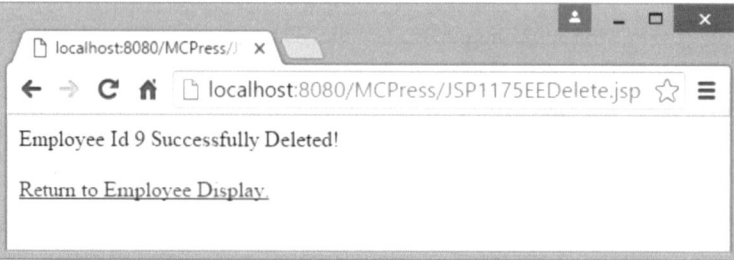

Figure 11.65: The deletion confirmation screen

When the user clicks the **Return to Employee Display** link, the application again returns to the main application page, shown in Figure 11.66. Notice that employee 9, Patricia Otulakowski, is no longer included on the list, so the total number of employees has changed from 9 to 8.

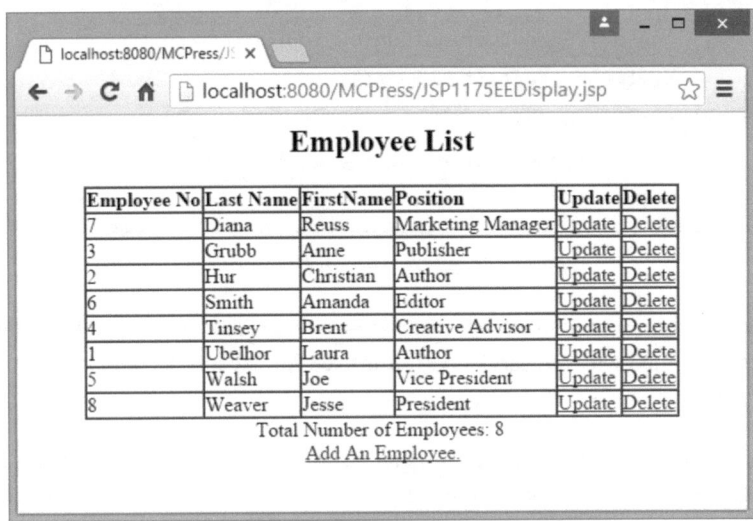

Figure 11.66: The employee list after a deletion

The ability to retrieve, display and update data is critical for business application developers. The examples in this section have shown some of the options for coding this functionality with JSP. As you have seen, JavaScript is often embedded within HTML and used with JSP to shift tasks such as editing fields to the client side, rather than using shared server-side resources.

Although these examples used MySQL, they will work with slight changes to access an IBM i DB2 database, SQL Server database, Oracle database, or other database sources. Similarly, although these examples used an employee update application, they could easily be changed to update other business databases, such as those for inventories, orders, or general ledgers.

Exception Handling

Exception handling is an important part of application development, as mentioned earlier in this chapter. An exception is an uncaught throwable object that results in an error. An exception might occur while connecting to a database when a server is down, when a buffer is full and overflows, or when a request method fails.

Exceptions can be caught by coding to throw an exception to a try and catch block. In the example in Figure 11.67, if an exception occurs while making the connection to a database, it is caught, and a message is displayed.

```
    try{
            String url="jdbc:mysql://localhost/Belhur?user=youruserid&pas
sword=yourpassword";
            con=DriverManager.getConnection(url);
            stmt=con.createStatement();
    }catch(Exception e){
                System.out.println(e.getMessage());
        }
```

Figure 11.67: A try catch exception

In the code, Exception is an implicit object that acts as a wrapper around underlying Java classes or interfaces typically defined with the servlet API. It is used for exceptions not caught by application code.

An exception may also be caught by designating an error page in the page directive. If an exception is thrown, the control will be transferred to the designated error page. Using this form of exception, you can provide a more meaningful error message for the user and also provide details for system administration about the exception encountered. Think carefully about whether or not to provide these system details. For exceptions that have a critical impact on the application, they may be more significant.

The example in the following pages illustrates the runtime error-handling features of JSP pages. The example includes three pages:

- The product list page (the main application page), JSP1196.html
- The form handler page, JSP1197.jsp
- The exception-handler error page, JSP1198.jsp

The HTML page in Figure 11.68 displays a form requesting the user to make a product selection. The page would also probably include code to list products, but this example has been kept simple to illustrate exception error-handling. The input field will be used in the form-handler page shown in Figure 11.69.

```
<!--JSP1196.html Exception Handling Example-->
<html>
<head>
Belhur Publishing Product List Page.
</head>
<body>
<form action="JSP1197.jsp" method="post">
                                                    Continued
```

```
Please Enter The Product Number:
<input type="text" name="product" />
<input type="submit" value="Submit" />
</form>
</body>
</html>
```

Figure 11.68: A product list HTML page

```
<%--JSP1197.jsp Exception Handling Form Handler Example--%>
<%@ page errorPage="JSP1198.jsp" %>
<html>
<head>
Belhur Publishing Product Selection Page.
</head>
<body>
<%
int product;
product = Integer.parseInt(request.getParameter("product"));
%>
<p>Thank You For Selecting Product Number <%= product %>.</p>
<p><a href="JSP1196.html">Return To Belhur Publishing Product List Page.</
a>.</p>
</body>
</html>
```

Figure 11.69: A JSP form-handler page

The JSP file in Figure 11.70 is the exception-handling page initiated when the user clicks the form's
Submit button.

```
<%--JSP1198.jsp Exception Handling Exception Handler Error Page Example--%>
<%@ page isErrorPage="true" import="java.io.*" %>
<html>
<body>
An error has occurred: the Product Selection is invalid! <br>
<%= exception.toString() %><br>
<%
out.println("<!--");
```
Continued

```
StringWriter sw = new StringWriter();
PrintWriter pw = new PrintWriter(sw);
exception.printStackTrace(pw);
out.print(sw);
sw.close();
pw.close();
out.println("-->");
%>
</body>
</html>
```

Figure 11.70: A JSP exception-handler page

When the application is initiated, the screen in Figure 11.71 will be displayed.

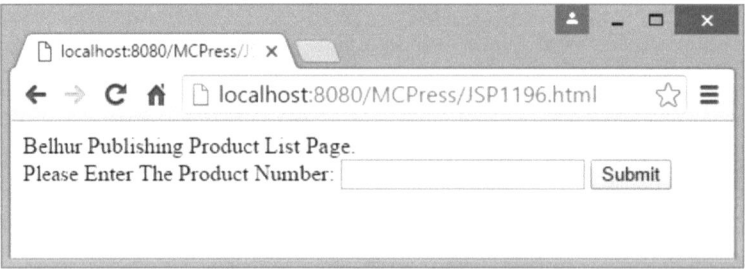

Figure 11.71: The main screen

The page prompts the user to enter a product number and click **Submit**. The input from the field is then received and used in the form-handler page. The first line of code on the page, shown in Figure 11.72, includes a directive to specify an errorPage.

```
<%@ page errorPage="JSP1198.jsp" %>
```

Figure 11.72: Specifying an error page

The page then declares the product as an integer variable. The entered value is parsed using the method Integer.parseInt() and the value is retrieved using the method request.getParameter(), as shown in Figure 11.73. The argument for the method is the name of the form field product.

```
<%
int product;
product = Integer.parseInt(request.getParameter("product"));
%>
```

Figure 11.73: Form-handler code for the get parameter request

Suppose the user enters *1* for the product number. This is a valid integer, so an exception will not occur. The page shown in Figure 11.74 will be displayed. The product number entered is displayed, and the user is provided a link to return to the main product list.

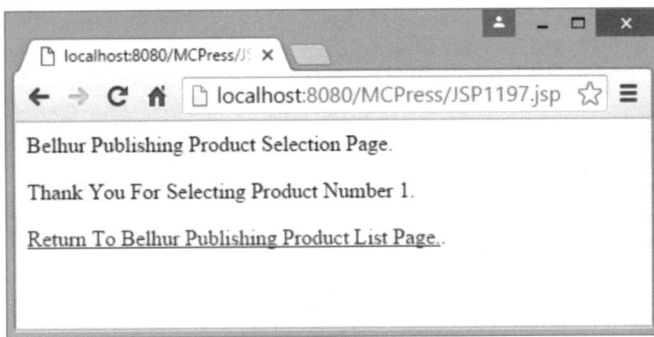

Figure 11.74: The result when no exception is thrown

Suppose, however, the user enters an invalid value. To make the JSP exception-handler error page, the isErrorPage attribute is specified, as shown in Figure 11.75.

```
<%@ page isErrorPage="true" import="java.io.*" %>
```

Figure 11.75: The isErrorPage attribute

In the declarative, the java.io class is also designated to provide functionality for the PrintWriter and StringWriter classes. Because errorPage has been declared, it has been made the name of the exception object of the type java.lang.Throwable.

In addition to the exception, a programmer-defined message has been provided for the user when an exception is encountered.

If the users enters *A*, an exception will be created, and the following message will be displayed:

An error has occurred: the Product Selection is invalid!
java.lang.NumberFormatException: For input string: "A"

The user is informed that an error has occurred. In addition, the stack trace information has been included inside HTML comment tags, so the user will see only the message and not the stack trace information. This information could be used by system administrators or developers to provide details about the exception error that occurred. Figure 11.76 is the code that creates the stack trace information.

```
<%
out.println("<!--");
StringWriter sw = new StringWriter();
PrintWriter pw = new PrintWriter(sw);
                                                    Continued
```

```
exception.printStackTrace(pw);
out.print(sw);
sw.close();
pw.close();
out.println("-->");
%>
```

Figure 11.76: Capturing stack trace exception details

To capture stack trace details, the PrintWriter and StringWriter classes are used. They are available because in the declarative, the import java.io* package was included. To view the stack trace, display the page source.

Exception handling is important. As you have seen, you can use JSP to control the messages displayed to a user and also to control how an application reacts when an error is encountered.

Summary

JSP is a widely used, proven technology for Web development. The language is very robust and can be used on a wide array of platforms and with a multitude of databases. JSP can be used alone or, more frequently, with other tools, including JavaScript and Java.

In this chapter, you have covered the basics of JSP. You have also seen how it can be used for dynamic tasks, including data retrieval and update. Other code examples can easily be found on the Web, and now that you have a basic understanding of JSP, you'll be able to understand and use these examples.

Fueled with the understanding of JSP provided through this chapter, you can determine how JSP can be used for your specific business application needs. You are now ready to take the next step: incorporating JSP into your Web application projects.

Key Terms

.jsp	expression	JSTL standard functions
actions	implicit object	JVM
application methods	import	predefined variables
bean	inheritance	query
cookies	Java Development Kit	request methods
cookie object method	Java servlet	response methods
database connection	JSP actions	result object
declaration	JSP servlets	session methods
directive	JSP syntax	scriptlets
driver	JSP tags	scripting elements
editor	JSTL	servlet API
exception handling	JSTL standard tags	SQL

submit	tag	tag libraries
superclass	taglib	XML tags

Discussion/Review Questions

1. Are JSP and Java the same thing?
2. What is a JSP action?
3. Is JSP compiled or interpreted?
4. What is a Java servlet?
5. Why would you use JSP instead of JavaScript?
6. What do you need to get started with and use JSP?
7. What are the two basic elements of the JSP page text document, and what are they used for?
8. How is a declaration tag used?
9. What is the difference between an expression tag and a scriptlet tag?
10. Explain what a JSP directive is and what include and page directives are.
11. Provide a list of JSP actions and an example of how they can be used within an application.
12. What is an implicit object? Provide three examples of implicit objects.
13. What is JSTL, and how is it used in JSP?
14. How can cookies be used in JSP?
15. Describe how JSP can be used to access and update a database.
16. What is a connection, and what is a driver?
17. How can you query data in JSP?
18. How can a submit button be used in a JSP application?
19. How are parameters passed between JSP pages?
20. Why would HTML, JSP, and JavaScript be used together in an application?
21. Why and how can exception handling be used?

Exercises

1. Complete all the necessary preparation to start coding with JSP, including installing the database, server, and editor.
2. Create a simple JSP script. Provide the script code and do a print screen for a page displayed in a browser.
3. Create an application that prompts for the site visitor's name and displays the entered name on the page after the user presses the Submit button. Provide code and print screens for the application.
4. Create an application that uses sessions. Provide the application's code and print screens.
5. Create a JSP script that uses cookies. Provide the script code and print screens.
6. Create a database, table, and a JSP script to display a list of table data. Provide the script code and print screens.
7. Create an add, change, delete application. Provide the application's code and print screens that show records being added, changed, and deleted.
8. Create a JSP script that includes exception handling. Provide the script code and print screens.

CHAPTER 12

Handling Browser Differences

An important part of your Web application project is how the site will appear to end users. It is unlikely all the visitors to your site will be using the same browser, the same browser version, the same hardware, and the same operating system and have the same browser configuration settings. You may view your site in one browser and have it display perfectly and view the same site in another browser and find the site looks quite different or doesn't work properly. There may be differences in how the margins, text, and images display. There is a long list of browsers available for use on the Internet. It would be an impossible task to code your site to work exactly the same with every possible browser combination. However, when you understand that browser differences exist, you can consider those differences when you design and develop your site, to ensure that your site's appearance is consistent for end users. Designers and developers should attempt to accommodate as many of your site's users as possible, working within the limitations of time, money, and resources.

As an application developer, you might reasonably ask: "Do I care about browser differences?" If you are an application developer and also are responsible for website design and appearance, certainly you care. If you're an application developer and another individual or group is responsible for site appearance, the answer is still certainly you care. Here, we will explore some of the most important browser differences, so you will better understand their impact on the code you develop for your business Web applications.

In previous chapters, we presented examples of website applications used for business by both internal staff and by external site visitors. Consider the example of the staff application used to check work schedules. When an employee cannot use the website because he or she is using a browser version that is not supported or cannot use some of the application's features, this means the application is useless for some of your end users—which is, of course, unacceptable.

Websites reflect your company's professional image. If your site displays and works improperly or not at all, your site visitors will leave with a poor impression of the site and of your business. In such a case, an external visitor may leave to visit another similar site and not return to your site. If your site has browser display problems, visitors and potential customers will easily leave your site and won't look back. If the site users are internal staff or external visitors, you want the site and applications to work properly for your audience. A professional-looking and functional site will leave visitors with a good impression and make them comfortable. If visitors are comfortable, they will likely stay on your site longer and browse more pages. A good impression will increase your site's credibility. If your site's purpose is to sell a product or service, a good impression and credibility will help make your site visitors more likely to purchase your company's products or services.

What Is a Web Browser?

Technically, what is a Web browser? A Web browser is a software application that enables a user to display and interact with text, images, and other information typically located on a Web page at a website on the World Wide Web or a local area network (LAN). Text and images on a Web page can contain hyperlinks to other Web pages at the same or a different website. Web browsers allow a user to quickly and easily access information provided on many Web pages at many websites, by connecting through these links. Web browsers format HTML information for display. Because they may and can work differently, a Web page's appearance may appear different from browser to browser.

Web browsers are the most commonly used type of Hypertext Transfer Protocol (HTTP) user agent. **HTTP** defines how messages are formatted and transmitted, and what actions Web servers and browsers should take in response to commands issued through a site. Browsers are typically used to access the Web. A browser can also be used to access information provided by Web servers in private local networks or to access data within file systems.

Browser Background and History

There is no longer support for graphical user interface (**GUI**) browsers older than the fifth generation. Within earlier versions of browsers (around version 4 and earlier), to accommodate differences in the proprietary Document Object Models (DOMs) of the popular browsers, developers were required to write website pages to work with a specific browser. At that time, developers' only choices to accommodate early versions of browsers were to either develop a different version of a site to work with each browser or to simply accept that the site's appearance would differ from one browser to another.

The Web and HTML have been around a long time. The language you use for writing a Web page is standardized by a group of around 500 member organizations from around the world. This group is the World Wide Web Consortium, or **W3C**.

What is **DOM**? It is a platform and programming-language–neutral interface that allows programs and program scripts to dynamically access and update the content, structure, and style of documents. The document can be further processed, and the results of the processing can be incorporated back into a presented page. "Dynamic HTML" is a term used to describe the combination of HTML, style sheets, and scripts that allows documents to be animated. The W3C has received several submissions from member organizations on the way in which the object model of HTML documents should be exposed to scripts. These submissions do not propose any new HTML tags or style sheet technology. The W3C DOM Activity is working hard to make sure interoperable and scripting language neutral solutions are agreed upon.

W3C was created in October 1994 by Tim Berners-Lee, the original architect of the World Wide Web. The W3C is an international consortium whose member organizations, staff, and the public work together to develop Web standards. W3C's mission is to lead the World Wide Web to its full potential by developing protocols and guidelines that ensure long term growth for the Web.

W3C Standards and Guidelines

W3C primarily pursues its mission through the creation of Web standards and guidelines. Since 1994, W3C has published more than 100 standards, called W3C Recommendations. W3C also engages in education and outreach, develops software, and serves as an open forum for discussion about the Web. For the Web to reach its full potential, the most fundamental Web technologies must be compatible with one another and allow any **hardware** and software used to access the Web to work together. W3C refers to this goal as "Web interoperability." By publishing open (nonproprietary) standards for Web languages and protocols, W3C seeks to avoid market and Web fragmentation. W3C's purpose is to develop open standards to enable the Web to evolve with interoperability. W3C is the reason the Web works no matter what business or organization builds tools to support it.

There are many different, and competing, browsers that offer different features. What these browsers have in common is they all can communicate across the Web. W3C publishes Web standards and guidelines that Web developers can use to build applications that conform to the latest W3C standards. Although creators and vendors of browsers are not required to follow the guidelines and standards provided by W3C, most current browser applications comply in varying degrees with standards set by W3C.

Most browsers are available for download from the Internet for no charge. The choice of browser is left to individuals and organizations to decide. Fortunately, W3C compliance has had an impact on the popularity of browsers used and has had a significant impact on the interoperability of current browsers. Although there are more commonalities among browsers than differences between them, the differences require attention from designers and developers of Web applications.

A sophisticated Web developer must consider the differences in **common browsers** and design Web applications to minimize the impact of those differences. One option, as mentioned, is to create several different versions of the same website to accommodate some of the various browser requirements. However, with this approach, it is next to impossible to address every combination of browser, browser version, and end user's system (operating system and hardware). Furthermore, taking this route can put a great strain on budget and resources and will still leave you open to browser variations and omissions of content. Another option is to create text-only versions of a site; this solution will have less effect on browser differences. The downside is that text-only sites are visually much less interesting and engaging than dynamic sites with graphics.

Addressing Differences in Common Browsers

The first step is to determine which browsers you should consider before coding, testing, and deploying your site. Identify the browsers to consider for your Web application project. Set a goal. If you feel you can expend the time, money, and resources, set your goal high. A good design should be able to work with about 90 to 95 percent of your audience's browsers. Test your website using the list of identified browsers. Understand that it is almost impossible to build a website that displays perfectly on every version of every browser running on every computer. If you tried to attempt this, you would likely leave out many features that you really want to include in your website.

A page written in pure HTML without any style sheets or scripts can look the same in almost any browser. However, upon closer examination, viewing the site pages in different browsers may reveal differences. Sometimes the differences may be so minor that you don't readily notice them. Other differences may be obvious. The more complex the pages on your site, and the more functionality the Web applications provide, the more likely there will be browser differences.

Browser Issues to Consider

Where do you begin? Within the constraints of time, money, and resources, it is usually impossible to design for all users. Therefore, identify the hardware and software used by your audience and design to maximize the effectiveness of your website. You must also take into account the constraints imposed by your site users' hardware, software, and **Internet connection speed**. Once you have created the list of browsers that your Web application or website must consider, you will likely be able to use the same list for all the website applications you will create. You or your development team should revisit the list every so often, to ensure that it accommodates changes in your site, changes in your application's purpose, and changes in common browsers.

The checklist below includes some important elements to consider in regard to your Web application's end users and browsers the application supports. Use this list as a guide (and adapt it to your purposes, as necessary) in the early stages of your Web application development project.

Web Application Browser Support Checklist

- ☐ Website audience
- ☐ Language
- ☐ Common browsers
- ☐ Browser features and settings
- ☐ Hardware
- ☐ Monitor settings
- ☐ Operating system support
- ☐ Internet connection speed
- ☐ Image format support
- ☐ How to minimize common browser difference impact
- ☐ Text format support
- ☐ Browser testing check list

Website Audience

Your **website audience** consists of the people who visit and use your website and use your Web applications. Always keep in mind that your site is for people. People are the key to your website's success. When visitors clicked a link to get to your site, that link very likely described something they are interested in. If your site is intended for users external to your organization, a topic on your site generates visits to your site. The purpose of your site should already be defined. The site's purpose will determine who your visitors and end users will be. To determine your site's audience, consider and answer questions such as these:

- Will employees visit your site during their work day, and at what times?
- Will visitors be customers who come to purchase items for sale?
- Will your company's existing customers visit your site to log a customer service request?
- Will internal customers use the site to order supplies or perform other business-related activities?

Let's use the example of Belhur Publishing to create a list of site users. Belhur Publishing's website consists of pages providing information about Belhur Publishing, a product-ordering application for customers, a customer service application, an application to update employees, and an employee work schedule inquiry. The audience for Belhur Publishing will include the following groups:

- Customers looking to order products
- Customers accessing the customer service requests application to log and view requests
- Employees accessing online information
- Internal staff updating employee data
- Internal staff updating product information

Next, you will need to consider how your site visitors and end users will access the Internet and what types of browsers they will use. We will again use the example of Belhur Publishing. We know most of our site visitors and users will be accessing our website from home. We know our customers and employees are accessing the site from diverse areas, including internationally.

Now that we know who our audience is, we are ready to do some research. We assigned our staff developer to research what kind of browsers the majority of our site end users will be using. The developer assigned to the task did research and reported the following: those accessing our site will be using newer browsers and likely will be using high-speed Internet connections. Our research also indicated customers looking to purchase our types of products likely have a higher income and are likely to be tech savvy (since they are using new browsers). Based on this research, we can determine our list of browsers to reach our goal of 90 to 95 percent of our target audience.

If the end users of your site are internal staff accessing the site through a LAN, your task would be easy, as you would likely know what kind of browser would be used for accessing your website. Other sites will be more complex, and you may not always be able to determine all of the types of browsers being used.

If you already have a website up and running, your log files will make it easy for you to know who your audience is. Most Web servers save access information to your site in a log file—typically derived from the W3C draft ELF, or Extended Log File Format. This log file includes significant information about your incoming visitors, including the user agent for the software used to access your site. This agent can help you identify incoming spiders and index crawlers, but it's also valuable for knowing the types of browsers being used to view your site.

If your site audience is external users and you don't readily know what kind of browsers users have, the log file will be very useful. The log file can be analyzed using any number of log analysis tools, or you can use a counting service to complete analysis and provide statistics. If external visitors are critical to the purpose of your site, using the log file can help you ensure that you don't exclude a significant percentage of your users or prevent wasting time on browsers that infrequently access your site. Some browsers, such as Opera, can spoof other user agents, so you may not get an accurate representation of all browser types. However, using the log file will enable you to determine most of the types of browsers accessing your site.

To whom do you want to target your site? The easy answer to this is: most of your users. You'll have to decide what your cutoff point is. Do you want to support "bleeding edge" users? Are you willing to risk that the 5 to 10 percent you exclude aren't a critical part of your audience? How much effort you spend on determining which users your site will and will not support will likely be determined by how much your site depends on external users whose browser types you cannot easily determine.

Language

Most browsers are available in more than one national language. Consider whether your site needs to be available in more than one language. Knowing this will help you narrow down the list of browsers to consider and test before you deploy your site. If your website or Web application will require multiple-**language support**, you will need to change the settings for your browser so that you can develop, test, and deploy the site or application with the correct language support. You can do this through your Internet options settings found in your PC control panel.

Screens similar to those in Figures 12.1 through 12.5 will be displayed, listing the languages supported by your browser and providing an option to specify your language preferences. The examples shown are Internet Explorer. Note that the option to specify language settings may look different depending on the browser that you are using.

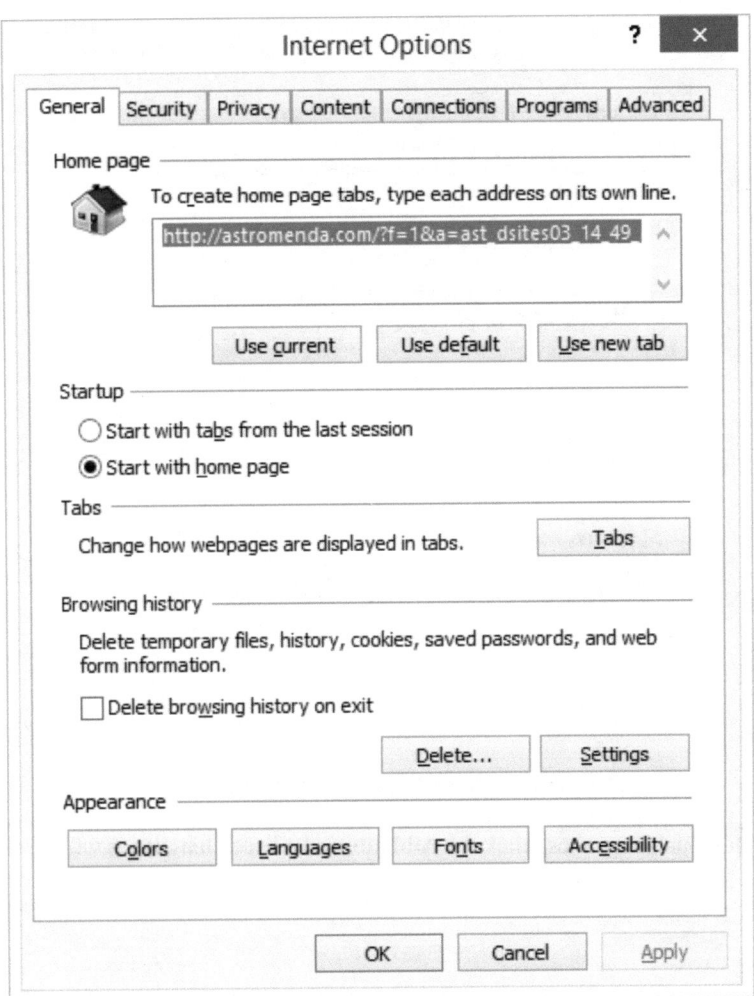

Figure 12.1: Selecting the languages setting in a browser

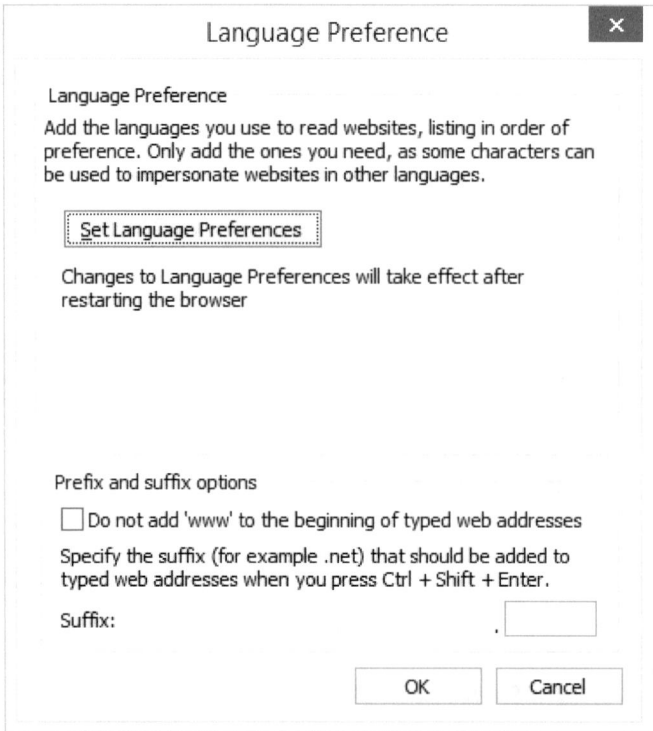

Figure 12.2: Specifying language preferences

If you require additional languages, click the **Add** tab, and a list of languages will be displayed.

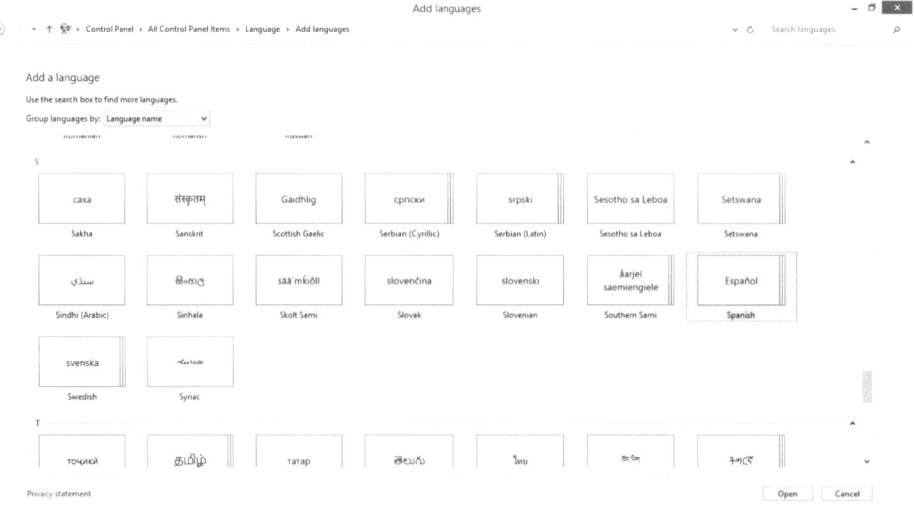

Figure 12.3: Languages list

Select the language you would like to include.

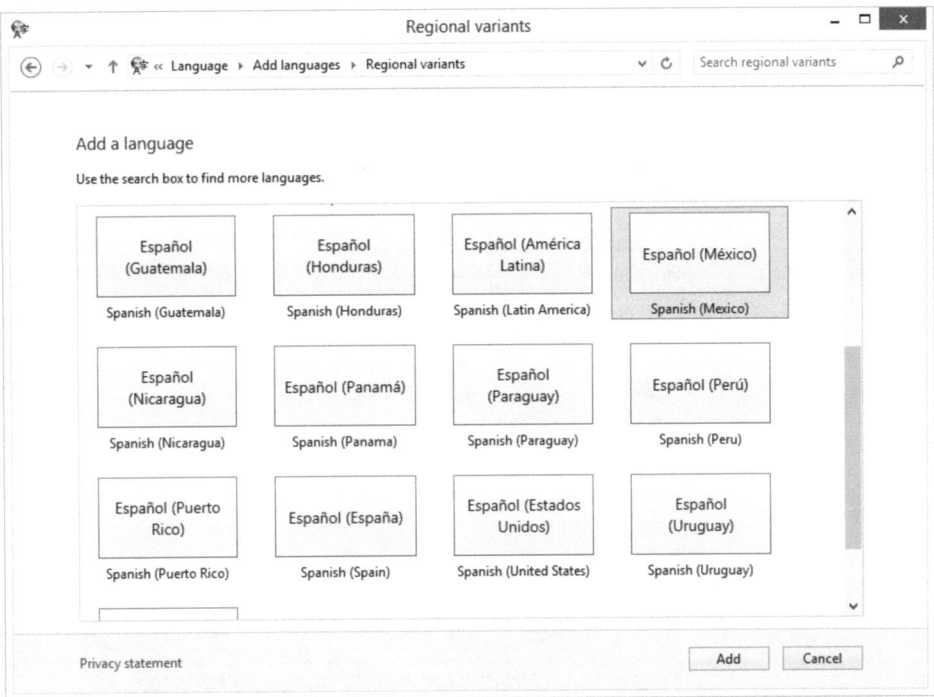

Figure 12.4: Adding a language

Double-click the language, and click **Add**, and the language will be added to the list of languages supported by your browser.

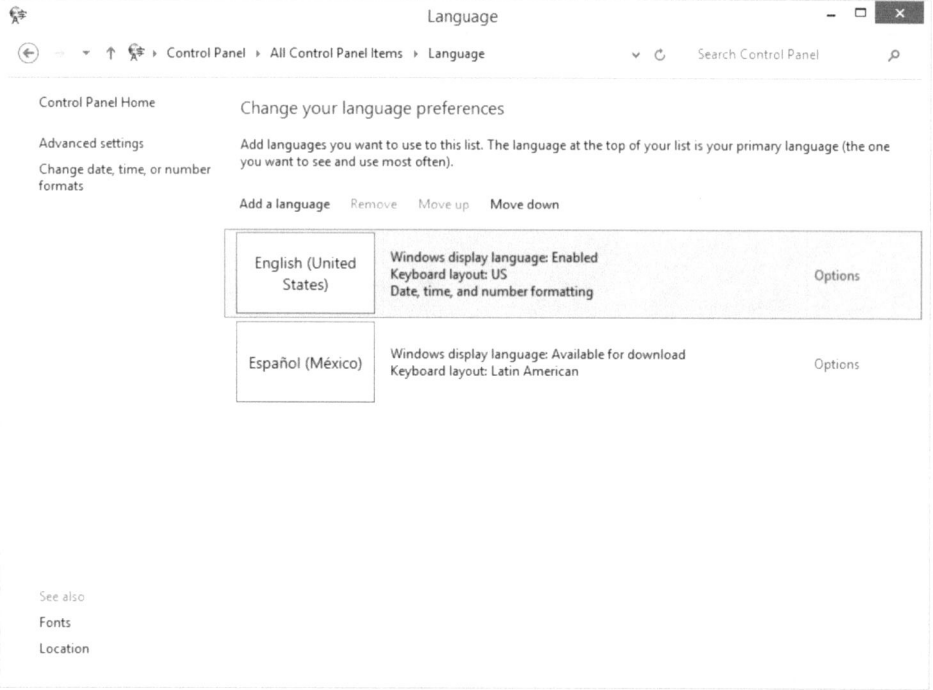

Figure 12.5: Updated browser language preferences

Repeat the process until your browser includes all the languages you would like to support for your site. Keep in mind you will need to perform this task on your system for each browser on your list that will be supported in your website or application.

Common Browsers

Many Internet browsers are available. Table 12.1 lists the most popular ones at the time this book was written.

Table 12.1: Commonly Used Browsers		
	Chrome	Browser developed by Google
	Firefox	Firefox (identified as Mozilla before 2005)
	Internet Explorer	Internet Explorer (IE), created by Microsoft and provided with Windows OS
	Safari	Safari, developed by Apple. Supports Mac OS and in January 2007 added support for Windows
	Opera	Developed by Opera Software

As of May 2016, Chrome is the most commonly used browser. Chrome has been the leader in browser usage for several years. When compiling your list of commonly used browsers, check several sources for statistics and also pay attention to browser versions.

Table 12.2: Browser Usage as of May 2016 Source: *www.w3schools.com/browsers/browsers_stats.asp*	
Browser	**Usage**
Chrome	71.4%
Firefox	16.9%
IE	5.7%
Safari	3.6%
Opera	1.2%

It is not correct to assume that the features a particular browser supports are standard features supported in all browsers. Different browsers may include nonstandard features not supported by other browsers. The true industry standards are those published by standards organizations such as ECMA, ISO, and W3C.

You'll also need to decide whether your website or application will support older browser versions. If you do not include older browser support, you may exclude some of your key market demographics. However, supporting older browsers will likely increase your maintenance costs, as you will need to duplicate some functionality to accommodate older browsers' features. Supporting older browsers may also affect your users' site experience, especially site visitors who use newer browser versions.

Also decide whether your site or application will support the very latest browsers. It is important to consider your site audience and how quickly they are adopting the new browsers. New browsers provide new features and can also present new considerations for development of your site. If you decide not to test with new browsers, you will not be prepared to accommodate functionality and features that may one day be required for your key audience.

Browsers support many different features that you will need to take into account before deploying your site to an audience. Do not assume that your site users will all have the same browser features and use the same browser settings. Accommodating browser features and settings can be a complicated task if your site is complex and uses advanced features like cookies, JavaScript, pop-ups, PHP, ASP.NET, or JSP. Keep it simple. If certain advanced browser features add important value to your site's audience, you may need to include additional code in your application to ensure that your site visitors have a pleasant experience.

Hardware

Is your website intended to be run on devices other than a PC—for example, smartphones or tablets? If so, this will certainly affect many decisions made in regard to compatibility. For many years, PCs running Windows were the dominant choice of device used to access the Internet. Today mobile devices with mobile OSs are used more than PCs to access the Internet. It would be easy if testing your site with a PC running Windows meant that it would work with Mac and other platforms, but unfortunately, it doesn't. Testing will increase significantly if you need to test support for multiple platforms. You may need to test several browsers on more than one machine. If your applications support mobile devices or other devices, this should and will impact testing. Excluding non-Windows operating systems may be a mistake if your audience includes users of devices other than PCs running Windows. Do you have staff on the shop floor using handheld devices? Or sales staff on the road using a smartphones or tablets to access applications through the Internet? To answer such questions and determine what devices your users will use to access your website or application, you will need to obtain data about your audience. Once you understand how your audience is likely to access your website, make a list of the devices your site will support. Be sure to include this device list in your site test plan.

Monitor Settings

Your audience will access your website using devices with many different screen sizes. If you design your site to be displayed on a monitor with 1920 × 1080 or 1366 × 768 resolution and some of your visitors have lower resolutions like 1280 × 1024 or 1024 × 768, they may have problems reading your website pages. Figures 12.6 through 12.8 show the same website viewed at different screen resolutions.

Figure 12.6: Website viewed at 1366 x 768 with browser in a maximized window

Figure 12.7: Website viewed at 1024 x 768 with browser in a maximized window

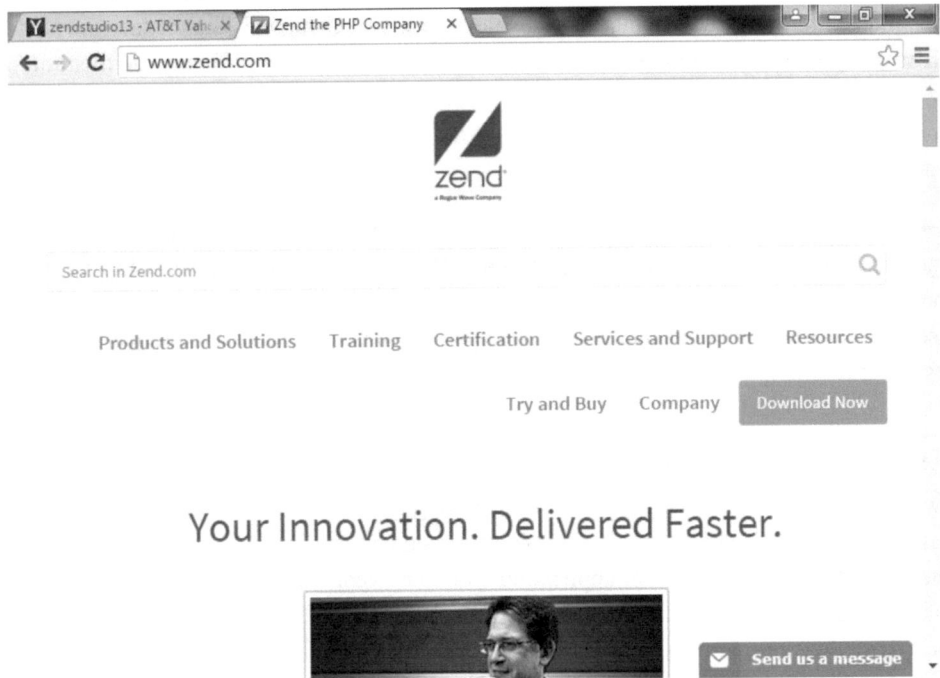

Figure 12.8: Website viewed at 800 x 600 with browser in a maximized window (Note a different page is displayed at this resolution.)

Those accessing your site on smartphones or tablets will have still lower resolution settings like 800 × 600, but the trend is toward higher resolutions. Make sure to test your site to display on different size monitors with different resolution settings. Site pages will look quite different using different resolutions. You can't control what resolution your visitors will be using. Given this reality, the safest way to ensure your pages will display well to the broadest audience is to test your site using each resolution. Table 12.3 lists the **screen resolution** sizes used to access *w3schools.com*, as of January 2016.

Table 12.3: Screen Resolutions Used to Access w3schools.com—January 2016 Source: *www.w3schools.com/browsers/browsers_display.asp*	
Resolution	Usage Percentage
1366 x 768	35%
1920 x 1080	18%
1280 x 1024	6%
1280 x 800	4%
1024 x 768	3%
800 x 600	0.3%
Lower	3%
Other (high)	30.7%

More than 50 percent of users have their monitors set to 1280 × 1024 or higher resolution. The common **monitor settings** will change as technology changes. Using this knowledge, you should include within your test plan the use of different resolution settings and different size monitors when testing your website or application. You can easily change monitor settings through your computer's Control Panel (Windows) or System Preferences (Mac). Plan to revisit your plan to make updates to accommodate technology changes.

Screen-resolution settings can affect the design and coding of a Web application, for example, a dynamic application that retrieves and displays data. Don't try to cram too much data on a page. Also, you may want to test the application using different resolution settings to ensure that what application users see is readable and not unexpected. If your application is, for example, a product catalog with images and text descriptions, you'll want to make sure different resolutions are tested.

Operating System Support

Your website visitors will be using a variety of operating systems on their computers or other devices. You need to understand which operating systems your audience is most likely to use and accommodate them in the website or application. For many years, the PC was the device most commonly used to access the Internet. Today, mobile devices are the most commonly used devices to access Web applications. If your application is intended for internal use only and everyone is using Windows 10, the task is easy. If your audience will include visitors who will access your site with devices other than a PC, be sure to include those devices in your list. Again, you will need to research your audience to find out what operating systems they are using. The list of operating systems you might consider includes, but is not limited to, the following:

- Windows 10
- Windows 8.*x*
- Windows 7
- Linux
- Apple OS X

Design your site to work well with the most popular operating system(s). Your goal is to accommodate as close to 100 percent of your audience as possible within the limitation of resources and time.

To compile a list of operating systems that should be tested for your site and for your Web applications, follow these steps:

1. Find out which operating systems are commonly available.
2. Collect and review statistics.
3. Draw conclusions from the statistics based on your audience.
4. Create a list of operating systems your site will support.
5. Make sure to have equipment available to test on.
6. Include operating system testing within your test plan.

Internet Connection Speed

Technology has changed greatly over the years, providing Internet users options for much quicker connections. Many Internet users have high-speed connections such as ADSL, cable (broadband), DSL, ISDN, OC3, satellite, SDSL, T1, T3, VDSL, and wireless; however, some users still have dial-up connections. Though not common, dial-up connections are still used in some rural areas or by those who haven't updated their connections.

If your target audience includes users who will access the Internet from home, and you have rural or international users, you may want to consider testing dial-up connections. For example, if your organization sells furniture over the Internet through a Web application, most of the site users will likely access the site from home. Even if your site loads quickly on your desktop, your audience may not have the same results. You should consider the lowest speed you will support and be sure to include this as a part of your test process.

Image Format Support

Images can be created in many formats, as discussed in chapter 3. The larger the image, the more resources will be required to display the image. Browsers do not all support the same image formats. GIF and JPEG are the most common formats. Usually, the better the image quality, the larger the image file. Vector files can minimize this impact but are not typically compatible with all browsers. The sizes of graphics can vary greatly when viewed on different computers. For applications and sites where images are critical, **image format** is very important. Almost all sites have some type of image, whether it is a company logo, product pictures, pictures of people, or site graphics. All graphics on Web pages are raster images with a fixed size in pixels. The size of the image varies on different computers according to the resolution of the monitor.

Minimizing the Impact of Different Browsers

It is easy to see that is important to recognize browser differences. The browser differences have a great impact on how our site will be displayed and the impression the audience will be left with. The goal is to design our site and applications so they have a consistent appearance for as many of the site visitors as possible, within reason. We will next consider things we can do to minimize the effects of browser differences.

Keep It Simple

Our first piece of advice is to keep it simple! Browser differences will create problems if the code or the page is needlessly complex. Simplicity will result in a site that is appealing and easier to use. This does not mean our site has to be plain. If it is too simplistic, we might not accomplish what we intended for our audience. A good site will leave our audience with a positive image.

Keeping things simple can be accomplished through using the available technology wisely. The best choice is usually to use HTML or XHTML to specify structure, and to use CSS to specify appearance, using carefully chosen CSS classes for page elements that recur throughout our site. If you chose to not use CSS, the result will likely be larger, harder-to-maintain sites with inconsistent pages. You must have a balance in your site design, and be sure to separate design and content. Large organizations with large websites and Web applications often have staff grouped so that one group takes care of appearance and site support and a separate developer group focuses on coding applications. Even if developers don't support the site design and are not entirely responsible for site appearance, they should understand conceptually the site's design, so that they code Web applications with the site design in mind.

Keeping it simple means focusing on effectiveness. This will result in a better site that requires less code and is easier to test. Before you incorporate a feature, consider the feature's impact on the site and end-user experience. Also take into account whether complicated code to provide an extra "wow" factor feature will return enough value for the site purpose and end user experience. Keeping it simple will result in a better experience for your site users. Your design should keep page appearance consistent. You don't want your site visitors wondering whether they are still on the same site, because the page they are on now looks much different from the previous page.

You should reuse common elements. If you have code that will be used on other pages within your site, be sure to reuse it rather than write all-new code for those pages. By using common elements, you'll reduce the need to recode and retest code when it is reused somewhere else on your site. Sometimes you can spend just a little bit of time making a component and perfecting a technique that is a bit more general, but doing so will pay off in allowing you to reuse and simplify application code. We touched upon this within the JavaScript and JSP chapters (chapter 8 and chapter 11).

Use Dynamic Components Carefully

Business applications will include programming languages like Java, JavaScript, PHP, and .NET. When using programming languages with your site, use standard, proven components and techniques.

Using **dynamic components** for your site adds an another level of complexity and increases the risk of having an unfavorable impact due to browser differences. Creating a dynamic page will increase development costs because it will take more time to code, test, and support your site. This is no different from the development costs that would be incurred for applications that are not Web-based.

Avoid Too Much Control

You should avoid trying to control your site's Web page layout too precisely. If you take an **over-precise control** approach, you may create fragile pages that break when browsers don't render the pages as expected. Imposing too much control over the page's appearance will also increase time spent resolving conflicts between how different browsers render Web pages and how user preferences will affect your website's layout. Browsers are just software that interprets HTML code and how a page is rendered. If you add too many formatting, feature, and appearance controls, your site or application may work fine in one browser—but you'll have spent a lot of time trying to make the controls render correctly with other browsers.

Trying to control layout precisely can result in problems such as overlapping blocks, vertical gaps appearing between rows because the graphic and text don't fit in the block, content being cropped if the content is too large to fit within the block, or a crowded page that site visitors have a hard time reading or finding what they are looking for. An over-precise layout may also impact applications. For example, an application that displays data may be fine for a simple display with a few columns but may not be able to accommodate all the information required for the application because the page layout does not allow flexibility for fitting the required content.

Browser Detection/Capability Testing

Most likely your site will be accessed and viewed in different browsers. To accommodate these differences, you can use any of a number of browser-detection coding techniques. Such techniques, which use a user agent (UA), are used to determine information about the browser being used. Coders have used and are using the technique because different browsers handle displaying pages and using features differently. This technique sometimes is used to work around a browser bug, check for a feature, or to provide different HTML for different browsers. The UA may be used to determine the browser name, browser version, rendering engine, OS, or what type of device the browser runs on.

Another option is to do **capability testing**. This means adding code in your application that tests the browser environment to determine whether it is capable of doing what you want it to do in the website or application when displaying the site pages. Then, based on the test results, initiate code. For example, if you have a video embedded and a non-standard font or image format within your HTML, this element may work fine in one browser and may not work with another browser. To ensure that a particular feature is included in your site or application, you can include code to check for browser capability to render or use the feature. Then, if the browser cannot support the feature, you can include additional code to provide an alternative compatible with the browser. For example, you may have a large image to display that looks fine within Chrome or IE but does not render with a mobile OS. The code could check for compatibility and provide a smaller image to render for mobile applications.

Developers disagree about the usefulness of **browser detection**. It can be argued that rather than using browser detection to work around browser differences, you can either use a bottom-up approach, where you start with a simpler site and build on features, or a top-down approach, where you build the best possible site, then make changes to enable it to work with older browsers.

Using Web standards can help you to minimize the impact of browser differences. It is a good policy to write code that supports established standards. The Web is intended to be accessible to everyone, regardless of the browser and device being used. Focusing on coding your site to use available features can prove to be a more effective strategy than targeting specific browsers.

Summary

Browser differences will always be an important factor that you will have to consider in your website development projects. Your site may be up and running well today, but at some point in the future, you will probably want to reevaluate its capabilities, make enhancements, and update the site to accommodate browser changes.

Browsers will continue to evolve. Who knows what features will be supported and what enhancements will be made in years to come? Even well-designed, simple code can be affected by changes in browsers. You should review your list of common supported browsers periodically and update the list when necessary—for example, when you update or revised and relaunch your website. Be sure to update your test plan to include any changes to your supported browser list.

You may also find it useful to capture website statistics. The statistics can help you to easily identify the types of browsers and operating systems used by your site's visitors.

It is a given that operating systems, screen resolution, the most popular browsers, and other factors affecting your website or application will change over time. By developing programming standards and coding proactively with consideration for different browsers, you will improve your site's quality and reduce the impact of browser differences.

Key Terms

browser detection	hardware	operating system support
capability testing	HTTP	over-precise control
common browsers	image format	screen resolution
DOM	Internet connection speed	website audience
dynamic components	language support	W3C
GUI	monitor settings	

Discussion/Review Questions

1. What is WC3, and what does it do?
2. Why are browser differences important?
3. What are some browser differences you should consider when developing a business website or Web application?
4. Which are the most common browsers used today?
5. What impact do screen size and resolution have on a website?
6. Why should the site user's OS be considered when developing a business website or Web application?
7. How can you minimize the effect of different browsers on your website or Web application?
8. What is browser detection?
9. What is a UA?
10. What is capability testing?

Exercises

1. Provide examples of the browser issues to consider when developing a business website or Web application.
2. Provide a list of 10 languages supported by browsers.
3. Provide examples of other browsers available today (other than the top five listed in Table 12.1) and their logos.
4. List six different devices that can be used to display and use websites.
5. Provide two examples of websites displayed in two different screen resolutions. Choose site examples and resolutions that show obvious differences.
6. Describe the difference in browser detection and capability testing and your opinion on which should be used.

13

SEO and SMO for Web Pages

By now, you've become familiar with some of the latest tools used in Web development. In the first few chapters, you learned the fundamentals of Web design with HTML5 and CSS3. You know how to create hyperlinks, add visual and multimedia elements to Web pages, and format HTML elements to produce visually pleasing Web pages. You've also learned how to create dynamic Web pages using both front-end and back-end Web programming languages, such as JavaScript, PHP, JSP, and ASP.NET. So, what's next? Understanding how visitors will find your website.

The first website went live in 1991. You can still access the site here: *http://info.cern.ch/*. The site still remains active with its original code. Since the launch of the first site, the number of websites published on the World Wide Web (WWW, or simply Web) has grown exponentially to over one billion sites. This chapter focuses on how visitors find these one billion websites and any new sites, once they are published on the Web.

Search Engines

Unless your business is already well established and well known, it's virtually impossible for people to find your business website on the Internet without relying heavily on the services of a **search engine** such as **Google**, Yahoo!, or Bing. We'll discuss search engines and the roles they play in Web development, and explore some techniques to optimize your business website for search engines: **search engine optimization (SEO)** and **social media optimization (SMO)**. Even if you are not an SEO guru and might not be responsible for search engines, an understanding of what they are, how they work, and what you can do to address search engine needs is important to ensure that you build websites and Web applications that are optimized for search engines and **social media**. This is especially important for sites and applications that will be accessed by the public on the Web. But even if the site is meant for internal use only, understanding Web pages' SEO and search engines will help you to understand the big picture of Web development.

What Is a Search Engine?

The history of search engines starts in the 1960s, when the concept originated. The first search engine was created in 1990, and it was called **Archie**—short for "archives." Archie was created to gather data and archive it into a database for quick retrieval. In a nutshell, that's exactly what search engines are. A search engine is simply any software system that is designed to search for information, particularly on the World Wide Web. A search engine might be used to search documents on a PC or network—for example, the Microsoft search tool used to scan documents within a system directory or folder. The user enters specific information, usually a word or several words and criteria to complete the search, and the search engine returns a list of matches. The results are returned sorted in order of relevance of the results based on the criteria. In this chapter the focus is Web pages and search engines and will be specific to Web searches.

The advent of the Web led to the development of some of the most powerful Web search engines today. Some of these popular search engines include Google, Yahoo!, Bing, and Ask. The top search engine today is Google, which comprises more than 60 percent of all online searches. Although most of the concepts discussed in this chapter can be applied to most search engines, we'll focus primarily on Google.

When developing a website and Web applications, you must design and build your applications with search engines in mind. Before considering the impact of search engines on your website, you will need to answer some basic questions. First, what is the site's purpose? Next, how will the site be used? And who will be using the site? A site that is used internally by corporate staff only could easily be set up as the default URL on a user's desktop. In this example, a search engine will have minimal effect on the website and your development project. However, for a site that is used to sell products or services in a marketplace and depends on bringing in new customers, search engines will have a critical impact on the site and development of the website and Web applications. SEO is what will enable visitors who do not already know your site or its URL to find the site easily in a keyword search in Google or another search engine.

People find your website on the Internet in several ways, usually by using a search engine, by word of mouth, or from another website. There are many search engines available on the Web, and their rankings change continually. The eBusiness MBA Guide (*ebizmba.com*) is a great source for statistics that show the relative popularity of various search engines. Table 13.1 lists the 15 most popular search engine providers at the time this book was written.

Table 13.1: Top 15 Most Popular Search Engine Providers		
Name	Searches	Alexa Rank
Google	1,100,000,000	1
Bing	350,000,000	22
Yahoo!	300,000,000	NA
Ask	245,000,000	31
AOL	125,000,000	NA
Wow	100,000,000	767

Table 13.1: Top 15 Most Popular Search Engine Providers (continued)		
Name	Searches	Alexa Rank
WebCrawler	65,000,000	674
MyWebSearch	60,000,000	405
Infospace	24,000,000	2,110
Info	13,500,000	1,938
DuckDuckGo	13,000,000	629
Contenko	11,000,000	4,505
Dogpile	10,500,000	3,084
Alhea	7,500,000	11,225
ixQuick	4,000,000	9,587

Although some search engines such as Google, Yahoo!, and Bing provide more universal searches, others provide very specific searches for particular niche markets. Figure 13.1 shows some of these popular search engines. Figure 13.2 shows Google's share of global search, according to Internet Live Stats (*www.internetlivestats.com*).

Figure 13.1: Some popular search engines

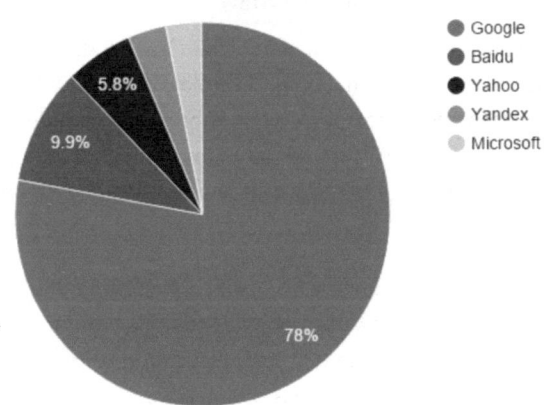

Figure 13.2: Google's share of global search, according to Internet Live Stats

Most Web search engines are commercial ventures supported by advertising revenue. Some search engine providers allow advertisers to have listings ranked higher for a fee. The providers that don't charge for ranking priority usually accept money for running ads alongside the regular search engine results and typically make money every time one of the ads is clicked. Most search engines are run by private companies; thus, detailed information that explains how the engine works is considered proprietary and is not disclosed to the public. However, there are few open source search engines that make detailed information about their inner workings publicly available.

How Does a Web Search Engine Work?

There are billions of pages available on the Internet, and most of the pages are titled by the page's author, often using a cryptic name that doesn't really portray the page's subject matter and content. In many cases, it would be nearly impossible to find what you are looking for on the Web without the help of a search engine. You simply enter a word or several words in a browser, and instantly a list of matches is displayed in a **search engine results page** (or **SERP**). Search engines sometimes return pages that aren't relevant, and you may need to do a little more searching to find what you're looking for.

The list of sites on the SERP is dependent on the methods, or **algorithms**, the search engines use. Google uses very sophisticated algorithms to determine which Web pages should appear at the top of the results page. This is why SEO plays a vital role in modern Web development. Overall, search engines do an incredible job of helping Web users find the information they seek, seemingly by "magic." How does the magic happen? There are differences in the way that different search engines work, but they all perform some similar basic tasks. All search engines search the Internet or select pieces of the Internet based on keywords, all engines keep an **index** of words they find and a reference to where they are found, and all search engines allow users to look for words or combinations of words found in an index. Today's most popular search engines index billions of pages and respond to billions of queries each day. Let's look more closely at the methods they use for performing those tasks.

Spiders and Web Crawling, Indexing, and Searching

For a search engine to tell you where a file or document can be found, the search engine must know where the file or document exists. To find matching information on the billions of Web pages that exist on the Web, a search engine uses special software robots called **spiders** (or **Web crawlers**) to build lists of words found on websites. When a spider is building lists, the process is called **Web crawling**. To build and maintain a useful list of words, a search engine's spiders have to look at a lot of Web pages.

A spider begins its travels through Web documents usually by starting with heavily used servers and popular Web pages. The spider will begin with a popular site, indexing the words on its pages and following every link found within the site. In this way, the spidering system quickly begins to travel, spreading out across the most widely used portions of the Web.

Spiders take Web page content and create key search words that enable users to use search engines to find what they are looking for on the Web. Figure 13.3 is a high-level example of how a spider uses Web crawling. Different search engines use different criteria, techniques, and proprietary algorithms (which are used for indexing and storing key values for Web search engines to use). Technically, the indexing process is much more complex than the overview portrays. (If you are familiar with data warehousing, it is akin to building a big data warehouse for quick information retrieval and fast performance.) Spiders can crawl many pages per second, and generate resulting data quickly. They may use data such as titles, subtitles, meta tags, links, and most frequently used words on a page in building the index and performing the search. For example, Google builds the index on every significant word, leaving out the words "a," "an," and "the." Other spiders and Web crawlers may use different criteria and approaches. The different approaches are attempts to make a spider operate faster and to allow users to search more efficiently. Some engines take the approach of indexing every single word on each page found.

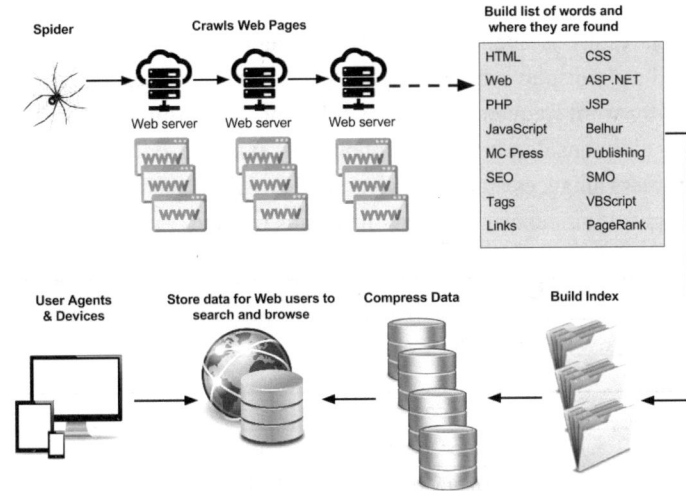

Figure 13.3: Spiders and Web crawling

Once a search engine index is built, it is available for use. Most popular search engines are continually rebuilding indexes so they can make the most current information available to users. Each search engine provider has its own schedule for rebuilding indexes, using its own techniques. Data about the pages is stored in the index database for use in search queries. Some engines will store all or part of the source page and information about the Web pages, while others will store every word of every page they find.

The searching process starts when a user enters a word, words, or phrases in the search box. Then the search engine matches the selection criteria by seeking in its database for those search words and their locations. The results are then automatically sorted by their probable relevance and presented with the most relevant results appearing first. A search engine may use various techniques to determine relevance. The goal is always to display the closest matches and best results first.

The content of a search engine is the resulting database containing words and websites where the words can be found. Each search engine has its own technology, style, look, features, and functionality that set it apart from other search engines. The search methods a search engine uses may also change as Internet usage changes and new search algorithms and programming techniques evolve.

Meta tags allow developers to specify keywords and concepts under which a page will be indexed. Such tags can be helpful if used in a manner that fits within the complex scheme of spider web crawling techniques. However, be aware that a search engine may overlook meta tags if they do not accurately reflect the content within a site's Web pages.

Search engines will continue to evolve as providers react to changes. Providers will continue to compete for top rankings, and some will focus on addressing the needs of niche users. The Web has grown very rapidly and continues to grow, so search engines will always be challenged to keep up with including new and updated page content.

Search engine providers do not usually disclose the techniques that their search engines use to rank sites in a listing of search results, or why one site may be listed in a higher ranking order. The information in a search results list includes a link to the matching site, allowing the user to click on the link, which immediately displays the linking site page. The search results listing usually includes website content logic for word frequency, location, relational clustering, and the site's design. The search results ranking also considers external content—for example, link popularity, click popularity, sector popularity, business alliances among services, and pay for placement rankings. Table 13.2 summarizes the factors that influence search engine results ranking.

Table 13.2: Search Engine Results Ranking Factors	
Factor	Description
Website content	
Word frequency	How often does a search word appear on a page in relation to other text?
Location	Is the search word in the title or near the top of a page or in meta tags?
Relational clustering	On how many pages on the site does the word occur?
Site design	Does the site use frames? How fast does the site load?
External Factors	
Link popularity	Sites with more links pointing to them are prioritized.
Click popularity	Sites visited more often by Web users are prioritized.
Sector popularity	Sites visited by certain demographics or social groups may be prioritized.
Business alliances	Results from a partner search service can be ranked higher.
Pay for placement	Site owners pay for higher rankings.

As you can see in Table 13.2, factors such as location of search words and how frequently the words appear near the top of a page, possibly in HTML title tags, in a headline or repeatedly found at the top of a page, are likely important in the rankings of items in a search results list. Location of words and frequency are major factors in how search engines determine relevancy. Words with a higher frequency are often considered more relevant than other words found on the page.

Indexing

The purpose of the index that a search engine builds is to allow information to be found as quickly as possible. This index is very much like the array indexes used in applications. There are many different ways an index can be built. Building a hash table or hash map is one of the most effective ways to build an index. There are some key differences between a hash table and a hash map, but the logic is the same. A hash table or hash map is a data structure that associates keys with values. The hash table is well suited for efficient lookups—for example, giving a key, such as a search word, and finding the corresponding value (e.g., URL links and Web page header information). A sample list of search words and their associate values is shown in Figure 13.4.

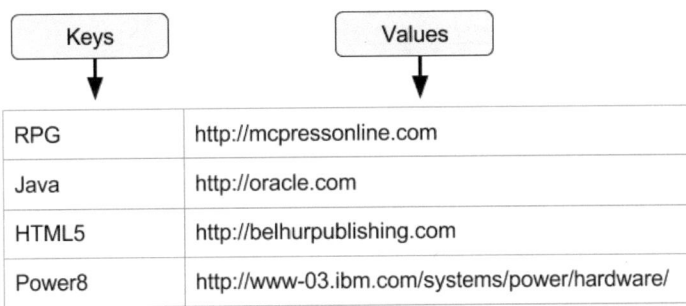

Figure 13.4 A sample list of key-value pair entries

The hash table works by using a hash function to transform the key into a hash. A hash is a number that is used to index into an associative array to find the location where the values should be. The process of creating the hash is called *hashing*.

In hashing, the search engine applies to entries a formula that attaches a numeric value to each word. The formula is designed to evenly distribute the indexed entries across a predetermined number of divisions. Compare this method to alphabetizing, where the corresponding distribution of words could be haphazard. In English or, for that matter, any language, there are some letters that begin many words and others that begin very few words. The numerical distribution using a number is much different from the distribution of words across the alphabet. For example, there are many words that begin with the letter "t" and many fewer that begin with the letter "x." Using an alphabetic distribution would create a lopsided list of entries, where many words with the most frequently found letters are grouped together. Hashing balances the list of entries, thereby reduces the average time it takes to find a matching entry. Hashing also separates the index from the entry. Figure 13.5 shows how the process of hashing works.

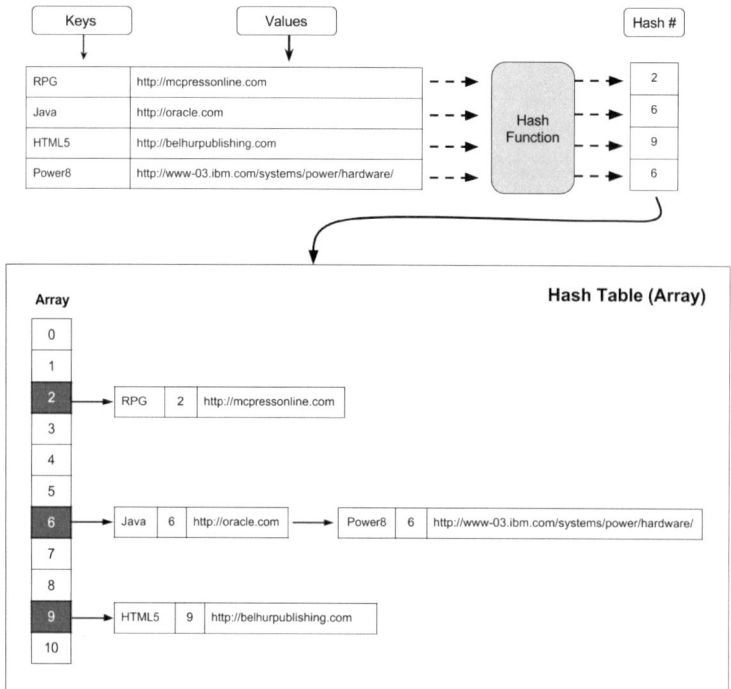

Figure 13.5 The process of creating a hash table

A hash table contains the hashed number and also a pointer to the actual stored data (entry). The stored data can be sorted in a way that allows it to be stored most efficiently. The efficient indexing and effective storage make it possible to retrieve indexed information quickly. The numeric distribution is the key to a hash table's effectiveness.

Spamming

Search engines may penalize or exclude references to pages or sites that exhibit characteristics of **spamming**. For example, a site that a search engine identifies as spamming may have multiple site pages that contain words purposely repeated numerous times to intentionally try to impact the page's ranking in search results. Another example is frequently rewriting pages in an attempt to gain ranking. Some webmasters have even tried to figure out search engine location and frequency logic and then use reverse engineering to improve their page rankings. Because of spamming, search engine providers use external factors, mentioned earlier, in their search algorithms. The external factors cannot be easily influenced by website owners, Web designers, or those who create Web pages for their sites.

Search Queries

A typical Web search, using a search engine that indexes pages, requires the user to build and submit a query through the search engine. A query can consist of one or more queries. Complex queries require the use of Boolean operators that allow the user to refine and extend the search. The most commonly used Boolean operators are *and*, *or*, and *not*, followed by *and near*. Using Boolean operators results in a more literal search that looks for the words or phrases as an exact match. Viewing search engine specifications will provide details on how a specific search engine is used. How often the information is refreshed and the technique used for indexing can impact the search results. Broken links and changed content can be the result. Search engines don't necessarily use the same collection or same number of Web pages to search through for index building.

Specialized Search Engines

In addition to the popular search engines most people are familiar with, there are a number of specialized search methods and engines. Following is a review of some specialized search methods and search engines.

Concept-based Searches

Searches that use Boolean operations are effective for most searches. But what happens when you search for a word that has multiple meanings? For example, the word "pen" can be a nickname for a prison, a writing instrument, a cage to house pigs, or a verb that means to write someone a letter. If you're searching on the word "pen," you may want to return results for only one of those meanings. You can either change the query to eliminate some of the unwanted meanings or use a concept-based search can eliminate some of the undesired information. Concept-based searching uses statistical analysis on the pages containing the words being searched for to find other pages that might be of interest. This means more information needs to be stored about each page and a lot more processing has to take place to return results. Search engine providers are working on making concept-based searches perform faster. Major general-purpose search engines, such as Google and Bing, already have this feature built in. Alternative to Google and Bing, there are some specialized search engines that perform concept-based searches. These include Dogpile, DuckDuckGo, and ChaCha.

Natural Language Queries

Natural language queries operate on the concept of entering a question in the same way you would ask someone a question. For example, at a library, when you ask the librarian to look for material related to a topic you are researching, you would not use just one word or a couple of words but would instead form your questions in complete natural language sentences. The most popular natural language search engine today is *Ask.com*, which parses each search query for keywords, which it then applies to the indexes built. Natural language search engines work only for simple queries. However, search engine providers are investing their efforts in developing natural language search engines that can be used for complex queries.

Internet Local Search

A fairly recent addition to search engine technology is the addition of Internet local searches. The processing of such searches is referred to as *geocoding* and *geoparsing*. The search builds indexes that enable search within a specified geographic area, locality, or region. The intent is to narrow the scope of the search and search results for users. The scope of area the search covers varies by search engine. Often these engines are targeted for product and service websites. For example, an Internet local search may be used to find all restaurants in an area that provide a barbecue menu or local companies that provide pest removal services.

Vertical Search Engines

Vertical search engines are a specialized search that is fairly new to the Internet search industry. Vertical search engines provide searches focused on specific businesses. The engines specialize in specific content categories or within a specific medium. Vertical search engines enable the Web surfer to find specific types of listings, thus making the search more customized to a user's needs. Some popular vertical search engines include Trulia, Yelp, WebMD, and Angie's List.

The vertical search engine gives companies that provide products and services an opportunity to be found by Web users. When a potential customer is searching for a specific product or service, marketers understand the searcher may be ready to make a purchase. Vertical search engines can assist likely buyers of products and services by providing accurate results for them. The companies that offer goods and services are happy to be on the receiving end of the traffic, whether the search listings are from unpaid or paid advertising listings.

Vertical search providers will play an important role in the paid search market in the future and will be a consideration for organizations as they develop their Web marketing strategies. Web and vertical search engines represent a large portion of consumer and business buyers and give businesses access to millions of potential customers.

Category-focused Vertical Search Engines

A category-focused vertical search engine includes sites, pages, and other Web content that fits within a specific category. Some examples include shopping, government, legal, travel, financial, and business search engines. *Educationworld.com* is a category-focused vertical search engine that focuses primarily on education and provides resources for teachers, administrators, and school staff. *Priceline.com*, *Hotels.com*, and *TripAdvisor.com* are category-focused vertical search engines that provide travel-related resources.

Media-focused Vertical Search Engines

A media-focused search engine is used to search within specific online media. Examples include forum or discussion groups, news groups, blogs, mailing lists, and chat search engines. These also are niche search engines. *BestEzines.com* and *AltPress.org* are among some of the popular media-focused vertical search engines.

Social Vertical Search Engines

Social vertical search engines retrieve and rank data taking into consideration the interactions and contributions of users via social media or other interactions on the Web. The user input could be bookmarking a site, sharing, tagging, or interaction with the search result—for example, promoting or demoting results that the user feels are more or less relevant to their query or webmasters linking to other content on the Web. The results gathered are used to establish algorithms or machine-based approaches where relevance is determined by analyzing the text of each document or the link structure of the documents. This is not a new technique; however, recently it seems to be impacting how search engines work.

A social search may analyze simple tagging of content or bookmarks or may use more sophisticated approaches based on the information gathered to combine human intelligence with computer-based algorithms. Many think social search can play an important part in cleaning up search engine spam problems. However, this type of search is a bit controversial because the technique can also be subject to inaccuracies, as the method does not take into account motives or authoritativeness of the users providing input.

Search Engine Optimization (SEO)

SEO deals with the visibility of your website in a search engine results page, specifically strategies and techniques that will make it more likely that your site will be listed on a search engine results page. The fundamental goal of SEO is to increase the number of visitors to your site, which will, in turn improve your search engine ranking—and the number of potential customers for your business. It was quite an easy task to trick search engines back in the early days of SEO. Then you didn't have to be an SEO guru to get a top ranking in the search engines. All you had to do was add a description and flood your Web pages with thousands of keywords arranged in different combinations, as shown in Figure 13.6.

```
<html>
<head>
<title>Belhur Publishing</title>
<meta name="keywords" content="Belhur publishing LLC,belhur,publish
ing,book,books,html,html book,html books,book publishing,html book
publishing,PHP,PHP book,Java,Java book,IBM,IBMi,IBM book,RPG,RPG
book,JavaScript,JavaScript book,Web Design,coding,programming"/>
<meta name="description" content="Belhur Publishing - your ultimate source
for technical publications. Where those in the know go to find eBooks and
hard copy books on technical topics. Whether you're a student or adding new
skills, we can help! "/>
<body>
```

Figure 13.6: Keyword and description metadata of a Web page

Search engines help Web users find information quickly. By adding your Web page to various search engines, you will make it more likely that the page will be easily found. Often search tools return the top 10 matching results ranked in order of relevance. Of course, everyone wants their site included in the top 10. Being listed in the 11th position and beyond could reduce your site's exposure through searches.

A site's or page's ranking depends on many factors, some of which are beyond your control. For example, a company selling a product in a competitive market with many similar products and many competitors will be less likely to be able to achieve a top 10 listing, while a company marketing a focused niche product or service will have a better chance of being in the top 10 search results.

Unlike in the early days of search engines, flooding your website with irrelevant keywords and metadata is no longer an effective way to improve your search rankings, as search engines have become smarter at flagging such efforts to undermine them. It is the Web developer's job to ensure the integrity of a website's metadata and content so it is searchable and SEO friendly. Fortunately, some factors in your website's or Web page's ranking are within your control. Let's look at how Google determines a page's ranking and then some things that you as a Web developer can do to affect your site's ranking in Google search results.

PageRank

PageRank is a part of Google's original algorithm that helps to determine the relative importance of a website. The way that PageRank works is that every website that a Google bot (or crawler) has gathered and archived is given a Google PageRank score between 0 and 10. Thus, PageRank doesn't pay attention to the page's content or URL, and also ignores whether a hyperlink is linked to an internal page and external links. In PageRank, what's important is how many inbound links a page has. The page has a high rank if the sum of the ranks of its inbound links is high. Figure 13.7 illustrates how a sample Web page gets its Google PageRank (PR).

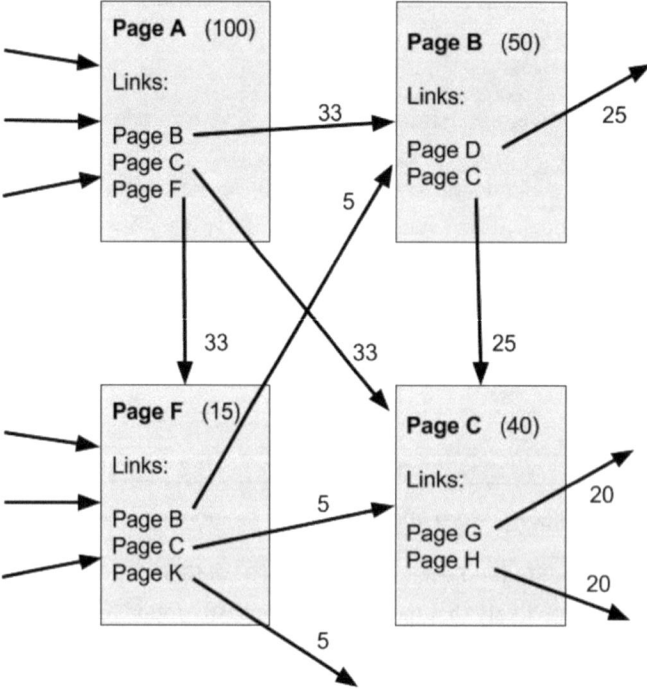

Figure 13.7: How Google PageRank works

In Figure 13.7, Page A has a total PR of 100 points and links to three pages: B, C, and F. Since Page A links to three pages, the total PR points will be divided by three; thus, each page has 33 points. When Pages B, C, and F receive a link from Page A, Google sees this as Page A endorsing them. Finally, Google takes into account all of these link points (or votes) in its algorithm and gives the entire website a PR. Of course, the actual calculations behind the Google's core algorithm are much more complex. There are other factors to consider, such as links with a "rel=nofollow" attribute, which affects how the link votes are transferred to the receiving pages. Since 2009, Google has introduced several new formulas into its original algorithm, which make it more difficult for Web developers to boost Google page rankings. Even so, as a Web developer, you have some options for optimizing your website for search engines.

Keyword Positions

Step back and put yourself in your users' shoes. Pretend you are a Web user looking for information. How do you envision someone would search for your site? What word or words would he or she type into a search engine prompt box to find your site? The words entered in the search are your target keywords.

The target keywords need to appear in specific locations on your Web pages. It is important to include the target keywords in a page's HTML title tag because search engines take the title tag into consideration when indexing and ranking Web pages. Not using the keywords in the title tag can result in a very relevant page having a poor ranking.

The <title> tag is an HTML metadata tag. The page title should include keywords and should consist of the top two or three search phrases that you expect visitors will use to find the page. Titles should be concise but provide enough page-specific information to accurately describe the page's content. Just as the title of this book, *Developing Business Applications for the Web*, represents the book's content, a Web page's title should represent the page's content and also make viewers want to look more closely at the content. Titles often appear in search engine listings. This is important because a quick glimpse of the title can trigger a viewer to visit your site.

Search engines may also look at content toward the top of a page. Keywords that appear closer to the top of a page will likely be considered for index building. Thus, keywords should appear in both your page title and the first paragraphs of your Web page. A good way to evaluate effective keywords and <meta> tags is to search using keywords and then look at highly ranked sites in the search results. Using your browser's view source feature, view each site's source and look at meta tags and page content.

Meta Tags

In earlier chapters you were introduced to <meta> tags, which are text information inserted into the head area of a Web page. Site visitors do not see the content embedded in the <meta> tags unless they view a page's source. The term *meta* comes from *metadata*, which means data about other data.

Search engines use <meta> tags to determine a page's content. Although a <meta> tag is optional in a Web page, it can affect your website's search engine ranking—so you will want to make sure you don't omit the step of creating the appropriate <meta> tags for your Web pages. The two primary types of <meta> tags are **meta description** and **meta keywords**.

Meta Keywords

It may be argued that **keywords** don't have the impact they once had. But they are still a critical element of SEO. Many search engine providers used keywords but have reconsidered because of the possibility of unreliable or misleading information and potential spamming. We don't know how many search engines use keywords, but it is possible that some may still use keywords if the words in the tag are found elsewhere on the page. So not using keywords could result in a missed opportunity to improve your website's SEO.

The <meta> keyword tag is placed in the head section usually after the <title> tag. When a user enters words in the search engine query window, the search engine considers the keyword tags in building an index. Within the keyword tag area, use both general and specific words to describe the page. For example, a Web page about this book should contain general keywords (such as book, coding, programming, Web) and specific words (such as HTML, CSS, JavaScript, Web development). You may also want to include keywords for commonly misspelled words. (Be aware, however, that some search engine providers may penalize sites that use words in the keyword tag that are not found within the page's content.)

How many keywords should you include? The best answer is enough to represent keywords that will likely be used to search for a site. This could be a few select words or many. Experts don't agree on the limit but often recommend including 500 to 1,000 keywords per website. Typically, sites don't use that many keywords. The most effective sites use meaningful, well–thought-out choices for keywords. As a general rule, flooding your <meta> tag and Web page with keywords will not increase your page ranking. In fact, Google might determine it to be spam, which will have a negative effect on your site's PR.

When choosing keywords, it's important not to duplicate words. The keywords are contained within quotation marks and separated by a comma. The value is not case sensitive. Also, keep in mind that quality outweighs quantity. Consider, for example, the list of keywords for our example website, shown in Figure 13.8.

```
meta name="keywords" content="Belhur publishing
LLC,belhur,book,books,html,html book,html books,book publishing,html book
publishing,publishing,PHP,PHP book,Java,Java book,IBM,IBMi,IBM book,RPG,RPG
book,JavaScript,JavaScript book,Web Design,coding,programming"/>
```

Figure 13.8: An example of weak keyword metadata for our sample Web page

The example in Figure 13.8 contains 24 search terms. Note that it's too long and includes too many repeated words, which should be avoided. Limit the number of keywords per page to 12 to 15 words or fewer, and be sure to use quality keywords rather than trying to fill up the list. A rule of thumb is to pick up to 10 best words that can describe the page. The keywords you choose should describe what your site or page is about. Avoid listing your website's name in the keywords, as it does not really describe your page. Also, don't put spaces between keywords or search terms. The list may be more human-readable with spaces, but Web crawlers prefer no spaces.

If we rework the list in Figure 13.8 and remove any redundancies, we can make the keywords much more effective for SEO. Figure 13.9 shows a revised list of keywords for our sample Web page.

```
meta name="keywords" content="book publisher,html,PHP,Java,IBMi,RPG,Web Des
ign,coding,programming,JavaScript,"/>
```

Figure 13.9: An example of strong keyword metadata for our sample Web page

The list has been shortened to only 10 search terms and has no repeated words. All spaces between the key terms have been removed except for the two-word terms "book publisher" and "Web Design." Notice also that "IBM" has been removed and only "IBMi" is listed. Keywords are not case sensitive, and search engines can search a whole word or only part of the word. For example, when you search for the word "IBM," the search engine will match the "IBM" portion in the word "IBMi." By the same token, we could remove the word "Java" and just leave "JavaScript." However, we'll leave that in because "Java" is such an important term. To help you pick out popular keywords, you can use the Google AdWords Keyword Planner (*https://adwords.google.com/ko/KeywordPlanner/Home*), as shown in Figure 13.10.

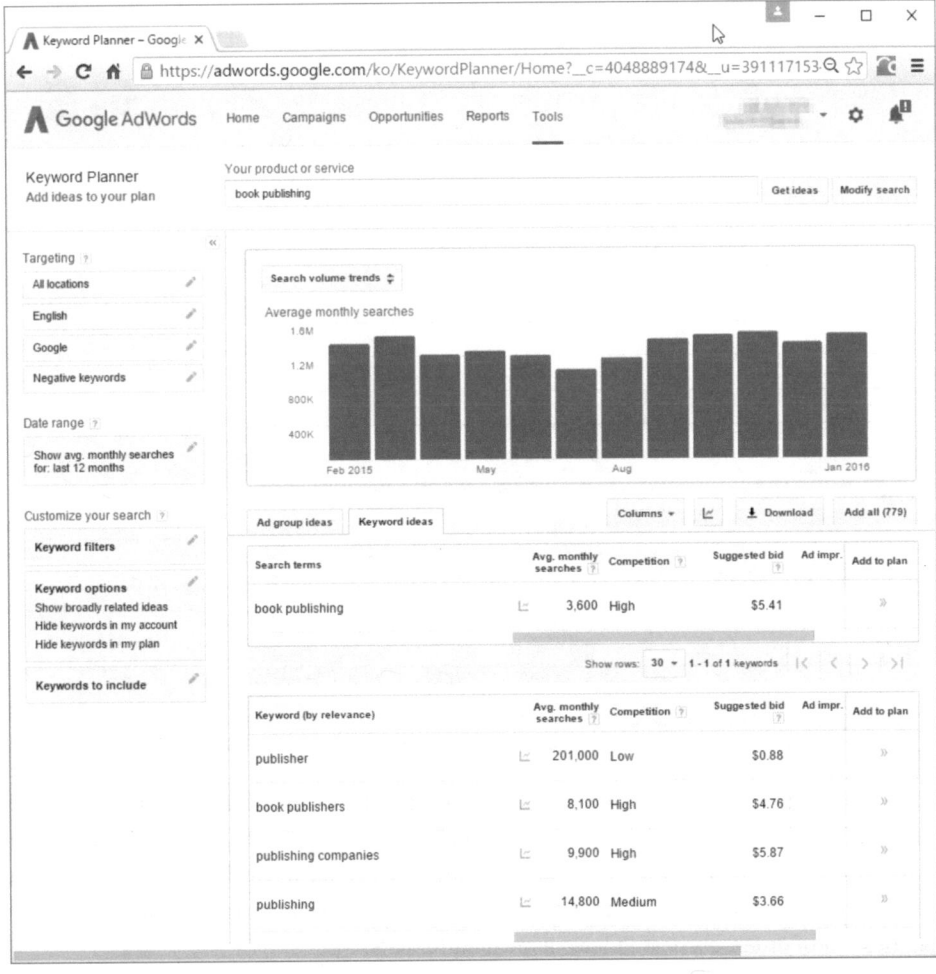

Figure 13.10: Google AdWords Keyword Planner tool

Page Title

In chapter 2, we introduced the <title> tag. The page's title is the text contained with the title tags and is perhaps the metadata that most clearly describes what your Web page is about. The title start and end tags (<title> and </title>) are placed in the head area of a Web page. The head area begins with the opening head tag <head> and the end head tag </head>.

Most search engines place emphasis on the title element on a site page. A title tag should accurately represent the page, so the search engine will assign it the correct relevance for ranking. A page's <title> tag is typically shown as the first line of the search result. It's also displayed in the browser title bar and will also be used for bookmarks and favorites, as shown in Figure 13.11. The title is often the first piece of information about a site that the searcher sees, and will use to decide whether or not to visit the site.

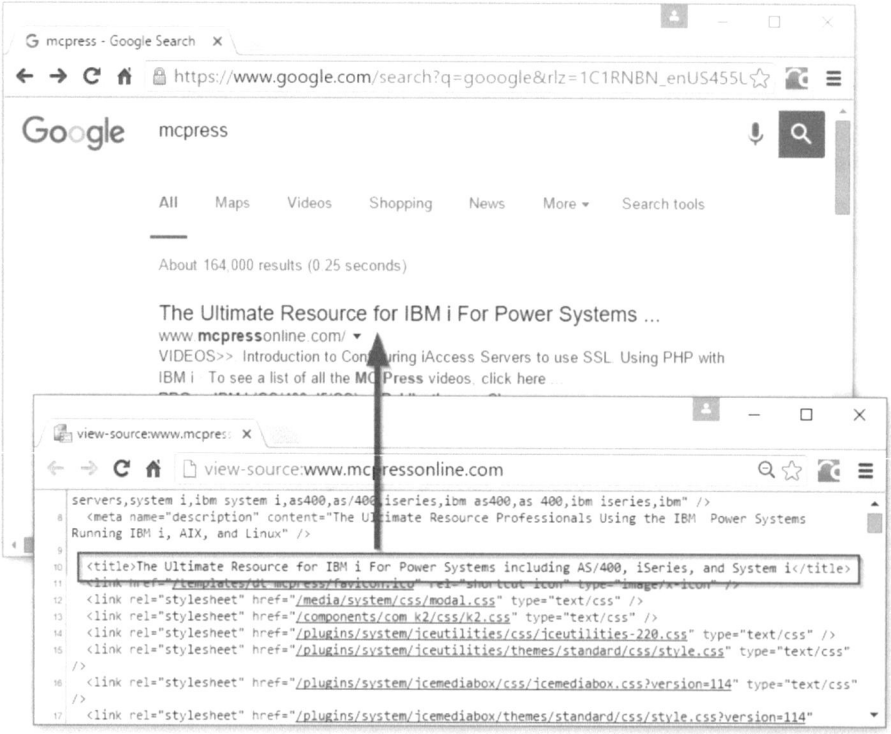

Figure 13.11: Sample page title from a search engine results page

As you can see, the title is an important part of a Web page. It should tell the visitor what the page is about and give a visitor an idea of what to expect to find on the page. A page title should be no longer than 65 to 100 characters long. Since most search engines can read words in any order, technically the order of words in your title isn't really important. However, because people are unlikely to search word phrases out of order, it's best to have a meaningful page title.

Meta Description

The meta description is used to describe a site. Search engines use this tag to match against the page title. Usually the better the match, the better the ranking results will be. If the meta description closely matches the title, chances are the content will be considered as a keyword. Figure 13.12 shows an example of a meta description that may be used for Belhur Publishing.

```
<meta type="description" content="Belhur Publishing - your ultimate source
for technical publications. Where those in the know go to find eBooks and
hard copy books on technical topics. Whether you're a student or adding new
skills, we can help!"/>
```

Figure 13.12: Meta description example

Meta tags will be placed in the head area following the title tag.

Meta Robots Tags

Meta robots tags are worth mentioning in regard to search engines. The meta tag is used when specific site pages are to be excluded from search engine indexing. This may be used to prevent spiders and Web crawlers from including the page—such as for pages on a site that are not intended for the general Web public. For example, an employee Web page may be intentionally excluded from indexing. The meta robots tag is also included in the head area of a page and usually follows the title tag. Figure 13.13 shows an example.

```
<meta name="robots" content="noindex">
```

Figure 13.13: Meta robots tag example to disallow a robot from indexing a page

In addition, a robots tag can be used to prevent robots from indexing and crawling any Web pages linked to the specific Web page. Figure 13.14 shows an example.

```
<meta name="robots" content="noindex, nofollow">
```

Figure 13.14: Meta robots tag with no link reference example

The nofollow is including within quotation marks and separated by a comma after the noindex. The noindex instructs robots to not index the page and the nofollow instructs robots to not crawl any links found on the page. The robots will still crawl the current page, but will stop there. It's important to note here that the nofollow value used in this context does not have the same implication as when it is used in the context of a hyperlink (as discussed in the Link Exchange and Banner Exchange section on page 516).

There are many other meta tags, among them the author and copyright tags. These other tags are less significant to spiders, Web crawlers, and search engines.

If you want help with creating meta tags, you can use any of the available meta tag generators, builders, and applications. Some of the software is free of charge, while other products are available for a minimal fee. You can easily find such software doing an Internet search, by using the keywords "meta tag generators, builders and evaluation software."

Using meta tags in your Web pages does not automatically guarantee that the site will soar to top ranking. Meta tags do offer a site developer some ability to impact the ranking and how a site is described by some search engines. However, meta tags are one of many factors that affect a site's search ranking.

Text Links and Image Links

A page may be designed using image map links from the home page to other pages within the site. Using image maps and image map hyperlinks (as discussed in chapter 5) can be an effective technique to enhance the appearance of your Web page while still providing links for a search engine to follow. However, some search engines aren't able to follow these links. This could result in having pages within a site being completely missed by some search engines. You can avoid this problem by adding **text links**, which are text hyperlinks on a website that can be linked to other Web pages, locations on the same page, or other content such as a PDF or movie file.

Figure 13.15 creates two image hyperlinks (or hot spots) around the authors' names on the book cover. Hovering over their names and then clicking on them will take the user to the target page. In addition to the image map hyperlinks, two text links are also provided. Using both types of links can also be a design technique you use to help your visitors maneuver through the site.

Figure 13.15: An image with an image hyperlink and a text link

A site map with text links to every page on the site can also be effective. The page with the text links can help search engines find and include pages within the site. Make sure to do a good job of linking site pages. That is, in addition to providing the main navigation links, use meaningful keywords or key phrases on a Web page to link to other pages within the site. Figure 13.16 illustrates this example.

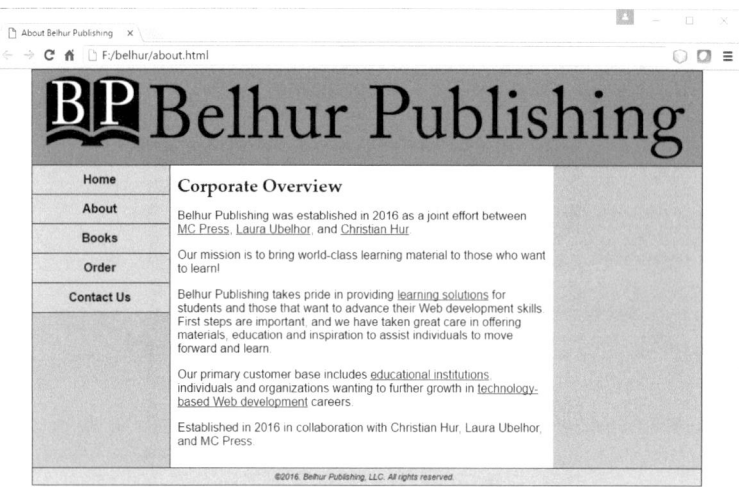

Figure 13.16 A Web page with meaningful keyword and key phrase text links

A design that includes meaningful links between pages within a site makes it more likely that search engines will find and use the links to all the pages on a site.

As discussed earlier, links matter the most to PageRank. They matter so much that having too few or too many can adversely affect the site's quality and ranking in a search results page. Keep in mind that regardless of which types of links you use, Google will credit your website with more inbound links than outbound links. In fact, the more inbound links your site has coming from other sites, the better your PR. Natural inbound links coming from sites that have high PR are ideal. By the same token, your outbound links (or external links) should also link to websites that are trusted by Google.

You may be wondering what a natural link is. A natural link is one that is not a paid link, such as a link you might buy through a network of link exchanges, which we will discuss shortly. An example of a natural link is one that is published on a trusted site such as CNN, USA Today, or ESPN and links to your site. Although it can be challenging to increase the number of natural, inbound links to your website, there are techniques that can help. One popular technique is SMO, which we will discuss later in this chapter.

Link Exchange and Banner Exchange

A common method that Web developers use to boost Google rankings is by using **link exchange** and **banner exchange**. A link exchange uses a text link while a banner exchange uses an image in the form of a banner ad that links to your site. Both options work the same. Link exchange is the bartering of links between your site and other sites. Basically, all you do is ask the owner of a website on which you'd like to have a link if they will add a text link or a banner link to your site on their website. In return, you would do the same and place a text or banner link to their site on yours. Figure 13.17 shows two sample banner ads that could be used as banner exchange to link to the fictitious website used in this book.

Figure 13.17 Examples of banner exchange ads

The advantage of this method is that it doesn't cost you anything. When you do a link or banner exchange, be sure to choose a site that is not in direct competition with yours and instead complements your site. For example, a publisher might exchange links with sites that sell books, such as bookstores. You should also be cautious and only exchange links with sites that you trust. One thing to watch out for are the **"nofollow"** links. A "nofollow" link that is one that's set with the attribute "rel=nofollow", which prevents any PR votes from being transferred over to the receiving page. If you are exchanging links with other sites, it's imperative that you check often to make sure that they don't use "nofollow" links for your links, or your inbound link-building efforts will be fruitless. Figure 13.18 shows an example of a "nofollow" link.

```
<a href="http://belhurpublishing.com" rel="nofollow">Belhur Publishing</a>
```

Figure 13.18: An example of a "nofollow" link

The downside of link exchange is that most search engines can easily distinguish a natural link from an exchanged link (or negotiated link). A *negotiated link* is a paid link: you pay another site owner to list a link on their site to link to your site. The whole idea is to mimic a natural inbound link in order to boost PageRank. Figure 13.19 shows an example of what a negotiated link might look like. One can quickly notice the irrelevance of the banner link about "Fishing Rods" placed on a page about Belhur Publishing. The exploitation of negotiated links and spamming to boost page rankings led Google to create the Penguin Update in 2012 to combat these SEO malpractices.

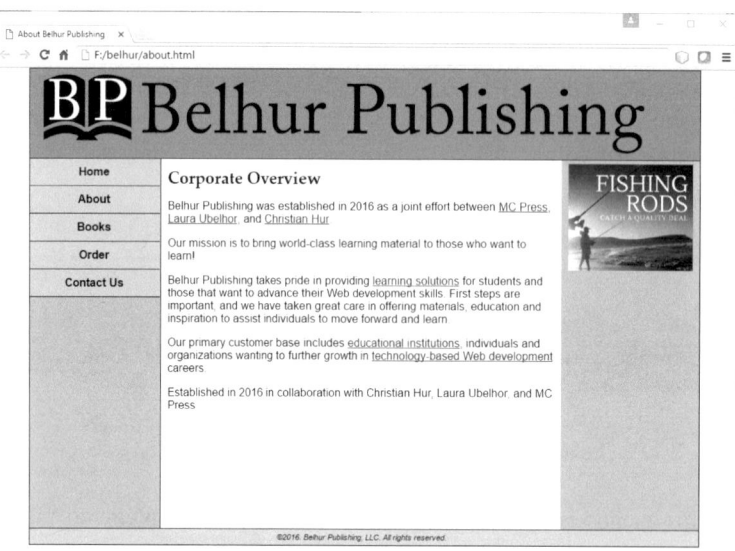

Figure 13.19 An example of a negotiated link (or paid link)

URLs

Although website owners and Web developers often have less control over their website's URL name than the other SEO elements we've discussed, if possible, make your site's URL SEO friendly and descriptive of the site's content. The name of your URL can well be reflective of the content of pages. One way to do this is to avoid using special characters in the URL name. URLs that include characters such as a question mark (?), exclamation point (!), tilde (~), or asterisk (*) can confuse search engines or even worse, be overlooked because the search engine isn't sure what to do with them.

TrustRank

To combat the problem of Web spam, researchers from Stanford University and Yahoo! developed a methodology called **TrustRank**. Like Google's PageRank, this technique gives a TrustRank score to every site that has been cataloged. Search engines use this score to decide the relevancy and the position of a particular site on a search engine results page. Two common elements that are factored into TrustRank are external links and content.

External Links

In their ranking algorithms, all the major search engines use logic that considers a page's external (outbound) links. Part of the reason search engines look at external links is to reduce the potential for site spamming. Links from other sites (made possible by outbound links in those sites) help legitimize the relevance of a site in regard to specific keywords and specific topics. Including links to legitimate, relevant sites in your website's pages can improve your site's search ranking. You don't want to simply include as many external links as possible, but rather include links from sites whose content is relevant to the specific topic or keyword. For example, an organization that is an IBM midrange system partner providing products and services to the IBM i market would find it very favorable to have a link on IBM's site or on a local user group site that has many members using the midrange platform.

What qualities make a site a good candidate to link to? The popularity of the site you're linking to is one quality that can affect your site's ranking. One way to find the most popular sites that are relevant to your keywords is to plug in target keywords in searches and see which sites appear in the top 10 results. The results may include your competitors; they may also include other sites you could approach to request a link exchange. By including outbound links to higher-ranking sites than yours, especially the top-ranked websites in your keyword-search results, you can improve your site's ranking and also likely increase traffic to your website coming from the sites you have linked to.

Popular relevant sites may also offer external link options for a fee. A site may offer banners or ads to be displayed on their site that link to your site. Investing in a banner placed on a high-traffic, relevant website may well pay off if it directs potential buyers or visitors to your company's website.

Here's how TrustRank works with links. Ideally, your links should link out to authority sites. An *authority site* is a site that Google deems authoritative and trusted. As discussed earlier, the sites that your site links to reflect on your site's search engine ranking. The farther away your site is linked to an authority site, the lower the TrustRank score.

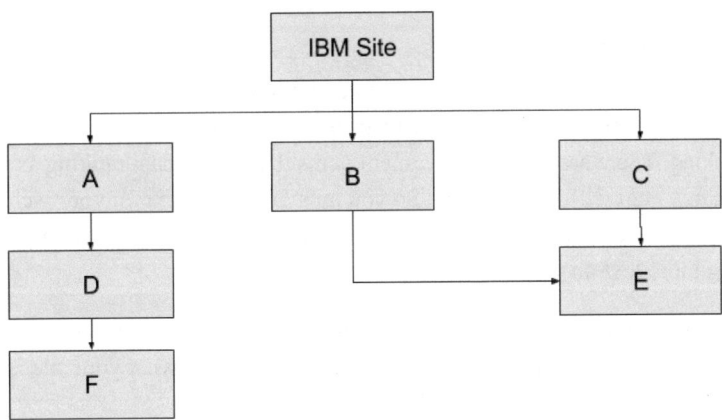

Figure 13.20 An authority site with six nodes in the link chain

For example, as illustrated in Figure 13.20, site **F** would have a lower TrustRank score than sites **D** and **E** because it is farther away from **IBM Site** (authority site) in the chain of links. Likewise, both sites **D** and **E** would have a lower TrustRank score than sites **A**, **B**, and **C**. Even if site **F** has a direct outbound link to the **IBM Site**, it's highly unlikely that its TrustRank score would increase because it's still farthest from the authority site. Hence, it's important to look at another site's link profile before taking the time to get a link from them. A site that has a good link profile is one that has no spammy links and many high-value and high-authority inbound links (also called *backlinks*). Since inbound links are coming from other sites, it can be difficult to know a site's inbound links to determine the site's link profile. One method is to visit the site to see if the site owner posts outbound links to an authority site that references their site. Another method is to use a search engine and inspect the top links listed on the search engine results page to determine the quality of those inbound links. For example, as shown in Figure 13.21, a search for "MC Press Online" on Google yields an article found on *www.zdnet.com* (an authority site) with an outbound link to MC Press. This link would be a quality inbound link for MC Press and thus improves the quality and health of its link profile. To increase our TrustRank score, you should have as many natural inbound links as possible.

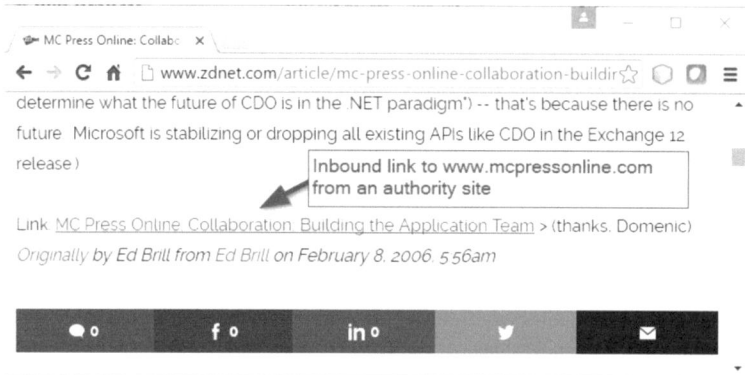

Figure 13.21 Example of an inbound link to MC Press from an authority site

Page Content Matters

As we've discussed, a title and keywords that accurately describe the page's content, as well as using keywords that are found elsewhere on the page (especially near the top of the page) affect a page's search engine ranking. There are other page content items that can impact ranking as well. Text, of course, is what search engines like to crunch. So you must make the text on your website's pages meaningful and reflective of the site's overall intent and content. Don't use text on your pages just for the sake of having more text on your page.

When it is appropriate to the content of a page and site, text references should be expanded where appropriate. Think about your audience and how they will search for what your site is providing.

Be careful to avoid spam in the content of your Web pages. Some webmasters have tried to spam search engines by repeating keywords in tiny font or in the same color as the background color of the page. The idea is that the text will be invisible to the browser but will show up for search engine indexing. More likely, this technique will result in the words being screened from indexing consideration. If the text isn't visible on the page, don't expect it to be picked up by search engines. Even worse, your site could be identified as one that uses spamming techniques and be completely dropped from consideration for ranking.

Dynamically Generated Pages

Pages that are dynamically generated using the CGIDEV2 utility or by using database information to build a page may well result in search engines not being able to index the content. Static pages are what search engines digest and use more easily. When Web ranking is very important, you may want to use database and CGI techniques to update specific content on static pages instead of generating pages.

Scripting in Web Pages

Embedding JavaScript or PHP scripting within Web pages can have the same impact as tables on your pages' search ranking, especially if your pages contain large sections of script code and the script is found near the top of a page. Of course, this doesn't mean you should not use script code. However, you should consider carefully where to position the script on your page.

Avoid Spamming

Say no to spamming. Not only is spamming unethical, it is usually a waste of time that can produce negative results for your website's search engine ranking. Search engine providers are always looking at new ways to avoid results tainted by spamming. Spamming doesn't always work, and in the worst cases can result in a site being penalized in ranking or even banned from being listed on a search engine.

Time would be much better spent on improving a site's design, features, or networking or finding other forms of publicity. Reaching users is the primary purpose of a site. Using spamming may well tarnish an organization's reputation and result in your site being blacklisted by search engines.

Consultants and Paid Rankings

When ranking is critical—for example, in a competitive high-volume market, you may find it worthwhile to look into enlisting an expert to help you make sure your website is optimized correctly so it will have the best ranking possible. There are many SEO organizations readily found on the Web that specialize in helping site developers to improve search engine ranking. When you evaluate such consultants, be sure to ask them for references, or seek recommendations from your colleagues.

Most SEO providers charge a fee for special ranking services, commonly known as *pay-per-rank* or *pay for performance*. While such services are synonymous with the pay-per-click (or cost-per-click) Internet advertising, the methods involved in improving a site's rank in the SERP can be tedious. Some common methods include keyword and meta tags optimization, relevant link building, blog postings, social media bookmarking, and relevant directory submissions. However, there are no guarantees that your ranking will actually improve, as many factors can influence search results. In a competitive market, if many of the players are paying for preferential ranking, doing so may not give you the results you're looking for or provide an equitable return on the investment. However, don't overlook paid ranking if your site's ranking has a big impact on your business.

Submitting Key Pages to a Search Engine

Most search engines allow you to submit pages for indexing. Most search engines will index other pages on a site by following links on the site pages. It is worthwhile to take the time to submit the top two or three pages that best summarize the site's content. Review the list of top search engines and take the time to manually submit your chosen site pages to each one. Doing so manually will allow for reviewing any errors encountered or problems reported.

If you want, you can submit all of your site's pages to the search engine. This may or may not affect whether those pages are indexed and your site's search ranking—it depends upon the technique the search engine uses for collecting information and building an index. It may take some time after a site is published before the major search engines have picked up the site through Web crawling and added the site pages to the listing. It isn't uncommon for this process to take a month or more. It is also wise to check to be sure your site is listed. Periodically monitor search results to make sure your site is listed when it should be. When a significant change has been made to a page or pages, you should resubmit those pages to the major search engines.

Social Media Optimization (SMO)

While SEO deals with the visibility of your website in a SERP, SMO deals with enhancing your business website's presence on the Web. Though still in its infancy, SMO's popularity is quickly growing. SMO helps give your website an online reputation through interactive communities such **Facebook**, **Twitter**, blogs, forums, and anywhere else your business is mentioned or linked to socially. Let's explore some of the important and common techniques to help optimize your website's SMO.

To improve your site's SMO, you should focus on engaging with relevant social audiences, contributing to online conversations, and posting your own shares through social media outlets to generate traffic for your website. SMO is becoming an important factor in SEO as search engines are increasingly utilizing the recommendations of users of social networks such as Facebook, Google+, **YouTube**, LinkedIn, Twitter, and **Pinterest** to rank pages. Figure 13.22 shows some popular social media icons.

Figure 13.22: Social media icons

SMO is considered an integral part of search engine reputation management (SERM) strategy for organizations or individuals who care about their online presence.

The key principle behind SMO is viral marketing. Social media sites like Facebook, YouTube, and Twitter have huge audiences in the hundreds of millions. Facebook alone has more than one billion users. Say you post a link to a video of your neighbor's cat doing an amazing acrobatic feat. The video is shared with your friends who in turn share it with their friends, and so on, multiplying into hundreds of thousands of shares and views. This outreach can result in high TrustRank links on your site.

Summary

You now have an understanding of what a search engine is, how it works, how search engines work with your published site, and how your site needs to respond to and interact with search engines. The purpose of your site is essential to its search engine strategy. To develop a search engine strategy for your business website, you must first know how much your business will rely on being listed in search engine results. Once you know this, you can determine how much time, money, and resources to invest in search engine ranking. Even if your site never makes the top 10, you can use the SEO and SMO techniques described in this chapter to attain the best possible ranking.

Key Terms

<meta>
<title>
authority site
banner exchange
category-focused vertical
    search engines
concept-based searches
Facebook
Google
hashing
inbound link
indexing
link exchange

media-focused vertical search
    engines
meta description
meta keywords
meta robots
negotiated link
nofollownoindex
outbound link
PageRank (PR)
pay-per-rank
search engine
search engine optimization
    (SEO)

search engine results page
    (SERP)
social media
social media optimization
    (SMO)
social vertical search engines
spamming
spider
TrustRank
vertical search engines
Web crawler
Web crawling

Discussion/Review Questions

1. What is a search engine?
2. How does a Web crawler index the Web?
3. What is the best method for indexing, and how does it work?
4. What are vertical search engines?
5. How are social vertical search engines different from other vertical search engines?
6. What is search engine optimization (SEO)?
7. What is the fundamental goal behind SEO?
8. Name seven major SEO techniques you can use to affect your site's ranking in a search engine's SERP.
9. What two primary meta tags search engines use to determine a page's content?
10. What are some similarities and differences between PageRank and TrustRank?
11. How does a search engine, such as Google, rank your Web page?

12. Are inbound links more important than outbound links? Why or why not?
13. In which section of a Web document should the meta keywords tag, meta description tag, meta robots tags, and title tag be included?
14. What are three reasons a page title is important for a Web page?
15. What are the recommended numbers of keywords page and keywords per site?
16. What is the main purpose of meta robots tag?
17. How do you prevent Web crawlers from crawling your website?
18. What are some pitfalls associated with using link exchange and banner exchange?
19. What is social media optimization (SMO)?
20. What is the key principle behind SMO?

Exercises

1. List 10 popular search engine providers.
2. Explain the processes of Web crawling.
3. Given the following key-value pairs and hash index values, construct a hash table.

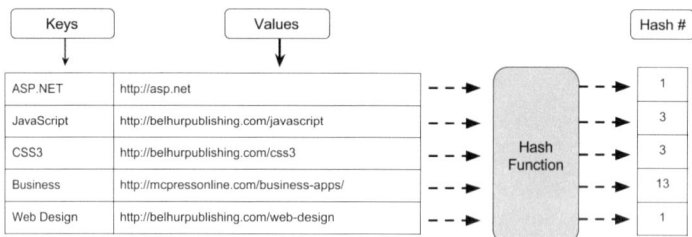

4. Compare and contrast one of the following vertical search engines with a general search engine: Trulia, Yelp, WebMD, CareerBuilder.
5. Visit two websites of your choice and determine whether or not the keywords and descriptions used are effective. If not, how could they be improved?
6. Write the HTML code for the following:

   a. Robots are allowed to index and crawl the entire website.
   b. Robots are allowed to index but not permitted to crawl the site.
   c. Robots are not permitted to index but permitted to crawl the site.
   d. Robots are not permitted to index or crawl the site.

7. Create a Web page about this book that includes an appropriate page title, a meta keywords tag with at least five keywords, a meta description tag, and a meta robots tag to allow indexing but not permit crawling of the site. Also provide one to two paragraphs of content with three relevant text links.

CHAPTER 14

Best Practices

There are a number of things to keep in mind to help make your website more effective and productive. Some of these best practices include keeping the site's overall purpose in mind, using a clear and easily maintained folder structure, and avoiding cutting-edge techniques. These and other important suggestions are discussed in this chapter.

Focus on the Site's Objective

When designing your site and Web applications, keep the focus on your business and technical objectives for the website. Don't add unnecessary components and content. A high-quality site should meet the following criteria:

- Offer site visitors what they want and need
- Be up to date
- Load and perform quickly
- Be easy to use
- Be simple

If your site has too much content, slow-loading pages, is hard to use, does not provide current information, or does not provide what visitors are looking for, not only will visitors have an unfavorable experience, but you will also increase the potential for unfavorable results due to browser differences.

Structure Your Site

Keep your site's file structure simple. Don't haphazardly structure your site files or use no structure at all. This is especially critical for larger sites, but it is also important for small ones. It is easy to have a Web application's structure get out of hand and become disorganized. Create a simple **site structure** to easily organize the components of your site. Use simple, meaningful filenames. For example, if you have a logo image, you might name the file *Logo.jpg*. Similarly, your "about us" Web page might be named *AboutUs.html*. Let's consider a site with the following components: HTML, CSS, JavaScript, images, and document files.

The example in Figures 14.1 and 14.2 is simplistic, but the message is clear: organizing your files in a simple structure makes it easier to locate them. If you put all your image files in an "images" folder, then you know any code that references an image file will use the format *images/imagefilename.xxx*.

```
C:\BelhurSite
Abc.html
Abc.js
Abc.jpg
BBQ.html
CC.html
CC.jpg
CC.doc
DD.doc
```

Figure 14.1: Unstructured site files

```
ABC.html
BBQ.html
CCC.html
\JSFiles
Abc.js
CC.js
\Images
ABC.jpg
CC.jpg
\Docs
CC.doc
DD.doc
```

Figure 14.2: Structured site files

When defining path naming and file naming conventions, remember that Windows is not case sensitive, but other operating systems are. For example, Windows would deem *Images* and *images* to refer to the same folder, but some other operating systems would not.

The design of your site and applications is critical. The more complex your site and applications, the more important it is to have a great design. The time and effort spent up front on design will result in a good end product and will also save you support time in the long run. Incorporate the file-structure definition and file naming conventions as a part of your development standards.

Avoid the Cutting Edge

It can be very tempting to use **cutting-edge coding techniques**. However, "cutting edge" can also mean "bleeding edge"; such techniques may end up causing unforeseen problems or be difficult to maintain or support. Be careful to choose your coding techniques and tools wisely. Choose proven tools that fit your business needs.

When choosing your Web development tools, don't reinvent the wheel. Research available tools before committing to a particular tool or set of tools. Also keep in mind the browsers you'll be developing a website or Web application for, and make sure your tools will work well on all of those browsers. Choose tools and technologies with a track record and proven capability for use in Web development—tools like JavaScript, PHP, JSP, .NET, HTML, and CSS. It is likely you'll use a combination of these.

Do not lose sight of your goal. Code to fit your application requirements, not to use technology for the sake of trying something new. If your company objective is to only use cutting-edge technology, be prepared to spend more time, money, and other resources on Web application development.

Use CSS

Use only CSS for layout consistency, and put the CSS in files that all pages share. Browsers have many properties whose default values are not defined in the specifications, and these properties can vary from browser to browser. You should, therefore, specify CSS properties fully to prevent differences in browser defaults. For example, default margins and padding are not defined in the specifications and may differ for different browsers; to ensure consistent results, your CSS should set both. Make sure designers and application developers work together in developing the CSS, and consider the business application requirements when you create your style sheets.

You might need to use different CSS code for different browsers and possibly for different versions of browsers. You can do this by detecting the version of the browser, as discussed in chapter 12, and coding to point to the CSS file designed for it.

Address Coding Issues

Coding errors are one of the leading causes of browser display problems. Making sure your code is error-free can have the biggest impact on preventing problems because of browser differences. Poor code can affect a page's look, performance, and errors encountered. Poorly coded sites will result in browser issues.

Use well-formed HTML. Tags should be nested properly. No end tags should be omitted. Some browsers will not display your site as desired if the HTML is not well-formed. The same applies to script and program code. You might want to use a code checker to identify and make corrections. **Code checkers** warn about irregular or faulty code.

Don't assume there are no coding errors in a page that appears correct. Some errors might not be obvious when you test your work. A browser that does not conform to the standards may produce the wrong results. Some browsers, most notably IE, try hard to recover from errors gracefully by guessing what the designer intended, which covers up errors. Often, the first sign of a problem with your code is that your page doesn't look right when viewed in a different browser or an updated browser. This also applies to Web application programming. Integrated development environments (**IDE**s) and other development tools like Dreamweaver, Eclipse, Komodo IDE, Microsoft Expression, Notepad++, Zend Studio, and many others can flag or help you avoid errors in your PHP, HTML, JSP, JavaScript, and .NET coding.

Coding to Specifications and Standards

As mentioned earlier, the W3C issues HTML specifications. You can find the specifications at *www.w3.org*. Design to the standards. Use a **DOCTYPE** declaration (DTD) within your HTML and XHTML. This declaration makes modern browsers honor standards more strictly, so that different browsers act more alike. Figure 14.3 shows the DOCTYPE reference for strict HTML 4.01 code.

A DOCTYPE declaration should appear at the beginning of an HTML or XHTML file to specify the standard applicable to the file. The declaration must be exact in both spelling and case, to be effective. You can find a list of valid DOCTYPEs on the W3C website.

```
<!DOCTYPE html PUBLIC "-//W3C//DTD HTML "http://www.w3.org/TR/html4/
strict.dtd">
```

Figure 14.3: A DOCTYPE example

Pay close attention to details to ensure that your site and application designs are efficient and effective. It is too easy to slap together page elements and overlook details. Being able to focus on the details is a skill that, as a Web application developer, you must continually practice. Learn from your mistakes. When you find an error, try to figure out where you went wrong. Every failure is an opportunity to learn.

Some people continue to use older, less capable browsers even when much better versions are available. Therefore, avoid using poorly supported elements of standards for several years, until so few people use the old browsers that you can reasonably exclude older browsers from your consideration. If you must use something that might not be supported, include a proven workaround that works with all browsers.

Code Checkers and Validators

Different browsers handle errors differently. You can find syntax errors during manual **testing** of your site or application, or you might decide to use a code validator or code checker to help you find errors prior to testing. *Validators* check your files to determine whether the CSS, HTML, XHTML, JavaScript, PHP, JSP, and ASP.NET syntax is correct and written in compliance with **coding specifications**. Using a validator is a fast and simple way to identify the most blatant errors. Before manual testing, fix all syntax errors and critical warnings found by the validator. Reviewing a validator's error messages will also help you to learn more about HTML, CSS, PHP, JavaScript, JSP, and .NET, which will help to improve the quality of your work.

Code checkers are sometimes also called *syntax checkers* or *lint checkers*. They check for problems in HTML or CSS. Some of the checks are similar to what validators do. Others go beyond what validators do, and check for browser incompatibility, broken links, missing files, missing tags, and other problems. For example, if an **<img>** tag's **src** attribute names an image file that does not exist, a validator will not report an error, because it does not violate HTML syntax to refer to a missing image file. A code checker, however, should report an error, or at least a warning, because it is very likely that the code specifies either the wrong file or one that has not yet been created.

It is easy to find **code validators** and checkers on the Web. Validators are often available for free. Code checkers are sometimes free, but are usually have a cost. The W3C website provides a free code validator and a free code checker for CSS and HTML. Code checkers and validators depend on the DOCTYPE line to determine the designated standards being used.

Use Accepted Coding Standards and Techniques

Every programmer has his or her favorite coding techniques. Whatever your preferred coding methods, make sure that when you create code you are mindful that someone else might have to maintain the application. Following accepted **coding standards** will minimize inconsistencies in code written by different programmers and will make it much easier to maintain and support the application in the future. This advice applies whether your organization is new to Web development or is experienced. The time spent on standards up front will minimize development and support requirements later.

When creating new pages or changing existing pages, do your work one step at a time, and after each change, verify that the code works as intended. This approach makes it easier to develop and test your work. If a new problem appears, you know that it is caused by what you have just done. Therefore, you only have to review the little bit of work done since your previous step. This process is called *incremental development*. Making massive changes before testing any of them can make testing and debugging a time-consuming and frustrating task.

Documentation

Documentation is an important part of developing and updating applications. A well-documented program is much easier to support and maintain than a poorly documented one. Documentation should not be an afterthought. Rather, you should thoughtfully create documentation that will enable another developer to easily understand the code. Having good documentation can be critical when incorporating new code or when debugging or correcting a programming error. Software design is an art in which great attention to detail is essential. Poorly documented software means that some details will be unclear, likely will be misunderstood, and often will cause errors.

Documentation embedded within an application should be used wisely because it will increase page load times in HTML, CSS, and JavaScript files. You might decide to have documentation stored in a separate file.

You must keep your documentation up to date. Incorrect or outdated documentation can be worse than useless, leading developers down the wrong path at a cost of time and effort.

JavaScript Support Coding

JavaScript will likely be one of the tools you will use for Web development. Most modern browsers support the use of JavaScript. Older browsers, however, might not support JavaScript, or a user might have disabled it. You can use coding techniques to accommodate browsers that are not JavaScript-enabled.

One possible method is to embed **<script>** tags within the HTML comment block. Browsers that don't support JavaScript will consider the code to be a comment and ignore it, while browsers that do support JavaScript will execute the code.

In Figure 14.4, when the browser in use supports JavaScript, an alert box like the one in Figure 14.5 will be displayed. When the browser doesn't support JavaScript, the code will be treated like an HTML comment and ignored.

```
<html>
<head>
<script language="javascript">
<!-- CS1404 - JavaScript Support Example -->
<!-- Just a comment to JavaScript Non Supported Browsers
alert ("JavaScript Is Supported By The Browser Being Used!");
-->
</script>
</head>
<body>
</body>
</html>
```

Figure 14.4: JavaScript support in an HTML comment

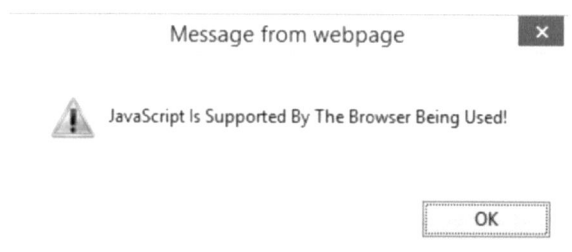

Figure 14.5: The alert displayed by a JavaScript-enabled browser

You might want to design an application to react one way when a user's browser supports JavaScript, and another way when it does not support JavaScript. This can be accomplished by using the **<noscript>** tag embedded within the HTML. JavaScript-enabled browsers recognize <noscript> and ignore everything from the beginning <noscript> tag to the ending </noscript> tag. When a browser doesn't support JavaScript, the browser ignores the <noscript> tags (because it doesn't recognize them) but not the contents within the <noscript> and </noscript> tags.

Figure 14.6 is another way to display the alert box in Figure 14.5 when JavaScript is supported. When JavaScript is not supported, the following message will be displayed:

The browser being used doesn't support JavaScript!

```
<html>
<head>
<script language="javascript">
<!-BP1406 - JavaScript Support <noscript> Example -->
<!-- Just a comment to JavaScript Non Supported Browsers
alert ("JavaScript Is Supported By The Browser Being Used!");
-->
</script>
<noscript>
The browser being used doesn't support JavaScript!
</noscript>
</head>
<body>
</body>
</html>
```

Figure 14.6: An example of <noscript>

These techniques can easily be used to incorporate code specific to your application. If the browser you are using is JavaScript-enabled, temporarily turn off JavaScript support, and run the examples.

Pages could get quite complicated and large if you incorporated JavaScript code to accommodate JavaScript-enabled browsers and other code for browsers that don't support JavaScript. Another possibility is to create separate pages for JavaScript-enabled browsers and for those not supporting JavaScript. For example, in Figure 14.7, when JavaScript is enabled, the page CS1326.html shown in Figure 14.8 will be loaded.

```
<html>
<head>
<!-BP1407 - JavaScript Support Example -->
<script language="javascript">
<!--
window.location.href="CS1326.html";
//-->
```
                                                                    Continued

```
</script>
</head>
<body>
<noscript>
The browser being used doesn't support JavaScript!
</noscript>
</body>
</html>
```

Figure 14.7: Loading a separate page for JavaScript-enabled browsers

```
<html>
<body>
<script language="javascript">
<!-CS1326 - JavaScript Support Example -->
alert ("JavaScript Is Supported By The Browser Being Used!");
-->
</script>
JavaScript Enabled Page!
</body>
</html>
```

Figure 14.8: The CS1326.html file

This example can be applied to most applications. Note that the code has been embedded within the HTML in a combination of **<head>** and **<body>** tags.

Fonts

You can minimize differences in common browsers by using any of the browser-safe **fonts**. Usually, using the native fonts provided as standard to the operating system is a reliable choice. Basic PC fonts include the following:

- Arial
- **Arial Black**
- Comic Sans
- Courier New
- Georgia
- **Impact**
- Lucida Console
- LucidaSans Unicode
- Palatino
- Tahoma

- Times New Roman
- Verdana

These fonts are commonly seen on Web pages. Font appearance can also be affected by size and color. Black is a pretty safe bet for consistent display, but other colors are often required to emphasize text. Using browser-safe fonts will make it more likely that text will be displayed consistently in different browsers. Test different browsers with the font types, sizes, and colors that have been chosen.

Text

You can put your pages' **text** in tables, which most browsers recognize. Then, you can control the width of the text on the page. This way, it won't matter what the visitor's browser is set at. It will look the same for everyone.

Test the Website and Code

Testing is a critical part of your Web project, just as it would be in any other application development project. Don't cut corners on this step. The goal of testing is to find any fundamental flaws in the design, to identify coding errors, and to ensure that your site displays as expected for your audience. The **test plan** should include testing of all pages in your website. If you have a large, complex site, we recommend that you complete the first round of testing after only a few pages have been coded. Initial testing will identify design flaws early on and minimize the time required to address them.

Testing needs to be comprehensive, and testers should try hard to make the design fail. A well-designed test plan will uncover flaws well before your audience views your site and Web applications. Test first with the browser most commonly used by your audience. After you are satisfied with your test results, move on to test the rest of the browsers your site will support. You might want to incorporate the use of automated tools to validate and test your site. As discussed earlier, a variety of automated tools are available, including code validators and checkers. The expense of such tools may well be justified by minimizing coding errors and saving time testing a large, complex site. Testing should not be considered complete until the problems identified have been corrected and retested.

Consider your tolerance for defects. It would be easy to say that you have zero tolerance for errors, but this is not practical, taking into consideration browser differences. If your website caters to a small or informal audience, your bug tolerance will be much higher than if your website represents your company to the public. The purpose and audience of your site will likely provide the key to determining your tolerance for errors and defects. You will have to consider how large an audience you will support and how much expense you are willing to expend to support it.

Make a formal test plan. Use your list of browsers, settings, hardware, and operating systems as a test checklist, as shown in Table 14.1. Incorporate the test plan as part of your standard development procedures. The test plan should be designed so it can be used for new development and for site changes. The test plan should include a detailed identification of the problems encountered, with planned actions to be taken to correct the errors.

Table 14.1: Test Plan Support Example				
Browsers Supported	Operating Systems Supported	Monitor Resolution Supported	Monitor Size Supported	Connection Speed Supported
Chrome	Windows 8	800 x 600	17"	Cable Internet
Firefox	Windows 7	1024 x 768	19"	DSL
IE	Windows 10	1366 x 768	14.1"	3G/4G Wireless
Safari	Apple Mac OS. 7.0.2	1280 x 1024	18.4"	Satellite
Opera	Windows 8.1	1366 x 768	15"	DSL

Figure 14.9 is an example test plan that includes support of the English language. This plan gives an idea of how the different combinations of criteria can be organized. The plan that fits your organization's needs might be more complex and include additional information. Your test plan should be based on the application audience. Completing testing at this level will eliminate user experience issues. Up-front investigation should be done to determine the appropriate criteria for testing. Periodically review and refresh the test plan criteria to keep the information current and relevant.

Site: Belhur Publishing
Site Page: Home Page
Language Supported: English (United States) [en-us]
Special Features and Notes:
Date: April 15, 2016
Name of Tester: Rickelle Walsh
Test Completion Date: April 16, 2016
Test Passed: No
Language Supported: English (United States) [en-us]
Instructions: If the test is valid, enter OK in the corresponding box. If the test fails, enter an X in the corresponding box and make a note identifying the description of the failure.

Operating System	Monitor Resolution	Monitor Size	Connection	Speed	Chrome	IE	Firefox	Safari	Opera
Win 8	1366 x 768	17"	Satellite	Ok	Ok	X	Text is hard to read	Ok	Ok
Win 8	1024x768	17"	Satellite	Ok	Ok	Ok	Ok	Ok	
Win 8	1280x1024	17"	Satellite	Ok	Ok	Ok	Ok	Ok	
Win 8	1366 x 768	17"	DSL	Ok	Ok	X	Text is hard to read	Ok	Ok
Win 8	1024x768	17"	DSL	Ok	Ok	Ok	Ok	Ok	
Win 8	1280x1024	17"	DSL	Ok	Ok	Ok	Ok	Ok	
Win 8	1366 x 768	19"	Satellite	Ok	Ok	X	Text is hard to read	Ok	Ok
Win 8	1024x768	19"	Satellite	Ok	Ok	Ok	Ok	Ok	
Win 8	1280x1024	19"	Satellite	Ok	Ok	Ok	Ok	Ok	
Win 8	1366 x 768	19"	DSL	Ok	Ok	X	Text is hard to read	Ok	Ok
Win 8	1024x768	19"	DSL	Ok	Ok	Ok	Ok	Ok	

Continued

Operating System	Monitor Resolution	Monitor Size	Connection	Speed	Chrome	IE	Firefox	Safari	Opera
Win 8	1280x1024	19"	DSL	Ok	Ok	Ok	Ok	Ok	
Win 10	1366 x 768	17"	Satellite	Ok	Ok	X	Text is hard to read	Ok	Ok
Win 10	1024x768	17"	Satellite	Ok	Ok	Ok	Ok	Ok	
Win 10	1280x1024	17"	Satellite	Ok	Ok	Ok	Ok	Ok	
Win 10	1366 x 768	17"	DSL	Ok	Ok	X	Satellite	Ok	Ok
Win 10	1024x768	17"	DSL	Ok	Ok	Ok	Ok	Ok	
Win 10	1280x1024	17"	DSL	Ok	Ok	Ok	Ok	Ok	
Win 10	1366 x 768	19"	Satellite	Ok	Ok	X	Text is hard to read	Ok	Ok
Win 10	1024x768	19"	Satellite	Ok	Ok	Ok	Ok	Ok	
Win 10	1280x1024	19"	Satellite D	Ok	Ok	Ok	Ok	Ok	
Win 10	1366 x 768	19"	DSL	Ok	Ok	X	Text is hard to read	Ok	Ok
Win 10	1024x768	19"	DSL	Ok	Ok	Ok	Ok	Ok	
Win 10	1280x1024	19"	DSL	Ok	Ok	Ok	Ok	Ok	

Figure 14.9: Test plan example

Summary

Web design projects have some similarity to traditional application design projects. There is no substitute for good planning, design, documentation, and testing. Developing and following coding standards improves your ability to create functional and easily maintained websites. Be sure to test your Web pages with the most common browsers. Also test them with the most common screen resolutions. We highly recommend using both CSS and JavaScript to extend the capabilities of your website and to make it easy to maintain.

Web development is a fulfilling, needed, and valued skill. The best practice is to enjoy what you do. Keep an open mind, because technology constantly changes. Don't fear the change; rather, embrace it. The skills you have learned in this book will prepare you to take the next step on your path to developing business applications for the Web.

Key Terms

<noscript>
<script>
code checkers
code validators
coding specifications
coding standards

coding techniques
cutting-edge coding techniques
DOCTYPE
documentation
fonts
IDE

site structure
test plan
testing
text

Discussion/Review Questions

1. What criteria should a high-quality website meet?
2. Why should you keep in mind a site's objective?
3. Should a website contain many or few files? How does the site's structure affect the Web application?
4. A new cutting-edge Web coding technique interests you. Does it make sense to use the technique within your business Web application?
5. Should you use CSS? What are the benefits to your choice of using or not using CSS?
6. How can you address coding issues?
7. Where can you find information about website coding specifications and standards?
8. Should you use coding standards? Why or why not?
9. What role does documentation serve in development of Web applications?
10. What coding techniques can you use to accommodate browsers that don't support JavaScript?
11. There are many fonts available for use on a website. How do you determine which font to use?
12. Why is testing a website important?
13. What criteria should you include within a test plan?

Exercises

1. Using the list of the criteria for a high-quality website, explain why each point is important for the user's site experience.
2. Describe an example business application website and provide an example of structured site files.
3. Research and provide a list of code checkers and validators. Create a list of at least three of each, including a URL link for each tool and its cost, if any.
4. Create an .html file that displays an alert *This is a test to show that JavaScript is supported by the browser being used*. Provide the .html file and a screen shot displaying the alert.
5. Create a simple .html document that lists the browser-safe fonts that can be used by common browsers. Provide the HTML code and a screen shot of the displayed Web page. The page should include each font name in that font—for example:

    Arial
    Arial Black
    Comic Sans

6. Create an HTML file using at least two uncommon fonts, and create a test plan using at least three different sets of parameters. Then test the HTML page and provide the filled-in test plan.

Index

Boldface numbers indicate illustrations, code, or tables.